CHILDHOOD AND ADOLESCENCE

CHILDHOOD AND ADOLESCENCE

A Psychology of the Growing Person

FIFTH EDITION

the late L. Joseph Stone
Vassar College

Joseph Church
Brooklyn College of the City University of New York

In collaboration with
Alexandria Church

Random House 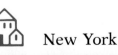 New York

Fifth Edition

9876

Library of Congress Cataloging in Publication Data
Stone, L. Joseph (Lawrence Joseph), 1912-1975
 Childhood & adolescence

 Bibliography: p. 595
 Includes index.
 1. Child psychology. 2. Adolescent psychology.
I. Church, Joseph. II. Title. III. Title: Childhood and adolescence.
BF721.S82   1983   155.4   83-21185
ISBN 0-394-33011-0

Manufactured in the United States of America

Cover Design: Linda Rettich and Joanne Stein
Cover photo: © Leonard Speier 1983.
Photo captions and summaries: Saralyn Esh

Text design: Nancy Sugihăra

Chapter opening photos: Chapter 1—© Lynne Jaeger Weinstein 1983/Woodfin Camp and Associates; Chapter 2—© Michael Heron 1980/Woodfin Camp and Associates; Chapter 3—© Peter Vandermark/Stock, Boston; Chapter 4—© Lilo Raymond 1980/Woodfin Camp and Associates; Chapter 5—© Paul Fusco/Magnum; Chapter 6—© Ted Koepper; Chapter 7—© Ken Heyman; Chapter 8—© Charles Harbutt/Archive Pictures, Inc.; Chapter 9—© Charles Harbutt/Archive Pictures, Inc.; Chapter 10—© Christopher Lukas, Rapho/Photo Researchers; Chapter 11—© Phoebe Dunn, DPI; Chapter 12—© Joe Church; Chapter 13—© Sepp Seitz 1978/Woodfin Camp and Associates; Chapter 14—© Jim Anderson 1981/Woodfin Camp and Associates; Chapter 15—© Peter Vandermark.

P R E F A C E

In this, the fifth edition of a textbook first published in 1957, we have tried to do several things. Our revision aims at preserving what is best from earlier editions, improving what needs to be improved, and incorporating significant new findings and insights.

As in previous editions, we have tried to present a portrait of the living, active child at successive periods of life. The child exists in a framework of family and community, of course, and we have tried to provide this framework, too. What is more, children have to be viewed in the framework of history. Childhood has some enduring features, but it changes as the cultural context of development evolves. This, too, we have tried to convey.

Our portrayal takes on deeper meaning when we adopt the special perspective of the scientist. Scientists work hard to uncover the facts of behavioral development and to formulate ideas and theories to make sense of the facts. Bear in mind, though, that scientific ideas also shift with the tides of history. New knowledge, and new ways of looking at established knowledge, may cause us to see our subject matter in an unexpected light. For instance, Thomas Szasz, a long-time critic of orthodox thinking about mental health and illness, has proposed that behavioral disturbances in adolescents may be a manifestation of unwillingness to accept the freedom and responsibility that go with being an adult (Miller, 1983). If this is true, the implications are dizzying. Until now, the emphasis has always been on the child and young person's striving for maturity, with only intermittent expressions of doubt about whether growing up is a good idea. If Szasz is correct, we may have to give increased attention to reluctance at all ages to move from one developmental status to the next.

Our task is to respect and preserve the insights of the past while integrating them with new facts and ideas. We try not to be slaves of either tradition or novelty, but to find an effective blend of the best of the old and the new.

We have tried to make our book accessible to the reader by combining its basic chronological approach with a topical one that deals with separate areas of behavior. Within each successive age period, we have first described the living child, feeling, thinking, perceiving, moving, growing, imagining, creating, and interacting with the human and nonhuman environment. We have then treated individual aspects of functioning as they appear at each age. When a topic is especially prominent at a given age, we have presented a general overview of that aspect of development in the chapter, elaborating in later chapters as appropriate. Thus attachment is crucial to infancy, so we consider attachment at length in the context of infancy and then follow it through in lesser detail at later ages. In each chronological chapter, we include the major applicable theoretical views and concepts, supported by research findings.

In prior editions, the book has opened with the birth of the baby and a discussion of the characteristics of the newborn, and then backtracked to the baby's genetic and prenatal history. We believe that there were sound reasons, in terms of engaging the reader's interest, for this order of presentation. However, we have moved this material back in response to the wishes of many users of the book who expressed a preference for a more strictly chronological arrangement. The book now opens with an introduction to the field of psychological development, its concepts, theories, methods, and principles. We do not simply present the material and assume that the reader will grasp its relevance at appropriate points later in the text. As we have said, we repeatedly review theoretical conceptions of successive age periods and make explicit the applicability of important principles to key features of the developmental process. In addition, our account stresses significant recurring psychological themes such as heredity and environment, individual differences, self-awareness and self-determination, identification and identity formation, the role of language, cultural differences, and competence. Thus our chronological organization includes the interweaving of many strands, topical, theoretical, conceptual, and thematic. But even as we anatomize children's behavior, we try to preserve a sense of their wholeness. Our description seeks to be systematic and integrated, covering all the essential factual information important to an understanding of childhood and development, but subordinated to an image of the child as a person in the world.

At two points in the book we interrupt the chronological flow to deal with topics of major significance. As in the last edition, Chapter 7 discusses research on the importance of early experience for later functioning. In Chapter 9, we give extended treatment to the beginnings of language, which many authorities see as the distinguishing characteristic of the human species. There is also a separate chapter on disturbances in development; this is a return to the organization of the first through third editions.

We have tried to include in this edition all the major topics of current interest, from cesarian births through day care and children's involvement with computers and video games to contemporary crises in adolescent values. We have also given special prominence to the still incompletely defined but rapidly growing field of social cognition as an added perspective on children's awareness.

The entire text has been thoroughly reviewed and, where necessary, rewritten and rearranged. We have tried to make our presentation as clear and simple as the present state of knowledge and understanding permits. Human psychological development is a complicated matter, but that is no reason to make our account as complicated as its subject. A principal goal of science is to simplify and dimensionalize, not to catalogue every last twitch and flicker. Nor is there any reason to be solemn about the study of human psychological development. It is possible to be a detached, dispassionate observer and still relish the emotional and logical convolutions of children's behavior.

In this edition, we have retained and improved the pedagogical devices that help readers understand, connect, and retain the many pieces of information given in the text. Additional headings and subheadings within chapters keep the reader oriented to the topic under discussion. An expanded photo program gives pictorial shape to verbal description, and tables, graphs, and diagrams illustrate important schematic relationships. At the end of each chapter there is a brief summary of the material contained in the chapter. A new feature is a list of the key terms introduced in the chapter, the words that seek to capture and communicate the central ideas of development. In addition, annotated suggested readings are given to supplement the material in the text; these range from fictional selections to highly technical surveys. In the back of the book, the reader will find a glossary giving definitions of the technical terms in which we talk about development, a bibliography that gives the sources for citations in the text, and an index. We have taken special pains with the index and recommend it to readers as a useful study guide.

Developmental psychology is not a finished science, a tidy collection of facts and principles to be dispensed according to formula. The study of development is itself a developing field, containing gaps and inconsistencies and ambiguities. Like other branches of science, it is not a stranger to controversy.

It would be surprising indeed if any textbook matched any instructor's needs exactly, and even more surprising if a textbook could be read through and grasped in its entirety by any student. Instructors have to do a certain amount of mediating between authors and readers. This gives instructors a chance to include additional material that they consider important, and to impart their own special emphases to the material in the book.

There are several approaches to the writing of textbooks. The one we have chosen seeks to involve the reader as an active participant in the quest for understanding. It is for this reason that we have not shunned the issues and controversies that sometimes trouble the field. We can present the facts and suggest how they might be organized into various patterns, but in the final analysis the reader has to become a party to the process of finding a coherent, sensible, satisfying synthesis. If science were all facts, it would not be a very rewarding enterprise. We have to ground our thinking on fact, but it is the meanings of the facts, and the still higher meanings they yield when joined to form patterns, that make the quest exciting.

Some instructors are interested only in textbooks that speak to an audience of future researchers and theoreticians. We welcome prospective colleagues and hope that they will find sustenance in these pages. At the same time, we make no secret of the fact that we resonate also to the concerns of those who want practical answers to the concrete problems of how to relate to children in assorted roles. Even though our knowledge is far from complete, we think we have helpful things to say to present and future parents, educators, social workers, nurses, doctors, clinical psychologists, children's court workers—anyone concerned with the welfare of children. We cannot guarantee that we know the solutions, but we are more than willing to talk about the problems.

A final point about the characteristics of our book. Ever since the first edition, we have made an effort to convey the great plasticity of young human beings, with all that this implies about both the dangers of damaging them and the opportunity and obligation to rear them to humane adulthood.

There remains the by no means empty formality of acknowledging our indebtedness to some of the many teachers and colleagues who have, by shaping our thinking, had a role in the writing of this book. We are deeply and permanently indebted to Barbara Biber, Otto Klineberg, Margaret Mead, Gardner and Lois Murphy, and Heinz Werner. The "we" that speaks from the pages of this book still very much includes L. Joseph Stone, whose influence lingers on and whom we recall with all the warm and vivid affection of years of sometimes contentious collaboration and unwavering friendship.

We are grateful to Evelyn B. Thoman and Jean Berko Gleason for comments on the fourth edition that helped plot the direction of this edition. A number of reviewers have read and commented on this book at various stages of completion. We have done our best to take advantage of their many helpful suggestions, but they are not to blame for any remaining shortcomings. We offer thanks to: Armin Arndt, Eastern Washington University, Everett W. Bovard, Queensborough Community College, C.U.N.Y.; Janet Burke, University of Lowell; Betty Franklin, Floyd Junior College; Charles E. Goldsmith, University of Wisconsin—Milwaukee; Gary W. Guyot, West Texas State University; Lillian Hicks, Houston Community College; Joan F. Henry, Los Angeles City College; James E. Hughes, Community College of Alleghany County; Mary M. Kralj, University of Maryland; Daniel Richards, Houston Community College; Tirzah Schutzengel, Bergen Community College; Randall L. Thomas, Ohio State University; and Alfred Weiss, City College, C.U.N.Y. We think these many cooks have helped us to make a nourishing broth.

Joseph Church
Alexandria Church

New York. N.Y.   September, 1983

CONTENTS

6

The Infant: Cognition 201

7

Early Influences on Development 235

12

The Middle Years of Childhood: Social, Emotional, and Physical Development 419

13

The Middle Years of Childhood: Cognitive Functioning 455

14

Adolescence and the Transition to Adulthood 497

15

Disturbances in Development 545

CHILDHOOD AND ADOLESCENCE

The Study of Development

This book is about the way people change in the course of growing up, the way they _develop_. There are a number of reasons for studying development. Some people are trying to construct a general theory of human nature, for which an understanding of development is indispensable. Others hope to find in the study of development the key to self-understanding, to knowing how they came to be the people they are. An understanding of development also contributes to the effectiveness of those concerned with the welfare of children—parents, teachers, social workers, medical personnel, among others. There are many who study development simply because it puts them in touch with one of the most delightful subjects imaginable—children.

Development as an object of scientific study is a relatively new discipline. People have been holding forth on the nature of childhood and how best to rear children for many years. Witness the biblical injunction to spare the rod and spoil the child. But there was no real awareness that childhood contained mysteries. Indeed, as the cultural historian Philippe Ariès (1962) points out, during the Middle Ages childhood was not viewed as a separate period nor were children seen as having a special way of feeling and thinking about the world. A primary concern of the times—and with good reason—was physical health and survival. People gave very little thought to children's psychological environment. Children were viewed as small-sized adults, and child-rearing methods were decreed by tradition, not by any attempt to find out what rearing conditions might be good or bad. By age seven or so children would take their preordained place in adult society, with children of the poor assimilated into the adult work force as early as possible.

The economic, political, and religious upheavals of the ensuing centuries brought new mobility in the social and economic roles people might assume. Gradually, childhood came to be recognized as a distinct period of life.

However, it was not until the middle of the eighteenth century that philosophers began to think seriously about the nature of childhood and the education of children. In 1762, the Swiss-French philosopher Jean-Jacques Rousseau published what was then considered to be a dangerous book in which a fictional child's education is put into the hands of a tutor (_Emile: Concerning Education_). The book was condemned as upsetting the natural order for two reasons. First, it held that children have capacities for thought and feeling different from those of adults. Second, it advocated a kind of education alien to the times, which stressed conformity to established values. Rousseau's "romantic naturalism" preached the inherent innocence of the child, which must be protected from the corrupting influences of society. According to Rousseau, children will by their nature seek those experiences needed for their own best individual development and fulfillment.

Educators like Johann Pestalozzi began in the late eighteenth century to translate and expand Rousseau's philosophy into educational practice. In a series of books on education for young children, Pestalozzi emphasized sensory experiences, observation, verbal expression, and the interrelationship of ideas, thus laying a foundation for the study of children's development.

In the last half of the nineteenth century, we had the first modern baby biographies, day-by-day records of infant development kept by a family member. Among these are Charles Darwin's account of his son (1877), William Preyer's of his son (1882), and Millicent Shinn's of her niece (1900). Darwin's account is particularly rich in its description of infant perception, early signs of emotional states, and language development. These biographies provided much-needed solid information about young children's capacities.

The late nineteenth century also saw the emergence of the man who has been described as the father of child psychology, G. Stanley Hall. Hall was among the first psychologists to describe children's views on a variety of topics, and how these changed with age. He solicited these views primarily through the use of questionnaires, a technique that he invented. Hall was also the first to give formal psychological recognition to the status of adolescence. His many writings were published in the early years of the twentieth century (e.g., 1904, 1907).

The literature in the field of developmental psychology has become so vast in the twentieth century that few people would claim to have a command of all the important facts and ideas. In this chapter and throughout this book, we will present a selection of what we consider to be the central facts and concepts in the field. We hope, too, to be able to convey some sense of the field as a continuing enterprise, with new ideas leading to research that in turn may force a reexamination of old concepts.

This book deals with development up to the attainment of adulthood. Needless to say, development goes on throughout life. However, we the authors are primarily concerned with what used to be known as the "formative years," the period of life in which growth and change are most rapid. Those who want to know about development in young adulthood, middle age, and old age will find a sizable literature awaiting their attention.

In this chapter, we look first at what people mean when they talk about development. We then examine some leading theories of development, together with some general concepts of how development takes place. Finally, we discuss the methods by which researchers gain new information about the facts and processes of development.

THE CONCEPT OF DEVELOPMENT

Before we can discuss the study of development, we have to say what we mean by development. This is not as easy as it sounds. Development means different things to different people, and whatever definition we give, it will not be universally accepted.

Development obviously is a process of change, but not just any kind of change. If you were to break your leg, your behavior patterns would be altered, but it is unlikely that you would think you had developed. Development refers to orderly sequences of change that go on throughout the life cycle, from conception to death, with the developing person functioning in new ways at different ages.

Some changes take place gradually, so slowly that they may go unnoticed until after the fact, while others occur with dramatic swiftness. Both kinds of

What is (develop ment?)

change, however, result in transformations such that during the life span we become successively quite different sorts of people. Emphasis on transformations views development as discontinuous. **Discontinuity** stresses the *emergence of truly novel behavior in the course of development*—talking as contrasted with babbling, drawing or writing as contrasted with scribbling—whether such changes take place slowly or swiftly.

There are, however, those theorists who insist on the **continuity** of development. Continuity theorists play down the appearance of novelty in behavior. They say, for instance, that talking is only a better organized, more effective form of babbling, or that writing and drawing are merely better controlled forms of scribbling. In addition, some thinkers view changes in behavior as discontinuous only if they occur very rapidly. For such thinkers, novel or transformed ways of acting must be considered as continuous if they occur gradually. We disagree with this view. The caterpillar does not metamorphose overnight into a moth, but moths are so qualitatively different from caterpillars that such change is a discontinuity.

We believe that all novel behavior is a product of discontinuity of development. At the same time, we recognize that there are continuous changes that do not result in transformations, but are simply accumulations of behaviors. For example, our vocabularies grow steadily, we acquire new skills and refine old ones, but we do not on that account become new sorts of people.

We have emphasized the continuity-discontinuity views of development because they underlie the thinking of the various theorists whose work we shall be discussing in sections that follow.

Although development is marked by a certain degree of regularity, there exists a wide range of individual differences, including both normal and abnormal ways of acting and reacting. For instance, all but a very few children between ages one and three progress from babbling nonsense sounds to speaking in complex, grammatically correct, sense-making sentences. But children of roughly the same age differ from one another enormously both in the number and the complexity of the words in their vocabularies, in their ability to formulate ideas, in their inclination to play with language, and in what they like to talk about. Some children develop very fast intellectually, and others not so fast. There are wide differences among young children in their ability to deal with numbers, with space and time, and with mechanical relations.

What we are saying is that our account of development must acknowledge the common path of human development, yet still recognize that there are many different ways of becoming human. We must also be aware that children grow up in diverse cultural settings, and that each culture calls forth certain human capabilities while neglecting or actively suppressing others. We have too little solid knowledge to talk a great deal about cultural differences in this book. We do know, however, that culture gets bred into the very marrow of our bones and that it is integral to the way we understand and evaluate the world. To dismiss it as a veneer of customs and manners would be a serious mistake. A cultural framework, then, whether it be the family, the neighborhood, or the larger society, is an inescapable fact crucial to our understanding of human development.

ISSUES IN THE STUDY OF DEVELOPMENT

The student of development confronts a number of problems. One of these is the matter of _description_. Good, objective description is an especially difficult accomplishment. To begin with, the observer must take note of the detailed, concrete specifics of behavior. At the same time, he or she must also be sensitive to the qualities of the behavior, the feelings it expresses. One must be careful to avoid interpreting behavior according to one's preconception of what it means. A gesture of annoyed impatience is not necessarily an expression of deep-rooted, chronic hostility, for example. Nor is an absent-minded scratching of the genital region likely to be an act of masturbation.

Another problem is that of _sequences_. Is there a constant, unchanging order in development, or is there a variety of possible sequences? As we shall see, for example, there seem to be certain fixed steps in the way children learn to count things. Beyond that, however, we know next to nothing about the order in which children can best learn to perform other arithmetical operations.

Yet another problem is that of _origins_—whether new abilities arise as a result of biological changes (according to this theory, nature is considered more important) or, at the other extreme, whether they are the product of experience (accordingly, nurture is more important). Here we see the ever-recurring nature-nurture controversy, which we shall examine in the next chapter.

There is a related problem. Do new, more mature forms of behavior depend on and incorporate earlier, more primi-

(© Jim Anderson 1981/Woodfin Camp & Assoc.)

Is a child's major inheritance genetic or cultural? A matter of biology—or society? Arguments abound over whether nature or nurture predominates in determining our development.

tive ones, do they replace them, or do old and new sorts of behavior continue to coexist? This question is central to education, which often seems to lead to new ways of behaving while leaving the person basically unchanged. During the past thirty years, for example, blacks and whites have learned to mingle freely on the job, to live in the same neighborhoods, to share certain social occasions, and to observe the accepted outward courtesies. Nevertheless, racial fears, hostilities, and stereotypes seem to linger unaltered just beneath the surface.

Another question applies to all of psychology and not just to development. This is the issue of whether behavior is the product of more or less fixed underlying traits—*dispositions*—or is a response to the demands of *situations*. Common sense is inclined to attribute behavior to the characteristics of the individual—his or her personality. On the other hand, psychological experiments often show that a person, without knowing it, is very much under the control of the situation, the pushes and pulls of stimuli. We think it is an error to take an extreme position on this issue. All of us, probably more than we realize, are pushed and pulled about by the situations in which we find ourselves. At the same time, most of us can, in varying degrees, take stock of situations and regulate our own behavior in keeping with our own notions of what is appropriate. In social situations the pressures to conformity are powerful. We sometimes find it convenient to keep our real thoughts to ourselves and to behave in ways that we find somewhat foreign to our own dispositions.

AN INTRODUCTION TO DEVELOPMENTAL THEORIES

A **theory** is an attempt to order and make sense out of related domains of reality, in this case human development. Theories make systematic statements about how facts are related. They help us understand what may look like a bewildering array of miscellaneous phenomena. Ideally, a theory will explain old facts and predict new ones. A good theory should enable us to control events, as in rearing or educating children or in setting right unproductive behavior such as delinquency.

Philosophers of science are generally agreed on the characteristics of a workable theory. A theory is supposed to be *inclusive*. That is, it should not leave important facts unaccounted for. A theory must be *internally consistent*. This means that it cannot contain general statements that contradict or are incompatible with each other. A theory should be *predictive*. That is, the principles contained in a theory should lead us by a process of logical deduction, which is called *hypothesis formation*, to find new, hitherto unnoticed facts. Another characteristic of a theory is a corollary of predictiveness. A theory should be *falsifiable*. That is, if its predictions do not work out, we know that the theory must be changed or, in some cases, scrapped. This can be stated another way, which is that a theory must be *verifiable*. It must be consistent with the facts that we discover through hypothesis testing. Verifiability and falsifiability are the two sides of *testability*. Finally, a theory must be *parsimonious.* That is, it should not include a great array of irrelevant, superfluous ideas. In other words, simple explanations are preferred over complicated ones.

In psychology, there is disagreement about whether the primary function of a theory is to *describe* or *explain*. Descriptive theories deal mainly in *principles*, and explanatory theories deal mainly in *mechanisms*.

Theories may be more or less ambitious. Some theories aim at an all-encompassing account of every aspect of human behavior. Others seek more modestly to account for a limited array of phenomena. Thus we have theories of learning, signal-detection theory, information theory, attribution theory, and theories of color vision.

None of the theories we are about to describe meets all the criteria of a good theory. We have chosen them as representative or influential ways of thinking. Others might choose different theories. The theories we shall present are interesting for two reasons. First, they help define the history of the field of developmental psychology. They illustrate how some very bright people have wrestled with the facts and tried to reduce them to a manageable system of ideas. Second, they contain a great many partial insights. These insights cannot be combined into a new theory, but all help us make sense out of at least some aspects of a rather difficult field of study. Even though they are not perfect, they may suggest new hypotheses and guide us to new discoveries.

Psychology has traditionally recognized three main areas of human functioning: _affect,_ or what we call feelings and emotions; _conation,_ will, or, nowadays, drives, motives, and intentions; and _cognition,_ knowing, thinking, and intellect. Since all behavior has components of all three, this is an artificial distinction, but it helps show the differing emphases of various theoretical orientations.

At present, three major orientations prevail. These are _psychoanalytic theory,_ exemplified by Sigmund Freud and Erik Erikson; _cognitive theories,_ exemplified by the teachings of Jean Piaget and Heinz Werner; and the theory of _behaviorism,_ nowadays identified with the name of B. F. Skinner. There is also an offshoot of behaviorism, _social learning theory,_ associated with the names of Albert Bandura and Richard Walters, which provides a convenient link to new ways of thinking about behavior and development that transcend current theories.

Psychoanalytic Theory: The Influence of Sigmund Freud

Freudian theory was very much a developmental system and has had a profound, pervasive, and enduring effect on the field of child development. However, Freud did not have a great deal of contact with children. He based his account of development on self-observations, observations of his own children, anecdotes from his friends, and reconstructions and recollections of his adult patients, all of whom were neurotic and most of whom were well-to-do females. Freud was trained as a neurologist, but shifted to the practice of psychiatry in the latter part of the nineteenth century. His theory and method of treatment, called **psychoanalysis,** emphasized conation and affection, although it contains some cognitive themes.

**The Libido.** Although Freud acknowledged a wide variety of human motives, he concerned himself mainly with the _libido,_ a person's sexual drive. Sexuality came to be called _Eros,_ after the Greek god of carnal love. Following World War I, Freud came to the conclusion that people are also driven by destructive urges, a death wish, which he called _Thanatos,_ from the Greek word for death. For Freud, instinctual drives were unconscious, so the individual might not be aware of his or her own true motives. In the course of development, different zones of the body become the focus for pleasure seeking. These are known as erogenous zones. As the libido, or Eros, changes its focus, gratification (deriving pleasure) in a particular area, or zone, is necessary for emotional well-being. Lack of gratification will have negative effects and interfere with the person's psychosexual development. The changing areas of gratification describe the first three of the so-called psychosexual stages of development: the oral, anal, and phallic stages (see below). Freud gave no systematic scheme for the development of the death wish, but he proposed that Eros and Thanatos work together to produce various complex needs and behaviors.

Freud's influence has been so extensive that many who would deny being Freudians nevertheless tend to apply his concepts to problems of emotions, motivation, and personality development. Freudian ideas underlie modern studies of the effects of maternal or paternal deprivation, of identification and its role in the formation of conscience, and of aggressiveness and its control.

Id, Ego, and Superego. Freud proposed a three-way conceptual partition of the person into *id,* the source of all the person's drives and impulses; *ego,* the rational, reality-oriented functions; and *superego,* corresponding approximately to what is called conscience, the moral and ethical sense. The baby at birth is considered to be pure id, a seething bundle of passions governed exclusively by the *pleasure principle,* which is the unbridled seeking of immediate gratification. Cognitively, the id is capable only of *primary-process thinking,* which is immune to fact or logic. Needless to say,

the greedy strivings of the id collide almost at once with reality. Out of this collision of forces and frustrations there emerges a layer of ego, made up of the practical strategies by which the developing person can take account of reality in the quest for gratification of the id. The ego, then, is thought of as governed by the *reality principle* and is capable of *secondary-process thinking,* which takes account of what is already possible or how things can be made possible. But note that the ego manipulates the id, getting it to postpone gratification for the moment. It also manipulates the environment, practicing deception or looking for detours, strictly in the interest of fulfilling the id's libidinal or destructive urges at the appropriate time. In the early childhood years, a portion of the ego is further differentiated as superego, adding an ethical-moral, socially responsible dimension to the purely hardheaded reality principle. The ego now has the tricky tasks of mediating among the conflicting demands of the ever-lusting id, the moral constraints set by the superego, and the practical demands of reality.

The most difficult job of the ego is to control the irrational id. To keep the forces of the id at bay the ego brings into play the *defense mechanisms,* ploys and stratagems that reduce the anxiety produced by severe inner conflicts. Among the better-known defense mechanisms are the following. *Repression* involves blocking unwanted ideas and cravings from consciousness. The deliberate forcing back of dangerous ideas and cravings from consciousness is called *suppression.* *Reaction formation is* going to the opposite extreme, as when one lavishes affection on a sibling one unconsciously wants to kill. _Projection_ means attributing one's own secret urges to other people, as when the rapist accuses his victim of seducing him. _Rationalization_ is inventing justifications for unjustifiable behavior. And _sublimation_ means finding socially acceptable ways of expressing forbidden impulses. A common mechanism is simple _denial of reality_, as when a woman, dying of cancer and asked by her friends what she would like for a present, replies that she would love a new set of luggage. Neither Freud nor his successors made clear what determines the ego's choice of mechanisms, or in what chronological order they develop.

The Psychosexual Stages. The differentiation of some of the id into ego and some of the ego into superego can be seen as a process of cognitive development. Side by side with this differentiation goes a series of motivational changes in what Freud called the _psychosexual stages_ of development. We have already briefly mentioned the first three of these in connection with Freud's concept of motivation.

The earliest of the psychosexual stages, the _oral stage_, coincides with infancy. The infant's main channel of gratification is the mouth and upper digestive tract, and the gratifying objects are the nipple and the mother who provides it (the thumb and pacifier can also serve as gratifiers, and later in infancy biting and chewing and swallowing solid food is a source of pleasure). For the infant, eating is less a survival function than a way of obtaining erotic pleasure. When the baby's teeth come in, biting serves the goals of both aggressive and sexual urges.

In the period we call toddlerhood, from about age fifteen months to two and a half years, the main channel of gratification ceases to be the mouth and becomes the lower digestive tract and anus, and the baby is said to be in the _anal stage_. This period, during which the baby gains control over the anal sphincter and becomes able to hold in, let go,

(© UPI)

Sigmund Freud, the founder of psychoanalysis. Freud contended that children normally pass through three early stages of psychosexual development centering around three different channels of gratification.

and actively expel feces, is supposedly marked by preoccupation with anal functions, to the point where the baby may even enjoy being spanked. Freud thought of the anal period as a time of inevitable conflict between parents and child over who is to regulate the time and place of defecation.

In the preschool years, the center of gratification shifts to the genitals, and the young child is said to be in the *phallic stage*—a designation betraying Freud's male-centered view. In the phallic stage, the child seeks genital gratification by whatever means. He or she has no concept of sexuality as the basis for a loving, caring, concerned, reciprocal relationship.

The phallic stage evolves into and culminates in the *Oedipus complex*. It is named for the tragic hero of Greek legend, King Oedipus, who unwittingly, but in fulfillment of a prophecy made at his birth, killed his father and married his mother. According to Freud, the boy directs his sexual strivings toward the mother, putting himself in direct rivalry with the father, whom he ambivalently loves, hates, and fears. Believing that his father will retaliate by cutting off the boy's penis, he develops what is called *castration anxiety*.

Moved both by castration anxiety and by love for the father, the boy, now about age five, renounces his desire for the mother's sexual favors and at the same time represses sexuality altogether. He begins to identify with the father and internalizes the father's moral code, which forms the superego. This resolution of the Oedipus complex moves the boy out of the phallic stage and into the phase of *latency*, corresponding in time to the grade school years, in which, ac-

cording to Freud, overt sexuality ceases to be a concern.

Girls go through a similar process known as the *Electra complex*. (Electra, according to Greek legend, conspired with her brother, Orestes, to kill Aegisthus, the man who, in cahoots with their mother, Clytemnestra, had murdered their father, Agamemnon, and usurped his throne.) However, Freud never formulated the Electra complex to his own or anyone else's satisfaction. It appears that for Freud all morality is transmitted from father to son, and feminists complain that Freud denied that women develop a superego.

Latency begins for the girl with the discovery that she lacks a penis. Disappointed, she renounces sexuality and enters the latency period. Notice that Freud did not regard latency as a psychosexual stage but, rather, an interval of asexuality separating the phallic and genital stages. It is the repression associated with the resolution of the Oedipus complex that accounts, in Freudian theory, for *infantile amnesia,* the fact that we can remember only isolated bits and pieces of our early childhood. It is not merely sexuality that is repressed, or desire for the parent of the other sex, but all of experience up to the trauma of real or threatened castration.

Latency ends when the physiological changes of puberty push sexual urges once more to the surface. The adolescent now enters the final stage of psychosexual development, the *genital stage*. In the genital period, raw sexual impulses and feelings can be combined with tenderness, romantic feelings, sustained love, the wish to give pleasure to another, and eventually the desire to have and rear children.

The usual progression from one psychosexual stage to the next is not automatic. It depends on the child's finding appropriate gratification at each stage. That is, in a given stage the child forms a *cathexis* (literally, an investment, in this case an investment of emotional energy) to the important gratifying elements of that stage. When the needs of a stage have been fully satisfied, the child withdraws his or her cathexis and reinvests energy in the components of the next stage. If gratification at any stage is either inadequate or too intense, however, the child may remain *fixated* at that level. A related notion is that of *regression*, development in reverse. When, having reached a new stage, the child finds that he or she cannot live up to the demands of the more mature stage, the child may regress—go back psychologically—to the last stage at which satisfaction could be found. The toddler who finds toilet training too stressful may regress to infancy, forgetting how to talk or use a spoon or perform the other usual functions of toddlerhood.

Freud spoke of adult character types that represented fixations at various stages of psychosexual development. Freudian thinking is so pervasive that adults often characterize their peers in Freudian terms. For instance, the *oral-acquisitive character* is a clinging, demanding, selfish, helpless, and an otherwise babylike person. Fixation at the anal stage comes in two varieties. The *anal-agressive character* seems still to be in rebellion against toilet training. Such people are marked by messy dress and grooming, personal disorganization, and language that resembles a hostile spewing forth of symbolic feces. The person with an *anal-retentive character*, by contrast, seems to have learned the lessons of toilet training all too well. He or she is meticulous in dress and grooming, compulsively precise in speech, thought, and action, miserly (money and other worldly possessions are said to symbolize grimly retained feces), and so unable to express feelings as to be describable as emotionally constipated. The person with a *phallic character* is the sexual exploiter, using others for selfish satisfaction and interested only in the taking of pleasure and not the giving of it: for example, the Don Juan, the sexual psychopath, or the rapist.

Another application of Freudian thought is interpreting the symbolism of dreams and fairy tales. Our dreams are full of sexual images, and our nightmares may express our most murderous impulses. Fairy tales likewise may lend themselves to psychoanalytic interpretation. Consider "Jack and the Beanstalk." What does the beanstalk itself signify? What was Jack *really* doing when he climbed heavenward on the beanstalk? What are we to make of the ogre's "Fee, fie, fo, fum"? Does the threat to grind up Jack's bones bear any resemblance to a castration threat? What significance should be attached to the ogre's wife hiding Jack in her oven? How do we interpret Jack's stealing the ogre's enchanted gold-egg-laying hen, chopping down the beanstalk, thus killing the ogre, and living happily ever after with his own dear mother and an inexhaustible supply of golden eggs?

From time to time we shall refer to Freudian ideas, sometimes to contradict them and sometimes to use them as helpful metaphors to describe and perhaps explain human behavior and development. Although Freud never stopped revising his theory, and his ideas have since been further modified by his psychoanalytic heirs, Freud formulated some powerful concepts that have been largely absorbed into our general culture. He made us aware of the pervasiveness of sexuality in human life and of the numerous disguises sexuality can assume. Nevertheless, Freud would be horrified by the sexual freedom prevailing in Europe and North America today. Freud was against hypocrisy and wanted people to stop denying motives that he found perfectly obvious. He wanted people to acknowledge sexuality, but not to practice it promiscuously. Freud was a proper, prudish Victorian who firmly believed in strict socialization, even at the risk of neurosis. His ideas underwent a reinterpretation in the course of being transported to America, where he was seen as an apostle of the uninhibited pursuit of Eros. Freud made us aware of the importance of the events and experiences of early life for the formation of adult character. And he forced upon us the realization that we often act for reasons of which we are not conscious and would prefer not to be, since we are ingenious in inventing defense mechanisms meant to deceive ourselves as well as other people about our true motives (for greater detail, see Freud, 1949).

Freudian theory has both continuous and discontinuous elements of development. Note that the driving forces in human behavior—Eros and Thanatos—remain constant throughout development. However, they become so disguised and transformed as to be unrecognizable except to the psychoanalytic eye. Note, too, that the ego has to learn a great deal to perform its nonstop juggling act, and

changes in the ego can be seen as discontinuous. Finally, the superego seems to be quite discontinuous from the self-centered, ruthlessly greedy id that is the starting point of development. This is particularly true as the superego becomes less rigidly sanctimonious and learns to tolerate reasonable departures from the strict paths of righteousness.

A Psychosocial Approach to Psychoanalytic Theory: Erik Erikson

One of Freud's best known followers is Erik Erikson. Erikson belongs to the school of psychoanalysis that emphasizes the person's rational capacities and thus is called **ego psychology.** Erikson stressed that development can be understood only in the context of society and culture. Accordingly, he proposed a series of *psychosocial stages* that represent the relationship between the developing ego and the social forces acting on it at different periods of development. Each period is characterized by an emotional conflict that must be resolved positively for healthy development.

Erikson (1964) gives us eight psychosocial stages of development covering the life span. The first five coincide in time with Freud's psychosexual stages (and latency), but the issues are not so much obtaining erotic gratification as coming to terms with the social environment and its demands. Thus feeding in infancy is viewed not in terms of oral satisfactions but of coming to have trust in the parents as reliable caregivers. The toddler does not fight the battle of the toilet so much as strive to become auton-

Table 1.1 Erik Erikson's Eight Stages of Psychosocial Development

Central Life Crisis	Positive Resolution	Negative Outcome
Birth to Eighteen Months Basic Trust Versus Basic Mistrust	Reliance on caregiver who has become an "inner certainty as well as an outer predictability" leads to development of trust in the environment.	Fear, anxiety, and suspicion. Lack of care, both physical and psychological, by caregiver leads to mistrust of environment.
Eighteen Months to Three Years Autonomy Versus Shame and Doubt	Sense of self as worthy. Assertion of choice and will. Environment encourages independence, leading to pride and good will.	Loss of self-esteem. Sense of external overcontrol causes doubt in self and others.
Three to Six Years Initiative Versus Guilt	Ability to learn, to initiate activities, to enjoy mastery and achievement.	Inability to control newly felt power. Realization of possible failure leads to guilt and fear of punishment.
Six Years Through Puberty Industry Versus Inferiority	Learns value of work; acquires skills and tools of technology. Competence helps to order things and to make things work.	Repeated frustration and failure lead to feelings of inadequacy and inferiority, affecting view toward life.
Adolescence Identity Versus Role Confusion	Experimentation with different roles toward formation of mature individuality.	Pressures and demands may lead to confusion over who one is.
Young Adulthood Intimacy Versus Isolation	Commitment to others. Close heterosexual relationship and procreation.	Withdrawal from such intimacy—isolation and self-absorption.
Middle Age Generativity Versus Stagnation	Care and concern for next generation of children. Widening interest in work and ideas.	Self-indulgence and possible social and psychological impoverishment.
Old Age Ego Integrity Versus Despair	Acceptance of one's life and death. Feeling of dignity and meaning in one's existence.	Disappointment with one's life and desperate fear of death.

Source: Adapted from E. H. Erikson, *Childhood and Society*, rev. ed. (New York: Norton, 1963), pp. 147–174.

omous, competent, and self-determining. At each stage there are opposing possible outcomes: *basic trust versus basic mistrust, autonomy versus shame and doubt,* and, in the preschool years, *initiative versus guilt.* A negative resolution of the conflicts of any stage can produce lasting inadequacies and insecurities.

We agree strongly with Erikson's views on infancy, toddlerhood, and adolescence (*identity versus role confusion*), and we will expand on his ideas in chapters dealing with these age periods. An outline of all eight stages is given in Table 1.1 (previous page).

The Cognitive Theory of Jean Piaget

Cognitive theory tries to explain behavior in terms of perceiving, learning, remembering, thinking, and perhaps language, rather than in emotional or motivational terms. The best-known cognitive theorist of recent times was Jean Piaget, originally a biologist who turned his attention first to philosophy and then to children's cognition.

Piaget's Stage Theory. Piaget believed that development consists of a series of stages, with behavior at each stage describable in terms of a single unifying theme. Thus the first two years are described as the *sensorimotor stage,* with behavior tied to the concrete here and now. The child learns about the environment by constant exploration and manipulation of materials. Ages two to six or seven are described as the *preoperational stage,* marked by growing proficiency with symbols. During this period the child can form inner representations of the world, as in drawing, dramatic play, and language. But he or she is still

not capable of systematic thought. From age seven till about eleven, the child is in the *concrete operational stage.* He or she begins to think systematically, but only with respect to the concrete world. For example, during this period, the child can begin to see relationships, but only as long as manipulable, concrete materials are available. The final stage, that of *formal operations,* begins around puberty and continues for the rest of one's life. The formal operational stage is marked by the ability to deal with abstractions, to form and test hypotheses, and to deal with the relations between relations. An outline of Piaget's stages is provided in Table 1.2 (pp. 18–19). We will talk in more detail about these stages when considering the pertinent age periods. (Also see Piaget, 1954, and Gruber and Vonèche, 1977.)

Equilibration, Assimilation, and Accommodation. Psychological development, according to Piaget, is largely under the control of physical maturation. However, the physical structures that govern knowledge and thought have to be activated by contact with things in the real world. The way the child comes to know objects is to bring ideas about things into balance with structures in the real world. The lack of fit between the child's expectations of what the structure of objects will be like and their actual characteristics creates a state of mental disequilibrium, or imbalance, which can only be set right by coming to terms with the object as it is, restoring mental equilibrium. This is called *equilibration.* Equilibration is often a two-step process. When children first encounter a new species of object, they are likely to react to it as a new example of something already known. This process is known as *assim-*

Piaget, an astute observer of children, watches spontaneous play in a Swiss park. Many of Piaget's theories first arose from naturalistic observations of his own and other children.

ilation. That is, children assimilate the object to what is familiar, distorting their perception of the object if necessary to make it fit. However, reality will tolerate only so much distortion. If the object persistently behaves in ways that it should not, children are forced to reevaluate their initial identification and modify their mental structures to take account of the special characteristics of the object. This changing of existing knowledge is known as *accommodation*.

That is, children accommodate, by modifying or reorganizing established ideas or even, if necessary, forming a new one.

On many occasions we have witnessed a baby's first encounter with a toy car, typically at age six or seven months. At first, babies treat this novel object as they would a block or a rattle. The car is scrutinized, mouthed, hefted, shaken, banged on the floor or table top, and rubbed back and forth across the surface. Up to this point, the baby has assimi-

---

Table 1.2 Jean Piaget's Stages of Cognitive Development

Stage and Age	Description	Major Developments
Sensorimotor Birth to Two Years	Development occurs through activity, exploration, and manipulation of the environment. Motor and sensory impressions form the foundation of later learning.	Begins to differentiate self from world—beginning sense of self-identity. Formation and integration of schemes—as in learning that sucking on a nipple produces milk or that shaking a rattle produces a noise. Achieves object permanence—that things exist even when not visible. Simple tool use.
Preoperational Two to Six or Seven	Child capable of symbolic representations of world, as in use of language, play, and deferred imitation. Still not capable of sustained, systematic thought.	Engages in symbolic play—can represent something with something else. Some decline in egocentricity—can take greater account of others' points of view. Develops language and drawing as modes of representing experience.

Source: Adapted from H. Ginsburg and S. Opper, *Piaget's Theory of Intellectual Development* (Englewood Cliffs, N.J.: Prentice-Hall, 1969).

---

lated the car to the general category of plaything. But now the baby notices something different. When the baby slides the car sideways, it drags, just like anything else. But when the baby slides the car forward or backward, it moves in an unexpected way: it rolls. The baby is now obliged to accommodate, to adapt previously formed ideas to take account of the special quality, rollability, of wheeled objects. Further accommodations take place, of course, as the baby encounters friction-motor and wind-up cars, which have properties different from those of free-rolling cars.

Accommodation assumes that the baby is maturationally ready to form an appropriate new concept. However, there are limits to the baby's ability to accommodate. For example, it is gener-

Table 1.2 (*continued*)

Stage and Age	Description	Major Developments
Concrete Operations Six or Seven to Eleven	Child becomes capable of limited logical thought processes, as in seeing relationships and classifying, as long as manipulable, concrete materials are available.	Becomes aware that some aspects of things remain the same despite changes in appearance (conservation). Can mentally reverse a process or action (reversibility). Can focus on more than one aspect of a situation at a time (decentration). Can deduce new relationships from sets of earlier ones (transitivity). Can order things in sequence (seriation). Can group objects on the basis of common features (classification).
Formal Operations Twelve Through Adulthood	Can reason logically and abstractly. Can formulate and test hypotheses. Thought no longer depends on concrete reality. Can play with possibilities.	Can deal with abstract ideas. Can manipulate variables in a scientific situation. Can deal with analogies and metaphors. Can reflect on own thinking. Can work out combinations and permutations.

ally accepted—although unproven—that young children are maturationally incapable of accommodating to written language, that is, learning to read.

The Schema. The term that Piaget used to describe a mental structure or idea was *schema* (plural, *schemata*), sometimes implicit, sometimes capable of being put into words, but experienced mostly as vague feelings. Schemata can embrace either segments of reality or reality as a whole. Partial schemata eventually become integrated into more inclusive patterns of knowledge, which eventually form a coherent (but not necessarily correct) framework for understanding the self and the world. Schemata generally lie outside awareness; they are the filters and frameworks that guide our perceptions and actions. We generally become aware of them when they are violated or clash with some aspect of reality. So, for example, we laugh when, at the circus, a tiny car stops and disgorges an endless throng of clowns. But violations of our schemata do not always provoke laughter; they can also move us to shock, nausea, and terror. Horror movies work because they violate our expectations—our schemata—of the normal. We acquire the ability to form sentences schematically. Long before we suspect that there is any such thing as grammar or syntax, we are applying grammatical and syntactical rules schematically. We develop a schema of our own body, so that if we lose an arm or leg, the schema continues to exist in the form of a _phantom limb_, which we continue to experience as part of the body.

Piaget also talked about a related concept, the _scheme_. A scheme was whatever structures underlay patterns of skilled action. The child was said to have a sucking scheme, for instance, or a grasping scheme. In any event, schemata referred to knowledge, schemes to action. Toward the end of his life, Piaget decided to collapse these two notions into one. He stopped talking about schemata and lumped everything under the heading of schemes. We have chosen to retain the earlier distinction.

Biological Maturation and Experience. We have already said that Piaget viewed development as an interaction between physical maturation and the environment, but we did not say what we meant by **maturation.** With the passage of time, children get bigger, they _grow_. In addition, they undergo organizational changes in anatomy and physiology. For instance, the nerves that lie outside the cortex acquire insulating sheaths that make possible finer, more precise forms of action. There are shifts in the way the brain functions, as indicated by changing brain wave patterns exhibited in the EEG (electroencephalogram). Our endocrine systems go through a succession of reorganizations. Perhaps the most dramatic manifestation of maturation is puberty, becoming sexually mature, but other, more subtle maturational changes go on throughout life. Although "growth" and "maturation" are sometimes used interchangeably, they stand for quite different aspects of physical development.

In the Piagetian view, the physical structures needed for certain kinds of thinking mature in a fixed sequence. This maturing of capacities does not automatically bring about new forms of behavior. Interactions with appropriate environmental situations activate these new capacities and make them a part of the child's functioning mental equipment. When enough such activations occur, the child enters a new stage of cognitive operations.

Stage-Free Concepts in Piagetian Thought. The disciples of Jean Piaget have become so preoccupied with investigating his stage theory that they forget that Piaget gave us a whole array of concepts (some of them borrowed from other workers) that simply describe primitive thinking in general and may extend over several stages. Thus, for instance, there is an evolution in thinking about cause and effect, from _dynamism_, where no explanations are called for, through _animism_, the idea that objects act under their own power, to _naturalism_, where one invokes the principles of science. (These concepts will be dis-

cussed in detail and in action in the description of cognitive functioning in preschool children, Chapter 11.)

There is also the phenomenon called by Piaget *primary adualism*, the experienced primitive intermingling of self and surroundings, as in the neonate's synchronous bodily movements to the cadences and rhythms of adult speech (see p. 132).

Another important concept that is not limited to a single stage is *egocentrism*, which means neither self-centeredness nor selfishness. Stated simply, egocentrism means that children have a hard time realizing that other people's views of and attitudes toward reality may be quite different from the child's own. What the child perceives is not *my* version of the world, viewed from a particular position in space and as a consequence of individual involvement, understanding, and values. Instead, it is simply *the* world, complete and obvious and absolute.

In fact, there are two types of egocentrism, one of which breaks down into two subtypes. The first type is *spatial egocentrism*, which refers to a limited ability to understand how different vantage points in space render various things visible or invisible. In the classroom, for example, the teacher typically can see the rear wall of the room, whereas the students see the front with its blackboards. The second type is *social egocentrism*, which takes the forms of, first, affective social egocentrism and, second, cognitive social egocentrism. Affective social egocentrism refers to limits on the child's ability to judge how others react emotionally to various situations. Cognitive social egocentrism refers to limits on the child's awareness of other people's psychological processes in general.

The problem is not that children are ignorant of things like remembering, having feelings about, thinking, wanting, and all the rest. It is that they assume that other people's reactions must be identical to their own. Children (and many adults) are indeed egocentric but probably less so than Piaget thought. We will have a great deal to say on how the child progresses from an egocentric to a relativistic orientation.

Realism is yet another concept that extends beyond a single stage. Like egocentrism, it does not mean what it at first seems to mean. Realism as a property of immature thought refers to the inability of children to distinguish clearly among differing sorts of realities, mixing them all together in a common sphere. Thus, dreams are not internal imaginings but real events taking place in real, external space. We shall see later that there are special varieties of realism such that pictures get confused with the things they represent, words have the same reality as the things they designate, and rules of moral conduct are a concrete part of the natural order rather than something created by human beings.

Note that Piaget's cognitivism addresses a somewhat limited and specialized domain—that of abstract logic, mathematics, physics, and chemistry. His focus was on children's thinking, with little regard for their motivations or emotions. His work on moral judgment rarely extended beyond minor infractions of convention. Most of the work on *social cognition*, which regards the child as a self-taught psychologist, has been done by Piaget's successors, not by Piaget himself (Flavell and Ross, 1981).

Piaget's theory of development is clearly discontinuous in nature. The child's entire approach to reality is transformed as he or she progresses from one stage to the next. Piaget's stage-free concepts likewise represent discontinuities. There is a qualitative difference, for example, between being egocentric and being nonegocentric (even though nobody is ever completely one or the other), or between a "realistic" view of the world and one that recognizes quite distinct levels of reality.

The Cognitive Theory of Heinz Werner

There is considerable overlap in the views of Piaget and Heinz Werner. However, Werner had no particular interest in stages and looked instead for general principles that could be applied to the overall growth of the organism (Werner, 1973, 1978). He proposed a number of developmental polarities to describe the contrast between immature and mature forms of thought. Werner also placed greater emphasis on the emotional components associated with cognition—for him an empathic fusion between self and world was a very important consideration. Werner termed his conceptual framework the _organismic-developmental approach_, which was in some ways far more ambitious than Piaget's. Werner sought not merely to describe individual human development but also to apply the same principles to the historical evolution of ideas, to the contrasts between "primitive" and advanced cultures, and to the understanding of human psychopathology.

Werner's central polarity was summed up in the _orthogenetic principle._ This principle says that development, whether of knowledge or of skilled action, "proceeds from a stage of relative globality and lack of differentiation to a state of increasing differentiation, articulation, and hierarchic integration" (Werner, 1957). To simplify this idea, we can say that, according to Werner, there are three stages in coming to terms with a new experience. At first we receive a global impression in which the various features and components are hard to distinguish. Next, we begin to sort out the different features that go to make up the whole. Finally, we reintegrate the separate features into a new, sensible, coherent whole. For instance, many of us can remember the first time we saw the engine of a car. At first encounter, it appears as a poorly differentiated, burbling, throbbing, ticking, whirring, faintly ominous metal mass enmeshed in a tangle of wires and sprouting mysterious pipes and hoses. With experience—and perhaps some instruction—we become able to differentiate the visible components: the engine block, the manifolds, the carburetor, the fuel pump, the distributor, the generator, the radiator, and so forth. And as we learn about the engine's functioning, including the movement of parts hidden from view, we become able to see the engine as an intelligible, orderly, stable, integrally functioning system. This now differentiated and articulated whole is quite different from the global, undifferentiated, and unarticulated mass with which we began. In later chapters, we will see other examples of the orthogenetic principle at work in human functioning.

Werner postulated a number of other developmental polarities. Certain of these, like the _egocentric-relativistic polarity_, are virtually identical to some of Piaget's concepts. Two other Wernerian polarities are closely linked to each other. These are development from *rigidity* to *flexibility* of thought and action, and from living in a *labile* (*unstable*) world to living in a *stable* one. In the unstable world of the young child, change can come without warning; there are no limits to what can happen, and safety can be achieved only by adhering to rigid, ritualistic patterns of behavior. The child is like an adult living in constant anticipation of earthquakes, landslides, volcanic eruptions, tornadoes, sinkholes, and so on, plus, in the child's case, the possibly malevolent workings of all kinds of supernatural forces. As the world becomes more stable, reliable, and manageable, the child becomes aware of new possibilities for effective action, and behavior can become more flexible and adaptive.

Werner, unlike Piaget, had a strong interest in language, its functions, and its endless convolutions and variations. He had a special interest in expressive language, language that tells us more about the state of mind of the speaker than about the objective realities surrounding him or her. Werner loved to study figures of speech such as metaphors. Werner, unlike the public Piaget, was very much aware of sexuality. More or less like Piaget, he paid little or no attention to the concept of learning. Piaget at least gives us equilibration, whereas Werner never mentions how knowledge or skills are acquired.

Note that both Piaget and Werner were discontinuity theorists. However, Piaget was a stage theorist, which implies periodic total transformations of the person's cognitive functioning, whereas Werner was a stage-free theorist. For Werner, different strands of functioning—motor development, language, social relations—could go their separate discontinuous ways, with little regard to what was happening elsewhere in the organism. That is, Werner did not think of various discontinuities as being necessarily synchronized. It was also Werner's view that discontinuous change can occur so slowly and gradually that it is only when we examine widely separated age periods that qualitative differences become apparent—for example, it may take years for the beginning reader's fumbling efforts to give way to the fluent literacy of the highly skilled reader.

Behaviorism (Learning Theory)

What is nowadays called **behaviorism,** or **learning theory,** has its historical roots in the doctrine of **associationism,** linked primarily to the seventeenth-century philosopher John Locke. The prevalent belief about human nature in Locke's day was the doctrine of innate ideas, according to which we are born with all our allotted stock of knowledge. In opposition to this way of thinking, Locke proposed that we think of the newborn baby as a *tabula rasa,* or blank slate, on which events write their lessons in the form of knowledge. This knowledge consists of associations, a set of connections between events that occur together in time and space. Notice that Locke, unlike today's behaviorists, gave people credit for piecing these recurrent associations into a coherent pattern that they could internalize and use in their thinking and behaving. Associationism was a first statement of what is now called **environmentalism,** assigning great weight to nurture (accumulated experience) rather than to nature.

Ivan Pavlov and Classical Conditioning.
The first scientific validation of associationism came from the work of Ivan Pavlov and his collaborators on conditioned reflexes. The model of **classical** (also called **Pavlovian**) **conditioning** is the famous experiment in which a dog is taught to salivate at the sound of a bell. It works like this: one begins with an *unconditioned stimulus (US)*, one that automatically brings about a particular reaction, the *unconditioned response (UR)*. For instance, a food pellet placed in the dog's mouth is a reliable US for the UR of salivation. Given such a US-UR sequence, one can then present a new, neutral, arbitrary stimulus (the *conditioned stimulus* or *CS*), which is, in this case, the bell presented before the US. By preceding the US-UR sequence with a CS, we now have a bell-food-salivation sequence. Repeat this often enough, and the bell alone, without any intervening food, will cause the dog to salivate. It is as though the bell has become a signal to the dog that food is on its way. More technically, the bell has become a conditioned stimulus for the *conditioned response (CR)* of salivation. This process is diagramed in Figure 1.1.

By the same logic, the mother becomes a potent CS for the baby because she is associated with need satisfaction, as in feeding. In this view, the mother begins as a neutral stimulus but soon comes to signal that feeding or other pleasant experiences will occur. Let us emphasize that classical conditioning implies passivity. Things are done to the organism which, in reacting, forms associations.

Hundreds of studies document that people can be classically conditioned. However, susceptibility to classical conditioning seems to require a certain degree of development since it seems not to occur in neonates, and, even when achieved in older babies, is often unreliable and transitory (Fitzgerald and Brackbill, 1976; Sameroff, 1971).

John B. Watson and Behaviorism. A somewhat stripped-down version of Pavlov's ideas was introduced into the United States by John B. Watson under the name of behaviorism (Watson, 1919). Watson (1928) made some rather extravagant claims about the powers of classical conditioning. One of his most notable claims was that if given exclusive care of a child during its early years, he could shape it into any kind of person imaginable. His prescriptions for child rearing included rigorous avoidance of strong emotional involvements, although in his later years he regretted the harshness of his early advice to parents.

Watson demonstrated conditioned fear in an eleven-month-old boy named Albert (Jones, 1974), a famous example of a classical conditioning experiment. Albert was shown a white rat of which he initially showed no fear. A loud noise (the US that caused a fear reaction [UR] in Albert) was sounded every time Albert reached out toward the rat. After repeated associations of noise and rat, Albert withdrew in fear from the rat, which had now become a conditioned stimulus (CS). Albert's fear of the rat was the conditioned response (CR). In fact, Watson's demonstration of conditioned fear was much less clearcut than he might have wished (Harris, 1979), but it is the best example available.

Edward L. Thorndike and Instrumental Conditioning. Thorndike (1911) was concerned with a form of associationism known as *instrumental conditioning*. Un-

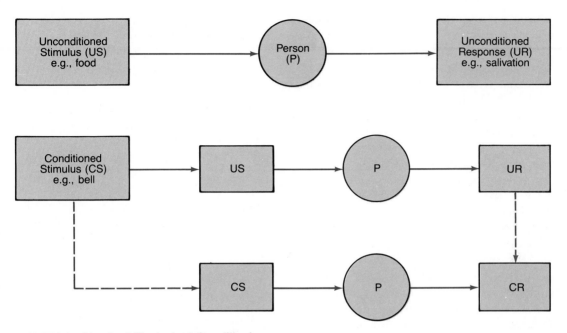

FIGURE 1.1   Classical (Pavlovian) Conditioning

like classical conditioning, which assumes an essentially passive learner, instrumental conditioning requires that the organism itself *do* something, which then produces favorable or unfavorable reactions from the environment. The basic notion is that when the organism is in a state of need, as when it is hungry, it becomes randomly active. Certain of its actions happen to produce need-reducing consequences, such as finding food. The consequences of action are called *reinforcers*. Pleasant consequences are called rewards or *positive reinforcers*. Unpleasant consequences are called punishments or *aversive reinforcers*. Thorndike tried to eliminate punishment ("annoyance," as he called it) from his theory of conditioning, but it kept cropping back up. Actions that receive positive reinforcement are retained, whereas the unproductive, unrewarded actions *extinguish*, or drop out. Thus

what began as mindless random activity can, through selective reinforcement, come to seem orderly, intelligent, and purposeful.

Unlike classical conditioning, instrumental conditioning can be demonstrated in the newborn baby. The newborn can, for instance, learn to turn its head to one side to obtain a mouthful of milk as a reinforcer. Indeed, newborns can learn to vary the rate or force with which they suck on a nipple so as to keep a picture in sharp focus. As this example illustrates, not all reinforcers are concrete satisfiers of tissue needs (thirst, temperature control, avoidance of pain, and so forth). Many psychologists have therefore come to prefer the concept of informative *feedback*, the environmental echoes of our own behavior that tell us how effectively we are acting. This process is diagramed in Figure 1.2 (over).

Although instrumental and classical

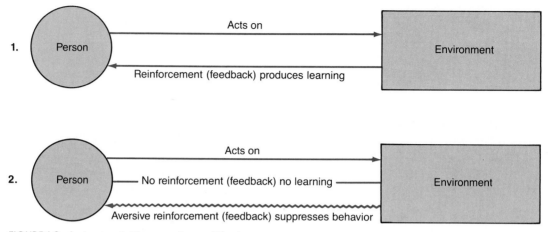

FIGURE 1.2   Instrumental (operant) conditioning

conditioning are usually talked about as different processes, they can be combined. For instance, a pigeon can learn, through instrumental conditioning, to peck a key to get food; but it can also learn, through classical conditioning, to wait until a certain light comes on or pecking will be in vain. The rat learning to find food in a maze is being active, but it is also learning to respond to cues, such as choice points in the maze, given off by the environment. The main difference is whether the association is between two external stimuli, as in Pavlovian conditioning, or between action and reinforcement, as in instrumental conditioning.

As a theory, behaviorism says that development is simply the accumulation of associations, whether acquired classically, instrumentally, or through some combination of the two types of conditioning. No known change takes place in the organism, since exactly the same laws of learning apply throughout life. As such, behaviorism preaches continuity of development. In sum, there is reason to question whether behaviorism can

be considered a developmental theory at all.

B. F. Skinner and Neobehaviorism. B. F. Skinner (1938, 1948), today's foremost spokesperson for what he calls **neobehaviorism,** has gone Locke's *tabula rasa* one better by giving us the doctrine of the *empty organism.* Remember that Locke's *tabula rasa* eventually gets filled in with knowledge, whereas Skinner's empty organism stays empty. The associations that guide the organism's behavior are all on the surface, in the form of reinforcement contingencies. Skinner's empty organism is of course a metaphor. Skinner recognizes perfectly well the physiology underlying behavior and even the existence of subjective states. However, the subjective states, according to Skinner, are under the control of reinforcers, past and present. At first, the organism acts blindly. It is only when the organism has learned which actions lead to pleasure or pain that it can act in anticipation of one or the other.

Skinner's thinking has closely followed Thorndike's, with a couple of exceptions. One exception is the distinction Skinner has drawn between instrumental conditioning and **operant conditioning.** Thorndike thought of instrumental acts as fixed, always involving near-identical sequences of neural discharges and muscular contractions and relaxations. This concept got him into trouble with those who took a more cognitive view of the learning process. For instance, it could be demonstrated that a rat that had learned a maze by running could still go to where the food was if the maze were flooded and the rat was obliged to swim. The concept of an *operant* gave the organism more flexibility. It did not matter what particular movement patterns were involved in obtaining reinforcement, it was only the consistency with which reinforcement could be obtained. Thus, the rat in a box could push a lever to get food, but it made no difference whether it worked the lever with its forepaw, its hindpaw, its nose, or its tail. An operant, therefore, is a whole set of instrumental acts, all of which produce approximately the same consequence. At the human level, the outcome is likely to be very much the same whether one says, "Pass me the salt, please" or "May I please have the salt?" These two somewhat different utterances are both equivalent and therefore constitute a single operant.

Behaviorism is nowadays being weakened from within. One of its strongest appeals has been that it offered practical applications in the real world, as in programed instruction or in what is called *behavior modification.* In fact, those who practice behavior modification not only deal with observable behavior but also act to change people's inner states—knowledge, ideas, attitudes, feelings.

(© Christopher S. Johnson/Stock, Boston)

Neobehaviorist B. F. Skinner developed the idea of the empty organism. He suggests that our behavior is guided not by anything innate but by reinforcement contingencies; that is, though we act blindly at first, experience soon indicates which actions lead to pleasure and to pain and we thereafter act in anticipation of them.

Pure behaviorism, however, would deny that such inner states can cause behavior. Behaviorism is also being undermined by one of its offshoots, social learning theory, to which we shall return in a moment.

Behaviorism has had one solid triumph. As the philosopher Gustav Bergmann (1954) has pointed out, we behavioral scientists have all become methodological (as opposed to metaphysical) behaviorists. That is, we will not accept as fact anything that cannot

(© R. Leavitt)

A parent talks to a two-month-old, who watches and listens intently. Modeling, a key tenet of social learning theory, has been shown to play an important role in children's acquisition of language.

be verified by observation. Behaviorism used to restrict verification to objectively observable and measurable actions and reactions, but today's behaviorists are willing to accept as legitimate data not only the expressive qualities that tell us how someone feels about what he or she is doing but even self-reports of feelings, attitudes, and intentions.

Social Learning Theory

The liberalization that has taken place within the behaviorist school helps explain the rise of **social learning theory** (Bandura and Walters, 1963; Bandura, 1977). Social learning theory has made two major contributions beyond conventional learning theory. First, it allows for *learning without reinforcement*. Second, it has given us the concept of **modeling**—

what used to be known as teaching and learning by example. For instance, parents who smoke cigarettes are very likely to have children who will later smoke cigarettes. Social learning theorists often equate modeling with imitation, which we do not consider quite accurate. In some experimental demonstrations of modeling, as when the child mimics the aggressive behavior of an adult model, the acquired behavior may be a very close copy of the original. But imitation includes the pointless repetition of senseless acts that seem largely irrelevant to normal development. In our view, modeling is more properly thought of as observational learning in which the learner picks up whole styles and categories of behavior rather than particular acts and action sequences. Indeed, in observational learning research with monkeys, the learner learns from the model's mistakes, which means learning by nonimitation. Modeling seems to be a key mechanism in learning to talk. The words the child learns are imitations, if only imperfect ones, of words he or she hears, but the use the child makes of those words is anything but imitative. Imitation will not account for the way babies absorb from those around them the rules of grammar and syntax and speech patterning so that children end up talking like other members of their community even when they are saying things that they have never before heard said.

In his presidential address to the American Psychological Association, Albert Bandura (1974) implied that he has taken social learning theory so far from its origins that it begins to sound like a description of recognizable human beings. In fact, it may no longer qualify as a theory but as one version of an expanding consensus among psychologists as to what is human in human behavior. A summary of the theoretical positions we have just described will be found in Table 1.3.

DEVELOPMENTAL PRINCIPLES AND MECHANISMS

In our discussion of theories of human development we have already alluded to a number of developmental principles, such as Werner's orthogenetic principle and all the polarities suggested by Werner and Piaget. However, there are several additional principles that do not belong to any one theory but that are important to an understanding of how development proceeds. Some of these

will come up in the context of later discussions, but others deserve treatment in their own right.

Principles are descriptive; they tell us *what* happens but do not tell us how it happens. In addition to principles, then, we need to be aware of the key explanatory *mechanisms* that tell us *how* things happen the way they do and help us understand the principles so that we can make sense out of the process of development. Modeling, for example, is a mechanism. Finally, we must examine some ambiguous cases, which from one angle look like descriptive principles but from another like explanatory mechanisms.

Principles. We begin with some principles that are perfectly objective and offer

Table 1.3 Theoretical Views of Development

Theoretical Orientation	Representatives	Emphases

Psychoanalytic	Sigmund Freud	Psychosexual stages
		    Oedipus and Electra complexes
		Structure of personality
		    Id, ego, superego
		Mechanisms of defense

	Erik Erikson	Stages of psychosocial development Successive resolutions of developmental conflicts
Cognitive	Jean Piaget	Cognitive stages and structures Equilibration through assimilation and accommodation Egocentrism and realism
	Heinz Werner	Orthogenetic principle of development (from global to articulated) Other developmental polarities
Behaviorism	B. F. Skinner	Operant conditioning
Social Learning Theory	Albert Bandura	Learning without reinforcement Modeling and identification

no ground for debate. The first of these is the double principle embodied in what are called the **growth gradients**—the directional components of growth. Growth before birth is governed by the *cephalo-caudal* (head-to-tail) *growth gradient* and the *proximo-distal* (near-to-far) *growth gradient.* The cephalo-caudal gradient describes the fact that the head end of the organism takes the lead in development, whereas the lower portions are elaborated later. The proximo-distal gradient tells us that growth proceeds outward, from the central axis toward the periphery. This gradient is most conspicuous prenatally in the development of the limb buds from the trunk and, in turn, of the still more remote hands and fingers and, later, feet and toes from the limb buds. We mention these phenomena of prenatal development because they seem to have some analogies in postnatal physical development. Babies control their heads before their arms, and their arms before their legs. Babies control the whole arm and hand as a unit before they can control their fingers (except, of course, for the well-sucked thumb).

A second noncontroversial principle is that of *asynchronous growth.* Asynchronous growth refers to the fact that different parts of the body (including the inner organs) grow at different rates at different times, leading to a constant shift in body proportions. It is the fact of asynchrony that keeps the adult from ending up with the same body proportions as the newborn baby. It is during adolescence that one becomes vividly aware of asynchronous growth, with the nose and chin sprouting to change the character of the face, and legs and arms projecting from dresses or trousers and sleeves that seem to have shrunk overnight.

A third principle is that of *discontinuity of growth rate.* Whereas asynchronous growth refers to the body's components, **discontinuity** refers to the size (primarily height) of the body as a whole. Human postnatal growth goes on in two spurts separated by a sort of plateau. Growth is very rapid in infancy but slows down by about age five and continues at a reduced pace until the time of the pubescent growth spurt, about age ten or eleven in girls and twelve or thirteen in boys. In late adolescence, growth again slows down and stops entirely somewhere around age eighteen or so in females and twenty-one or so in males.

We now enter the realm of the subjective, where the principles have to be taken partly on faith. It is our view that human development brings with it both *an increase in self-awareness* and an accompanying *increase in self-direction and self-control.* We will describe in later chapters the expansion and elaboration of self-awareness. Self-awareness implies two sorts of differentiation. It implies an increased differentiation of self from environment. This means a decrease in instantaneous, unthinking responding and an increase in reasoning about situations. It also brings with it a detachment of self from self, a capacity for *duplicity.* In ordinary usage, duplicity means deceit, but that is only part of the meaning intended here. Here it means that one self watches and analyzes the second self in action, which means that we become capable of self-criticism and even of laughing about ourselves. It also means that we are capable of keeping our true thoughts to ourselves while we act in keeping with the demands of situations.

We have spoken, too, of the schematization of self and world, mentioning that the body schema can survive the loss of some portion of the anatomy, as in the preservation of a lost extremity in the form of a phantom limb. This, as we have noted, is an experience in which the missing part of the body seems to be functional and capable of feelings. Here we want to mention a contrary phenomenon, that of the **phantom environment.**

There are two sorts of phantom environments. The first is the product of schematizations so strong that we are unable to perceive that external reality has changed. Skinner, in *Walden Two* (1948), describes how one can fence in a flock of sheep with electrified barbed wire. After the sheep have had a small bit of experience with the noxious results of touching the wire, one can substitute plain string for the wire and the sheep will continue to avoid the string just as they did the now-vanished wire. Carr and Watson (1908) taught white rats to enter one arm of a T-shaped maze to find food. Once the rats had learned which way to turn, the experimenters blocked the previously correct arm and moved the food to the other one. The rats went on indefinitely banging up against the barrier that kept them from their accustomed feeding place and never did find the food that was now easily accessible to them elsewhere. Human beings likewise fail to adapt to changing circumstances; when we say that a person "is living in the past," we mean that person inhabits a long-gone phantom environment. But there is a second kind of phantom environment. We have already spoken of realism and have mentioned that one particular form of realism is called *symbolic realism.* Symbolic realism is also known as *verbal realism, word realism,* and *linguistic realism.* That is, we can create a whole imaginary universe out of words and then act as though that universe actually exists. People take seriously no end of entities and forces that exist only by virtue of having been indicated symbolically. We take it for granted that children believe in Santa Claus or the Tooth Fairy, but we rarely acknowledge that adults can build their lives upon a belief in deities and demons, none of which to the best of our knowledge has ever actually been observed. Political leaders find it easy to create phantom environments in which our feelings and actions can be easily manipulated. They populate the world with diabolical enemies and portray themselves as angelic beings of superhuman status. We emphasize this to remind you that our own image of cognition includes the human capacity for highly irrational behavior.

Mechanisms. We now switch to concepts that offer, however vaguely, explanations of developmental change. We have already mentioned **maturation,** the systematic reorganization of anatomical and physiological subsystems that permits the emergence of new, unprecedented behaviors. Children can have sexual intercourse from an early age, but it is only after the maturational changes of puberty that males can ejaculate sperm, females ovulate, and conception take place. But maturation is not a wholly **autogenous** (self-generating) process. It is at least partly under the control of environmental factors, permitting us to speak of *stimulation-induced maturation.* In animals, rearing conditions can affect brain development and function and endocrine activity (Wallace, 1974). Female

Learning is much more than the principles of learning described in learning theories. It comprises a variety of kinds of learning—about our environment, about values and judgments about sources of information, about causes and effects, and about the people around us.

rats raised in an all-female environment reach puberty at a significantly later age than those raised in mixed company (Vandenbergh, 1974). The fact of stimulation-induced maturation becomes an important consideration when we return in Chapter 2 to the collaboration between nature and nurture in development.

Modeling is an important mechanism of development, but not all by itself. Modeling leads to a more general state of affairs called *identification*, where we come to think, feel, and act in harmony with one or more members of our community, where we feel at home with them, where we have the sense of being ourselves an essential element in the communal totality. Note that identification is a concept common to both psychoanalysis and social learning theory. However, there is a world of difference between identification through modeling and identification through frightened submission to a father who threatens castration.

Learning theories have given us some important principles of learning, but only of a rather narrow kind. *Learning* as a mechanism of development has to embrace a great variety of learnings, such as learning about space and time, learning values and how to make value judgments, acquiring facts, information, knowledge, and ideas, and understanding relationships ranging from kinship systems and authority relationships to the many kinds of cause and effect. We have to learn something about history and government and economics and the way people live around the world. Most basically, perhaps, we have to learn enough about how people function to be able to live with them without endless friction, conflict, and unhappiness.

One mechanism of learning about which we will be saying a great deal is *role playing*. This ranges from the make-believe of the toddler and preschool child to the adopted personalities of adolescents. Role playing permits one to understand how another sort of person feels from the inside by becoming—almost—that other person. Adults do their share of role playing, too, but for somewhat different reasons, such as projecting a socially desirable image.

One issue about learning remains. According to Piaget, learning always requires activity, initially motor activity and later on symbolic substitutes for actual doing. On the other hand, classical conditioning tells us that learning can be passive, the product simply of things done to the organism. It is also obvious that children can learn from watching television, although not necessarily the things we would like them to learn. But there are both passive and active approaches to watching television or a movie or a play, or for that matter to reading a book. In the passive mode, one simply surrenders and lets images have their will of one's inner life. In the active mode, one watches critically, letting one part of the self react while the other part thinks about both what is being offered and how it is reacted to. We must note further that much learning is unconscious. We learn the rhythms of our days and the layouts of familiar spaces without taking any special note. Indeed, many of our most basic and fixed values are absorbed without an explicit awareness. Piaget is probably correct in contending that intellectual knowledge is best acquired by active or symbolic manipulation of materials. On the other hand, passive learning can and does go on, perhaps accounting for the great bulk of what we think we know.

The Ambiguities. At the beginning of this section, we said that there are some developmental concepts that might, according to how one viewed them, seem to refer to either principles or mechanisms. One of these is *attachment*. As a principle, attachment simply means that babies and parents normally fall madly in love with each other and that this love is an important ingredient in everything they do. As a mechanism, attachment can be seen as vital to complete identification, which in turn seems essential to sound development. We must note that young people, in asserting their mature independence, often go through a period of *counteridentification*, in which they try to be as unlike their parents and other identification figures as possible, but this does not weaken the basic argument. If they had not formed deep identifications to begin with, they would not have to battle so ferociously to assert their own individual uniqueness.

This brings us to a related ambiguity. Not only must babies and parents become solidly attached, but there also comes a time to undo the old attachments so that new, more appropriate ones can take their place. The relationship between parents and child has to change constantly to take account of the child's growing competence and independence. There is, in other words, a developmental principle-mechanism of *letting go*, in which the parents relinquish some of their authority and children transfer to others some of their attachment. Letting go is not easy, but unless it comes to pass, new and equally satisfying kinds of parent-child relationships will not have a chance to emerge.

We have spoken of self-awareness and self-control. What do they tell us about the limits on our ability to define the kind of person one wants to be and then to set out to become that person? We think that a certain amount of *self-shaping* is visible in almost everybody—that, after all, is what role playing is about—which qualifies it as a principle. The mechanism of self-shaping remains undefined. One could call it will power, but that would be to resort to symbolic realism. Let us simply accept that people can do it—some more than others, but nobody completely. The most autonomous of us are to some extent a product of forces over which we have near-zero control.

Our final ambiguity is what Robert W. White (1959) called *competence motivation* or *effectance*. White was battling the then-prevalent notion of deficiency motivation, whereby one became active only in response to some physiological need or tension. Once all one's physiological needs were seen to, it would seem to follow, one would slip off into a blissful nothingness. In fact, as White pointed out, the well-satisfied human organism has an urge to be up and doing. And one of the things we like doing best is to cultivate our skills, to become competent. Despite a wide range of individual differences, in most people an urge to do things well appears to be a major mechanism in development (Harter, 1981). On the other hand, almost everybody's competence improves with the passing of time, which would make the idea of competence motivation redundant and make increased skillfulness a rather minor descriptive principle. Whether effectance is viewed as a universal motivating force may depend on how one defines competence. Things that other people get excited about set our heads to nodding, and things that we find exciting seem to induce deep somnolence in others. If our students spend a lot of their time in class sleeping, it may be because they are exhausted from their pursuit of competence in other realms.

We now leave off theorizing and turn to the methods by which people gather information about human psychological development.

METHODS IN DEVELOPMENTAL RESEARCH

Theories require facts, and the way to obtain facts is through research. In this section, we shall look at some of the techniques by which researchers gather factual material. In the chapters yet to come, we will be drawing on a considerable body of research and will occasionally describe a study in some detail. You will be able to infer from the discussions a great deal about how developmentalists go about the job of gaining knowledge. But some points about these methods should be made explicit in advance.

Naturalistic Observation

We must stress first of all that accurate, objective observation is at the heart of all useful research. We recommend that all students receive supervised practice in the arts of observing and recording behavior. At first, one learns to observe whole individuals in whole situations, capturing the total flow of behavior as it is happening. A basic check of accuracy is to compare observations made of the same event by two or more people. Videotapes and films are extremely useful, since one can compare what one thinks one has observed with an unvarying record that can be repeated indefinitely. However, making films and videotapes requires skill. One must be close enough to the person to capture telltale changes of facial expression or posture, but far enough away to include a goodly part of the background, which often gives clues to the causes of the person's behavior. Good observing and recording are useful not only to prospective scientists, teachers, and clinicians, but also to future practitioners in such fields as art (even abstract artists begin by learning to draw), police work, and journalism. Indeed, all of human communication has as its starting point the accurate perception and interpretation of the words, manner, gestures, facial expressions, postures, and body cues of self and others. Supervised practice in observation can enhance such perception and interpretation. Thus, if there is a competence of almost all-purpose applicability, it is skilled observation (Almy and Genishi, 1979; Cohen and Stern, 1978; Irwin and Bushnell, 1980).

The scientific study of development derives, as we have said, from baby biographies, observational records of single children over a span of time. Among the best-known of the baby biographies are those kept by Charles Darwin (1877), Wilhelm Preyer (1882), and Millicent Shinn (1900). These accounts today have a charming, antiquated quality. They are longer on interpretation than on actual observation, but they still contain much useful information.

Observational records take four main forms. First, there is the *running record,* a narrative account that tries to capture everything that happens within a given period. Such records can often be analyzed selectively for items of particular interest. Second, there is the *anecdotal record,* an account of behavior episodes that illustrates special aspects of functioning. Third, there is the *impression record,* a summary of the total flow of events, with those events that typify the group style and emotional atmosphere treated in some detail. Fourth, specifically for research purposes, there is the *selective record,* which focuses exclusively on some preselected form or aspect of activity, such as sharing, block building, fighting and quarreling, dominance, and, increasingly, facets of parent-child interaction. A number of devices are used to help the observer keep track of the occurrence of the behavior(s) under study. One of these is the precoded *checklist,* which enables the observer simply to make a mark next to the code number for a given behavior. An *event recorder* is in effect an electronic checklist, with the observer pressing precoded buttons to make a record on a moving tape. *Rating scales* allow the observer to assign a numerical value to such traits as emotionality, involvement with the group, or quiet versus active play (see Figure 1.3 on p. 36 for a sample rating scale). Rating scales can be applied to things as well as to people, and one can assign ratings of maturity or creativity to things children make, such as block structures or paintings. When necessary for research purposes, an observer can use *time sampling,* observing each child in a group for a fixed period and then moving on to the next child, in either a random or predetermined order. This ensures that all members of a group contribute equally to the accumulated observations. And, of course, observers now have at their disposal a great array of observational technologies, from videotape equipment to electronic eavesdropping devices, which permit them to spy on and record behavior inaccessible to the unaided senses. Some researchers even attach tiny radio transmitters to their subjects' clothing.

An important part of learning to observe is learning to be unobtrusive, so that the subjects soon lose interest in the

	1	2	3	4	5	
A. Cooperative						Uncooperative
B. Leader						Follower
C. Generous						Selfish
D. Clumsy						Adroit
E. Timid						Aggressive
F. Energetic						Lethargic
G. Involved						Detached

FIGURE 1.3 Sample Rating Scale

observers and their equipment and treat them as part of the background. Even though the skilled observer can tell when children are putting on a performance for his or her benefit, it is better to arrange conditions so that the children can behave spontaneously and unselfconsciously. Luckily, children adapt quickly to the presence of the experienced observer who knows how to melt into the woodwork.

An excellent example of observational research is John Gottman's study (1983) of how children aged three to nine get to know each other. Two sorts of artifice were involved in the research project. First, pairs of unacquainted children were brought together in the home of one member of the pair. Second, all the observations were made via audiotape recordings. Gottman was able to arrive empirically at such scoring categories as communication clarity and connectedness, information exchange, establishing a common-ground activity, exploration of similarities and differences, conflict

resolution, positive reciprocity, and self-disclosure. Note, though, that it took some 800 hours to transcribe 80 tapes, and 4,200 hours to code the transcripts.

Correlational Studies

Much of our knowledge about child development is based on *correlational studies.* In strict usage, correlational studies permit one to calculate a **coefficient of correlation,** a numerical statement of how subjects' distribution of scores on one variable is related to their distribution on another variable. (One can also do calculations involving several variables, but let us stick to the simple case.) For this purpose, one obviously needs measures that yield a range of values—age, height, weight, IQ, temperament, socioeconomic status, and so forth. The value of a correlation coefficient can vary from +1.0, indicating a perfect positive relationship between two variables, through 0.0, indicating that the variables have nothing to do with each other, to -1.0, indicating a perfect negative, or inverse, correlation. For example, until adulthood there is a strong positive correlation between age and height; a child's IQ cannot be predicted from his or her height (no correlation); the more cigarettes a pregnant woman smokes per day, the less her baby will weigh at birth (a strong negative correlation). In human affairs, perfect correlations are almost unheard of, so one must consult a table to find out what values of correlation are needed for samples of a given size before the relation can be trusted.

Note, too, that statistical significance of correlations does not imply psychological significance. With a large enough sample of subjects, correlation coefficients on the order of .05 become statistically reliable, but we would hesitate to postulate a strong connection between variables yielding so low a coefficient. It is for this reason that we prefer "statistical reliability" to "statistical significance."

Obviously, the most widely used variable in developmental studies has been age, but one can of course study children all of the same age and look at the correlations between other measures, as between socioeconomic status and intellectual functioning.

We must repeat the oft-stated warning that correlation does not imply causation, although it is tempting to find a cause-and-effect relationship in a high correlation. For instance, parents who batter their children turn out in many cases to have been battered children themselves. Otherwise stated, there is a high correlation between being a battered child and, once grown up, being a child batterer. But it is not safe to infer a simple causal link. It may indeed be true that the experience of being battered teaches one that this is how one deals with children. However, others might interpret this correlation to mean that the tendency to wreak violence upon immature human beings is transmitted via the genes from generation to generation. Furthermore, there may be no direct link at all between two things that covary; poverty is inversely related to IQ, but the actual causal links have to do with nutrition, mobility, and other factors that limit learning possibilities.

The Formal Experiment

The scientific ideal in research is the *formal experiment* (which does not have to be carried out in a laboratory). The point of an experiment, as contrasted with a correlational study, is precisely to attempt to isolate a causal agent. For instance, there is a correlation between violent behavior and watching TV programs that portray violence (Liebert, Neale, and Davidson, 1973). If, however, we want to know whether watching TV violence makes children more aggressive, we would have to carry out an experiment more or less along the following lines. First, one would have to find a group of children of reasonably similar backgrounds and determine, during a period of observation, that they were all about equally likely to practice violence in everyday situations (any child who deviated too greatly from the group would probably have to be eliminated). This group of children would then be randomly assigned to either an **experimental group,** which would be exposed to one or more films depicting violence, or to a **control group,** which would spend an equal amount of time watching nonviolent films, or even in doing something else altogether, like going for a walk. After the treatment period, the experimental and control groups would be compared to see if either showed a greater inclination to aggressive behavior. This could be done either by observing the children in a free play situation or by testing them in a situation designed to provoke an aggressive response. The variable under study (in this case exposure to aggression in the film) would be the **treatment** or the **independent variable,** which is the hypothesized cause, whereas the changes observed in the subjects' behavior as a result of watching the film would be the **outcome** or **dependent variable.** In fact, an experiment similar to the one just described has been carried out (Friedrich and Stein, 1973). We shall talk about it later because its fascinating but complex pattern of findings would take us too far afield from our discussion of methods (see Chapter 10).

There are two approaches to selecting subjects for an experiment. One is to match experimental and control subjects as closely as possible on all possibly relevant variables. This is not always easy. In the study we have just described, for instance, it would be very difficult to know how much time the various children spent at home watching TV, and who watched what kinds of programs (Friedrich and Stein did their study in a camp setting, where they had direct control over most of the variables). An alternative is to draw random samples of children from a larger, heterogeneous population. It is important that we learn to work with large and truly heterogeneous samples. The smaller and more homogeneous the group from which we choose, the more likely it is that we will select biased, not truly comparable samples. In fact, much of our knowledge is questionable because it is based all too heavily on white, middle-class American samples, which we have tended to accept as representative of an abstraction called the Universal Child. Small samples are all too likely to be unrepresentative, and the statistical tests that we use tell us only that differences between experimental and control groups have thus-and-such a likelihood of being due to chance, and not whether either group is truly representative of the population at large. People are not fully sensitive to the peculiarities of sampling (Nisbett and Ross, 1980), and we suspect that many of the controversies and contradictions in psychology arise from our practice of using too-small samples and assuming that subjects are more or less interchangeable.

In designing an experiment, both independent and dependent variables must be *operationalized*—that is, defined in terms of concrete, observable manipulations and behaviors. If the dependent variable is to be some sort of subjective state, whether anger or contentment, we have to say in advance how these will be manifested. Following treatment, experimental and control groups are compared, often in terms of statistical tests, to determine the *significance* or *reliability* of differences between the average performances of the two groups. These terms refer simply to the probability that an observed result is merely the product of chance fluctuations. In general, psychologists accept a probability of .05 as justifying confidence in a finding.

Having said this much, we must go on

to say that the formal experiment is used less in developmental studies than in other areas of psychology. There are several reasons for this. The formal experiment varies only one independent variable at a time, holding the others constant. We have now come to recognize that important behavior is rarely under the control of a single variable, and we have to find ways to keep track of the numerous forces that may be at work in any given situation. Further, the one-variable-at-a-time approach assumes that the various independent variables are indeed independent of one another, so that one can be changed without affecting the rest. This, too, is rarely the case; changing the main variable alters the meanings of the variables supposedly left untouched. In fact, they are all part of a system, and changes in one part of the system inevitably affect the others: one cannot shorten one side of a square and expect the square to retain its squareness. The use of control groups loses much of its meaning when one is interested only in age differences. One allows nature to take care of the independent variable, age, and tests successive age groups on the same measure.

If one really wants to study a treatment effect with members of a single age group, it often seems more economical to use two *comparison groups* in place of an experimental and a control group. Such an arrangement is called a *quasi-experimental design*. Each of the comparison groups receives a contrasting but related treatment. A quasi-experiment that used comparison groups was carried out by K. E. Nelson (1977) in a developmental study derived from social learning theory. Nelson wanted to study learning through modeling of linguistic forms. He undertook to teach two new

syntactical forms, one each to two groups of two-and-a-half-year-olds. In interacting with one group, the experimenter made it a point to use complex verb forms, statements involving future, conditional, and past tenses. In interacting with the second group, the experimenter made frequent use of so-called tag quesitons, which add emphasis to what has been said, as in "That certainly jumped high, *didn't it?*" or "That didn't work, *did it?*" Each group consisted of three boys and three girls, all at approximately the same level of language development as judged from conversations tape recorded in the children's homes. The children were exposed individually to five one-hour treatment sessions spread over two months. The treatment—the independent variable—consisted of inserting the syntactical forms into normal conversational exchanges while the child and the experimenter played together. The outcome measure—the dependent variable—was the children's spontaneous use of the forms to which they had been exposed. To make sure that the outcome observations were the result of the experiment and not simply of normal developmental progressions, Nelson had to test both for the treatment given and for the treatment withheld in each group. All six children in the tag question group acquired tag forms, but none began using the complex verb forms. By contrast, all six children in the complex verb group picked up the verb forms, and one subject also began using tag questions.

One cannot draw any sweeping conclusions from a study based on twelve children without follow-up studies on retention. The examples given of posttreatment utterances suggest, however, that the children had learned new speech forms and were not merely parroting things the experimenter had said. Thus one more empirical block has been added to the structure of social learning theory as a basis for the acquisition of new syntactic forms.

Another problem with formal experiments is that of **ecological validity,** whether the treatments to which children are exposed and the tasks on which they are tested bear any resemblance to or have any relevance for real life. Merely placing a subject in a laboratory setting may significantly alter his or her behavior. Belsky (1980) conducted a study ostensibly directed at styles of mother-infant interaction but in reality meant to compare behavior at home and in the laboratory. The setting apparently did not affect the babies, but in the laboratory, mothers showed a marked increase in attending to their babies, talking to them, responding to them, and stimulating them. This does not imply that laboratory research cannot be ecologically valid. It is less a matter of the setting than of the stimuli or tasks to which the subject is asked to respond, although, as in the Belsky study, setting and task may interact.

Yet another problem is that of time. Experiments, by definition, are short-term enterprises, whereas significant developmental change takes place slowly, and cause and effect may be widely separated in time. (However, we should note that some experiments providing intellectual and emotional enrichment for children from less-favored backgrounds extend over a period of years.) One cannot as a rule confine young human beings in specially designed environments that will mete out constant treatments.

The problem of time merges with the problem of ethics: what sorts of manipulations of development are legitimate, whether simply to satisfy scientific curiosity or to look for improved methods of child rearing and education? To some extent, the problems of time and ethics can be solved by using animal subjects. Even though there are some fascinating analogies between animal and human development, many people balk at extending findings from animal studies to the human level. Animal research has its ethical problems, too. All in all, a number of developmental researchers seem to be turning from formal experimentation, in which they are in charge of the experimental manipulations, to the natural experiment in which one capitalizes on the independent variables that arise by accident in the everyday world.

The Natural Experiment and Related Methods

The **natural experiment** (sometimes called the **experiment of nature**) differs from the formal experiment in that the experimental treatments are not under the researcher's control. Certain conditions happen to occur, and the experimenter takes advantage of the opportunity to assess their impact on the individual(s). For instance, studies of the effects of traumatic birth, of drugs given during labor, of fetal malnutrition, of abuse or neglect, of home versus adoptive versus foster-home versus institution rearing, of brain damage, of separation of identical twins early in life—all are done as natural experiments, with the investigator using independent variables that he or she could not ethically bring to pass. This does not mean that natural experiments have to be done ad hoc, like crisis research. We know that certain experimental conditions occur all the time, and it is merely a matter of stationing ourselves at the points of most likely occurrence. One difficulty, of course, is that the variable under study may be confounded with endless extraneous variables. For instance, in studies of abnormal behavior, possible psychological causes are usually intermingled with possible physical causes, making it hard to draw conclusions. Consider the many studies that have been done on the babies of mothers who drank heavily during pregnancy, with such consistent results that we now speak of the Fetal Alcohol Syndrome (which we shall describe later). But heavy drinkers tend to be light eaters, so possible malnutrition has to be taken into account. Heavy drinkers are also likely to be under psychological stress, which affects physiology, leading to another possible complication. And so on.

All comparisons between children of differing backgrounds can be seen as variations on the method of the natural experiment. Thus comparisons on a common measure of children differing with respect to sex, socioeconomic status, race, or culture have as their antecedent variables conditions that the experimenter can select but not bring into existence.

Cross-Sectional Versus Longitudinal Studies

For a long time, age differences alone were considered a significant independent variable in developmental research. In recent years, we have become aware of the necessity of taking into account a great many additional background factors. Nevertheless, age differences continue to be the defining feature of developmental research.

There are two main approaches to studying behavioral differences associated with age differences. The **cross-sectional method** compares the performance of representative groups of children differing in age. All subjects are tested on the same measure or set of measures, such as word knowledge, problem-solving ability, or motor skills. Differences in performance are assumed to reflect differences in mental maturity. For many years, developmentalists were content to make age comparisons with regard to anything that came to mind, sometimes with a view to constructing age-graded tests. Such studies produced a great deal of knowledge about the average age at which children could do various things. These averages were called *norms,* and studies seeking such averages were called **normative studies.** We should be grateful for the information available to us about norms of child development (even though they may change with the passing generations), but normative studies have gone out of fashion for two reasons. First, they were unrelated to any particular theory and second, being cross-sectional, they gave little hint of the mechanisms involved in progressing from one developmental level to another.

Contrasted with the cross-sectional approach is the **longitudinal method,** by which researchers trace development in the same child or group of children over an extended period of time. Longitudinal studies can follow development in general or some special aspect of development. For instance, there is great interest in relating conditions present at birth to later functioning. Such research is of necessity longitudinal. Many recent studies of language development have been longitudinal, since many changes take place very rapidly and it would be very difficult to plot out developmental sequences using data from cross-sectional samplings. However, one of the more ambitious longitudinal studies, the so-called *Genetic Studies of Genius*, set out to scrutinize all areas of functioning over the life span of a set of gifted children. This study was launched in the 1920s by Lewis Terman and Catherine Cox and is still going strong under the supervision of a group at Stanford University (Terman, 1925; Terman and Oden, 1959; Oden, 1968; Sears, 1977).

The cross-sectional method has the clear advantage of being less expensive and time consuming than the longitudinal method, but it has drawbacks in addition to those already hinted at (lack of theory, disregard of developmental mechanisms). For one thing, cross-sectional studies are plagued by the problem of representativeness. Even when one controls for all the obvious background variables in forming comparison groups, individual differences may still be so great as to cast doubt on one's findings. A related problem is that of historical change. Childhood is not the same from era to era, and eras change fast among children. For instance, we know a girl who, when in the sixth grade, would not, like her classmates, think of going to a party that included boys. Two years later, when her brother was in the sixth grade, mixed-sex parties, including a goodly amount of necking and cheek-to-cheek dancing in the dark, were taken for granted. We can only guess at the

mental functioning a few years hence of children who have grown up with access to the family's computer.

A different kind of historical change menaces the longitudinal study. Apart from fads in research, there are some enduring changes in what researchers consider to be important strands to follow. Thus a longitudinal study designed in the 1920s holds little interest for us today. There used to be heavy reliance on IQs, and past longitudinal researchers have been somewhat bemused to find that this supposedly stable measure of intellectual ability could fluctuate over a wide range in some individuals (Anastasi, 1982). Nowadays almost anyone plotting a longitudinal study would build in measures to trace the development of Piagetian thought. The *Genius* study failed to include a control group of average-IQ subjects whose development could be compared with that of the gifted group.

In general, people have become reluctant to make long-term commitments to longitudinal studies. Any given longitudinal study is for keeps, and if you realize somewhere along the way that you have chosen the wrong variables for study, there is no way to get your subjects to go back and start over. However, less ambitious longitudinal studies, lasting two or three or five years, make sense. Over such a relatively short time, one can trace in detail a number of significant transitions. A study of the first three years of life, for example, can enable us to follow a great many interesting developments, including some important strides toward the mastery of language. The longitudinal method allows us to see subtle changes that might be missed or averaged out in cross-sec-

(© Christopher K. Walter/The Picture Cube)

A family in the Toros Mountains of Tashkent. The barriers to cross-cultural research appear almost insurmountable when attempts are made to study development in less familiar settings.

tional studies. In addition, only by studying the same individuals over time may we gain insight into the detailed processes of change. Furthermore, a number of people have been working on ways to combine the cross-sectional and longitudinal methods, so that the researcher can cover a wide range of ages with only a few years of study. We are not yet aware of any major findings from this approach, but it holds a good deal of promise.

Cross-Cultural Studies of Development

Anthropology has been with us for a long time, but it has seldom been particularly developmental in its orientation (the work of Margaret Mead [e.g., 1930] comes to mind as a notable exception). For a long time, the only interest of developmentalists in non-Western cultures seemed to be in proving the inferiority of these cultures. More recently, there has awakened an enlightened, sympathetic concern with development in a variety of cultural settings. This concern has led to a great deal of research of rather dubious significance. There seem to be two problems. One is whether to study each culture on its own special terms, without making comparisons with other cultures, or else to take Western norms as one's standard and compare children from non-Western cultures on standard test procedures. The second, interlocking problem is the language barrier, which can be circumvented only imperfectly by working through an interpreter. For example, several investigators have reported that African children follow the Piagetian sequence of cognitive development, but much more slowly than Western children. However, a study by Nyiti (1976), who is a native speaker of the Kimeru dialect of the Meru people of Tanzania, shows that Meru children, schooled or unschooled, when interviewed in their own language showed concrete operational thought at roughly the same age as European children. Cole and Scribner (1974) report that they can find no consistent or characteristic cognitive differences between young Western and non-Western children, although their common human capacities are eventually elaborated or transformed according to the teachings of their various cultures. We continue to accept Joseph Glick's (1975) gloomy conclusion that the barriers to cross-cultural research appear almost insurmountable.

Clinical Approaches to the Study of Development

All the methods we have discussed so far are addressed to discovering general facts, principles, and mechanisms of development, with individual subjects serving merely as representatives of whatever category of people they belong to. Gordon Allport (1942) called such studies **nomothetic.** The **clinical approach,** by contrast, is **idiographic,** aimed at the understanding of one particular, unique, idiosyncratic individual. Let us avoid a possible misunderstanding. Clinical studies should not carry the connotation of the study of disturbed individuals. Clinical psychologists do indeed deal mainly with people troubled by some malfunction, but the clinical method can be applied to the study of anybody at all. We must also point out that nomothetic methods, such as standardized tests, can be applied to idiographic studies. Part of the vocabulary of idiographic description necessarily consists of comparisons with other people. Conversely, idiographic studies may have nomothetic implications. A thorough understanding of one person may suggest new ways of thinking about people in general. In fact, very few people other than clinical psychologists (and biographers) spend a major part of their careers doing idiographic studies, but it remains as a legitimate and interesting field of endeavor.

The basic tool of the clinical investigator is the *interview,* encouraging the individual to reveal his or her inner universe. Obviously, no one knows himself or herself so thoroughly, or can verbalize so well, as to be able to tell all to an interviewer, even if he or she wanted to. Thus the interviewer is forced to draw out the subject, make interpretations, and be sensitive to nonverbal cues to feelings. Note that not every inconsistency in people's accounts of themselves is an indicator of deception. Some inconsistencies may indicate ambivalence, shifting attitudes, or an ill-defined domain of experience. To help the process along, the clinical investigator gives the subject toys, puzzles, questionnaires, and tests to elicit information that is not accessible in direct oral question-and-answer form.

Two main sorts of tests are used. One is the **psychometric test,** which yields a numerical score (or a set of scores called a *profile*) that can be compared with norms derived from a supposedly representative sample of the population at large. (In fact, the normalization samples used for most tests underrepresent poor people and members of racial minorities.) Intelligence (IQ) tests are the best known of the psychometric instruments, but there are also psychometric tests of such personality factors as dependence, initiative, ability to concentrate, sex-role identification, and self-esteem. The second sort of test is the **projective test,** which asks the subject to make sense out of unstructured or unorganized stimulus materials. Examples of projective tests are various sets of ink blots (of which the Rorschach is the best known) in which children are invited to find depictions of things or events; thematic apperception tests (TAT), in which subjects are asked to make up stories about pictures; and world tests, in which subjects are asked to arrange figures and models representing different sorts of people and things—family members, police officers, animals, furniture, houses, cars, barns, fences, and the like—into whatever patterns they wish. Scoring systems have been devised for some projective techniques—the task of drawing a person can be treated and scored as either a psychometric or a projective test—but the main emphasis is on the clinician's intuitive judgment of what subjects are revealing about themselves. Other ways to keep people talking are to play games with them, to share work projects, or to introduce supposedly remote topics of conversation.

The clinical investigator, like a detective, can turn to people other than the subject for important information. Par-

(© Robert V. Eckert Jr./The Picture Cube)

Testing in kindergarten. Both psychometric tests, which yield numerical scores that can be compared with supposedly representative norms, and projective tests, which ask for an interpretation of unstructured materials, are administered.

ents, teachers, the family doctor, all can be sources of important insights. Many clinical investigators see the logical last step of their inquiries as a *case history,* an integrated word portrait of the individual from all the information gathered from the various sources used. The case history may contain diagnostic clues, pointing to major areas of concern, and it may also suggest therapeutic or educational means to help the individual function more effectively.

Piaget's studies evolved from observations of his own children to what he called his *clinical method.* Initially, he used interviews, but he soon began to supplement them with concrete tasks, like sorting toys into categories or interpreting drawings or making drawings. But almost from the beginning Piaget's goal was nomothetic. He used idiographic methods, but only as a way to capture general principles. Indeed, it is one of the shortcomings of Piaget's work that he gave very little attention to the fact of individual differences. It is our strongly held opinion that a complete view of the human condition must be aware both of shared humanity and of personal individuality. This is not to say that all manifestations or individuality are equally admirable; it is merely to point out that the theorist who ignores them does so at his or her own peril.

ETHICAL CONSIDERATIONS IN RESEARCH WITH CHILDREN

We have mentioned the ethical problems raised by certain kinds of experimental manipulations, but all sorts of research and clinical work with children are subject to ethical abuse. The generally accepted code of ethics governing work with children is the one adopted by the Society for Research in Child Development (1982). The Society's code is to be found in the back pages of its membership directory, of which new editions are published from time to time.

We intend only to point to some of the highlights of this code. The important thing is for prospective researchers to be aware that there are deep ethical problems in working with children and to make sure that they understand them thoroughly before embarking on a project.

The core precept of the Society's code is that the child's welfare must take absolute precedence over the investigator's curiosity or convenience. No matter how scientifically crucial the research problem, it cannot be studied if its procedures threaten the child with the slight-est physical or psychological harm. In general, research projects are subject to prior review by boards (set up by either the fund-granting agency or the investigator's home institution) competent to judge their value, procedures, and potentialities for harm. Note that the board is not expected to do a cost-benefit analysis, weighing the worth of the knowledge to be acquired against the risks of damage. If there seem to be serious risks, the project, no matter what its worth, has to go.

The child (beyond infancy) must be told in advance about the procedure of the study so that he or she can make a considered decision whether to take part. Further, the child may withdraw from the study at any time, even though such a withdrawal might send the researcher into a deep depression. Parents or guardians must of course be fully informed and their consent obtained; this takes on special importance in research with babies.

Some research involves deception, as when subjects are given false information about how well they did on a task. Such misinformation is given to affect the child's feelings of self-worth in order to see how such feelings influence other behavior, such as aggression. However, deception is legitimate only when no other approach is feasible. The child who has been deceived must have the deception explained immediately afterward to remove any ill effects. For instance, children told that they performed poorly on a task may be told that the apparatus was not working right and then given a second chance, this time achieving a perfect score. (One might question, though, whether a second deception is a satisfactory undoing of the first one.)

The code of ethics forbids the release of information about any identifiable individual. There is one exception. If a child shows signs of serious problems, the parents should be told and steered to possible sources of help.

Some researchers dislike these restrictions, either because they feel that they can safely be guided by their own ethical sense and resent what feels to them like unnecessary regulation or because they feel that too great a concern with ethics can stifle scientific creativity. However, there have been enough abuses to make a codified set of rules desirable, and the torrent of new research shows no signs of abating.

We turn in Chapter 2 to the debate over the contributions of heredity and environment to development and offer our own suggestions about how to reconcile this issue.

SUMMARY

1. Development is the way in which people change with age, i.e., the orderly sequence of changes that occur throughout the life cycle.

2. Development can be considered to be continuous, with behaviors emerging simply as more evolved forms of earlier behaviors, or discontinuous, with qualitatively new behaviors emerging, whether slowly or swiftly.

3. When studying development, the following are desirable: good objective descriptions of the behavior to be studied; the sequence involved, if any; origins of the behavior (nature or nurture); whether new behaviors replace older ones or coexist with them; and whether behaviors represent the workings of underlying dispositions or responses to situations.

4. A good theory helps make sense of reality, explaining known facts and predicting new ones. Theories should be inclusive, internally consistent, predictive, testable (falsifiable and verifiable), and parsimonious.

5. Psychology recognizes three main areas of human functioning: affect, or feelings and emotions; conation, or drives, motives, and intentions; and cognition, or knowing, thinking, and intellect.

6. Three main orientations prevail in psychology today: psychoanalytic theory (Sigmund Freud, Erik Erikson); cognitive theories (Jean Piaget, Heinz Werner); and behaviorism (B. F. Skinner). Social learning theory (Albert Bandura, Richard Walters) is an offshoot of behaviorism.

7. Freud's psychoanalytic theories have profoundly affected the field of child development, and his theory of unconscious drives has influenced modern thinking about emotion, motivation, and personality development. Freud acknowledged many human motives, but emphasized the libido, that is, the sex drive, or pleasure-seeking impulse. He believed that personality has a three-part structure: id (instinctual), ego (realistic), and superego (moral-ethical). The ego controls what it perceives to be dangerous impulses by various defense mechanisms. Freud proposed that our well-being depends on gratification experienced in particular zones of the body during the course of psychosexual development, that is, the oral, anal, phallic, and genital stages.

8. Erik Erikson divided the life span into eight stages of psychosocial development. Each stage is characterized by an emotional crisis with two possible outcomes, one favorable and one unfavorable. The resolution of each crisis determines subsequent development.

9. Cognitive theory explains behavior in terms of internal processes, especially those involved in knowledge and thinking. Jean Piaget, the best-known cognitive theorist of our day, divides cognitive development into four distinct stages: the sensorimotor stage (from birth to two years), the preoperational stage (from two to six or seven years), the stage of concrete operations (from six or seven to about eleven years), and the stage of formal operations (from about age twelve on).

10. Piaget's general mechanism for the formation of new knowledge is equilibration, the resolution of cognitive imbalance by a new balanced organization at a higher level. Equilibration involves two processes—assimilation and accommodation. As children develop, they integrate various schemata into organized, inclusive patterns of knowledge, which eventually form a coherent vision of self and world. Piaget regards development as an interaction between physical maturation (organizational changes in anatomy and physiology) and experience.

11. The cognitive theory of Heinz Werner overlaps that of Piaget. The focus of Werner's approach is the orthogenetic principle, which states that development is a movement toward increasing differentiation, articulation, and integration.

12. Behaviorism, or learning theory, views development as the accumulation of associations acquired through conditioning. In Pavlovian (classical) conditioning, an organism forms an association between an unconditioned stimulus and a neutral stimulus so that the neutral stimulus becomes able to elicit the previously unconditioned response.

13. Unlike Pavlovian conditioning, operant (instrumental) conditioning, proposed by Edward L. Thorndike, assumes that an organism is active, producing favorable or unfavorable reactions from its environment. Through selective reinforcement, desired behaviors can be elicited. B. F. Skinner believes that the developing organism learns a repertory of responses linked to reinforcement contingencies, the patternings of actions and reinforcers.

14. Social learning theory, as seen in the work of Albert Bandura, has developed out of the behaviorist school. Its chief departure from operant theory is that it allows for learning without reinforcement and through modeling, or observational learning.

15. Certain principles (descriptions of what happens) and mechanisms (explanations of how things happen) are important to an understanding of development. Some principles are objective; growth gradients, for example, describe the directions in which growth occurs. Other principles are subjective and must be taken partly on faith; symbolic realism, for example, describes the fact that we can create an entire, imaginary universe out of words and then act as if that universe actually existed.

16. Mechanisms explain developmental change. Role playing, for example, is one important mechanism of learning.

17. Some developmental concepts can be principles or mechanisms; attachment, for example, can describe what happens between parents and children as well as how identification occurs.

18. Accurate, objective observation is at the heart of all useful developmental research. Observational records take four main forms: running records, anecdotal records, impression records, and selective records. Checklists, rating scales, and time sampling are useful supplements to observation.

19. The correlational study has always been a popular method of developmental research. It attempts to gauge the relationship between two variable factors, expressed in terms of a coefficient of correlation. This type of study only reveals observable relationships; correlation does not imply causation.

20. The classical experiment attempts to isolate a causal agent in behavior by studying a control group and an experimental group. Experimental and control groups should be matched according to all relevant factors so that observed differences can be safely attributed to experimental

manipulation, or the independent variable. The dependent variable is the change in the subject's behavior as a result of the independent variable. The classical experiment in its ideal form has severe limitations for the study of development.

21. In the natural experiment, the independent variables are not under experimental control. The investigator takes advantage of circumstances that he or she could not control, for ethical or practical reasons.

22. The cross-sectional method compares the performance of children of different age groups on the same measure or set of measures. The longitudinal study traces development in a given individual or group over an extended period.

23. Cross-cultural studies of development have been attempted, but the barriers to effective research of this kind still appear to be insurmountable.

24. The clinical approach aims to understand one particular individual. Its basic tool is the interview, in which the subject is encouraged to talk about himself or herself and the world. The clinical investigator gives two main kinds of tests—psychometric, which yield numerical scores comparable to norms derived from a representative sample, and projective, which require interpretation or arrangement of unstructured or ambiguous stimuli. Based on this information, the clinician assembles a case history.

25. The generally accepted code of ethics governing work with children is the one adopted by the Society for Research in Child Development. Its basic concern is that the child's welfare is of the utmost importance. No matter how urgent the research problem, it cannot be studied if the techniques involved threaten to harm the child physically or psychologically in any way.

KEY TERMS

associationism, 23
autogenous, 31
behaviorism (learning theory), 23
classical (or Pavlovian) conditioning, 24
clinical approach, 44

coefficient of correlation, 36
continuity, 6
control group, 38
cross-sectional method, 41
discontinuity, 6

ecological validity, 40
ego psychology, 14
environmentalism, 23
experimental group, 37
growth gradients, 30
idiographic study, 44
longitudinal method, 41

SUGGESTED READINGS

Bandura, A. *Social Learning Theory*. Englewood Cliffs, N.J.: Prentice-Hall, 1977. The latest version of social learning theory and its implications by one of its founders.

Erikson, E. H. *Childhood and Society*. Rev. ed. New York: Norton, 1963. Although we often disagree with Erikson, he is a stimulating writer with many provocative ideas.

Flavell, J. H., and Ross, L. (eds.). *Social Cognitive Development: Frontiers and Possible Futures*. New York: Cambridge University Press, 1981. Under the auspices of the Social Science Research Council, several social scientists discuss social cognitive development in terms of their own theoretical positions and research and the implications of their work for the field of social cognitive development.

Freud, S. *An Outline of Psychoanalysis*. New York: Norton, 1949. Freud was always his own best advocate, and here is his summing up, completed shortly before his death in 1939. Note his difficulty in coming to terms with the Electra complex.

Gruber, H. E., and Vonèche, J. J. (eds.). *The Essential Piaget*. New York: Basic Books, 1977. A detailed scholarly analysis of Piaget's contribution. Contains many selections from Piaget's own writings.

Lerner, R. *Concepts and Theories of Human Development*. Reading, Mass.: Addison-Wesley, 1976. An excellent survey of the technical issues in theory building and research.

Phillips, J. L., Jr. *Piaget's Theory: A Primer*. San Francisco: Freeman, 1981. An introduction for the layperson to the cognitive theories of Piaget.

Piaget, J. *The Construction of Reality in the Child*. New York: Basic Books, 1954. A presentation of the fundamental ideas developed by Piaget in his period of systematization.

Pulaski, M. A. S. *Understanding Piaget*. Rev. ed. New York: Harper & Row, 1980. Unlike Freud's and Skinner's, Piaget's theoretical writings are highly obscure, and are best approached through an interpreter. This book, and that by Phillips listed above, offer excellent introductions.

Skinner, B. F. *About Behaviorism*. New York: Knopf, 1974. A heroic and ingenious, if largely unsuccessful, attempt to fit a wide spectrum of human behavior into the Procrustean framework of operant conditioning principles.

Werner, H. *Developmental Processes: Heinz Werner's Selected Writings*. Vols. 1 and 2. S. S. Barten and M. B. Franklin (eds.). New York: International Universities Press, 1978. An excellent collection of some of Werner's important but sometimes inaccessible writings.

CHAPTER 2

Heredity and Environment in Development

In Chapter 1, we identified the question of *origins* as one problem in defining development. Is development to be considered the unfolding of a scenario laid down in the structure of our genes? Is development the gradual accumulation and reworking of experience? Thus posed, the question resolves itself into the nature-nurture controversy. Nowadays most developmentalists would reject an either-or answer to the nature-nurture controversy. Instead, they would insist that the only sensible stance is acceptance of interaction, the working together of heredity and environment in the course of development. Nevertheless, occasional thinkers crop up espousing one extreme or the other of the nature-nurture debate. For this reason, the issue cannot be ignored.

The study of biological inheritance belongs to the science of **genetics.** Genetics aims to make clear the mechanisms by which characteristics are transmitted from one generation to the next.

This chapter is an attempt to show how genetic mechanisms and the environment interact in the course of development. However, it should be made clear that we are not seeking to specify the respective contributions of heredity and environment to development. Statements assigning percentages to the role of genetics and environment are meaningless. We start with Donald Hebb's (1953) conclusion that behavior is determined 100 percent by genetics and 100 percent by environment. We then indicate our agreement with Anne Anastasi (1958b) that the question to be answered is not *how much* but *how*? Note that the concept of interaction does not describe the actual back-and-forth workings between genes and their developmental context. We are not in a position to do

so in any detail, either, but we have tried to draw a first rough sketch. We begin by looking at some basic ideas in genetics.

THE BASIC MECHANISMS OF HEREDITY

The field of genetics has become so vast that it defies condensation into a brief section. However, we shall try to give you some basic genetic information that is probably in the process of change even as this book is being written.

Each individual human life begins with the fertilization of an **ovum** from the mother by a **sperm** from the father. Sperm and ovum fuse to form a new one-cell organism called a **zygote,** which will develop into a human baby. The nucleus of the sperm and the nucleus of the ovum each contains twenty-three **chromosomes.** These combine in the nucleus of the zygote, which then has a normal human complement of forty-six. (Chromosomes are shown in the accompanying photos on p. 55.)

Each chromosome is made up of **genes.** The genes consist of molecules of **deoxyribonucleic acid (DNA).** The genes are the primary units of heredity and contain the genetic code that determines the transfer of characteristics from one generation to the next.

The zygote develops from a one-cell organism into a multicellular organism through repeated cell division, or **mitosis.** In mitosis, the chromosomes split down the middle and the two halves separate. Each half then is a complete chromosome, so that as the cell is about to divide there are briefly ninety-two chromosomes within the cell. Matching pairs of chromosomes then migrate to oppo-

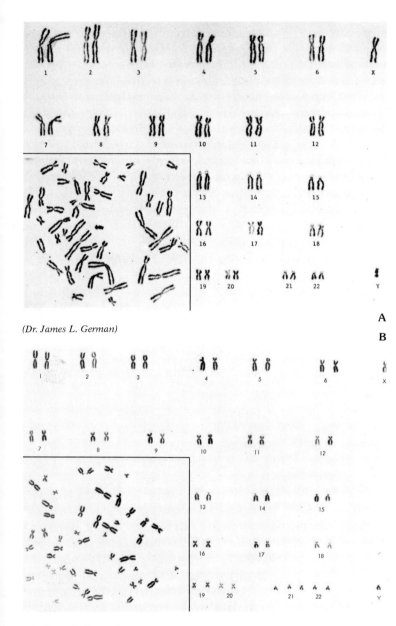

(Dr. James L. German)

(Dr. James L. German)

FIGURE 2.1 Mitosis

Human chromosomes of a single cell. The lower left corner of each photo shows the chromosomes before they are sorted, as they look when arrested during the process of cell division, or mitosis. The numbered displays are karyotypes, with the chromosomes arranged according to type. **A.** Normal male chromosomes. Note the 22 paired types, plus the X and Y chromosomes, which determine sex. **B.** Chromosomes from a male with the genetic abnormality known as Down's syndrome, in which there are three, instead of the usual two, number 21 chromosomes.

site regions of the cell, the cell divides down the middle, and each resulting "daughter" cell has its correct complement of twenty-three pairs of chromosomes, or forty-six in all. All the body cells contain identical sets of chromosomes and genes. Cell division through mitosis occurs in all the so-called body or **somatic cells,** those that make up the bones, nerves, glands, and muscles of the organism.

There is, however, a major exception to what we have just described. Reproductive cells, or **gametes** (the sperm in the male, the ovum in the female), have a peculiarity. In the early stages of their formation, they too divide by mitosis. As the sperm and ovum mature, they undergo a special final stage of cell division known as **meiosis,** or **reduction division.** At this point, the individual chromosomes do not double and separate into two complete sets; instead, the chromosome pairs split up, with one member of each of the twenty-three pairs going to one new cell and the other to a second new cell. Thus the mature human gamete, unlike the somatic cells, contains only twenty-three chromosomes. When in due course sperm meets ovum, each brings only half the usual chromosome complement. To return to where we began, when sperm fertilizes ovum, their nuclei fuse, and the resulting zygote has a normal complement of forty-six chromosomes, twenty-three from the mother and twenty-three from the father.

Dominant and Recessive Traits

In the traditional view, particular traits are associated with particular gene pairs, and variations in these genes account for trait variations. This means that subtle differences in the composi-
tion of the pertinent gene will determine the different forms that a structure can take: noses can be straight or hooked or turned up, broad or narrow, with or without a marked indentation at the brow; hair can be blond or red or brown or black, straight or wavy or kinky; and so forth for all the varieties of human constitution. In fact, many physical characteristics do have such a stable pattern of inheritance. These are the so-called **assortative** or **discontinuous traits,** the ones that can be categorized in terms of qualitative differences, such as eye color. (Assortative traits are contrasted with **distributive traits,** those that vary in terms of more or less, but without qualitative differences.) For each assortative trait, there are two genes, one on each of the appropriate paired chromsomes. Certain traits develop given the presence of a single gene, which suppresses the action of the second, counterpart gene. Such traits are called **dominant.** Other characteristics cannot appear unless the two controlling genes are both of the same kind. These traits are called **recessive.**

When a gene producing a dominant trait is paired with a gene for a recessive trait, only the dominant trait is expressed. For instance, the person who has a gene for brown eye color and another for blue eyes will have brown eyes, brown being dominant. This leads us to the distinction between **genotype,** the individual's underlying genetic make-up, and **phenotype,** the observable trait or characteristic. Phenotypically, a person may have brown eyes. Brown eye color may, however, represent two different genotypes. The person may have two genes for brown eyes, or one dominant gene for brown eye color and one recessive gene for blue.

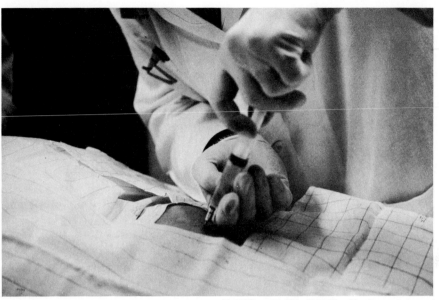

(© William Hubble 1983/Woodfin Camp & Assoc.)

Amniocentesis, a technique for the diagnosis of genetic disorders, incidentally reveals the sex of the unborn child. (See p. 99.)

Genetic Sex Determination

There is an exception to the rule that there are two genes for each assortative trait. In general, the two members of a chromosome pair are very much alike. This is not true in males, one of whose chromosomes, called X, is paired with a smaller, quite dissimilar one, called Y. It is the Y chromosome that determines maleness. Following reduction division (meiosis), then, the human sperm are of two kinds. About half carry an X chromosome, and half carry a Y. Females, by contrast, have two X chromosomes, and all ova thus carry Xs. When an X-bearing sperm joins with an ovum, the result is XX, and a female has been conceived. When a Y-carrying sperm fertilizes an ovum, producing XY, a male zygote is formed. Note that it is the father's sperm that determines the child's sex. Until late

in the embryonic period we are all female in phenotype. Then in males the Y chromosome acts by differentiating the primordial *gonads* (sex glands) as testes rather than as ovaries, and the testicular hormones govern the further elaboration of the male's genital organs and reproductive tract.

The Y chromosome is a shorter chromosome than the X chromosome and carries many fewer genes than does the X, so that there are genes on the X that have no counterparts on the Y. Certain of the genes that occur only on the X chromosome are responsible for what are called **sex-linked recessive traits.** That is, they are recessive in females, for whom the gene responsible for the trait must occur on both Xs or the trait will not appear. In males, whose Y chromosome completely lacks the corresponding gene, the trait occurs whenever the specific gene is present on the X chromosome. The best-known of the sex-linked recessives are red-green color blindness (other forms of color blindness are only partially sex linked) and hemophilia, or bleeder's disease, in which the blood lacks the usual clotting mechanisms. Remember, these same conditions are found in females, but only when the same gene occurs on both X chromosomes. For instance, red-green color blindness is found in some 8 percent of males, but in only .4 percent of females. It should be remembered, too, that the male always inherits his sex-linked recessive traits from his mother, who supplies his X chromosome.

GENETIC AND ENVIRONMENTAL INFLUENCES ON BEHAVIOR

Remember that this is a book about behavioral development. Genes never directly determine behavior. Genes are essential to the making of the organism, and it is the structural character of organisms that may have an influence on behavior. Do not be taken in by such metaphors as "the genes create the person." Genes process the raw materials that go into the making of the person, but how they do so is governed by at least four things. First, operator genes, by virtue of their structure, are programed to turn out various proteins. Second, regulator genes "supervise" and coordinate the workings of the operator genes. Third, what the operator genes actually produce depends on the kinds of raw materials it has available. Normal genes operate abnormally when they do not have the right materials to work

with, either because of a deficiency or because anomalous materials, such as x-rays or viruses, are introduced into the system. A fourth consideration is that we react physiologically to meaningful stimulation, and modifications in our physiology can influence the workings of the gene—remember, the genes do not go into retirement as soon as the baby is ready to be born, but participate throughout life in the processes of growth, maturation, tissue replacement and repair, aging, and dying.

It is obvious that relating particular genes or groups of genes to variations in the structure and behavior of complex organisms is a very ambitious enterprise. Two approaches are possible. First, one can look for the genetic correlates of particular kinds of behavior. This approach has proven quite fruitful in localizing the genes associated with certain abnormalities of function. It has worked hardly at all in dealing with normal variations: We think it is safe to say that the only significant normal variation that we know about is the sex chromosomes X and Y. Even eye color, which used to be thought of as a simple trait governed by a single pair of genes, has now turned out to be something of a puzzle. It is even reported that two blue-eyed parents occasionally produce a brown-eyed child, although we would investigate the question of paternity before discarding all our genetic lore. The second approach is to try to sort out the relative contributions of heredity and environment to variations in a measurable trait. It is this approach that we will be discussing.

Note that this approach makes no attempt to specify which genes account for behavioral variations. It simply seeks to show that the variation is most easily accounted for in terms of either genetic factors or environmental ones. We cannot emphasize too emphatically that these studies are concerned only with people with no demonstrable genetic abnormalities. In Chapter 3, we will talk about genetic abnormalities, but here we are talking about people with ordinary sorts of genes. The studies we discuss fall into two main areas: the origins of intellectual differences (more precisely, differences in IQ scores) and the origins of mental illness, particularly schizophrenia. A third area of interest is behavioral differences between the sexes, but we reserve detailed treatment of this topic to a later chapter.

Intellectual Differences

It is with regard to differences in intellectual ability that the nature-nurture controversy has raged most bitterly. One's views on this matter are likely to be closely related to one's political ideology, with conservatives embracing a strong genetic position and liberals rallying around the environmentalist flag. It is perhaps because this is as much a political arena as a forum for scientific debate that fireworks constantly erupt. We do our best to give a rational summary of this area of wholesale unreason.

A Brief History. We need to begin with a bit of history to put the question of intellectual differences into perspective. When psychologists speak of differences in intellectual ability, they usually mean differences in performance on so-called intelligence tests, as measured by the IQ. The modern intelligence test was created around the turn of the century by Alfred Binet in collaboration with Théophile Simon. Binet had received a mandate from the French Ministry of Education to devise an instrument that would distinguish between "the indolent and the inept," it being a relatively recent notion that some children did poorly in school because of limited ability (ineptness) rather than laziness (indolence). The origins of the intelligence test should be kept firmly in mind: It was a means of predicting success or failure in school, regardless of what other academically less relevant characteristics the child might have. The basic score on the Binet-Simon test was expressed as **mental age,** defined as equivalent to the average score of a group of children the same age. Thus a child of a given chronological age might obtain a mental age score higher or lower than his or her chronological age. This fact inspired Wilhelm Stern in 1912 to invent the concept of **intelligence quotient,** or **IQ:** divide the child's mental age by his or her chronological age and multiply by 100 (to get rid of any decimal points). The child whose mental age and chronological age were the same would have an IQ of 100, which expresses the average performance of each age group. The child whose mental age exceeded his or her chronological age would have an IQ greater than 100; whereas if mental age were lower than chronological age, the IQ would be less than 100.

The IQ, unlike a simple mental age score, seeks to state whether a child's mental development is fast or slow, and precisely how fast or slow. The IQ is no longer calculated by the formula MA/CA × 100, but is expressed in terms of deviation from the mean score of each age group.

The Binet test was first adapted for American use in 1916 by Lewis M. Terman, and it formed the basis for the much-discussed Alpha and Beta tests given to soldiers during World War I. The Terman adaptation of the Binet test came to be known as the Stanford-Binet test. It has undergone several revisions and has spawned a host of imitators and competitors. Terman and a great many of his contemporaries were convinced that the tests measured "native" or "innate" endowment, unaffected by the environment. In time, this view came to be challenged, and for some years practically all psychologists professed to believe that IQ was born out of some kind of interaction between native ability and life experience. Nowadays many testers use one or another of the Wechsler scales, such as the Wechsler Intelligence Scale for Children (WISC).

The rather vague interactionist resolution of the issue served well enough until an article by Arthur Jensen, "How Much Can We Boost IQ and Academic Achievement?" (1969) brought the whole nature-nurture controversy boiling to the surface once more. Jensen claimed that the available evidence (all of it rather ancient) showed IQ to be overwhelmingly determined by heredity, with only a minor share attributable to experience. He further argued that groups that showed consistent average differences in IQ did so because the groups had differing genetic endowments. Basically, Jensen's position was that blacks are genetically inferior to whites in intellect. Jensen pointed out that the average difference in IQ between blacks and whites is some fifteen points. The same difference is found between middle-class and working-class white children. Jensen's thesis drew an outpouring of support from the popular press and from academic colleagues holding similar views. It also brought forth enraged opposition from those in the academic community who strongly questioned Jensen's assessment of the evidence.

We can see that opinions on this matter have serious social consequences. People get tracked into different educational sequences and career opportunities on the basis of presumed intellectual ability. In many countries, including the United States, the supposition that certain racial groups are superior and others inferior is invoked to justify perpetuating long-standing practices of discrimination. Even within the dominant racial group, the assumption of genetically fixed differences helps keep people frozen into established patterns of social and economic stratification.

Jensen's opening argument was that remedial education for disadvantaged children had been tried and had failed. Furthermore, it was doomed to continue failing because economically disadvantaged children were genetically unsuited to academic learning. Jensen and other hereditarians base their conclusions about the preeminence of genetic factors in intellectual development on two sorts of evidence derived from two main approaches to sorting out the relative contributions of heredity and environment. First, there are studies of the degree of similarity in *identical (monozygotic or MZ) twins*, who come from the same original egg and have identical genetic make-ups, as compared to *fraternal (dizygotic or DZ) twins*, who come from two different eggs. A variant on this approach is to compare MZ twins reared apart from each other. The second main approach is to study the resemblance of adopted children to their biological parents and their adoptive parents. Note that most of the evidence available to us from these two kinds of sources is quite old, but we have to settle for what we have.

Studies of Twins. Comparisons of MZ and DZ twin pairs are rather easily summarized. Bouchard and McGue (1981) have surveyed all the reliable studies on consanguinity (degree of kinship) and report the averages and ranges of IQ correlations for different relationships. The average correlation in IQ between monozygotic twins reared together is .86. The range from thirty-four studies of 4,672 twin pairs is from .58 to about .95. The mean correlation from forty-one studies of 5,546 DZ pairs reared together is .60, with a range from about .20 to just under .90; eliminating an extreme case at either end, the range is .30 to .75. The average correlation for MZ twins reared apart falls to .72; but note that there are only three studies of a total of only sixty-five MZ pairs. There are no studies of DZ twins reared apart. Siblings who, like DZ twins, have about 50 percent of their heredity in common, and whose IQs should correlate about .50, have an average correlation of .47 when reared together and of .24 when reared apart. In the case of DZ twins and nontwin siblings, it made no difference whether the twins were of the same or opposite sex. Bouchard and McGue (1981) conclude:

> Although the data clearly suggest the operation of environmental effects, we found no evidence for two factors sometimes thought to be important—sex-role effects

(© Elizabeth Crews)

Monozygotic (identical) twins have identical genetic endowments. Psychologists have studied identical twins in an attempt to understand the extent to which genetic structure and environmental factors affect intelligence and other areas of development.

and maternal effects. That the data support the inference of partial genetic determination for IQ is indisputable; that they are informative about the precise strength of the effect is dubious (p. 1058).

Bouchard and McGue point out that the data point to a **polygenic** (many-gene) **mode** of inheritance for intellectual abilities. It is an axiom of genetics that polygenic traits are much more susceptible to environmental influences than are assortative traits. This is because each gene can vary in its operation according to both environmental conditions and the workings of neighboring genes. This capacity for variable operation is called the gene's **range of reaction** (Dobzhansky, 1973). The more genes there are involved in a trait, the more combinations of ranges of reaction are possible, and so the greater variety of expression of the same set of genes.

There is a further problem in interpreting studies of identical twins reared apart. This is the fact that physically separate environments may be psychologically quite similar. When one looks more closely at the environments in which MZ twins were raised apart from each other, one finds that they vary in their resemblance. If one takes years of schooling of the twin pairs studied by Newman, Freeman, and Holzinger (1937), it appears that differences in IQ correlate .79 with differences in years of schooling (Anastasi, 1958a). See Table 2.1.

Thus the resemblance in IQ between separated MZ twins depends to a large extent on the degree of resemblance in their educational environments—the greater the disparity in these environments, the greater the difference in IQ. Even if we turn the correlation on its head, as we are logically permitted to do, and say that the twins with the greatest difference in native IQ had the great differences in schooling, we would then be obliged to seek out a new factor to account for the initial difference in IQ. In either event, the data of Newman *et al.* do not support the strong genetic position that most textbooks attribute to them. In keeping with an interactionist position, monozygosity means little un-less we take account of the rearing environment.

Studies of Adoption. During the 1920s and 1930s there were a number of studies comparing the IQs of adopted children with the IQs of their biological and adoptive parents. With one exception, a study by Snygg (1938) which has somehow been dropped from the literature, the adoption studies seemed strongly supportive of the hereditarian position. However, Kamin (1974) has pointed out a number of flaws in these studies which, while not refuting the hereditarian view, render their conclusions moot. As Kamin points out, comparisons between natural and adoptive families can yield valid results only if the comparison families are highly similar in means and in ranges of variation on all the relevant variables, such as parental age, family size, economic status, and education. Typically, adoptive parents are older than natural parents, have only a single child rather than the two or more typical of the biological families, are on the whole more affluent, and have markedly higher levels of education.

The most widely cited adoption study is one by Skodak and Skeels (1949). This study involved 100 adopted children. It compared the IQs of sixty-three of these children with the IQs of their biological mothers and with the estimated intellectual levels of their adoptive mothers. Hereditarians attach great significance to the finding that the IQs of the children correlated much more highly with those of their biological mothers (.44) than with those of their adoptive mothers (.02).

There are three facts that cast doubt on the meaningfulness of these correla-

Table 2.1 Resemblances in IQ and Rearing Environment of Identical Twins Raised Apart

Pair Number	Estimated Differences in Educational Advantages (Maximum Possible Difference = 50)	IQ Differences
11	37[a]	24[b]
2	32	12
18	28	19
4	22	17
12	19	7
1	15	12
17	15	10
8	14	15
3	12	−2[c]
14	12	−1
5	11	4
13	11	1
10	10	5
15	9	1
7	9	−1
19	9	−9
16	8	2
6	7	8
9	7	6
20[d]	2	3

[a] This figure represents in part a difference between two years of schooling and graduation from college.
[b] This value is five times as great as the average difference found between nonseparated twins, and three times as great as the average difference in this study.
[c] A negative sign indicates a difference in direction opposite to that reflected by the Differences in Educational Advantages.
[d] This case was not part of the original sample but was added later.

Source: Adapted from A. Anastasi, *Differential Psychology,* 3rd ed. (New York: Macmillan, 1958a), p. 299. Based on the data of H. H. Newman, F. H. Freeman, and K. J. Holzinger, *Twins: A Study of Heredity and Environment* (Chicago: University of Chicago Press, 1937).

tions. In the first place, the adoptive mothers were not even tested—their IQs were estimated by the researchers. The second point is more technical and deals with the problem of what is known as the **restricted range.** All correlation coefficients are based on a rank ordering of subjects along a given dimension, such as IQ. With imperfect measuring instruments, subjects are sometimes ranked wrongly. This makes little difference as long as the subjects' scores fall across a wide range. However, when the subjects occupy only a narrow or restricted range—that is, when they are relatively homogeneous with respect to the trait being measured—a few misrankings will destroy whatever actual relations exist. In the Skodak and Skeels study, we have the dual fact that the adoptive mothers were uniformly bright and that their brightness was simply estimated, a rather cruder technique than giving a test. Thus the low correlation between their intelligence rankings and those of the adopted children has no meaning whatsoever. What is more to the point is fact number three, that the biological mothers had a mean IQ of 86 whereas the children they gave up for adoption had a mean IQ of 106. This twenty-point difference seems to reflect the beneficial effect of living in homes that offered a large portion of developmentally beneficial conditions.

The only mystery to be explained is how the correlation between biological mothers and children happened to be so high (.44) in the Skodak and Skeels study, whereas the four correlations cited by Bouchard and McGue (1981) for parents and children living apart range from under .0 to under .40, with the average at about .20. One expects statistically a .50 correlation between the IQs of parents and their offspring. At this late date we can only guess, but it seems plausible that the brighter of the biological mothers sought and received better prenatal care.

More recently, Schiff et al. (1978) compared thirty-two school-age children who had been born to low-socioeconomic-status (SES) mothers and adopted before age six months into professional families, with twenty of their siblings who had been raised by their own mothers. On two IQ tests, the adopted children had averages of 111 and 107, whereas the children reared by their biological mothers had averages on both tests of about 95. The school-failure rate for the adopted children was about 15 percent (comparable to that of children born into families at the same socioeconomic level). The rate for their siblings was 55 percent, somewhat higher than for the general run of low-SES children.

Let us comment in passing that in these studies, and in others to be mentioned later in this chapter, there are unresolved questions about the nature of the adoptive relationship. A thorough study still needs to be made of how well adoption works and what factors help and hinder the process, notably in the area of reciprocal attachment between parents and child. Such research will add new dimensions to studies where adoption is a key variable.

We defer the topic of interracial adoption (which usually means adoption by white parents of children of different racial backgrounds) until we have had a closer look at the thorny matter of racial and social-class differences in IQ.

Group Differences: Race and Social Class. Those who see evidence of a large genetic component in normal variations in intelligence (let us repeat that we will discuss genetic abnormalities later) have sought to generalize their thesis to differences in average IQ between subgroups in the population. There are two main sorts of studies. The first concern themselves with socioeconomic and class differences, and the second with race differences.

Studies of social-class differences have compared average IQs of poor children with IQ averages supposedly derived

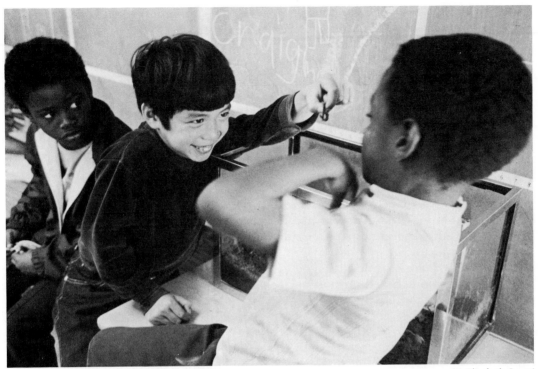

(© Elizabeth Crews)

Although ethnic prejudice is far from dead, many stereotypes fade as new generations become assimilated. Many children and grandchildren of racial and ethnic minority groups have risen socioeconomically and have adapted to mainstream American culture.

from a random sampling of the total population. Children from Appalachia, from the canal boats of England, and from the slums of Edinburgh have all been tested and found wanting. The children of impoverished immigrants to the United States have likewise been tested and marked as inferior, sometimes in total disregard of the fact that the testees had a severely limited command of English. Thus at various points in our history we have been told that the Irish, Italians, Jews, and Eastern and Central Europeans are made of genetically inferior stuff and could never hope to rise to the level of those of British and Northwestern European stock. The social and economic inferiority of these groups was seen as a natural consequence of their biological inadequacies, with no thought given to the possibility that the causal relationship might be the other way around: Poverty and associated deprivations could impair both physical and intellectual development. Nor was much attention given to the fact that many of the poorer immigrants had cultural backgrounds incompatible with the assumptions built into our testing instruments. If the poor, in desperation, turned to crime, this was taken by prosperous people as further proof of biological inferiority.

In the past hundred-odd years, the tides of history have washed away most of these stereotypes, although ethnic prejudice is far from dead. Large numbers of the children and grandchildren of the poor have risen in the socioeconomic system and have mostly accommodated to American cultural thinking. It is especially interesting to note that the Chinese and the Japanese, who were once regarded as subhuman, have now come to be seen as exemplifying many of the nation's highest ideals.

There is one group of Americans, however, against whom hereditarians periodically unleash campaigns of systematic defamation. We are speaking, of course, of people of tropical African ancestry, most of whom are descended from involuntary immigrants, the slaves. Much is made of the fact that in study after study blacks score, on the average (with, of course, considerable overlap), about 15 IQ points, equal to one standard deviation, below whites. This difference is interpreted as clear evidence of a genetic difference beween blacks and whites. Once again, the champions of racial differences have chosen to ignore the fact that American blacks, with some obvious exceptions, have been economically deprived, and that IQ is correlated inversely with poverty, regardless of race. The twin and adoption studies tried, however crudely, to incorporate measures of environmental influences into their designs. However, the studies of group differences, whether of social class or race, have been resolutely nondevelopmental. That is, they considered only the end product, IQ, and not the developmental histories

of the individuals being tested. The members of disfavored groups, as closer scrutiny quickly shows, have learning opportunities quite different from those of members of favored groups. In the case of black Americans in particular, it appears that a distinct culture has formed, with its own special beliefs, values, practices, music and dance, and even language. Slum children of all ethnic backgrounds learn a set of survival skills attuned to poverty, run-down housing, high crime rates (some learn to be criminals, others to avoid being victims), widespread drug use, temptations to early sex, an atmosphere of violence, and outwitting the often unsympathetic agencies of government. But the street smarts of the slum child, black or white, are of little use in dealing with either the abstractions of intelligence tests or the academic and nonacademic demands (punctuality, quiet immobility, obedience, attentiveness) of the standard school classroom.

Such considerations do not, of course, constitute an argument that there are no racial or social-class differences in genetic endowment. They only serve to put the matter of assessment in a different perspective. Even the question of race is full of ambiguities. It is the convention in the United States to designate as Negro anyone with any known degree of black ancestry, which means that "Negroes" represent a broad spectrum of racial intermixture. Moreover, very few "blacks" can lay claim to anything like a pure African lineage. The European practice of lumping together all black Africans as Negroes does little justice to the realities of African racial diversity, which ranges from the Bushmen to the Ibos to the Watusi to the Masai.

One study addressed the question of

Table 2.2 IQ Scores of Four-Year-Old Children of Black–White Matings

	Parental Race			
	Black Mother/ White Father		White Mother/ Black Father	
	Sex of Child		*Sex of Child*	
Marital Status	Male	Female	Male	Female
Married	88.4 (9)	105.1 (11)	100.8 (20)	103.8 (19)
Unmarried	67.5 (2)	88.6 (5)	94.7 (7)	100.3 (15)

NOTE: Numbers of cases are given in parentheses.

Source: Adapted from L. Willerman, A. F. Naylor, and N. C. Myrianthopoulos, Intellectual Development of Children from Interracial Matings, *Science*, 17 (1970), 1329–1330.

racial mixing directly, testing the four-year-old offspring of black-white matings (Willerman, Naylor, and Myrianthopoulos, 1970). The independent variables in this study were race of the mother (and by implication that of the father), marital status, and sex of the child, yielding eight categories. The dependent variable was IQ. The groups were all roughly equated in term of the average education of both parents. The study has some serious flaws, such as the widely uneven number of cases per category, but the results are nevertheless intriguing and baffling. These results are summarized in Table 2.2.

As we can see from Table 2.2, the eight groups of children, in ascending order, had the following IQs: sons of unmarried black mothers, 67.5; sons of married black mothers, 88.4; daughters of unmarried black mothers, 88.6; sons of unmarried white mothers, 94.7; daughters of unmarried white mothers, 100.3; daughters of married white mothers, 103.8; and daughters of married black mothers, 105.1. Even if the numbers in

each category were big enough to permit statistical comparison, the averages found in adjacent categories would probably not be reliably different. Still, the total spread of averages from 67.5 to 105.1 is very striking. Drawing infer-

(© Cynthia W. Sterling 1981/The Picture Cube)

Mother and child. It is difficult to determine the effects—if any—of racially mixed marriages upon children's IQ scores.

Vietnamese children with their adoptive parents. Studies of interracial adoption have not yet answered the question of whether racial and social-class differences are genetic or environmental.

ences is risky, and the most we can make of these findings is that living with both parents and being female helps, and that the race of the parents is of little consequence.

Scarr *et al.* (1977), using blood group markers as an index of racial mixing, found that intellectual skills did not vary consistently with the degree of black or white ancestry in a group of racially mixed children. We are not sure how much confidence can be placed in this system of measuring racial proportions in one's forebears. In addition, all the subjects were twins. It is beyond the scope of this book to talk about all the subtleties involved in being a twin, MZ or DZ, but they are serious enough to make generalizations from a sample consisting entirely of twins rather shaky.

Interracial Adoption. William Shockley (e.g., 1968), well known as a firm believer in race differences, has several times proposed an experiment in which black children be adopted into Jewish families to see if any of the assumed Jewish intellectual superiority would rub off on the black adoptees. No one has ever carried out Shockley's proposal, but Scarr and her associates (Scarr and

Weinberg, 1976; Scarr, 1981) have conducted the natural experiment of measuring the IQs of black and other non-white children adopted into middle-class and upper-middle-class white families. All the adoptees had lived with their adoptive families for at least five years. There comparability ended. The children's age at adoption ranged from birth to age sixteen, and age at testing ranged from five to twenty-one. Children of black or mixed black-white descent had an average IQ of 106.3 (range 68 to 144); adopted white children had an average of 111.15; and children of Asian or American Indian origin averaged 99.9. Considering only those children who were adopted when they were very young, black and mixed children had an average IQ of 110.4, and white children, 116.8 (there were no early-adopted Asian or Indian children). The black means are definitely higher than those of black children drawn from the general population and are even somewhat higher than the national average of 100. At the same time, adopted black children scored well below their white step-siblings, who had mean IQs on two tests of 114 and 119, and a range from 68 to 150. Here again we mention the unknowns in the matter of adoption, with the added complication of interracial adoption.

Thus with regard to racial and social-class differences, we are left with a frustrating ambiguity, unchanged from the conclusions of Walter Neff's (1938) panoramic survey of research on group differences in IQ. Neff rendered what he called a "Scotch verdict": not proven. This ambiguity is nonetheless instructive: It tells us that strong assertions about either the genetic or the environmental origins of racial and social-class differences have only a feeble foundation in fact.

Intelligence Tests

The studies we have described above have based their results on IQ scores. To say that the origins of differences in IQ are obscure is not enough. Down through the years, the value of the IQ tests themselves has been called into radical question. Psychological research is plagued with the problem of finding satisfactory assessment techniques, and many of the ambiguities and contradictions we shall encounter along the way spring from inadequate measures.

Intelligence tests, however, provide a special problem because, despite never-ending barrages of criticism, they have marched grandly ahead, accepted by large numbers of psychologists and lay-persons as objective, accurate measures of "intelligence," that ineffable something that eludes definition but that almost everybody assumes he or she understands.

To appreciate how fundamental the criticisms of intelligence tests are, it might be well to look at how the tests are constructed. Since the pioneering days of Binet, test construction has begun with the collection of a large miscellany of test items that presumably have some bearing on intelligence. From there on, test construction is a highly pragmatic procedure, with little regard for theory or even logical coherence. The pool of test items is given to a sample of the population for which the test is intended and is then boiled down to those items that work best. These are the items that are passed by a growing proportion of children as age increases. In practice, as the tests have multiplied, latecomers to the business have borrowed heavily from the items collected by their predecessors, lending a certain similarity to a variety of tests.

The usefulness of the items is then further tested by trying them out on a large number of subjects, a process called **standardization.** It thus becomes a vital matter that the standardization group be representative of the same population from which the individual test taker comes. In practice, this requirement is seldom met. In fact, meeting it is all but impossible in a pluralistic society such as ours. Each of our many subcultures provides its children with somewhat different environments and somewhat differing interpretations of the environment. Thus while tests may purport to measure the child's innate intellectual ability, they are comparing his or her mastery of one culture with an ideal mastery of a supposedly common culture. In sum, test makers have abandoned the original goal of measuring native ability and instead test what the child has learned of some more or less representative features of mainstream culture.

The most widely used tests average out performance on very diverse sorts of measures—from word knowledge to mental arithmetic to repeating strings of numbers backward and forward, from knowing certain facts to being able to spot absurdities—into a single IQ score. This masks what in many cases are highly uneven patterns of performance. For instance, the Wechsler Intelligence Test for Children—Revised (Wechsler, 1974) consists of eleven subtests. Correlating performances on these tests, two at a time, yields sixty-six correlation coefficients. For the standardization sample of seven-and-a-half-year-olds, ten of the sixty-six fall at or below .25. The lowest (.13) is between Coding (which requires the child to match familiar forms like a star with a simple mark such as a wavy line) and Picture Completion (in which the child is asked to specify what is missing in pictures of familiar objects). Twenty-one of the correlation coefficients fall between .36 and .45. Ten fall between .46 and .55. Only six fall between .56 and .64. The highest value, .64, is between Block Design (which requires the child to reproduce a printed geometric pattern using colored three-dimensional blocks) and Object Assembly (which is a species of jigsaw puzzle). The Information subtest (which is a test of general knowledge) correlates most highly with the others, and Coding correlates the lowest with the other subtests. Clinicians using the Wechsler Scales can take account of variations among the subtest scores and perceive patterns of strength and weakness in the subject's functioning. However, the total IQ score derived from so heterogeneous an assortment of tests is very hard to interpret. Extremely high and extremely low IQs necessarily reflect a homogeneous level of functioning. However, scores in the middle range can reflect a great many diverse patterns.

The content of the standard tests has been criticized on several grounds. It has been faulted for being **culturally biased,** being based on material familiar to middle-class subjects but remote from the experience of other groups. Vocabulary is at the heart of intelligence testing. Even an information test that asks you to identify the Koran or explain a lien is in fact a vocabulary test. Vocabulary and the stock of common knowledge vary greatly from group to group. Identifying the author of *Romeo and Juliet* or the composer of *Faust* is not likely to be equally relevant to all segments of society.

In addition to being culturally biased, the content of intelligence tests may be highly conventional. A typical question asks what the correct thing to do is if one finds a sealed, addressed envelope with a fresh stamp. The correct answer is to drop it in the nearest mailbox. The answer closer to the run of human actuality, which is scored as being wrong, is to see if the envelope contains money.

Intelligence tests given to subjects past age five are good predictors of academic success in school (McCall, 1977). As we stressed earlier, this is precisely what they were meant to do when they were first devised. But this means only that schools and IQ tests are both concerned with the same sorts of skills and knowledge. It is hardly safe to generalize from either IQ scores or academic performance to all of intellectual ability. The tests cover only a narrow range of cognitive skills. None of the major tests, for instance, has yet incorporated any of the wealth of material produced by Piagetian research or even cognitive findings from outside the Piagetian camp. The tests call only for *convergent thinking* (Guilford, 1967), following a set routine to a single correct answer, as in doing arithmetic problems. They ignore the opposite process, *divergent thinking*, playing around with the possibilities of problems that may have many solutions or none at all. A typical divergent task, designed as part of a test of creativity, calls for the child to think of all the different uses to which one could put a common object such as a paper clip.

An attempt has been made to by-pass the criticism that diverse skills are treated as equivalent in the summary IQ score. This attempt is embodied in **factorial theory,** which assumes the existence of quite distinct kinds of intellectual competence, or "factors," and tests for each separately. The result is not a single score but a "profile" of many scores, each standing for a separate factor. On the face of it, this approach seems more sensible than using a composite IQ score. In practice, the factorial approach to measuring abilities has been beset by as many disagreements and confusions as the unitary IQ approach.

The Concept of Intelligence

From what we have said, we might conclude that we are not too sure what we are talking about when we try to discuss intelligence. This book will continue presenting research in which IQ is the dependent variable, but the reader should be aware of our skepticism regarding IQ as a valid estimate of intellectual ability. We think that part of the problem lies in a general cultural worship of efficiency and quantification, which leads to ill-conceived attempts to find shortcuts to understanding and describing how people function. To say this is not to denounce the quest for ways to define intellectual differences among individuals or for ways to measure them. We are simply asserting that our science is less than perfect and can be improved.

Ours is a classifying society, bent on typing and labeling people, with very little concern for human complexity and diversity. Perhaps some reader will take this message to heart and take a new direction in research into human differences. Meanwhile, we think we could strike a blow for semantic purity by abolishing the noun "intelligence," which through word realism gives the impression that something called intelligence really exists. This process is known as *reification*, converting an abstract and perhaps meaningless concept into a solid and perhaps potent entity. It would still be legitimate to use the adjectives "intelligent" and "unintelligent," and the adverbs "intelligently" and "stupidly." These are very useful terms for describing particular bits of behavior with respect to various situations, but they should be used with great caution in describing individuals or groups.

We now turn to the influence of biology and experience on the development of mental health and illness, with special reference to schizophrenia.

HEREDITY AND ENVIRONMENT IN MENTAL HEALTH AND ILLNESS

The second most discussed area of dispute over the relative role of nature and nurture is in the origins of mental health and illness. If the discussion of nature and nurture in intellectual development has given us an intimate introduction to ambiguity, when it comes to mental health and illness, the reader should be prepared to savor chaos. The students of "intelligence" at least have a generally used measure, the IQ test, whatever its shortcomings. In the field of mental health, no such widely accepted measure exists. All is subjectivity, with psychiatrists at odds over definitions of normal-ity and abnormality and where to draw the boundaries, and over which diagnostic categories to use and how to apply them. The particular form of mental illness most often singled out for debate is schizophrenia, a group of conditions with diverse manifestations that may include delusions, hallucinations, near-total withdrawal or lethal assaultiveness, garbled langauge and thought processes, and spells of total lucidity. We will concentrate on schizophrenia simply because it has been studied the most.

A great many authorities seem to agree that there is some genetic predisposition to schizophrenia, in the form of a lowered threshold for breakdown when under stress. One source of this belief is, as in the IQ controversy, studies of **concordance** in MZ versus DZ twins. Concordance is simply the observed percentage of cases in which both twins are diagnosed as schizophrenic. There is less insistence here on comparing separated and nonseparated twin pairs. It strikes a blow for hereditarianism when two long-separated twins both erupt into schizophrenia, but the numbers are necessarily small. After all, the entire literature of IQ differences in separated MZ twins rests on a total of only sixty-five pairs (Bouchard and McGue, 1981). Whereas every twin has an IQ of some sort, only a small percentage of twins becomes schizophrenic, decreasing the opportunities to measure concordance. In any event, the published estimates of concordance for schizophrenia in MZ twins range from a high of 85 percent to a low of zero. Again as in the case of IQ studies, early separation of MZ twins does not imply psychological dissimilarity of environments.

(© Michael Weisbrot & Family)

An autistic child with his parents. Whether emotional disturbance in children is the product of nature or nurture is an open question. In fact, there is no widely accepted measure of mental health or illness.

A more promising strategy for assaying the genetic contribution to schizophrenia is, as you may have guessed, the adoption approach. One can compare the children of schizophrenic parents adopted into normal families with adopted children whose mothers were not schizophrenic. (The schizophrenic parents in this study were overwhelmingly mothers since schizophrenic males rarely become parents.) Here again we run into a problem of numbers. Just as schizophrenics make up a relatively small proportion of the population as a whole, women make up only a small proportion of schizophrenics; we have no way of knowing what proportion of schizophrenic women have babies. In any case, the most ambitious adoption study yet reported (Rosenthal *et al.,* 1974) had a total of seventy-six offspring of schizophrenic mothers and sixty-seven controls. Measures of environmental variables were out of the question since the subjects were all studied as adults, ranging in age from twenty to fifty-two, with a mean of about thirty-three. Another problem with the study was that there was no way of knowing whether the adoptive parents had been aware of the schizophrenic or nonschizophrenic history of the mothers whose children they adopted. Such knowledge might serve to generate a self-fulfilling prophecy. In any event, Rosenthal *et al.* found that about a third of the offspring of schizophrenic mothers showed signs of psychiatric disturbance (two were actually diagnosed as schizophrenic), as contrasted with less than a fifth of the children of normal parents (no diagnoses of full-blown schizophrenia were reported in these children). This difference, favoring a genetic interpretation, is statistically reliable, but it leaves several questions unanswered. What are we to make of the two-thirds of the children of schizophrenic parentage who escaped any detectable abnormality? How are we to account for the incidence of serious symptoms in almost 18 percent of the children of normal parents? This project, which took a number of years, was expected to provide some clear answers to the problem of the origins of schizophrenia, but we seem to know little more than when it was begun. That there is a genetic component in schizophrenia seems hard to doubt, but we are far from understanding what it is and how it operates.

The larger program of which the schizophrenia study was a part has now drifted into such areas as psychopathy (inability to identify with the feelings of other people), criminality, and alcoholism, which contribute little to our understanding of schizophrenia. We seem once again to be left with a "Scotch verdict": Not proven.

The same applies to the origins of psychological differences between the sexes. Differences do exist, but apart from those directly involved in reproduction, we cannot say with confidence whether they originate in the differing anatomies and physiologies of the two sexes or in the differing modes of socialization to which they are exposed. We shall have more to say about psychological sex differences in Chapter 14.

THE FUSION OF NATURE AND NURTURE—THE PSYCHOBIOLOGICAL ORGANISM

It seems obvious to us that the reason research on the relative contributions of nature and nurture to human functioning dissipates in a cloud of ambiguity is that the question is incorrectly put. There can be no answer because there is no question. Twenty-five years ago in an article titled "Heredity, Environment, and the Question 'How?'" Anastasi (1958b) made clear that biology and experience are always totally interdependent, so that it becomes impossible to assess how much each contributes. A great many people have cited her article, but very little progress has been made in reformulating the problem. Indeed, an entire issue of *Child Development* (1983) has been devoted to what is called "developmental behavior genetics." It appears that practitioners in this "new" field are once again trying to measure the respective contributions of nature and nurture, as though Anastasi's logic had somehow been invalidated. It has not been.

We propose that we begin by erasing the accepted boundary between biology and psychology. They are not two separate subject matters, but two perspectives on the same subject matter. Now

(© James R. Holland/Stock, Boston)

Nature or nurture? Actually, the dichotomy is false. They are interdependent. Our genes interact with one another and with our environment. The organism takes biological and psychological shape through interaction with a material and psychological environment.

that we have had a brief look at genetic mechanisms in development, it should be easy enough to see that genes interact with one another and with environmental processes to shape a human being and that they do not stop operating at birth. They play a role in development throughout the life of the organism.

After birth, the developing organism is able to take in information through the sense organs from the surrounding world, retain it, rework it, combine it with other batches of information to construct a world view, and thus becomes able in turn to act on the environment.

To move away from this somewhat computerlike vision of experience, we say the child perceives the world, has feelings about it, acquires knowledge, forms opinions and attitudes, learns skills, and in some measure controls him- or herself. In fact, everything we think of as psychological—self-awareness, creativity, courage and cowardice, generosity and selfishness, our ability to fabricate science and art and culture and delusion—is in fact a biological property of the human organism. All our psychological potentialities are in fact biological potentialities. Which potentialities get realized, and in what forms and combinations, is a product of our opportunities for different kinds of learning. Obviously, other environmental factors enter in, such as nutrition and exposure to and protection from disease. But we are primarily concerned with our responses to *meaningful* stimulation. For it is the *meaning* of events to which we react and on which we nourish ourselves.

Some parts of the world seem to be meaningful at birth—human faces and voices, human contact, being rocked. Other aspects of reality take on meaning through associative learning, as when the baby raises its head to meet the approaching nipple. Still other parts of reality take on meaning as derivatives of the world view (the schematic framework) that takes shape through experience, as when the baby shows fear of strangers or is puzzled by a plaything's refusal to be assimilated to existing structures. It is *meanings* that are the key to feelings and action. Standard theories of perception try to tell us how we recognize and classify objects, but they do not explain why we do things to or about the objects we perceive—approach them, grasp them, embrace them, eat them, laugh at them, or run away from them.

We have said that the boundary between psychology and biology is an arbitrary one, drawn for the convenience of specialists. So also is the boundary between organism and environment. Biologists have long recognized that what are referred to as organism and environment are an interpenetrating, interacting system. For instance, the air and carbon dioxide in our lungs and the food in our digestive tracts are technically part of the environment. The biologist Claude Bernard hypothesized that our bloodstreams are internalized versions of the aquatic environment from which terrestrial life emerged. Our bodies make continual homeostatic adjustments to environmental variations in temperature. But there is behavioral homeostasis as well: If it gets too hot, we move into the shade; too cold or wet, and we seek shelter; hunger and thirst impel us to seek out food and drink. Psychologically, too, we and the environment are initially one. Part of the process of development is learning to detach ourselves from the environment so that we can act according to thought-out plans instead of reacting automatically. Whether we are acting or reacting—or, as is more often the case, engaging in a sequence of action and reaction—it is through the medium of our bodies. Emotional reactions, after all, are not mere feeling states. They involve changes of physiology. To put it another way, psychological development and somatic development are part and parcel of the same process.

This is a **psychosomatic** view of behavior and development. It is unfortunate that the term "psychosomatic" has come to be associated so exclusively with illnesses—in our terminology, with disagreeable *meanings* and the unfortunate physiological and anatomical reactions they produce. Psychosomatic illness is an indisputable reality, but so are favorable psychosomatic reactions. Take the opposite of psychosomatic illness, the psychosomatic cure, otherwise known as the *placebo effect* (Moerman, 1981). A certain proportion of very real somatic pathologies can be cured by the ingestion of inert substances with no intrinsic curative properties whatsoever. Norman Cousins (1979) claims wonders for the therapeutic power of laughter against cancer. In any case, laughter is one of our more common positive psychosomatic responses. In April of 1982, the New York Academy of Sciences sponsored a conference on Mind and Immunity, specifically concerning the way our thoughts and feelings influence our susceptibility to disease. If a description of a delectable meal makes our mouths water, that is a psychosomatic reaction. Sexual arousal in response to sights and sounds and smells is a psychosomatic reaction. An odd sort of psychosomatic adjustment is seen in female hamsters caged together. First, their menstrual cycles are roughly halved, from ten days to five; second, they menstruate simultaneously. It has also been observed that female college roommates experience a shift toward menstrual synchrony (McClintock, 1971). Finally, as was suggested earlier, psychological stimulation can be shown to play a role in the maturation of the brain and the endocrine glands. Thus the development of our bodily structures and the way they function is under the joint control of our genes and the meaningful stimulation—positive and negative—to which we are exposed. How genes operate is determined by the biochemistry of the raw materials they are given to process, and our responses to meanings are as much biochemical as psychological. Psychologically, the joke strikes us as funny; biologically, we laugh. We submit that these are only two aspects of a single psychobiological event.

This view of development as having both genetic and experiential components, without trying to assign primacy to either, is usually called **interactional.** However, interaction implies the working of two distinct sets of forces. To call behavior and development **psychobiological** means that the biological organism is more than merely biologial. It contains all our psychological potentialities for feeling, knowing, thinking, and acting.

To repeat, which psychobiological possibilities develop, which are left latent, and which are actively suppressed is a product of our varied learning opportunities as well as of nutrition, disease, and so forth. We nourish ourselves on meanings, we formulate meanings of our own, and we try to impose our meanings on the world we are part of even as we try to detach ourselves. We do not react to each event afresh, but as part of a coherent, comprehensible, manageable system of events. When something truly unprecedented happens, as when we are caught in an earthquake, our view of world and self is threatened with disintegration.

The psychobiological view that we propose is **ecological,** since all behavior has to be considered in terms of its context, a view shared by such thinkers as Bronfenbrenner (1977). Behavior is always directed toward an object, real or imagined, including the self as object. However, we shift with situations, at the extreme becoming different personalities to meet the demands of changing circumstances. Obviously, the environment with which we deal is to a large extent a human and cultural environment which can modify not only our immediate behavior but our general frame of reference. This carries the implication that the very nature of human nature can change from one historical era to the next and from one cultural setting to the next.

The psychobiological view is developmental, since we do not spring into the world full blown but take shape as human beings through our encounters with material and personal and ideational worlds. Development, after all, is what this book is about.

SUMMARY

1. Genetics, the study of the way physical characteristics are passed from one generation to another, is an essentially developmental science. Genes have significance only as they interact with each other and with environmental conditions throughout life to produce a functioning organism.

2. The trait-carrying elements of heredity are genes; composed of DNA molecules, many genes make up each chromosome.

3. When a sperm and an ovum combine, each contributes a set of 23 chromosomes to the resulting zygote, and these two sets of chromosomes pair up and undergo repeated mitosis, or cell division. Through the process of mitosis, the unborn baby grows and takes shape. In gametes, or reproductive cells (the sperm and the ovum), a special final stage of cell division called meiosis, or reduction division, occurs, so that the mature gamete contains 23 chromosomes, half the normal complement.

4. In the traditional view, particular traits are associated with particular genes, and variations in these genes account for trait variations, such as eye color. Thus subtle differences in the composition of genes determine the different forms that a structure can take. Traits that follow a stable pattern of inheritance and can be categorized in terms of qualitative differences, like eye color, are called assortative traits. Dominant traits are those which develop due to the ability of a particular gene to suppress the action of its counterpart gene. Recessive traits are those that will not appear unless the controlling genes are both of the same kind.

5. The genotype is the precise genetic makeup of an individual. It is to be distinguished from the phenotype, which is the observable trait, such as brown eyes. Thus a brown-eyed person genotypically may possess either two genes for brown eyes, or a dominant gene for brown eyes paired with a recessive gene for blue eyes.

6. The sex of a person is determined by the presence or absence of the Y chromosome. Males have one X chromosome, paired with a smaller, dissimilar chromosome, termed Y. Females have two X chromosomes. Until late in the embryonic period we are all phenotypically female. Then the Y chromosome acts by differentiating the primordial gonads as testes rather than as ovaries. The testicular hormones then govern further development of the male characteristics. Certain sex-linked recessive traits appear predominantly in males.

7. Polygenic (multigene) models are used in attempts to explain the genetic basis of individual differences in intellectual ability and in other complex human traits and characteristics. Polygenetic traits are more susceptible to environmental influences than assortative traits. The genes involved have more potential combinations of ranges of reaction.

8. Genes never directly determine behavior, but through complex interactions with their environments, help shape the structure, physiology, and functioning of an organism. In most cases, the gene-behavior linkage becomes so complex that it is impossible to try to assign quantitative weights to the relative contributions of heredity and environment. The greater the number and diversity of interactions among genes and between genes and environments in the course of development, the less predictable the outcome. Some areas that have been explored in relation to genetics and behavior include the origins of intellectual differences and the role of heredity in mental health and illness.

9. Through adoption and twin studies, as well as through studies of race and class differences, psychologists have sought to discover the link, if any, between genetics and intelligence. The results of the research have been inconclusive, and the value of the measuring instruments themselves has been questioned. Thus not only do we know nothing for sure about the origins of differences in intelligence, but we are not even sure what we are talking about when we discuss, and try to define, intelligence in the first place.

10. The study of the origins of mental illness is even more chaotic. All is subjectivity in this area, with psychiatrists at odds over definitions of abnormality and normality. However, many authorities do seem to agree that there is some genetic predisposition to schizophrenia in the form of a lowered threshold for breakdown under stressful conditions.

11. Many psychologists are rethinking the problem of nature and nurture and are now focusing on the interaction of each individual's biological and psychological potentialities. Support for this psychobiological theory comes from examples of psychosomatic reactions, in which a psychological stimulus produces a physical response. This psychobiological outlook is ecological and developmental. It views organisms as sensitive to meaningful psychological stimuli, which can, in turn, change or create biological reactions. Behavior is also affected by situational demands and behavioral models within the environment. All our encounters with objects, people, and ideas throughout our lives affect the psychobiological process of development.

KEY TERMS

assortative traits (discontinuous traits), 56
chromosomes, 54
concordance, 72
cultural bias, 70
deoxyribonucleic acid (DNA), 54
distributive traits, 56
dominant trait, 56
ecological, 77
factorial theory, 71
gametes, 56
genes, 54

genetics, 54
genotype, 56
intelligence quotient (IQ), 59
interactionism, 77
meiosis (reduction division), 56
mental age (MA), 59
mitosis, 54
ovum, 54
phenotype, 56
polygenic (multigene), 61

psychobiological, 76
psychosomatic, 76
range of reaction, 62
recessive trait, 56
restricted range, 63
sex-linked recessive traits, 57
somatic cells, 56
sperm, 54
standardization, 70
zygote, 54

SUGGESTED READINGS

Jacob, F. *The Logic of Life: A History of Heredity*. New York: Vintage Books, 1976 (originally published, 1970). A Nobel prize-winner's account of modern genetics for the lay reader.

Lerner, R. M. *Concepts and Theories of Human Development*. Reading, Mass.: Addison-Wesley, 1976. Includes a detailed discussion of the nature-nurture controversy.

Lewis, M. (ed.). *Origins of Intelligence*. New York and London: Plenum, 1976. A thorough survey of infant intelligence, including historical background, by many of the major figures in the field.

McBroom, P. *Behavioral Genetics. National Institute of Mental Health Science Monographs 2*. Washington, D.C.: U. S. Government Printing Office, 1980. A simple but thorough treatment. Note that it gives somewhat different figures from those in the text for the incidence of psychiatric symptoms in adopted children, but it does not cite a published source.

Winchester, A. M. *Heredity: An Introduction to Genetics*. New York: Barnes & Noble, 1977. An excellent introduction, although fast becoming obsolete. For instance, it makes no mention of gene splicing.

For a critical examination of the evidence concerning the relationship between race and intelligence as well as an analysis of the social and political implications of this issue, we suggest the following books:

Block, N. J., and Dworkin, G. (eds.). *The IQ Controversy*. New York: Pantheon, 1976.

Kamin, L. J. *The Science and Politics of IQ*. Potomac, Md.: Lawrence Erlbaum, 1976.

C H A P T E R 3

Prenatal Development and Birth

We now turn to the chronology of development, beginning at conception. Remember, the baby at birth is already nine months old, and we wish to sketch some features of development during those nine months.

The total **gestation period,** which we will describe in its various stages, is estimated at, on average, 266 days. However, it is usually impossible to date conception exactly, so pregnancy is reckoned from the beginning of the last menstruation, adding about two weeks, for a total of 280 days, or forty weeks, or ten lunar months.

The successive metamorphoses by which a single cell becomes a human being form a remarkable history, and we urge you to consult a specialized text for more detail than we can offer here. We stress only a few highlights important to our understanding of later development.

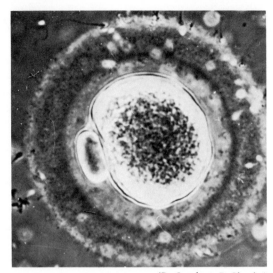

(Dr. Landrum B. Shettles)

A living human egg at the instant of fertilization.

CONCEPTION

The sexually mature human female ordinarily produces one ovum per four-week lunar month, at about the midpoint of her menstrual cycle, which extends from the beginning of one menstruation to the beginning of the next. The egg is expelled from one of the two ovaries and is drawn into the nearby Fallopian tube. It then begins its journey to the uterus (taking from three to seven days), helped along by hairlike cilia that line the tube. The egg remains fertile for only a short time, so if it does not encounter a horde of sperm shortly after entering the tube, it begins to break down. Conception can no longer take place, and the egg disintegrates in the uterus. (However, sperm can live for several days within the uterus, so intercourse does not have to coincide with ovulation to cause pregnancy.)

During sexual intercourse, the male ejaculates semen containing several hundred million sperm into the vagina. The sperm, by lashing their tails, swim upstream through the cervical opening, across the uterus, and into the Fallopian tubes. The casualties are enormous, but a swarm of sperm eventually surrounds the descending ovum.

By a selection process that is not fully understood, one and only one sperm is able to penetrate the ovum. As described in the previous chapter, the two cells break down and reorganize as a single cell, a zygote, complete now with forty-six chromosomes, twenty-three from the mother's ovum and twenty-three from the father's sperm, and a new individual has been launched.

THE GERMINAL PERIOD

The zygote travels down the Fallopian tube and embeds itself in the lining of the uterus. In the process, it is transformed, through a series of cell divisions, into a **blastocyst,** a hollow sphere of cells with an inner cell mass at one side. It is from this cell mass that the baby itself will develop. By age ten days, there is differentiation of the cell layers into *ectoderm* (from which the skin and nervous system will develop); *mesoderm* (the future skeleton, muscles, and supporting tissues); and *endoderm* (the future mouth, throat, and digestive tract). Most of the blastocyst is for the baby-to-be's housing and life-support systems. The key structures that develop are the *placenta,* by which the baby is attached to the mother via the **umbilical cord,** and the double-walled balloonlike sac in which the unborn baby floats in a bath of **amniotic fluid,** which serves to protect it from mechanical injury. The inner membrane of this sac is called the **amnion** (whence, amniotic fluid), and the outer one the **chorion.** The structure and function of the placenta are important to understand, and we will return to this topic after following the future baby's own development into the next stage.

THE EMBRYONIC PERIOD

The six weeks following the formation and embedding of the blastocyst are known as the **embryonic period.** Along with the placenta and umbilical cord (which at first is more like a stalk), the embryo emerges from the inner cell mass of the blastocyst, and during this period all the future baby's characteristically human anatomy takes rudimentary shape. The various tissues differentiate very rapidly, with the nervous system leading the way. It is important to understand that the embryo's various organs and organ systems develop in a fixed sequence according to a strict timetable. That is, each system has its own set time in which to develop, which is known as its **critical period.** During a system's critical period, that system is developing fastest, is most sensitive to growth-inducing forces, and is most vulnerable to the sorts of damaging agents that we will discuss later in this chaper. It should not be inferred that only one organ system is growing at any one time. The critical periods for various systems overlap. But if anything goes amiss during a particular system's critical period, it gets no second chance. The schedule of development slides relentlessly along. (Some idea of the embryo's appearance and development can be gained from the accompanying photographs.)

About two weeks into the embryonic period, or four weeks following conception, the woman becomes aware of being pregnant. Most obviously, by that time menstruation is about two weeks overdue. In addition, the woman may feel a heaviness and a fullness of the breasts, and see an enlargement and darkening of the nipples and their surrounding areolas. She may have to urinate more often than usual because of pressure on the bladder from the expanding uterus. She may have morning sickness, the nausea that afflicts some two-thirds of women in the early weeks or months of pregnancy. Most women, given that their pregnancy is voluntary, find the experience a mixture of discomfort and re-

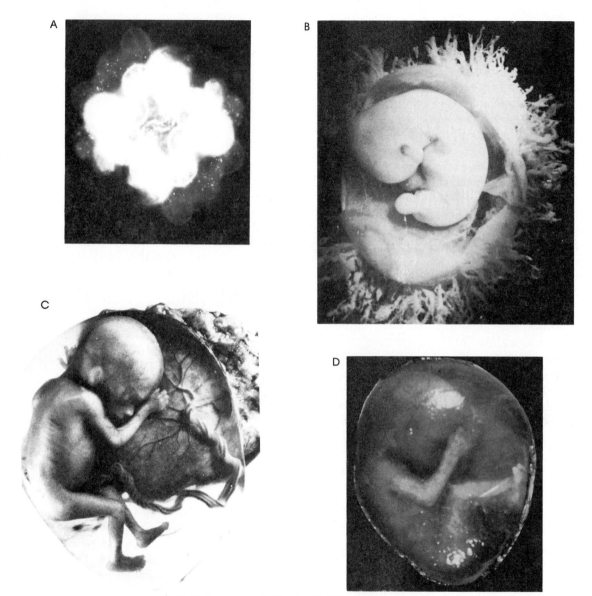

(A, B, D: Dr. Landrum B. Shettles; C: Edith L. Potter, Fundamentals of Human Reproduction.*)*

Stages in prenatal development. **A.** A three-and-a-half-day-old fertilized cell mass. **B.** An embryo at six weeks. Note the placenta and blood vessels developing around the embryo. **C.** A sixteen-week-old fetus. Note the umbilical cord and the well-developed arms, legs, and rib cage of the fetus. The body structures are becoming defined. **D.** A twenty-four-week-old fetus in utero.

wards, hopes and anxieties, pain and delight. Many women report late pregnancy as a time of unparallelled physical well-being.

Toward the end of the embryonic period, around eight weeks, the baby-to-be is about 1.6 inches (4 cm) long. It has limbs and digits and humanlike facial features. The endocrine glands have formed, and the male embryo's testes produce androgens. However, there still is no visible difference between the sexes. Note that all human beings begin life as females. As we said earlier, those who carry a Y chromosome develop gonads that secrete male hormones, and those hormones govern the elaboration of the male sexual apparatus and secondary sex traits. An embryo removed from the womb will show a few isolated reflex movements when stimulated, indicating some degree of neural transmission.

THE PLACENTA

The placenta begins taking shape during the first three weeks of the embryonic period. When fully developed, it is a disk-shaped fleshy slab, 6 to 8 inches (15 to 20 cm) across, slightly more than 1 inch (2.5 cm) thick, and about 1 pound (slightly under .5 kg) in weight. On the side attached to the uterus, it is a spongy-surfaced mass of blood vessels implanted in the lining of the womb and, in some cases, penetrating into the wall of the womb itself. The placenta is smooth on the side where the umbilical cord connects it with the baby. The cord is a rubbery tube enclosing two arteries carrying waste-laden blood to the placenta and a vein carrying fresh blood from the placenta back to the baby. Within the placenta, the umbilical vein

and arteries branch out into a network of roots that are bathed in pools of maternal blood. The embryo's heart, which begins beating three or four weeks after conception, pumps blood through the body, the cord, and the placenta.

Note that the unborn baby's and the mother's blood never normally mix. Substances are exchanged through the walls of the placental blood vessels which, it should be remembered, are outgrowths of the baby's body. The tissues through which materials are exchanged are known collectively as the **placental barrier.**

Wastes, such as carbon dioxide, are absorbed from the arterial vessels into the mother's blood, and the cleansed blood draws from the mother's blood nutrients—oxygen, water, sugars, fats, amino acids, minerals—and other substances such as hormones, antibodies, viruses, and blood fractions (that is, platelets and red and white blood cells) for the return trip via the umbilical vein.

Note, too, that there are no neural connections between mother and baby. However, the placenta has another function besides cleaning and refreshing the baby's blood. It serves as an endocrine gland, secreting hormones that become an integral part of the mother's physiology and presumably help regulate the baby's own development. Some authorities believe that it is the slowing down of placental hormone secretion that helps trigger the birth process.

THE FETAL PERIOD

From about eight weeks after conception, the developing creature is known as a **fetus.** Now all the essential anatomy has been sketched in and we have a quite human-looking being. The fetal period is given over to the growth and elaboration of the structures laid down in preliminary form during the embryonic stage.

By age ten weeks, when it is less than 3 inches (7.5 cm) long and weighs less than 1 ounce (28 g), a surgically removed fetus makes breathing movements. It also makes sucking movements if the lips are stimulated, and the feet show a reflexive fanning out of the toes when the sole is stroked. By about twelve weeks, an expert can distinguish the sexes, although the male's testes do not descend from the abdominal cavity into the scrotum until age twenty-eight weeks or later. Before age sixteen weeks, reflex swallowing begins, and the fetus takes in small amounts of amniotic fluid. Between twenty and twenty-eight weeks, the fetus comes to be densely covered with lanugo hair, which is shed, although not always completely, shortly before birth. With the help of a stethoscope, one can hear through the mother's belly the twenty-week-old fetus's heartbeat. It is about this time that the mother first experiences **"quickening,"** fetal movements that she can feel. "Quickening" is felt first as a mild fluttering, but later in pregnancy as good solid kicks. Twenty weeks is the midpoint of pregnancy, and the mother's condition will usually be apparent to other people. Any morning sickness is likely to be over, and the woman will be entering what is usually the most comfortable time of pregnancy. A fetus born at this time is likely to die quickly, but heroically elaborate (and formidably expensive) techniques have been devised to save the lives of ever-tinier babies.

Toward age twenty-four weeks, the eyelids, previously fused shut, separate, and the fetus opens and closes its eyes. The sebaceous glands—glands deep in the skin that secrete a fatty substance—start operating and produce the *vernix caseosa*, a cheeselike coating that covers the baby at birth. A twenty-eight-week-old fetus, some 15 inches (38 cm) long and weighing 2.5 pounds (1 + kg), stands a fair chance of surviving birth. However, if supplementary oxygen is needed, it has to be given with great care to avoid the blindness associated with *retrolental fibroplasia* (a thickening of the inner eye).

THE BIRTH PROCESS

During the final weeks of pregnancy, the mother will probably feel healthy, but she is likely to suffer some discomfort of mechanical origin. Her inner organs are being crowded by the expanding uterus. She must make postural adjustments to a new distribution of weight—note the sway-backed stance of many women in late pregnancy. In the final few weeks, a number of women experience their bodies as awkward and cumbersome and look forward to giving birth as a welcome liberation.

Toward the end of gestation, the fetus turns head down and comes to rest with its head in the lower part of the uterus, by this time well down in the mother's pelvic basin. The baby is then in position for the usual headfirst passage through the birth canal. As the fetus shifts, the woman's high-prowed profile sags. Pressure against her upper body is eased, and she breathes more freely. This relief from pressure gives the name of the *"lighten-*

ing" to the baby's change of position. The "lightening" may come any time from four weeks before birth until the actual onset of **labor,** the process by which the baby is expelled from the mother's body. The muscles in the uterus contract, squeezing the baby out into the open. The decline of placental hormone production has been cited as one possible initiator of labor, and other hormonal influences are known to be involved. Labor can also be artificially induced by a variety of techniques and substances, but as we shall see shortly, such induction is for use in out-of-the-ordinary situations.

The Three Stages of Labor

There are three different signs that may alert the woman to the onset of labor. One is *labor pains,* produced by recurrent contractions of the womb, initially of mild intensity and spaced fifteen to twenty minutes apart. The pains steadily increase in frequency, sharpness, and duration. They may begin in the back, but they migrate forward as they continue. (False labor pains, which cannot always be distinguished from the real thing, have sent many a woman on a wasted trip to the hospital.) Another first sign may be a *showing,* the emergence from the vagina of a small clot of mucus brightly spotted with blood. This is a plug that had formed in the cervical opening of the uterus and is now released as the cervix begins to relax and dilate in preparation for birth. Yet another sign may be a gush of clear fluid from the vagina. This is amniotic fluid released following the *"bursting of the bag of waters,"* the rupture of the membranes enclosing the fetus.

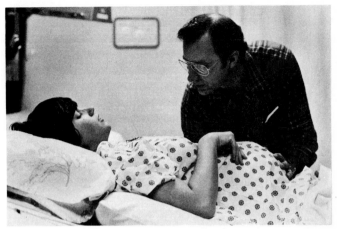

(© Mimi Forsyth/Monkmeyer Press)

A woman with her husband serving as delivery coach at the onset of labor. Initially mild and spaced widely apart, labor pains steadily increase in frequency, sharpness, and duration.

There are three stages of labor. The first and longest is marked by the passage of the baby's head through the dilating cervical opening. The mother is usually encouraged to remain active during the first stage, since there is nothing she can do to help the process along, since activity distracts her from pain and discomfort, and since, according to current obstetrical lore, lying on her back may impede the fetal circulation. If she wishes to rest, we are told, she should sit in a chair or lie on her side. The first stage of labor typically lasts ten to twelve hours for first babies and considerably less for later ones, as police officers and taxi drivers well know.

The second stage of labor involves the baby's passage through the vagina and into the outside world. This takes from twenty minutes to an hour and a half. During the second stage, the mother is often urged to "bear down," tightening her abdominal muscles in concert with the uterine contractions. The exercises that many women now take in anticipation of childbirth include practice in bearing down. The baby's head turns so that the back of the skull, the *occiput*, appears first. The vaginal and surrounding tissues have softened during pregnancy and can be stretched considerably. If, however, the tissues seem in danger of tearing, the attendant may make a lateral cut in the lips of the vagina *(episiotomy)* to enlarge the opening. Such a cut, properly stitched, heals neatly, as a tear might not. Once the occiput has been forced out, the rest of the baby's head quickly comes free, face down and draining. The attendant supports the head with one hand and draws gently. The baby's shoulders are aligned with the long axis of the vulva, and the rest of the baby's body slips out rapidly and easily. The baby's first breath is marked by the birth cry, a thin, reedy wail. Most babies breathe spontaneously, but if breathing has not begun within a few seconds of birth, the baby is massaged or otherwise stimulated to get breathing started. In the hospital, a suction device is used to clear mucus from the baby's nostrils and upper throat. The umbilical cord is clamped and cut. Silver nitrate drops are put into the baby's eyes to prevent infection with gonorrhea—at one time and perhaps still a serious source of blindness. An identifying band is fastened around the baby's wrist or ankle, and the baby's footprint is inked onto a card bearing the mother's thumbprint, as insurance against mixing up babies.

The third and final stage of labor is the delivery of the *afterbirth*, the placenta with its attached membranes and cord. This takes less than twenty minutes and is moderately painful. The afterbirth is carefully inspected to make sure that it is all there (pieces left in the uterus can cause infection) and that there are no abnormalities. In the hospital, the mother is given hormone injections, which hasten shrinkage of the uterus, squeezing shut any broken blood vessels. In many cases, the attendant will knead the mother's belly to restore tone to the uterine muscles.

Some authorities would add a fourth stage of labor: the mother's, father's, and baby's first coming to know one another. Whether or not one considers it a part of labor, this first getting acquainted is a powerful emotional event that may play a significant role in parent-child attachment (Klaus and Kennell, 1982; Kaplan, 1978).

The mother loses a pint (250 cc) or less of blood in giving birth—about what one would donate to a blood bank. For ten to fourteen days after birth, the uterine lining disintegrates and is shed in a process resembling menstruation (the **lochia**).

Atypical Births

What we have just described is the usual pattern of events involved in giving birth. Not all births, however, follow the usual pattern. Some babies fail to turn head down and are delivered in what is called a **breech presentation;** that is, they emerge buttocks first. (The standard headfirst attitude is called a **vertex presentation.)** Some babies are delivered surgically, by cesarian section; we will have more to say about this in a moment. If the contractions weaken or stop during delivery, the mother may have to be given a hormone injection to restart the contractions. If that does not work, the baby may have to be delivered by forceps, tongs that are inserted into the vagina and fit around the baby's head. These complications sometimes lead to harm, but individual prediction is far from easy.

THE MANAGEMENT OF BIRTH

Down through the years, childbirth has become increasingly a medical problem, even though most mothers are healthy and give birth to healthy babies. At one point, it seemed that the mother had no role to play except to submit passively to the doctor's ministrations. Fathers and other family members were rigorously excluded from participation. It became routine to anesthetize the mother totally, use forceps to remove the child, to induce labor at a time convenient to the doctor, to keep mother and baby apart except at feeding times, to discourage breast feeding, and in general to give many parents a sense that the baby belonged to the hospital rather than to them.

There now appear to be four competing systems, with some areas of overlap. At one extreme, a fair number of couples are deciding to have their babies at home, sometimes with a doctor in attendance, sometimes with a midwife, and in a few cases going it alone. The role of the nurse-midwife has grown, not without some active resistance from physicians. A second trend appears in the guise of birthing centers, specialized settings devoted entirely to the needs of parents and babies. Some birthing centers are located in or next to hospitals, whereas others are free-standing but have hospital affiliations in case of emer-

gency. A third trend is simply a continuation of having the baby in the hospital, with modifications. A number of obstetricians, for instance, are willing to dispense, as far as possible, with anesthetics and analgesics during delivery. A great many hospitals have now adopted the practice of **rooming-in,** whereby the mother is allowed to spend as much time as she wishes with her baby, and the father, too, is actually allowed limited contact with the neonate. An increasing number of hospitals is willing to allow fathers in the delivery room, and some will even permit fathers in the operating room during a cesarian. Many hospitals are now willing to cooperate with mothers who wish to breast-feed, instead of more or less subtly discouraging the practice. Fourth and finally, there is the ultimate technologization of the birth process, exemplified by induced labor and, even more, by the increasing resort to *cesarian sections*, removing the baby surgically from the mother's body. Induced labor, which allowed the doctor to schedule deliveries tidily, has received a bad press and seems to be on the decline. Surgical births are still on the increase, though, and deserve further discussion.

Cesarian Childbirth

In 1980, the National Institutes of Health (NIH) convened a group of authorities to consider the facts and implications of the rise in surgical deliveries (U.S. Department of Health and Human Services, 1982). Between 1968 and 1977, the rate of birth by cesarian section almost tripled, from 5.5 percent to 15.2 percent, and is rising still. Similar trends are seen in Canada, a slighter rise is found in most Western European countries, and

Norway has the highest cesarian rate of all. Let it be said to begin with that a certain, quite small number of births call for cesarian section: the baby should be delivered early in cases of maternal diabetes or hypertension. Cesarian section may be desirable when there is danger of erythroblastosis, a blood disorder caused by incompatibility of blood type between mother and child, the most common being Rh incompatibility. However, most cases of Rh-induced blood disorder can be prevented by treatment of the mother with gamma globulin, and erythroblastosis is a rare menace.

Among the reasons given for performing a cesarian are the following: dystocia (we shall talk about this in a minute), 31 percent; repeat cesarian (following the theory that once a cesarian, always a cesarian), 31 percent; breech presentation, 12 percent; and fetal distress, 5 percent. Some less overt reasons for the cesarian option may be that there are fewer children being born than formerly, so greater concern can be lavished on the few; increased use of fetal monitoring, which may reveal otherwise hidden fetal distress; the use of cesarian delivery as an alternative to forceps delivery, which carries a certain amount of risk; the practice of defensive medicine, inspired by a fear of malpractice suits if any harm comes to the baby in the course of a vaginal delivery; the potentially greater profit to the doctor (surgical births are more costly than ordinary ones); and the emphasis given in some residency programs to the desirability of the cesarian option. Avoiding exposure of the baby to genital herpes has become a fairly common reason for cesarians.

Dystocia can mean either abnormal positioning of the fetus in the womb or a disporportionately large baby relative to the mother's reproductive apparatus. The NIH panelists found this definition somewhat vague, and called for more precision in invoking it as a reason for doing a cesarian. The panelists also found that most breech births could safely be handled vaginally by an experienced obstetrician. The panelists conceded partial validity to the repeat cesarian logic. Older cesarian methods entailed a vertical incision in the uterus, and healed vertical incisions are liable to tear under pressure. Nowadays, however, most cesarian sections involve what is called a low-segment transverse incision, which means a horizontal cut in the uterus. Such incisions, once healed, are thought to be less likely to tear under pressure than are vertical ones, but the facts are not yet all in. The panel recommended clinical trials, which means that some women who have had transverse cesarians be allowed to deliver vaginally; the panelists acknowledged the ethical questions raised by research that places human lives at risk, but felt that the risk here was low enough to justify the knowledge gained. In general, the panel came down on the side of vaginal delivery except in some well-specified cases. It was pointed out that mothers who have cesarians are twice as likely to die as mothers giving birth vaginally, and cesarians carry a significantly greater risk of infection. The panel definitely recommended against an immediate cesarian when labor is interrupted.

There is no substantial evidence on the developmental effects on babies of delivery by cesarian section. For instance, a study by Field and Widmayer (1980) found that at four months babies born by the vaginal route performed better on formal measures than did babies born by cesarian section, but the cesarian mothers expressed more satisfaction in their babies than did the noncesarian mothers. At eight months, there were no differences on formal measures, but cesarian mothers continued to rate their babies more highly.

Cesarian births require that the mother be anesthetized, either wholly or partially, and the role of anesthetics in childbirth has long been a matter of fierce controversy. No one doubts the desirability of alleviating the mother's pain during delivery, but a great many people fear that the relief of pain is bought at the expense of the baby's welfare. The research findings are contradictory, but on balance there is reason to think that drugs given to the mother during delivery—which find their way via the placenta into the fetus's system—pose some risk to the baby. A study by Murray *et al.* (1981) examines the effects of epidural anesthesia (drugs injected or dripped into the region of the lower spine) on the development of babies during the first month. The babies of drugged mothers showed poor **state stability** during the first five days (state stability refers to the consistency of sleep and waking patterns from day to day). By one month of age, there were no detectable differences between the babies of drugged and undrugged mothers. However, the mothers who had received no medication, as compared to those who had, reported that their babies were more sociable, more rewarding, and easier to care for; the investigators also found that the nonmedicated mothers were more responsive to their babies' cries than were the mothers who had had drugs. Murray *et al.* echo the feeling of quite a few observers that the drugs themselves may have no lasting effects on the babies, but that drugs can interfere with the parent-child bonding that begins right after birth (Klaus and Kennell, 1976). Others (e.g., Haire, 1980) question the adequacy of the government's screening methods for both drugs and fetal monitoring devices such as ultrasonic scanners, and feel that supposedly benign medical technology may be more hazardous than is usually recognized.

Prepared Childbirth

Earlier in the century, there arose a movement associated with the name of Grantley Dick-Read known as **natural childbirth.** This approach emphasized educating the prospective mother so that she could understand and participate intelligently in the birth process, exercises that would limber the mother's body and ease delivery, no use or only sparing use of anesthetics, and, well in advance of its time, the participation of the father throughout pregnancy and birth.

Nowadays, the emphasis is on **prepared childbirth,** combining the teachings of Fernand Lamaze (1958) and of Frederick Leboyer (1976). Lamaze emphasizes the preparations for birth, the education and exercises and care of the body, whereas Leboyer focuses on the birth process itself. Lamaze, unlike most advocates of causes, has published some figures. He rated the results of his methods with 4,487 births as good to excellent in 65.23 percent of the cases, and as fair to failure in the remaining 34.77 percent.

Leboyer views the birth process as traumatic for the baby. He has in effect resurrected the psychoanalyst Otto

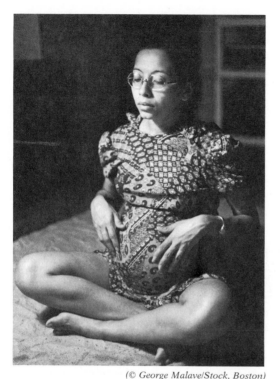

(© George Malave/Stock, Boston)

Practicing breathing exercises, one of the skills developed in prepared childbirth classes. Combining the insights of Fernand Lamaze and Frederick Leboyer, prepared childbirth emphasizes preparations for birth, care of the body, and the birth process itself.

Rank's theory of the trauma of birth, which says that the sudden change from a warm, dark, silent, protective universe into a clamorous world of light and activity and heat and cold is so devastating that many people spend the rest of their lives symbolically trying to climb back into the lost Nirvana of the womb. In fact, Otto Rank abandoned his theory, but it is alive and well in the writings of Leboyer. To minimize the trauma of birth, Leboyer keeps the lights turned dim, the room silent, and the air warm, and handles the baby very delicately. Immediately after birth, the baby is placed for a short resting period on the mother's body, and the mother gently massages the neonate. The baby is then immersed in a bath at body temperature, simulating the wet warmth of intrauterine life. As the baby is dried and folded in warm wrappings, with head and arms left free, and given to the mother or father to hold, there is a gradual introduction to the new, more turbulent reality of the postnatal environment.

As a variant on prepared childbirth procedures, Odent (1982) encourages women in labor to experiment with different positions to reduce pain. He finds that kneeling during the first stage brings considerable relief, and squatting with support during the birth facilitates delivery, reduces the need for episiotomies, and makes some cesarians unnecessary.

Note that prepared childbirth lends itself most easily to home delivery or the birthing center. It works in a hospital setting only if the staff is receptive and promises to keep hands off except in case of emergency. We do not know how many parents follow the various paths to childbirth (except in the case of cesarians, not all of which are planned for), but it is our impression that college-educated young people are now coming to take prepared childbirth as the norm. The medical profession may end up split right down the middle, with one half going along with the low-technology approach and the other half insisting on its right and duty to pour on all the high technology it can muster.

The prepared childbirth movement finds a natural extension in the early

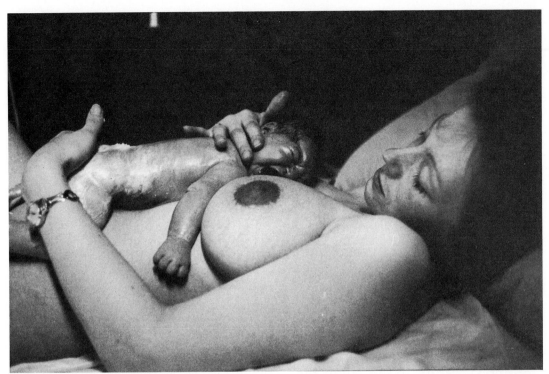

With the Leboyer method, the baby—umbilical cord uncut—is placed on the mother's body for a short rest immediately after birth, and is gently massaged by her. Dimmed lights, a warm, quiet room, and delicate handling all help to minimize the trauma of birth.

contact movement. A series of studies by Klaus and Kennell and associates (Kennell *et al.,* 1973, 1974; Klaus and Kennell, 1976; Ringlet *et al.,* 1975) arranged to have the baby placed naked in bed with its naked mother, the father when possible also being present, for one hour within the first three hours after birth, and then for another five hours daily for the first three days. The mothers were encouraged to nurse their babies. Although the mother's breasts do not begin to produce milk until a day or two after delivery, they secrete a substance called *colostrum,* which is thought to be good for the baby. In addition, the baby's sucking on the nipple may hasten actual lactation in the mother. This treatment was said to result in intensified mother-infant involvement, which was still apparent two years later. A number of critics have questioned whether the effects of immediately postnatal bonding are that much greater than those of bonding that takes place during the first few days and weeks (Brody, 1983). Klaus and Kennell (1982) have themselves moderated their initial claims.

NEONATAL PATHOLOGY

All but a few babies are born sound of body and capable of full psychological development under ordinary conditions, but we must take note of the exceptions. There are four main sources of disorder in the neonate. First, there are genetic disorders, some negligible and some life threatening. Second, there are disorders associated with the action of prenatal environmental influences. Third, there is premature birth. Fourth, there are disorders related to events during the birth process itself, referred to as *perinatal disorders.* In addition, there are disturbances of unknown origin. We begin with genetic abnormalities. We give only a few examples. You will find a more detailed account in, for instance, Hendin and Marks (1979).

Genetic Disorders in the Newborn

Two kinds of genetic disorder may be present at birth. There are, first, true hereditary traits that are passed down from generation to generation. Second, there are genetic disorders that seem to be the product of environmental forces—notably x-rays and viruses, which disturb the normal structure of the chromosomes.

Most chromosomal abnormalities result in spontaneous abortion, but several permit survival to birth and beyond. These are generally traceable to the mother, who carries her lifetime supply of ova from birth. The longer she lives, the more likely it is that the genetic material in one or more ova may be damaged by some environmental agent. Since the man's sperm supply is constantly renewed, he is less likely to pass on a damaged chromosome. Note, however, that veterans who were exposed to the defoliant Agent Orange during the Vietnam war report that they are fathering an unusually large proportion of defective babies. There may be mechanisms that affect the sperm that we do not yet understand.

Inherited Genetic Disorders. The largest group of hereditary disorders is called the **inborn errors of metabolism,** of which more than 125 are known. The best known of these is *phenylketonuria (PKU).* PKU and other diseases related to errors of metabolism are traceable to a deficient enzyme. In the case of PKU, the defective enzyme is the one that metabolizes phenylalanine, and all babies born in American hospitals are routinely screened for excess phenylalanine in the blood or urine. The baby with PKU is placed on a special diet that excludes milk and other high-protein foods, but includes enough phenylalanine to meet the body's minimal requirement. Given such a diet starting in the first few days of life, PKU children can develop normally.

Cretinism, a form of severely retarded mental and physical development associated with diminished thyroid gland activity, was long a mystery. It is now known to be caused by an enzyme deficiency, and its symptoms can be prevented by regular treatment with thyroid extract, especially if detected early.

Another enzyme-deficiency disease is **Tay-Sachs,** which is found almost exclusively in Jews, especially Jews from Eastern Europe. Tay-Sachs is marked by early and rapid brain deterioration and death; there is no known treatment. A recently discovered enzyme-deficiency disease is *familial hypercholesterolemia (FH)* (Rosenfeld, 1981). FH is caused by an error of fat metabolism, which leads to arteriosclerosis (fatty deposits in the blood vessels and hardening of the arteries) and heart attacks in children and young adults.

Hemophilia, or bleeder's disease, is well known at least partly because of its mode of inheritance. It is one of the so-called sex-linked recessives, caused by a gene on an X chromosome inherited from the mother, and found most often in males, whose much smaller Y chromosome lacks a corresponding gene. Females carry the trait, but ordinarily they have only one abnormal gene, which is counteracted by the normal gene on the second X chromosome. However, an occasional female inherits two of the abnormal genes and develops hemophilia. A far less serious example of sex-linked recessive inheritance is red-green color blindness, which is found in some 8 percent of males but only .4 percent of females. Other forms of color blindness may be inherited, but they are only partially sex linked.

We have heard a great deal in recent years about *sickle-cell anemia*, a condition found primarily in blacks of West African extraction but to a lesser degree in people from the Mediterranean basin and the Middle East. Sickle-cell anemia requires two like genes. It is marked by sickle-shaped red blood cells that can impede circulation, causing pain, sickness, and even death. It used to be thought that sickle-cell carriers, those who have only one gene for the trait, could also develop anemia under conditions of severe oxygen deprivation, such as great physical exertion, excessive consumption of alcohol, or being at high altitudes. For this reason, the U.S. Air Force Academy would not accept sickle-cell carriers as air-crew trainees. It turned out that carriers do not develop anemia at high altitudes, and the Academy has now changed its policy. Sickle-cell anemia is thought to be a mutation that survived because it confers partial immunity against malaria.

We should note that not all genetic disorders are apparent at birth. *Huntington's disease* (formerly known as Huntington's chorea from the dancinglike movements of its victims) may not appear until middle age, when the sufferer may already have passed the disease along to offspring. Huntington's disease is a progressive deterioration of the central nervous system, marked by grimacing and the dancing movements mentioned above. It sometimes involves impaired mental functioning, but not always. Woody Guthrie the folk singer, who died of the disease in 1967, was one of the most widely known victims.

Chromosomal Abnormalities. We now turn from the gene-borne diseases, most of which are truly hereditary, to the **chromosomal anomalies,** most of which are genetic without being hereditary. Chromosomal abnormalities are associated with the action of external agents on the chromosomes in the mothers' ova (with the reservation about effects on the sperm noted above). Among these agents, x-rays and viruses are the chief suspects, but some of the many toxic chemicals in the environment may eventually be implicated. In rare instances, in the formation of the germ cells, errors in cell replication occur and a gamete ends up with abnormal chromosomes or an abnormal number of chromosomes. These so-called **errors of dysjunction** are of two kinds: either a chromosome is omitted or extra ones are included. Most

(© Bruce Roberts/Photo Researchers, Inc.)

A little boy with Down's syndrome. Note the child's physical appearance: the fold over the eyelids and the thick, protruding tongue, which are common in those born with an extra chromosome number 21.

chromosomal anomalies are fatal to the organism. However, a few of the chromosomes can appear in abnormal numbers without killing the individual, although there is almost always some disruption of normal functioning.

The most widely known of the conditions due to chromosomal anomalies is *Down's syndrome* (formerly called mongolism). Most cases of Down's syndrome are associated with an extra chromosome number 21, for which reason it is often referred to as *trisomy-21* (trisomy means three bodies). The condition is

marked by a number of physical stigmata, the most conspicuous being the extra, epicanthic folds of skin that cover the eyelids, giving the eyes an Oriental appearance. It used to be thought that Down's syndrome automatically implied severe mental deficiency, but special training and stimulation may bring the IQs of victims up to the range of the 70s or 80s (Rynders, cited in Scarr-Salapatek, 1975). The life expectancy of children with Down's syndrome, once no more than about ten years, has increased with care and education so that some live into the thirty- and forty-year range (Smith and Wilson, 1973). An experimental program begun in Germany performs cosmetic surgery on children with Down's syndrome to make them look normal. It seems that the change of appearance creates a social climate much more favorable for development ("Mongoloid Children in Israel," 1982).

Another group of conditions reflects abnormalities of the sex chromosomes. Some of the atypical sex-chromosome combinations that have been observed are XXY, XYY, XXX, XO (the O stands for a missing chromosome) and *mosaicism*—in which the individual has two kinds of cells, each with a different complement, as in XX/XO or XXY/XO. All these anomalies except XYY are accompanied by various physical abnormalities and sexual underdevelopment, although hormone therapies may help (Reed, 1975).

The only outward sign of an XYY abnormality is unusual tallness. The XYY combination has received much attention because for a while it was believed that this condition predisposed men to violent criminality. In 1968, one Daniel Hugon received a reduced sentence for murder in a French court on his plea that because he had an XYY-chromosome abnormality he could not be held fully responsible for the crime (McBroom, 1980). In fact, more careful study has made the XYY-violence link seem most unlikely. For instance, one study found that men having an XYY-chromosome combination are more likely than those with an XY combination to run afoul of the law, but for petty, nonviolent offenses (Witkin et al., 1976). The authors of this study found that men with XYY-chromosome abnormalities scored lower than those with XY combinations on a crude intellectual screening test used by the Danish armed forces, and thought that the XYYs' minor brushes with the law might be attributed to low intelligence. However, another large-scale study in Britain found that its sample of seven boys with XYY combinations (out of 7,849 boys examined, indicating the rarity of the condition) had an average IQ of 99.5 (which is normal) and a nondeviant range from 78 to 130 (Ratcliffe, 1976). These studies indicate the sum of our knowledge of the XYY combination. We know remarkably little about where the extra Y chromosome comes from except that mothers cannot be held accountable for its presence.

Genetic Counseling. We digress for a moment to talk about **genetic counseling,** expert advice on reproductive matters for parents or prospective parents. People who are thinking of having a child can seek genetic counseling before marriage, before conception, during pregnancy, or when the birth of a child has revealed an unsuspected genetic problem. The first tool of the genetic counselor is the family history, which can show whether genetic disorders have occurred on either side. The next step is a genetic examination of the parents themselves, from biochemical assays to chromosome studies. For instance, Tay-Sachs disease, being recessive, can be foretold when both parents are carriers. For this reason, it is urged that all Jewish couples be tested for Tay-Sachs. If either parent is a noncarrier, they can have children without fear of transmitting this disease to their offspring. If one parent is a carrier, however, the children in due course will have to be alerted that they in turn may be carriers. If both parents are carriers, they then have to decide whether they want to run the 25 percent chance of having a child affected by the disease.

Another procedure in the case of high-risk pregnancy is **amniocentesis.** This routinely includes women past thirty-five years of age, since, as we have said, the longer a woman lives, the greater the likelihood that one or more of her ova will have sustained chromosomal damage. Between the sixteenth and twenty-second weeks of pregnancy, samples of amniotic fluid can be drawn directly from the womb with a hollow needle. This fluid contains shed skin cells from the fetus that can be cultured. The cells can be **karyotyped**—that is, their chromosomes made visible and sorted—to detect any gross anomalies such as Down's syndrome. (One can also, of course, identify the baby's sex and any abnormalities of the sex chromosomes.) The skin tissues can be analyzed biochemically to reveal various enzyme abnormalities. Not all genetic disorders can be detected this way. For instance, potential disorders of kidney function are not detectable in skin tissue. Tay-Sachs disease cannot be diagnosed before birth. However, it has now become possible to spot sickle-cell anemia in the course of tissue analysis. Amniocentesis occasionally leads to miscarriage, but most studies show the rate to be hardly higher than spontaneous abortions.

British doctors have developed a test for neural tube defects in the unborn baby. These include *anencephaly* (lack of a brain, which is quickly fatal) and *spina bifida* (failure of the covering of the spinal nerves to develop normally). The test consists of examining the mother's blood for the presence of *alpha-fetoprotein (AFP),* the only component of fetal blood that is detectable in the blood of the mother. However, the test had just begun to be used in the United States when it was discovered that the procedure yielded too high a proportion of *false positives,* indications that something is wrong when in fact nothing is. Now more elaborate procedures are used in Britain to screen for neural tube defects (Kolata, 1980). If the mother's blood contains AFP, she undergoes ultrasound scans to check for the presence of twins or triplets, fetal death, or miscalculated gestation, any of which can lead to overproduction of this substance. If the fetus is anencephalic, the sonogram will reveal that directly; however, it is not likely to pick up spina bifida. Provided the sonogram reveals none of the foregoing, the amniotic fluid is assayed for a high level of AFP and also for *acetylcholinesterase,* a nerve enzyme that may indicate neural tube defect. Kolata points out that in 20 percent of cases of spina bifida, skin covers the incomplete neural tube, and, with the help of surgery, development can be essentially normal. Of the remaining 80 percent, children whose open spines remain exposed, some may have *hydrocephaly* (water on the brain); many (but not all) are mentally retarded; many (but not

all) are permanently incontinent (that is, they cannot control elimination); nearly all require medical and surgical treatment; and most suffer some paralysis of the legs. This more elaborate screening is now available in Great Britain, but the American medical profession has not yet adopted it.

Thus prenatal diagnosis can reduce (but not eliminate completely) the likelihood of bearing a genetically abnormal child. (There was fear briefly that parents would exploit these techniques to control the sex of their children, but it has turned out that American parents are inclined to accept whatever sex fate deals them, and many do not even want to be told in advance, preferring to be surprised.) New techniques are being devised, although some of them, such as ultrasound monitoring, are probably best reserved for special situations, since they may involve risks to the fetus (Haire, 1980). We should also note that prenatal surgery is being tried experimentally to correct some defects.

In recent years, genetic counseling has branched out into all areas of reproduction. For the couple made infertile by Fallopian-tube blockage, there is now the possibility of test-tube conception. An ovum is removed surgically from the mother, inseminated with the father's sperm, and reimplanted surgically in the uterine lining. If either parent is deficient in gamete production, there now exists the possibility of artificial insemination. If it is the woman who cannot conceive, the couple may choose to find a surrogate willing to carry to delivery an infant conceived with the father's sperm.

In this context, we mention a debate that grew out of the nature-nurture controversy. This was between advocates of

eugenics, those who propose to better the species through controlled breeding, and the partisans of **euthenics,** those who favor improving the species by improving the environment in which children are reared. Hitler's program of genocide was the ultimate exercise in eugenics. Less ghastly but still sickening enough was a program in Lynchburg, Virginia, in which 4,000 men, women, and children were sterilized on the ground that they were "misfits" ("50-Year Sterilizing in Virginia Decried," 1980). Most of those sterilized were supposedly mentally retarded, but the program also reached prostitutes, petty criminals, and maladjusted children. The sterilizations ended in 1972, but a state law still authorizes them. According to the *New York Times* report cited above, Virginia ran second to Delaware in the number of sterilizations performed on so-called misfits.

Obviously, genetic counseling is a form of eugenics, but counseling is based on sounder scientific principles than the Holocaust and the sterilization of "misfits," and it is, besides, totally voluntary. In any event, the battle between the eugenicists and the euthenicists has been misdirected, since it is obvious that eugenics and euthenics can go hand in hand. Meanwhile, somewhere off on the horizon, lies **euphenics,** control via the manipulation of the genetic material itself. Euphenics has a forerunner in gene splicing. Gene splicing promises us such wonders as manufactured insulin and interferon, which once looked as though it might be an all-purpose antibody.

Prenatal Influences on Development

A second source of neonatal pathology is the action of unfavorable forces on the child before birth. The intrauterine en-

(© Leonard Speier)

Environmental hazards could threaten this woman's pregnancy. No matter what our genetic endowment, teratogens—that is, environmental agents that induce variations in embryonic and fetal development—can radically alter normal intrauterine development.

vironment is generally quite stable and favors normal prenatal development of the kind we have described. However, departures from normality in the prenatal environment can produce a variety of consequences. Note that the general channel for these disruptive agents is the placental barrier. However, some agents, such as ionizing radiation (as in x-rays), can act directly on the developing organism. We talk about the effects of prenatal influences not to frighten prospective parents but as part of our description of the developmental process.

The study of prenatal environmental influences carries a potent theoretical implication: The deformities we are talking about are produced through the action of perfectly normal genes, genes that are themselves unaffected by the agents that are responsible for the deformities. Our genetic endowment is not a fixed blueprint for development. It is, instead, a very flexible system that can manufacture many different variations on the human theme, according to the inputs it receives. Indeed, some of these variations are so extreme as to fall outside our usual definitions of what is human. The study of these environmentally induced variations is called **teratology,** literally the study of monsters. The word **"teratogen"** has entered the common language, along with **"mutagen"** (an agent that causes changes in the structure of genetic material) and *"carcinogen"* (a cancer-causing agent) to describe various toxins and their possible effects. Perhaps the best general survey of teratology for the lay reader is still the volume by Ashley Montagu (1962).

Two different sorts of effects appear, depending on whether the disturbing agent intrudes during the embryonic or the fetal period. During the embryonic period, the actual design of the organism, its basic morphology, can be radically altered. Later, during the fetal period, the baby can suffer various degrees of damage, but without changes in his or her very design.

Embryonic Period. The *embryonic period*, as we have said, lasts from two weeks to eight weeks after conception. The following agents are among those that have been implicated in embryonic malformations: poisons; drugs; viruses (such as *rubella*—German measles); x-rays and other forms of ionizing radiation (radiation can also be a mutagen, but its role here is as a teratogen); abnormal blood conditions in the mother (hormonal imbalance, anemia, or the presence of unusual proteins); gross excess or deficiency of certain vitamins; protein deficiency; and iodine deficiency (agents do not have to be abnormal forces; they can also be the absence of normal ones).

Among the deformities produced during the embryonic period are the following: *anencephaly* (lack of a brain); *harelip* (an opening in the upper lip); *cleft palate* (a split in the roof of the mouth); *phocomelia* (the "seal flippers syndrome"— the stunted arms and incompletely differentiated fingers—associated with, among other possible agents, the drug thalidomide); *syndactyly* (failure of the digits to separate); extra members or missing members; reversal or ambiguity of sex; and a host of other conditions sufficient to fill a textbook.

What we do not know enough about is whether, in contrast to these teratogens, there are anomalous agents or influences that exert a favorable effect beyond that which is produced by the normal prenatal environment. For the time being, it seems safest to say that the normal environment, free of teratogens, is the ideal environment.

Fetal Period. During the *fetal period* (from eight weeks after conception to birth), the developing organism can become addicted to alcohol or narcotics if the mother is a frequent user of these substances. Experts have now come to recognize the **fetal alcohol syndrome (FAS).** Alcoholic babies are reported to show growth deficiency, slow motor and intellectual development, small head size, heart defects, and mild abnormalities of the face and limbs. One survey (Abel, 1980) concludes that the most serious consequence of prenatal exposure to alcohol is mental retardation. Abel joins others in pointing out that some of the effects of maternal drinking may also be the effects of malnutrition, since people who drink heavily are liable to neglect their diets. Mothers who are heavy drinkers are also likely not to have good prenatal care, and, if they continue to drink after birth, may not make the most effective rearers of children.

Babies whose mothers are addicted to narcotics are themselves born addicted and show a consistent picture. They do not manifest any detectable physical or intellectual impairment, but various emotional disturbances are common, even when the babies are reared in what seems to be good environments (Strauss *et al.*, 1975; Wilson, Desmond, and Verniaud, 1973).

There is growing agreement that cigarette smoking by pregnant women is harmful to the fetus, being linked especially to low birth weight.

A syphilitic mother may give birth to a syphilitic child who contracted the disease in the uterus. Gonorrhea, on the other hand, is most likely to be transmitted during passage through the birth canal. It appears that genital herpes is also likely to be transmitted during birth rather than earlier.

The evidence of adverse effects on the fetus from maternal malnutrition is a matter of some dispute, although malnutrition seems to be an important factor in premature birth and low birth weight and their associated risks. A problem is that most studies of the effects of maternal malnutrition are of necessity retrospective—that is, we are presented with the end product of a history at which we can only guess. Animal studies can, of course, be prospective and deliberate, and they have consistently found fetal deficiencies, such as decreased brain weight, when the mothers are kept on low-protein diets (Zamenhoff, van Marthens, and Grauel, 1971). A much-discussed retrospective study at the human level is a follow-up examination of children carried during the Dutch famine of 1944 to 1945 (Stein *et al.*, 1972). Using Raven's Progressive Matrices, a single, rather limited measure of IQ, the Stein group found no lasting untoward consequences of prenatal malnutrition. There are weaknesses in the study beyond its choice of measuring instrument, however. The subjects were candidates for the draft, and so were exclusively male. The study did not cover persons in institutions or, of course, those who had emigrated or died. And there is no sure way of knowing what pregnant women actually experienced in 1944 and 1945. It is not beyond imagining that their relatives, friends, and neighbors skimped on their own short rations to share them with the mothers-to-be.

In general, obstetricians nowadays encourage pregnant women to eat an ample diet and not to be afraid to put on some weight. This runs counter to the conventional wisdom of twenty-five years ago, when women were counseled to gain as little weight as possible during pregnancy. It is now generally accepted that brain development is most rapid just before and after birth, and it is essential that the brain have adequate protein. Apart from the issue of nutrition, some people are concerned that the many food additives found in today's diet may have harmful consequences for mother and child.

A matter of concern is that as many as 1 percent of American babies are born infected with cytomegalovirus (CMV). We might note that the incidence changes from 0.5 percent to 2 percent as one descends the economic scale. CMV is a poorly understood disease. Some infected babies show no symptoms, but in those cases where the disease is active, the symptoms are many and varied, and there is danger of deafness, blindness, and mental retardation. CMV is thought to be the most common viral cause of retardation, affecting about one of every thousand American infants, or a total of 3,000 babies a year. No preventive or treatment has yet been found (Marx, 1975).

Although the problem of Rh blood incompatibility is mostly of historic interest these days, it is during the late fetal period that its effects start to become evident. *Rh factor*, a blood protein first discovered in rhesus monkeys (whence Rh), is present in some 85 percent of Caucasians and about 99 percent of other racial groups. It can cause trouble only when an Rh-negative woman mates with an Rh-positive man (Rh is dominant, so we would have to know the man's genotype to know the child's chances of getting an Rh gene). If the child should be Rh positive, any intermingling of maternal and fetal blood, as through a rup-

tured vessel, most often during birth, would cause the woman to start producing antibodies against the Rh factor. Antibody production is too slow to affect a first child. If, however, the woman carries a second Rh-positive child, and if there once again is mixing of the blood, her Rh antibodies can destroy the fetal blood. However, most cases can be prevented by treatment of the mother with gamma globulin.

Variables in Prenatal Environmental Influences. Whether potential teratogens have an effect, and what the effect is likely to be, vary with certain conditions: (1) the point in development at which the agent is introduced; (2) how large a dose is present; and (3) species, strain, and individual differences in susceptibility.

1. Timing. We have already mentioned the fact of critical periods during the embryonic phase, when each organ system has its one allotted developmental period in an unchangeable timetable, and when it is most sensitive both to growth-enhancing and to growth-damaging influences. Thus the timing of the introduction of a teratogen may determine its effect.

The principle of timing is illustrated by *rubella* (German measles) infection. Depending on when the virus strikes, it can cause brain damage, blindness, deafness, or peripheral deformities, as of the extremities. An interesting if somewhat frightening feature of prenatal rubella is that the baby remains infectious for some weeks after birth and has to be kept apart from other newborns and from pregnant women who have not had rubella. The use of thalidomide, which is a tranquilizer, also illustrates timing. It is teratogenic only during a brief period of the embryonic stage; at other times it has no effect at all.

The critical period principle tells us that the same deformity can be caused by a variety of teratogens depending on the timing. For instance, deafness can be caused by rubella, x-rays, or some other teratogen that strikes during the auditory apparatus's critical period of development.

We should also note that some systems are more central to total functioning than others. The nervous system, digestive tract, circulatory system, and endocrine system are most important. If these are damaged, other, secondary deformities are likely to follow. Thus endocrine abnormalities in the mother can reverse the baby's sex. If, by contrast, one of the peripheral systems is affected, then the damage may be quite minor, such as incomplete separation of the toes.

Finally, we should be aware of long-delayed teratogenic effects. The hormone diethylstilbestrol (DES), formerly given to prevent miscarriage, has been associated with cancer of the genital tract in the adolescent daughters of women given DES in pregnancy.

Reinisch (1981) has reported that children of both sexes whose mothers were treated with progestins such as DES to prevent miscarriage show greater aggressiveness in a test situation than do untreated controls. Reinisch found that sons of treated mothers were more aggressive than the daughters of treated mothers, but that sons of untreated mothers also were more aggressive than daughters of treated ones. Although the daughters of treated mothers were more aggressive than girls in general, they showed no visible signs of physical viril-ization—that is, they appeared to be completely female in their anatomy.

2. Dosage. Some teratogens have no effect unless they surpass a certain minimum dose. On the other hand, there may be a dual threshold: Either too little or too much vitamin A, B_6, D, or K for instance, can cause harm to the embryo. There is endless debate about whether ionizing radiation has a threshold effect; some people hold that a small dose may do just as much harm as a large dose. Until the debate is settled, it is probably the better part of wisdom to make sure one's unborn child is irradiated as little as possible. It is probable in the case of radiation that, even if no damage occurs immediately, it is cumulative, and repeated doses can be "stored" until they reach an effective mass.

3. Species, strain, and individual differences. What is a teratogen for one species may not be for another. This makes for difficulty in screening new drugs for safety. The test animals may show no effect, but when a different species is exposed, the chemical turns out to be harmful. Thalidomide seems to affect only humans. But even within a given species, some strains are more vulnerable than others to particular agents. And within a given strain, some individuals are more or less susceptible than others. When new compounds are tested on dogs or rabbits, some members of the litter may be affected while other members of the same litter go untouched. We have no way of accounting for these differences.

Old and New Conceptions of Prenatal Influences. The prenatal environmental influences we have been discussing are, of course, quite different from those that have always figured in old wives' tales: the pregnant woman who sees a tree struck by lightning gives birth to a child who will one day have a blaze of white in his or her hair; the woman who listens to good music throughout pregnancy will have a musically gifted child; by resolutely thinking only pleasant thoughts, the mother guarantees a child of cheerful disposition. Unlike these magical influences, the ones we have been talking about involve direct physical action on the tissues of the unborn child. (Remember that the nervous systems of the fetus and mother are unconnected.)

However, there is one respect in which the old wives' tales may contain a grain of substance. There is firm evidence from animal experimentation, and suggestive evidence from human studies, that chronic stress in the mother can affect fetal development and lead to difficulties during pregnancy and delivery (Copans, 1974). As we know, emotional arousal involves physiological changes, such as release of adrenalin into the bloodstream, and the chemicals produced by emotional upheavals can cross the placental barrier. Stress, of course, may also go hand in hand with poor eating habits, drug use, drinking, and smoking. The exact relationships are still unclear, but it is evident at the animal level that severe or extended stress to the mother can affect the infant's body size; adrenal gland size and activity (the core of the adrenal gland is the source of adrenalin); learning ability; and longevity. Needless to say, if one wants to study the effects of stress on pregnant women, one has to stick to the model of the natural experiment.

Another point that should be emphasized in reviewing the effects of environmental factors on embryonic and fetal development is that the malformations produced by teratogens are not inheritable. The teratogenic agents we have been talking about alter the developing physical structures of the unborn child. They do not, however, directly modify, or "mutate," the child's genes. Therefore, these **congenital** (present at birth) **anomalies** are not inherited by the next generation. People with physical defects produced teratogenically are capable, provided they attain sexual maturity, of having normal children. The affected persons have perfectly normal genetic make-ups but develop in a severely distorted manner in the presence of teratogens.

Premature Birth

It is estimated that 6 to 8 percent of babies are born prematurely (twenty to thirty-seven weeks instead of the usual forty) or have low birth weight (under 2,500 g or about 5 lb.; Brody, 1982). **Premature birth** was once thought to lead almost inevitably to less than satisfactory development. In fact, premature and low-birth-weight babies account for about 85 percent of neonatal deaths. However, premature and low-birth-weight babies who survive and are given extra care seem to develop well in about 75 percent of cases. Part of the problem used to be one of attitudes. The premature baby was regarded as though he or she were still a fetus and was treated more like a vegetable than a human being. Nowadays, preterm babies are treated as much as possible like normal

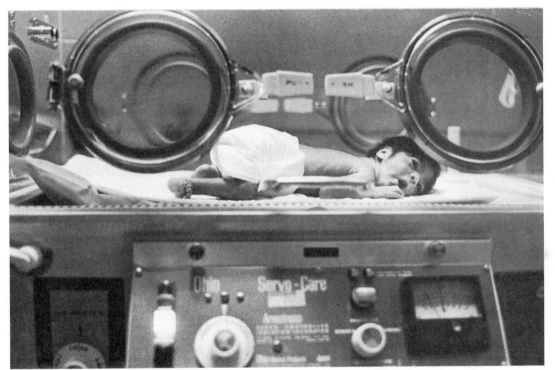

(© Mimi Forsyth/Monkmeyer Press)

A premature infant. Premature and low-birth-weight babies who survive and are given extra care seem to develop well in about 75 percent of cases. Preterm babies are nowadays treated as much as possible like normal babies.

babies, with gratifying results. In one study, special counseling was given to the mothers of premature babies who seemed to be at especially high risk: the children of lower-class, black, teenage mothers (Field *et al.,* 1980). At least at age eight months, these babies were thriving. Cohen and Parmalee (1981) studied cognitive functioning in five-year-olds who had been born prematurely and found not only a negligible relationship between birth factors and IQ but concluded that: ". . . we cannot predict intellectual development from obstetrical and postnatal hazardous events" (p. 2).

Brazelton (1982) speculates that one source of difficulty for premature babies is that parents need the usual full nine months of pregnancy to mobilize themselves to play the parental role. If in fact the baby arrives ahead of schedule, the parents are unprepared and disoriented. Brazelton also notes that premature babies are precariously organized and can wear themselves out trying to respond to excessive stimulation.

Prematurity and low birth weight are

often associated with prenatal malnutrition. Zeskind and Ramey (1981) worked with a population of fetally malnourished babies. All the babies were given standard medical care, but half were given cognitively oriented day care beginning at three months. At age thirty-six months, the enrichment group had IQs just below 100, whereas untreated babies had IQs averaging between 70 and 85.

Perinatal Causes of Neonatal Pathology

A fourth source of neonatal pathology is the actual circumstances of birth—the so-called **perinatal** influences. Breech delivery inexpertly managed can cause complications. The mechanical damage sometimes inflicted by forceps can lead to brain damage. Some babies are partially strangled by having the umbilical cord wrapped around their necks. *Anoxia,* deprivation of oxygen associated with partial strangulation, with premature separation of the placenta, or with delayed breathing can produce brain injury and perhaps *cerebral palsy,* a severe impairment of motor control.

Pain-relieving drugs given to the mother during delivery may do harm to the baby. As we said earlier, obstetrical medication derived from the mother's body does not seem to have a lasting effect on the baby's physical well-being, but if it makes the newborn sluggish and unresponsive, this may retard and even impair bonding with the parents. It seems to be an unfortunate fact of life that some proportion of mothers are permanently alienated from babies who do not respond fully to early maternal initiatives. This applies with particular force to the feeding situation and is fur-

ther amplified when the mother tries to breast-feed an unresponsive baby (Hubert, 1974).

In general, the United States has little to be proud of in its record of child health, which is generally taken as a major index of societal well-being. Although the United States has pioneered in medicine, including neonatal and infant care, our advanced technology runs well ahead of the statistics. The infant mortality rate (deaths before age one per 1,000 live births) has been dropping steadily, but our 1979 rate (the latest figures available) of 13.1 ranked tenth among the world's nations, well behind Sweden's 8.0 and the 9.0 found in Japan, the Netherlands, and Switzerland. White infants in the United States had a death rate of 11.4, whereas nonwhites had a rate of 21.8, about the same as Bulgaria's.

Continuum of Reproductive Casualty Versus Continuum of Caretaking Casualty

It was once believed that congenital defects, whether genetic, teratological, or perinatal, led invariably to later psychological difficulties. Pasamanick (Kawi and Pasamanick, 1959; Pasamanick and Knobloch, 1963) formulated the concept of a **continuum of reproductive casualty,** which said that the more severe the congenital problems, the more severe the later psychological problems. Unfortunately, the studies by Pasamanick and his associates were all done retrospectively, after the fact.

Prospective studies—those that look forward in time rather than back—tell us that early impairment is likely to become permanent if the child fails to receive a full ration of the love, stimula-

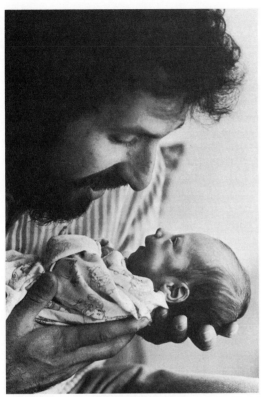

(© Mark Antman/The Image Works)

Father and baby. While it was once felt that congenital disorders caused irreversible psychological damage, recent studies have shown that good, loving parenting can overcome most negative effects of birth complications.

tion, and discipline necessary to sound development. The notion that the degree of impairment varies inversely with the adequacy of parenting has been summed up by Sameroff and Chandler (1975) as the **continuum of caretaking casualty,** which includes the notion of self-righting tendencies in high-risk babies. The difference between reproductive casualty and caretaking casualty is not to be thought of as the difference between nature and nurture. Reproductive casualty refers to congenital disorders of all sorts—genetic, teratological, perinatal influences, the effects of prematurity—and should therefore not be taken as hereditary. To emphasize caretaking casualty does not deny the importance of organic factors. It merely says that good caregiving can go a long way toward overcoming organic handicaps (Werner and Smith, 1982). In thinking about this issue, we must insist on the reciprocity of parent-child relations and note that children with congenital organic disorders may fail to trigger the kinds of parental responses that make up beneficial caregiving.

Disorders of Unknown Origin

Some newborn babies manifest organic conditions that may or may not be significant but the origins of which are not known. The two that we discuss are minor physical anomalies—unusually large head circumference, widely spaced eyes, a curved fifth finger, wide gaps between the first and second toes—and *state stability*, consistency or inconsistency of patterns of sleep and alertness from day to day.

Halverson and associates (Halverson and Victor, 1976; Jacklin, Maccoby, and Halverson, 1980; Waldrop *et al.*, 1978) have sought to link minor physical anomalies with various forms of problem behavior. The number of anomalies found in newborn baby boys (girls were not studied) correlated highly (.86) with problem behavior at age three (Waldrop *et al.*, 1978). However, this seemingly strong relationship, approaching the power of individual prediction, was all but invisible in Jacklin *et al.*'s later study of preschool children. Links (1980) found minor physical anomalies in a few autistic children (see Chapter 15), but the presence of anomalies seemed to be related only to age of the mother and not to psychiatric status. In general, if minor physical anomalies have any behavioral significance, it is probably because odd-looking children receive less positive emotional stimulation than do ordinary-looking children.

Thoman and associates (Thoman, 1981; Thoman *et al.*, 1981) have used the stability of patterns of sleep and arousal to predict later malfunctioning. They took four weekly measures of how much time each newborn spent in each of six states: active waking; quiet alert; fuss or cry; drowse or transition (being on the borderline between sleep and waking); active sleep (asleep but with much movement); and quiet sleep. From these measures they derived an index of consistency. Babies who showed a great deal of stability in their state patterns were assumed to have good prognoses, whereas those low in stability were considered to be at risk. In fact, the four lowest scoring babies of twenty-two had later difficulties. The lowest was diagnosed at two and a half months as having aplastic anemia (red blood cell deficiency, with associated pallor and weakness, caused by defects in the bone marrow). The second lowest at six months developed epilepsylike convulsions with abnormal brain-wave patterns. The third lowest baby succumbed at age three and a half months to *sudden infant death syndrome (SIDS)* (crib death). The fourth lowest was diagnosed at age two and a half years as possibly hyperactive. This approach is the only one so far that

promises to yield individual predictions. Note two things, however. It predicts only that trouble lies ahead, and not the particular kind of trouble. Second, the study involved only twenty-two children. The value of the technique can be demonstrated only with a consistent record of accuracy when used on a large scale. We might note in passing that group predictions of SIDS can be made on the basis of unusually long interruptions of breathing (such interruptions are called *apnea*) during sleep. Several babies have had their lives saved because they slept hooked into monitors that sounded an alarm when breathing was too long suspended.

Let us end, then, on a note of reassurance. Even damaged babies—no more than 10 percent of those who survive birth—possess powerful self-righting tendencies, especially if they are given strong emotional support and adequate intellectual stimulation. Parents who give up on impaired babies are in danger of launching a self-fulfilling prophecy. We do not know the secret of how to make it possible for parents to love babies who are slow to respond or who carry the visible signs of some organic condition such as Down's syndrome. Perhaps they have to discipline themselves to play the part of loving, involved parents. Role playing sometimes evolves into the real thing. In any event, it is incumbent upon medical personnel to give parents every reasonable encouragement about the future of less-than-perfect newborns. Professionals often fail to appreciate how ignorant, confused, and frightened new parents can be, even when their babies are wholly normal. If the professionals were to take full account of the parents' insecurity, they would be more likely to give badly needed emotional reassurance and con- crete guidance. Flawed babies can reach full humanity, and they deserve the right to do so.

SUMMARY

1. The successive metamorphoses (or changes) by which a single cell becomes a human being are a remarkable process. During the germinal period (the first two weeks of gestation), a series of cell divisions occurs, and the resulting blastocyst embeds itself in the uterine lining. The key structures that nourish and house the baby during pregnancy are the placenta, umbilical cord, and amniotic sac.

2. During the next six weeks of development, called the embryonic period, all of the baby's characteristically human anatomy is taking rudimentary shape. The baby's organs and organ systems develop in a fixed sequence according to a strict timetable. During the time that a particular system is set to develop (its critical period), this system is particularly sensitive to growth-inducing or growth-damaging influences. If anything goes wrong during this critical period, there is no second chance to correct it during prenatal development.

3. The placenta and umbilical cord have the important functions of carrying fresh blood to the baby and carrying waste-laden blood away from the baby. The placenta secretes hormones which are part of the mother's physiology and presumably help to regulate the baby's growth. These exchanges of wastes, nutrients, and other materials take place via the placental barrier. The baby's and mother's blood normally never mix.

4. During the fetal period (from eight weeks until birth) growth and elaboration of the structures laid down during the embryonic stage occurs. Doctors can now hear the fetal heartbeat, and by twenty weeks, women can feel the fetus's movements. If all goes well, the baby is fully developed and ready for birth after approximately 266 days of gestation.

5. The signs that birth is near are labor pains, "showing," or the "bursting of the bag of waters." There are three stages of labor. The first and longest involves the passage of the baby's head through the dilating cervical opening. The second stage includes the baby's passage through

the vagina and into the outside world. The final stage is the delivery of the afterbirth, the placenta with its attached membranes and cord.

6. Some babies fail to follow this normal pattern and have atypical births. Some babies are breech births, others must be delivered by cesarian section or forceps.

7. Recently, there has been a movement to view the birth process less as a medical procedure and more as a normal and natural event. Dr. Fernand Lamaze has developed a widely used method of prepared childbirth which involves both parents and uses a series of physical and breathing exercises to reduce pain, fear, and tension during delivery. Some hospitals use "rooming-in," which allows the mother and child to be together as much as the mother desires, and also gives fathers contact with mother and baby. Dr. Frederick Leboyer has developed a method of minimizing the shock of birth for the baby by using lowered lights, quiet, and continuous human contact immediately following delivery. These new methods seek to humanize the birth process for both parents and child. There has also, however, been a counter-trend toward greater medical control of the birth process, as seen in the increase in cesarian sections.

8. Unfortunately, some babies are born with impairments. There are four types of abnormalities: genetic disorders, conditions caused by prenatal environmental influences, disorders caused by premature birth, and disorders caused by events during the delivery itself.

9. There are two kinds of genetic disorders. First, there are hereditary traits which are passed down from generation to generation, such as hemophilia, sickle-cell anemia, diabetes mellitus, PKU, and cretinism. Second, there are genetic disorders which seem to be the product of environmental forces (for example, x-rays and viruses) which disrupt the normal arrangement of chromosomes. These disorders, such as Down's syndrome or unusual sex-chromosome combinations, are genetic but not hereditary. They often result in sterility, but if not, they supposedly could be passed on to the next generation, as in the case of XYY.

10. At present there are many ways of detecting or predicting before birth the likelihood of congenital flaws. Genetic counseling, amniocentesis, AFP, sampling fetal blood, and ultrasound techniques are some methods of detecting certain genetic or developmental abnormalities.

11. A healthy environment is essential for normal prenatal growth. Negative environmental influences (called teratogens), such as poisons, drugs, viruses, x-rays, abnormal blood conditions in the mother, gross excess or deficiency of certain vitamins, and protein deficiency, can cause embryonic malformations. Alcohol, narcotics, cigarette smoking, or malnutrition can cause premature birth, low birth weight, and a variety of other complications. Prolonged stress on the mother also is thought to have a negative effect on the fetus's development.

12. The type and extent of damage caused by teratogens depends on several factors: the time in prenatal development at which the teratogen is introduced, the amount or dosage present, and individual differences in susceptibility to the agents.

13. Premature birth is no longer synonymous with less than satisfactory development. Premature babies are now treated as much as possible like normal babies, except that they are given extra care.

14. A fourth source of neonatal pathology is the actual circumstances of birth. Breech delivery, anoxia, damage inflicted by forceps, and medication given to the mother during delivery can all have short- or long-term harmful effects on the infant.

15. It appears, despite previously held ideas, that perinatal complications do *not* inevitably lead to developmental disorders. The effects of such complications depend largely on the caretaking that the child receives.

KEY TERMS

amniocentesis, 99
amnion, 85
amniotic fluid, 85
blastocyst, 85
breech presentation, 90
chorion, 85
chromosomal anomalies, 97

congenital anomalies, 106
continuum of caretaking casualty, 109
continuum of reproductive casualty, 108
critical period, 85
embryonic period, 85
errors of dysjunction, 97

eugenics, 100
euphenics, 101
euthenics, 101
fetal alcohol syndrome (FAS), 103
fetus, 87
genetic counseling, 99
germinal period, 85
gestation period, 84

inborn errors of metabolism, 96
karyotype, 99
labor, 89
mutagen, 102
natural childbirth, 93
perinatal, 108

placental barrier, 87
premature birth, 106
prepared childbirth, 93
quickening, 88
rooming-in, 91
state stability, 93
teratogen, 102

teratology, 102
umbilical cord, 85
vertex presentation, 90

SUGGESTED READINGS

Berezin, N. *The Gentle Birth Book*. New York: Simon and Schuster, 1980. A guide for parents-to-be to the birthing techniques based on the teachings of Lamaze and Leboyer.

Hendin D., and Marks, J. *The Genetic Connection*. New York: New American Library—Signet, 1979. A useful popular guide to genetic abnormalities and genetic counseling.

McBroom, P. *Behavioral Genetics*. Washington, D.C.: U. S. Government Printing Office, 1980. A good, medium-difficult survey of the field.

Montagu, M. F. A. *Prenatal Influences*. Springfield, Ill.: Thomas, 1962. An excellent guide to the subject. More recent topics, like prenatal diagnosis, genetic disease, and neonatal pathology are best kept track of through current articles in newspapers and magazines and some of the suggested readings included herein.

Nilsson, L. *A Child Is Born*. New York: Delacorte/Seymour Lawrence, 1977. A stunning account in photographs and text of human reproduction.

Russell, K. P. *Eastman's Expectant Motherhood*. Boston: Little, Brown, 1977 (originally published, 1940). This guide for prospective parents is probably the layperson's best introduction to prenatal development.

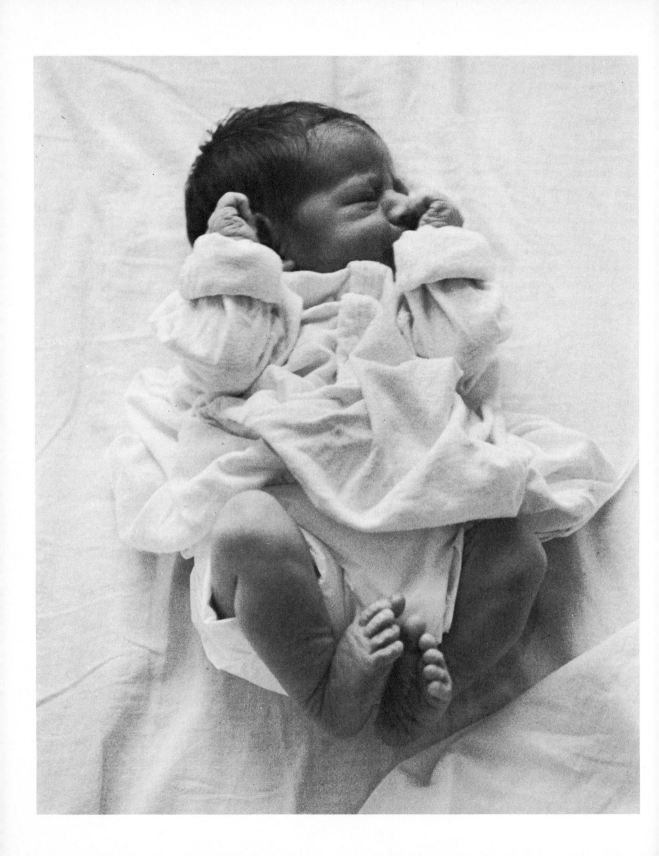

CHAPTER 4

The Newborn Baby

One of the odd by-products of our urban-suburban civilization is that many people never see a newborn baby—a **neonate**—until confronted with their own. The result is often a sense of shock. Parents-to-be are rarely told what their newborn will look like and so base their expectations on the idealized "newborns" (usually babies two or three months old) shown in advertisements. Most actual neonates are tiny, wet, sticky, and possibly red (it may take a while for skin pigments to develop in babies who will have dark skin). It is because so many people are unfamiliar with neonates that we begin with a description of the baby's physical appearance. Newborns have their special individual identities, but they share a quality of newbornness, a still somewhat fetal look.

Note that here and throughout this chapter we speak of neonates not only as they are right after birth but also during the first few weeks of postnatal life—experts disagree on the precise length of the neonatal period.

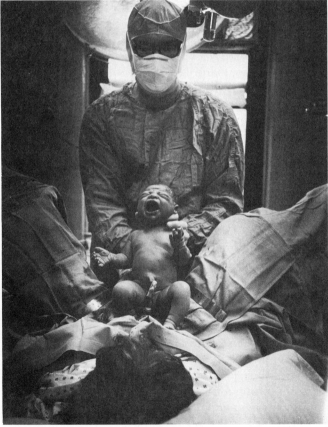

(Daniel Benevento)

In our society, many people never see a newborn baby until the birth of their own. Tiny, wet, sticky, and possibly red, most neonates still display a somewhat fetal look.

PHYSICAL APPEARANCE OF THE NEONATE

Newborn babies seem incredibly small: average weight 7 pounds (3+ kg), average length 20 inches (51 cm); since they keep their legs drawn up, they look even smaller. Their proportions are very different from those in later life. The head makes up about a quarter of the total length (try to picture an adult with these proportions) and seems to rest directly on the puny shoulders, the neck being visible only when the baby's head is bent back. The almost useless legs are about a third of the overall length. When the neonate is held vertical under the arms, the head lolls to one side and the bowed legs hang helplessly. The baby's feet, which are strikingly long, are bent inward at the ankles so that the soles are almost parallel. Facial proportions also will undergo many changes. The cranial dome is well developed and the eyes are relatively large. The ill-defined nose may have been flattened and the head squeezed out of shape in passing through the birth canal. This "molding" disappears within a week or two. Many neonates have a beautifully formed rosebud mouth, but they seem virtually chinless. Neonates may still be wearing some of their fetal hair *(lanugo)*, dark and ranging from coarse to downy, not only on the crown but sometimes low across the brows or far down the back. The fetal hair, if present, will eventually be replaced by a regular crop, either gradually or after an intervening period of baldness.

The neonate at birth is still wet with the amniotic fluid in which it was immersed during gestation, and the skin is coated with a cheeselike substance *(vernix caseosa)* which when it dries takes on a chalky cast. (Before birth, the vernix caseosa acts as a protective coating on the fetus's skin.) Depending on how much time the baby has had to mature within the womb, and also on how well he or she was nourished, skin color may range from ashen to rosy pink or red. Eye pigments, too, are slow to develop, and virtually all babies are born with smoky blue eyes. (Remember that newborns have drops of silver nitrate solution put into their eyes as protection against gonorrhea, and the film of silver nitrate may deceive parents into thinking their baby has brown eyes.) The baby's skull has six soft spots, or *fontanels*. These are openings covered with a tough, resilient membrane just beneath the skin. The most easily noticeable fontanel is at the very top of the head; it may not close over completely until age one and a half. The fontanels serve two functions. During birth, they permit some compression of the baby's skull to ease the passage.

After birth, they allow space for the baby's rapidly growing brain.

The newborn's genitals are surprisingly large. Both boys and girls have enlarged breasts that may secrete a whitish substance called "witch's milk." Girls may have a brief "menstrual" flow shortly after birth. These phenomena are caused by hormones absorbed from the mother and subside rapidly.

Neonates are likely to look scrawny because they have not yet fully developed their layers of body fat, except for the fat pads that fill out the cheeks. The fat pads play an important part in sucking and, incidentally, keep the baby's toothless mouth from having the withered look of some old people. Premature babies are likely to have underdeveloped fat pads and so look remarkably like old people. At the other extreme, very mature newborns may be well plumped out with body fat and so resemble the pudgy "neonates" seen in advertisements.

We should not be misled by the almost larval look of many neonates. They are genuine human beings physically and psychologically, with all the potentialities associated with the human condition. They are ready for vital if basic interactions with other people. They respond to a variety of human and nonhuman stimuli. The major body structures are already present, even if only in immature form. Virtually all the brain cells are present at birth, although a good deal of development lies ahead. Between birth and age one, and again by age six, the brain doubles in size as its various structures take shape and become organized. This growth is accomplished by increases in the size of nerve cells, by the development of insulating sheaths on cells outside the cortex, and

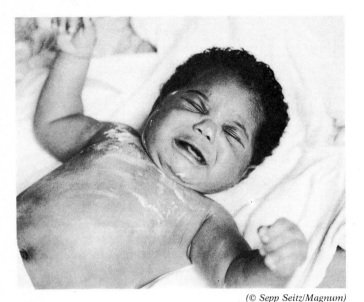

(© Sepp Seitz/Magnum)

A crying neonate. This well-developed, plump neonate is communicating its distress by tearless crying. Note the fetal hair (lanugo) on the forehead, the seeming lack of a neck, and the chalky remnants of the vernix caseosa on the chest.

by the growth of glial cells that regulate both development and function in nerve cells. The newborn comes into the world complete with eyebrows and eyelashes and with tiny, paper-thin fingernails and toenails (many mothers find it convenient to keep the nails trimmed by biting them). In the neonate's jaws are buds for two sets of teeth. The newborn girl's ovaries already contain, or soon will, her lifetime supply of rudimentary ova, or eggs. By contrast, sperm do not form in the testes of the boy until he approaches puberty.

The feel of a neonate is something to be experienced. A practiced adult can hold a newborn with one hand and forearm, fingertips bracing the back of the baby's skull, the heel of the palm holding the baby's shoulders, the forearm supporting the almost nonexistent buttocks (remember what we said about body fat). But not all neonates feel the same when held. Some remain compactly and comfortably curled like kittens; others sprawl like loosely joined bundles of sticks; some are tense and stiff; and others squirm and writhe or flail. Bear in mind that the basis for these individual differences dates from the moment of conception, since each fertilized egg is genetically unique.

BASIC LIFE PROCESSES IN THE NEONATE

This book is about psychological development, but we have to know something about biological development as well. The neonate has just undergone a dramatic transition from prenatal life in total darkness and near-total silence to life as a semiautonomous being in the light and air.

Before birth, the fetus received all the necessities of life—oxygen, water, foodstuffs, and various other substances—from the mother's body. Wastes from the fetus's body likewise were absorbed by way of the placenta into the mother's blood. This statement needs some qualifying. Once the fetus's kidneys are working, small amounts of urine are excreted directly into the surrounding amniotic fluid. In addition, the fetus excretes mucus and sheds skin and hair into the amniotic fluid. Small amounts of fluid are swallowed, and the solid wastes are stored in the bowel as a tarry substance tinged greenish black by bile from the liver. These fetal feces, or *meconium*, are

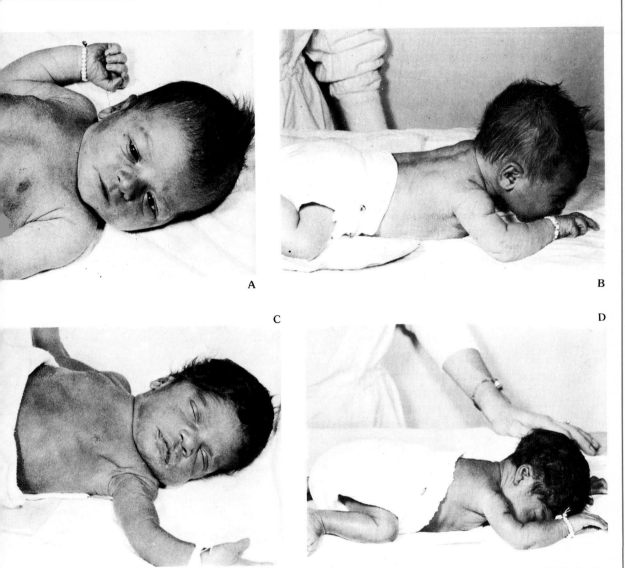

*(Dr. Frances K. Graham/*Courtesy, Journal of Pediatrics)

Contrasts between full-term (**A** and **B**) and premature (**C** and **D**) neonates. Note the limp sprawl of the baby in **C** and the difficulty in raising the head to clear nose and mouth in **D**.

not ordinarily excreted before birth.

The neonate now handles his or her own *digestion*. Unlike the fetus, the baby must take sustenance through the mouth, digest it in the stomach and intestinal tract, and eliminate wastes by urination and defecation. At first, some newborns may be unskilled eaters, taking fluids in one- or two-ounce doses, part of which may be promptly regurgitated. One reason that young babies vomit is that they swallow a fair amount of air with their milk, and when they belch up the air, milk is carried along.

Respiration, as we have said, is a new activity for the neonate. Once born, neonates have to get their oxygen by breathing. The baby's first breath may be stimulated simply by exposure to air; it may be set off by a sneeze or a yawn; or it may be brought on by more strenuous measures, such as the once-traditional slap on the bottom. The birth cry initiates the whole complicated reflex pattern of lifelong inhalation and exhalation.

A total shift in the pattern of blood *circulation* takes place. Once the umbilical cord is cut, its blood vessels are squeezed shut and the navel heals completely in about five days. The stump of umbilical cord dries and shrivels and drops off in a week or two. Blood is forced to flow through the lungs where it exchanges carbon dioxide for oxygen to be carried throughout the body.

Furthermore, the neonatal body must now begin to *regulate its own temperature*. This is a slow process. At first, the baby's body temperature is at the mercy of environmental fluctuations, and the neonate easily becomes chilled or overheated. There are several mechanisms for temperature regulation that are not yet fully operative in neonates. The capillaries do not readily approach the skin to radiate excess heat or shrink to conserve heat. The baby's sweat glands do not begin working until about age one month. Nor can neonates engage in behavioral thermoregulation, such as moving to where the temperature is more agreeable.

A legacy of prenatal life helps babies survive through the early months. Among the many things absorbed from the mother's blood are her antibodies against viruses. (Most antibodies against bacteria are too large to pass through the placental screen.) Thus, although babies are vulnerable to and have to be protected from a great many diseases, they are not likely to develop any of the common viral diseases until around age six months, when the maternal antibodies have been lost. During this early period, then, the baby has a mixed pattern of *immunity* and *susceptibility*, resistance to common viruses but vulnerability to bacterial diseases.

From a psychological standpoint, the most important change is that the neonate is for the first time bombarded with sensory stimulation. (There may be prenatal responsiveness to sound, vibration, and pressure, and if sugar is injected into the amniotic fluid, the fetus increases its swallowing; but the fetus is largely buffered by amniotic fluid against external stimulation.) Most of the equipment for receiving information is in place and functioning at birth, and people spend a major part of their lives trying to make sense of and organize all the information that the environment supplies. This leads us to an examination of the psychological capacities of the newborn baby.

NEONATAL PSYCHOLOGY

During the past twenty-five years there has been a revolution in the study and understanding of the neonate as a psychological being, capable of learning, of feeling, of processing information, and of interacting with other people. When we consider that people have been having and rearing babies throughout the history of humankind, our earlier ignorance seems incredible. Once psychologists (and psychiatrists and pediatricians) got around to discovering the neonate, there began an outpouring of research by investigators too numerous to list. A number of factors seem to have helped bring about this revolution: (1) growing interest in development as a key dimension in human behavior, which led to the logical realization that one had to study development from its very beginnings; (2) sharpened observations, ingenious procedures, and sophisticated instrumentation, including recording devices for what are called **indicator responses,** the physiological reactions that tell us that stimuli are having an impact on the baby; (3) recognition that the baby's state of arousal at the moment of testing makes a considerable difference in whether and how he or she will react; (4) use of subdued stimuli and gentle handling so as to avoid overwhelming neonates with more stimulation than they can manage; and (5) recognition that neonates **habituate**—that is, stop responding to the same stimulus after repeated exposures—so that lack of consistent response does not by itself mean that the baby is insensitive to a particular stimulus. Habituation has turned out to be very useful in the study of perception. Since babies resume responding when the stimulus changes, we can see what sorts of differences the baby is capable of detecting.

Newborn States

The baby's momentary condition, such as degree of arousal, hunger, health, or whatever else may affect receptivity to outside stimulation, is called a **state.** The chief state dimension for research purposes is that of arousal—sleep and wakefulness. At least seven different ways of classifying neonatal states have been proposed, but all of them have *deep* or *regular sleep* as their starting point. Deep sleep is marked by even breathing and a minimum of grimacing and body movement. *Irregular sleep* is marked by uneven breathing, much movement, changes of facial expression, and, in some cases, starts and tremors and twitches. An intermediate kind of sleep in which the baby moves little and the eyes open and close is variously called *light* or *transitional sleep*, or *drowsiness*. *Rapid eye movements (REMs)*, which frequently accompany dreaming in older children and adults, are found in both irregular sleep and drowsiness (one can see the eyes moving behind the closed lids). Although we do not understand the significance of REMs in neonates, they occur with greater frequency right after birth than at later periods of life. These classifications of sleep remind us that neonates spend most of their time—as much as twenty hours a day—asleep. During sleep, particularly REM sleep, boy neonates have cyclical erections of the penis. There is some evidence that girl neonates have analogous cycles of erections of the clitoris.

Depending on whose system we follow,

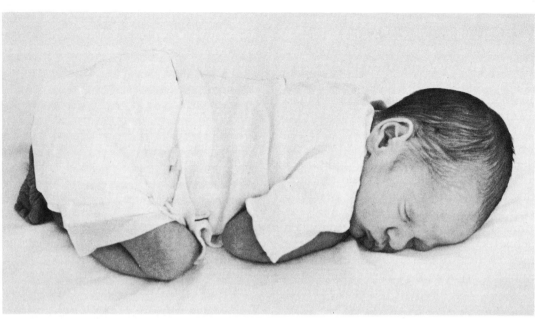

(© Mimi Forsyth/Monkmeyer Press)

A sleeping neonate in the prone position. Newborns spend as many as twenty hours a day asleep. This neonate appears to be in a deep sleep, with even breathing and lack of movement. Babies go through a variety of sleep states and may even dream. Notice the common sleep position of arms and legs curled under the body and the turned head.

we can recognize either two or three waking states. First, there is *alert inactivity*, which means that the baby is awake, comfortable, and ready to make contact with the world, which also means that this is the ideal state for both psychological testing and interaction with parents. Alert inactivity is most often found after the baby has been fed, has eliminated and has had his or her diaper changed, and is not yet ready to go back to sleep. Second, there is *active wakefulness*, characterized by considerable movement of the arms and legs and twisting of the head and trunk. Finally, active wakefulness shades into *agitation*, during which the baby may become distressed and begin to cry.

Young babies cry for two main reasons. The first is hunger. Hunger crying can be temporarily allayed by picking up and snuggling and rocking the baby, or by giving a pacifier. However, these measures will satisfy the baby only briefly, and the only effective answer to hunger crying is to feed the baby. The second major cause of crying is *colic*, which, beginning at any age from a few days to a few weeks, afflicts a sizable proportion of babies and about which we have little understanding at this time. Its most common form is several hours of intense screaming, usually at a particular time of day, most often the evening hours. A bout of colic ends when the baby drops off to sleep. There are no reliable remedies for colicky crying, just as there is no sure knowledge of its cause. In addition to crying, the symptoms of colic are a swollen belly, suggesting painful distension of the bowels by "gas," doubling up of the body, and breaking wind. A pacifier may help, rocking the baby in one's arms or the bassinet may do some good, and some experts propose that the sure-fire treatment is to drive the baby around in a car. Parents driven to their wits' end by colicky crying can take solace from the fact that colic almost always ends right on schedule, at age three months, vanishing as mysteriously as it appeared.

Reflexes

A wide array of what are called reflex actions can be fairly reliably stimulated in the newborn. **Reflexes** are predictable, unlearned, automatic, and involuntary responses to particular forms of stimulation. The reflexes are of three main kinds. First, there are the physiological reflexes, such as changes in the pupil of the eye to changing levels of light, which play a part in sustaining life. Second, there are reflexes that serve no known function, such as the familiar knee jerk, but that may be useful in detecting neurological abnormalities. Third, there are complex behavioral responses to stimulation. Although these are quite predictable when we know the baby's state and provide the right stimulus, their complexity suggests that the baby is acting intelligently, cooperating in having his or her needs taken care of.

The baby comes into the world equipped with such important physiological reflexes as vomiting, sneezing,

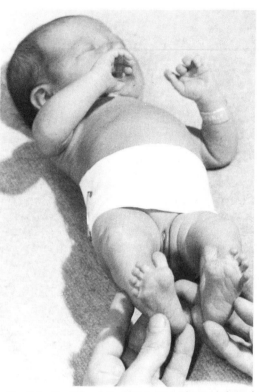

(Dr. Heinz Prechtl and David Beintema, The Neurological Examination of the Full-Term Newborn Infant.*)*
The Babinski response.

hiccoughing, yawning, and blinking. The neonate's pupils dilate and shrink as the illumination changes. The baby's tear ducts do not participate in his or her crying, but the tear glands do bathe the eyeballs continuously and will step up their activity to wash away irritants. However, the automatic focusing functions of the eyes on a nearby object are not yet present. The newborn salivates reflexively when anything is put into its mouth.

The reflexes with no known physiological or behavioral function are important as indicators of the newborn's neurological maturity. One of these is the familiar

(© Michael Weisbrot & Family)

Nursing. The sucking response is one of the neonate's reflexes; touching the baby's lips or cheek causes the head to turn toward the stimulus and the mouth to try to take it in. If the stimulus is a milk-producing nipple, a fairly well coordinated sequence of sucking, swallowing, and breathing ensues.

knee-jerk (patellar) reflex. Another such reflex is interesting because it changes with age. This is the *plantar* (sole of the foot) *response.* If one strokes the neonate's sole from back to front with a firm instrument (a thumbnail will do), the toes fan up and outward in what is known as the *Babinski response.* Later in infancy and thence throughout life (except in conditions of brain damage or stupor), the toes have the opposite reaction—they curl downward. The *Babkin response* is produced by pressing on the neonate's palms while he or she is supine (lying face up). Before describing the reaction, we have to note that the reclining neonate typically keeps the head turned to one side. When one presses on the palms, the supine baby's head turns to the midline, the mouth opens, and sometimes the head is raised.

We come now to the third type of reflex, those that seem to have some behavioral relevance. The most important of these is the **rooting response.** Lying alone on a table or in a bassinet, the neonate is virtually helpless. However, when held in close contact with a responsive adult body, the newborn becomes a very different creature (this is an example of how behavioral capabilities vary according to the situation). A hungry neonate, like the young of other mammalian species, "searches" the adult body with his or her mouth as though trying to find a nipple. The baby clutches at whatever handholds are available—clothing, hair, folds of skin—and propels him- or herself so actively with trunk, arms, and legs that the adult may wonder if, like the Duchess's baby in *Alice in Wonderland*, the baby is not changing into a small pig. Some writers equate the rooting response with what is really only one of its components, the *sucking response*, which can be brought about in isolation from the larger pattern. Touching the baby's lips or cheek causes the head to turn in the direction of stimulation and the mouth to try to take in the stimulating object. The response can be set off with a finger, but if the stimulus is a milk-producing nipple, the baby will take it in and begin a fairly well-coordinated sequence of sucking, swallowing, and breathing. Neonates show wide and consistent individual differences in the rate and force with which they suck. The head-turning portion of the sucking response implies that if one wants the young baby to face in a given direction, as when one wants to take a picture, it does no good to push against a cheek. The baby's head turns toward the push instead of away from it. One has to touch the cheek on the side toward which one wants the baby to turn.

The **grasping reflex** seems to be a legacy from our apelike ancestors. When the baby's palm or fingers are stimulated (neonates typically keep their hands lightly fisted), the hand reacts by taking a firm grip on the rod or finger used to stimulate it—so firm in some babies that they can hang by their hands for as long as a minute. Reflex grasping gives way to voluntary grasping between three and four months of age, but even then, once the baby has picked something up, the still persistent grasp reflex makes it impossible for the baby to let go. It is around age six months that the baby can voluntarily let go of what he or she is holding.

Newborns react to sudden intense stimulation with their own special version of the adult startle. This is called the *Moro response* and can be triggered by a loud noise, a flash of bright light, or an abrupt loss of support (put the baby on his or her back on a fluffed-up pillow and then press quickly down on both sides of the pillow). The baby reacts by stretching the arms and legs wide, often crying at the same time, and then hugging the extremities inward against the trunk.

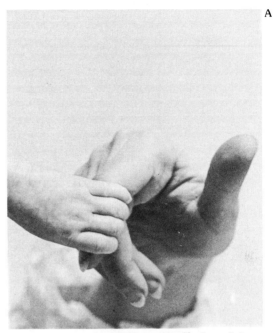

Martin Weaver, Woodfin Camp & Assoc.

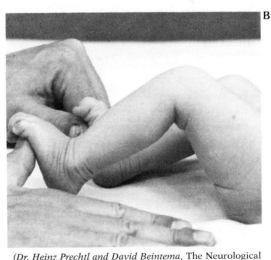

(Dr. Heinz Prechtl and David Beintema, The Neurological Examination of the Full-Term Newborn Infant.*)*

A Grasp reflex of the hands. **B** Grasp reflex of the toes.

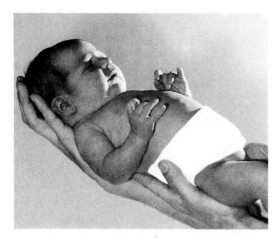

The Moro response.

(Dr. Heinz Prechtl and David Beintema, The Neurological Examination of the Full-Term Newborn Infant.*)*

If the baby is supported horizontal on the belly, he or she makes swimminglike movements *(swimming reflex)*. If he or she is held vertical with the feet lightly touching a firm surface, feet and legs move up and down as though walking *(stepping reflex)*. This response disappears shortly after birth, to emerge again in middle to late infancy in more mature form in readiness for walking. There is evidence that giving babies practice in walking can accelerate the development of walking ability (Zelazo, Zelazo, and Kolb, 1972). If the neonate is lying prone and the bottoms of the feet come in contact with a solid surface, the feet push against it, sometimes with enough force to move the baby's body; this *push-back response* probably explains reports of newborn babies' "crawling." At a slightly older age, the baby pushes back when supine.

Posture and Movement

Most babies quite early have a preference for lying either on their backs or on their bellies, as shown by agitated movements or actual crying when placed in the less favored position and by relaxation in the preferred one. Since neonates cannot roll over by themselves, parents need to be sensitive to such cues. This is part of the larger issue of parent-child communication, and of learning to understand the baby's "language of behavior," about which we shall say more later. On back or belly, babies keep their arms and legs flexed, the fingers curled into fists, and the head turned to one favored side (one cannot predict from the baby's head preference whether the baby will be left- or right-handed). Babies who regularly lie on their backs are likely to develop a bald spot (assuming they have hair) and some flattening of the skull where it meets the mattress. This flattening is harmless and goes away, although not always completely, after about age six months, when babies can roll over and begin spontaneously to vary their sleeping positions.

When in distress, newborns squirm, twist the head from side to side, and flail the limbs—not randomly but, as shown by high-speed movies (which can slow down the action), in a rigidly consistent pattern.

In some cultural settings, people learn child-care practices through lifelong observation. In our society, the opportunities for such learning are limited, and new mothers who want to breast-feed their babies have to be shown how to position themselves and their babies for nursing and how to put the nipple and surrounding area into the baby's mouth. However, as long as the mother plays her part correctly, the baby knows how to behave reciprocally. We might note that breast-feeding is becoming increasingly popular in the United States, but that nursing mothers are often reluctant to suckle their babies in public, and the public in turn looks askance at the nursing mother who does.

High-speed movies show the details of another postural interaction. When picked up to be carried against an adult shoulder, the neonate presses his or her cheek against the adult's. The usual adult reaction is to press back, which only pushes the baby's head to the other side. New mothers, by contrast, seem to know that if they tilt the head away from the neonate's, the baby's head slides down to the base of the mother's neck; when the adult straightens up, mother and baby are perfectly interlocked. Holding the baby in this position stimulates the inner ear, and this vestibular stimulation soothes the baby and enhances alertness. Many such patterns of reciprocal adjustment can be seen in both humans and animals. In species such as sheep and goats, these interactions, so uniform as to appear ritualized, are essential to the early formation of the

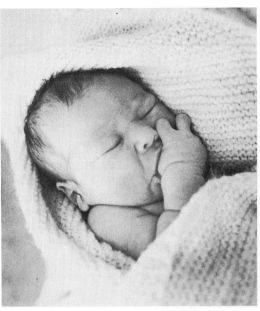

(© Elizabeth Crews)

Some neonates suck their thumbs from birth; some cannot find their mouths with their hands; and some hook the whole hand into the mouth when hungry.

mother-offspring attachment on which depends the young animal's survival and even mental health (nonhumans too can develop neuroses and psychoses).

Newborns have only limited control of their hands. People learn to use their hands in a great variety of ways, but the entire neonatal repertory can be specified quite briefly. Neonates may, in waving their arms, scratch their face with their fingernails, for which reason the nails have to be kept trimmed. But babies must be at least one month old before they can effectively scratch at an insect bite or a patch of eczema. Neonates grasp things that come in contact with their hands, but are unable to reach out and grasp things that are merely seen. Bower (1974) reports visually guided grasping from a few days of age, but others have been unable to confirm this finding (Ruff and Halton, 1978). The newborn clings when rooting and soon begins to clasp breast or bottle when nursing. Some neonates can suck their thumbs at birth (and some fetuses do so prenatally), but many newborn babies cannot find their mouths with their hands, try as they will, whereas others, when hungry, hook the whole hand into the mouth.

So far, we have touched only lightly on a central topic, the social life of the neonate. Good interpersonal relations are vital to the baby's development, but we want to begin by cataloguing the neonate's psychological capacities.

Emotions in the Neonate

The newborn baby's emotional expression is often intense, but it lacks variety. Distress, whether from hunger, pain, or other causes, is expressed as tearless crying, thrashing, and turning red all over; this whole-body crying eventually gives way to the more circumscribed crying found in older children and

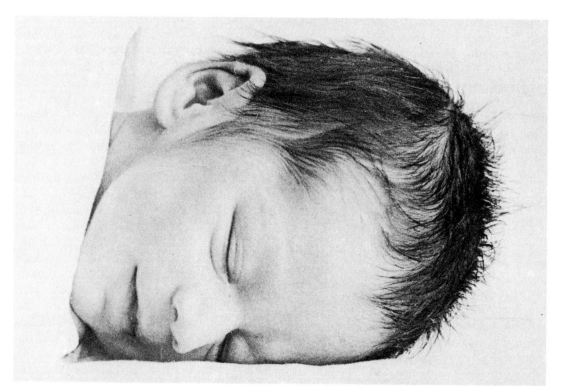

(Courtesy, Altyara Sarabhai)

The pleasure smile in a moment of placid rest. This common neonatal smile precedes the social smile.

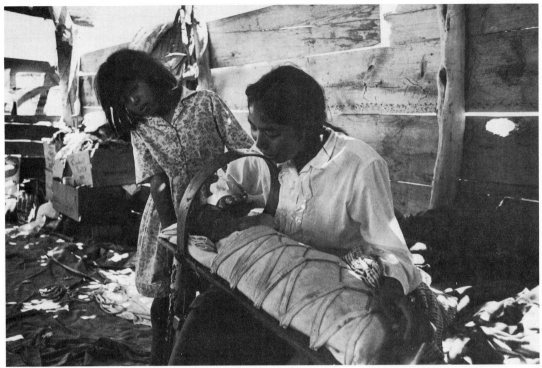

(© Michal Heron 1982/Woodfin Camp & Assoc.)

A swaddled Native American baby. Although partial immobilization causes neonates to kick and cry vigorously, total immobilization has a paradoxically calming effect.

adults. Distress also increases the electrical conductivity of neonates' skin by stimulating light sweating (which heat will not do), just as in the so-called *galvanic skin response (GSR)* of adults who are upset. Asleep or awake, newborn babies in moments of well-fed, placid repose show a reflexive **pleasure smile.** This must be distinguished from the *social smile* that appears at about age six weeks in response to the human face or voice.

Most of the time, however, neonates are blankly unemotional. Thus we can recognize only three basic affective states: contentment, neutrality, and distress. We cannot tell one kind of neonatal distress reaction from another, so there is little point in talking about fear or rage or grief in newborns. Loss of support will indeed produce a Moro response (as will other abrupt, intense forms of stimulation), but it is going a little far to equate a Moro response with fear. If one partially immobilizes neonates, they respond with vigorous kicking and crying. But snug **swaddling,** with the baby wrapped up like a mummy, the ultimate in restraint, has the opposite effect: It calms the infant. As adults, we find being restrained quite disagreeable, but it is easy to establish that this is not the case in newborns. Indeed, swaddling is standard practice in some societies, including the Soviet Union.

There is no indication that newborns feel affection for anybody or anything, although affection develops rapidly in the early months. This is not to say that neonates are closed off from social influences. Several phenomena bridge social responsiveness and perception. First, there is evidence that babies as young as one day cry in response either to the crying of other neonates or to a simulated cry having some of the tonal characteristics of ordinary newborn crying (Sagi and Hoffman, 1976). Second, there is the newborns' sensitivity to human touch and snuggling. Third, there are studies—which need to be repeated with more careful controls—suggesting that newborn babies move synchronously with the speech rhythms of an adult who is talking to the baby (Condon and Sander, 1974a, 1974b). Fourth, there is evidence of early imitation of adult facial expressions.

Neonatal Imitation

In speaking of imitation in newborn babies we have entered upon an area of debate. Neonatal imitation of tongue protrusion was first reported by René Zazzo (1957). Meltzoff and Moore (1977) reported that babies twelve to twenty-one days old imitated adult tongue protrusion, mouth opening, lip pursing, and finger movements. However, recognizing a possible procedural flaw in their first experiment, Meltzoff and Moore repeated the study using only mouth opening and tongue protrusion as models for imitation. The results were reliable for these two behaviors.

Meltzoff and Moore's findings have met a good deal of resistance. We believe that the greatest source of skepticism is that such imitation goes contrary to a belief by Piaget that imitation begins with parts of the body visible to the person doing the imitating. Thus one should be able to imitate hand movements long before being able to imitate facial movements. Further, many psychologists conceive of imitation as involving complicated thought processes that are far beyond the neonate's abilities.

Anisfeld (1979) demonstrated that with a different scoring system the imitation reported by Meltzoff and Moore seemed to be only random movement. Masters (1979) noted that both mouth opening and tongue protrusion play a part in feeding and proposed that Meltzoff and Moore had happened to choose stimuli that triggered off a feeding response. Jacobson and Kagan (1979), using six-week-old subjects, found that adult tongue protrusion produced tongue protrusion in infants, but that some tongue protrusion could also be stimulated by moving either a closed black felt pen or a dimpled white ball in the direction of a baby's mouth.

On the other hand, Burd, Milewski, and Camras (1981) tested babies two, six, and ten weeks old for imitation of tongue protrusion, mouth opening, and eyebrow raising. Following Jacobson and Kagan, they also used a felt pen as a stimulus. In all three age groups, adult tongue protrusion reliably produced infant tongue protrusion, and adult eyebrow raising produced infant eyebrow raising. Mouth opening was imitated, but not reliably. The felt pen was an ineffective stimulus, producing infant tongue protrusion only 13 percent of the time as compared with 61 percent in response to adult tongue protrusion. Brazelton (1973) has developed a test for neonates. He uses the test as a means of demonstrating to new parents the remarkable range of behaviors of which their babies are capable. Brazelton (1981) reports that he has made it part of his demonstration to stick out his tongue at the baby, because he discovered more or less by accident that neonates most of the time respond in kind. Most recently, Tiffany Field and associates (Field *et al.*, 1981) have shown that neonates seem capable of imitating such global adult emotional expressions as happiness, sadness, and surprise. There is no reason to think that neonates experience the emotions whose expression they mimic.

We think that the fact of imitation has been adequately demonstrated. The problem remains of how to understand it. We believe that the anti-imitation school makes a basic conceptual error. Its adherents think of imitation as a complex cognitive act, as though the baby is reasoning along lines such as "What is that person doing? Maybe he or she wants me to do it, too. Let's see, now, where do I keep my tongue? OK, there it is; now all I have to do is figure out how to. . . ."

There is a much simpler explanation available. This is the phenomenon of **empathy.** Most basically, empathy points to a close behavioral link between person and environment, as though the material boundaries had been blurred. If you yawn when other people do, if you try to clear your throat when listening to someone with a frog in his or her throat, you have experienced empathy first hand. We have already seen evidence of empathy

in neonates in the contagiousness of infant crying and in the way neonates move their arms and legs in rhythm to an adult's speech.

Sensory and Perceptual Capacities

The neonate's sense organs are in good working order but, as we have said, it takes a long time for babies to acquire the skills with which to organize and make full use of the information carried via the senses, including those that tell them about events in their own bodies.

Vision. For perhaps a day after birth, babies' eyelids tend to be puffy and their eyesight blurred by the drops given right after birth, which makes immediate visual testing unreliable. By the second or third day, though, neonates can track a slowly moving object with their eyes. A few babies right after birth can turn their heads to follow a moving object, and most can do so within a few weeks.

Babies as young as two weeks show the **looming effect** (Ball and Tronick, 1971; Schiff, 1965). When what looks like a large object rapidly approaches on a collision course, babies react by throwing back their head, raising their arms, and probably crying. In fact, the oncoming large object is simply a rapidly expanding shadow rear-projected onto a screen placed directly in front of the propped-up neonate. If the shadow expands symmetrically, babies see it as approaching head-on and react as described. However, if the shadow expands asymmetrically, babies simply watch the thinglike shadow without emotion, as though perceiving it moving on a course that will miss them. Note that babies must be propped up for the looming effect to occur. By the same token, propped-up babies will blink when a small object approaches their eyes, whereas supine—lying on the back—they will not. These observations carry an implication: At least when in a semivertical position, newborn babies may be sensitive to depth.

It is worth noting here that the newborn's eyes have a fixed focal point at about 7.5 inches (19 cm), so stimuli have to be presented at about this distance if neonates are to see them clearly. Accommodation of the lens—changes in lens shape to bring objects at various distances into sharp focus—and convergence of the eyes on nearby or approaching objects develop during the first few months.

Physiological evidence suggests that the newborn baby's nervous system is equipped for discrimination of different wavelengths of light, corresponding to different colors. However, behavioral evidence of color discrimination does not appear until around age four months.

Neonates seem to prefer patterns of intermediate complexity to either very simple or very complex ones, and they prefer patterned to featureless surfaces. Neonates spend more time looking at a facelike arrangement of shapes than at the same shapes arranged randomly (Fantz, 1963). Even when there is nothing to look at, awake, alert neonates scan the environment, but mostly from side to side and hardly ever up and down. For instance, if a card half black and half white is shown to babies so that the dividing edge is vertical, the neonate's wandering eyes take hold of the edge and explore it briefly. However, if the card is turned so that the edge is horizontal, babies, scanning from side to side, are

likely to miss the edge altogether (Kessen, Haith, and Salapatek, 1970). Using a special television camera that translates infrared light into visible images, one can observe that when the visible light in a room is turned off, neonates, even if asleep, open their eyes and scan the darkness (Haith, 1969).

Hearing. The use of *indicator responses*—physiological responses to stimuli, such as change in heartbeat or in breathing rate—has made it possible to study the newborn's hearing. For instance, heart rate varies directly with loudness within the normal range, becoming more rapid as the sound gets louder. Very young babies discriminate both pitch and loudness. Neonates perk up at the sound of the human voice, and fussing neonates find the human voice soothing. Indeed, babies as young as three days show recognition of and preference for their own mothers' voices (De Casper and Fifer, 1980). By sucking on a nipple with a switch inside, neonates were able to turn on and off tape recordings of their own mothers' or strange females' voices. By day three, they consistently spent more time listening to the voices of their own mothers. Note, though, that babies will suck simply for the sake of hearing a human voice, familiar or not.

Recall the fact of habituation, the way babies stop reacting to the same stimulus repeated over and over. When the oft-repeated stimulus is changed in some way, babies once again pay attention. This gives researchers a method of finding out just how great a change has to be for babies to take notice. It turns out that neonates make rather fine auditory discriminations. Using the habituation technique, it can be shown that within the first month babies can distinguish between artificially generated speech sounds as close as "puh" and "buh" (Eimas *et al.*, 1971; Eisenberg, 1969; Stratton and Connolly, 1973).

Psychophysical studies of the kind we have been describing promise to make possible the early detection of visual and auditory impairments. Remember that deafness and blindness need not be all-or-nothing conditions, but can vary in severity. There is also good reason to believe that the earlier such problems can be caught and dealt with, the less serious their eventual impact.

The Coordination of Sight and Hearing. The usual adult reaction on hearing a new sound is to look and see where it is coming from. That is, auditory space is coordinated with visual space. There has been confusion and conflicting evidence whether such coordination exists in newborns. For instance, Brazelton's (1973) newborn assessment scales include a test for orienting to a sound source, but since the manual gives no norms, there is no telling how many babies, if any, show the response. The Bayley Scales of Infant Development (Bayley, 1969, p. 51) give age 3.8 months as the average for orienting to a sound (range 2 to 6 months). Our own observations (Church, 1970) indicate that babies turn to the sound of the mother's voice at about two months, and search for the source of inanimate sounds at about four months. Research by Darwin Muir and associates seems to have cleared up the mystery, although still leaving a residual puzzle. Muir and Field (1979) have shown that most newborn babies do indeed orient to a sound source, provided: (1) the babies are in a state of alert inactivity; (2) the sound

(from a rattle) is kept up for a while (up to 20 seconds); (3) the babies are held supine on an adult arm and hand (the adult's ears are muffled so that he or she cannot be unwittingly cued to manipulate the baby's head); and (4) one is prepared to accept a delay of as long as 2.5 seconds before babies respond. Too many testers have tried to evoke orienting with only brief bursts of sound, and have ascribed the baby's lack of response to a failure to connect hearing and vision. However—and here is the puzzle—orientation to sounds declines during the second and third month (except for reactions to the mother's voice at two months), and then recovers in the fourth month (Muir *et al.*, 1979). We do not know the reason for this pattern of decline unless it is a generalized sort of habituation to all but the most compelling sounds. Note that sight-sound coordination, like the looming effect, points to early perception of depth.

The Other Senses. Psychologists have devoted the bulk of their attention to the study of seeing and hearing, but they have also examined neonates' capacities in other sense modalities. We now summarize these findings.

We begin with the *position sense*, sensitivity to body cues—especially from the semicircular canals of the inner ear—that tell us how we are oriented in space. As far as we can tell, neonates have only a very weak position sense. They make postural adjustments to keep their balance when they are held or moved around in an adult hand, but they seem thoroughly indifferent to whether they are held head down or head up. However, neonates show the same sort of jerky eye movements (*nystagmus*) as adults after being spun on a turntable. Such eye movements suggest an effort to anchor oneself in the visual environment to compensate for the disorientation of being spun around.

The baby's *sense of touch* (which includes four subsenses: pressure, texture, shape, and temperature) is obviously important in our ability to soothe by stroking or snuggling or swaddling. The tactile sense also plays an obvious part in rooting behavior.

As for the *sense of smell,* neonates react negatively to some odors that adults regard as unpleasant, such as ammonia and other ill-smelling substances, but they show no signs of delight at what adults consider highly agreeable fragrances. Later in infancy, babies do enjoy sniffing flowers and they approach new foodstuffs with an exploratory sniff. Also later in infancy, however, babies seem indifferent to smells that adults find offensive, such as the odor of body wastes. We do not know whether or to what extent rooting behavior is guided by the sense of smell. Biologists have been much intrigued by *pheromones,* airborne chemical messages secreted by an organism (plant or animal). For instance, practically everyone has heard of insect sex attractants, which can be used to lure crop pests into traps. There is speculation that body odors (fresh, not stale) may serve as sex attractants in humans. The manufacturers of perfumes and various aromatic substances like musk have long assumed, along with their customers, that odors influence mating behavior. In the case of newborns, one might assume that milk or other substances from the mother's breast guide rooting, but in our experience, neonates root as readily at a male body as at a female one, and touch seems to take precedence over smell.

In the *taste sense,* it can be shown that neonates react to differences in flavors. Neonates let us know very quickly that they do not relish the bitter taste of quinine. Babies given a choice of nipples reliably choose the one delivering milk over the one producing a weak solution of dextrose (one kind of sugar). However, neonates do like small doses of sweet-tasting substances, and they can discriminate among various concentrations of glucose and sucrose (other kinds of sugars) (Engen, Lipsitt, and Peck, 1974; Nowlis and Kessen, 1976).

Sensitivity to *pain,* as measured by reactions to pin pricks or mild electric shock, increases rapidly during the first few days after birth. Circumcision on day three, routinely carried out without anesthetic in American hospitals, is being called into question as serving no useful purpose. While we doubt that the operation leaves any lasting psychic scars (psychoanalysts hint darkly of long-lasting castration fears), there is clear evidence in physiological changes of brief pain and stress (Emde *et al.,* 1971). The neonate's reactions to internal pain, as of colic or hunger cramps, are even more pronounced than those to externally produced pain.

If the baby's nose and mouth are blocked, thus interfering with breathing, the neonate may try ineffectually to remove the obstruction by wagging the head or waving the hands in the general vicinity of the face. Neonates cannot get rid of a cleaning tissue spread over their face, and pediatric lore has it that babies should sleep without a pillow lest they suffocate.

Whatever the sense organ, we should

note that stimuli that are noxious to newborns may be noxious because of their strong intensities rather than their specific qualities as perceived by adults. Well into infancy, babies react aversively to bright lights and loud noises and, as solid food is added to an all-milk diet, to strongly flavored foods.

Neonatal Learning

Using the methods of *classical conditioning* (see Chapter 1), psychologists some years back set out to study learning in neonates. The results were so unsatisfactory that the field of neonatal learning fell into neglect for a long time. During the renaissance of neonatal studies since 1960, people have relied increasingly on the methods of *instrumental conditioning*, whereby the baby's own actions produce a reward (*reinforcement*, or, in today's cognitively oriented climate, *feedback*). We have seen how babies suck to hear a human voice and suck selectively to hear their own mother's voice. We have already encountered examples of neonatal learning that do not fit neatly into either the classical or instrumental framework. For instance, habituation can be thought of as a form of learning, since babies have become familiar with the characteristics of one stimulus and can distinguish it from another.

The two acts of which just about all neonates are capable are sucking and head turning. For instance, we have spoken of neonates' preference for milk over sugar water. This was determined by giving babies milk as a reward for turning their head to one side or sugar water if they turned to the other. Babies quickly learn which way to turn their heads.

Similarly, babies suck on nipples that

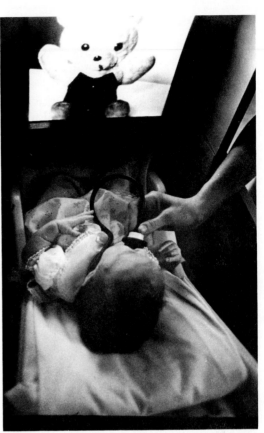

(Jason Lauré/Courtesy, Dr. Lewis P. Lipsitt)

Siqueland's apparatus, which permits the baby to control a visual display by varying his or her sucking.

deliver no milk but that contain switches controlling pieces of the environment. By sucking or not sucking, or by varying the speed or intensity of sucking, babies can make things happen. Prearranged sorts of sucking behavior can turn on pictures, or make a slide projector change pictures, or raise or lower the room's level of illumination. Babies very quickly learn to vary their sucking to obtain the desired result. For instance, babies learn to adapt their sucking so as to keep a picture in sharp focus (Siqueland, 1969). Thus, from the beginning, perceptual clarity seems to be important. We are still waiting for someone to find out whether babies will perform the auditory equivalent, sucking in just the right way to keep a radio sharply tuned to one station.

What we have been talking about is the process known as **contingent reinforcement,** in which the things that happen in the environment bear a direct, predictable, and immediate reaction to the baby's own actions, thus providing feedback about the baby's own behavior and power to control events. Babies who are reared by loving, attentive adults receive a lot of contingent reinforcement, conveying to them that they are to some degree autonomous agents and not mere passive playthings of fate. This is not to say that homes have to be rigged with exotic electronic equipment for babies to manipulate in search of feedback. The great bulk of contingent reinforcement comes about in the course of social interchanges between infant and family, and a great deal comes too in explorations of the material environment of household goods and of playthings.

That neonates can learn should not really surprise us. Everyday observation tells us that by age twenty or thirty days babies have learned to recognize the nursing bottle: When held in the feeding position, babies open their mouth and raise their head to meet the approaching bottle (at this age, though, babies are easily tricked, and will make this same response to just about anything held as though it were a bottle). Babies have to begin at some point to take in and master unmeasurable quantities of experience, and as far as we can tell, the process begins immediately at birth.

Limitations of the Neonate

We have been stressing that newborn babies are far more capable than people used to give them credit for. They attend selectively to sensory information, they learn, and they show a primitive but vital capacity for participating in social interactions.

Despite these capacities, most neonates are remarkably passive, placid, and malleable. Most of the newborn's response capabilities are likely to go unnoticed by parents. At the same time, parents may project upon the baby remarkable qualities of mind, morality, and purpose that are totally alien to the neonate's competence.

For all their rudimentary humanity, newborns still lack a great many abilities. The only vocal sounds they make are crying and the noises that go with breathing, digestion, and indigestion. All but a very few neonates are unable to raise their head. They cannot roll over (except by accident) or move thumb and fingers separately. They do not reach out to things at a distance. They have no control over elimination. They begin almost at once to pay attention to human faces, but cannot tell one face from another. They do not even know that they have feet. Contrary to some opinions, there is no evidence of memory of life before birth. The neonate's life is governed largely by the rhythms of the digestive tract and the closely linked rise and ebb of wakefulness, the triggers that set off reflex discharges, and the kind mercies of adult caregivers. Here we must mention two points that cannot be stressed too often. The character of caregiving is determined not only by the character of the giver, but also by the characteristics, real or imagined, that the caregiver perceives in the baby. Thus relations between adult and child are, from the very beginning, a back-and-forth interaction in which each person's response becomes the stimulus to the other person's reaction (Osofsky and Danzger, 1974). This is particularly important in the case of unresponsive babies, such as those made sluggish by drugs given to the mother during birth. The second point is that the earlier such interchanges begin, the better. This means that parents should avoid being discouraged if the baby fails to be fully responsive during early encounters. There are times, as when a baby is born extremely prematurely, that normal interactions cannot take place immediately between parent and child. In such cases, extra understanding, patience, and perseverance are called for in establishing the usual cycle of reciprocal communication.

(© George Zimbel/Monkmeyer Press)

Mother and baby. In the relations between parents and children, the responses of each become the stimulus for the reactions of the other. The sooner these interchanges begin, the better. In some circumstances, the cycle of reciprocal communication may require extra understanding, patience, and perseverance.

INDIVIDUAL DIFFERENCES AND PREDICTING THE BABY'S FUTURE

Right from birth each baby manifests a uniqueness that is the product both of his or her special genetic make-up and of conditions in the uterine environment. To the unpracticed eye "all newborns look alike," but a small amount of experience makes clear that neonates vary strikingly in innumerable ways, such as muscle tone, the intensity with which they react to stimulation, the speed with which they move their limbs, the zeal and vigor with which they attack the nipple, the patterning of bursts of sucking, their sensitivity to light or sound or touch, their irritability, the volume and persistence of their crying, their alertness, their sleeping rhythms, and their acceptance or rejection of new experiences (Birns, 1965; Escalona, 1968). They differ in the competences that we have been describing. They differ in size and shape, in the absolute and relative size of body organs, in blood chemistry, and in hormonal balance. Within a short time, the very proteins of their bodies become so individualized that they reject tissues transplanted from other persons. Note that we are speaking here only of the wide range of normal variations, not abnormal conditions of the kind discussed in Chapter 3.

One would assume that from such traits, or combination of traits, some solid predictions could be made about a baby's future characteristics. In fact, such predictions are very difficult to make with any degree of confidence. We have already spoken of Brazelton's (1973) Neonatal Behavioral Assessment Scale. This scale covers almost the entire range of newborn competences and, as we would expect, yields a wide range of scores. These scores, however, have a predictive value approaching zero (Kaye, 1978; Sameroff, 1978). Apgar (1965) has developed a method to evaluate the newborn's physical condition along five different dimensions: breathing effort, muscle tone, heart rate, reflex irritability, and color (from grayish to rosy). Newborns receive a score of 0, 1, or 2 for each dimension, with 0 indicating severe physical problems and 2 indicating an absence of physical problems. The scores for the five dimensions are then added to give the **Agpar Score** (which can range from 0 to 10). Of the babies receiving scores of 0 through 3 (of a possible 10), 96.5 percent develop normally (Nelson and Broman, 1977). Note that these low-scoring babies are twenty-two times as likely as higher-scoring babies to develop abnormalities, which points to the fact that one can identify low-risk and high-risk *groups*. However, our concern here is with being able to foretell *individual* patterns of development. Bee *et al.* (1982) also report that measures of perinatal physical status have only a weak relationship to IQ and verbal ability at age four, whereas characteristics of the human environment make a considerable difference (see Chapter 7).

Setting aside individual differences, we might take a moment to consider a major group difference easily observable at birth. This is the difference between the sexes. The obvious anatomical differences apart, what can we say about the two sexes at birth? Boys are a tiny bit longer and heavier on average than girls, but these differences seem nothing to get excited about. We know that males, as a general rule, will be more prone to physical and mental illness than females and are likely to die younger. (The sex ratio, the number of males per 100 females, varies from place to place and era to era, but currently is about 105 in American newborns; between ages twenty-five and twenty-nine the ratio shifts in favor of females and continues to increase in their favor thereafter.) We can also predict in general that boys and girls will have quite distinct patterns of upbringing and, barring a cultural revolution, will end up having quite different psychological make-ups. But what of psychological differences at birth? Many have been reported, but none have been confirmed. Kaye (1978) demonstrated that there are absolutely no sex differences in performance on the Brazelton scale.

Whatever the facts of inborn psychological sex differences, parents ascribe very different traits to boys and to girls (Rubin, Provenzano, and Luria, 1974). Fathers and mothers agree in their stereotyping, except that fathers view little girls, and mothers little boys, as more cuddlesome. Condry and Condry (1976) had college students rate the videotaped reactions of a baby to various test situations. It was always the same baby, but half the raters were told that it was a boy, and half that it was a girl. The complex analysis of results (involving sex of rater, experience of rater, "sex" of baby, and test situations) yielded reliable but not very striking differences in ratings. The most impressive differences were not in ratings of the baby's reactions to the tests but in the more global ratings of temperament. The "boy" baby was rated consistently higher than the "girl" on scales of activity and forcefulness. The assigned sex made no apparent difference in ratings of liking or disliking. Haugh, Hoffman, and Cowan (1980) repeated Condry and Condry's eye-of-the-beholder study with three- and five-year-old children, and found sex stereotyping at least as strong as in adults. It appears that we are still a long way from treating boys and girls as individuals rather than as members of groups.

In these first four chapters we have tried to describe the enterprise of studying human psychological development. We have introduced you to its motives, its methods, its major theories, and its chief governing principles. We have discussed the contributions of heredity and experience to development and have offered a psychobiological view that we think takes full account of how nature and nurture work together in development. We have talked about development before birth, environmental influences on prenatal development, the birth process, the abnormalities found in a small proportion of newborns, and modern-day genetic counseling. In Chapter 4 we have set forth the pattern of psychological competences found in newborn babies. We now move on to the dramatic story of development during the rest of infancy.

SUMMARY

1. All newborn babies have their individual identities from the moment of birth, but they share a fetuslike quality of newbornness.

2. Neonates are functioning human beings physically and psychologically, with all the potentialities associated with the human condition, and they respond to a variety of human and nonhuman stimuli. All of the major body structures are present at birth, at least in rudimentary form.

3. Before birth, fetuses receive all the necessities of life from, and discharge most wastes into, the mother's blood. Once born, neonates must begin to breathe, eat, eliminate waste, and gradually regulate body temperature. Babies are helped in their survival during this crucial period by antibodies they have absorbed from the mother's body during prenatal life.

4. During the past two decades there has been growing interest in the study of the neonate's psychological capacities. Psychological study of the neonate depends on the use and knowledge of infant states (degree of arousal, hunger, comfort or discomfort), on the use of mild stimuli, and on ingenious instrumentation.

5. Newborns show three major categories of reflexes: physiological reflexes, such as vomiting; nonfunctional reflexes, such as the knee-jerk response; adaptive behavioral reflexes, such as the rooting response.

6. The newborn baby's expression of emotions is often intense, but most of the time the neonate is blankly unemotional. However, we can recognize three basic affective states: contentment, neutrality, and distress.

7. Babies' openness to human contact, whether direct or at a distance, is essential to the development of attachment, and this is, in turn, essential to all other development. Attachment and identification are the vital bases of sound psychological development in all areas.

8. Babies have been shown to be capable of imitation, responding in kind to tongue protrusion, mouth opening, and eyebrow raising. Imitation probably represents an instance of empathy.

9. It takes a long time for the neonate to acquire the skills with which to make full use of and organize the information carried via the senses. In the first few months, the baby seems to be able to perceive depth and pattern and responds to human faces. Young babies discriminate pitch and loudness within the normal range, and the baby alerts to and is soothed by the human voice. Neonates can learn to recognize their mothers' voice. Studies suggest that auditory–visual coordination is built into the newborn but still has to develop over several months.

10. Newborn babies seem to have a rudimentary positional sense and make postural adjustments when supported. The baby's sense of touch is important in our ability to soothe by stroking, and, in rooting, touch seems to take priority over smell. Neonatal sensitivity to pain is present at birth, and it increases rapidly during the first few days.

11. In recent explorations of neonatal learning, psychologists rely on instrumental conditioning. They have found that infants will learn for the sake of cognitive reinforcement, such as clarity. Contingent reinforcement, of which babies should get a lot, communicates to babies that they have some control of events and that they are not passive playthings of fate.

12. Habituation refers to the tendency of babies to stop responding when the same stimulus is repeatedly presented. Habituation may be viewed as a form of neonatal learning, in that it implies memory and recognition of repeated stimuli. Habituation can also be used to study sensory discrimination.

13. For all their rudimentary humanity, newborns still lack a great many capacities. Their lives are governed largely by the rhythms of the digestive tract and other physiological events, the rise and ebb of wakefulness, the triggers that set off reflexes, and the mercies of adult caretakers.

14. One cannot safely predict much about an individual baby's future from neonatal traits or combinations of traits. What seems most important to the neonate's future development is not the baby's characteristics but how parents perceive and react to those characteristics. This is true in the areas both of sex differences and of organic impairments.

KEY TERMS

Apgar Score, 140
contingent reinforce-
   ment, 138
empathy, 133
grasping reflex, 127

habituation, 123
indicator responses,
   123
looming effect, 133
neonate, 118

pleasure smile, 131
reflexes, 125
rooting response, 216
state, 123
swaddling, 131

SUGGESTED READINGS

Escalona, S. K. *The Roots of Individuality: Normal Patterns of Development in Infancy.* Chicago: Aldine, 1968. Gives a sensitive account of parent-child interaction and reciprocal adaptation from birth on.

Stone, L. J., Smith, H. T., and Murphy, L. B. (eds.). *The Competent Infant.* New York: Basic Books, 1973. A compendium of research on all aspects of infancy, includ-ing the neonatal period, together with a rich commentary and analysis by the editors.

Tronick, E., and Adamson, L. *Babies as People.* New York: Collier Books, and London: Collier Macmillan, 1980. A sensitive, up-to-date summary of knowledge about the capabilities of neonates and young infants.

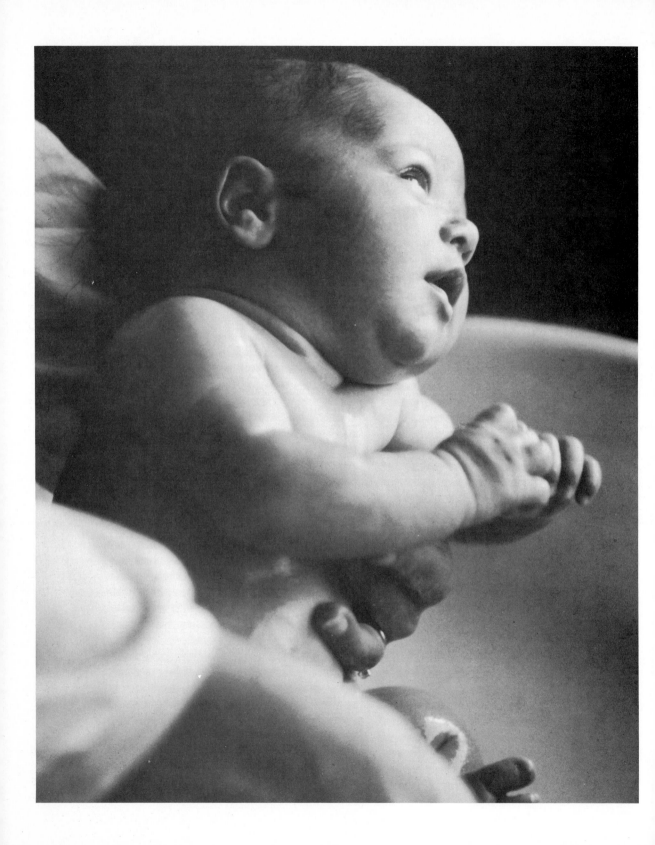

CHAPTER 5

The Infant:
PHYSICAL GROWTH AND MATURATION, FINE AND GROSS MOTOR CONTROL, SOCIAL AND EMOTIONAL DEVELOPMENT

Development during infancy—from the age of a few weeks until fifteen months or so—is a dramatic thing to watch. Striking and radical changes take place within this relatively brief period. During these first fifteen months outside the womb, the baby changes from an almost helpless—if sometimes noisy—neonate to a high-powered, willful pedestrian exploring and exploiting everything within reach in the most active way possible—tasting, chewing, fondling, probing, tugging, pushing, pounding, and tearing. By the end of infancy, most babies are walking securely and are on the threshold of talking. These behavioral changes are made possible, of course, only through equally dramatic changes in size, strength, skills, proportions, and physiology, the last including stabilization of daily rhythms. But we must note the inescapable circularity of such changes. Normal physical development can take place only when the child's physical and psychological needs are adequately met.

Socially, infants' behavior progresses from blank, unblinking staring at faces to smiling at people, to demanding company, to actively participating in social games. Early in life babies learn to distinguish between familiar and unfamiliar faces, voices, and touches (and probably smells), and in middle to late infancy many come to fear unfamiliar people, places, and things, turning away and shrieking in dismay.

The limited emotional repertory with which babies begin life differentiates during infancy into about a dozen recognizably distinct feeling states and their expressions: pain, surprise, aversion, anger, fear, loneliness, affection, elation, curiosity, disappointment, per-plexity, and perhaps others. This list is not a chronology. Not all the emotions of which a baby is capable have been tied to particular ages.

The word "infancy" comes from the Latin *infans*, which means "not speaking." No matter how much infants vocalize, or how much their vocalizations change during this period, their babblings stop short of true speech. Before age one, though, most babies can understand a great many words and phrases, listen attentively even to those they do not understand, and react most sensitively to the emotional shadings of language. In rare cases, "infants" may use a few words of their own. We choose to use "infancy" in the strict sense.

From being neonates whose existence is dominated by their own volatile inner processes, with only transitory communication with their surroundings, infants move on to a quite elaborate knowledge of the familiar world—of people and things and their attributes, of space and the relationships among objects in space (known as spatial relations), of how to make things happen, of their own body and the sensations it provides, and of a sense of self as a distinct person. But these awarenesses develop only by virtue of the emotional attachments and meanings that are formed in this crucial period.

In this chapter and the next, we give a descriptive account of developmental landmarks, the conspicuous transformations of body and behavior, that appear in a fairly stable sequence during the first year or so. For the sake of simplicity, we talk about different areas of development separately—physical growth, motor development, social and emotional development, and so forth.

The *sequence* of behavioral development within each area is fairly stable, but the particular *ages* at which given forms of behavior emerge are highly variable. For physical and motor development especially, we give approximate ages. We realize that they are based on norms derived years ago from inadequate samplings of children, which assumed that development in a Western setting is representative of development everywhere. Existing infant scales (Bayley, 1969; Catell, 1940; Gesell, 1925; Griffiths, 1954), from which many items of behavior are drawn, also assume that development during infancy is in large part **autogenous,** that is, a simple product of spontaneous growth and maturation. (The Brazelton Scale, it should be remembered, is a neonatal assessment scale and does not purport to measure development during all of infancy.) Up-to-date norms would have to take account of a huge array of background influences, so that new, more sophisticated normative studies have become a formidable task.

There seems to be general agreement that babies reared in Western societies develop faster than they used to. This apparent acceleration may be related in part to improved diet, sanitation, and medical care, including immunization against what used to be called "the common diseases of childhood"—whooping cough, scarlet fever, measles, and all the rest. Of equal importance, we believe, is a spreading recognition of the baby's psychological needs, which is leading to better parenting.

This expanded awareness of the baby's needs has not been without its costs. Ever since the popularization of psychoanalytic theory in all its varieties, with a further boost from behaviorist teachings, from John B. Watson to the current flood of child "training" books supposedly based on behavior-modification principles, we have lived in an "age of self-conscious parenthood." Parents, bombarded with sometimes conflicting dictates from the Experts, often were so concerned that they might be doing something dangerous to the child's future mental health that they sometimes seemed afraid to act at all, or at least not until they had consulted the "Gospel according to the latest Authority." There are still some thoroughly self-conscious parents. There are also parents so profoundly ignorant of the needs of babies that it never occurs to them that what they do may have lasting psychological effects. By and large, though, it is our impression that today's parents have learned to be more relaxed about their babies, to take babies' resilience more for granted, and, with greater understanding, to find more pleasure in the role of parent.

PHYSICAL GROWTH AND MATURATION

Physical growth and maturation may not sound very much like a psychological topic, but it is relevant to psychological development in at least two ways. First, there is a reciprocal relationship between physical development and the babies' expanding repertoire of abilities. Normal physical development is essential to the appearance of the usual motor skills. The exercise of early motor skills facilitates the development of later ones.

Furthermore, growth and maturation are dependent on conditions in the material and human environment. Second, in later years the sense of being physically normal is a vital part of self-awareness and the ability to maintain sound social relations.

We begin with a distinction that is often blurred. As we said earlier, **growth** and **maturation** are not the same thing (nor is "maturation" a synonym for "maturing"). Growth refers simply to increases in size and the changes in body proportions associated with the asynchronous growth of the various parts of the body. Maturation, by contrast, refers to the subtler anatomical and physiological reorganizations through which the individual passes in the course of becoming older. For instance, the peripheral nerves develop insulating sheaths, which permit more differentiated forms of action. New enzymes appear in the digestive tract, sometimes in response to the challenges of a changing diet. There are changes in the internal temperature-regulating mechanisms, including activation of the sweat glands, that enable babies to adapt to fluctuations in heat and cold in their surroundings. The endocrine glands constantly form new patterns of organization, culminating in that most dramatic of maturational changes, puberty—becoming a sexual adult.

The many facts of physical growth in the first year can be summarized as follows. Between birth and age one, the average baby grows about 8 inches (20 + cm), increasing in overall length by some 40 percent. In the same period, the baby gains about 15 pounds (7 kg), tripling his or her birth weight. Even though virtually all the brain cells are present at birth, the brain doubles in size in the first year, and again by age six. The brain cells and their outgrowths increase, myelin sheaths coat the axons of cells outside the cortex, and the glial cells grow. Full brain (and skull) size, of course, is not reached until adulthood. During infancy, most babies grow a full head of hair. The facial proportions change, from the fetal look of the newborn to the smooth roundness characteristic of the infant.

Maturational changes are often less noticeable but are just as important. The baby's diet changes, from pure liquid to mush and from mush to just about everything older members of the family eat. By age three months, most babies have lost their need for a late-night feeding. By five months, they can wait four to five hours between daytime feedings, and longer during the night. By six months, babies have adapted for the most part to their families' meal schedule, plus an occasional snack and a bedtime nursing. These shifts in diet correspond both to new digestive capacities and to the need for new kinds of nutrients to meet the demands of developing tissues. They also reflect the stabilization of the baby's daily activity cycle. As the baby is introduced to new foods, he or she has to adjust to novel consistencies, flavors, textures, and temperatures, and learns new techniques of swallowing. Many babies develop strong food preferences, and most American mothers have learned to accept these. In some societies, though, such preferences are ignored, and the adult relentlessly crams the baby's mouth full of mush.

We mention in passing one small but noticeable maturational change. At about six to eight weeks, just about the time babies first smile at faces, they begin to shed tears when crying. The baby's earlier crying was real enough and abundantly vociferous, but tearless.

The age of three months is, in many ways, a turning point. A change comes over babies that can be summarized by saying that they are "becoming human." It is hard to define the subtle ways in which becoming human manifests itself, but parents have no trouble recognizing the transition. By this age, babies have lost their neonatal look and are highly individualized infants. The head is now normally held in the midline while awake, instead of being turned to one side. Babies seem to be newly alert and responsive and give the impression of having a beginning inner life. There even seems to be a shift in brain-wave patterns at this age. Of no small consequence in terms of babies' and parents' emotional states, any bouts of colic end about now. Likewise, as babies give up late-night feedings, the parents' disposition improves. As a further sign of a new awareness, many three-month-olds show angry resentment during a feeding when a parent turns his or her attention from the baby to address a visitor. Indeed, this is the age at which the first major emotional struggle between parents and child may be acted out, as we are about to see.

Sleeping, Bedtime, and Waking

Sleep patterns change, probably reflecting changes in neural organization. Neonates drift into and out of sleep around the clock. During infancy, sleeping and waking come to be sharply defined, and babies sleep twelve to fourteen hours during the night and take a couple of naps during the day. In early infancy, eating and sleeping are closely intertwined, and only hunger seems to bring babies fully awake (the pattern of colicky babies obviously differs). Sometime between two and three months of age, many babies sleep through the night, from an evening feeding to five, six, or seven in the morning. The age at which babies sleep through seems to be a matter of physical maturity, general stabilization of physiological rhythms, and also of parental experience, since, according to Moore and Ucko (1957), second and subsequent babies sleep through at younger ages than first-borns. Experienced parents recognize that the late-night feeding (usually around 2 A.M.) interests the baby less as an occasion for nourishment than for play and socializing, and stop responding to the baby's signals for a feeding time; the signals, unreinforced, soon stop coming.

Coincidental with beginning to sleep through comes the first real crisis in parent-child relations: the baby's resistance to evening bedtime. Daytime naps present no problem. The baby becomes tired and simply goes to sleep. Previously when the baby was being put to bed for the night, there was likely to be some brief fussing and whimpering before the baby drifted off. Now, however, the baby seems to be aware that evening bedtime is the end of company and play and attention, and screams in anger and protest. This bedtime screaming, incidentally, may be the first voluntary, intentional use of the voice for communication, since it is not an accompaniment to crying. In addition, the baby does not merely scream and go on screaming. Instead, the baby yells and then stops, as though listening for a reaction. Indeed, in our experience, if a parent starts walking toward the baby's sleeping place, the baby will stay quiet as long as the parent keeps moving in the right direction. If the parent, heartened by silence and hopeful that the baby has gone to sleep, stops to listen, there will be a series of howls, punctuated by silences, each howl more forceful and prolonged than the one before. This is apparently a way of insisting that the parent keep coming to the child.

There are several ways to ease this crisis. One is simply to let the baby fall asleep in the midst of adult company and then move him or her to the regular sleeping place when asleep. There are, however, two possible drawbacks to this procedure. First, the baby may get so used to going to sleep in the middle of the household bustle that he or she becomes unable to drop off when the house is quiet. Second, the baby may wake up while being moved, starting a new round of protest. Another approach is for a parent to stay in the room after putting the baby to bed, patting and stroking the infant's back and crooning softly until he or she falls asleep. The chief difficulty with this tactic is that it may take half an hour or longer, which is no great fun for an already weary parent. This kind of bedtime soothing is likely to evolve into a fixed ritual, lasting into the preschool years, which must be faithfully observed. Another way of easing the baby's sense of isolation is to leave a soft light burning in the baby's room. Total darkness may threaten the baby with a dissolution of identity, whereas visual contact with familiar landmarks helps the baby stay oriented. This is an extension of the principle of **field dependence,** according to which the organism relies on cues from the environment rather than on internal cues for orientation in space (Witkin *et al.*, 1954). Reliance on internal cues constitutes **field independence.** Normal development entails a shift from field dependence to field independence, indicating an increasing awareness of self.

The time will inevitably come, however, when, the rituals having been performed and the night light left on, the adult will have to leave and, if necessary, let the baby cry himself or herself to sleep. This requires considerable fortitude on the part of sensitive parents, who imagine all sorts of things—an open diaper pin (if pins are used), the baby's head wedged between the crib bars—that might be causing the baby distress. In fact, parents can readily tell from the quality of the baby's cries whether a real emergency has arisen. Even the most indulgent parents find that they have to draw a line between times they are available to the baby and times they reserve to themselves. In any event, it takes only a few evenings for babies to get the message that screaming is of no use, although each moment may feel like an enternity to loving parents. After this, babies usually go to bed without any further significant protest. To the surprise and relief of guilt-ridden parents, the baby awakes the next morning with no trace of rancor or resentment and greets the parents with the customary broad grin. When babies are sick, of course, parents have to go in to them during the night. Once the sickness is past, the baby will have to relearn the lesson that bedtime is for sleeping and not for seeking attention.

Yet another change with social implications takes place around age four months. At younger ages, babies announce their morning awakening with howls for instant attention. Once a bleary-eyed parent appears, the baby calms down and greets the parent with a loving smile. At four months or so, instead of screaming for the parents, the baby wakes up and lies softly crooning and crowing for a while. Parents often become aware of this change almost as of something wrong. For the first time in months, they wake up of their own accord to a somewhat uncanny quiet hardly touched by the baby's vocalizations. Some babies come to insist on a period of solitude before being picked up. They scan the room, inspect and play with their hands, pick at the designs of the crib bumper or play with its strings, and shout angrily if the parents approach too soon.

The four-to-six-month period is the beginning of a time, before babies become mobile and increasingly self-reliant, when the baby can be left contentedly alone in a bassinet or carriage at least long enough for a parent to complete a few household chores. It helps if the baby has something to look at and handle, such as a cradle gym or a suspended cloth doll, or to listen to, such as music or a family conversation or a news broadcast on the radio or TV. It helps, too, to keep the baby in the room where adult activity, including frequent contacts with the baby, is centered.

By age six months, as we noted above, the (American) baby eats three meals a day plus occasional snacks and a bedtime nursing. The bedtime nursing not only staves off hunger pangs during the night but also, and perhaps more important, provides a final period of social contact, cuddling, and soothing before the day's activities end. However, unlike eating schedules, most babies' sleeping patterns resist synchronization with the parents'. Children are early wakers until the school years, when, as parents soon learn, it can be a major enterprise to get them out of bed and off to school.

The stabilization of the baby's eating and sleeping rhythms illustrates the phenomenon of *biological clocks*, the mechanisms that govern our daily cycles of activity and repose, of hunger and thirst, ingestion and digestion and elimination, and of such physiological changes as rises and falls in body temperature. These cycles seem to be set initially by events in the outside world, but they stabilize and become semiautonomous, resisting day-to-day variations in schedules and routines. A great many species, from flowering peas to oysters and bees also develop regular daily (and, in some cases, seasonal) cycles. It is our biological clocks, of course, that account for what is known as jet lag, the disorientation in time that afflicts us when we cross several time zones rapidly to east or west.

In our view, the stabilization of the baby's body rhythms has emotional and cognitive implications. There are now longer periods for play, exploration, and socialization free from the distracting demands of unscheduled physiological processes.

Teething

Another important physical change, celebrated by all parents, is the appearance of the first teeth, usually between six and seven months. The two front lowers are usually the first to erupt, soon followed by the two front uppers. The teeth con-

(© Shelly Rusten)

Teething causes the baby discomfort in the gums, which it relieves by chewing on whatever is available.

tinue to sprout in pairs, spreading toward the back, with the lower teeth taking the lead, at intervals of about a month. Thus by age one, the baby has about a dozen teeth. Teething continues, although not so visibly, until about eighteen months, when the child has a full set of twenty baby teeth. It is interesting that when the baby teeth are shed, beginning around age five or six, they are lost and replaced in the same order. Again in old age, when the teeth begin to loosen, it is still in the original order.

It used to be thought that teething caused sickness. Many babies do indeed have their first illness just about the time they are teething. However, we now know that teething simply coincides with the wearing off of antibodies absorbed before birth from the mother. There is no causal connection between teething and sickness. It is worth noting that sickness in babies and young children is often marked by raging fevers. Sickness can also be the occasion of delirium or, in toddlers and preschool children, distorted perception or hallucinations. Frightening though these manifestations may be, most children given decent medical care seem to survive undamaged.

Teething is of some psychological interest. Teething causes a certain amount of discomfort in the gums, which babies relieve by chewing on teething rings, pacifiers, or whatever else is available. Apart from the chewing caused by discomfort, the new teeth apparently demand to be used, and babies begin to chew their meals, including baby food and milk. They also bite down hard on anything that comes into the mouth, which probably explains why nursing mothers often find it convenient to wean the baby from the breast at this time. Some psychoanalysts, for whom infancy is the oral stage, interpret babies' biting at the breast as an expression of ambivalence or even hostility. We prefer the simpler explanation that developing systems demand to be exercised, and that biting is a form of exploratory behavior. Biting the breast may also be an evolutionary adaptation, since mother's milk no longer meets all the nutritional needs of babies older than about six months.

Growth and maturation obviously continue past age seven months, but at this point it seems to make sense to relate them more closely to behavioral development, particularly in the realm of motor control. We next focus on the baby's control over the hands, as in prehension (grasping and holding) and manipulation **(fine motor control),** and over the body as a whole, as in posture and locomotion **(gross motor control).**

FINE AND GROSS MOTOR CONTROL

Motor control in infancy ordinarily follows so stable a pattern of development that it was long assumed to be *autogenous,* a simple product of maturation. We now know that behavioral development, like physical growth, requires emotional and cognitive support and stimulation. For instance, Dennis and Najarian (1957) set out to study the role of practicing preliminary skills in the emergence of autogenous functions, using as subjects babies in a foundling home. They were surprised to discover that babies in this institution were greatly retarded in their supposedly autogenous development, apparently due to lack of stimulation. Indeed, a goodly proportion of the children were not walking even by age three. This was especially unsettling to Dennis, who had first proposed the concept of autogenous development.

We must be aware that motor development overlaps and is interwoven with cognitive and perceptual development,

about which we talk in Chapter 6. When babies reach out to grasp something, it is to grasp something perceived. The baby who can sit up commands a very different view of space than the one who spends most of the time lying down. Space as something to move around in is very different from space for a baby who cannot yet creep or walk.

Fine and gross motor control develop together and sometimes cannot even be distinguished. Although we associate fine motor control with use of the hands, sucking also involves complex "manipulation" of an object, the nipple. Head turning would ordinarily be seen as gross motor behavior, but when head turning is instrumentally conditioned so as to yield a reward, head turning becomes a fine motor act. At times, as we shall see, the feet act as auxiliary hands, so that these tools of locomotion likewise can be tools of manipulation. What can be said is that fine motor control often develops from rather gross forms of action to much more highly differentiated and skilled ones. When babies begin to reach out to things at a distance, it is first to bat at them with the whole hand, then simply to grasp them, and finally to manipulate them. Let us somewhat arbitrarily, then, begin with prehension and manipulation.

Prehension and Manipulation

Fine motor control refers generally to the use of the hands in seizing and manipulating objects. Recall that the grasping reflex is present from birth, and babies take hold of anything that accidentally comes in contact with their hand. Thus babies may clutch and fondle the edge of a blanket. In no time, they clasp in

(© George Zimbell/Monkmeyer Press)

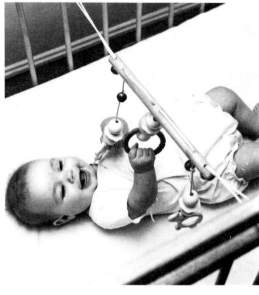

(© Lew Merrim/Monkmeyer Press)

Visually guided grasping. The infant may at first reach out to objects slightly too far away to touch, but its distance judgment develops rapidly. Note that once the baby has grasped something, it finds it hard to let go.

both hands the breast or bottle from which they are receiving milk. But it is only toward age three months that babies reach out to make contact with things at a distance, with things given purely visually rather than by direct contact.

The baby begins merely by batting at dangling objects, and if successful sets them swaying. The infant may at first reach out to objects slightly too distant to touch, but there is remarkably rapid adjustment of distance judgment, so that the baby soon learns to see that an object is out of reach. Beginning at about age three months, the baby not only bats at dangling objects but tries to grasp them. **Visually guided grasping** is usually well established by age four months. Such grasping at first has a spastic quality that unprepared parents may find quite alarming. The thumb is aligned with the other fingers rather than opposed, and the baby's hand bends backward at the wrist as it awkwardly clutches the object.

Visually guided grasping is one of the maturation-based skills that appear on schedule only in the presence of normal stimulation. In a study by White and Held (1966), it was found that institution-reared babies were one to two months retarded in visually guided grasping.

In Chapter 4 we spoke about the looming effect, distress caused by the apparent rapid approach of a large object toward the baby, and we remarked that this effect might be taken as an early index of depth perception. Reaching out to things at a distance definitely implies perception of both depth and solidity. However, objects do not have to be solid for babies to see them as solid. Babies try to grasp sunbeams and tobacco smoke. They also try to pick up two-dimensional designs and pictures, scratching vainly at figures on their crib mattresses or bumpers.

Another interesting feature of early grasping is that once babies have something solid in their hands, they are unable to let go of it again. It seems that babies' still-active grasp reflex keeps the fingers clenched around anything that stimulates the palm. Either the object eventually falls out of the baby's gradually relaxing fingers or, if the baby is really eager to get rid of the object, he or she learns to force it loose by rubbing it against the chest.

Between five and six months of age, babies become able not only to grasp but also to let go of, hold on to, and manipulate rings and rattles and rags. Needless to say, everything goes into the baby's mouth for sampling. Babies use both hands in a coordinated way to handle objects, for example, to stretch out a piece of cloth while inspecting its intricacies, and they can transfer things from one hand to the other. Babies turn any new object around so as to examine the far side, indicating, as does reaching out to grasp, that objects do not exist for babies as flat projections but instead are seen as continuing around out of view, like proper solid things (Piaget, 1932). This is an example of *implicit perception*, awareness of the hidden parts of objects that cannot be viewed all at once in their entirety.

By the time babies are old enough to be fed in a highchair or feeding table, usually around six months, they use their hands to feed themselves. When eating mushy foodstuffs, they slap a hand into the dish and then scrape the mush off against a wide-open mouth. Babies can hold a cracker and gum off mouthfuls for chewing and swallowing. Babies may at first have trouble aligning the cracker correctly to go into the mouth; many babies have to learn by trial and error that a cracker held at right angles to the mouth will not fit. With square crackers, babies like to consume the corners one after the other, leaving a final mouthful of center. The baby who has known nothing but square crackers will be totally at a loss the first time he or she is given a round cracker to eat. The baby searches in vain for the nonexistent corners. Once babies have teeth, they can bite off mouthfuls of more substantial foods, such as apple slices.

Around age eight months, the thumb becomes fully opposed, and accurate pincers grasping between thumb and forefinger becomes possible. Now, at mealtimes, babies are able to pick up a pellet of food, such as a pea or a bit of meat, and pop it into the mouth. But use of the pincers grasp is not limited to eating. As with all new skills, babies practice this one industriously, picking up minute granules, bits of lint or dust, snippets of thread, whatever. Some babies even go so far as to pick up imaginary particles, storing them in the cupped other hand or giving them to a cooperative adult.

When babies are as young as seven

(© Elizabeth Crews)

Once the thumb has become fully opposed, babies can pick up bits of food between thumb and forefinger and pop them into the mouth.

months, the parents may find themselves obliged to give them a spoon to hold while being fed, or else, once the first ravenous pangs of hunger have been appeased, babies may be more interested in grabbing the feeding spoon than in eating the food it contains. With a spoon of their own, babies can go through the motions of scooping up food while parents take care of the practical business of transferring food from dish to mouth. By nine or ten months, babies may try to feed themselves with a spoon, making a splendid mess of food, self, and surroundings. Effective self-feeding with a spoon does not usually come until toddlerhood.

A manipulative skill of late infancy is rotary movements of the hands, which permit babies to unscrew caps from bottles and toothpaste tubes (often with messy results), to turn knobs to open cupboards, to switch on radio and television sets, and to twist the knob to control the volume. Some babies we have observed prefer the right hand for clockwise rotations and the left for counterclockwise. Babies learn that there may be a delay between turning on a television set and the emergence of picture and sound, although infants obviously have no concept of the set having to warm up. Babies may magically seek to hasten the warm-up process by turning the volume full on, and then be so frightened by the ensuing blast that they cannot approach the set to turn it down.

We will encounter other instances of fine motor control in other contexts, but we have said enough here to give the general picture. We now turn to the development of *gross motor control*, posture and locomotion.

Posture and Locomotion

Just as manipulation evolves from prehension, so does locomotion evolve from the baby's developing control over posture and changes of posture. Newborn babies stay where they are put. Although they can wave their arms and kick their legs freely, they usually keep their legs flexed, knees spread, and heels together, as though squatting. Transported on an adult hand and forearm, neonates show signs of maintaining balance. And the full-blown rooting response has elements of crawling. By age one month, many babies, when prone, can raise their head enough to clear their chin. (A few especially mature babies can do this at birth, whereas some perfectly normal babies cannot do this until age two months or later.) By age two months, babies cannot really change position, but, when supine, they arch their body and flail from side to side, sometimes in distress but sometimes also as an expression of pleasure.

For the first five or six months, babies are essentially horizontal creatures. The widespread use of baby seats allows babies to be propped up comfortably from

(© Suzanne Szasz)

The five-month-old can push its chest and shoulders clear and hold its head erect, as in this classic family album photograph.

an early age, but we do not know how this affects babies' postural or motor development. Without a baby seat, four-month-olds can be held briefly in a seated position before their head lolls helplessly. By age five months, babies can sit propped up, the head supported, more or less indefinitely. Prone five-month-olds can push chest and shoulders clear and hold the head erect, as in the classic family album photograph of the nude baby on a shaggy rug. At this age, if something is too big or heavy to be brought to the baby's mouth, the baby can grab hold and pull his or her mouth to the object. By age five months, the baby's ankles have begun to straighten, so that the feet no longer stare each other in the face.

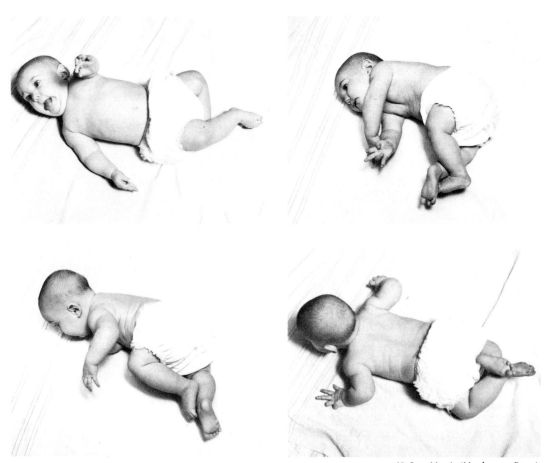

(© *Lew Merrim/Monkmeyer Press*)

Rolling over from back to belly.

At age six months, babies still cannot get into the sitting position unassisted, but if placed sitting they can remain that way without support—which makes possible the use of highchair or feeding table. Babies have to be strapped in; otherwise, seated babies often just relax and go sliding down out of their chairs or tables. Around age six months (with wide individual variations), babies become able to roll over, usually first from back to belly and then from belly to back. Once able to roll over, they begin to vary their sleeping positions, so that those who slept consistently on their back, head to one side, flattening the skull and wearing off the hair at the point of contact with the mattress, begin to regain the lost hair and rounded skull. The stepping reflex, set off by supporting the baby upright with the feet lightly touching a firm surface, returns about now, having disappeared shortly after birth. A fair number of six-month-old babies can lock their knees and stand on an adult lap, supported by the adult's encircling arm.

Sitting infants assume a characteristic

Buddha-like pose, and as they play with something on the floor, six- to seven-month-olds may droop forward until they are helplessly nose against floor.

By age eight or nine months, babies outgrow the folding bath or dishpan or kitchen sink and will have to be moved to the family tub for bathing. This provides endless opportunities for play, reciprocal interaction, and learning, especially if infants are given a supply of washcloths, sponges, plastic cups, floating rubber animals, and wood or plastic boats. Babies will inevitably swallow some of the bath water—after all, it is a great discovery that one can squeeze water from a soaked rag or sponge into one's mouth—but we have never known this to cause any harm. Nevertheless, a couple of cautions are in order. The water should be kept shallow, or the infant, whose buoyancy works against the sense of balance, will topple. Even in shallow water, babies can never be left alone. Far too many untended babies have drowned.

Crawling and Creeping. Toward seven months, prone babies begin to make crawling movements. (Usages differ, but we try to distinguish between **crawling,** in which the torso touches the ground, and **creeping,** in which the torso is clear of the ground.) The movements are mostly abortive, but babies may succeed in propelling themselves short distances—forward, sideways, or backward, more as chance dictates than from any intention of their own. Infants who can roll over sometimes learn to use rolling as a means of self-propulsion.

Somewhere between ages six and eight months, babies become able to hold on to an adult's forefinger and half pull themselves, half let themselves be pulled

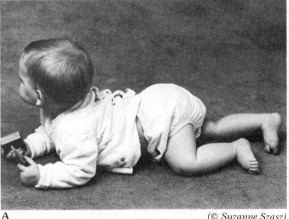

A   (© Suzanne Szasz)

B   (© Elizabeth Crews)

C   (© John Fay)

A Crawling. **B** Creeping. **C** Bear walking.

into a sitting position. Between eight and nine months, on the average, babies become able to sit up without help. Different babies accomplish this in a variety of ways. Some, from a prone position, walk their hands under the chest until the trunk is almost erect, simultaneously swinging their legs from back to front. Others lie on one side, knees drawn up, and half rock, half push the body into a seated position. Once the baby can get up on hands and knees, it is a simple matter to ease or plop the backside between the legs onto the floor.

Toward eight months, the baby's attempts at crawling have become quite effective. Typically, babies crawl by dragging themselves with the forearms and pushing with legs and feet, with a fair amount of incidental wriggling and writhing. Some babies, though, crawl feet first, pushing with their arms or hands; some travel by swiveling on their arched bellies; and some, as we have said, roll from place to place.

Starting around nine months, babies can get onto their hands and knees, either by pushing up from a prone position or by tilting forward from a sitting position. At first, they can only rock back and forth, but they soon figure out—and one can see them concentrating hard—how to shift their weight so as to free one limb (or pair of limbs) after another and begin to creep.

As with crawling, various individual styles of creeping can be observed. The usual pattern is the simultaneous advance of one hand and the opposite leg in alternation. Some babies, though, leapfrog forward, moving both hands together in alternation with both legs. Bear walking, with the legs held straight and the feet rather than the knees touch-

ing the ground, is another common variant. One little girl we know used her hands in the regular way, but used one leg simply for support and poled herself along with the other, like a gondolier. Some babies move seated, hitching their bottom along with the help of hands, feet, or both. One such baby used her feet oar fashion, placing them forward and then sliding them outward to the sides, dragging her rump forward. At a more advanced stage, on a smooth floor, babies may push themselves along with their legs while sliding their hands on a sheet of paper or a rag.

Creeping babies may take several approaches to carrying something. They may simply drag it along in one hand, or hold it off the floor and travel on all threes, or carry it in the mouth dog-style. Creeping babies enjoy wending their way snakelike through the rungs of chairs, under tables, and through whatever passageways space offers for investigation.

Standing and Walking. As we have said, the published norms of development are out of date, but the sequences remain stable. So with walking. We will follow the Bayley Scale of Motor Development (Bayley, 1969), but in full awareness that the standardization sample was largely based on urban middle-class children. According to the Bayley norms, the average age at which children can pull themselves to a standing position is 8.6 months, with a range from 6 to 12 months. The first few times babies pull themselves to their feet, they do not know how to get back down and may cry in alarm until an adult comes to the rescue. Very soon, though, babies learn to simply let go and thud onto their seats—

A   *(© Vivienne/DPI)*

B   *(© Margaret Mead)*

D

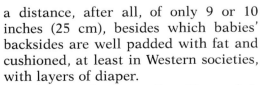

Progress toward walking. **A** Pulling oneself to standing. **B** Balinese walking rail. Compare with the more familiar enclosing playpen. **C** Taking steps assisted by mother. **D** A toddler toddling.

C   *(© Shelly Rusten)*   *(© George W. Martin/DPI)*

a distance, after all, of only 9 or 10 inches (25 cm), besides which babies' backsides are well padded with fat and cushioned, at least in Western societies, with layers of diaper.

At 9.9 months (range 7 to 12 months), babies can walk with slight adult help. At about the same age, babies become able to *cruise*, side-stepping while they shift their grip from support to support, such as tables and chairs and anything else they can reach. By 11 months (range

9 to 16 months), babies can stand alone. Free-standing babies like to bounce in place, either to music or just for the fun of it.

And then, one day—parents often sense it coming and wait expectantly—babies gather themselves together, raise their hands for balance, and toddle a few steps. In a matter of seconds, a major transition has taken place. Bayley places this momentous event at 11.7 months, with a range from 9 to 17 months. Once they have walked, babies almost immediately learn to stand up without gripping anything. Seated, they may draw their feet together and simply push upward. On hands and knees, they shift their weight backward from knees to feet, producing a squat, and then straighten up. For another month or more, babies may prefer to creep when they have a definite destination, but they periodically practice walking—often only a few steps at a time before they collapse on their bottoms. There then comes a time when they creep only as a clearly intended joke, a joke that tells us something about their self-awareness.

Bear in mind that a newly walking baby stands some 29 inches (74 cm) tall, which means that in Western households the top of the baby's head comes just about even with an ordinary table top. By stretching, the baby can barely see what is on the table. It will be almost a year before he or she can grasp a doorknob, some 38 inches (96.5 cm) above the floor.

As walking becomes more assured, babies love to lug, haul, and shove outsize objects. Babies will rearrange as much of the family's furniture as they can move. Carrying is at first enjoyed for its own sake. Later it will be integrated into complex functions, such as building with blocks. Babies' first carrying preference seems to be for large objects hugged to the body with both arms, failing which they will carry two smaller things, one in each arm. Apparently the urge to carry is great, for we have many times observed a baby pick up something tiny like a scrap of paper, hug it to the chest, and walk around with it.

SOCIAL AND EMOTIONAL DEVELOPMENT

Although neonates are essentially asocial creatures, they come into the world with a special sensitivity to the human face, voice, and physical contact, which provides channels through which social communication can take place and develop. At first, while their very survival depends on care by adult human beings, they are scarcely aware that such beings exist. By the end of infancy, however, babies are highly social creatures, at least with the people they know well, and are capable of complex social interchanges (Honig, 1982).

Erikson and Basic Trust

The key to social and emotional development in infancy is to be found in Erik Erikson's (1964) notion of **basic trust versus basic mistrust,** the first of his eight psychosocial stages. Basic trust refers initially to confidence in providers as reliable, consistent, and sensitive meeters of **basic needs.** Babies' basic needs include, of course, material needs for food and shelter and the like, but they also include psychological needs for love, attention, play, contact, stimulation, and, at various times, discipline and control. Basic trust expands to trust in the world at large as a safe, reliable, predictable, manageable place in which to live. It also works its way inward, giving the baby a feeling of self-worth, competence, and self-confidence. Basic mistrust arises when a baby's needs are not met in a way that leads the baby to trust the parents, the world, and the self. The mistrustful baby experiences the self as helpless and the world as a source of misery, frustration, and uncertainty. The sense of trust or mistrust applies also to the parents' view of themselves as competent caregivers and of the baby as satisfying, reasonable, and lovable.

Note that meeting needs, especially as the baby grows older, does not always mean instantly giving whatever is needed. A reasonable delay in feeding or in picking the baby up after sleep is not going to produce damage, even if the baby acts as if the world were coming to an end. It is when gratification is too long and too consistently delayed that panic sets in. The baby has no time perspective, the crisis seems to drag on interminably, the baby is helpless to do anything about it, and a tiny seed of mistrust has been planted.

It is not only the actual meeting of needs that counts, but the quality of the attention given to the baby. If parents are grudging, if they are hostile or impatient, their movements are likely to be rough, jerky, and abrupt. If they feel anxious, their movements may be hesitant, fumbling, and erratic. Babies are sensitive to such qualities, just as they are responsive to handling that expresses love and confidence. With dependable, self-assured care, a fair amount of normal hardship and the time needed for practice by inexperienced parents are easily tolerated.

Erikson places feeding experiences at the center of the development of basic trust or mistrust, which should remind us that his view of infancy is derived from Freud's idea of infancy as the *oral stage of psychosexual development*. Even if we do not accept orality as an expression of sexual drives, there is no denying that oral experience is very important for infants. Some observers have gone so far as to say that babies are "all mouth," although parents will be vividly aware that the digestive tract has two ends. Apart from the pleasures associated with feeding, babies find sucking and, later, biting and chewing to be highly pleasurable activities in their own right. (Adults who chew gum are indulging the same sort of drive.) Further, the mouth serves babies as an important prehensile tool and also as an organ of cognition—the baby's mouthing of objects is a way of gaining information about their shape, consistency, texture, and flavor.

The Development of Emotional Expression

Crying as an indicator of distress is present from birth and serves as the first, uncontrolled signal to the parents that the baby is in need of attention. Hunger is the most common form of early distress, but the baby's crying rapidly comes to convey pain, anger, and frustration.

We have already spoken of the neonate's *pleasure smile*, which seems to express placid contentment. **Social smil-**

ing, stimulated by a face or voice, first appears between ages six and eight weeks. The most potent stimulus for a social smile is a human face seen in front view, preferably nodding. However, babies will also smile at a crude approximation of a human face, such as a cloth wrapped around the straws of a broom and daubed with a pair of "eyes" (Spitz, 1946; Ambrose, 1961). There is also evidence that at least some young babies smile in response to a familiar voice (Kreutzer and Charlesworth, 1973). As a rule, though, social smiling is usually delayed in blind babies (Fraiberg, 1977). Social smiling is a clear indicator of babies' pleasure at the sight of a human face or the sound of a familiar voice (Sroufe and Waters, 1976). It also serves as a powerful reinforcer for parents, who will go to great lengths to elicit smiling from their babies, babbling nonsense, making faces and silly gestures, and engaging in various kinds of physical play.

At about age two months, vocalization other than crying or the sounds that accompany digestion begins. The first vocalizations have been accurately described as "small, throaty sounds" (Gesell, Thompson, and Amatruda, 1938). These thereafter evolve into highly complex patterns of babbling—but not yet, in infancy, true speech. However, parents often react to their baby's babblings as though they were divinely sent messages.

Before age two months, babies (except those in the grip of colic) stop crying at the sight of a parent. This does not necessarily imply individual recognition of the parent, and may be a case of conditioning to the human face as promising relief from distress. By two months, many babies stop crying at the approach of parental footsteps, again perhaps as a product of conditioning.

It is around age three months that babies show the first clear signs of distinguishing between familiar and unfamiliar people, a vital landmark in social relations. Familiar people are greeted with smiles and coos and gurgles and wriggling (Kreutzer and Charlesworth, 1973), whereas unfamiliar ones are met with a solemn stare, a frown, or an expression of vague puzzlement. This guarded reaction to strangers has been given the name of **wariness** (Bronson and Pankey, 1977). In cognitive terms, wariness implies the beginnings of an internal representation—a *schema*—of the primary figures in a baby's life. Let us recall, incidentally, that age three months marks the stage of infants' "becoming human" and also is the age at which infants seem to achieve voluntary control of the voice, as when they resist evening bedtime.

Around age four months, to the surprise and delight of parents, babies produce a genuine laugh, in the form of a hearty chuckle. Perhaps the most reliable stimulus for laughing is nuzzling the baby's belly. Along with gurgling and cooing and babbling, laughing soon becomes a recurring ingredient in playful interchanges with adults. By age six months, babies are highly sensitive to parental moods and emotions, and may laugh and cry empathically as parental feelings shift.

Stranger Anxiety. Beginning anywhere from age five months to one year, many babies show a pronounced fear of unfamiliar people, or **stranger anxiety.** Remember that stranger anxiety has a precursor in the wariness found in three-month-olds. Now, at the approach of an unfamiliar person, babies are likely to scream, bury their face in the parent's neck, clutch at the parent, and put as much psychic distance as possible between stranger and self. (For those babies who can creep or walk, the refuge of the parent's arms offers more safety than running away).

Stranger anxiety is of both practical and theoretical interest. On the practical side, we have the hurt feelings of loving but unfamiliar grandparents, aunts and uncles, and family friends who cannot understand why the baby should reject their advances and who may suspect, however irrationally, that the parents have taught the baby to dislike them. A baby's developing fear of medical personnel can be seen as a case of stranger anxiety aggravated by fear of the pain of immunizing injections, and by the unpleasantness of having incomprehensible things done to one, sometimes by force. There is the further practical problem of leaving the baby with an unfamiliar sitter or of placing the baby in day care with unfamiliar adults.

It should be stressed that stranger anxiety is a reaction not only to unfamiliar people but also to strange settings or objects. Even familiar objects acting in unaccustomed ways may trigger fear. One eight-month-old girl had a self-righting roly-poly doll; a visitor turned the doll on its side and set it spinning, which so terrified the baby that it was some months before she could even bear to look at the doll. Indeed, babies may not recognize, and thus show fear of, their own mother the first time they see her dressed up (and made up) to go out for the evening, or their own father with a face disguised by shaving cream.

(© Michael Weisbrot & Family)

By six months, babies are highly sensitive to parental moods and emotions.

At the practical level, stranger anxiety is easily dealt with. The wise stranger knows that the baby's fear is at least partly counterbalanced by curiosity, so the thing to do is to remain quiet and at a safe distance. In a short while, the baby begins stealing furtive glances at the stranger, then, reassured, gives him or her a steady scrutiny, and finally may make overtures of actual friendship, smiling and perhaps even reaching out to be held.

On the theoretical side, stranger anxiety is interesting first because it tells us that the infant, out of repeated exposure, has built up a stable mental framework of the familiar, against which strangeness stands out by contrast. There is the further theoretical question of why some babies show stranger anxiety and others do not. Some years ago, Bettye Caldwell (1963) established the basic principle: Those babies who have been exposed to only a limited variety of caregivers are much more likely to show stranger anxiety than babies who have had a great variety of caregivers. For instance, kibbutz children, who are reared in groups by a number of different caregivers, rarely show stranger anxiety (Spiro, 1958). Note, though, that we are talking about diversity within a fairly limited range, since very few children have close contact with people representing all the variety to be found in humankind.

Stranger anxiety can be seen as a special case of babies' general reaction to novelty. Here we encounter the **discrepancy hypothesis** (McCall and Kagan, 1967; Welsh, 1974), according to which small deviations from the familiar are attractive, whereas greater departures from the familiar produce increasing fearfulness. Various levels of the familiarity-strangeness polarity have been proposed, but we think three are enough for most purposes. The first level is the everyday, including both the intimate and affect-laden, whether parent or security blanket, and the merely humdrum familiar, so much taken for granted as perhaps not even to be noticed. The second is the novel, which is enough like the familiar not to arouse fear but different enough to stir up curiosity and exploration. The third is the unprecedentedly strange, so different from what we are used to that it can arouse negative feelings ranging from apprehension to horror to nausea—the extremes of strangeness are the weird and the bizarre.

We must also note that discrepancy sometimes works in the opposite direction. That is, when our framework of familiar expectations, our schemata of reality, are violated, we experience positive feelings. We may laugh. Indeed, the very essence of a joke is to lead us to expect one outcome and then, at the punch line, to substitute another, discrepant one. We find exotic, unfamiliar landscapes beautiful as often as threatening, and certain unfamiliar conditions can move us to something like religious awe. No one has yet come up with a satisfactory explanation of our varied reactions to differing sorts and degrees of strangeness.

A consideration that is both practical and theoretical is that stranger anxiety is a good indicator of attachment to and identification with the family. This is a theme on which we shall dwell at some length later in this chapter.

A further question is: When do we outgrow stranger anxiety? The answer in many cases seem to be never. Many of us have identified with the ways of those familiar to us to the point of **ethnocentrism,** an unquestioning acceptance of our own society's ways of doing things as the only truly human way. This acceptance may be so deep that the behavior of people from different backgrounds strikes some adults as perverse, depraved, and even subhuman. Ethnocentrism can be seen as the extension of both egocentrism and stranger anxiety. It may lead to fear and distrust of foreigners, called *xenophobia*, to racial and religious prejudice, and to prejudice against the handicapped. Prejudice has some of its roots in the cradle.

Stranger anxiety in infancy indicates strong attachment, and as a precursor of later capacities for strong feelings is undoubtedly good. But parents and educators would be well advised to make sure that children receive the diversity of experience that will enable them to accept, value, and enjoy unfamiliar people, places, customs, and foods simply as manifestations of our varied yet common humanity. We want our children to generalize basic trust to people at large.

Separation Anxiety. Yet another manifestation of early attachment is **separation anxiety,** a child's distress when shut off from the parents for any length of time. Once babies can creep, even though they play all over the house, they return at frequent intervals to look at or touch a parent, often hugging the parent's legs. Here we can see at work the competing urges to move away and explore and at the same time to maintain close contact. We spoke above of how a baby might not recognize his or her parent dressed up for an evening out. This soon changes to a realization that the dressed-up parent is about to be separated from the baby, which provokes a squall of protest. This reaction makes it a good idea to have a steady sitter whom the baby will accept as a temporary parent surrogate. If an unfamiliar sitter has to be hired, he or she should arrive enough in advance of the parents' departure to establish a relationship with the baby, in company with a parent, that will make distress-free separation possible.

A more serious case is when a parent has to be away for an extended period, for example, a hospital stay. The remaining parent, unless he or she is free to take over the entire task of caregiving, must assure an ample supply of caregivers and make sure that the baby accepts them. Even so, it is not uncommon for a returning parent to be greeted as a stranger. This does not imply nonrecognition, but resentment at having been deserted. If the child has to go to the hospital, a disturbing blend of separation anxiety and stranger anxiety is liable to arise. Even when frequently visited by the parents, a baby who has to undergo extended hospitalization is likely to suffer a period of inconsolable anguish followed by dull, apathetic withdrawal This is sometimes unavoidable and simply has to be dealt with as best the parents can. However, a number of enlightened hospitals now permit or even encourage a parent to stay with the baby or young child throughout hospitalization, taking over some of the duties of nurses and aides.

It is hard to study separation anxiety apart from stranger anxiety, although they are clearly distinct states. Our best formulation of separation anxiety is that the baby's still immature sense of identity is threatened when out of contact with an attachment figure that serves as the baby's reference point—we see here another instance of our extended definition of field dependence (see p. 150).

Development of Social Relations in Infancy

It is obvious that the baby's first social relations are likely to be with family members—parents, of course, but also older siblings and sometimes other relatives, and even household pets. All these become objects of reciprocal attachment.

During the baby's first couple of months of life, social relations are likely to revolve around the routines and mechanics of caregiving—feeding, changing, bathing, putting to bed and taking out of bed, outings and the bundling and unbundling of the baby to suit the temperature. However, there is no reason for routines or mechanics to be routine or mechanical, and a good deal of affective interchange goes on in the course of care-giving. During nursing, for instance, parent and baby can snuggle close, each studying in great detail the other's facial features, and the adult, as often as not, can keep up a train of largely nonsensical small talk.

Increasingly during infancy the pragmatics of life are interspersed with episodes of play. Perhaps the most basic form of play between parent and baby begins when the infant is about two months old, in the form of what J. S. Watson (1970) has dubbed "the game." The parent leans face-to-face over the baby and talks to him or her. The baby responds with smiling and delighted wrigglings and mouth movements that appear to be an effort to answer back. The parent responds with smiling, further vocalization, and physical handling, and a back-and-forth movement of communication has begun. In less than no time, the baby's smiling and wriggling become his or her own way of signaling to a parent that it is now time to play "the game."

Whether through smiling or crying or more advanced forms of signaling, babies begin at a very early age to learn that they exert a degree of control over the social environment. The responsive parent, in other words, provides **contingent reinforcement** (Horowitz, 1968). *Contingent reinforcement,* or *feedback,* consists of environmental events that are clearly produced by the baby's own actions. Contingent reinforcement contributes significantly to the baby's sense of competence, to feeling that he or she can control things.

"The game" is only one of the many *social games* through which parents and babies come to know one another and

further cement attachment. From the beginning of infancy, parents play "This Little Piggy" with the baby's fingers and toes. By age three months, babies enjoy the mock fright that comes when parents say "Boo!" and then smile and tickle the baby. This is an early example of what is nowadays referred to as **nonliteral behavior**. At the literal level of behavior, the parent offers a threat when saying "Boo!" but as the baby perfectly well understands, the parent is instead engaged in a nonliteral act of play. Make-believe, then, is usually understood by children, even when they take it seriously, not to refer to the real world. Lies, of course, are nonliteral statements intended to be taken literally.

An important activity that is sometimes incorporated into social play is *imitation*. We have seen that imitation probably appears right after birth, but it is in the second half of the first year that imitation comes into full flower. Babbled conversations between infant and parent begin with the adult imitating the sounds the baby makes, but soon the baby in turn is imitating—no matter how imperfectly—new sounds introduced by the parents. Babies blindly imitate such gestures as those involved in breaking an egg into a bowl or in brushing away a fly. Blind imitation begins to shade into observational learning—and presumably modeling—as the baby begins to perform functional acts such as using a cleaning tissue to mop up spilled liquid. The baby tries to blow out a match, going "Puh, puh, puh." Through imitation, babies quickly learn the behaviors that will stimulate parental participation in social games: slapping the highchair tray or feeding-table top, sham coughing, sniffing, puffing out the

(© Leonard Speier)

Imitation comes into full flower during the second half of the first year. In time, blind imitation shades into observational learning.

cheeks to have the air squeezed out, puckering the lips in a vain attempt to whistle (many babies enjoy using a forefinger to plug up and so shut off parental whistling). The baby joins in heartily when the parents laugh, even though the infant can have no idea what the joke is about. Babies try to start a new round of merriment by making a strained laughing sound.

The parents are not the only models for the baby's imitations. From watching television, older babies learn—obviously again without understanding—to go through the motions of dancing, conducting an orchestra, or doing calisthen-

ics. When babies see television audiences applauding, they too clap their hands, although for the most part soundlessly. Nor is all imitation social. Babies learn to mimic the sound of car and airplane engines, the ding of the kitchen timer, and the hum and hiss of the vacuum cleaner.

Social games feed into attachment and identification, and most are fun for parent and child alike. However, one social game of late infancy is a lot more fun for the baby than for the parent. Since it seems to make a contribution to the baby's cognitive development, though, it probably has to be endured. This is the

(© Clif Garboden/Stock, Boston)

One social game that is more fun for baby than for parent is drop and retrieve. An example of the baby's fascination with repeating new activities until they are mastered, drop and retrieve contributes to cognitive development.

game of *drop and retrieve*. At first the baby seems to drop things overboard from the feeding table as a form of spatial exploration, first listening for the sound of impact and then searching the floor for the dropped object. The realization soon dawns, however, that getting the parent to pick up the dropped object is great sport. This activity is a good example of the baby's fascination with repeating new activities until they are fully mastered. Such repetition is likely to seem boring, foolish, and perverse to parents. They might bear in mind two things. First, they themselves behave in exactly the same way when they acquire a new gadget. Second, the drop-and-retrieve game, by letting the infant control the parent, provides contingent reinforcement and bolsters the baby's sense of competence. It is easy for parents to forget that the world they take for granted is a place full of fresh and novel experiences for the baby, a place teeming with things to discover, experiment with, and digest. It might help if the parent can remember discovering the way raindrops trickle down a window pane, fusing and sticking and accumulating and branching, and how the better part of a childhood day could go to tracing the movement of the raindrops, or discovering how one can fog a window pane or mirror by breathing on it and then draw designs in the mist.

Among the common social games of middle to late infancy are peekaboo, swinging the baby between the adult's legs or jiggling the child high overhead, and bouncing the baby on the adult's knee to the tune of "To Market, To Market" or "Ride a Cock Horse." A perennial favorite is the game of give and take: "Now I'll give it to you," "Now you give it to me," handing a plaything back and forth. As Ross and Kay (1980) point out, turn alternation of this sort, along with the parents' being willing to respond to cues from the baby, are among the earliest defining features of social games.

When we discuss object permanence in Chapter 6, we will talk about the game of hiding a trinket in one hand and asking the baby to guess which hand is holding the object. Once babies can creep, they enjoy being chased to the accompaniment of "I'm gonna getcha, getcha, getcha," with the adult at the climax scooping up the baby with a great hug. Babies like to feign deafness and invisibility while the parent keeps calling the baby's name, searching in wastebaskets and drawers for the "missing" infant. When they are able, babies like to hide behind a door or in a closet while a parent carries on an elaborate search. Babies, of course, betray their hiding place by fits of giggling, and it will be a couple of years before they grasp the notion that true hiding requires silence. Note again the nonliteral character of the baby's "invisibility."

Note, too, how such play implies the sense of a separate self. However, the sense of self is still unstable. Suspense games like peekaboo, chasing, and being unable to find the invisible baby cannot go on too long. What begins as an enjoyable playing with the baby's sense of identity can become a threat to continued existence. In keeping with our extended version of the concept of field dependence (see p. 150), babies need a good deal of testing of the world's and their own durability before they can tolerate more than a brief denial of either.

A common social activity of late infancy is the baby's exploration with the fingers of a parent's facial features (babies respond quite readily to the admonition "Gently, gently"). If the baby explores one adult ear, he or she is sure to turn the adult's head to check on the other one. Babies soon adopt the pattern of touching an adult feature and then feeling for the same feature on their own faces. This may take some groping, since babies have not yet developed a complete schema of their bodies. If the adult names the features as the baby explores them, the infant may by the end of the first year be able to respond correctly to requests to "Show me your (eyes, tongue, teeth, or other feature)." Here we have touched on the development of the baby's detailed knowledge of self, to which we return in Chapter 6.

Not all parent-child relations are pleasant. Every so often the parent has to hold the struggling baby immobile while the doctor or nurse gives the injection. Sometimes babies have to be warned away from breakable or dangerous objects. However, such disagreeable interludes get lost in the larger pattern of loving, well-synchronized interchanges. Late in the first year babies begin to wean themselves from total human involvement and turn their attention increasingly to the wonders of the nonhuman environment. At this point parents learn not to be overly intrusive, to leave babies to their own devices while remaining ready to respond to their calls for help, attention, or participation.

The Language of Behavior

To say that parents learn to respond appropriately to cues and signals from the baby is another way of saying that they learn to read the infant's **language of behavior.** This language takes two forms. First, there are the spontaneous manifestations of distress, and parents must learn to distinguish special expressive qualities that identify the nature of the particular distress. From a rather early age, the baby's cries of hunger, fatigue, anger, loneliness, pain, and so forth are fairly easy to tell apart. Sometimes there are postural cues. For instance, it is sometimes hard to tell whether the baby's cues signal hunger or colic, but the baby tends to stretch out with back arched when hungry and to double up when in the throes of colic.

The second form taken by the language of behavior is the feedback a parent receives from babies when trying to meet their needs. If the parent tries to feed a colicky baby, the baby may indeed try briefly to nurse, but after a few swallows will spit out the nipple and resume crying, indicating that the parent has not yet singled out the right need and its remedy. Of course, it is not merely the cessation of crying that guides parental behavior, but also the baby's smiles and gurgles of satisfaction. The language of behavior is an early form of what is called "body language." People often betray their inner states by postures, gestures, and styles of movement. In general, we respond not only to the words people speak but also to the total array of information they transmit in everything they do, including the play of facial expression and tone of voice. We read their motives, pretensions, doubts, bravado, and insecurity—and they, ours. In the same way, we can take cues from the behavioral qualities of the still wordless baby. To anticipate later discussion, we might say that older infants transcend body language and invent means of preverbal communication—grunts, shrieks, gestures, pointing, and tokens, like the dog that signals its desire to go out by bringing its leash.

We do not want to idealize the realities of early parent-child relationships. The first few months involve feeding around

the clock, which has brought more than one set of parents to the verge of nervous breakdown, bouts of colic for some babies when nothing the parents can do seems to soothe the distress, and frequent immersions in saliva, mucus, urine, feces, and vomit. The baby's language of behavior sometimes defies interpretation, and even the most loving of parents are sometimes clumsy, impatient, and even resentful. Families may have money troubles, medical problems, or fallings-out with relatives or neighbors, and all such distractions take their toll on parent-child relations. Luckily, most parents cling to a few threads of sanity and are able to take advantage of tranquil interludes to dispense love and stimulation. And when the baby smiles lovingly, the agonies and fatigue recede into the background and it all seems worthwhile.

In describing the course of parent-child relations during the first year, we have implicitly been describing the formation of attachment. The study of attachment has become a major part of the developmental enterprise, and it is to this topic that we now turn our attention.

ATTACHMENT

Attachment is important for several reasons. First, the positive emotional arousal involved tones up the baby both physically and psychologically, contributing to sound development. It is the raw material for later affection for people outside the immediate family. It provides the foundation for the entire process of humanization and socialization, including, where necessary, discipline and control. It gives the baby a secure emotional base from which to turn attention and curiosity outward and to explore and learn about the world. And, in time, it liberates the baby to strive for and assert autonomy (Tronick, 1982).

Attachment refers to the powerful emotional bonds that develop between the child and, initially, the parents and other household members, and which, in time, can be generalized by the child to a great array of individuals. The parents' attachment to the neonate begins almost instantaneously, in the upwelling of a unique and potent feeling that comes with their first view of the new creature. The parents' initial feeling is elaborated and modified during the course of their child's development, but it immediately motivates them to establish and maintain contact with the baby.

On the side of the baby, attachment evolves more gradually. Its foundation, as we have said, is basic trust, which takes shape as the baby's physical and psychological needs are met. At first, the baby's responsiveness to people is fairly undiscriminating, and it is the emergence of differential responding toward particular individuals that tells us that attachment is taking place. The baby's emotional expression, whether as stimulus or response to parental behavior, plays an important role in attachment formation. The end product of attachment, as we have said, is identification, taking on the ways of and feeling at home with the people among whom one lives and develops.

The literature on attachment has grown to such proportions in the past few years that we can hope only to touch a few of the high points. Most of the major contributors to the growth of the field

are represented in a volume edited by Emde and Harmon (1981), and you are urged to go to this source for more detail.

Circularity in Attachment Formation

We have already said that parent-child relations are a two-way street, and we take a moment to elaborate on this point. How babies are treated by their parents is in some measure a product of the baby's own perceived qualities, real or imaginary. We cannot assume that caregiving patterns always spring directly from the personality characteristics of the parents. Control by the infant is a phenomenon common to many species (Harper, 1971). Different babies evoke different feelings in their caregivers (Bell, 1971). The baby's age, sex, and momentary states modify parental behavior (Moss, 1967). Fathers and mothers react differently to sons and daughters—in general, fathers are indulgent toward daughters, and mothers toward sons (Rothbart and Maccoby, 1966). Some babies relish cuddling, and others actively resist it (Schaffer and Emerson, 1965). Babies vary in physical attractiveness, too. It is not enough to say that there are some babies only a mother could love. There are some babies who, for whatever reason, do not call forth love even in their own particular mothers and fathers. In other words, attachment is not always an automatic event that occurs between parents and infants (Brazelton, 1981).

Apart from characteristics of the baby, parents may have reasons of their own for not responding fully or appropriately. They may be so immersed in other concerns that they are insensitive to whatever charms their baby may possess. The baby may have arrived at the wrong time in the marriage or may symbolize the end of carefree youth and beauty. And such influences may be powerful without ever becoming conscious. Fortunately, such reactions are the exception. As one investigator put it, babies socialize their parents as much as the parents socialize their babies: "Of men and women [the baby] makes fathers and mothers" (Rheingold, 1969).

The Study of Attachment

One obvious way to study attachment is through repeated observations of parents and infants in everyday settings, notably the home. This is the method used by Schaffer and Emerson (1964), who observed sixty babies for more than a year, recording their interactions with family members and other people at regular intervals. Their findings indicate that attachment to specific people, especially the mother, is formed by approximately nine months.

The British psychoanalyst John Bowlby (1969) is widely regarded as a leading authority on attachment formation. He argues strongly that attachment to a specific, stable mother figure is crucial to sound development. His conclusions are based on observations of normal mothers and infants; on studies of the disruption or failure of attachment in children in hospitals or other institutions where a stable mother figure was not available; and on the literature on attachment in nonhuman species as described by students of animal behavior. Note that Bowlby's thinking has not yet been adapted to the current era in which fathers share parenthood with mothers,

where almost half of married mothers hold jobs, and where day care is a booming phenomenon. We believe that Bowlby's basic ideas still hold good, but also that attachment has to include fathers and caregivers from outside the immediate family.

More systematic observations of attachment have been made in experimental settings. Pioneering experimental work was done by Rheingold and her associates (Rheingold and Eckerman, 1969) and by Ainsworth and her associates (Ainsworth, Bell, and Stayton, 1969). Such experiments take place in what are called **strange settings** or **strange situations,** a room or pair of rooms constructed within the laboratory. Some of the independent variables are presence or absence of toys, presence or absence of one or both parents, presence or absence of a stranger, departure or return of any or all the adults, and degree of involvement with the baby by any or all the adults. Some of the dependent variables are the baby's emotional reactions, approach to or retreat from toys or people, amount of exploration, and attempt to make contact with any or all the adults.

Rheingold and Eckerman showed that attractive toys can lure a baby away from his or her mother into an adjoining strange room, especially if the baby is given time to warm up to the novel situation. In such tests, as in everyday life, babies typically return often to check on the mother's continued presence. Ainsworth and Bell (1970) found that one-year-old babies engaged in the exploration of space and objects most when the mother was present and least when the baby was left alone or with a stranger. Feldman and Ingham (1975) found that all their one-year-old subjects showed

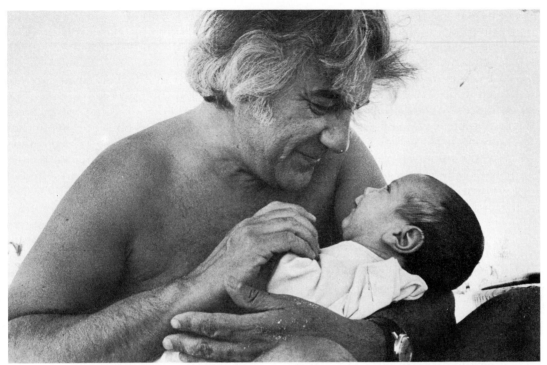

(© Abigail Heyman/Archive Pictures)

Father and baby. The continuing cultural shift in conceptions of male and female will undoubtedly alter how fathers and mothers regard child care and parent-child relationships.

anxiety when placed alone with a stranger in a novel setting. Ross and Goldman (1977) found that, the mother being present, one-year-olds responded more favorably to a stranger who made active attempts to capture their interest than to a stranger who waited passively for the baby to make overtures.

Fathers and Attachment

For reasons that we find hard to understand, for most of its history child psychology has overlooked father-child attachment. The larger culture, of course, assigned to the mother the primary responsibility for the care of children and assumed that "mother love" or the "ma-

ternal instinct" was the main source of bonding (Parke, 1981). The father was seen in the role of provider and, as occasion required, disciplinarian. Indeed, it was thought almost unmanly for fathers to wax sloppy and sentimental over their children. Horses and dogs, yes, but hardly children. There is, of course, one widely accepted exception. Fathers are expected to be indulgent with their little girls, who notoriously are able to wrap daddy around their little finger. Freud perpetuated the cultural stereotype, casting the father as the heavy who told his son to shape up or lose it. A good deal of study was devoted to the lack of a father on children's, especially boys', development, but again largely in terms of what happens to children deprived of a male role model and authority figure.

But even before fathers became so actively engaged in infant caregiving, bonds of attachment formed between male parent and baby. Michael Lamb (1978) has surveyed the research on father-infant attachment and concludes that babies become attached to both parents at about the same time. Fathers and mothers have different styles of interacting with their babies, however, and the nature of the resulting bonds is therefore different. Some representative studies of father-infant attachment are summarized below.

Kotelchuck (1973), using the strange situation approach, observed babies at three-month intervals between ages six and twenty-one months. The most striking behavioral changes emerged between fifteen and eighteen months. Play increased whenever the stranger left the room and decreased when either the mother or the father went out. Crying increased with the departure of either parent and decreased when the stranger left. Babies old enough to be mobile followed their departing parents toward the door and touched them when they returned. The reactions were greater to mothers than to fathers, but not impressively so, and seemed to be independent of father-child and mother-child relations as reported by the parents. Lamb (1976) found that twelve-month-olds paid equal attention to both parents when no stranger was in the room, but immediately oriented to the mother rather than the father when the stranger entered.

As part of a longitudinal study conducted by Ainsworth and associates (Ainsworth and Bell, 1970; Ainsworth, Bell, and Stayton, 1969, 1972, 1974; Tracy, Lamb, and Ainsworth, 1976), Lamb (1977) specifically compared mother-infant and father-infant interactions with babies from ages seven to thirteen months. He found that babies were equally attached to both parents and at first shunned the strange observer. However, as the stranger's strangeness wore off, babies showed signs of attachment to the stranger, too. The key difference between mothers' and fathers' interactions with their babies was that mothers held the baby most often for purposes of caregiving, while fathers held the baby to play with him or her. In his survey of research on father-infant attachment, Lamb concluded, as we said above, that attachment to both parents occurs at about the same time but is different in nature. Thus each parent should have his or her own special influence on the child's personality development.

Weinraub (1978) believes that such differences should be kept to a minimum, and that both parents should play essentially equivalent roles. While it seems unlikely that Weinraub's ideal will ever be fully attained, the continuing cultural shift in conceptions of male and female roles will undoubtedly work toward greater interchangeability of father and mother in the way in which they relate to their children.

Cross-Cultural Perspectives on Attachment

The heading on this section should not lead you to expect a rich fund of information. Our knowledge of attachment formation in cultures other than our own in quite limited.

The importance of enjoyable social interaction and of attachment has been demonstrated by Mary Ainsworth (1967), who studied infant care in a tribal setting in Uganda. Her observations showed that most Ugandan infants were attached to their mothers by the middle of the first year. However, she also found that the quality of mothering beyond the mere satisfaction of physical needs played a vital role in depth of attachment. Attachment was strongest with mothers who described breast-feeding as a warm and pleasurable experience. These mothers were the ones who were most likely to spend the most time interacting with their babies and who showed sensitivity and appropriate timing in their responses.

Frodi (1980) surveyed father-infant attachment in a number of settings and found great cultural variation in the degree of father-infant involvement. Frodi concluded that father-infant bonding at its strongest calls into question the idea that women's hormonal equipment makes them especially fit for the care of children.

The Work of Harry Harlow

Harry Harlow and his associates have carried out one of the best-known series of studies of social learning in nonhuman infancy. The first report of this work (Harlow, 1958) was of special importance in challenging the conditioning theory of attachment, which says that babies come to love their mothers as conditioned stimuli for need satisfaction, especially feeding.

Harlow studied the development of attachment in rhesus monkeys. He began by placing newborn rhesus monkeys with two different kinds of dummy surrogate mothers. One kind of dummy was made of bare wire mesh and was warmed from within by a light bulb. The other kind was covered with sponge rubber and terry cloth and was likewise warmed from within by a light bulb. Half the wire-mesh and half the terry-cloth surrogates were fitted with nursing bottles from which the monkeys could obtain milk. The dependent variable was the amount of time per day spent in contact with each kind of mother. The monkeys, regardless of which dummy supplied milk, showed an overwhelming preference for the cuddlesome terry-cloth mothers, which provided warmth and what came to be called **contact comfort.** Indeed, when possible, the monkeys clung tenaciously to the terry-cloth surrogate while stretching over to nurse from the wire-mesh one.

Monkeys placed in an unfamiliar environment with a terry-cloth mother for company were able to venture forth to explore their surroundings. With a wire-mesh mother, however, the monkeys simply huddled fearfully. In a study by Harlow and Zimmerman (1959), a fear-inducing mechanical toy was placed in the cages of monkeys housed with either a terry-cloth or wire-mesh surrogate. The monkeys with terry-cloth mothers at first clung to the mother but gradually approached and explored the strange object. Those with wire mothers, however, either dashed wildly about the cage or huddled forlornly, rocking back and forth. There was no comfort to be gained from the wire-mesh dummy.

The sense of affection and security gained from contact comfort proved, however, to be an insufficient base for sound development (Harlow and Harlow, 1962). The monkeys reared by both wire-mesh and terry-cloth surrogates grew up to be neurotic and sexually inadequate—they obviously experienced sexual urges but would try to copulate with just about any region of the partner's body but the correct one.

Further study (Harlow and Harlow, 1969) suggested that the missing vital ingredient was social interaction. Monkeys raised in complete isolation from monkeys and people showed apathy, unprovoked aggression, self-aggression, and various sorts of bizarre mannerisms, such as endless rocking. However, monkeys isolated for six months or less were able to make a good recovery when returned to monkey society. Those kept in isolation for a year, by contrast, were profoundly impaired, although some forms of therapy brought about decided improvement (Novak and Harlow, 1975; Ruppenthal *et al.*, 1976). By the same token, attachment in human babies is only

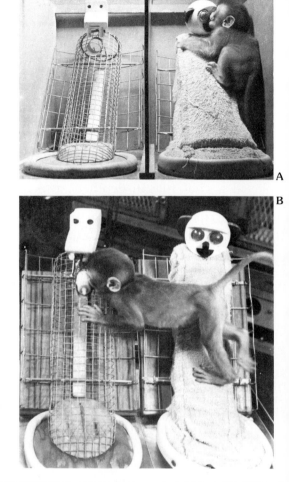

A

B

C

The research of Harry Harlow demolished the conditioning theory of attachment. **A** One of Harlow's monkeys lavishes affection on its terry-cloth surrogate mother. **B** A monkey stays in contact with the terry-cloth mother even as it nurses from the wire mother. **C** Typical posture of a monkey raised in isolation.

(University of Wisconsin Primate Laboratory)

a necessary first step in normal psychological development.

A Critical Period for Attachment?

We have spoken of critical periods in embryonic development, and many authorities believe there are analogies in postnatal development, including attachment.

To begin with, the standard concept of a critical period assumes a biologically fixed interval of maximum sensitivity and vulnerability. In keeping with our psychobiological view, we find it hard to accept any period as defined purely by biology without regard to environmental circumstances. However, we cannot escape an avalanche of evidence that attachment delayed may be attachment lost, or at least weakened. In Chapter 7, we shall consider some studies suggesting that children deprived of normal opportunities for attachment early in life may nevertheless make some degree of recovery when given such opportunities later on. These studies, however, are rarely based on detailed accounts of parent-child interaction, and we cannot be sure what mechanisms are operating.

It is our opinion that one does not need a theory of critical periods to say that children develop best when, from an early age, they are given the loving, strong, responsive attention we have described. The longer they are deprived of such attention, even when all their basic physical needs are met, the more difficult it is for them to form attachments. This is not because a critical period has expired but because babies' capacities for positive emotional responding waste away when unstimulated—which is another way of saying that they develop basic mistrust. This implies some degree of across-the-board impairment when the conditions for early attachment are absent, but it does not deny the possibility that heroic expenditures of love can remedy some or most of this impairment. In sum, we do not think a critical-period hypothesis for attachment can be either proved or disproved. Imagine a natural experiment in which long-deprived children are now given a long regimen of what we suppose to be appropriate sorts of stimulation. Only if these children were made whole could we say that the critical-period hypothesis must be discarded. If, as seems more likely, our efforts led to only partial improvement we would not know whether it was because we did the wrong things or did not do enough of the right ones, or because the critical period had come and gone.

Attachment and Imprinting

Some developmentalists are inclined to equate attachment to what students of animal behavior call *imprinting*. In its strict sense, imprinting refers to the fact that newly hatched fowl (chicks, ducklings, goslings, and so forth) will follow the first moving object they encounter and thereafter show unswerving filial devotion to that object. The first moving object is usually the mother, but it can also be a football dangling from a trolley or even Konrad Lorenz (a pioneer in the study of imprinting) waddling along, flapping his arms, and honking like a goose to his gaggle of goslings. The imprinted object seems to define the young bird's species identity. At maturity, the human-imprinted bird tries to mate with humans instead of with another bird (Lorenz, 1952; Schein and Hale, 1959).

We find the analogy between imprinting and attachment charming but unpersuasive. First of all, nonhuman attachments take at most only a few hours, whereas human attachment develops over months. Animal attachment, moreover, does not involve the elaborate interplay between parent and young found in humans, nor does it permit the verbal interchange, both playful and serious, that becomes a vital part of human attachment. Both imprinting and attachment contribute to identification, becoming like one's models, but the entire course of human identification is likely to include a phase of **counteridentification,** or rebellion, a phenomenon unknown in other species. Thus one is free to speak of human imprinting metaphorically, but we must be careful not to take our metaphors literally.

In closing this section, we should make it clear that there is no one right way to love a baby. Babies are individuals and need different kinds and amounts of affection. Parents, too, are individuals and have their own styles of expressing love. Some are lavish with physical demonstrations; others are not, but still manage to convey their affection. Some are soft and tender, some are bluff and hearty, others are sober. What is more, no parent can love a baby equally at all times and in all circumstances. What is important in terms of the baby's sense of trust is the reliability of parental love, the clarity with which it shines through the transitory vicissitudes and the inevitable strains and anxieties of everyday life.

PRACTICAL ISSUES IN INFANT CARE

People have been giving and receiving advice on how to rear children at least since biblical times, as witness the injunction to "spare the rod and spoil the child." (This is actually Samuel Butler's rephrasing of Proverbs 13:24.) Until relatively recently, though, people have simply taken for granted, on the basis of tradition, what should be done to and for children. Let us make clear that those givens of folk wisdom were by no means the same from society to society, or from era to era, but each group had its own tradition-sanctioned ways.

In what we like to think were simple societies, there were abundant opportunities to observe and absorb the accustomed ways. People were not guided by theories of how earlier experience shapes later character. Instead, they knew intuitively what to do and assumed that children, if they survived, would turn out all right. A number of things have happened to change traditional views of child rearing around the world. European explorers, traders, colonizers, missionaries, and slave buyers helped disrupt familiar patterns and undermine accepted customs. For instance, missionaries forbade infanticide, which in many cases was used to keep the population in balance with food supplies. In some tropical areas, ending infanticide meant premature weaning of an older baby if a new baby was born. The older baby would then be put on a low-protein diet and develop *kwashiorkor,* a protein-deficiency disease that can lead to brain damage.

The United States probably led the world into the era of self-conscious parenthood. Following World War I, improved diet, sanitation, immunization, limitation of family size, and the preachings of child psychologists were turning parents away from their preoccupation with simply keeping children healthy and alive—and obedient—toward a new concern with children's psychological welfare. It is said that we gave up living in extended families and began to live in nuclear families—consisting of mother, father, and children, with few if any links to grandparents, uncles and aunts, or cousins. There is some question about how much of a reality the extended family ever has been in American life, but originally there was a shared body of assumptions about correct child rearing, and relatives, neighbors, and friends were likely to help out. Keniston (1977) asserts that the key change in family life has been the increasing isolation of the nuclear family from this informal human support system. This isolation has meant the end of learning the traditional ways through lifelong observation and participation and has made parents ever more dependent on the Expert for guidance. The Experts have been around at least since medieval times, but they have multiplied rapidly in recent years with the spread not only of self-conscious parenthood but also of literacy. Most of what the early Experts had to say was based on superstition, but their writings could do little mischief because so very few people could read them.

Parents have always been ambivalent about Experts, but advice to parents has always been a readily marketable commodity and is supplied in never-abating plenty—along with the latest gadgets— to an insatiably avid public. The apparent paradox between disdain for the ex-

pert and a servile seeking for guidance can perhaps be reconciled by noting two things. First, parents are truly uncertain of themselves and badly want counsel. Second, they seem to seek out and attend to those Experts, or those parts of a given Expert's preachments, that confirm and sanction what they are already doing. Parents want advice, but they are most receptive to advice that fits their preconceptions. David Levy (1954) has shown how mothers both fail to understand pediatricians' recommendations and act on only so much of what they comprehend as suits their own inclinations. Even when they try, people are likely to grasp unfamiliar notions in distorted ways— that is, they assimilate them rather than accommodate to them—and we the authors, when cast in the roles of experts and teachers, have seen our ideas come back to us in some very strange guises indeed. As one student told us on an examination paper, "According to Freud, all children are either oral, anal, or Gentile."

A Brief History of Modern Trends in Child Care

The past sixty years have seen some strange twists and turns in the guiding themes of advice to parents.

Freud, for instance, was an influential figure who became a force in American child psychology in the 1920s. However, Freudian doctrines underwent a subtle change in traveling from Europe to North America. Freud had a pessimistic, Victorian, moralistic outlook and saw people fated by their animal nature to live in lust and violence until the slow process of human evolution remade them into true human beings. Americans misinterpreted Freud's emphasis on instinctive drives as an endorsement. In the American version of Freud's teachings, people are made neurotic by the artificial restraints imposed by society on the expression of impulses, and the secret of successful child rearing as popularized in the 1930s and 1940s was to avoid frustrating and inhibiting the child.

By contrast, John B. Watson, the father of behaviorism, taught that the main goal of child rearing is to instill the proper habits and to avoid teaching undesirable ones. It is not simply that love and affection were left unemphasized: they were regarded by the early Watson and like-minded thinkers as downright insidious. Watson represented the ultimate in American dedication to machine-like efficiency. His prescriptions for raising children without poisoning them with sugary sentimentality sound almost like a formula for rearing children to have no concern for the feelings of others, much like the psychopathic personality. As we said in Chapter 1, he later regretted some of his teachings.

A blend of psychoanalytic thinking and social anthropology (the names of Ruth Benedict and Margaret Mead come to mind) fostered a return to more "primitive" ways of child rearing—carrying the baby in a sling with free access to the mother's breast, or backpacking the papoose while the parent bicycled on his or her daily rounds. Here there were overtones of *Romantic Naturalism*, first set forth by Jean-Jacques Rousseau, according to which the ideal condition for human beings is that of the happy, noble savage living in a state of nature.

Another trend that should be mentioned is John Dewey's *pragmatism*, which said that much of what we teach children is obsolete and of no earthly use to them, but which some people took as an injunction to teach children only practical skills, as in life adjustment courses or in vocational education. Although Dewey was not particularly concerned with infancy, his teachings were very much in the air in the 1920s and 1930s and then again in the 1960s.

B. F. Skinner proposed another ideal system of child rearing in *Walden Two* (1948), his utopian novel based on operant conditioning. Human behavior is to be thought of as shaped by forces lying outside the organism. Notions of self-control, self-determination, will, and purpose are delusions with which people needlessly torment themselves. One behaves as one does because initially random acts set off by states of need are selectively reinforced according to whether they serve to reduce the need. Eventually, the organism learns which acts work and in what circumstances, and behavior becomes orderly, effective, and seemingly purposeful. Children are taught by being rewarded for socially useful behavior, whereas aberrant behavior receives no response of any kind and so withers away for lack of feedback. Like many utopia makers, Skinner paints a coolly rational or rationalistic world without guts, without strong passions, without illness or grief or jealousy, without responsibility or the need to make decisions. More than a few people have found Skinner's vision appealing enough to want to found Walden Twos of their own. Such ventures have not worked out too well. The bland bliss of Skinner's utopia is probably unattainable by Skinner's means, since his principles of learning, while highly useful and correct for application to a narrow range of conditions, are hopelessly inadequate as a general theory of human nature.

By the late 1940s, doctrinaire approaches to child rearing were almost a thing of the past, and a large measure of eclecticism permeated the field, exemplified by Benjamin Spock's *Baby and Child Care* (1976). There is still a torrent of books promising salvation through a single formula, such as behavior modification, and traveling seminars spring up about the land professing to unlock the secrets of effective parenting for those who attend. But it is our impression that self-conscious parenthood is on the wane, and today's parents are more sensitive to scientific knowledge about child development and less receptive to the appeals of the wonder workers.

In the discussion that follows, we shall try to dissociate ourselves from our predecessors. Two things need to be said. First, one cannot derive a sound course of child rearing or education from any single formal theory. Second, any set of recommendations that seeks to squeeze all parents and children into a single rigid mold is a doomed enterprise. We therefore try to stick to general principles that permit flexible application. What we have to say is not always based in theory and research. Some of it is grounded in our own experience as parents and clinicians. At the same time, we will present some relevant facts that are best learned in the context of practical issues. A word of warning: We do not want to draw too sharp a boundary between physical care and psychological cultivation. Some of the most important emotional and cognitive interchanges take place in the course of routine care—

in other words, routine care need not be merely routine.

Some General Considerations

There are a number of principles of child care that seem applicable at all ages. The first of these is *timing*. It is futile, and hence frustrating for parent and child alike, to expect of children behavior of which they are not yet capable. Sometimes children's readiness or unreadiness to undertake something new is a matter of motor control or proficiency, and sometimes a matter of what they can understand. Although developmental readiness is a necessary condition for learning certain things, two points should be emphasized. In some cases, the only way to find out whether a child is ready to learn something is to try teaching it, being prepared to abandon or postpone the attempt if it becomes evident the child is not yet ready. A related point is that our attempts at teaching, if carried out in a relaxed way, may in fact induce the necessary readiness. We also have to beware of holding children back when they are eager and ready to move ahead.

A second, related principle is *gradualism*. Babies tend to be conservative, to resist innovations. In introducing something new, parents should avoid abrupt transitions and cannot expect immediate results. Parents have to watch the baby for feedback and adapt their tempos to the baby's reaction. It is all right to try, as long as trying does not turn into forcing. Too hurried an approach may be self-defeating, since it can provoke resistance. Even the most adaptable children need time to come to terms with new experiences.

Third, there is *avoidance of moralism.* We want our children to grow up moral, but the way they acquire morality is not through parental outrage, scoldings, and preachings. One teaches morality through modeling, demonstrating care and concern and decency and generosity. The infant has no sense of sinfulness or wickedness. Even so, babies can act in ways that try the limits of parental patience. This brings us to the related principle of *parental self-confidence.* When the exercise of authority is called for, parents must be able to act decisively, secure in their own maturity and love for the child; but moral indignation is out of place in dealing with babies.

The behaviors that parents try consciously to teach their children (such as manners) are known collectively as **socialization.** These explicit teachings of socialization are contrasted with the much broader, often unconscious process of **enculturation,** the various mechanisms by which we communicate to the child the shared meanings of the group. Whereas socialization is in large measure conscious and deliberate, much of enculturation takes place outside the sphere of anyone's awareness and is the work of many agencies beside the parents, from television to peers to schools. Needless to say, the better parents understand their own culture and its sometimes groundless assumptions about reality, the better prepared they will be to modify their behavior in the direction of sound developmental practices. Some parents believe that they can teach morals through the process of socialization, but this would require that they be able to formulate beliefs so deeply ingrained that they may not even know what they are.

Feeding

The first responsibility that falls to parents is feeding the baby, and the first decision they make about feeding the baby is whether it will be by breast or by bottle. First, if the parents are poor and live in unhygienic conditions, breast-feeding is the only safe way to nourish a baby. Public health specialists consider bottle feeding one of the major scourges inflicted by Western invaders on people in the poor nations of the world. The problem is a dual one. Mothers tend to overdilute the prepackaged formula—it *looks* the same as properly diluted formula—thereby saving money but reducing the nutritive value. They also dilute the mixture with water that is all too likely to be contaminated, thus feeding disease-causing agents directly to their babies. With no knowledge of sterilization and no facilities for refrigeration, mothers who are seduced into the "modern" technique of bottle feeding are being persuaded to risk their babies' health and even life.

Second, even for parents living in sanitary conditions logic is all on the side of breast-feeding. Human milk is as nearly perfect a foodstuff for young babies as can be imagined. Breast milk contains antibodies that help protect the baby against infections. Of considerable importance for a number of babies, mother's milk seems to be almost totally non-allergenic, whereas cow's milk is anything but. Some mothers describe nursing as a pleasurable experience and to some it has, on occasion, been reported to lead to orgasm. If there is a drawback to human milk, it is that there is some risk—we have no idea how great—that toxins such as DDT may be lodged in the breast fat and may find their way into the milk. This slight reservation aside, we repeat that logic is in favor of breast-feeding.

However, logic is not everything. The final choice really depends on psychological factors, attitudes toward nursing, and reactions to the actual experience. Attitudes range from the profoundly enthusiastic through the noncommittal to the thoroughly antagonistic. Some mothers feel that nursing gives them an unparalleled sense of intimacy with their babies. On the other hand, some mothers do not find any special joy in breast-feeding, and some are repelled by it. As a further complication, attitudes interact with lactation: The more favorably inclined a woman is to breast-feed, the more abundant her milk supply, whereas those who find nursing unpleasant may produce insufficient milk.

If, for any reason, a woman chooses not to nurse, it is not wise for anyone else to reproach her. Babies do perfectly well on the various synthetic formulas now available, and a bottle can be given with the same sort of physical closeness as a breast, including the same sorts of visual and vocal stimulation. What is more, a bottle can be given by the father or a sitter or an older sibling, who may welcome this chance to take part in the baby's rearing. It thus follows, given good hygienic conditions, that women who find satisfaction in nursing should nurse, and those who do not should not.

Nutrition and the "Wisdom of the Body."
Nutritionists have come to take it for granted that babies offered a nourishing diet can pretty well govern their own intake and that parental worries about whether babies are getting enough of the right foods are groundless. This generally relaxed attitude toward feeding probably accounts for the virtual disappearance of the once-common "feeding problem." At one time, parents, grimly determined that their child consume a full complement of everything wholesome, would find themselves confronted with an equally grimly determined child who, in the escalating battle of wills, would flirt with starvation rather than give in to attempted force feeding, even if the force took the form of cajolery. Fortunately, such scenarios seem to be largely a thing of the past.

Relaxed attitudes toward feeding are based on the assumption that children are guided in their choice of diet by what the physiologist Walter B. Cannon called the "wisdom of the body." Body wisdom is thought to sensitize us to the nutrients needed by our bodies, so that we can adapt our intake accordingly. Thus the patient with Addison's disease, which interferes with salt metabolism, spontaneously increases salt consumption to compensate. Animals kept on a salt-free diet show a clear preference for weak saline solution over plain water. In a famous but poorly described series of studies, Clara Davis (e.g., 1939) claimed to show that just-weaned children, given an array of basic foodstuffs to choose from, would select a balanced diet. Davis's subjects did not eat the right proportions of the right foods every day, as on a dietitian's chart, but over a span of weeks they kept their consumption balanced.

We should not, however, have exaggerated faith in the wisdom of the body at the human level. There are at least two ways in which it is unreliable. The first

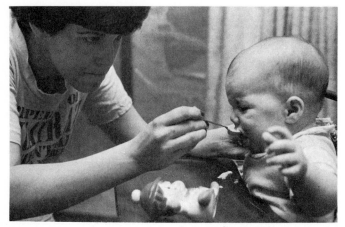

(© Pat Coffey 1981/The Picture Cube)

An introduction to solid food. Babies may accept solid foods without resistance or slowly, a taste or two at a time.

problem with body wisdom is that it is easily overridden by cultural tastes in food, which do not always represent the best diet available. Fortunately, the general public has become more aware of the importance of good nutrition for good health in recent years, and groups are lobbying to ban chemicals in foods and to provide more nutritious meals to children in schools.

Note, though, that following a culturally defined diet may in fact change the body's digestive capacities so that alien foods not only look unappetizing but are in fact dangerous. The abrupt introduction of protein-rich food into the diet of a person who lives on low-protein foods can cause depletion of vitamin A and consequent impaired vision. It has been said that there are racial differences in tolerance to milk, but the weight of evidence points to cultural differences and the practice of drinking milk after early childhood (Johnson *et al.*, 1980).

The second problem with body wisdom is that it does not warn us away from harmful substances. Nothing in our physiology tells us which is the delectable mushroom and which the deadly toadstool. Nor does it keep countless children from sampling the paint thinner, detergents, insecticides, and medicines about the house. It is for this reason that potential poisons must be kept well out of the reach of children, that especially stringent taboos have to be imposed on the locations where such things are stored, and that parents should keep taped to the telephone the number and address of the nearest poison-control center.

Weaning. We must also touch upon the topic of *weaning*, which used to be a source of great stress but nowadays appears to be achieved matter-of-factly. Weaning really means two things. One is the transition from nipple to cup, and the other is the transition from a purely liquid diet to one that contains solid foods—more accurately, in the beginning, strained, mushy foods that were once solid. The latter transition begins around age four months or earlier. Here, as elsewhere, parents and children must synchronize their tempos. Babies may show no resistance to solid foods or they may come to accept them slowly, a taste or two at a time. It is probably not a good idea to try out new foods at the beginning of a meal, when the baby is extremely hungry and has no patience with experiments. Some pediatricians recommend that one introduce only one new foodstuff at a time, allowing several weeks to pass to make sure that the food agrees with the baby before moving on to the next one. One incidental observation is that adults, spooning solids into young babies, cannot resist making empathic mouth movements, as though magically but unconsciously helping the baby eat. Many babies develop strong food preferences, and these have to be respected. Babies can try drinking from a cup as early as six or seven months, but an adult has to hold the cup and regulate the flow. Many babies can hold their own cup with both hands by age one, and with one hand by eighteen months.

Spoiling and Discipline

There are still parents who think that giving infants too much attention will "spoil" them, meaning that the baby will end up clinging, demanding, and forever whining for attention. Such thinking is thoroughly and perhaps dangerously wrong. With one exception, one cannot give the baby too much attention. (The exception is evening bedtime, a matter we dealt with earlier.) If anything, the greatest danger during infancy may be the failure to satisfy the baby's cravings for attention. The baby who gets a grudging or erratic ration of attention develops an increased need which, like the neurotic needs of adults, may indeed become insatiable. Premature attempts to cultivate the baby's "powers of self-reliance" may have exactly the opposite effect.

When babies cry, it is because they need something, not that they, or we, always know what. If what the baby is crying for is human contact and attention, then that is what should be given. Babies who are given an abundance of attention do eventually develop some powers of self-reliance (although no one ever wholly outgrows his or her craving

for an occasional dose of concentrated attention), and there comes a time when children can stave off loneliness or boredom with toys, some TV watching, or a good book, and older babies and children learn to tolerate delay until the adult can turn from more pressing concerns.

Let us qualify further our statement that one cannot give babies too much attention. Some well-meaning but over-solicitous parents hurry to do something about every expression of discomfort before either the baby or the adult has a chance to find out what, if anything, is really called for. In this way, the wrong need may be gratified, leaving the baby with a vague, restless dissatisfaction that may later come out as "spoiled" behavior. A similar pattern may originate in parental insecurity: The parent feels so inadequate, or is so afraid of losing the baby's love, or is so guilty about not loving the baby enough, that he or she overwhelms the baby with unwanted gratifications. Spoiling may also result from capricious teasing, offering children something and then snatching it away, leaving them fearful that they may never get what they want, and dissatisfied when they finally do.

The baby who receives lots of sensitive attention is the one who develops basic trust and strong attachment, and with this as a foundation moves toward independence. The bonds of attachment greatly simplify communication in general and discipline in particular.

We must remember that babies show little self-control, delay of gratification, and anticipation of consequences. They may be affectionate and even sympathetic to parental distress, but they have virtually no ability to understand parental thoughts and needs. Therefore, a large measure of control—*discipline*— has to come from outside, notably the parents.

The question of discipline is open to a great deal of misinterpretation. By discipline we mean only necessary control. It is by no means a synonym for punishment. In general, punishment plays a very minor role in controlling children and teaching them self-control. Nor should we think of punishment simply in terms of physical punishment: One can inflict as much pain on a baby with a loud yell or a cold withholding of affection as with an angry slap.

Even when we define discipline simply as the minimum of necessary control, parents still feel ambivalent about it. On the one hand, lack of discipline calls forth images of tyrannical, egotistical monsters who rule with a whim of iron and bulldoze their way through life. On the other hand, parents feel that discipline will mar and embitter their child, stifle initiative and curiosity and creativity, and produce a cringing, servile, and authoritarian person. It is further feared that discipline will teach the child to hate the parents, who thirty years later will be exposed and blamed on a psychoanalyst's couch.

Such feelings are groundless. Remember, we have had our first encounter with discipline at bedtime. Once babies come to terms with the fact that they have no choice but to relax and go to sleep, they do so, and greet the parents in the morning with no traces of resentment.

The issue of discipline becomes more prominent as the baby's mobility grows. There are three guiding themes in discipline. First, one must protect babies from doing themselves harm through their own clumsiness or ignorance. Second, one wants to avoid damage to the family's more precious possessions. And, third, one wants to preserve the parents' peace of mind. Once the baby can move around, taboos must be imposed, but they should be made as few as possible. The first step is to remove from the baby's reach fragile or dangerous objects that are not needed for everyday use. The things that are needed for daily use should, so far as is practicable, be grouped in a few locations, so that a few wholesale taboos can take the place of numerous specific ones. Once the house has been child proofed, the baby is free to explore and manipulate and gratify its insatiable curiosity. The experienced visitor to a family with a baby learns to recognize the "high-water mark" of breakables that defines the baby's scope. Whatever the baby's cognitive limitations, parents should not underestimate his or her growing resourcefulness and ingenuity. One little girl we know used the drawers of a bureau to form a staircase that gave her access to the bureau top and all it contained. Numerous babies have learned to scale the toilet seat, climb from there to the sink, and so be able to reach the medicine cabinet. It is in such cases that one appreciates the child-proof caps that adults often find hard to manage. By the time they can walk, some babies learn to move footstools and small chairs to where they can stand to reach forbidden objects. Thus, child proofing a house can never work perfectly, and parents have to exercise a certain amount of vigilance.

The best and simplest way to impose a taboo is by mild punishment—*aversive conditioning:* a sharp bark of "No!" whenever the baby reaches for a prohib-

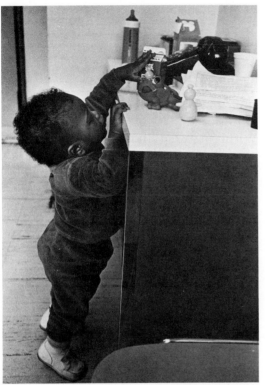

(© Lawrence Frank 1981)

As mobility grows, taboos are required, but they should be kept to the minimum possible. Although a home can be child proofed, with fragile or dangerous objects removed to a few taboo areas and the baby otherwise free to explore and gratify its curiosity, child proofing can never be perfect.

ited object. Timing is important. The "No!" should come at the very beginning of reaching. Once the object is grasped, the reaching has been reinforced and the taboo becomes that much harder to impose. The well-timed "No!" is usually sufficient, but if the baby persists, the verbal command can be supplemented with a gentle slap on the back of the hand. This is not to advocate corporal punishment or child battering; no force should ever be applied to a young child that is in any way likely to cause physical injury.

When the baby persists in reaching for a taboo object, the wise parent can be aware of the following possibilities. Sometimes the baby is seriously testing the limits, to see how strongly the parent feels about this particular taboo. In such cases, the parent must be prepared to stand fast. Often, though, what seems like testing the limits is merely teasing, turning discipline into a social game. This is revealed by the baby's sly smile when reaching toward the forbidden object. In such cases, the proper response is probably mock ferocity to match the baby's mock naughtiness, perhaps culminating in a wrestling game. Remember that babies are capable of nonliteral action. But there is another possible answer to serious testing of the limits. One can give the baby a permitted plaything as a substitute for the forbidden one, or one can move the baby to another, safer location.

Babies quickly learn which things and areas are off limits, and they also learn to wait until they are alone to explore them. When caught in the act, babies show clear evidence of guilt in a fascinating variety of ways. Some hurry to finish playing with the forbidden object before they can be separated from it. Others simply wail piteously. Some feign sweet innocence, turning away from the taboo object and acting as though they were unaware of its proximity. Others hand the object to the adult as though proffering a gift. And there are those who turn to the adult and begin lavishing great affection on him or her. In any event, when the baby is in another room, prolonged silence is likely to be an ominous signal of forbidden activity. It is worth emphasizing that the baby's guilt reactions to being caught out show the beginnings of a conscience, long before there can be any Oedipus conflict to be resolved.

We have been talking about restrictions on the baby's behavior on the assumption that he or she has many things to be busy with, not only toys but also ordinary household articles of some sturdiness or of no great value. A certain amount of breakage is inevitable, and it serves no purpose if the adult has a temper tantrum when something gets broken. Remember, too, that children themselves suffer a number of minor cuts, bumps, and bruises, which, as long as they are minor, are educational.

Finally, it is important to give babies supervised access to fragile things that they find attractive but are not ordinarily allowed to play with. Parent and child can sit side by side while the child explores the object. As we have already said, the infant responds to admonitions of "Gently, gently." Once the object's possibilities have been exhausted, the child will either hand it back to the adult or try to fling it into space. Parents have to be aware of this second possibility and be alert to stop it.

Thumb Sucking and Comfort Devices

Sucking is an important part of the baby's equipment for survival. In addition, it becomes during infancy a need that demands gratification in its own right. Babies who do not get enough sucking during nursing make up for it by sucking on other things—a thumb, a corner of a blanket, a rattle, whatever they can fit into the mouth.

If we accept sucking as a need that, when fulfilled, will cease by itself, then thumb sucking no longer appears a dirty, disgusting "habit" that the child will maintain throughout life if not stopped early. An alternative to the readily available thumb is a pacifier, provided it is kept reasonably clean.

There is very slim evidence connecting thumb or pacifier sucking with crooked teeth. The air pressures associated with mouth breathing, which usually implies blockage of the nasal passages, are more likely to distort the dental arch than is any amount of thumb sucking. But crooked teeth mostly mean a misfit between big teeth and small jaws, which may be a genetic condition that cannot be prevented but only corrected by orthodontia.

Thumb or pacifier sucking is one of the many sorts of comfort devices employed by the baby who is feeling out of sorts or as a way of closing off contact with the outside world at bedtime so that sleep can come. Some of the common bedtime patterns are, along with sucking, twisting a lock of hair, holding on to an ear, fingering a blanket, or clutching a favorite—often tattered and disreputable—doll or toy animal. Some children, day or night, are never without their treasured security blanket. Parents used to worry about their children's attachment to a security blanket, but the blanket-trailing Linus of the "Peanuts" comic strip has helped to make such a habit acceptable around the globe. Bedtime masturbation is quite common after age one and can be viewed as yet another way of shutting out the world. Years ago, when people worried about thumb sucking and masturbation as moral issues, child-care manuals would solemnly instruct parents to put the baby's hands under the covers to prevent thumb sucking, and then, a few pages or paragraphs later, tell them to keep the hands outside the covers to prevent masturbation.

Sex Typing

In Chapter 4, we said that parents perceive boys and girls differently, which would imply that boys and girls receive different sorts of treatment from birth on. Note that the first question parents ask, if the birth attendant has not already made haste to tell them, is "Is it a boy or a girl?" When they know the answer, and not before, there is language available to talk about the baby. Once they know the sex of their child, a whole set of attitudes falls into place and subtly governs their actions and reactions from then on. There is one note of anxiety that seems to characterize parents' feelings about the sex of their child. They are concerned more about the boy's masculinity, and less about the girl's femininity, and fathers are more concerned about their sons' masculinity than are mothers (Lynn, 1976).

Although parental attitudes are changing, the sex stereotyping of tradition is not easily discarded. It sometimes appears that parents operantly condition their baby into a sex role, reacting with delight to expressions of "sex-appropriate" behavior and ignoring "inappropriate" behavior. In general, boys still are given "masculine" playthings and girls "feminine" ones. Boy babies can be handled boisterously; girls are treated more gently. One takes pleasure in the delicate contour of a daughter's mouth; one takes delight in a vigorous and sturdy son.

The strength of parental attitudes toward the sex of their child can perhaps be gathered from these lines from Ogden Nash's "Song to Be Sung by the Father of Infant Female Children":

My heart leaps up when I behold
A rainbow in the sky;
Contrariwise, my blood runs cold
When little boys go by.
For little boys as little boys,
No special hate I carry,
But now and then they grow to men,
And when they do, they marry.
No matter how they tarry,
Eventually they marry.
And, swine among the pearls,
They marry little girls.*

Despite the paucity of research on sex typing during infancy, even the most casual observation shows that it goes on. The important practical issue is that we do not want to close off any developmental options for either boys or girls. We cannot call for identical emotional reactions to boys and girls during infancy, but we can hope for a broader range for each. Boys need tender, gentle hugging and kissing as much as girls do, and girls need to be wrestled and roughhoused with as much as boys. Both sexes need access to all sorts of playthings and full encouragement in trying out playthings and activities without regard to traditional associations. One important point that has been overlooked is that female liberation has until now been defined largely as obtaining for women the same things that have always been available to men. This implies that the ideal woman is the most nearly masculine one

*Copyright 1933, by Ogden Nash. From *Verses From 1929 On* by Ogden Nash, by permission of Little, Brown and Co.

(© Mimi Forsyth/Monkmeyer Press)
Father and daughter. Girls enjoy wrestling and roughhousing as much as boys.

possible. It may turn out that the most sought-after female identity will have little or nothing to do with traditional views of either masculinity of feminity. The same applies to the future of the male. In any event, sex roles and sex typing are topics to which we will return throughout this book.

Day Care

Whatever tomorrow's version of the female role, today's, for practical reasons, increasingly includes working outside the home. And for those females who have children, working means turning over the care of the children to someone else while mother earns her daily bread. According to the U.S. Department of Labor (1977), mothers of more than 6 million children under the age of six hold jobs. This number has most likely increased dramatically since then. Some mothers, working or not, can afford to hire nursemaids or nannies. A few have agreeable parents of their own who will take responsibility for the children. Sometimes husbands and wives work different shifts so that one is free to play parent while the other is toiling in the vineyards. But for the overwhelming majority of working mothers, the only answer is day care, if they meet the eligibility requirements. Day care today has expanded from infant programs to after-school programs for school-age youngsters. It takes the form of group day care or family day care. Family day care is by far the largest provider of care for children outside their own homes. In this type of program, children are cared for in the homes of provider adults (usually women). Group centers for the most part operate in separate quarters, with children grouped according to age. Centers are operated somewhat like preschools, although the range in quality of care is vast. Licensing for family day care differs from state to state, and many family day care homes have no licensing at all. The ratio of number of children to a single adult and the qualifications of the adults vary widely—from barely being able to read to having some training in child development. Many programs are custodial at best, with notable exceptions in both group and family day care. For a survey of day care in the United States, the report of The National Council of Jewish Women (Keyserling, 1972) continues to be an excellent source, both for its findings and recommendations. Most of these recommendations, made in 1972, still need to be acted on. The most fundamental issue in day care today remains that of quality versus cost. There is an increasing literature to help parents choose the form of care most suitable for them and to identify what to look for in day care for infants, preschoolers, and school-age children (e.g., U.S. Department of Health and Human Services, 1980; Willis and Ricciuti, 1978; Glickman and Springer, 1978; Provence, Naylor, and Patterson, 1977).

We would like to dispel the myth, propagated largely by psychoanalysts, that day care threatens the mother-infant tie and thus the baby's mental health in general. Belsky and Steinberg (1978), while noting the dearth of good research on day care, concluded from a survey of the field that *high-quality* day care: (1) has little impact either way on children's intellectual development; (2) does not interfere with parent-child bonds; and (3) fosters interactions with peers. Zigler and Gordon (1982) provide another excellent survey of day care, including its current status, options for current and future programs, and a synthesis of research that analyzes the effects of day care on children by examining the interaction of children's personality, parenting practices, characteristics of the day care teachers, and the materials available in the day care centers. This analysis enables the reader to understand the complexity of day care rather than focus on any single variable.

As we said above, the growth of day care has provided new opportunities to study peer interactions among young children, especially toddlers, and we shall return to this topic in Chapter 8.

Toys for Babies

We look now at the world of inanimate objects with which the child interacts. In general, sound cognitive development seems to be related to the variety and accessibility of objects to explore, experiment with, and come to know—watching, listening, tasting, smelling, touching, manipulating, hefting, setting in motion. In fact, access to playthings seems to be highly correlated with the accessibility of adult caregivers who make objects available, respond to the child's response to them, encourage further exploration, and talk about what is going on. Thus playthings can be important in themselves, but they take on special importance in a context of social interchange.

Often the first playthings of the infant are soft cuddly objects, such as a teddy bear or a blanket, which share some of the properties of the parents' and child's bodies. Later, such objects are supplemented by others that are not toys in any formal sense but are found as a matter of course in many homes. Babies find paper a fascinating play substance, something they can crumple and flatten and tear and suck and chew on. Rags serve many of the same purposes but offer some interesting contrasts. Babies like plastic dishes to bang on the table top or floor, mirrors in which to watch and eventually identify themselves, paper bags and empty boxes to put things into and take things out of, including, in

(© John Fay)

Babies find paper a fascinating play substance—it can be crumpled, flattened, torn, sucked, and chewed on.

late infancy, grocery cartons for climbing into and out of and hiding under. Babies take great delight in kitchen utensils and pots and pans, which they use in myriad ways. Messy though it may be, babies profit from the chance to play with their food, slapping and smearing and squeezing handfuls. Regardless of how parents feel about it, babies will experiment with pouring milk from a glass or cup—eventually from container to container but at first into the void— for the sheer pleasure of seeing it pour.

Besides what the household provides, toy makers have come up with some ingenious and useful devices (and also with loads of unspeakable junk, some of which is not even safe to give babies). It should be emphasized that homemade equivalents are often easy to make and are every bit as good as the commercial product. In any event, it is not a good idea to overwhelm the baby with toys. Mobiles that hang above a bassinet or crib seem to fascinate very young babies,

but soon it becomes important that the baby have dangling toys to bat and grasp and manipulate. Cradle gyms serve the purpose well, especially if they are hung on springs, and even more especially if by moving them the baby can activate a bell or rattle. Rattles and cloth dolls suspended from a length of elastic give the baby something to set swaying, to grasp, to pull and release, and to mouth and chew on. Babies past six months can operate the sort of music box that is wound by means of a drawstring. There is no reason similar contrivances could not be built to yield all manner of sound effects.

We have already described the pleasure babies find in the family bathtub. Water itself is an elemental play material. Outdoors, in warm weather, water, sand, dirt, stones, containers, and spoons and small shovels offer endless opportunities.

During late infancy and early toddlerhood, babies become increasingly adept at playing with blocks that can be fitted on rods. Small wagons and cars and trucks are perennial favorites and also lend themselves to increasingly mature uses. The rubber ball is so basic a toy that it hardly needs mentioning, except for one thing—the smaller the child, the bigger the ball should be.

So-called activity panels, or gadget boards, equipped with knobs and latches and cranks and gears, and doors that open on mirrors or pictures or simply the world on the far side of the board, are appealing to babies and young children. One that we built for research purposes included a low-wattage bulb for the baby to turn on and off, and a battery-powered doorbell activated by a pushbutton. Such activity boards are easily built, and making one could be a worthwhile and enjoyable project for a parent and an older sibling.

These, of course, are only a small sample of things that babies enjoy and learn from. We should repeat that babies on their own find many intriguing activities. They learn to open and empty out drawers and cupboards. They learn to unscrew the cap on the toothpaste and to squeeze out the paste. They discover the possibilities of rolls of toilet paper and boxes of cleaning tissues. Parents are sometimes hard put to know whether to laugh or cry. In any event, such escapades help teach babies about the properties of the universe and help develop motor control.

It appears, then, that babies thrive when they have loving, responsive caregivers (who are not afraid to exercise needed discipline); when they are well nourished and kept safe and healthy; and when they have ample opportunity to explore the wonders of the environment and discover some of its many possibilities.

SUMMARY

1. During the first fifteen months, the infant develops from a helpless neonate into an active explorer. This growth is marked by developmental milestones—conspicuous physical and behavioral transformations. Physical development entails growth, or increases in size and changes in body proportions, and maturation, or the often subtle physiological and anatomical reorganizations through which the individual passes while growing up. Growth during the first year is marked by a 40 percent increase in length, a threefold increase in weight, a doubling of brain size, and growth of a full head of hair. Facial proportions change as well. Maturational developments include changes in digestive capacities, shedding tears, and generally "becoming human" at around three months.

2. Sleeping patterns change. During infancy, sleep and waking become sharply defined, and between two and three months many babies begin to sleep through the night. The development of the baby's eating and sleeping rhythms represents the stabilization of biological clocks. Between four and six months, the baby becomes more self-reliant and can be left alone for longer periods. The first teeth appear between six and seven months.

3. Motor development, like physical growth, demands emotional and cognitive support and stimulation. Advances in fine motor control include visually guided grasping, or reaching for visible objects (the grasping reflex is present from birth), which is usually well established by age four months. By age six months, babies can generally eat with their

hands and at around age eight months, their thumbs become fully opposed, allowing for accurate pincers grasping. A manipulative skill of late infancy is rotary movement of the hands.

4. There are also significant developments in gross motor control during infancy. For the first five or six months, babies are essentially horizontal creatures. Toward seven months, they begin to attempt crawling, and between eight and nine months, they can generally sit up without help. Creeping begins at around nine months. By eleven months, the baby can stand alone, and it first walks around age one.

5. Erikson's concept of basic trust versus mistrust illuminates the social and emotional development of infants. Erikson proposed that during infancy, the baby learns whether the world is good, reliable, and satisfying or painful and uncertain. Basic trust is essential for positive development. In Freud's view, infancy corresponds to the oral stage of psychosexual development.

6. Social smiling, vocalizing, and laughing are forms of early emotional expression in the infant. Stranger anxiety (a pronounced fear of unfamiliar people and surroundings, which often develops between six and twelve months and generally subsides by age two) is seen at this time. Separation anxiety also appears during this period. Ethnocentrism, prejudice, and xenophobia may be outgrowths of stranger anxiety.

7. Opportunities for social relations, especially play, develop as well. Imitation flowers during the last half of the first year, and social games develop throughout infancy. Imitation begins to shade into observational learning.

8. A key factor in child development during infancy is thought to be parental responsiveness to the baby's signals. The responsive parent provides contingent reinforcement that not only satisfies a momentary need but also feeds into the baby's sense of competence.

9. Parents gradually become aware of the baby's language of behavior—the cues it gives to indicate the kind of attention it wants. This "language" takes two forms: manifestations of distress and reactions to parental attempts to meet its needs.

10. The baby develops strong bonds of attachment to its family and other familiar people during infancy. Attachment is important because it reinforces sound physical and psychological development and provides

the foundation for the processes of socialization and cognition. Studies have confirmed the power of attachment during the first year. More recently, greater emphasis has been placed on the father's role in infant development.

11. The formation of attachment has been examined by a number of researchers. Harlow's experiments with rhesus monkeys proved that attachment is not a conditioned response and that normal development depends on strong attachments.

12. There have been opinions about child care since biblical times, but this century has seen the emergence of many formalized, and often conflicting, theories. Instead of learning through lifelong observation of caregiving practices, American parents have come to rely on the advice of Experts for guidance in child rearing. Freud, Watson, Mead, Dewey, Skinner, and Spock are among the thinkers whose work influenced child rearing between the 1920s and the present.

13. Good child care observes the principles of appropriate timing, gradualism, and avoidance of moralism. Parental self-confidence is also important.

14. The first responsibility that falls to parents is feeding the baby. In conditions of relative affluence and sanitation, the choice between breastfeeding and bottle feeding is a matter of personal preference. Attitudes toward feeding have relaxed, and diet and scheduling now tend to rely more on the child's innate "wisdom of the body." Of course, parents need to make sure that children stay away from harmful substances and maintain a healthy diet.

15. In general, one cannot give babies too much *sensitive* attention, but oversolicitousness or overwhelming, unwanted gratification is not appropriate. Discipline—that is, necessary control—is required, and it becomes an issue of increasing importance as the baby's mobility increases. Discipline is not synonymous with punishment (nor is punishment necessarily physical). Some taboos must be imposed, but the number should be kept to a minimum. The best and simplest way to impose a taboo is through aversive conditioning: A sharp, well-timed "No!" is generally sufficient.

16. Although parental attitudes are changing, parents still tend to treat girls and boys differently from birth; sex stereotyping is not easily discarded. In order for all developmental options to be kept open for

boys and girls, both sexes need access to a broader range of physical and emotional stimulation.

17. Day care, which has become tremendously more prevalent within the past decade, can provide high-quality care for children and can foster peer interaction.

18. Since sound cognitive development appears to be related to the variety and accessibility of objects to explore, experiment with, and come to know, playthings are important—especially in a context of social interchange.

KEY TERMS

attachment, 173
autogenous development, 147
basic needs, 162
basic trust/basic mistrust, 162
contact comfort, 177
contingent reinforcement, 168
counteridentification, 180
crawling, 159
creeping, 159
discrepancy hypothesis, 166

enculturation, 184
ethnocentrism, 166
field dependence/independence, 150
fine motor control, 153
gross motor control, 153
growth, 148
imprinting, 179
language of behavior, 171
maturation, 148
nonliteral behavior, 168
separation anxiety, 167
sex typing, 191
social smile, 163–164

socialization, 184
strange settings (strange situations), 174
stranger anxiety, 164
visually guided grasping, 154
wariness, 164

SUGGESTED READINGS

Church, J. *Understanding Your Child From Birth to Three*. New York: Pocket Books, 1973. One psychologist's account of the early years, with special attention to practical issues in infant and child care and including a section on social development.

Emde, R. N., and Harmon, R. J. (eds.). *The Development of Attachment and Affiliative Systems*. New York: Plenum, 1981. An up-to-date and comprehensive survey of attachment.

Escalona, S. K. *The Roots of Individuality*. Chicago: Aldine, 1968. A collection of different approaches in viewing normal development in the first half year of life.

Fraiberg, S. *Every Child's Birthright: In Defense of Mothering*. New York: Basic Books, 1977. A passionate account of the need of babies to forge loving attachments to a caring, committed person as the foundation for future healthy development.

Richards, M. P. M. (ed.). *The Integration of a Child Into a Social World.* London: Cambridge University Press, 1974. A British perspective on the socialization process.

Stone, L. J., Smith, H. T., and Murphy, L. B. (eds.). *The Social Infant.* New York: Basic Books, 1978. A collection of research studies on infants' social development, with extensive commentaries by the editors.

CHAPTER 6

The Infant: Cognition

Basic trust and attachment underlie sound emotional development, and sound emotional development is essential to normal development in all spheres. However, with children as with Harlow's monkeys, emotional security is not enough. The developing human being has to learn to cope with and adapt to a huge variety of situations, and the basic processes of making sense of the world so that one can act effectively are what we call **cognition.** We have already seen cognition in action. Stranger anxiety is possible only because the baby has formed an image of the familiar. The baby's gross and fine motor development involves a changing view of space and objects and new ways of adapting to them. Recall that we can make a logical distinction between cognition and other aspects of functioning, but in reality cognition is only one aspect of the person's general orientation to self and world.

Hence the study of cognitive development does not restrict us to the study of dry-as-bones logic. Human beings are seldom coolly rational in their dealings. Their knowledge is embedded in and saturated with feelings and values. Some of their knowledge is in fact delusion, but delusions, too, are a part of cognition. Some spheres of human activity, like falling in love, lie outside the scope of rational analysis. We all have areas of profound ignorance, about which our reasoning is hardly better than an infant's. We all have irrational fears, some of them remnants of periods of our lives lost to memory. We are all subject to vanity and want to present ourselves to the world in the most favorable light possible. We all have our jealousies, rivalries, animosities, pettinesses, and selfishness. We all know feelings of self-doubt. The bravest among us have tasted cowardice.

In sum, our thinking and perceiving can be badly distorted, but they still qualify as cognition.

Piaget and his followers have focused almost exclusively on the development of rational thought. They have analyzed children's logical inadequacies, but without reference to possible emotional factors that can distort thinking. Piaget has written about the development of moral judgment (1965), but in terms of how children conceptualize morality rather than of how they feel about it. Like other writers of textbooks, we single out cognition as a major topic, but we beg the reader to bear in mind that pure cognition is a rarity indeed. Even the study of social cognition (Flavell and Ross, 1981; Shantz, 1975) shows few signs of the emotional and even passionate contexts in which social cognition often operates.

PIAGET ON INFANT COGNITION

You are invited to turn back to Chapter 1 for a general introduction to the ideas of Jean Piaget. Briefly, Piaget describes children's cognitive development in terms of a series of fixed, unvarying stages, with each stage characterized by a cohesive set of abilities and limitations. Although Piaget feels the ages at which the stages emerge may differ somewhat, there is no flexibility in their sequence. Piaget's stage theory has come under attack as being inadequate to the facts (Case, 1980; Flavell, 1981) and will probably not survive. However, it still provides a convenient framework for describing cognitive functioning at various periods of life. Piaget's enduring contribution is in demonstrating that there are profound differences between the thinking of children and that of adults and that the world experienced by the child is a very different place from the one grownups take for granted.

For Piaget, infancy extends from birth to age two, overlapping the age period that we call toddlerhood (Chapter 8). The infant is said to be in the **sensorimotor stage** of cognitive development during this period, pointing to the fact that babies are guided more by stimuli in the environment than by inner mental structures. Piaget proposes six major achievements that appear during the sensorimotor stage.

1. Knowledge of the properties of familiar objects. As we have seen, infants come to recognize the members of their own household and to recognize strangers as unfamiliar. Babies also know their own dwellings and the furnishings they contain, their regular playthings and the household objects that serve as playthings, and so on with all those things with which they have frequent contact. Babies know key locations and the routes between locations, although they are some years away from being able to construct a coordinated image of all those locations and routes. Babies usually know the stores they are taken to on shopping trips, the family car or other means of transportation, and the doctor's office. It is not merely that infants recognize these things; babies know what sorts of interactions they can expect to have with them, from social games with the parents to being scrutinized and injected at the doctor's office.

2. Means-end relations. Infants develop a rudimentary sense of cause and effect. They learn that if they pull the cat's tail, the cat will bite or scratch.

(© Frostie 1982/Woodfin Camp & Assoc.)

Though infants do not yet *think* in terms of cause and effect, they acquire a rudimentary understanding of means and ends.

They become able to push aside an obstruction to reach some desired article. They perceive directly that they can obtain an object resting on a sheet of paper by pulling the paper. They figure out, at first by trial and error, how to bring an unreachable object closer by pulling on an attached string. They can perceive through mental operations the possibility of using a stick to rake in an otherwise unattainable plaything. They can switch radios, television sets, and lights on and off. Note, though, that babies do not yet think about cause and effect. Their knowledge is purely pragmatic:

Event A is very likely to be followed by event B. The development of causal reasoning is discussed in later chapters.

3. Intentionality or purposiveness. Goal-directed behavior appears during infancy. This is illustrated by such actions as the baby's pushing against a barrier to reach for a toy or removing a cloth from a hidden object. One can observe a baby at play stop what it is doing, think a few seconds, and then head off to where some particular plaything is kept or has been left. In the sphere of communication, babies find ways to let their parents know that they want some particular thing, and what it is they want. Note the concreteness, the focus on immediate goals. Babies have a very restricted image of the future, although they have to have some ability to anticipate consequences in order to act purposively.

4. A sense of a separate identity. An important part of infant development is detaching self from environment, particularly the human environment. By late infancy, babies have consciously defined many areas of their own bodies, although their body awareness is far from being well organized and integrated. Babies acquire a sense of themselves as distinct people, as shown by their ability to play with their own identity. In toddlerhood, as we shall see, babies struggle for autonomy and assert themselves through negativism. We are speaking here of beginnings: The sense of identity evolves throughout life, and the puzzle of who I am is sometimes never satisfactorily resolved.

5. The beginnings of language. Infants and their parents establish increasingly complex means of communication until, by late infancy, babies are able to understand a certain amount of true language. Early in the second year of life, babies begin to talk and, by the end of the sensorimotor period, some babies have become highly proficient users of language. We know of one twenty-month-old boy who placed his lollipop on the kitchen counter and announced, "I'll leave it here so I can have it after my bath." Piaget, it should be noted, says little about early language, treating it as subordinate to the child's evolving "intelligence," or "logic," which is contained in the mental structures built up through concrete experiences.

6. Object permanence or the object concept. Young infants seem unaware that things that disappear from view may nevertheless go on existing. During late infancy and into early toddlerhood, babies come to terms, one step at a time, with the notion that objects can have a stable, independent existence regardless of whether the baby can see the object, and regardless of any particular location in space.

All these developments, and some others as well, will be treated at greater length in the sections that follow. Let us first remind you of some Piagetian concepts that were defined in Chapter 1. We spoke there of schemata and schemes, of equilibration and its constituent processes, assimilation and accommodation, and touched upon such notions as egocentrism and realism. It might be helpful to remind you briefly of what these concepts represent. As we said, the basic unit of knowledge is the **schema** (pl. **schemata**). A schema is a simplified image of some aspect of reality. Schemata are generally unconscious, but we become aware of them when they are violated. For instance, we develop a schema of our own bodies such that, if we should lose an extremity, we go on acting as though the extremity were still there. A **scheme,** on the other hand, is the mental pattern that underlies the performance of a skilled action. Thus the baby has or acquires schemes for sucking, for grasping and manipulating, for primitive tool use, and so forth, even though there is not yet a schema of cause and effect. Schemata are for knowing and thinking; schemes are for doing. **Equilibration** has two components, assimilation and accommodation. **Assimilation** refers to the fact that the baby tries to fit new experiences into already established schemata, if need be distorting perception of the new thing to suit. For instance, a baby may surrender himself or herself to a stranger's arms, unaware temporarily that the stranger is an unknown quantity. However, if reality resists too much distortion, and if the misfit between schema and reality is severe enough, mental disequilibrium or imbalance results. To restore equilibrium, the baby must **accommodate,** either altering the old schema or forming a new one. In the case of the stranger, the baby modifies its people schema so as to include further human qualities. Equilibration seems to be the closest thing for Piaget to development through learning. It will be helpful to bear these notions in mind as we talk about various aspects of infantile cognition, beginning with perception.

PERCEPTUAL DEVELOPMENT IN INFANCY

Perception is our primary source of knowledge, supplemented as we go along by both the ability to learn vicariously, through what other people tell us, and the ability to reorganize what we already know to produce new knowledge. That is, we can find new patterns, see new connections, draw inferences, project events into an image of the future, and form hypotheses. We do not want to draw too sharp a line between perception and other aspects of cognition. As we shall say at greater length in later chapters, all but the earliest beginnings of perception are filtered through our system of knowledge, beliefs, attitudes, and feelings. Note that such filtering can enrich and deepen our understanding of what we perceive. But note, too, that it can badly distort our perceptions, investing them with irrelevant and sometimes destructive meanings.

Characteristics of Early Perception

Piaget and Werner have pointed out that immature perception is distinguished from that of adults by a number of special characteristics. Note that the distinction between child and adult is not hard and fast; we can find plenty of lingering immaturities in adult perceiving and thinking. Let us now take a closer look at these characteristics, to most of which you had a first introduction in Chapter 1.

Empathy. Babies come into the world with all their senses in good working order, but with a severely limited capacity for processing and organizing information. We can specify some of the baby's limitations. First, there is difficulty distinguishing between self and world. That is, the primary mode of perceiving is **empathic.** Empathy is often used to signify projection of our own feeling states onto objects. We stress a second meaning that refers to an interpenetration of self and surroundings, such that we participate in external events as though they and we were all portions of the same organism. We have already seen empathic behavior in the newborn. There is empathic crying, as can be readily observed in the nursery of any maternity ward. There is some evidence of synchrony of movement on the part of the baby in time with the rhythms of adult speech when an adult leans over to talk to the baby face to face. And there is early imitation, as of tongue protrusion, lip pursing, and eyebrow raising.

The basic fact of empathy can be made clear by its persistence into adult life. As we have noted, many of us are susceptible to the yawns of other people. When listening to a speaker with a frog in his or her throat, we clear our own throats. The body English by which we try to steer a pool ball or bowling ball or golf ball is an empathic reaction. When, in a movie, the hero totters on the brink of a cliff, we lean away from the precipice. When we watch a fight on television, we writhe and grunt in unison with the combatants. However, as adults, we can also stand back and contemplate the world objectively, analyzing situations and forming judgments, and even being aware of our own empathic vibrations.

Egocentrism. As we have said, egocentrism is not to be confused with either selfishness or preoccupation with self. Egocentrism is rooted in lack of awareness of the self. Most adults find it hard to understand that although the baby relates everything to "my" wants and feelings, there is at first no *me*. There simply are states of hunger or wetness or discomfort, all in a context of familiar persons and places. But there is no *I am* hungry or *I feel* tired. The baby's experience is personal because it is the only experience of which he or she is aware, but babies have not yet defined themselves as entities, just as at first they have no awareness of a world that exists apart from their own feelings, actions, and experiences. This is the state that Piaget (1954) has labeled **egocentrism.** In sum, babies accept their own view of the world as the absolute and only possible view, simply because they are unaware of themselves at the receiving end of the stimulation.

Note that it is possible to be egocentrically generous. When the baby offers a parent a bite of its saliva-soaked toast, it is in a spirit of loving altruism; the baby simply has no idea that this well-meant gift might appear somewhat revolting to the intended recipient. The boy who gives his mother a pocket knife for her birthday is probably displaying a mixture of egocentrism with the suspicion that his mother will find a way to give it back to him.

Even as the baby develops a sense of a separate identity, he or she cannot be aware both of the world and of himself or herself as perceiver. That is, babies perceive themselves at the center of the universe and are unable to take anyone else's point of view. As adults, by contrast, we are aware of ourselves as perceivers and are better able to take account that other perceivers with different vantage points in time or space or values will perceive the same situation very differently. Egocentrism is not an absolute. Children and grownups can

(© Stephen Shames 1982/Woodfin Camp & Assoc.)

Like adults, babies perceive the world physiognomically, responding to the global, overall, unanalyzed qualities of objects and situations. The physiognomics of objects elicit emotional and behavioral reactions. A muzzle demands to be patted; fur demands stroking.

behave more or less egocentrically, which has led some observers to question whether there is such a condition as egocentrism.

Physiognomic Perceiving. At all ages, but particularly in infancy, we perceive the world **physiognomically,** responding to the global, overall, unanalyzed qualities of objects and situations, with little regard to how they are actually formed (Kemler, 1982). For instance, by age one month babies held in the feeding position open their mouths and strain toward the approaching bottle. This indicates learning and suggests recognition of the nursing bottle. In fact, though, the

baby reacts in the same way to all sorts of approximations of the nursing bottle (Church, 1970). As stimuli we have used crumpled up cleaning tissues, gray and white spheres, a gray cylinder, and a gray cone, all roughly equal in volume to a standard nursing bottle. It takes several months for the baby to learn to open its mouth only when a real bottle with the nipple properly aimed comes into view. Here is an example of physiognomic perception in a four-month-old girl:

[Debbie] mistook a curly fabric black jacket on a chair for her black dog [real] and reached and strained toward it from across the room, uttering something suspiciously like "dg, dg, dg," over and over again and with increasing confusion in her facial expression when it didn't come to her as her dog does (Church, 1978).

Physiognomic perceiving gets its name from the way we see human faces, or physiognomies. We have no trouble recognizing individual faces, although we may find it very hard to specify how one face differs from another. We have already seen how infants smile at imitation faces defined only by a couple of daubs for eyes. The physiognomies of inanimate objects may convey to the child the objects' "feelings"—an overturned cup may be perceived as "tired" (Werner, 1948). Young children learn to recognize geometric forms by their physiognomies: The child can correctly name "star" and "triangle" long before he or she can draw either or say how many sides a triangle has.

The physiognomies of objects have expressive properties called **demand qualities** or **characters**, which elicit emotional and behavioral reactions even in the absence of learning (Werner, 1973). In fact, these demand characters seem very close to what we mean by an object's "meaning." For the baby, knobs come to have the demand quality of graspability and twistability, crevices demand poking, and novel textures ask to be felt. For the adult, the baby's cheeks (both kinds) demand to be pinched, fur to be stroked, or wet paint to be tested. But to speak of demand qualities, as we hinted above, is only another way of speaking of *meanings*, which we perceive and react to. As adults, of course, we can study objects and situations before we decide how to react to them, but the baby lacks this option. Physiognomies

and their meanings must be considered primary.

Realism. We spoke in Chapter 1 about **realism**, the fact that children have trouble distinguishing different kinds of reality. A thought is just as real as a solid object, but they belong to two different orders of reality, the mental and the material. Young children experience their dreams not as internal events but as actual happenings taking place in the real world; children have been known to ask their parents to close the bedroom door "so the dreams can't get in." Or they may object to sleeping in a particular room because it is too full of dreams.

Piaget postulated several specialized forms of realism. We have already spoken of *symbolic realism* in our discussion of phantom environments, our ability to conjure up verbal entities and then act as though they were real—Santa Claus and the tooth fairy are purely verbal creations, but young children believe in them faithfully and may stoutly resist older children's attempts to disillusion them. We shall talk later about *moral realism*, the idea that the rules of moral conduct are a part of nature rather than human conventions. **Picture realism** is easily seen in infancy, as when babies pet a pictured animal, lower an ear to hear the ticking of a pictured watch, sniff at a pictured flower, or try to pick up designs on their crib bumpers. Here is a mother's account of picture realism in her daughter at age four months, nineteen days: "Ruth became very excited today. She tried to pick up the colored pictures in her story book. She tried and tried. Then she tried to eat them and scratch them. She couldn't understand why she couldn't grasp them" (Church, 1978). In a test of depth perception in infants, Yonas, Cleaves, and Peterson (1978) showed babies pictures of a rectangular lattice rotated 45 degrees so that it appears to have a nearer, larger edge and a distant, smaller edge. Infants aged twenty-six to thirty weeks tried to grasp the "near" side.

As adults, we fall victim to a combination of picture realism and verbal realism when we become so absorbed and emotionally involved in a movie or television drama that we forget that "it is only a story."

Phenomenalism. Another important principle governing primitive perception is **phenomenalism,** which refers to the fact that children and quite a few adults respond only to the surface aspects of things, never wondering what lies behind appearances.

A simple test of phenomenalism, which can be played as a parlor game, is to equip people with pencil and paper and give them the following instructions:

> I want you to draw me a picture of an island. Not an island as shown on a map, looking down on it from above, but an island seen in profile, from the side. I want you to draw the entire island, what's under the water as well as what's above. Begin by drawing a line across the page representing the surface of the water.

All the children we have tested through third grade draw islands that float, not as the peaks of mountains thrusting up from the ocean floor (Mitchell, 1934). This applies to children living on the island of Oahu, in Hawaii, as much as to children in Poughkeepsie, New York. A survey done some years ago indicated that 14 percent of college men and 40 percent of college women drew

floating islands. More recently, virtually every college student, male or female, to whom we have given the task has produced either a floating island or a drawing so ambiguous as to defy interpretation, with the lines fading out or running off the sides of the page, leaving the task unresolved.

We shall be talking shortly about the development of **object permanence,** the baby's growing awareness that objects can continue to exist even when they are out of sight. *Object impermanence*—the baby's lack of awareness that the object is still there even though out of sight— can be understood as a manifestation of phenomenalism.

Synesthesia and Intersensory Effects. Another characteristic of early perception is **synesthesia,** the fact that stimulation in one sense modality produces effects in another (Marks, 1975). One of the most common forms of synesthesia is color hearing, so that various sound patterns produce the experience of seeing colors. We have an example of confusion between sight and hearing in the case of a little girl holding a watch against her closed eyes to hear the ticking (Church, 1978). As adults, we all know the synesthesia of taste and smell (the way aroma contributes to flavor), as we become aware when our noses are stopped up by a cold and foods lose their familiar "taste."

Synesthesia has a reciprocal, the so-called **intersensory effects** (Birch and Lefford, 1963; Blank and Bridger, 1964). Babies have to overcome synesthesia and learn to distinguish among the different kinds of information carried by the various senses, but they also have to learn how experience in one modality is coordinated with experience in the others.

The baby apparently sees spontaneously that sandpaper is rough to the touch, but to judge by the baby's surprise when a soap bubble bursts, the bubble's fragility is not automatically visible to the baby. Babies have to learn what kinds of sounds various materials make when struck against other kinds of materials. We know that rapping our knuckles against a board produces a knock, but babies do not. Babies have to learn that, in general, size is correlated with weight, but also that there are exceptions: There are big, light things like balloons and styrofoam rafts and down pillows, and there are small, heavy things like chunks of lead. Transfer of knowledge among modalities is a complicated matter, still incompletely mapped.

Some Landmarks in Perceptual Development

You may wish to return to Chapter 4 and review the section on the newborn baby's perceptual capacities. We begin here after the neonatal period.

Before age two months, babies can track a moving person or a dangling trinket through an arc of 100 degrees or more (some babies swivel their heads to look over their shoulders), but if the object is lost sight of, the baby does not search for it. It is at about age two months that the supine baby first blinks in response to an object rapidly approaching the eyes (White, 1963).

Some babies at three months begin to croon to music, suggesting that for babies as well as adults music has special qualities that set it apart from other sounds. Babies' crooning is not particularly musical, but it is quite distinct from the other vocalizations they emit.

By age three months, accommodation of the lens of the eye is essentially complete. The fixed-focus gaze of the neonate is past and the eyes now show improved convergence on nearby objects.

We noted in Chapter 4 that there are physiological indications that the baby's eyes and visual cortex are ready from birth onward to make color discriminations, but that color does not become prominent for the baby until later. One study indicates that neonates may make color discriminations, but the author herself points out that they may be reacting to brightness rather than color (Jones-Molfese, 1977). Pending further data, we abide by the conventional idea that babies show pronounced color preferences beginning in the four-to-six-month range (Bornstein, 1981; Spears, 1964; Staples, 1932; Valentine, 1913–1914). A study by Bornstein, Kessen, and Weiskopf (1976) finds that four-month-olds show a preference for blue over yellow-green, and, in general, for pure colors rather than those that merge with adjacent hues; for instance, they prefer red to red tinged with orange. Those who want to establish very early color discrimination might want to use the technique of some ancient research by Raehlmann and Krasnogorski alluded to by Werner (1948). These experimenters gave babies (age not specified) a salty formula in a bottle of one color and a normal formula in a bottle of another color; babies very quickly learned to reject, on the basis of color, the salty formula.

The Visual Cliff

We have already pointed to the looming effect and visually guided grasping as early indicators of depth perception.

However, one technique for demonstrating depth perception in infancy has become so well known that it deserves special treatment. This is Walk and Gibson's (1961) **visual cliff effect.** In its original form, the effect could be demonstrated only with babies old enough to creep. The baby is placed on a raised platform with guard rails on two of its four sides. On one unguarded side of the platform there is a shallow drop-off, and on the opposite side a deep one. Both drop-offs are in fact covered with sheets of heavy plate glass, making the cliffs visual rather than real and falling off impossible. Mothers summon their baby first from one side and then from the other. When a mother calls from the shallow side, the baby scurries directly to her. However, when a mother calls from the deep side, the baby turns to her but is stopped by the apparent drop-off. The baby's avoidance of the deep side is taken as evidence of the innateness or very early development of sensitivity to depth in humans and a number of other species. By itself, though, the visual cliff effect is not conclusive, since by the time babies can creep they have had abundant opportunities to learn about depth. More convincing is the fact that babies too young to creep, when placed face down on the glass over the deep side, show by their change in heart rate that they are reacting to the changed situation (Campos, Langer, and Karowitz, 1970).

The baby's perception of the visual cliff is thought to be based on motion parallax, the fact that objects at different distances have different rates of displacement on the retina (an airplane appears to be traveling much faster when seen close up than when seen at a dis-

(© Dr. Richard Walk)

A child peers cautiously at the deep side of the visual cliff.

tance) (Bower, 1965). Binocular cues are not necessary for the visual cliff effect; Walk and Dodge (1962) demonstrated the effect in a ten-and-a-half-month-old who had been blind in one eye since age five and a half months.

We must modify this description of the visual cliff effect. For some babies, and for some puppies we have tested just after their eyes had opened, the cliff appears to be inviting rather than repellent, and these babies and pups cannot wait to hurl themselves into space. We have named this reaction the "Geronimo response" (Church, 1970). In addition, some of the puppies have shown fear of the drop-off coupled with acrophobia (fear of heights). That is, they wanted very badly to get down but were deterred by the drop. This conflict was expressed behaviorally: the front legs were braced stiffly against going over the edge, while the hind legs churned to propel the puppy over the precipice.

Babies who can creep learn very quickly to climb stairs. Once at the top, though, they turn around and find themselves blocked by the visual cliff effect from going back down. One can teach babies to descend a flight of stairs by bumping on their seat from step to step, but it is not a good idea to have babies unattended by adults on stairs or other high places. Some, let us remember, may be of the Geronimo persuasion. Also, on a bed or changing-table top, babies like to roll over, and they may roll over the edge before they see it. Many babies like to play the game of flopping backward from a sitting position onto a bed, and they are liable to flop with their back at the very edge. If a surface is no more elevated than the baby's own height, as in the case of many couches, babies by eleven months can be taught by manipulation to slide feet first to the floor. The reminder of "Piggies first" seems to help.

So far, we have been talking mainly of the baby's perceptual capacities. In the rest of this section on perception, we want to describe how the baby actually explores objects and their relations in space, including the achievement of object permanence.

Exploration of Objects and Relationships in Space

From the time babies reach out to grasp, and most especially from the time they become mobile, they are relentless explorers of whatever comes within their reach. Once babies have hold of an object, they inspect it from all sides, suggesting that babies have some rudimentary idea of how solid objects are constituted. Here, as we said before, we have the principle of *implicit perception*, awareness that a thing seen only partially continues on out of view; the hidden portions may even contain some interesting surprises. In one mother's words, Debbie, age nine and a half months, "peers around labeled jars and cans to see the design on sides and back and tries to turn them herself, with uncertain control" (Church, 1978).

From late infancy through toddlerhood, a favorite activity of babies is emptying pots and pans and utensils from the cupboards, banging them together, mouthing their handles or other protuberances, and disassembling complicated pieces like double boilers and percolators. (Progress note to young parents: If you are devoted to electrical appliances, try to keep on hand a few antiques such as percolators or dripolators and crank-operated beaters for the baby to play with.) The infant has neither the inclination nor the ability to put things back together, but the toddler can and does.

By late infancy, the baby can stack pierced blocks on a peg. However, if the blocks are graduated in size, infants ignore the "right" sequence, while toddlers gradually learn to stack the blocks in order of decreasing size. (We have observed just one fifteen-month-old ordering the blocks, but he started with the smallest and built upward to the largest.) Babies are sensitive only to gross differences in size. They enjoy putting things on top of things, and putting things into and taking things out of containers, but they may be completely baffled to find that they cannot fit a large object into a small container.

However, babies do make a discovery about quantity during late infancy—at least those babies who still wear diapers fastened with pins. Babies older than about nine months resist holding still while having their diapers changed and have to be given something to play with to keep them quiet. The something is often the diaper pins—closed, we hope we need not add. When babies are given only one pin, or when they drop one, they search about for the missing member of the pair, indicating a rudimentary awareness of two-ness. Indeed, a study of ten- to twelve-month-olds by Strauss and Curtis (1981) indicates that babies may have more advanced numerical skills than we are used to giving them credit for. The basic tool was habituation, the baby's losing interest in a repeated stimulus but perking up when the stimulus is changed in some perceptible way. In the Strauss and Curtis study, the contrast was between collections of different numbers of objects: two versus three, three versus four, and four versus five. In half the trials, the larger number was presented for habituation, and in half the trials the smaller number; which came first made no difference in the results. In half the trials, the collections were of homogeneous objects, and in half, heterogeneous. In the two-versus-three condition, both males and

females made the discrimination with both homogeneous and heterogeneous sets. In the three-versus-four condition, males made the discrimination between homogeneous sets, whereas females made the discrimination between heterogeneous sets. What, if anything, this early sex difference means eludes us. In the four-versus-five condition, the babies showed no signs of discrimination.

Babies have to learn by trial and error that they cannot rest a plaything on a vertical or steeply sloping surface. That is, they do not see the visual cliff as it applies to things other than themselves. Although they soon learn not to try to rest things on tilted surfaces, this learning does not suggest to them the possibility of rolling a toy car down an incline, a discovery that comes at about eighteen months.

It sometimes seems that babies have a hard time perceiving extended plane surfaces, since we have observed babies trying to pass a spoon from one hand to the other through a feeding-table top and creeping head on into a wall as though unaware that it existed, like a trapped wasp that seems to be trying to fly through the ceiling. It is possible that such surfaces seen close up have for the baby (and the wasp) something of the character of a *Ganzfeld*, a homogeneous surface that fills the field of view and gives the impression, according to adult subjects in experiments, of a space-filling fog (Cohen, 1957).

Babies in late infancy explore apertures and crevices with a probing forefinger, and many go through a period where the forefinger leads the way through the world. With palms and fingertips, babies caress interesting textures, learning the feel of surfaces such as fur and fabric and

(© Dani Carpenter/The Picture Cube)

Some babies seem indifferent to the up-and-down, front-to-back orientation of books and magazines; others learn to position them carefully before "reading."

brick and glass and wire screening. Not only does such textural exploration give the baby pleasure, it probably helps in the intersensory coordination mentioned earlier.

Late in the first year, babies become aware that some objects have a "correct" vertical orientation and go through a period when they almost compulsively set upright the overturned things they encounter as they creep about the house. In observations we have made, graduated disks on a central spindle of the kind mentioned above, and even such unfamiliar abstract forms as a wooden cone, are set on their base.

While some babies seem indifferent to the up-down, front-to-back orientation of books and magazines—perhaps depending on how much exposure they have had to such articles—others quickly learn to position them conventionally before "reading." At first, babies turn pages handfuls at a time, but they soon master the trick of separating and turning single pages. One of the earliest manifestations of picture realism is trying to pick up printed matter from surfaces, but this applies to all sorts of forms and not only pictures. We do not know at what age babies begin to recognize the subject matter of pictures. One knows that they do recognize pictures when they rock to a picture of a rocking horse, meow at a picture of a cat, or make motorlike sounds at a picture of a car.

Object Permanence. To understand **object permanence,** or the *object concept,* one must first understand *object impermanence.* Up to a given age, in the six-to-eight-month range, babies seem to be totally unaware that an object continues to exist after it has passed from view. Babies watch intently, for instance, as a plaything is slowly lowered behind a screen. The moment the object disappears, the babies' expression goes blank and their eyes drift elsewhere. There is no sign of surprise or bewilderment or curiosity, and babies make no effort to find the vanished object.

The acquisition of object permanence, the realization that objects continue to exist even though they can no longer be seen, is not an abrupt, all-or-nothing transition. Rather, it develops gradually over a period of some ten or more months. We believe that certain privileged "objects," such as the parents, take on permanence long before other, less emotionally charged things. For instance, the three-month-old screaming in protest against having been put to bed in the evening seems fully aware that the parents are still there, within range of the baby's voice. In any event, strong attachment is highly correlated with the development of object permanence as measured by formal procedures (Bell, 1970).

There are several competing systems for tracing the evolution of object permanence, but we will not try to describe them all in detail (Kramer, Hill, and Cohen, 1975; Mehrabian and Williams, 1971; Uzgiris, 1973). The sequence goes approximately thus. A four-month-old is able to retrieve a toy that is only partly hidden—that is, the exposed portion implies the presence of the remainder of the toy. If the toy is completely covered, of course, the four-month-old loses interest; if the baby was reaching for the toy when it was covered, the baby will immediately withdraw his or her hand. Indeed, at six months, if the baby is already holding the toy when it is covered, he or she releases the toy and withdraws the hand, with no apparent distress (Gratch, 1972).

As permanence becomes more stable, beginning around seven or eight months, the vanished object will continue to exist for the baby, but only in the location where it was last seen. One can demonstrate this by playing the hand-hiding game with a seven- or eight-month-old. Bring your hands together over a small trinket, close one hand around the trinket, and extend both fists for the baby to choose. If the baby picks the fist holding the trinket, fine. If not, open the correct hand to show the baby where you have hidden the trinket. Continue to hide the trinket in the same hand for a number of turns. The baby will consistently choose the correct hand. Then switch hands. When the baby discovers that the usual hand is now empty, show the trinket in the other hand and continue to hide it there. For a number of trials the baby will first go to the originally correct hand and only then to the other. After perhaps a dozen repetitions, the baby will simply touch the original hand before going on to the other one, but the touching is obligatory—the baby seems absolutely unable to go directly to where he or she knows the trinket to be.

At the next stage, the baby can watch an object being moved from one hiding place to another and looks in the place where the object made its final disappearance. Then the lure is moved from

A

B

*(©George Zimbel/
Monkmeyer Press)*

C

(© Elizabeth Crews)

(**A, B**) Note how the baby loses interest
in the elephant the moment it is concealed
from view, turning instead to the camera as a
promising object of interest. (**C**) Certain privileged "objects," such as the parents, take on
permanence before other, less emotionally
charged phenomena.

hiding place to hiding place without the
baby being able to see the successive dis-
placements. When, usually at about
eighteen months, the baby more or less
systematically explores all the likely hiding places, he or she can be said to have
achieved full object permanence: The object now exists independent of the baby's

being able to perceive it, or of the baby's
actions with regard to it, or of any particular location in space.

One ingenious test for permanence is
to hide one toy and have the baby find a
completely different one in the same
place (LeCompte and Gratch, 1972). The
baby's surprise, as measured both by

emotional expression and by active investigation of the hiding place, is a good indicator of the solidity of the concept. The six-month-old seems unaware of the switch. From nine to eighteen months, babies show a steady increase in expressions of incredulity.

We have two descriptions of eleven-month-olds playing their own games of object permanence:

Games: Dropping bits of paper or a block off the back of the couch, then getting down, walking around the couch, and finding it. This sometimes entails considerable skill since her toy box and its attendant mess and accumulation of objects is behind the couch, so that searching, sorting and choosing has to occur for her to find the object she has dropped. This she does very well.

. . . . I noticed him one evening standing on one side of the bench in front of the sofa. He had some small object in his hand. He leaned way over the bench and dropped the thing. He looked at it for a moment, then got down on the floor, crawled around the bench to get it, crawled back to where he had been before, stood up, leaned over, and dropped the object again, crawled around after it, and this time shoved it under the sofa and left it there (Church, 1978, pp. 47, 139).

By late infancy, babies can hide a plaything under or behind a couch or in a closet and then retrieve it a day or so later, indicating permanence linked with location. This is a real-life equivalent of the **delayed-reaction experiment,** which had its heyday between 1910 and 1920, long before most psychologists had ever heard of object permanence. The delayed-reaction study tests the child's (or animal's) ability to remember the location of a concealed object. Young children do not perform well in delayed-reaction tests, but in real life it is the baby rather than the experimenter who does the hiding, and in general babies do best on tasks they set for themselves. The difference between home and laboratory settings may also be significant. Indeed, DeLoache and Brown (1979) have shown that toddlers eighteen to thirty months old did very well on delayed-response (three to five minutes) tests that consisted of finding an attractive plaything hidden in the children's own homes. Informal tests of a few toddlers showed an ability to delay thirty to sixty minutes, and even overnight. Children tested with three hidden objects did almost as well as with one. On "surprise trials," in which the toy was secretly removed from its original hiding place, the babies showed amazement at not finding the plaything. Following the initial surprise, two sorts of reaction were noted. The older (twenty-five- to thirty-month-old) babies went searching in likely places for the missing toy, whereas the younger ones simply wandered about aimlessly. Note the analogy with the LeCompte and Gratch study described above.

We should make clear that permanence does not apply across the board. As far as the evidence of the senses goes, many substantial material things (not to mention dreams or aches and pains or mist or lights or sounds) are unstable: Milk disappears from the bottle and food from the plate, fat cools and congeals, ice melts and water evaporates, balloons shrink and shrivel, flowers bloom and wither, and logs are consumed by fire. Children, then, have two cognitive problems. They have to sort out stable objects from unstable phenomena, such as those we have just mentioned. In addition, they have to recognize the permanence of stable objects, from parents to toys. But even stable objects change—they age, they wear out, they get broken. We will see later that even preschool children can accept seemingly magical transformations, which leaves them with the further problem of sorting out possible and impossible sorts of metamorphoses.

Size-Distance Constancy. There is one aspect of infant perception that has long been hotly debated. This is whether babies exhibit size constancy, or, more accurately, **size-distance constancy.** *Constancy* in general refers to the fact that an object retains its stable identity, size, shape, and color under a wide range of viewing conditions. (There are also constancies in the other senses, but vision is easiest to talk about.) To adults, an object at a distance looks almost the same size as when it is close up. This is in spite of the fact that every time the distance between viewer and object doubles, the diameter of the retinal image of the object is reduced by half. It is our hypothesis that the infant shows size constancy within a small circle, and that this circle expands with age and experience.

Our evidence is indirect. It is common for a toddler, seeing people at the far end of the block, to exclaim, "Look at the *little* people!" Zeigler and Leibowitz (1957) compared size constancy in seven- to- nine-year-olds and adults. Both groups showed almost perfect constancy to a distance of 10 feet (3m); beyond that distance constancy deteriorated, but much more so for the children than for the adults.

Note that size constancy applies only in the horizontal plane. When we look any distance up or down, things lose their constancy. We are subject to the moon illusion, the fact that the moon looks larger just above the horizon than high in the sky, although the retinal image is the same size in both cases. Most of us know the sensation of watching an airplane come in to land and seeing it jump from toy size to real-life size as it nears the ground. Similarly, we know that people and cars lose their identities viewed from a tall building. Returning to babies, they reach up to embrace their mother as she leans out of a third-story window, and they try to grasp the moon.

Orientation in Space. Three studies by Linda Acredolo give us some clues to egocentric spatial orientation in infants. The basic situation is the same in all three studies: The baby is induced to make a left-right differentiation and then is turned to face in the opposite direction. The baby responds egocentrically by turning either left or right as the original situtation dictated, or responds objectively by reversing the direction of his or her gaze to compensate for the reversal in orientation. In one study (Acredolo, 1970), nine-month-olds were asked to find an object hidden under a cloth either to their left or right. However, there was a second independent variable besides turning the baby to face the other way. This was testing babies in both laboratory settings and at home. In the laboratory, the babies behaved egocentrically, that is, they did not compensate for having been turned around. At home, presumably thanks to the wealth of familiar landmarks, babies were aware of their reversal of position and behaved objectively.

In another study (Acredolo, 1978), a

conditioned association was established between the sound of a buzzer and the appearance of a face at a window to either the baby's left or right. Once the conditioned response was established, the baby was rotated 180 degrees, and the buzzer sounded to elicit a head turn to the window. At ages six months and eleven months, babies responded egocentrically, even when the target window was marked by a star to make it more easily recognizable. However, the star made the conditioning easier and also increased objective responding in a sample of sixteen-month-old subjects. In variations on the experiment, nine out of thirteen different sixteen-month-olds responded objectively even without the star, while changes in procedure did nothing to eliminate egocentrism in young subjects. Using a similar situation, Acredolo and Evans (1980) made the target window even more conspicuous with lights and stripes, reducing egocentric responding at six, nine, and eleven months. However, when it was the nontarget window that was made salient, only the eleven-month-olds could make use of the information.

Means-End Relations. One of the key achievements of the sensorimotor period is awareness of **means-end relationships,** or cause and effect. This does not mean that babies try to make sense of causal relations. Rather, they learn pragmatically how to make some things happen. Also, they form associations between events that occur together, which may be the beginning of causal thinking. However, there is not yet even a glimmering of wonder about the deeper structure of how the world works. Note that we are still in the domain of perception: seeing how things go together.

Perhaps the first manifestation of means-end behavior, which appears around age seven months, is moving a barrier to reach some desired object. Piaget described such behavior in his son and judged it to be both intelligent and intentional. In our observations, it is also at about seven months that babies learn to use a string to bring an attached object within reach. Many babies discover the use of the string only by accident. They tire of stretching directly for the lure (the desired object), and play with the string instead. In so doing, they may notice that movement of the string causes movement of the lure. They then come to realize that pulling the string will bring the lure within reach. However, babies attempt to retrieve things tied to a string by giving only a single yank, which is as likely to send the object flying as to bring it near. It is an advanced skill to be able to reel in a length of string hand over hand.

A related task is getting an out-of-reach object by pulling on a cushion or a piece of cloth or paper on which the object rests. In this case, however, the baby seems to perceive the relationship in advance, without benefit of trial and error, and to solve the problem directly. It is conceivable that, when the lure rests on an extended surface such as a piece of paper instead of being attached to a length of string, the object is seen simply as the far part of a totality whose near side is within easy reach.

A more advanced form of tool use is using a stick or a small rake to procure an otherwise unreachable object. This skill supposedly emerges without prior experience around two years of age, but we have observed its spontaneous appearance in a one-year-old girl, and have found it possible to teach to some babies, one as young as thirteen months. One teaches by demonstration, reaching around the baby from behind to show how it is done. Such a demonstration is, of course, *applied modeling*. Not all babies learn this trick, however, and we have no way of explaining the success or failure of the teaching method.

This is about the limit of development of means-end relationships in infancy as such, although other manifestations appear later in the sensorimotor period.

THE ROLE OF INSTRUCTION

As we know, a great deal of emotional and attitudinal and cognitive learning goes on in infancy, but it involves very little conscious instruction. Here we would like to talk about approaches to deliberate teaching of new abilities to babies, conscious attempts to improve their competence. To illustrate, we mention an aspect of spatial perception that we intentionally omitted from our earlier account. Until somewhere between ten and twelve months, babies find it impossible to solve what looks to adults like a ridiculously simple problem, reaching around a transparent barrier to get an attractive toy. The standard barrier is a small sheet of glass or Plexiglas or coarse wire mesh. Younger babies persistently try to penetrate the barrier, apparently unable to comprehend that a visible object can be untouchable. We have used a variant of this problem that makes even more vivid the baby's inability to deal with transparency. A lure is placed in a wide-mouth transparent container that is then set in front of the baby. This variant illustrates two things. First, the container-barrier is perfectly

(© Stephen Shames 1982/Woodfin Camp & Assoc.)

A great deal of emotional and cognitive learning occurs in infancy without conscious instruction. Nevertheless, studies demonstrate that babies can be deliberately taught simple tasks.

visible to babies, because they often grasp the rim with one hand to steady the container while trying vainly with the other hand to go directly to the lure through the container's side. Second, while wrestling with the problem, babies are likely to spill the lure out of the container's open mouth, but this experience teaches them nothing. One simply replaces the lure and the baby goes on as before trying to reach the lure through the unyielding side.

Using a standard transparent screen, Kenneth Kaye (1976) gave mothers the task of teaching their six-month-old babies how to solve this problem. Three different teaching strategies emerged (it was rare for any mother to try more than one): *"shoving," "shaping,"* and *"showing."* "Shoving" consists in moving the baby's hand around the barrier and putting it in contact with the lure. "Shaping" consists in moving the lure a little bit at a time from full accessibility to partial accessibility to a position behind the barrier. "Showing" was simply demonstrating to the baby how to get the lure, and it was the only technique that worked, pointing again to the power of observational learning, or modeling. Kaye emphasizes that all the mothers, successful or not, were highly responsive to feedback from their babies.

We have used "showing" to teach babies to pour a Ping-Pong ball from cup to cup (a Ping-Pong ball was used in preference to water or sand, which could have made a mess). Babies learning this skill were sometimes impeded by either of two considerations. First, some babies grasped the general idea but could not see the necessity of positioning the second cup accurately to receive the ball. Second, some babies physiognomically perceived the white Ping-Pong ball in the cup as milk and tried to drink it. We mentioned a moment ago that we have had some success with the "showing" technique in teaching babies to rake in a lure with a stick.

For some kinds of teaching, however, "shoving" seems to work well. We have spoken of how one teaches an infant to slide down feet first from a couch by manipulating the baby. We have had considerable success teaching babies past the age of one year to turn a light on and off by folding the baby's hand around the string that controlled the switch, folding our hand around the baby's, and then moving the hand to make the light go off and on. A few babies learned this through observation, but most needed to be "shoved." It is worth mentioning that "shoving" has a very central part in the teaching of young Balinese children, especially in dancing and in playing the gamelan, a xylophonelike instrument. When chimpanzees are taught sign "language," the primary method is "showing," but when the chimp has particular trouble with one or another sign, its hands are manipulated by the instructor until the chimp gets the gesture right.

We cannot think of any effective applications in infancy of "shaping," although operant conditioners shape—in a somewhat different meaning of the word—all kinds of behavior in animals, as when Skinner taught pigeons to play Ping-Pong.

So far, we have been talking about the teaching of specific competences to babies, but in at least one case there has been a program to teach the very broad skill known as linguistic proficiency. Metzel (1980) taught parents techniques of verbal enrichment, beginning at birth. She used three groups: one of controls to whom no instruction was given; one of mothers who were taught enrichment techniques; and the third of both mothers and fathers instructed in language enrichment. On the Bayley Scale at six weeks and six months, all the babies showed gains, but they were greatest for babies whose parents had both been trained. The babies of trained parents also had higher HOME scores (to be discussed in Chapter 7), indicating that the training may have led to a general improvement in the home environment.

SELF-AWARENESS AND THE SENSE OF A SEPARATE IDENTITY

Yet another achievement of the sensori-motor stage is the *sense of having an identity of one's own*, apart from those of other people. The infant makes considerable progress toward knowing himself or herself as a distinct person. At the core of the infant's self-awareness is basic trust, feeling good about people in relation to oneself and about oneself in relation to the world at large. As we have said, the sense of a separate self requires gradual detachment from a primitive fusion of self and world. According to Margaret Mahler and her followers (Kaplan, 1978), babies have to detach themselves from a total fusion of identity with the primary caregiver, usually the mother. We agree that strong attachment and identification imply some intermingling of identities, but the empathic phenomena that we have emphasized suggest that self-world fusion exists from birth, before attachment has had a chance to form. There can be no doubt, however, that the emotional charge that comes with attachment helps define the baby's sense of self.

In any event, whether one is a psychoanalyst or a cognitivist, one has to recognize and remember the duality of experience: The external world is the world as perceived by me, and self-awareness is awareness of me, the person, situated in the world. We must mention further that the self acquires its own duality or, as we have called it, duplicity, but not yet in infancy. The egocentrism of babies implies that they cannot yet contemplate self and world, or be aware of the self as contemplator of the world,

imparting an inescapable personal bias to what is perceived. The sense of a separate identity is an important milestone in the lifelong development of self-awareness and understanding.

Much of the infant's developing self-awareness centers on the discovery, part by part and region by region, of the body, and the integration of these discoveries into a schema of the body as a whole. Anatomically and physiologically, the infant's body is a fairly well-integrated system from shortly after birth. Psychologically, however, it has to be brought into awareness through experiencing its various regions both in isolation and in relation to one another.

There is not much we can say about bodily awareness during the first three months. Babies obviously experience hunger, fullness, pleasure, pain, and fatigue. Notice that such experiences come from sense receptors attuned to bodily states, but they are experienced as states and not as mere sensations. Babies also receive tactile sensations from being touched and sensations of movement from being carried about and rocked and jiggled. These experiences undoubtedly contribute to a beginning definition of the body, a first step in developing a sense of self.

Our story properly begins when the baby is about three months old and is said to be "becoming human." This coincides with reaching out to things at a distance, which implies a beginning transition from a passive to an active orientation toward the world. This leads us to our first point. Parts of the body may become functional before the baby becomes clearly aware of them. Babies often develop good command of their hands before they notice the hands them-

One achievement of the sensorimotor stage is the sense of having an identity of one's own. With the development of the sense of a separate self comes an ability to appreciate others for their unique selves.

selves. When they do take notice, one hand grasps the other, turning it about for visual inspection, and the hands bring each other to the mouth for oral exploration—remember that babies can suck their thumbs without taking any particular note of the hand to which the thumb is attached. The baby watches fascinated as the hands open and close and the fingers wriggle, dimly aware, if at all, that he or she is actually producing these movements. For a span of several days, the baby may periodically interrupt play with objects to contemplate these newly discovered portions of the self. Then the hands seem to be accepted as the baby's own, and the infant

matter-of-factly resumes using them to explore and manipulate.

Three months is also the time of the evening bedtime crisis, which suggests some degree of self-awareness. By age four months, the hungry baby, if held by an adult, waits to be fed. It is a very active kind of waiting, marked by bodily tension, occasional escaping bleats, and straining toward the feeding place, but it expresses a primitive degree of conscious self-control in anticipation of satisfaction to come.

We have already described the baby's self-feeding, but an elaboration is called for here. Making direct manual contact with the mouth, whether in thumb sucking or smearing soft food into the mouth, is no problem. But now an object, whether an apple slice or a cracker or a spoon, intervenes between hand and mouth, and the baby has to learn afresh where the mouth is, poking about until the opening is found. When the baby tries to use a spoon, there is the further problem of keeping the spoon upright until it gets into the mouth.

A simple test of early self-awareness is to drape a piece of cloth over the baby's face. At age three months, babies respond to being thus shut off from the world by turning their heads from side to side and waving their arms ineffectually in the general vicinity of the head. By age four months, babies can wipe away the cloth with a hand or an arm. By five months, babies can reach up, grasp the cloth, and lift it off the face. However, the baby may first sit quietly for as long as thirty seconds, as though thinking about what is wrong and what to do about it. Some five-month-olds, having removed the cloth, will then put it back again, as though playing peekaboo (Church, 1970).

At six or seven months, babies discover their feet. You should bear in mind that at this age babies spend much of their time supine and that their well-rounded bellies may block their view of their feet. The feet first appear as strange objects that swim into view above the horizon of the belly. The hands clutch at them and, with persistence, capture one or both. The captive foot is brought to the eyes for viewing and to the mouth for tasting and chewing. Remember that the baby is just now getting teeth. Hence, when the baby bites down on the foot, he or she gives a look of painful surprise. The baby obviously had no idea

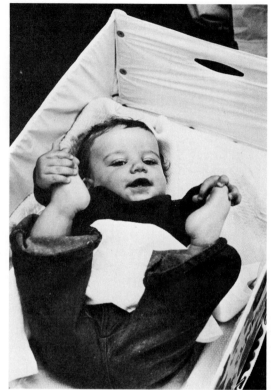

(© Susan Dryfoos/Monkmeyer Press Photo)

Babies discover their feet at six or seven months. Swimming into view above the belly, the feet are brought to the eyes for viewing and to the mouth for tasting and chewing.

he or she was about to bite a part of itself. The progressive integration of the feet into the body schema becomes apparent as the feet become more cooperative about being caught. First, they stop kicking when the baby reaches for them, and then they move within easy grasping range. In a matter of weeks, the feet are acting as prehensile tools, assistant hands that fetch things the hands cannot reach or that support an object while the hands play with it.

It is around this same age that babies

play a curious sort of peekaboo without an adult partner. They seem to take pleasure in covering their face with a corner of a blanket, peering out from time to time as though to see whether anything has changed. This may in fact be a step in the development of object permanence, a testing of the world's continuity and stability. And it may also be a step in the development of self-permanence, a testing of one's own continuity and stability.

Around nine months of age, many babies learn to scream (as contrasted with crying) as a way of announcing that they want something, such as dinner. In the course of screaming, babies may discover their own voice. Losing interest in whatever they originally wanted, babies follow a pattern of screaming and listening, screaming and listening, as though attending to the internal reverberations of the sounds they have just produced.

An important stage in self-knowledge comes when babies learn to recognize their own reflection in a mirror. This recognition develops through several stages. From five or six months, babies show interest in their reflection and reach out to explore it manually, often patting or slapping at the image. Next, there are manifestations of strong affection: Babies lean over and lavish kisses on their reflection. Then comes recognition of the reflection of the adult who is holding the baby. The baby looks back and forth, from image to person, making comparisons. Self-recognition is shown when the baby compares image and some aspect of the self, reaching up to touch the hat reflected in the glass, or looking back and forth between the patch on the overall knee and its reflection in the mirror. This discovery comes

somewhere around ten months, although it may be delayed in babies who have limited experience with mirrors.

One experimental study (Amsterdam, 1972) studied self-recognition by adapting a technique used by Gallup (1970) with chimpanzees. Gallup had already observed that his chimps recognized their own image; for instance, if an animal saw a seed lodged in its reflected teeth, it would reach up to fish it out. However, for a more rigorous test, he anesthetized the chimpanzees, shaved patches on their brows and upper ears, and stained the shaved places red. When the chimps saw their altered appearance in the glass, they showed great distress. In working with babies, Amsterdam surreptitiously applied a spot of rouge on each subject's nose. It was only between twenty-one and twenty-four months that babies reached up to touch the spot of rouge, from which Amsterdam concluded that this is the age of self-recognition. These observations differ from our less formal ones (Church, 1978), but we are willing to stand by our conclusions based on everyday observations. We might mention here that orangutans (Gallup, 1977) and gorillas (Hayes, 1977), but not rhesus monkeys, also share the capacity to recognize their own reflections. We do not take seriously Skinner's attempt to demonstrate self-recognition in pigeons, since it involved elaborate training and was quite unlike the spontaneous self-recognition found in higher primates (Epstein, Lanza, and Skinner, 1981).

Babies who have learned to recognize their own reflections take great pleasure in making faces at themselves. They also discover self-reflections in every shiny surface, including automobile hub caps.

It is not until toddlerhood, though, that babies learn to drape themselves in odds and ends of cloth and clothing and to posture before the looking glass.

We have mentioned manifestations of guilt in babies caught at some forbidden activity, such as poking at an electrical outlet. Such indications of a dawning conscience can be regarded as part of the developing sense of self.

At some point in late infancy, babies discover the navel, poking and stretching and working about this curious bit of anatomy. We have already talked about the social game of exploring the parent's facial features and then comparing them with the baby's own. This seems to carry one step further the self-awareness that babies gain in learning to recognize their own reflection in the mirror.

It is around age one that babies discover their genitals. This discovery seems to come earlier in boys than in girls, probably because the boy's penis is more visible to him than is the girl's vulva to her. The little boy typically discovers his penis while taking a bath. He notices something floating between his thighs, seizes it, and is pleasantly electrified by the resulting sensation. We have not observed little girls discovering their vulva—and presumably clitoris—for the first time, but assume that they do so while manually exploring the body.

In any event, both boys and girls past age one engage in occasional masturbation. It seems to occur most often at bedtime, perhaps as one more comfort device for shutting out the world and letting sleep come, but it can also be observed at miscellaneous moments during the day. This is not an issue for parents to become worked up about. Babies who have plenty of activities and playthings and adult attention and affection are not likely to become preoccupied with masturbation.

We do not know whether discovery of the genitals and erotic sensations comes earlier in societies in which babies are soothed by having their genitals fondled. Nor are we sure at what age genital experience becomes intense enough to produce orgasm. One authority states that at least some boys and girls are capable of full climax by mid-infancy, but he does not cite the source of his information (Pomeroy, 1971, 1973). Little boys, of course, cannot ejaculate before the approach of puberty, but ejaculation is not necessary for orgasm to occur.

When the baby is between one and two years old, if one peers at the baby's eye through a tube (we use the cores from rolls of paper towels), holding the tube slightly away from one's own eye so that the eye is illuminated and visible to the baby, and says something like "Hi!" to make sure the baby is paying attention, the baby will be delighted and will want to do likewise. One hands the tube to the baby, who plants it squarely between the eyes. The baby knows something is wrong but is unable to do anything about it. Babies of this age generally know that they have two eyes, but they apparently experience seeing as being centered between the eyes. We have named this behavior the *Cyclops effect* (Church, 1970). It is around age two that the baby becomes able to peer monocularly through a tube.

The degree of body integration achieved by late infancy or early toddlerhood does not provide a map adequate for the child to localize pain. There is no doubt that the pain is felt, but the child has no idea of its location. Parental questioning is likely to be of little avail, and only if the adult can see the source of the pain can anything be done about it immediately. Pediatricians learn to question babies and young children not with words but with probing fingers.

We have been emphasizing babies' discovery and integration of the body, but this by no means exhausts the sense of self. Infants are also developing a sense of self as person. One cannot quiz infants about their sense of personhood, but one can read it in their independence or dependence, in their self-assurance and assumption of competence, in their easy giving and receiving of affection. Babies find their qualities as persons reflected in the ways people act and react to them and very early learn a sense of worth or worthlessness.

Finally, let us remember that play patterns in late infancy can express a sense of self. The older infant may pretend to be a dog, or may simulate distress to get adult attention and petting. Note here the nonliteral quality and also the baby's readiness to accept the mock sympathy offered by the adult. Babies may pretend, or go along with adult pretense, to be invisible, or may hide just for the sake of being found. Such play with one's own identity implies that one has an identity to play with, a secure sense of self that one can set aside in full confidence of being able to return to it at any time. The self will undergo many elaborations and transformations in the years ahead, but it gets its start very early.

Another achievement of the sensorimotor period is the early development of language. Infants by definition cannot speak, but we can see in their behavior many precursors of spoken communication.

THE FOUNDATIONS OF LANGUAGE IN INFANCY

Beginning right after their baby's birth, most parents routinely and without thinking talk or sing to their baby while carrying out the business of caregiving. Babies, in short, serve as stimuli to adult vocalization—often, in fact, vocalization that parents would be most embarrassed to have overheard. One father we know changed his baby's diapers to the accompaniment of the Declaration of Independence, "Columbia, Gem of the Ocean," and "Ol' Man River," interspersed with doggerel rhymes based on the baby's name, and was quite mortified to learn that his performances were fully audible to the downstairs neighbors. We take it for granted, even though we have no hard evidence, that such parental vocalizing contributes to the baby's own eventual vocalizing and talking. At the very least, it can convey to the baby that the voice is a primary means of communication.

Up to the age of six or eight weeks, as we have said, babies themselves do not vocalize. This is not to say that they are soundless. They cry, fuss, belch, and hiccough, but they do not make voluntary vocal sounds. Around six to eight weeks—which coincides with the first social smiling—babies begin to produce what Arnold Gesell (Gesell, Thompson, and Amatruda, 1938) accurately de-

(© George Malave 1981/Stock, Boston)

Communication with an older sister. At around two months, infants respond to being spoken to and begin to vocalize. At three months, babbling matures from cooing and crowing to gurgling to a variety of vowel sounds; consonants then emerge and, by late infancy, long strings of diversified sounds.

scribed as "small, throaty sounds." Around age two months, when an adult leans over and talks to the baby face to face—it matters little what is said, and gibberish works as well as speech—the baby writhes around and works his or her mouth as though struggling to answer. Some babies, as we have said, even squeeze out a few strangled sounds. We have two mothers' accounts of their baby's beginning vocalizations:

> She [age two months, three weeks] has begun to practice hearty crows of glee when approached or offered food, or at the dog. She also makes guttural sounds of all volumes when playing by herself, along with sounds of impatience when she can't reach or do a thing she wants to.

> Ruth [age two months, six days] makes cooing noises, but only when she is being played with and spoken to, and on these occasions only when she is comfortable, happy, and very engrossed in the person playing with her. Ruth has to work herself up before she coos. First she has to be totally engrossed in the person talking to her, then she smiles, then she strains her head, mouth, and body, opens her mouth soundlessly several times, and then, finally, coos. The later coos come easier and closer together (Church, 1978, pp. 10, 168).

Later, these exchanges become the foundation for babbled conversations between parent and infant.

At about three months, the baby's babbling starts to mature in a fairly stable sequence. Cooing and crowing give way to gurgling, and gurgling to a variety of vowel sounds. Consonants emerge among the vowels, and by late infancy the baby produces long strings of diversified sounds, including, as we have said, imitations of inanimate sounds. Around six months, many babies begin to indicate hunger or mild distress by sounds made up of *m*'s and *n*'s ("mnamnamna," for instance), which some observers consider to be precursors to the universal "Ma-ma" for "mother." Indeed, many mothers are totally convinced that the baby is now calling them by name.

There is a long-standing belief that babies all over the world make the same babbling sounds in the same sequence. However, by late infancy we can observe *phonetic drift;* that is, babbling begins to take on the intonations and rhythms of the baby's native tongue.

Games of imitation between parent and infant undoubtedly feed into linguistic development. Parents usually begin by imitating the sounds their babies make, but babies end up imitating sounds—eventually words—that their parents produce. Remember that we have no real explanation for imitation. We have related it to empathy but, since we have no explanation for empathy either, this is simply to substitute one mystery for another.

Although babbling may be a forerunner of speech, it is not an effective means of communication. The baby's first form of communication is crying, which in the beginning is nothing more than an automatic, uncontrolled outpouring of distress. The angry crying of resistance to evening bedtime seems closer to true communication, but it does not last long. More nearly deliberate communication appears at about nine months when babies begin screaming as a way of letting the world know that they want something. This screaming is often accompanied by straining with arms and body in the general direction of what it is the baby wants. Characteristically, the adult responds by offering the baby likely satisfiers. Wrong guesses are met by brief, angry shrieks. When the right object is provided, the baby accepts it with a grunt of satisfaction.

At a more advanced but still prelinguistic stage, babies communicate with concrete behavior or with tokens. When a baby tries to climb into its highchair, this signifies hunger. The baby may bring an adult a phonograph record it wants to hear played—babies are remarkably accurate at recognizing individual records, presumably on the basis of each label's unique physiognomy. Or babies may bring a coat or sweater as a way of saying that they want to go outside. Notice the analogy here with the dog that scratches at the door to be let out, brings its leash to be taken for a walk, or brings its dish as a way of asking to be fed.

Even though the baby does not yet speak, language learning has begun to take hold in late infancy. This is shown in the baby's **receptive language,** the ability to understand a great deal of what it hears. Babies respond appropriately to key words signaling routines ("bath time") or standard games ("Where's the baby?") and to simple or even rather complex commands and requests ("Please hand me my socks"). We have a mother's account of her daughter at ten months, one week:

> Debbie surprised us today by bringing "Red Fox" on request from her room to the dining room (a distance of 40 feet [13m] through several rooms—and a major feat for her to creep the distance both ways, dragging this 12-inch-high [30+ cm] animal with her on the return trip). We had not realized she knew its "name" or that she could distinguish between it and "Bear" and "Heffalump," but she demonstrated to us then that she knew each of these equally well by bringing them, too (Church, 1978, p 42).

There is yet another potential form of language learning in late infancy that many parents fail to detect and so fail to provide appropriate contingent reinforcement for. This is the baby's asking for the names of things. Babies do this by pointing at something and making an interrogatory sound like "Ugh?" or "Duh?" The observant parent supplies the name, and the baby gives a small grunt of acknowledgment. This behavior may not be essential for later language learning, but it provides one more occasion for meaningful and satisfying interaction between parent and child. It also suggests that the baby has arrived at a truly basic insight: Things have names.

Our account of language in infancy ends here. We shall pick up this strand again in Chapter 9, where we introduce you to **productive language**, actual talking, and to some of the complexities in theorizing about language. In later chapters, we shall talk about the special features of language characteristic of successive age periods.

At the beginning of this chapter, we listed six accomplishments that Piaget assigns to the sensorimotor stage. We have talked very little about one of these, *intentionality* or *purposiveness*. The reason is that this is a quality of behavior rather than a category of action. We hope it has been obvious throughout this chapter that a good part of what the baby does is done intentionally and purposively.

INFANT COGNITION AND INFANT "INTELLIGENCE"

We cannot close this chapter without further mention of infant scales, some of which purport to measure the baby's current intellectual status and even to predict future ability.

Most infant scales were spawned during the psychometric era, 1900 to 1940, when attention was given mostly to the easily observable and scorable physical and motor aspects of development. For this reason, baby scales are better measures of physical well-being than of intellectual ability. (The few cognitive measures in such scales, such as reaching around a transparent barrier, have been included in our description of infant cognition.) Most scales were conceived before the Piagetian revolution and so have not had the benefit of more recent discoveries about early cognition. Remem-

ber that some of Piaget's most important observations were made during the 1920s and 1930s, but his ideas did not gain acceptance and respectability in the United States until the 1960s.

Infant tests may be useful in detecting severe organic impairment (Escalona, 1954; Honzik, 1976; McCall, 1977; Stott and Ball, 1965; Yang and Bell, 1975). This may mean that they have a latent predictive value that is masked when they point to a problem that then gets solved, spoiling the correlation between infant-scale score and measures made later in life. On the other hand, there are a great many reasons to suspect that infant scales give far from valid measures of intellectual ability. Stranger anxiety, we can say from experience, can be an impediment to valid testing. Babies vary greatly from day to day in their alertness, their good cheer or irritability, and their interest in the test materials. The functions tested in infancy bear little perceptible relation to the problems that tax our wits in later years. Perhaps most important, the tests are insensitive to individual differences in rates of development, which vary widely. The concentration on averages may obscure important differences. For instance, the curve of average growth does not show the universal discontinuity of growth rate; it was only when investigators began looking at individual growth curves that discontinuity became obvious.

More recent tests for infants and young children have incorporated Piagetian tasks, such as measures of object permanence and tool use, and may eventually offer useful assessment techniques for infant functioning (Mehrabian and Williams, 1971; Uzgiris and Hunt, 1974). Until someone has demonstrated beyond question the validity of infant tests, they should be taken seriously only when they point to problems that something can be done about. If they are used merely to classify babies, they may generate a **self-fulfilling prophecy.** Parents' treatment of their children is influenced by the parents' hopes and fears. Especially in the case of fears, the way parents treat their children may make their most doleful expectations come true. Therefore, babies classified in some way as defective by such techniques as infant tests may simply not receive the tender loving care they need and may end up truly defective.

In Chapter 7, we interrupt our chronological account of development to take a closer look at how a wide range of environmental conditions may be associated with a wide range of developmental variations. We ended Chapter 2 with the conclusion that genetic endowments work together with environmental influences in regulating development. In the next chapter, we hope to demonstrate the potency, for better or for worse, of several environmental forces.

SUMMARY

1. The developing human being has to learn to adapt to and cope with a huge variety of situations. The basic capacity for making sense of the world in order to act effectively is called cognition.

2. Jean Piaget designates the first two years of life as the sensorimotor stage of cognitive development. He assigns six major cognitive achievements to this period—knowledge of familiar objects, means-end relations, intentionality, the sense of a separate identity, the beginnings of language, and object permanence. Piaget proposes that equilibration, or preserving balance between established knowledge and new experiences, is a key mechanism for mental change.

3. Empathy is the earliest mode of perception. There is no differentiation between self and surroundings, so that we participate in external events as if we were a segment of a universal organism. Another characteristic of early perception and thinking is egocentrism; the baby relates everything to its own wants and feelings, although there is only a limited sense of self. Infants display physiognomic perception, or a reaction to the global, overall, expressive qualities of things and situations. Infants also display realism, that is, difficulty distinguishing different kinds of reality: Experiences, dreams, pictures, and objects are intermingled into one domain. Picture realism—petting a pictured animal, for example— is particularly characteristic. Phenomenalism characterizes the sensorimotor stage as well: Children (and quite a few adults) never wonder what lies behind appearances. Object impermanence is one form of this:

Until around six or eight months, babies seem unaware that an object continues to exist once it has passed from view. Synesthesia is also present: Sight and hearing may be confused, for example. Conversely, the sense modalities need to be coordinated; the fragility of a soap bubble is not automatically apparent to an infant. Caressing textures and learning the feel of surfaces enhances such intersensory coordination.

4. By age two months, the baby can track a person or object within a 100-degree arc and coordinate sight and sound. At this time the baby begins to blink in response to an approaching object, even when supine. The visual cliff effect demonstrates the baby's early depth perception.

5. Once babies reach out to grasp—and especially when they become mobile—they are relentless explorers of everything within their reach. They are sensitive only to gross differences in size, and they have to learn a great deal by trial and error. Size-distance constancy is an aspect of infant perception. Probably, the infant exhibits it within a limited range that expands with increasing age and experience.

6. At about age seven months, infants first manifest means-end behavior by showing the ability to move a barrier to reach a desired object. They also begin to acquire object permanence—the realization that objects exist even when they are not in view. By late infancy, babies can hide an object and retrieve it a day or so later. Intentionality, or purposiveness, also becomes more and more evident during this period. Babies can be instructed by "showing" (observational learning, or modeling) or "shoving," manipulating the baby's body to achieve the desired result. "Shaping" (approaching a solution by stages) has not yet been shown to be an effective teaching technique.

7. Much of the infant's developing self-awareness centers on the part-by-part discovery of its body and the integration of these discoveries into a schema of the body as a whole. The process begins at about three months and progresses gradually. One especially important step is the infant's recognition of its reflection in a mirror, which occurs generally at around ten months. The infant also develops a sense of itself as a person, based largely on the way other people act and react to it.

8. During infancy, the baby begins to acquire the foundations of language. At about three months, babbling begins to mature in a fairly stable sequence—first combining vowel sounds, and then adding consonants. By late infancy, the baby produces long strings of diversified sounds that begin to take on the rhythms and intonations of its native tongue. The games of imitation that parent and child play undoubtedly feed

into linguistic progress. Older infants have acquired receptive language—the ability to understand much of what they hear said.

9. Infant scales have been devised to measure current intellectual status and even to predict future attainment. Most of these tests predate Piaget's work and thus do not benefit from his insights. While infant scales may depict developmental status, their long-range predictive value is limited.

KEY TERMS

accommodation, 205
assimilation, 205
cognition, 202
delayed-reaction experiment, 217
demand qualities or characters, 208
egocentrism, 206
empathy, 205
equilibration, 205

intersensory effects, 209
means-end relationship, 219
object permanence, 209
phenomenalism, 209
physiognomic perceiving, 207
picture realism, 208
productive language, 230
realism, 208

receptive language, 229
schema (schemata), 204
scheme, 205
self-fulfilling prophecy, 231
sensorimotor stage, 203
size-distance constancy, 218
synesthesia, 209
visual cliff effect, 211

SUGGESTED READINGS

Church, J. (ed.) *Three Babies: Biographies of Cognitive Development.* Westport, Conn.: Greenwood Press, 1978 (originally published, 1966). Diary accounts kept by their mothers of three babies' development to age two, with commentary by the editor.

Church, J. *Understanding Your Child From Birth to Three.* New York: Pocket Books, 1973. One psychologist's account of the early years, including practical issues in child care and sections on intellectual development.

Ginsburg, H., and Opper, S. *Piaget's Theory of Intellectual Development* (2nd ed.). Englewood Cliffs, N.J.: Prentice-Hall, 1979. A good general introduction to Piaget with detailed treatment of the sensorimotor stage of cognitive development.

Stone, L. J., Smith, H. T., and Murphy, L. B. (eds.). *The Competent Infant.* New York: Basic Books, 1973. A comprehensive handbook of research on infancy, including more than two hundred selections on all aspects of development during infancy. The book is being reissued in shorter editions dealing with specialized aspects of infant development.

CHAPTER 7

Early Influences on Development

235

" **J**ust as the twig is bent, the tree's inclined." Alexander Pope's eighteenth-century dictum nicely sums up an article of faith among many thinkers, that events in the child's earliest months and years can have important and enduring consequences for the whole of development. This is not a restatement of the environmentalist position in the nature-nurture controversy. It takes for granted that experience has an effect, but it stresses the significance of early experience as a foundation for later development.

Not everyone has shared this belief. During the 1930s and 1940s there were a number of **co-twin control studies,** in which one member of a pair of identical twins was given special training to see if this gave him or her a developmental advantage over the other twin. Prominent among such studies were those by Myrtle McGraw (whose identical twins turned out not to be identical; 1935) and by Arnold Gesell (Gesell and Thompson, 1941). The general conclusion from these studies was that special training gave only a temporary advantage, to be obliterated as soon as the untrained twin caught up maturationally. In fact, the training in motor skills, such as climbing, given by Gesell did not give the trained twin greater physical agility, but it seemed to give him a lasting edge in self-confidence and venturesomeness. Wayne Dennis, who propounded the concept of *autogenous* (that is, self-generated, or maturationally determined) *development,* tried a somewhat different approach (Dennis, 1941). Dennis simply withheld all extraneous stimulation, such as smiling at or talking to his twin pair on the basis of his theory that de-velopment was autogenous and that behavior would appear when the child was maturationally ready. Such stimulation was withheld until the children had spontaneously manifested whatever form of behavior was being studied. Dennis was convinced that his nonstimulation approach did not impede normal development; one of the twins turned out to be retarded, but Dennis wrote this off to congenital defect. As we shall see, Dennis radically changed his thinking in later years.

This special emphasis on the effects of environmental variations is of great practical concern to parents and educators and pediatricians. So too is the closely related issue of whether damage inflicted early in life can later be reversed. This question is of special significance for psychiatrists and clinical psychologists, whose work is often concerned with undoing the effects of unfavorable early experience.

The accumulating evidence has gradually strengthened the belief that at least extreme variations in early life can have marked effects on what kinds of people we become. Sigmund Freud found the secret of adult neurosis locked in the repressed memories of childhood events. Harry Harlow (1958, 1962), as we have seen, found that contact comfort was essential to emotional security in infant monkeys, but that normal social and sexual development further required play with peers. A group of experimenters working at the University of California at Berkeley (Bennett *et al.*, 1964; Krech, Rosenzweig, and Bennett, 1960; Wallace, 1974) demonstrated that rats' and mice's brain size and brain chemistry vary according to whether the animals are raised in psychologically stimulating or barren conditions. In general, we have come to view mammalian babies as highly plastic, to be shaped for better or worse by experience. Let us not forget, though, that the baby's own characteristics, actions, and reactions help determine the world's actions and reactions and how the baby incorporates various experiences.

As we pointed out in our discussion of attachment, some thinkers have proposed what is called the *critical-period hypothesis*. You will recall that during the embryonic period of prenatal development, each organ system has its own critical period in the developmental timetable, during which its formation is most rapid and is most susceptible to stimulating or damaging influences. By analogy, some theorists have reasoned that there are critical periods in postnatal development—critical periods not only for attachment, but also for toilet training, learning to talk, and learning to read (Scott, 1962). According to this view, once the critical period for a given function is past, that function must already have developed or it will be seriously impaired. Insofar as the critical-period hypothesis assumes a fixed biological timetable of psychological development, we beg to differ, and before this chapter is over we hope to have shown why.

We prefer to follow the reasoning of Theodore Schneirla and Jay Rosenblatt (1963), who hold that there is a fairly stable sequence of normal development, but that this sequence is accounted for by the fact that new capabilities depend on the presence of earlier ones. Here the matter of precise timing is of less impor-

tance. This leads to an optimistic view of the possibility of compensating for early deficiencies and reversing the effects of damaging experiences.

We now come to the question of what sorts of variation in early experience make a difference, and the following sections are organized around the themes that researchers have singled out for study. By rights, the first of these should be cultural and subcultural variations in patterns of child rearing and the difference these make in emotional and cognitive outlooks. It is obvious that members of different cultural groups can have profoundly differing world views, but we lack the information needed to make reliable generalizations about how these differences are related to child care practices. We therefore begin with variations within the normal range in Western-style cultures.

There is great room for argument about what is meant by the "normal range." We choose to by-pass this argument and define normality negatively. We use "normality" to refer to ordinary family life *un*marked by signs of gross pathology, *un*likely to run seriously afoul of the law, and sufficiently well socialized to avoid ostracism or hostility from neighbors. In short, normal families are those that manage to remain, despite inevitable tensions and animosities, a functioning part of their community. Even so, wide variations are possible. These variations have been studied in terms both of broad sociocultural factors, such as economic status, and of specific child-rearing practices such as toilet training, weaning, discipline, or responsiveness, singly or in combination.

We then move away from normal var-

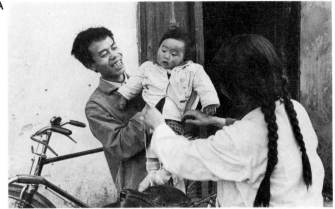

*(© Eric Kroll
1979/Taurus Photos)*

A. A Bushman mother and child. **B.** A Puerto Rican family in New York City. **C.** An Asian family. Although different cultural groups have different world views, we do not have sufficient information to generalize reliably about how these differences influence child-care practices.

(© Melvin Konner)

(© Jim Anderson/Woodfin Camp & Assoc.)

iations and discuss the effects both of severe restrictions on the child's early experience, as in institution rearing, and of less massive restrictions, as in congenital blindness or deafness. Next, we look at the spectrum of neglect, rejection, and abuse. We continue with a discussion of the evidence that the effects of such early distortions of experience can be wholly or partially overcome. After that, we look at studies designed to enrich the early experience of children whose chances for full development are in jeopardy.

NORMAL VARIATIONS IN CHILD REARING

One has only to think of the adults one knows to realize how diverse people from the same cultural community can be. It would be all too easy to surmise that such diversity is the simple product of hereditary variations. However, when we compare differences in approaches to child rearing, we find systematic differences in such areas as intellectual ability and temperament clearly related to rearing conditions. As we have said, there are two approaches to studying normal variations. One focuses on broad sociocultural conditions and the other on the specifics of child rearing. We begin with the former.

Sociocultural Surveys

There can be no doubt that social conditions such as wealth or poverty have profound effects on children's development. However, to say this is none too illuminating psychologically. It points only to general statistical trends and not to psychological processes. It does not help us understand why some children from economically and socially deprived backgrounds make out just fine, and why children who, given every imaginable advantage, make total messes of their lives. Even when we narrow our focus somewhat, as in studies of family size or birth order, we still come up with reliable statistical relationships and a minimum of psychological insight. Just for the record, children from big families are less likely to be bright (as measured by IQ and academic achievement) than are children from small families, and first-born children fare better psychologically than later-born children. In general, that is. There are exceptions, and we do not pretend to understand either the exceptions or the main trends.

We believe that the closest link between psychology and sociological surveys is to be found in the work of Bettye Caldwell and her associates (Bradley and Caldwell, 1976, 1977, 1979; Elardo, Bradley, and Caldwell, 1975, 1977). These workers have devised an instrument called **Home Observation for Measurement of the Environment (HOME)**, which seeks to define favorable and less favorable family settings. The HOME inventory, in its most recent version, rates family environments along eight dimensions: (1) stimulation through toys, games, and reading materials; (2) language stimulation; (3) properties of the physical environment such as safety, cleanliness, cheerfulness, pleasantness of outdoor surroundings, and spaciousness; (4) pride, affection, and warmth; (5) stimulation of academic behavior (color naming, rhymes, spatial vocabulary, counting, word recognition); (6)

modeling and encouraging socially mature behavior; (7) variety of stimulation (music, art materials, outings, and the like); and (8) the sparing use of physical punishment (Bradley and Caldwell, 1979). Ratings on these scales are good predictors of IQ: HOME scores at ages five to six correlate .58 with IQs at ages six to ten. In a study of fifty low-income children, HOME scores at age one correlated significantly with school achievement five to nine years later, yielding correct classifications in 68 percent of the cases; the HOME scores of siblings tested at least ten months apart correlated .86 (van Doornick *et al.*, 1981). Frankenburg (1981) asserts that the HOME scale is the best predictor available, and can be further enhanced by including such easily overlooked factors as plants and pets and whether the mother has ever tried new recipes gleaned from the newspaper. It is clear that the HOME inventory shades into our next category, that of observed child-rearing practices.

Studies of Child-Rearing Practices

For a number of years, investigators concentrated on the possible effects of single, isolated child-care variables, such as breast-feeding versus bottle feeding, age at weaning, timing and manner of toilet training, styles of discipline, and so forth. As Bettye Caldwell (1964) pointed out, this proved to be an unproductive strategy. No single variable seemed to have a reliable effect on the child's subsequent development. What was needed was study of the whole complex pattern of interactions in order to understand what makes child rearing go well or badly.

One set of studies, focusing on the concept of **competence** (to be defined in a moment), has been carried out by Burton White and associates (White, 1975; White and Watts, 1973). The chief conclusion of these studies was that competent mothers produce competent children. Competent mothers are described as those who enjoy being with their children, who are readily available when needed, who are able to structure the material environment in keeping with their children's interests and capacities, and who respond verbally to their children's preverbal signals. Less competent mothers either give their children insufficient time or else overwhelm them with unwanted attention and intrusions. Note here the importance of letting the child set the pace and exercise an appropriate degree of control. Competent children are well developed cognitively and linguistically, show planning and persistence in their activities, make their feelings known, and are effective in getting the attention and help of adults.

Although the White studies have received a great deal of respectful attention in the public press, they have come under increasing criticism from developmentalists. For instance, White (1975) asserts without qualification that children spontaneously and autonomously toilet train themselves at age two, an assertion that many professionals and parents have cause to question. White enjoins parents not to let their children have temper tantrums, but he does not tell them how to accomplish this near-miracle. White almost espouses the doctrine of autogenous development for the first eight months of infancy, whereas his own research demonstrates the importance of early social stimulation, as in the development of visually guided reaching and grasping. We also know that these early months are crucial in the formation of attachment. White's definition of child competence has been called into question as giving insufficient weight to a capacity for caring, cooperation, and similar virtues.

A smaller, more sharply defined study of competence by Alison Clarke-Stewart (1973) was based on home observations and tests, analyzing mother-infant interactions from nine to eighteen months. The subjects were thirty-six low-SES mothers and their first-born babies. As expected, maternal competence was highly correlated with the competence of babies at eighteen months. In this study, the child's competence was defined in terms of consistently high scores on measures of intellectual ability, language skill, adaptability to new situations, positive emotions, and strong attachment to the mother. Maternal competence was defined in terms of being warm and loving, stimulating and enriching, and—once again—contingently responsive, that is, showing appropriate and well-timed responses to the baby's behavior. *Contingent responsiveness* is another way of saying that mothers can let the baby take the lead in achieving synchrony, in learning to dance well together.

The less competent mothers spent more time attending to their babies' physical needs and restricting their babies' activities, to the neglect of "educational" interactions.

Girls were judged more competent than boys, being more socially oriented, linguistically advanced, and positively involved with the mother. On the other hand, mothers of boys expressed more

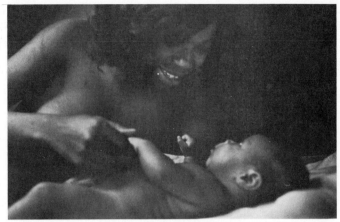

(© Marlis Müller)

Maternal competence is considered to be a combination of factors. Being warm and loving, as well as stimulating and enriching, contributes to competent mothering. Also important is the mother's ability to be contingently responsive, that is, to show appropriate and well-timed responses to the baby's behavior, at times taking the baby's lead in communication.

positive attitudes toward their sons than did mothers of girls toward their daughters.

Note that this excellent study has its limitations. It deals only with low-SES subjects, follows children only to age one and a half, and does not consider the role of fathers. In a later paper, Clarke-Stewart (1978) hypothesized that the influence of fathers is mainly indirect, in terms of the emotional interactions between them and their wives. This may apply in families where the major responsibility for child care is assigned to the mother, but we need more information about the growing number of families in which the father, too, is a significant caregiver.

Various attempts have been made to formalize the description of differing patterns of child rearing. Perhaps the best known of these is Earl Schaefer's (1965) *spherical model.* In this scheme, the parents' treatment of the child is scored on three intersecting dimensions of acceptance–rejection, psychological control–psychological autonomy, and firm control–lax control. Within the "conceptual space" defined by these three dimensions, one can locate points standing for such parental orientations as acceptance of individuality, loving involvement, protectiveness, intrusiveness, and hostile indifference. Ingenious as this scheme is, it is obviously incomplete. It leaves out of account cognitive stimulation, language, and the baby as stimulus *to* as well as object *of* parental behavior.

DEVELOPMENT IN CONDITIONS OF SEVERE DEPRIVATION

The model for studies of the effects of growing up in conditions of extreme psychological **deprivation** is the comparison of children reared in foundling homes and similar institutions with children reared in normal family settings. Pioneering studies in this field, notably those by René Spitz (1945, 1946), emphasized the theme of "materal deprivation," the devastating effect on babies of not having a stable one-to-one relationship with a loving adult (see also Goldfarb, 1945; Provence and Lipton, 1962). Critics of this view pointed out that institution-reared babies were deprived of a great deal more than mother figures. They lacked varied sensory stimulation, playthings, opportunities to explore interesting spaces, stimulation of

positive emotions, and models for language development. However, in the absence of one-to-one attachment, babies seem unable to take advantage of opportunities for stimulation. Provence and Lipton (1962) observed that institution-reared children responded little or not at all to stimuli unless there was an adult with whom to share them. We shall talk later about a partial exception to this principle. First, however, we examine the general picture of deprivation.

The sort of natural experiment in which institution-reared babies are compared with home-reared ones has a thirteenth-century antecedent in an account by Salimbene of an experiment by Frederick II of Sicily that had unforeseen results:

> . . . He wanted to find out what kind of speech and what manner of speech children would have when they grew up if they spoke to no one beforehand. So he bade foster mothers and nurses to suckle the children, to bathe and wash them, but in no way to prattle with them, or to speak to them, for he wanted to learn whether they would speak the Hebrew language, which was the oldest, or Greek, or Latin, or Arabic, or perhaps the language of their parents, of whom they had been born. But he laboured in vain because the children all died. For they could not live without the petting and joyful faces and loving words of their foster mothers. And so the songs are called "swaddling songs" which a woman sings while she is rocking the cradle, to put the child to sleep, and without them a child sleeps badly and has no rest (Ross and MacLaughlin, 1949).

There have been numerous well-documented accounts in recent times of children growing up in institutions that offered them a minimum of psychological stimulation, but all such studies have been subject to serious methodological criticisms of one kind or another. We shall therefore cite in detail the findings of only the most recent such study, executed with great care but still open to criticism for its almost exclusive reliance on infant-scale scores and IQs as dependent variables. This study, carried out by Wayne Dennis (1973) and his associates, is notable because it fairly well confirms the findings of earlier studies that Dennis himself had once dismissed as worthless.

The *Crèche* Study

Crèche is the French word for crib or cradle, as in Nativity displays at Christmas, and, by extension, for any institution for the care of young children. In his book *Children of the Crèche* (1973), Dennis compares the development of children and of a sample of female adults raised almost from birth in the well-meaning but psychologically barren environment of a Lebanese foundling home with that of children reared in more favorable circumstances.

To get an idea of what psychological barrenness consists of, you should know that the foundlings from birth to age one spent most of their time in bassinets. They were fed by bottle in the bassinets and were removed only for daily bathing and changing. There was a ratio of about ten infants to one caregiver. Dennis describes the caregivers as "ignorant, indifferent, and apathetic." Even after the babies were liberated from their bassinets, they had few playthings, a minimum of human contact and snuggling,

and little emotional and linguistic stimulation. They had virtually no contact with the world outside the walls of the *Crèche*.

To measure intellectual status, Dennis used the Cattell Infant Scale, which is essentially nonverbal, with babies up to age two, and a Lebanese adaptation of the Stanford-Binet test with children past age two. These tests yielded score distributions with home-reared Lebanese children just like those of normal American children. The foundlings, illegitimate or otherwise unwanted babies abandoned on the *Crèche* doorstep shortly after birth, could thus be compared with established developmental norms. A second comparison group consisted of "dependents," babies and young children who had spent varying periods in ordinary circumstances but who were lodged temporarily in the *Crèche* for family reasons such as parental illness or an economic crisis.

The foundlings had an average IQ or DQ (developmental quotient, as baby-test scores are usually called) of about 53, as compared with 92 for dependents and 100 for the general population of children living at home.

To understand the findings that follow, you should know that the foundlings were transferred from the *Crèche* to boarding schools at about age six. The girls were sent to a drab, cloistered institution run, like the *Crèche*, by nuns. There they received a smattering of academic instruction and a great deal of training in domestic chores of the kind needed to operate the *Crèche* or the boarding school itself. The school also enrolled dependents and day students, or externs, who were given standard academic programs. The girl foundlings showed an eventual rise in IQ, by age fifteen or sixteen, to an average of 59, as compared with 85 for dependents and 96 for externs.

Conditions were very different in the boys' boarding school. There they had lay teachers, male and female, as well as nuns and monks. They learned both academic and vocational skills and had considerable contact with the outside, everyday world, in which they expected in due time to find a place. The stimulation in the boys' school did not completely undo the effects of the first six years, but male foundlings tested at age ten had a mean IQ of 81, statistically reliably higher than that of the girls. Male dependents at the school had a mean IQ of 95.

Dennis was able to trace into adulthood (ages sixteen to thirty-five) thirty-five females who had lived at the *Crèche* and graduated from the boarding school. These women had a mean IQ of 59, with a range from 30 to 77. They showed a high incidence of psychiatric disturbance, and most lived and worked in institutional settings. Comparable follow-up data for males were not available, apparently because the young men were simply absorbed into Lebanese society and so lost to view.

In 1956, Lebanon legalized adoption, and the *Crèche* thereafter served mainly as a way station between abandonment and adoption. Boys and girls adopted into Lebanese families had an average IQ of 85 when first tested and of 92 two years later. Those adopted by American families could be tested only once and had a mean IQ of 85. However, age at adoption—which obviously relates to the length of time spent in the foundling home—proved an important variable.

Those adopted before age two into Lebanese families had a mean IQ of 95, and those adopted before age two into American families averaged 97, not greatly different from the American national mean of 100. The differences in IQ between girls and boys in boarding school, between adopted and nonadopted children, and between early- and late-adopted children all bear on the topic of overcoming the ill effects of early deprivation.

Effects of Rearing in Less Barren Institutional Settings

It should not be concluded that all foundling homes are like the *Crèche*. In Great Britain, for instance, the findings from early studies of institution rearing were taken seriously (in the United States, unfortunately, there has been more debate than action), and far more humane and homelike institutions have evolved. Children raised in such institutions have normal IQs. Indeed, in certain institutions where staff members are given a great deal of autonomy in their dealings with the children, the children's mean IQ is 112.9, well above the average. There is one inescapable weakness in these institutions, however. There is lack of continuity in relations with caregivers, which limits opportunities to form one-to-one attachments. As compared with a sample of home-reared working-class children and with another sample of children who had been adopted from the institution or reclaimed by their parents, four-and-a-half-year-olds who had been reared in institutions from shortly after birth showed such problems as shallow emotions, poor peer relations, temper tantrums, clinging, and poor concentration

(Tizard and Rees, 1975). The other groups were by no means problem free, but the difficulties listed above stood out among the institution children. This does not point to the effects of "maternal deprivation" as such, but it does suggest the need for stable attachment figures. We have spoken of one-to-one relationships, but of course a single adult can serve as attachment figure for several children, and children can form multiple attachments, as in an ordinary family. The key issue here appears to be continuity of interaction with a particular caregiver or set of caregivers.

The best institution care, however, probably cannot substitute for adoption. The British institution children were probably doomed to stay put until adulthood because they bore the "stigma" of being black or racially mixed. Fortunately, we are witnessing a slow change in consciousness on the part of adults, who are becoming willing to adopt previously "unadoptable" children—not only those who differ from the adult in racial or ethnic background, but also those who are physically or mentally impaired. Adoption agencies, too, are becoming more relaxed about their standards for "acceptable" adoptive parents. All the evidence indicates that the sooner we can remove children from institutions and place them into private families (including those headed by single adults), the better off we all will be. Apart from compassion for the blighted lives to which many institution children seem fated, we must reckon on the fantastically high costs to society at large of caring for them. As a corollary, it seems a good idea to spend what is needed to provide more and better pregnancy counseling and services, including sex education and birth control.

(© Ken Heyman)

An orphanage in the U.S.S.R. No matter how good the institution, the lack of continuity in relations with caregivers creates such problems as shallow emotions, poor peer relations, tantrums, clinging, and poor concentration.

Feral Children

Down through the years, there have appeared in the popular and learned literature numerous accounts of *feral children*, thought to have been reared by wild animals (Romulus and Remus of

Latin legend are the prototypes), and of the characteristics they have acquired as the result of animal rearing. All such accounts seem to be erroneous or downright fraudulent (Evans, 1958; Ogburn and Bose, 1959). By all means enjoy movies like *The Wild Child*, but do not imagine that you are witnessing the attempted humanization of a feral child. There are, of course, well-documented cases of **"closet children,"** those who have been reared in isolation, and we shall talk about them when we discuss the possibility of reversing the effects of unfavorable rearing conditions. But we will waste no more time on phantom feral children.

Blindness and Other Obstacles to Normal Stimulation

The kinds of deprivation we have been talking about so far are imposed from without, but there are other sorts that are organically built in. Such is the case with blindness, deafness, and other sensory defects (Fraiberg, 1977; Freedman, 1975). Taking blindness as representative, we have first to make a distinction between congenital blindness, which is present at birth, and adventitious blindness, which is caused at later ages by illness or accident. Some experts would extend the congenital period to as late as age three or four, reasoning that visual experience of lesser duration does not allow the child to form a stable image of reality. In any case, adventitious blindness is inevitably physically and psychologically traumatic, but, with emotional recovery, the person who has lost his or her eyesight can learn to lead a normal life. It is quite different with

(© Mitchell Payne, Jeroboam)

Congenitally blind children are liable to suffer serious developmental impairment unless they are given early special care focusing on tactile, oral, and auditory experience.

the congenitally blind, who are liable to suffer serious developmental impairment unless they are given early special care and training focusing on tactile, oral, and auditory experience. Parents of congenitally blind children are often unaware of the need for such extra early stimulation. Fortunately, congenital blindness is a rare condition and total blindness even rarer—only about 10 percent of those classified as legally blind are totally without sight.

Most of the restrictions imposed by blindness can be overcome, and so can those associated with other impairments—deafness, being crippled, being born without arms or legs. What is essential in all sorts of organic defects is the recognition that special help is needed from the beginning. We have to beware the self-fulfilling prophecy and bear in mind that, in keeping with the principle of caretaking casualty, good care can offset all sorts of potential handicaps.

THE IMPACT OF NEGLECT, REJECTION, AND ABUSE

In general, growing up in an institution is less desirable than growing up in a family, but some well-run institutions offer more benign developmental environments than do some families.

Some parents, simply because they do not understand the needs of infants, neglect those needs. This lack of understanding may extend to not even knowing when one's baby is sick. Other parents, more self-centered or beset by one or more problems, cannot be bothered with giving their infants proper care. Going a step further, there are parents who, for whatever reason, resent or dislike their babies and want no part of them. Such parents grudgingly give the baby the necessary minimum of physical care, but nothing more. And then there are parents who actively inflict physical harm on their babies, beating and battering them, sometimes to death.

Failure to Thrive

Both neglect and emotional rejection can have grave consequences. The most common is called **failure to thrive.** Neglected or rejected babies with no detectable organic pathology do not grow or develop normally. Instead, they show signs of wasting and misery and are unable to make human contact. Most cases of failure to thrive are clearly related to psychological disturbance in the parents, often chronic marital discord. Note that failure to thrive may entail malnutrition, itself a serious threat to development.

However, here as elsewhere we must look for circularity. Parental disturbance is likely to interact with some infant characteristics to produce the neglect and rejection that underlie failure to thrive. Sameroff and Chandler (1975) report two typical patterns, although there are probably numerous others. First, babies with a high level of energy seem to have an abrasive effect on chronically tense mothers. Needless to say, the baby's energy level will decline markedly if failure to thrive sets in, but by then it may be too late. The second pattern results from the pairing of a passive baby with a passive, depressed mother. We do not know what becomes of babies who suffer failure to thrive, but we may be excused for feeling pessimistic.

Child Battering

Beyond neglect and rejection lies a problem of scandalous dimensions, the **battered child syndrome** (U.S. Department of Health and Human Services, 1981). Child battering has been with us from the beginning of human history, but in recent years, in countries that pride themselves on being civilized, it has attracted great public attention and dismay (Kempe and Kempe, 1978; Kempe and Helfer, 1980).

Many theories and observations have been published on the subject of child battering. We begin with the finding that a large proportion of child batterers were themselves battered children, and its converse, that battered children grow up to be child batterers (Spinetta and Rigler, 1972). Note again that this correlation can equally well support a biogenic and an environmentalist interpretation of child battering.

Yet another finding leaves us with a chicken-and-egg dilemma. This is that battered children tend to be below average in intellectual ability. Does this mean that battering produces retardation or that children of low ability invite abuse? The only sure fact is that some parents beat and even torture their children (Fraser, 1974).

Clinicians working with women who have seriously harmed their children report consistently that such mothers are emotionally immature (Helfner, 1973), have poor control over aggressive impulses when under stress, and complain about their babies' crying. The crying seems to the mother to signify rejection, and she, already low in self-esteem, reacts with anger. Battering mothers report a sense of betrayal, in that their babies have failed to give them the love they expected and deserved.

A pair of studies (Smith and Hanson, 1974; Smith, Hanson, and Noble, 1974) examined the characteristics of 134 English children battered seriously enough to land them in the hospital. These studies also examined the characteristics of the children's parents. The experimenters used as a comparison group children hospitalized for other reasons and the parents of these chil-

dren. The studies do not settle the question of causality, but the findings are intriguing nonetheless. They dispel two misconceptions that were common for some years: first, that fathers (or other men attached to the mothers) are more likely to be serious batterers than are mothers; and second, that the battered child is unlikely to have battered siblings. According to the data of these studies, mothers are at least as likely as fathers to batter their children, and 31 of the 134 children had a sibling who was known to have been battered (the authors suspected additional, unreported cases).

We look first at the characteristics of the battered children. It has been proposed that battered children are "different," and that it is this differentness that provokes battering. The data of the studies provide some support for the hypothesis. As compared with the nonbattered hospitalized children or with children in general, the battered children had lower average developmental scores (similar to IQs): 89 versus 97; 16 percent showed failure to thrive as compared with 2 percent of the comparison group; 24 percent were of low birth weight as compared with the national rate of 5.6 percent; 7.46 percent had serious birth defects as compared with 1.75 percent in the general population; and the battered children cried more than the comparison group. Also, the battered children were less excitable and lively, and they slept better and were less tired during the day.

The battering parents, as compared with the comparison parents, were of lower SES; they were younger; 29 percent of the fathers and 14 percent of the mothers had criminal records; they had

(© David R. White 1980/Woodfin Camp & Assoc.)

Child battering is a widespread problem that in recent years has attracted great public attention. Significantly, many child batterers were themselves physically abused as children.

lower IQs; and they scored higher on measures of neuroticism. Children under age two are more likely to be battered than older children.

To judge by these studies, battering seems to occur at the intersection of parental characteristics, child characteristics, and situational stress, such as marital strain or prolonged crying or fretfulness on the part of the child. A study by Kadushin and Martin (1981) emphasizes the many interacting factors. Kadushin and Martin point out that many abusive parents first try nonviolent but ineffective methods of control and only then, in desperation, become severely violent.

A smaller study examined interactions between mothers and their battered babies in a controlled situation (Dietrich, Starr, and Kaplan, 1980). The experimental group consisted of fourteen low-SES mother-infant pairs who hospital personnel suspected were cases of abuse. The controls were fourteen comparable pairs in which the child had been admitted to the emergency room for non-traumatic reasons. Each group consisted of ten black mothers and four whites, and of six boys and eight girls. The mean age of the battered children was 5.1 months, with a range from 3.0 to 8.5 months; the control babies had a mean age of 5.4 months and a range of 3.0 to 9.1 months. There were no differences between the groups with respect to the number of mothers pregnant, the birth order of the baby, the babies' Apgar scores at birth, or the babies' birth weights. The mother-infant pairs were videotaped during ten-minute sessions in an observation booth, the mother having been instructed first to feed the baby and then to talk to or play with him or her. The control mothers provided more, and the experimental mothers less, tactual and auditory stimulation; varied tactual stimulation (patting, stroking, squeezing); rocking of their babies; and more baby talk. The battered babies had a mean score of 90 on the Bayley Mental Scale, as compared to 106 for the control-group babies; both groups, however, had a wide range of scores. Both groups of children were in poor physical condition, but the battered group had a significantly lower red blood cell count than the controls, suggesting iron-deficiency anemia, which may have meant that they were being fed nothing except milk. The authors point out that hemoglobin level correlates .53 with measures of motor development.

A Study by the National Center on Child Abuse and Neglect (1982) reports that there is also a high level of neglect and abuse of adolescents. This deserves to be noted but is not specifically germane to the present discussion of early influences.

We must also take note of a quite different sort of brutality that rarely comes to the attention of the medical or police authorities. Even today, there are parents who systematically beat their children, not in retaliation for wrongdoing but in the honest belief that it is their duty to "break the child's spirit," much on the analogy of "breaking" a wild horse. Implicit here is the notion that children are by nature evil and uncontrolled, and that without the early and unquestionable establishment of parental (especially paternal) authority the child will run diabolically wild.

We now face the problem of what can be done to help battered children. There is evidence that psychotherapy with the parents works in some cases. It seems to work best when the therapist fills the role of the understanding, accepting parent that the batterer never knew. The most effective kind of therapy may be to work with groups of parents who have voluntarily joined together to seek new ways of coping with child rearing. But therapeutic and educational measures do not always work. What are the alternatives?

One obvious answer is to remove children from their abusive parents. This simple solution runs head on into several difficulties. First, improbable though it may seem, battered children and battering parents may love each other very deeply, and to separate them is to damage them both. It is probably only in the most extreme cases, when the child's actual survival may be at stake, that removal should be considered. But here we meet a second difficulty: What does one do with the children who have been taken away from their dangerous parents? Even the best of foundling homes are hardly a promising refuge, although, as we have said, they may be preferable to the worst parental homes.

Foster care is a possibility, although some basic structural problems have been turning up in our systems of foster care. Most obviously, some foster parents are in the business only for the money, and they provide minimally for the child's material needs and not at all for emotional or intellectual ones. Another problem is that, as long as there is a chance that children will be returned to their biological families, or that they will be adopted by someone other than the foster family, systematic attempts are made to keep children and foster parents from becoming too closely attached. This is accomplished by setting a time limit on any child's stay in a particular foster home. Many children spend their childhoods being shuttled from foster home to foster home, and many are wrecked in the process. This is not because there is anything wrong with any of the individual foster homes, but because the child is denied a chance to form lasting emotional bonds. In fact, after a few years of pillar-to-post treatment, the child may become incapable of forming attachments, and may become a chronic discipline problem who has to be shipped from placement to placement. We can think offhand of several criminals who had such backgrounds, and we wish some budding young investigator would discover whether there is a link between repeated changes of foster homes and a career as a criminal.

All in all, we see only limited hope for today's generation of battered children. We can only continue to pray and preach that parents have children only when they fully understand the often harsh demands of parenthood and are willing to endure them for the sake of the rewards that successful parenthood brings. Meanwhile, we can wish for a more humane society, one in which violence is not celebrated as the quick and easy solution to problems. From youth gangs to organized crime to the "warfare state," we are immersed in a climate of violence, and we can take it for granted that this will affect parents' dealing with children—even children whom the parents basically love.

REVERSIBILITY OF EFFECTS AND PREVENTION OF DISTURBANCE

We now turn to the related topics of what can be done for children who have already been damaged by deprivation and how we can intervene in advance to give children from unfavorable environments a good chance to develop well.

Reversibility

Despite our gloom about the fate of children who have been physically or psychologically deprived, neglected, rejected, or abused, we have already seen in Wayne Dennis's *Crèche* findings how some degree of improvement can be achieved by moving children from an un-

satisfactory environment to a better one. We do not know that the boys who spent their first six years in the *Crèche* ever fulfilled all their human potentialities, but their boarding school experience at least helped them live ordinary lives. Those children who were adopted into families showed even more striking gains in IQ, although we must remember that adoption before age two worked appreciably better than adoption after age two. We do not know in detail how the adopted children fared in their new homes, but the indications that Dennis gave us suggest that they did well.

A special kind of deprivation is experienced by *closet children*, those brought up at home in conditions of severe isolation. Two cases illustrate the possibility of recovery from this sort of mistreatment.

One closet child, Isabelle, was first discovered after she had been shut away with her deaf-mute mother between birth and age six and a half. As a result of devoted treatment and teaching (Mason, 1942), Isabelle made a good recovery and was leading a normal life at age fourteen (Davis, 1947).

A more recent case involves a girl, Genie, who spent her life until almost age thirteen in a small room with a minimum of human contact, much of which was abusive. She spent her waking hours strapped in a potty chair and slept in a sleeping bag in a covered crib. In warm weather she was exposed to two sorts of attractive stimulation: When the window was open, the curtains waved in the wind, and Genie could sometimes hear music from a nearby house. When first discovered, she was grossly retarded, with a developmental level of slightly over one year. After some five years of intensive treatment, Genie showed considerable improvement: She was toilet trained, spoke reasonably well, and had gained good motor control. There were still vestiges of her early confinement: She seemed acutely sensitive to music and stared fascinated at undulating patterns of movement like those of the curtains at her open window (Curtiss, 1977).

Two things need to be said about reversibility of early deprivation and abuse in closet children. First, such children acquire behaviors at ages well beyond what would be considered the critical periods for such acquisitions. Second, they receive the concentrated, highly individualized attention of doctors, speech therapists, nurses, psychologists, and other professionals. This latter consideration leads us to suspect that adoption from a foundling home would be even more beneficial than usual if the normal family environment were to be supplemented by extra professional care suited to the particular needs of the children and their families.

The Skeels Study

There is one classic study that has elements of deprivation, enrichment, and remediation. This is the remarkable thirty-year natural experiment by Harold Skeels (1966). Skeels began with a group of twenty-five babies who had been institutionalized because they were deemed mentally retarded and therefore unsuitable for adoption. Skeels had thirteen of the babies (the experimental group, chosen on the basis of their being the only ones legally eligible for transfer) moved to an institution for retarded women, where the babies were "adopted" by small groups of eighteen- to fifty-year-old inmates and became the object of much care by the institution's attendants, such as taking them on errands and outings. The other twelve children (the control group) were simply left where they were. After two years, the transfer group had gained an average of 27.5 IQ points, from 64.3 to 91.8, whereas the controls had lost 26.2 points, dropping from a mean of 86.7 to one of 60.5.

Thirty years later, Skeels did a follow-up study of the original twenty-five children. He found that eleven of the children in the experimental group had in fact been adopted from the institution into families. Twelve of the thirteen experimental children grew up to become adults who were self-supporting, held responsible positions, and had achieved the average educational level of the population. Their own children had average IQs. There were eleven survivors of the twelve in the control group. Only one of these had risen beyond marginal social status. Of the remaining ten, four were inmates of institutions of one kind or another, one was employed as a gardener's assistant at an institution, three worked as dishwashers, one was a part-time worker in a cafeteria, and one was a vagrant. The one marginal member of the experimental group was an unmarried female domestic who had several strikes against her from the beginning: She was born two months premature and was never given incubator care; she had congenital syphilis (she was cured by age one); and she was hospitalized at four months for accidental poisoning by her drunken parents.

There are some flaws in this study. The

experimental group, by the luck of the draw, was overweighted with females, and the control group with males, and males are generally considered more vulnerable to psychological damage than are females. Even so, it would be hard to ignore the findings. There seems to be little room for doubt that some form of individualized care in the early years can reverse the effects of deprivation and start the child on the road to normal adulthood. Just as important, the results demonstrate stunningly that early diagnoses of mental retardation should be treated with the utmost skepticism.

Preventing Psychological Impairment: Early Enrichment Studies

It is a depressing fact that children from low-SES backgrounds do not fare as well—by the criteria of middle-class society—as children from high-SES backgrounds. There have been numerous attempts to **enrich** the early experience of low-SES children to forestall the expected consequences of growing up in disadvantageous circumstances (Horowitz, 1980). Most of these studies sought primarily to improve the cognitive status of poor children, but they also tried to help out in all areas of the children's lives—decent shelter and clothing, access to medical and dental care, improved nutrition. Parents—usually mothers—were taught homemaking, child-rearing, and job skills, and were given help in coping with the welfare authorities and in finding employment. The many pioneering studies in this field, including the nationwide Head Start program (Zigler and Valentine, 1979), have had mixed results. The Head Start program, which began in 1965 under federal funding, set out to prepare five-year-olds from disadvantaged backgrounds to succeed in elementary school. The general pattern of the program was a gain in IQ or academic achievement that faded away as the children grew older and were no longer in enrichment programs.

Zigler and Trickett (1978) criticized the studies' emphasis on cognitive change and called for better measures of all-around social competence. A group of researchers in the field pooled all the available data to determine long-range effects of early intervention (Darlington et al., 1980; Lazar et al., 1982). They were able to obtain information on 1,599 youngsters out of an original total of 2,700. They confirmed that the initial IQ gains had disappeared by follow-up. What they chose as a measure was the proportion of experimental and control subjects who had had academic difficulties, defined as being held back one or more years or having had to be placed in special education classes. The percentage of experimental subjects with academic difficulties was 24.1 (range 17.2 to 52.8), and of control subjects, 44.7 (range 11.1 to 68.4). Horn (1981) pointed out that these figures applied only to performance in grade school, but Darlington (1981) said that the additional data showed that the effect continued into high school. It seems clear that most (not all) of these early ventures into enrichment had a positive but short-lived effect and fell far short of what was envisioned by enthusiasts.

Three main lessons were learned along

the way in conducting and evaluating the first batch of studies. First, it became obvious that it is essential to involve parents as deeply as possible in enrichment programs (Bronfenbrenner, 1974). Second, programs should start with children as young as possible. Third, programs should continue well into the school years, when the initial benefits of enrichment begin to be lost.

An additional lesson that might have been learned is that many of the public schools, especially in poor neighborhoods, do little to contribute to the continuing mental and emotional development of students. This leads us to the question of what we mean by enrichment. The very concept seems to connote cultural deprivation among its beneficiaries.

We consider the notion of cultural deprivation to be both insulting and incorrect. Children growing up in economically deprived neighborhoods most certainly absorb a culture. The problem is that the culture they absorb may be very much at odds with the modal, dominant culture of the larger society. Thus if they wish to participate in the mainstream culture and share in its reward system, they are obliged to learn and abide by its conventions. So-called enrichment programs, then, are really programs of cultural indoctrination. In itself, this is not too bad, but many people are beginning to express dissatisfaction with the way the mainstream culture functions. The critics come from within the mainstream as well as from outside it. The rhetoric of the dominant culture paints it in rosy colors, but the realities, especially for those in the lower reaches of the socioeconomic hierarchy, can be

(© Mark Cohen)

Children growing up in economically deprived neighborhoods most certainly absorb a culture. The problem is that the culture they absorb may be very much at odds with the dominant culture of the larger society.

murderously harsh. It follows, then, that in "enriching" the lives of poor children we are equipping and inviting them to move into the jungle of mainstream life. Obviously, the alternative for many poor children is simply a different sort of jungle, which confronts us with a powerful moral ambiguity. Because we retain a fundamental, and perhaps foolish, optimism about American society's capacity to cleanse itself, we vote for enrichment, but not without misgivings.

Of the second generation of enrichment studies, perhaps the most ambitious was Rick Heber's Milwaukee Project (Heber, 1972). Heber's subjects were the children of mothers whose IQs averaged around 75. Taking account of the statistical tendency for children of both high-IQ and low-IQ parents to have IQs somewhat closer to the mean, these children, without special intervention, would be expected to have IQs averaging around 90. Heber supplied his experimental subjects with a great diversity of enrichment experiences beginning when they were three months old. (The control group was made up of children from similar backgrounds who received no special treatment.) The mothers of the experimental children were given extensive training, and the children received superior diets, good health care, and intensive intellectual and emotional stimulation, at first in the home and then in small day-care groups. After the first six years, the experimental group had IQs averaging above 120. At age seven, when the program ended, their average IQ was reported to be around 125. The untreated control group, as predicted, had IQs averaging around 90. After the program ended, however, the frequently observed erosion set in, and the experimental group's IQs began to sink (Clarke and Clarke, 1976). Heber promised that

a complete report would appear in 1974, but it has not yet been published.

A similar study by Ronald Lally and Alice Honig (1977) in Syracuse dealt with children from age six months to age five years. Their experimental subjects showed gains on a number of intellectual and personality measures. For instance, at age five, 92.1 percent of the experimental group had IQs within or above the average range, as compared with 79.2 percent of the controls (no means are given, but the experimental group's distribution of scores is markedly higher than the control group's). Unlike Heber, Lally and Honig had a high-SES contrast group that far outstripped both the other groups on all measures.

Lally and Honig may have been a little more realistic than Heber about some of the difficulties of doing enrichment studies. For instance, they make clear that their parent population included many diverse types—from stable to disorganized, from concerned to indifferent, and from proper to promiscuous—which made for differing degrees of parental involvement.

A study carried out in Colombia (McKay et al., 1978) compared the effects of varying periods of enrichment, starting at age three, on improvement in cognitive functioning. The longer the period of enrichment, the greater the improvement. However, this relationship is complicated by the fact that those children who received the most enrichment were the ones who started at the youngest ages. Thus the effect may as easily be due to age at which enrichment started as it is to duration of enrichment. The rate of cognitive development tended to level off after about age seven. However, the enrichment groups retained their improvements until age eight, the oldest age at which they were tested. As in the Lally and Honig study, though, a group of untreated high-SES children consistently outperformed the groups made up of poor children.

It seems safe to conclude that we can remedy and prevent a large measure of psychological malfunctioning. At the same time, we must recognize that we are a long way from working magical transformations. We think it is obvious that the child's family culture is a far more potent force than any enrichment techniques that we have so far been able to invent. Note, too, that we have not even touched upon the problem of undoing the serious psychopathologies, neurosis and psychosis. In general, the early-experience hypothesis is upheld: A person can in part overcome the effects of early experience, but events (or voids) early in life have a powerful effect on what the person is likely to become.

SUMMARY

1. The degree to which early influences affect our development into adulthood has been widely discussed. There is a fairly stable sequence of normal development, in which new capabilities depend on the development of earlier ones. But many factors, such as intellectual ability and temperament, are variables that depend largely on rearing conditions. In general, children from big families are less likely to be bright (as measured by IQ and school achievement) than children from small families, and first-born children fare better psychologically than later born children. (There are, of course, exceptions, and neither the exceptions nor the main trend is understood.)

2. Studies of parent-child interaction reveal subtler variations in child-rearing patterns. The HOME inventory is one tool that allows researchers to evaluate the adequacy of family environments; it has been a good predictor of school achievement.

3. No single variable—such as style of feeding, weaning, toilet training, or discipline—explains what makes child rearing go well or badly: The whole complex pattern of interactions must be studied. One main conclusion of such studies is that competent mothers produce competent children. Competent mothers enjoy being with their children, are available when needed, can structure the material environment according to their children's interests and capacities, and respond ver-

bally to preverbal signals. Less competent mothers either give their children insufficient time or overwhelm them with unwanted attention and intrusions. More information is needed about the growing number of families in which the father is a significant caregiver, too.

4. A psychologically barren environment can hamper normal development. Studies of children who were raised in foundling homes and other institutions reveal a lack of stimulation and stable attachment figures. The *Crèche* study, conducted in Lebanon, is a notable example.

5. The spherical model represents an attempt to formalize descriptions of different patterns of child rearing; in it, the parent's treatment of the child is scored on three intersecting dimensions of acceptance–rejection, psychological control–psychological autonomy, and firm control–lax control. The scheme does not account for factors such as cognitive stimulation, language, and the baby as a stimulus to (as opposed to being the object of) parental behavior.

6. Some forms of deprivation are organically imposed—handicaps such as blindness, deafness, or physical deformity. In such cases, proper care and positive parental attitudes can help to offset potential developmental problems.

7. Parental neglect, rejection, or abuse of children can have severe developmental consequences. The most common problem is failure to thrive, characterized by abnormal growth, misery, and withdrawal. The battered child syndrome has also become a phenomenon of serious dimensions.

8. The harm that children suffer can sometimes be reversed if they are moved into a more favorable environment. The Skeels study showed quite conclusively that some form of individualized care in the early years can prevent or correct the effects of deprivation.

9. There have been attempts to enrich the early experiences of low-SES children in order to improve their cognitive status. Such experiments have had mixed results. Because the desirability of mainstream culture as opposed to other cultures has been questioned, this area of research is controversial.

10. Even in humane institutions, the lack of continuity of interaction with the children's caregiver or set of caregivers is the key weak point.

Adoption into a private family—including those headed by a single adult—is almost always preferable to institutional care.

11. In general, the hypothesis that early experience acts as a foundation for later development has been upheld; although early experiences can in part be overcome, events (or voids) early in life have a powerful effect on what a person is likely to become.

KEY TERMS

battered child syndrome, 247

closet children, 246

competence, 240

co-twin control studies, 236

deprivation, 242

enrichment, 253

failure to thrive, 247

Home Observation for Measurement of the Environment (HOME), 239

SUGGESTED READINGS

Brown, C. C. (ed.). *Infants at Risk*. Skillman, N.J.: Johnson & Johnson Baby Products Company, 1981. A guide for both professionals and parents to very early assessment of organic disabilities and attempts to counteract them.

Gerbner, G., Ross, C. J., and Zigler, E. *Child Abuse: An Agenda for Action*. New York: Oxford University Press, 1980. An overview of the problem of child abuse, proposed solutions, and obstacles to a coherent policy.

Kempe, R. S., and Kempe, C. H. *Child Abuse*. Cambridge, Mass.: Harvard University Press, 1978. A survey of the problem and a critical discussion of proposed solutions.

Lewis, M., and Rosenblum, L. A. *The Effect of the Infant on Its Caregiver*. New York: Wiley-Interscience, 1974. Variations on the theme that parent-child interactions must be understood in terms of reciprocal stimulation.

CHAPTER 8

The Toddler

Between the ages of about fifteen months and two and a half years, the baby lives a style of life that is called *toddlerhood*. This period is marked by its own distinctive cluster of emerging abilities. Toddlers make distinct progress in the mastery of **productive language**; that is, they begin to talk—as opposed to the **receptive language**, the ability to understand some language—of infancy. They complete the transition from quadruped to biped; walking and trotting are now the normal means of locomotion. They begin to form attachments to and interact with peers, others of the same age. They strive, although not always consistently, for psychological **autonomy**—self-determination and freedom of action. The striving for autonomy that marks this age expresses and further enhances the sense of a separate self and an increased degree of self-control, including sphincter control. Toddlers are still babies, but walking, talking, self-assertive babies quite different from what they were as infants.

Recall that as an infant the walking baby in a hurry to get someplace might revert to the speed and security of creeping. But the toddler is truly up and away—exuberantly, doggedly, or timidly, according to temperament—legs apart but pumping steadily. Now the baby creeps only in play, pretending to be an infant or a dog, and displaying an advanced capacity for nonliteral thought. Toddlers fall down a lot, tripping or stumbling or simply losing their balance. But they rarely hurt themselves seriously. This is because they have not yet learned the maladaptive reaction, found in older children and adults, of going stiff when they fall. Instead, toddlers tumble limp and relaxed and resil-

ient. In any case, they do not have far to fall.

The babyish charm of toddlers is indicated by the fact they they, rather than infants, were the models for the cherubs and cupids of Renaissance paintings. Their small size means, of course, that they still view much of the adult-scale world in terms of its undersides. They see the bathroom sink, for instance, with its pipes and drains, rust and scale and cobwebs. Much of this is usually hidden from adult vision. On walks, the pint-size toddler often pauses to examine some detail on the ground—a fallen leaf, a tiny worm, a feather, a broken bit of sidewalk—almost invisible to the adult but highly appealing to the toddler's still-fresh openness to novelty.

In much of their behavior, toddlers betray their babyishness. Every new object is seized, inspected, waved about as though to sample its heft and discover what sounds it will make, and, as often as not, stuffed as far as it will go into the baby's mouth. At least in early toddlerhood, children are still babies in that they deal with people more on a motor than on a verbal level. The young toddler, like the older infant, still may take two naps a day, shifting to a single nap around age two. With time out for naps, the toddler's waking hours stretch from perhaps five in the morning to as late as eight in the evening.

THEORETICAL VIEWS OF TODDLERHOOD

For Freud, let us remember, toddlerhood corresponds to the **anal stage** of psychosexual development. Freud considered this a time when the child's greatest pleasure derives from the anal area, as in moving or not moving the bowels. This is indeed the age for toilet training. However, in Freudian thought toilet training always meant a fierce battle of wills between parent and child. How this battle is resolved is central to the meaning of the anal stage and can be expected to have repercussions even into adulthood. This part of Freud's thinking may have been made obsolete by today's more relaxed, humane approaches to toilet training.

In Erikson's reinterpretation of Freud, the battle over sphincter control is only one instance of a larger struggle in which toddlers try to assert their autonomy, their ability to think and act for themselves. The failure to achieve autonomy leads to **shame and doubt.** Erikson's stages and their key crises imply a critical-periods view of development. While we do not accept the notion of critical periods, we are sympathetic to the idea that the toddler's assertion of autonomy is vital to the formation of a sound sense of self. We shall return to this topic later in the chapter.

Piaget does not recognize toddlerhood as a distinct period of life. Toddlers straddle two of Piaget's stages, the *sensorimotor period* of infancy and the *preoperational stage* of the preschool years. The preoperational stage is characterized by **symbolic functioning**—the internal representation of experience through mental symbols, such as words and images. Thus the child is no longer tied to the present (and only to those aspects of the present that can be known through the senses and through concrete action), as in the earlier sensorimotor stage.

Toddlers show at least the beginnings of preoperational thought. They can remember and anticipate, which implies some capacity for inner representation. Toddlers can store information in words. They are capable of **deferred imitation,** the ability to witness some act and then, at a later time, to reproduce it. Indeed, this capacity is essential to the acquisition of language: The child does not automatically parrot each new word, but files it away until a suitable occasion arises for its use. Since late infancy, the baby has been engaging in simple **dramatic play** (which Piaget calls **symbolic play** and others call **fantasy** or **pretend play**). Examples of early dramatic play are pretending to be a dog, pretending to be in pain, and enacting simple themes from everyday life, such as feeding a doll or holding a make-believe telephone conversation. From these behaviors, we can infer that the toddler's activity is in some part guided by internal images.

Toddlers show signs of emerging from egocentrism. John Flavell and associates (Flavell, 1977) have made a number of interesting observations on the toddler's escape from egocentrism. For instance, when eighteen-month-olds want to show someone a picture in a book, they typically "share" the book by positioning themselves next to the other person. By age two years, the toddler simply turns the book so that the picture faces the other person. If the intended viewer of a picture covers his or her eyes, the eighteen-month-old will move the obstructing hands away. Yet another problem is knowing whether a given object is visible to another person. Young children were tested by being asked to put an object where another person in the same room could not see it. It is not until about age three that children can perform this task. However, toddlers can find the object to which another person is pointing. They can also detect where someone's gaze is directed, but only if face and eyes are aimed in the same direction. If the other person looks at something by turning the eyes but not the head, the toddler will be unable to guess what the other person is seeing.

The one preoperational skill completely missing in toddlers is representational drawing (although toddlers love to scribble). Piaget places the beginning of pictorial representation at age two or two and a half (Piaget and Inhelder, 1969). In our experience with American children, representational drawing does not begin until age three or later. Although toddlers are entering the preoperational stage, they do not yet think like preschool children. The differences are vast. But according to Piaget's criteria of preoperational thought, toddlers are well on their way.

Piaget, as we know, was a cognitive theorist. However, for him cognitive structures and processes were the same regardless of what the person was thinking about. Most of Piaget's investigations of children's thinking were addressed to the understanding of physical phenomena and mathematical and logical reasoning. Piaget's successors (e.g. Case, 1980; Flavell, 1981; Siegler, 1981), however, have taken note that our thinking changes according to the domain being considered. They have recently been giving special attention to the domain of human relations and the special kinds of thinking that are called for in dealing with other people. This is what is referred to as **social cognition,** which is now contrasted with **physical cognition.**

This chaper does not have a section devoted to physical cognition. The toddler's physical cognition is revealed in concrete behavior. It can be inferred from play patterns, skills, self-awareness, and self-control. In Chapter 9, where we discuss language, we will talk about how language gives us clues to the child's cognitive processes, physical and social.

PLAY AND ACTIVITIES IN TODDLERHOOD

A goodly portion of the toddler's day is taken up by the mechanics of life—eating, napping, being bathed and cleaned and changed, dressing and undressing. Even so, the toddler has several hours a day free for other sorts of activities. Prominent among these is what we call **play,** which is essential to sound development (*Play,* 1971; Garvey, 1977). The distinctive feature of play is that it has no goal or motive other than the satisfaction derived from the activity itself. (We will have to qualify this later when we talk about competitive games and winning and losing, but the definition will do for now.) The sustenance-producing or otherwise useful activities of the adult are considered serious work, whereas the activities of the child are viewed as frivolous play. In fact, however, the baby's play is not always as frivolous as it may appear. In the course of playing, babies work hard at mastering and perfecting new competencies. Even those bits of play that seem aimless to the adult feed into the baby's expanding awareness of self and world.

Note, though, that babies are not oriented to achievement. They have no sense of any future benefits to be gained from present play. Such benefits are incidental by-products. Nor do babies, practicing and acquiring skills, feel any need to have final products as monuments to what they have done. Preschool-age children delight in showing off their paintings or block buildings, but toddlers are seldom aware of having produced anything. They enjoy, and sometimes even demand, adult attention to what they are doing, but more for the sake of companionship than for demonstrating their skills. Toddlers are likely to abandon projects midway as their attention shifts or new impulses arise. They drop the doll they were about to put to bed, toss aside the crayon with which they were scribbling, or let the tune they were humming trail off. Older children and adults seem to have an urge to carry an activity through to completion, but toddlers seem to feel no such need. Parents may feel empathically frustrated by the toddler's indifference to unfinished business. For the toddler, it is the activity itself that counts, not the completion of a total task.

It is often said that toddlers prefer gross motor (large muscle) activity to fine motor (small muscle) activity, and boisterous play to quiet play, that they would rather deal with large things than with small ones, that they would rather send their whole bodies hurtling through space than engage in sensitive manipulations. This has a large measure of truth. In the playground, toddlers love the spring of a bouncing board underfoot (but they want to hold an adult finger); the swooping movement of a swing (but not too high); the tug and jounce of riding in a wagon; the unwieldy weight of

(Courtesy, Dr. Lois B. Murphy)

Riding a tricycle is a typical activity for a toddler.

big objects to lift and haul and shove. They like to hammer, and pound tirelessly at the sort of bench that allows pegs to be driven through to the other side and then back again. They trot about pushing or pulling a roll toy. They revel in splashing in water and digging in sandboxes. They explore tunnels and try out—very tentatively when coming down—ramps and catwalks. They learn to ride tricycles and to climb up a rung or two on the jungle gym. They drift about aimlessly, staring wide-eyed at other children at play, often moving in empathic rhythm with them. They set off in pursuit of rolling balls, close doors that they find open or ajar, and, when they become tall enough to manage the knob, open closed doors. They squeeze into narrow crevices, step up onto large blocks and then step down again. They join in clusters with their peers around every new activity.

But this is only part of the story. Toddlers have their quiet, moments, when they squat down to follow the progress of a beetle or an ant, or savor the feel and taste of snow, or listen to music (usually bouncing to the beat). They sit on the floor and scribble (it is a good idea to give toddlers drawing materials only when there is an adult around to keep watch; otherwise, their experiments are likely to overflow onto floor, walls, and furnishings). They like to look at picture books, spend long minutes in examination and exploration of a new object, or relish the flavor of food. By age two, American toddlers may sit quietly hypnotized for a while in front of the television set, or trot in from the next room for a favorite commercial. There can be no doubt that toddlers find certain changing patterns of sight and sound fascinating—toddlers memorize commercial jingles from an early age—but there is reason to question what sense they make of television programs. We even know of one two-year old for whom watching television was a comfort device. When he felt out of sorts, he sat on the couch, put his thumb in his mouth, and stared at the blank and silent set.

Toddlers, as the saying goes, are "into everything." Some part of their day is likely to be spent emptying toy boxes, closets, drawers, and cupboards. Sometimes this is done with a view to playing with the contents, as when toddlers drape themselves in odds and ends of clothing and parade around the house or admire themselves in various poses in front of the mirror. As often as not, though, it is simply for the pleasure they find in each step of the emptying-out process, each novelty, each familiarity. From the time a child is a year old until almost school age, reasonably permissive parents must resign themselves to a daily clean-up of a household that seems to have disintegrated into fragments that must be collected, sorted, reassembled, cleaned, and put away. Toddlers are perfectly willing to help, but they are liable to lose sight of the goal and begin taking things out as fast as they are put away.

Dramatic Play

Toddlers (boys and girls) play with dolls, trundling them in their carriages, feeding them, petting them, scolding them, wiping their noses, putting them to bed, and so forth. In the toddler's play with dolls, we see the further flowering of **dramatic play,** the acting out of scenes and events, real or imaginary, from everyday life. In dramatic play, children try out roles taken from the models with whom they identify, even if only momentarily. Early dramatic play is likely to be solitary and episodic, limited to simple unelaborated themes from domestic life: telephoning, answering the door, rocking the baby to sleep, pouring tea or coffee. It is not always possible to draw a line between dramatic play and simply mimicking the behavior of adults. Thus, shaving: Little girls as well as little boys go through a pantomime of removing whiskers; and little boys as well as little girls go through the motions of shaving legs

(© Melvin Konner)

(© Melvin Konner)

(© Elizabeth Crews)

An African toddler "makes a fire"; an American girl "drives a tractor"; an American boy "navigates." Dramatic play often involves simply mimicking the behavior of adults, but it also can verge into functional behavior, as when a child attempts to help with household chores.

and armpits. More than one eighteen-month-old has been found with a cigarette or cigar or pipe shoved deep into his or her mouth, trying valiantly to strike a match. Toddlers go through the motions of driving or fixing the car. They may trail a parent around the house, either playing on their own or copying the adult's activities. They may even pitch in as best they can with household chores, a shading of dramatic play into functional behavior.

SOCIAL RELATIONS

So far, we have emphasized the toddler's solitary activities, although we trust you have been aware of an adult or two always lurking nearby. The toddler is better equipped than was the infant to play alone for extended intervals. However, as we have said, frequent doses of adult attention are welcomed and sometimes demanded. In addition, as we might expect, there is a good deal of direct playful interchange between adult and child. Some of this goes on in the context of routine care, such as feeding and dressing, but much of it is purely social. Many of the social games of infancy, like hiding and peekaboo and roughhousing, continue largely unchanged into toddlerhood and beyond. Toddlers and older children delight in the game in which the child curls up in a parent's chair, and the parent, seemingly oblivious of the child's presence, tries to sit down and goes through an elaborate ritual of trying to find out why the chair is so lumpy. Toddlers love to snuggle up with an adult to hear a simple story read from a book with lots of pictures or with three-dimensional insets such as snaps or zippers to work, or textured animals to pet. We cannot overemphasize the importance of reading to toddlers, and of reading well, at a measured pace and with plenty of feeling. Toddlers are not too young to grasp that marks on paper can carry meaning.

Lap sitting is a special activity of toddlerhood. Toddlers do not try to climb into an adult lap but hold their arms aloft as a signal to be lifted up. Sometimes lap sitting is for the sake of cuddling and comfort or of reading, but most of the time it is a very lively activity. Toddlers delight in jiggling or being jiggled, bouncing, and dipping outward into space while lightly encircled by the adult's arms or firmly holding hands with the adult. The adult has to do most of the work, but the activity originates in the toddler.

Peer Relations

In late infancy, babies notice other babies, but they seem to regard each other as curious specimens of alien species, to be poked and prodded but hardly to be related to. During toddlerhood, there develops a recognition that other toddlers are creatures much like oneself. Two toddlers, meeting for the first time in the park, may warily circle each other, reach out to touch, smile, and perhaps embrace. One toddler we knew developed the habit of going directly up to any young child she encountered and giving him or her a hug—sometimes to the amazement and even consternation of the other child. A rudimentary friendship is formed between toddlers who come to know each other well, and they enjoy visiting back and forth. They play side by side with very little interchange—there may be an occasional wordless struggle over some disputed plaything, perhaps ending in tears from the one who loses out—but obviously taking pleasure in each other's company. This is known as **parallel play,** the earliest form of play with other children.

A study by Carol Eckerman and associates (Eckerman, Whatley, and Kutz, 1975) traces the development of social play during the second year. This study documents the rise and decline of play with parents, and the increasing interest in peers. There is an increase in such social behavior as smiling, vocalizing (not to be confused with speaking), imitation, and struggling over a toy. Positive reactions were far more common than negative ones. A study by Harriet Rheingold and associates (Rheingold, Hay, and West, 1976) demonstrates sharing in eighteen-month-olds. *Sharing* is defined as showing, giving, or *"partner play"* between two toddlers meeting for the first time. "Partner play" was scored when

> The child manipulated an object that he had given to the person and was still in contact with the person. An episode of partner play began when the child manipulated the object and faced, looked at, or vocalized to the person. The episode ended when the child turned away from the person or released contact of the object.

Note that such sharing was between strangers. A widespread social change has caused us to revise our thinking about social relations between toddlers. This is the rise of day care, which gives toddlers a chance to see the same children day after day and explore new forms of social interaction. Rubenstein

(© Frank Siteman/The Picture Cube)

Two friends with a toy. Sharing consists in showing, giving, or "partner play."

and Howes (1979) compared toddler behavior in day-care centers and at home. In the day-care center there is greater peer interaction, play with toys, and adult-toddler interaction, play, physical contact, and reciprocal smiling. In the home, there is greater verbal responsiveness by toddlers to their mothers' speech, more crying, and more maternal restrictiveness. Among the peer interactions noted are vocalizing, smiling at or touching, exchanging or sharing objects, and imitation. Conflicts occurred, but only rarely. Ross and Hay (1977) likewise report a low incidence of conflicts in day-care centers. Eight-seven percent of disputes were over toys, and in 56 percent of the cases the child who grabbed the toy retained possession. A few conflicts were caused by intrusive acts such as trying to put a hat or a bucket on another child's head.

Goldman and Ross (1978) studied interactions between babies of differing ages. They paired unacquainted eighteen-month-olds with either twelve-month-olds or twenty-four-month-olds. In the company of twelve-month-olds, eighteen-month-olds engaged in such activities as ball rolling, ball bouncing, imitation (kicking a barrier, foot taps, faked laughter), and removing blocks from the other baby's mouth (only one interchange was initiated by a twelve-month-old). The twenty-four-month-olds paired with eighteen-month-olds engaged in such actions as putting their legs across the other child's lap, performing "silly" movements or uttering nonsense vocalizations, and touching and tickling the other child. Ross (1982) found that adults could do little to influence social interactions between toddlers. She also added two new toddler games to the catalogue: using a piece of furniture to play peekaboo, and chasing. Brenner and Mueller (1982) contribute the further category of "motor copy": making marks on a blackboard, banging a radiator with a stick, tongue protrusion, pulling on window shades, rocking in the rocking boat, putting sticks in the mouth, and hammering on a xylophone, all in imitation of a companion.

Social Cognition

The important point about the toddler's social relations is that they imply a degree of awareness of human beings as a special breed of objects with qualities quite different from nonhuman entities (Gelman and Spelke, 1981). Thus we speak of social cognition. According to Golinkoff and Harding (1980), however, the animate-inanimate distinction is not altogether clear in early toddlerhood. Two-year-olds showed surprise when a chair appeared to move about spontaneously, but sixteen-month-olds took no notice.

We have described infantile perception as *egocentric* and *phenomenalistic*. Infants react only to the surface features of things, with no apparent regard to hidden structures. However, we must make at least a partial exception for infants' awareness of people. Regardless of what sixteen-month-olds think about chairs being able to move on their own, very young infants are aware that people feel and act. Infants and adults may have very little understanding of how they and others operate psychologically, but they know that something is going on. Ross and Hay (1977) report that toddlers may try to resolve a conflict by distracting the other child's attention from a contested object. Hoffman (1981) gives the example of a twenty-month-old who had been trying without success to take a plaything from her older sister. Inspired, she mounted the sister's rocking horse, which was strictly off limits to all but its owner. The sister rushed to the defense of her territory, and the twenty-month-old quickly took possession of the now-abandoned toy. An even more remarkable example of nonegocentrism is given in Hoffman's account of a battle for a toy between two fifteen-month-olds. One of the combatants started to cry, whereupon the other let go of the contested toy. The crying continued, so the other child offered his teddy bear as solace. This didn't work, so the other child, after a moment's reflection, fetched the crying child's security blanket from another room and peace was restored. Mueller and Musatti (1981) raise the question of whether toddlers playing together share a concept of what is really going on. They answer their own question in the affirmative, citing as evidence the note of conscious playfulness or nonliterality, planfulness, ritualization, and the use of vocal signals, as in imitation of sounds.

Obviously, toddlers' intuitions about people will eventually be translated into ideas that can be articulated. These will focus on similarities and differences in feelings, knowledge, interests, traits and dispositions, learning and remembering, foresight, and cognitive capacities in general. Social cognition expands to include a recognition of deception, acceptance of conventions, a grasp of moral principles, and an awareness of social institutions that transcend individual behavior. It is obvious that our awareness of other people's inner workings plays a crucial role in being able to communicate. Since it is far from easy to know what other people are thinking or how they will react to this or that initiative, it is a wonder that communication ever takes place. In fact, a number of authors have said that successful communication often rests on egocentrism. Lacking information to the contrary, we assume that other people will react to things pretty much the way we ourselves

do. A fair amount of the time, the egocentric assumption proves out. Not always, as everyone should know, but reasonably often.

Sibling Rivalry

There is a traditional belief, dating back at least to the story of Cain and Abel, that there necessarily exists among siblings—children of the same family—a spirit of competition, jealousy, and hos-

(© Elizabeth Crews)

The idea that a spirit of competition, jealousy, and hostility necessarily exists among children of the same family is called sibling rivalry. Parents should take care not to become so engrossed in the arrival of a new baby that the toddler's continuing needs for affection and attention become lost.

tility. This idea was made into a formal psychological concept by Alfred Adler, who named it **sibling rivalry.** For instance, an older child, and especially a first-born who for a while was an only child, may feel that a new baby has deposed him or her from a reigning position in the parents' affection. A younger sibling, on the other hand, may feel resentfully envious of an older sibling's size, strength, and privileges. Adler and others have plotted out what they believe to be the typical patterns of sibling rivalry that go with particular birth orders (or positions in the *"family constellation"*), modified according to the sex of the siblings. However, for our purposes we need be concerned only that a toddler may be upset by the arrival of a new brother or sister.

Experts have proposed various ways of forestalling or holding to a minimum a toddler's jealousy toward a new baby. If the toddler is old enough—two and a half rather than one and a half—he or she should be told in advance so that the baby does not come as a total surprise. However, the toddler should not be told so far in advance that he or she forgets about it or that it becomes unreal with the slow passage of time. Within the limits of their competence, toddlers can be given a share in preparations for and care of the newcomer. This way they can feel that the baby is in some sense theirs—or the family's—as well as the parents'. It is important that the parents not become so engrossed in the care and appreciation of the new baby that they lose sight of the toddler's continuing need for affection and attention. The friends and relations who come to admire the new baby can help in this respect, too.

However, it is doubtful that these and related measures, no matter how diligently and skillfully practiced, can altogether prevent the older child from becoming jealous of the new intruder. Nor is it certain that all jealousy ought to be avoided, if we want children to know a full range of emotions. After all, ambivalence is a fact of life, and sibling rivalry does not mean that brothers and sisters cannot love one another. We might also note in passing that the family dog or cat may exhibit a certain amount of jealousy toward a new baby.

There are several ways in which toddlers may show jealousy of a new sibling. They may regress, turning back to more infantile ways of behaving. They may begin to whine or to cry easily. They may cling possessively to the parents. Their speech may become more babyish or even disappear. They may lose control over the bladder. Such regression often indicates that the toddler feels left out, and that the only way to get attention is to be an infant. In such cases, it may be necessary to give the toddler an especially generous ration of love, together with whatever hints are possible that he or she can safely act his or her age. Another way in which toddlers may show jealousy is by trying to injure or get rid of the new baby. (Older children have been known to suggest to the parents that they dispose of the baby, perhaps by flushing the newcomer down the toilet or by returning the baby to the hospital.) Sometimes toddlers will try to take matters into their own hands with the frank intention of doing away with the interloper. Here is one mother's account of the reaction of a seventeen-month-old boy to the arrival of a baby sister:

When I came home with Jenny, Mark stared at me at first as though I were a complete stranger. He cried bitterly when his father carried Jenny from the car to the house. He was somewhat aloof for several hours. I was prepared to see some jealousy in Mark, but somehow I thought it would be subtle, or directed against me. Not so at all! The first chance he got, he went right for the baby, with the most agonized expression, and tried to sock her. He looked grimly determined to smash this little bundle of trouble, and yet he was obviously terribly upset by his own impulse and sobbed, "No, no," even as he went for her. . . . The ice finally broke one day perhaps a week after Jenny and I came home. I was diapering Jenny, and Mark was watching from his grandmother's arms. Jenny made some little noise, I imitated her and said to Mark, "Doesn't that baby make *silly* noises?" Suddenly Mark smiled broadly and said, "Silly!" It must have been a revelation to him that I was on his side. Here we all were together, laughing at the baby. From then on, there was almost no more trouble. Gradually we let Mark loose in Jenny's presence, and it was practically no time before he was admiring her "tiny toes," kissing her, and patting her ("Gently, gently," he would remind himself).

Such peaceful solutions do not always come to pass, in which case the toddler must continue to be restrained from harming the baby. But there need be no suggestion that the toddler is wicked or depraved. A formal, inflexible, categorical, and even angry prohibition can be imposed in full understanding of how normal the toddler's feelings are, and without denying the toddler the full measure of love to which he or she continues to be entitled. As in all discipline, the emphasis must be as much as possible on the act, and not on the toddler's worth as a total person. Especially in the matter of jealousy, an excessively moralistic approach can reinforce the toddler's conviction that he or she has been displaced. There are bound to be times when the new baby has to be given a disproportionate share of attention, as when he or she is sick. At such times, the toddler will inevitably feel like a second-class citizen in the parents' affections. But such temporary strains, as long as they are the exception rather than the rule, will probably do as much in the long run to strengthen as to weaken the bonds between toddler and parents. It is only when toddlers are consistently relegated to second place that they come to think of love as something that has to be earned or stolen or fought for—or regressed for—rather than as something that is simply there, stable and to be counted on.

Sibling rivalry may be peculiar to small, nuclear families of the kind Westerners take for granted. In large or extended families, or in communal societies where the children belong to everybody, sibling rivalry may not develop or may take quite different forms.

LOCOMOTION, POSTURE, AND ORIENTATION IN SPACE

As the very designation "toddler" implies, one important difference between older babies and infants is the former's bipedal mobility. In general, the toddler's motor skills are more advanced than the infant's. It is to these that we now turn our attention.

Locomotion

Although walking begins in infancy, the toddler's walking is marked by a qualitative change. Walking becomes the regular mode of travel (as we have said, the toddler may still creep in a spirit of play). Toddlers gain in stability, and they no longer need to use their arms for balance.

Even so, early in this period, children have to warm up to walking by first rocking from foot to foot. Such preludes to action are called *intention movements.* They are seen in a variety of situations, from the dog's circling before it lies down, to the pitcher's winding up before throwing the ball, to the singer's preliminary "mi-mi-mi-mi."

Before long, toddlers not only walk but trot. One has the impression, as suggested earlier, that toddlers are constantly in motion. They are often described as clumsy, but this applies only when they are all bundled up. Lightly clothed and barefoot, the toddler, like Tuesday's child, is full of grace. Once toddlers can trot, this becomes their favorite mode of locomotion, and they run trippingly, on spread toes. One can see the beginnings of preschool-age styles of movement in how they turn a corner. Toddlers and preschool children negotiate a bend in a corridor by running straight ahead into the wall, changing direction as they bounce off, and then resuming their run. Toddlers become able to hop on both feet and perhaps to stand on one foot. However, hopping on one foot does not come until about age three. Toddlers also learn to walk backward.

When babies first begin walking, they have to toddle laboriously through a change of direction. In a short time, however, they learn to pivot on one foot. Toddlers "dance" to music, at first by bobbing up and down in place, and then by moving their feet in a crude imitation of adult dancing. But note that children growing up in societies in which dancing is an integral part of life become proficient dancers at an early age. The same is true of skiing and skating. Toddlers enjoy being danced around in an adult's arms to the tune of singing or humming or to music from record player or radio.

As we have said, toddlers love to carry, shove, trundle, or otherwise set objects in motion, the bigger the better. This is the age at which children trot about pulling or pushing mechanical ducks or corn poppers that produce a pattern of sound and action. Toddlers may try to give their dolls a ride in a coaster wagon. However, they often have trouble because the handle and pivoting front wheels are designed for pulling, not pushing, whereas toddlers want to push so that they can see their dolls riding.

You will recall that older infants can figure out or be taught how to bounce from step to step down a flight of stairs. By toddlerhood, backing down on hands and knees is the most common technique of descending a staircase. This method entails a lot of hesitation, of twisting and craning to see where one is and where one is going, of easing knees and hands warily from step to step. Somewhere around age two, the toddler may be able to walk downstairs clinging to an adult finger—but here, as in other situations, toddlers may be overwilling to surrender all their weight to the adult and end up dangling helplessly. By age two and a half, some children can walk both up and down stairs, one step at a time, holding on to a railing.

Young toddlers have to climb up not

A mother helps her toddler walk on a railing. Many motor skills evolve rapidly during toddlerhood, for example, the ability to hop on both feet and perhaps stand on one, to walk backward, and to turn by pivoting on one foot.

only onto a full-sized chair but also onto a toddler-sized one. They do this by sprawling on their belly or climbing on their knees to the seat and twisting themselves around until they work their feet into place and are triumphantly seated facing forward. At a more advanced stage, toddlers back toward a child-sized chair or bench. They aim themselves at the seat by peering between their legs or over their shoulder until they make contact and can let themselves down. Here, as in the feet-first creep down a staircase, it is obvious that space behind the toddler is less well

defined and manageable than the easily visible space in front. By late toddlerhood, the baby, like the adult, can walk up to a chair, turn around, and plump confidently and casually down on the seat.

Posture

Now that we have found a break in the toddler's seemingly perpetual motion, it is time to examine the baby at rest. When, as sometimes happens, toddlers stay in one place, their posture is very different from that of younger or older children. For brief periods of contemplation or play, toddlers drop into an easy squat. For longer periods of quiet pursuits, toddlers typically sit with legs forward, a book or plaything on the lap or between the thighs. Note the contrast here with both the Buddha-like pose of infancy and the forelegs folded back, heels-to-buttocks sitting posture of the preschool child. We have described how toddlers get onto chairs, but they rarely stay in them for long, much preferring the floor or the ground. The toddler, and only the toddler, is so proportioned as to be able to bend at the waist, rest head on floor, and look through straight legs at the upside-down world. Assuming this position is a favorite occupation of toddlers, and becomes even more enjoyable when a parental face appears between the legs and offers greetings.

When toddlers keep an adult company, they characteristically lean limply against the adult's knee or shoulder (depending on whether the adult is sitting in a chair or on the floor), so limply that they may slide into a heap to the floor. This draping of self against adults may continue into the school years, but past-toddlerhood children maintain better muscle tone and balance. When toddlers are not directly engaged with other people, they are likely to treat them less as people than as things: as obstacles to be shoved aside, as climbing apparatuses, as resting places. In general, the toddler's posture and movements are marked by *symmetry*, a limited differentiation of the two sides of the body. When beating time or kicking heels against the side of a box on which the child is seated, both arms or legs move as one rather than in alternation. Indeed, if the toddler gets a Band-Aid on one finger, a second Band-Aid may be demanded for the matching finger on the other hand.

(Anna Kaufman Moon/Stock, Boston)

Space can be explored in a variety of ways.

Awareness of Space and Spatial Relationships

Throughout all these activities we can see the toddler's increasing familiarization with and mastery of space and its possibilities. Toddlers know by heart the layout of familiar regions, such as house and yard. They may even cry out in protest when, on the way to Grandma's, Mother makes a left turn where she customarily makes a right. Toddlers know where all the household goods are kept, including the taboo objects.

However, it is important to understand the nature of the toddler's knowledge of space. What they know is a great many specific locations and routes linking these locations—from living room to bedroom, from bathroom to kitchen, and so forth. However, they have no notion of how these segments of space are related to one another as parts of a coherent whole. In other words, the toddler has schematized some regions of space,

but is incapable of weaving part-schemata into a larger, unified guiding mental map. In this, toddlers are very much like "space-blind" adults, who learn to get from place to place but are incapable of inventing an alternate route, cannot map larger spaces mentally, and become lost if they deviate even slightly from their customary paths. Even when toddlers think they see a possible alternate pathway, as when, out on a walk with an adult, it occurs to them to detour around a bush and rejoin the adult on the other side, as soon as they lose sight of the adult they become disoriented and panicky.

Even though toddlers have well-developed object permanence, they do not yet appreciate that one object cannot be in two places at the same time. For instance, the family of one two-year-old had a rather unusual automobile. One day, while out on a drive, they passed another car just like it. The father jokingly remarked, "Look, somebody stole our car." The two-year-old responded by bursting into tears, unmindful of the "obvious" fact that their car was still safely in the family's possession.

The toddler's orientation in space can be summarized by saying that the child inhabits what Werner (1973) called **action space**, defined not by its maplike relationships and coordinates but by its possibilities for movement, the dynamics that push and pull and steer and channel the toddler's active migrations. These spatial dynamics are strictly equivalent to the demand qualities or meanings found in objects—just as knobs invite twisting and tugging, so do configurations of space invite exploration. Action space is very different from the **map space** that begins to appear in the late preschool and early school years. At this time, the child forms integrated schemata, not merely of routes and pathways but of whole regions of familiar space.

What we have been talking about is the larger, enclosing space in which we all dwell and move about. But spatial relations apply also to the internal structure of objects, such as the way a piece of machinery is put together and comes apart. We shall look at the toddler's dealings with small-scale spatial relations in the context of manipulation of objects.

MANIPULATION OF OBJECTS

We have compiled a list of commonplace skills that appear during toddlerhood in American babies. It is during this period that babies become able to feed themselves with a spoon (Chinese and Japanese children, we are told, master chopsticks by age three). They can chew gum without swallowing it. They are able to drink through a straw. They can blow their nose into a handkerchief or tissue held by an adult (when toddlers try blowing their noses unaided, the results are extremely messy). They can eat an ice cream cone (a skill best acquired outdoors in warm weather, to simplify cleaning up). Toddlers are able to work simple record players, switching on the power, selecting the particular record they want to hear, placing it on the turntable, moving the tone arm into position, and adjusting the volume. They generally keep it turned low, suggesting an aversion to loud sounds. In learning to ride a tricycle, they may at first try to push with both feet at once and have some trouble getting the knack of alternating thrusts—symmetry again.

It is not until the preschool years that Western children learn to put on and fasten their own clothes, but toddlers are highly adept at removing them. An otherwise occupied parent may be startled to look down and find a nude baby. Toddlers imitate the superficial aspects of grooming, chewing on toothbrush bristles and going through the motions of combing or brushing their hair. We even have a record of a seventeen-month-old trying to trim her nails with a pair of pruning shears. By age two, Japanese babies have learned to bow properly to an adult.

Toddlers not only take apart things like cooking utensils but also begin putting them back together again. Infants can unscrew container caps, but toddlers can screw them back on, provided they

(© Suzanne Szasz)

(© Vivienne/DPI)

(© Michael Weisbrot & Family)

Toddlers love to explore and examine their environment. They begin to stack objects, they investigate bugs and they delight in water play.

are of a manageable size. Although most toddlers cannot yet pile pierced disks on a peg in order of size, by age two many can fit together a series of nesting boxes or eggs. This may require some trial and error. Toddlers, like infants, perceive size relations imprecisely and may try to fit big things into little containers. Two-year-olds can match solid shapes to the spaces in a form board, but they may have trouble orienting the pieces so that they will slip into place. Toddlers are able to make block towers several blocks high, but they never seem to imagine them as anything other than a stack of blocks. Preschool children, as we shall see, use blocks to represent all kinds of structures, and incorporate such structures into their dramatic play.

SELF-AWARENESS: AUTONOMY VERSUS SHAME AND DOUBT

In Erikson's scheme, the chief issue of toddlerhood is to develop *autonomy* or become mired in *shame and doubt*. The main ingredient in autonomy is the sense of being in charge of one's own life, making one's own decisions and carrying them through. Another important component is a sense of competence, having what it takes to be in charge. Shame and doubt, by contrast, mean fear of taking charge, a sense of incompetence and impotence, and generally negative feelings toward one's own body and functioning. Obviously, no toddler achieves full autonomy. But, if the child in infancy acquires a sense of basic trust, he or she as a toddler, with new powers of mobility and communication, develops an ever more refined awareness of a separate identity, with individual wants and sensitivities and capabilities.

New possibilities for action emerge, matching the toddler's new patterns of competence. Toddlers want to try out new things for themselves, without help or hindrance or coercion from others. Successful ventures fortify the toddler's developing autonomy. Excessive restraint, chronic failure, and, above all, parental emphasis on failure and failure to recognize the toddler's successes, undermine the toddler's autonomy strivings. They breed feelings of worthlessness and incompetence. We agree with Erikson that these opposing orientations can be crucial to all of later development.

We know that toddlers have certain capabilities and limitations. We know also that they are not always very good judges of what they can and cannot do. We further know that they are subject to **growth ambivalence**, conflicting feelings of wanting to reach out and test themselves and at the same time wanting to play it safe, to preserve the status quo. The role of the parents, then, is to allow the toddler every reasonable opportunity for self-testing—the urge to hover protectively is almost irresistible—while preventing the more foolhardy ventures and standing by to give comfort and reassurance when things go wrong. For toddlers are extremists. At one moment they cherish notions of omnipotence, which can crumble abruptly into feelings of despair and impotence. Just as toddlers are most vigorously asserting their autonomy, their vulnerability comes to the fore. They may suddenly want to be helped or carried, to be babied and cuddled and protected. But as long as there seems to be a fair chance that the toddler can successfully face some new challenge, it is a good idea to urge the toddler to go ahead and try.

Negativism

Two words dominate the toddler's battle cry for autonomy. "Me!" and "No!" "Me!" means that I want to do it myself, without even helpful interference. "No!" accompanies one of the visible manifestations of the drive to autonomy, **negativism**—resistance to control by other people. However, negativism does not need verbal expression. The toddler may go rigid or limp; he or she may kick, bite, scratch, run away, or throw a temper tantrum. Strong adult reactions to negativism seem to act as reinforcers, increasing its frequency and force. In

(© Lew Merrim/Monkmeyer Press)

Negativism is a normal and perhaps essential part of developing autonomy. Unless it is inflated into a major issue between parent and child, it is soon integrated into the more constructive, competence-building aspects of autonomy.

contrast, nonreinforcement, ignoring the display, lessens negativism.

Negativism is vivid behavior and so is likely to warp our perception of toddlerhood. When we look closely, we find that most of the time toddlers cooperate cheerfully, automatically, and casually with adults. Even when negativism does erupt, it usually means that the child wants to try to handle a situation in his or her own way, and unless physical danger is involved, it is a good idea to let the toddler try. If toddlers find that something is indeed beyond their competence, then they usually revert to co-operation. Sometimes, of course, a real battle of wills develops, in which case the adult has to be prepared to assume full authority. If need be, a squalling toddler can be carried away from the scene of conflict in the crook of one adult arm, with the toddler's arms and legs flailing harmlessly. In the aftermath of confrontations, however, the adult has to ease the sting of authority with extra affection, a period of play, and the offering of a substitute activity. Otherwise, the toddler perceptibly loses face, which can happen at a very early age and is always damaging.

It is important to point out, too, that many times the toddler's seeming negativism is in fact nothing more than play acting. The toddler is trying out how it feels to say no. A parent who continues unperturbed to dress the child or tuck it into bed finds the toddler cooperating through a refrain of verbal resistance. If the parent fails to detect the playful quality of the child's negativism, an actual crisis of authority may be generated where none existed before.

Negativism is a normal and perhaps essential part of developing autonomy. Unless it is inflated into a major issue between parent and child, it is soon integrated into the more constructive, competence-building aspects of autonomy. If toddlers have ample opportunity to practice things on their own, balanced by the support they sometimes need and by a few necessary restrictions, they emerge from this period with a sound sense of their own abilities and a readiness to tackle the new problems of later ages.

Growth Ambivalence and Dual Ambivalence

We have just spoken of the child's growth ambivalence, the conflict between progressive urges, a desire for mastery and competence, for trying out the new and challenging, and a conservative streak, a desire to play it safe and avoid risks and possible failures. Such growth ambivalence characterizes all ages from toddlerhood on. The adult given a golden opportunity for a new job hesitates and vacillates and cannot decide whether he or she is really up to the challenge.

The situation is made complicated because parents, too, feel ambivalent about their children's development. They applaud the child's first steps, first words, first day at school, but at every major developmental juncture they are assailed by misgivings which are best summed up as "I'm losing my baby!" The combined growth ambivalence of children and of their parents is called **dual ambivalence.** It can mean the parents pushing hard when the child would rather take it slowly, or the parents holding back a child who is eager to strike out on a new path. When the conservative side of parental growth ambivalence predominates, it can lead to a subtle sabotage of the child's progress. Psychiatrists call this *infantilization.* As a further complication, the two parents may have different patterns of growth ambivalence, with one parent urging the child on and the other clinging hard to prevent movement.

Dual ambivalence reaches a searing climax at adolescence, when the young person is moving toward true independence from parental support and authority. Here we must emphasize a point that should be self-evident but is often overlooked: The parental role has to keep shifting as the child develops. The older the child, the more parents need to practice a hands-off policy that allows the child to try things out and make mistakes. Mistakes can be instructive, too.

The toddler's manifestations of growth ambivalence are everywhere to be seen. Out on a walk, the child may plunge off in pursuit of a pigeon or go scuttling into an alluring hallway, only to stop short and come hurtling back to the security of parental contact. Toddlers may strike out on their own to explore the wonders of a store, and then burst into tears at the realization that the hand they are reaching for belongs to a stranger. When trying out some new feat, such as jumping from a step, the toddler makes a great show of boldness but still clings tightly to an adult finger.

The very fact of growth ambivalence points to the toddler's developing self-awareness. Note that self-awareness is an important component in the social cognition discussed earlier. Children's ability to make sense of other people's behavior cannot exceed their comprehension of their own workings.

Other Aspects of Self-Awareness

As we have said, young children are egocentric, and a key feature of egocentrism is the inability to be simultaneously aware of oneself and the outside world. Toddlers have no sense of themselves as obstacles: They block doorways or passages and seem unable to comprehend why other people cannot get by. Indeed, toddlers have no sense of themselves as obstacles to their own actions, as when they tug heroically to pick up a length of rope on which they themselves are standing. Toddlers seem to have no awareness of their own weight, as when they try to walk up a sheet of cardboard leaning against a wall and are startled to find it giving way underfoot. Their subjective weightlessness also shows up in the way they fling themselves about when lap sitting. As long as children are involved in their surroundings, they may not even notice being chilled or overheated or sick. Toddlers do, of course, take note of extremes of heat and cold and severe sickness, and they are most certainly sensitive to acute pain. Like infants, though, toddlers are unable to localize pain.

A lack of differentiation between self and world may account for the toddler's reaction to things that are broken. Toddlers react quite passionately to breaking things or to finding them broken. It is as though brokenness in the environment is a threat to their own bodily integrity. Toddlers may refuse a broken cookie, even though they themselves are ready to demolish a whole one. They may refuse to play with a broken doll, even after it has been repaired.

Toddlers sometimes have an almost compulsive concern with neatness and cleanliness. They love to squash cereal or mud through their fingers, but afterward they want their fingers wiped clean. It is as though any clinging remnants of muck are distracting and interrupt smooth communication with playthings.

Young toddlers seem unaware of needing to eliminate, of being in the process of eliminating, or of having eliminated.

However, in the course of a few months, they become aware, first, of having eliminated, then of being in the process of eliminating, and finally of being about to eliminate. It is at this last point that children are most easily toilet trained. The child's new control, first of defecation and then of urination, marks a major advance in the development of the self. We will talk more about toilet training in a moment.

Toddlers can name their own major facial features and body parts. There are occasional confusions, as when a two-year-old girl was asked where her body was, and she spread her legs and pointed to her vulva. Some such confusions may be the product of adult euphemisms or avoidance of any reference to things sexual. Toddlers are able to follow such instructions as "Let's see you open your mouth" or "Let's see you close your eyes." A few toddlers may be able to answer such questions as "What do you smell with?" or "What are your eyes for?" But verbal knowledge of sensory functions does not usually appear until the preschool years.

We have already seen how toddlers like to adorn themselves and pose and posture in front of a mirror. We mention it again as an indicator of developing self-awareness. As their language skills increase, toddlers begin to instruct and direct themselves, to keep up a running commentary on their own activities, and to regulate their own behavior verbally in keeping with parental commandments and taboos (not that toddlers always obey themselves).

Toddlers become vividly aware of ownership, or at least of what goes with whom, and fiercely resist the use of any object by someone with whom it is not associated. Toddlers as a rule are defensive about the property rights of other members of the family before they begin to assert their own. The time comes, though, when toddlers enter a period of determined possessiveness lasting into the preschool years. This often shocks altruistic parents who want to raise their children in a spirit of sharing. However, the child's possessiveness probably means that his or her belongings are an integral part of the self. Remember that adults' self-images include things like clothing, cars, and houses.

A major factor in how children come to view themselves is the way other people regard and treat them. Other people's feelings may be reactions to what the toddler does, but there are also more constant and pervasive communications of affect unrelated to particular events and circumstances. That is, a well-loved toddler feels parental affection even through occasional scoldings, whereas the rejected toddler will feel little satisfaction even in occasional praise.

The way our self-image is shaped by the way other people treat us is revealed in the following exchange between a mother and her almost-two-year-old daughter:

> I was telling Ruth how proud I was of her for going on the potty. She said, "Sometimes I wet my diaper and you are not proud of me. Now you are proud of me." She thought for a moment and added, "and I am proud of myself, too" (Church, 1978).

Just as toddlers' self-respect depends on the world's respect for them, their esteem for others is contingent on their own self-esteem. Hostility, viciousness,

and evil seem to originate in one's own sense of worthlessness. Whether one is caught in a vicious circle of hatred or a benign cycle of love, one cannot escape the circularity of development.

PRACTICAL ISSUES IN THE CARE OF TODDLERS

Because toddlers live in such intimacy with their parents, much of this chapter has necessarily been about how to handle the mechanics of caring for the toddler. However, there still remain several topics of practical interest. The remainder of this chapter will be devoted to setting limits, toilet training, and sex typing. Day care for toddlers would also be a legitimate subject for discussion; but, since infants and toddlers tend to share the same physical quarters in day-care facilities, we feel that we have little to add to what we have already said in Chapter 5.

Setting Limits

Despite our desire to encourage toddlers in their quest for autonomy, it is necessary to impose certain restrictions on their behavior. There are several reasons for this. One is to protect young children from their own impluses and to keep children from being injured or from injuring themselves. Another is to preserve the rights and feelings of others. And still another is to protect such fragile valuables as cannot conveniently be kept out of the child's reach.

When limits are necessary, they should

be firm and definite. The toddler has little comprehension of subtlety or tolerance of ambiguity, and finds comfort and security in clear-cut guidelines. Some parents seem so afraid of losing their babies' love that they end up begging heedless monsters to behave. Tentative, hesitant commands invite toddlers to test and probe limits, partly in teasing, which they enjoy, and partly in uncertainty, which they do not. Much misbehavior looks to the expert eye like pleas to parents to exercise a control of which children themselves are not yet capable.

There is little place for "reasoning with" the toddler. Indeed, "reasoning" may be far less satisfying to a toddler than an abrupt command. The underlying menace in much of adult reasoning is conveyed in a preschool child's tirade against a comrade: "I'll hit you! I'll cut you up in little pieces! I'll—I'll—I'll *explain* it to you!"

In the matter of physical safety, toddlers are relentless explorers and experimenters, and their enthusiasm and curiosity far outstrip their prudence. This is partly because their perceptual capacities have not yet been enriched with extensive knowledge. For instance, toddlers do not foresee what will happen if they tug hard at a lamp cord.

Toddlers may egocentrically forget about themselves as objects of harm. They may be so absorbed in watching a car back out of the driveway that they fail to realize that they themselves are in its path. Toddlers simply do not see the menace in speeding cars and their capacity for mangling flesh and bone. Thus, ways have to be found and enforced for keeping toddlers out of the street.

Unlike adults, toddlers have not yet learned to adjust to the changing field of forces in a moving car. They have to be firmly anchored so that they are not flung across the car when it turns a corner or sent smashing into the windshield by a sudden application of the brakes.

Toddlers love water and have no idea that pond or ocean or swimming pool can engulf them. This means that toddlers cannot be left alone in any body of water deeper than a small mud puddle. They do not see the cutting qualities of knives or the piercing qualities of things like sticks and scissors.

In the matter of protecting breakables, the same principles apply that we discussed in connection with infancy. Those things that have to be left where the toddler can reach them have to be made taboo through aversive conditioning. As in infancy, toddlers can sometimes be given supervised access to fragile objects, if only to satisfy the toddlers' curiosity and reduce the objects' allure.

The greatest menace to other people's mental health is a child's temper tantrums. In general, adult excitability tends to breed tantrums, making for a vicious circle in which adult and child feed the flames of each other's passions. Away from home, prompt removal of the child from the scene is usually the best treatment for tantrums. At home, non-reinforcement is usually the best medicine, as illustrated in the following description:

Ruth [age fifteen months] has tried tantrums to get her way. She lies on the floor and cries. If I ignore her and leave the room, she stops crying, comes to the room I am in, lies on the floor and screams. I go into another room and she follows. When she discovers she cannot get any attention this way, she comes over to me, puts her head in my lap and puts her arms around my legs and says, "Hug" (Church, 1978).

Toilet Training

A number of parents have reported to us in recent years that their children have toilet trained themselves. We think what parents are saying is that they gave their children total freedom to observe the parents using the toilet and that the children learned through modeling to do likewise. We suspect also that there was a modicum of verbal encouragement to try to use the toilet like a big boy or girl. If this nondirective approach works, fine. What follows is written for those parents whose children have shown, along about age two, no inclination to abandon their diapers.

Attitudes toward body functions have changed down through the years. Very few people nowadays regard elimination and its products as dirty, shameful, disgusting, and unmentionable. To those parents or day-care workers who have inherited or retained Victorian attitudes of revulsion toward the processes of urination and defecation we can say only that they should try hard to overcome them.

In the interests of safeguarding the child's autonomy, it is a good idea to work cooperatively with the toddler in achieving sphincter control, and to avoid any suggestion that you are preempting his or her dominion over his or her own body. No matter what Freud said, there is no need to make the potty chair a battleground.

Toilet training is one area in which parents have to take seriously the matter

(© Michael Weisbrot & Family/Stock, Boston)

A toddler teaches his "Digger Dog" to use the potty. With many toddlers, a nondirective approach to toilet training works fine; by around two, through modeling and verbal encouragement, the children have virtually trained themselves.

of maturational readiness. If a toddler is unable to control elimination—holding on, letting go, expelling—then no techniques of training are going to work. We repeat the indicators of readiness: first the toddler becomes aware that elimination has just taken place; second that elimination is in progress; and third that elimination is about to take place. It is at this last point of awareness that the child is ready to learn control. It helps if toddlers are switched from diapers to training pants during their waking hours.

As a rule, we do not favor baby talk, but a standard vocabulary of child elimination has developed and most parents feel comfortable using and having their toddlers use such designations as "BM," "caca," "doo-doo," "pee-pee," among others. More precise language does not come easily to everybody's tongue. Whatever words one chooses, one should feel free to talk about elimination with the toddler.

Parents have an important asset working for them in the process of toilet training. Parental approval is a powerful reinforcer. Combined with children's normal tendency to emulate parental behavior, their desire for praise contributes mightily. Parents are advised not to use material rewards, such as candy or other treats. There is a considerable literature saying that extrinsic rewards depress intrinsic motivation to learn (Lepper and Greene, 1978); and there is no good reason to fly in the face of what looks like one of psychology's few stable principles. Once ready, toddlers may be on and off in their cooperation, but once they know what is wanted and get used to the idea, they are willing to try.

A vital ingredient, of course, has been parental openness about their own elimination practices. From the time they can move around, babies love to trail after their parents as they go through their bathroom routines. This should give babies ample opportunity to see their models ridding themselves of body wastes. If parents feel self-conscious about exposing their intimate anatomy to inspection by their young children, they may be retarding the process of toilet training. On the other hand, parents may have a strong need for privacy, and we can hardly recommend that people go against their personal inclinations.

Bowel training usually comes first. Let us for once be dogmatic: Do not try to schedule your child's bowel movements by giving either laxatives or enemas. Either

may be necessary in times of sickness, but both can be physically and psychologically harmful when used routinely.

We recommend the use of a potty chair for the simple reason that the child can get in and out of it without help. Whether in keeping with the toddler's schedule or in response to signals of an approaching bowel movement, the child can be led gently to the pot. The child should have the right and responsibility to lower his or her training pants. If nothing happens and the child becomes restless, there is nothing to do but let him or her go. If, a few minutes later, the child has a bowel movement in its pants, the parent can only take it in stride and wait for the next time. If the child succeeds in having a movement in the pot, praise is in order. The parent should not rush to empty the pot down the toilet. This conveys the idea that what the baby has produced is revolting. The pot can wait while the parent cleans the baby's bottom, preferably to the accompaniment of words of satisfaction at the new sign of maturity.

Progress is more a matter of parental attitudes than of techniques. A casual, cheerful manner throughout, concern for the baby's comfort, abundant expressions of affection, and praise for success all contribute to the success of the cooperative enterprise. Anxiety, haste, prolonged confinement, strain, disgust, or punishment or moral outrage when the child falters can only be disruptive. We might note that some children master bowel control and then, satisfied, cannot be bothered to use the pot again until, at a somewhat later age, they realize that going in their pants is just too babyish. Also, although we are talking about bowel control, bowel movements are often accompanied by urination. This makes no difference in the case of little girls, but boys who are about to urinate are very likely to have an erection. The parents who note such an erection are well advised to aim the penis down into the pot.

Bladder control comes in two stages, waking control and sleeping control. Waking control usually comes first, somewhere around age two. Sleeping control may lag some months behind. The internal signals of impending urination may be less well defined than those of defecation, and the mechanisms of muscular control are more elusive. Therefore, parents have to take an active role. The child's readiness becomes evident when there is an increase in the intervals between urinations. When the child has not urinated for a while, the parent can invite him or her to try.

At first, both girls and boys urinate sitting down. Remember that the boy's penis has to be aimed downward, especially if he has an erection. Both boys and girls, assuming that they have observed their father urinating, may want to urinate in the fashion of older males. Explanations about why this will not work are likely to have slight impact, and both boys and girls may have to learn from sad, wet experience before they are willing to sit down again. Azrin and Foxx (1974) propose a somewhat different approach to bladder training, based on behavior-modification principles. This approach seems to work well with retarded children. We do not know how effective it is in everyday circumstances.

Nighttime bladder control usually follows almost automatically, with a delay of a few months, as a consequence of daytime control. It appears that the child's practice in controlling the urinary sphincter reverses the reflexive response to bladder tension, from relaxation and expulsion to contraction and retention. If nighttime control seems to be too long in coming, the parents can awaken the child before they go to bed and let the child urinate in a hand-held vessel. However, such measures are not usually necessary.

It is important to realize that practically all well-trained children have occasional lapses. During the day the child may be so preoccupied with some activity that the warning signals go unnoticed, or responding to them is delayed until it is too late. Sleeping control sometimes gets lost in times of illness, special excitement, novel situations, or unusual strains. Even older children under severe stress may revert to bed-wetting. During the evacuation of children from London during World War II, school-age children separated from their parents were reported to wet their beds in such numbers that, as one observer put it, "half of England was awash." The only cure we know of is to remove the stress.

Sex Typing

Psychological sex differences constitute one of the major areas in which the nature-nurture controversy rages. Biological differences between male and female undoubtedly account for some of their differences in behavior. At the same time, we must acknowledge that **sex typing**—casting the child in the role thought appropriate to his or her sex—begins at a very early age. Three studies by Beverly Fagot (1973, 1974, 1978) illustrate how the toddler's sex influences parental attitudes and behavior. In one study, Fagot (1973) asked a sample of well-informed but childless adults to rate thirty-eight behaviors in terms of their appropriateness for one sex or the other. Only six of the thirty-eight activities were judged as sex typed, and one of these only marginally. Roughhousing, playing with transportation toys, and aggressive behavior were seen as more masculine. Playing with dolls, dressing up, and looking in the mirror (the marginal case) were judged to be more feminine. There were statistically reliable differences between male and female raters on five of the six items. However, only the differences with respect to roughhousing and playing with transportation toys seem of sufficient magnitude to be worthy of attention. Women viewed these as more feminine appropriate than did men.

In another study (Fagot, 1974), observations were made in the homes of twelve pairs of parents and their singleton (only child) toddlers, six girls and six boys. To quote from the author's abstract:

> Boys played with blocks and manipulated objects significantly more than girls. Girls asked for help, played with dolls, danced, and dressed up significantly more than boys. Both parents gave girls more praise and more criticism than boys, and both parents joined boys' play more often than girls' play. However, boys were left to play alone more than girls (p. 554).

Some other findings were: (1) mothers tended to use physical punishment on both sexes more than fathers did (although the literature tells us that boys get more physical punishment than do girls [Maccoby and Jacklin, 1974]); (2) fathers rated more behavior as sex appropriate than did mothers (this time on a forty-six-item list); and (3) parents of daughters saw father and mother roles as much the same, whereas parents of sons saw father and mother roles as quite different, with the mother doing the caretaking and the father playing with and providing a model for his son. This ties in with the general findings that fathers are more concerned with cultivating masculinity in boys than femininity in girls (Maccoby and Jacklin, 1974)—although they definitely reinforce their daughters' displays of affection.

Fagot (1978) found that parents react differently (positively, negatively, or neutrally) to various behaviors in their twenty- to twenty-four-month-old toddlers, depending on the "sex-appropriateness" of the behavior. Aggression provided the only real surprise: It occurred rarely, was equally common in both sexes, and provoked very little reaction in parents.

Children also begin at an early age to sex type themselves through observational learning and modeling. At first, both boys and girls imitate both fathers and mothers. Soon, though, through mechanisms that we do not entirely understand, little girls come to identify with their mothers and little boys with their fathers.

It seems to us that nothing can be done, or should be done, to change the differential sorts of affection that parents feel toward sons and daughters. At the same time, the cause of women's liberation demands that we stop stereotyping our children according to sex. We think that there are two ways parents can avoid stereotyping. First, they can be emotionally open with children of both sexes, and they should encourage the same degree of emotional expression and control in both sexes. Second, they can supply children of both sexes with the same range of playthings, learning opportunities, experiences, and discipline. The idea is not to abolish differences between the sexes. It is to make it possible for children of both sexes to grow up to be the kinds of persons they feel most comfortable being. Children need to be socialized so that they can operate as part of the larger group. But there should not be two sets of rules, one governing the permissible limits for males and the other for females. We can begin by dropping words like "unmanly" and "unladylike" from our vocabularies. A key principle should be that what is sauce for the goose is sauce for the gander.

As we said earlier, one of the defining features of toddlerhood is the child's coming to share one of the defining features of humankind—language. It is to this topic that we turn in Chapter 9.

(© Elizabeth Crews)

We can stop stereotyping children according to sex by encouraging the same degree of emotional expression and control in both sexes and by supplying both with the same range of playthings, learning opportunities, experiences, and discipline. There should not be two sets of rules, one consisting of permissible limits for females and the other, for males.

SUMMARY

1. Between the ages of about fifteen months and two and a half years, the child goes through a period called toddlerhood. During toddlerhood, the child masters productive language, walking, and trotting; forms attachments to peers; begins seeking psychological autonomy and increased self-control; advances his or her capacity for nonliteral thought.

2. For Freud, toddlerhood corresponds to the anal stage of psychosexual development. Erikson regards toddlerhood as a critical period for the resolution of a conflict between autonomy and shame and doubt. Piaget does not recognize toddlerhood as a distinct period; toddlerhood straddles the sensorimotor and preoperational stages.

3. Toddlers can remember and anticipate and can store information; their play shows that they are guided in part by internal images.

4. Toddlers spend a great deal of time engaged in play activities. These behaviors help them to master new skills and to heighten their growing awareness of self and world. At this stage, they are not oriented toward achievement, however, and are not motivated to complete the projects they begin. Toddlers delight in gross motor activities, but they are also able to examine new objects and materials quietly and intently.

5. During toddlerhood, we see an increase in dramatic play, or imitation of role models. Such play is generally based on simple themes of domestic life. Toddlers also enjoy roughhousing with their parents, and they begin to recognize their similarities to and become interested in their peers. Parallel play, the earliest form of play with other children, develops. The toddlers play side by side, but rarely interact.

6. Toddlers' social relations imply a degree of awareness of how humans can be expected to behave. Children's social cognition eventually expands to include a recognition of deception, an acceptance of conventions, a grasp of moral principles, and an awareness of social institutions that transcend individual behavior.

7. A toddler may be upset by the arrival of a new sister or brother. Though all jealousy cannot be avoided—nor ought it, if children are to know a full range of emotions—a prohibition against harming the new arrival can be imposed without denying how normal the toddler's feelings are and without denying the toddler the full measure of love to which she or he continues to be entitled.

8. One of the key developments during toddlerhood is the adaptation to pedestrian life. Early in this period, toddlers need to warm up to walk, but soon trotting becomes their favorite mode of locomotion. They also learn how to pivot on one foot, go down a flight of stairs, and sit down on a chair, stool, or bench. Toddlers have several characteristic postures—squatting, sitting with legs forward, bending at the waist with head on the floor, and leaning limply against an adult. They also develop a broader familiarity with space and spatial relationships. They can master action space, but cannot yet grasp map space.

9. During toddlerhood, American children acquire a great many commonplace skills. They can feed themselves with a spoon, chew gum without swallowing it, blow their noses, eat an ice cream cone, operate a simple record player, ride a tricycle, take off their clothes, and take utensils apart and then reassemble them.

10. Toddlers are extremists, feeling omnipotent one moment and crumbling into despair and impotence the next. As long as there's a fair chance that a toddler can face a new challenge successfully, however, it's a good idea to encourage the child to try.

11. Although "Me" and "No" dominate the toddler's quest for autonomy, negativism is not actually a predominant part of toddlerhood, and much of the negativism is play acting, soon integrated into the more constructive, competence-building aspects of autonomy.

12. Growth ambivalence characterizes the toddler's experience; parents have their own ambivalent feelings toward their children's growth as well, making for dual ambivalence. As the child develops, the parental role must keep shifting, practicing an increasingly hands-off policy that allows the child to try things out and make mistakes. Mistakes can be instructive.

13. Toddlers are egocentric: They have no sense of themselves as obstacles, no awareness of their own weight, and, although they are sensitive to acute pain, they are unable to localize pain. However, they are increasingly able to take account of other people's points of view, as in showing a picture or knowing where someone is looking.

14. There is little place for "reasoning with" a toddler, and they must be protected from the danger inherent in their nature as relentless explorers and experimenters. Toddlers do not foresee problems; they must be firmly anchored in cars; they love water but have no idea that a pond or a pool can engulf them; nor do they see the cutting qualities of knives.

15. Readiness for toilet training—if the child doesn't do it spontaneously through modeling by about age two—depends on one condition: the toddler must know when elimination is about to take place. Whatever words one chooses, one should feel free to talk about elimination with the toddler.

16. Bowel training usually comes first. An accessible potty chair is helpful. Emptying it immediately, however, may suggest that what the child has produced is revolting; praise and cleanup for the child should precede it.

17. Bladder control comes in two stages, waking and sleeping; the latter may lag by some months. Practically all children have lapses.

18. Although nothing can—or should—be done to change the differential sorts of affection parents feel for daughters and sons, they can stop stereotyping children according to sex. They can be emotionally open with children of both sexes and can supply both sexes with the same range of playthings, learning opportunities, experiences, and discipline—not two sets of rules, one for males and one for females.

KEY TERMS

action space, 277
anal stage, 262
autonomy, 262
deferred imitation, 263
dramatic play (symbolic,
   fantasy, or pretend
   play), 263

dual ambivalence, 281
growth ambivalence, 279
map space, 277
negativism, 279
parallel play, 269
physical cognition, 264
play, 264

productive language, 262
receptive language, 262
sex typing, 287
shame and doubt, 263
sibling rivalry, 272
social cognition, 264
symbolic functioning, 263

SUGGESTED READINGS

Brazelton, T. B. *Toddlers and Parents*. New York: Delacorte, 1974. An account of toddler behavior in case-history form by a well-known pediatrician-educator.

Church, J. *Understanding Your Child from Birth to Three*. New York: Pocket Books, 1973. One psychologist's account of the early years, with special attention to practical issues in infant and child care.

— (ed.). *Three Babies*. Westport, Conn.: Greenwood Press, 1978 (originally published, 1966). These diaries, kept by the babies' mothers, offer an unusually intimate view of the everyday life of infants and toddlers, with illuminating comments by the editor.

Fraiberg, S. H. *The Magic Years*. New York: Scribner's, 1959. This psychoanalytically, clinically oriented classic offers a vivid portrayal of child life.

Rubin, R. R., Fisher, J. J. III, and Doering, S. G. *Your Toddler*. New York: Macmillan Collier, 1980. A guide to parents. The text is sound and the pictures by Bill Parsons are superb.

Woodcock, L. P. *Life and Ways of the Two-Year-Old*. New York: Dutton, 1941. This classic is out of print, but if you can find a copy, read it for a delightful description of toddlers in a preschool setting.

CHAPTER 9

The Beginnings of Language

In this chapter, we discuss the earliest manifestations of language and the leading theoretical views of this essential human capacity. Other important features of language development will be described as they emerge at particular ages. For instance, toddlers work hard at talking, but they seem unaware of language as something to contemplate. Preschool children become aware of language as something to be thought about, and they consciously manipulate it and play with it. Here, as the chapter title indicates, we are concerned primarily with the beginnings of language.

One of the more remarkable achievements of the developing human being is becoming able to understand and use language. It takes about two years to learn the fundamentals, after which further elaboration of linguistic abilities can go on lifelong. Children learn the fundamentals with a minimum of help. They make very few mistakes of meaning, that is, mislabeling aspects of reality. They make numerous mistakes in assembling words into sentences. However, these mistakes, when examined closely, turn out to be the products of logic, a logic shared by practically all children. What is more, children gradually eliminate their peculiarly childish constructions and come to make utterances following the same rules as do the people among whom they are growing up. One of the most amazing features of this whole process is that children can use the resources of language creatively. That is, they can combine words into sensible utterances quite unlike any they have ever heard. They can formulate ideas of their own and give voice to them.

STRUCTURAL ANALYSIS

An account of learning to talk has to begin with a chronological description of the steps that babies and young children go through as they work toward proficiency. To give such a description, we must invoke some of the formal tools of **structural analysis**, dissecting language into its components. There are four levels of structural analysis: (1) *phonetics,* the sound patterns that are found in spoken language; (2) *grammar* and *syntax,* the rules by which words are shaped and combined to form typical, correct sentences; (3) *semantics,* meaning the way words and word combinations "stand for" states of affairs ranging from material objects to vampires or relativity theory; and (4) *pragmatics,* the techniques we use and the rules we follow in order to communicate.

Phonetics

Phonology is the study of speech sounds and, often, of the structure and function of our vocal and auditory apparatus. It seeks to specify the phonetic features of language (de Villiers and de Villiers, 1978; Dale, 1976, Miller, 1981). It should be obvious that using language consists in producing and understanding sound patterns. Variations in sounds mark the differences among words, among different versions of the same word (e.g., plural versus singular form, past versus present tense), and among combinations of words such as sentences. However, in producing or understanding sound patterns, the child is far more concerned with the meanings carried by sounds than with their physical composition. That is, the analysis of sounds into either the muscular movements by which they are produced or such physical characteristics as pitch, tonal quality, abrupt versus crescendo onset or abrupt versus diminuendo termination, does not describe the psychological reality of the child. Children at first hear and speak globally rather than analytically. Only later do they come to some awareness of the fine points of how speech sounds are constructed.

Phonologists recognize several levels of phonetic analysis and description. We begin with *phonemes,* the units of sound of which language is composed. Alphabetic representation of sound is very often incomplete. We have only twenty-six letters to represent the forty-odd speech sounds that are important in English. To solve such problems, phonologists have devised the phonetic alphabet. This contains characters to represent all the speech sounds found in all the known tongues. Then come *morphemes,* the smallest sound units that carry meaning. A single word can be a morpheme, such as "ball" or "car." Then there are parts of words that are morphemes and carry meaning. Take the word "misunderstanding." This includes three morphemes, *mis, understand,* and *ing. Mis* reverses the root meaning of *understand,* and *ing* converts it to a participle or a gerund, a verb made into a noun. You may object that *under* and *stand* are also meaning-bearing units. However, their meanings as separate words bear no direct relationship to their meaning when combined.

We now jump from the level of the phonetics of words to the phonetics of sentences. Here we enter the realm of *prosody,* the melodic structure of utterances. Listen to someone speaking one of the Scandinavian languages, or French, or Japanese. Note how different their flow is from that of someone speaking English. Prosody includes such features as cadence, intonation, and emphasis. It tells our listeners that our words are to be construed as a command or a question (listen to yourself saying "He's coming, too!" and "He's coming, too?"). Prosody conveys attitudes such as playfulness or contempt, and emotions such as joy or anger.

We do not yet know how children come to master all the subtleties of phonetics. In a very few years, though, they progress from the phonetic crudeness of baby talk to rather well-articulated speech. And for all their fumblings and occasional stutterings, they do it on their own, with little or no help from adults. Most of what we shall have to say in the remainder of this chapter will simply take for granted children's phonetic development.

Grammar and Syntax, Semantics, Pragmatics

Grammar refers to the ways we represent such characteristics of words as tense or number; how we classify words into parts of speech such as nouns, verbs, adjectives, adverbs, and conjunctions; how we classify sentences as declarative versus interrogative, affirmative versus negative, indicative versus imperative, and so forth; and the functions of words within sentences, such as subject, object, complement, qualifier, modifier, and the rest. *Syntax* is that branch of grammar that specifies how words can be assembled to form meaningful utterances such as phrases, clauses, and sentences. For instance, in a declarative sentence the subject usually precedes the verb and the object, as in "The dog bit the man." However, we can in some cases reverse the order by using a passive-voice construction: "The man was bitten by the dog." Syntax allows the speaker to form a huge range of messages from a multitude of single words. Grammar and syntax merge into semantics.

Semantics is the study of what words and longer utterances are about, what they mean. We do a reasonably good job in day-to-day communication of making other people aware of our meanings and of deciphering their meanings. However, years of work have not yet told us how to define or describe or explain how bundles of words can stimulate us to particular ways of feeling, acting, thinking, and answering back. Nor do we know how words can enlighten us by giving knowledge and understanding, or delude us by giving us believable but incorrect information. Add to this that we do often misunderstand each other, try as we may to make ourselves clear. You can see why the study of meaning has not advanced very far.

Pragmatics seeks to identify the means, linguistic and extralinguistic (gestures, pointing, facial expression, prosodic manipulation) by which we communicate. For instance, communication demands that we transcend egocentrism to the extent of judging our listener's need for information, his or her ability to grasp certain relationships, the values he or she will attach both to what is said and how it is said, and so forth. In conversational contexts we have to learn to take turns. Effective communication depends on our ability to listen as well as to speak. We learn the tricks of prosody. We learn to convey implications and draw inferences. We learn to speak in a variety of registers: We speak in a casual way when conversing with family and friends. We use more formal but still colloquial language on the job. A business letter or report requires even more formal language. The awed commoner might address royalty in highly stilted language.

FUNCTIONAL ANALYSIS

The line is blurred between structural analysis, particularly semantics and pragmatics, and another, contrasting approach, **functional analysis** (de Villiers and de Villiers, 1978). Structural analysis, as we have said, concerns dissecting language into its components, whereas functional analysis focuses on the uses to which language is put (Karmiloff-Smith, 1979). It is commonplace to say that language is a means of communication, but that is only part of the story. We use language to stir people up emotionally, as when we tease them or tell them a joke. We can use language as a weapon or as a means of calming down a troubled situation. We use language to order and make sense out of reality, to formulate theories and principles, or to try out different arrangements of reality in a process called thinking. We also use language magically, hoping to change brute facts by talking them away, or by invoking supernatural help. This does not exhaust the functions of language, but indicates their diversity.

RECEPTIVE AND PRODUCTIVE LANGUAGE

Now to the chronology of language development. Language learning begins in late infancy, in what is called **receptive language**—that is, children begin to understand what other people say before they themselves begin to speak. We have seen, too, that the infant develops nonverbal means of communication: shrieking, pointing, and using tokens.

Babies vocalize a great deal from an early age, and it seems probable that preverbal vocalizing plays its part in readying the child to speak (de Villiers and de Villiers, 1978). Exchanges of babblings between parent and child can easily be seen as the forerunners of conversation.

In toddlerhood, the baby begins not only to understand a certain amount of language but also to produce language, to talk. Talking is referred to as **productive language,** in contrast with the receptive language of comprehension. Note that our power to understand always outruns our powers to formulate statements, just as reading is easier than writing. The baby talks first in single words. Some of these early "words" are in fact fusions of commonly linked word groups: the familiar "awgone" (the French toddler's equivalent is *yapu* from *il n'y en a plus*); "whadda?"; "goodboy" and "goodgirl"; "not-in-the-mouth"; "what-a-pity"; enough is enough, pronounced "enuss-enuss."

The Beginnings of Productive Language

There has been a great deal of debate about children's first words, in an at-

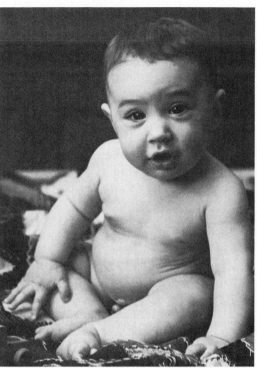

(© Leonard Speier 1983)

While an infant's babbling may sound meaningless, it very likely serves the practical purpose of preparing the child for speech.

tempt to deduce the motivational basis for speaking. For instance, it seems reasonable to suppose that babies speak in order to have some want fulfilled. However, the attempt to identify children's first words seems hopeless. For one thing, it is not always easy to tell whether a child is actually using a word. For instance, many parents develop a game in which they ask the baby "Where's the (whatever)?" and the child, pointing, responds, "There!" (pronounced "dhzare"). We cannot be sure whether the baby's "there" is a word or merely a sound that is part of the ritual of the game. Or a child may use in an appropriate context a sound that occurs regularly in its babbling. Thus the child responds to the sounds of water flowing into the bathtub by trotting tubward and exclaiming "Ba! Ba!" But since "ba" peppers the daylong stream of nonsense sounds, it is not unambiguously being used as a word.

We can be certain that the baby has begun to talk only on the day he or she points to some object and says its name, although the pronunciation may be far from perfect. A clear instance of this is when a toddler, who had been making all the sounds mentioned above for some time, one day pointed to a Japanese paper fish hanging on her wall as decoration and clearly said "Heefsh."

This rules out as first words all parts of speech except concrete nouns, although the baby may previously have used verbs or adjectives without these being noted by anyone. The identifiable first words are in fact so varied that they will support no theory of motivation for speaking (Greenfield and Smith, 1976). It is our position, to be elaborated shortly, that word realism makes speaking intrinsically satisfying, in that speaking creates realities. No other motivations are needed.

Holophrases. The child's one-word utterances may serve several purposes. Sometimes toddlers make the rounds of the house naming things, as though rehearsing their vocabulary. Sometimes the toddler's saying a name seems to be an invitation to a parent to look at the object in question. Toddlers may speak an object's name with a questioning tone, as though asking a parent to verify that they have the name right. All such functions seem to express a one-to-one relationship between word and thing. However, some of the toddler's one-word utterances seem to imply an entire sentence. Such utterances are called **holophrases** (singular, **holophrasis**). Thus, "Up" means "I want to be picked up"; "Out" means "I want to go out"; "Daddy," while pointing to a shoe, means "That is Daddy's shoe." By noting the context and the child's manner, one can distinguish between the several kinds of naming and a holophrasis or one-word sentence.

Children are insatiably word hungry and seek the names of things as though compiling a catalogue of the universe. "Whadda?" is a dominant theme of early language. As suggested by "up" and "out," toddlers use parts of speech other than nouns. They also use a fair number of interjections ("hi," "bye-bye," "ouch"); verbs ("go," "carry," "eat"); and adverbs ("up" and "out," of course, and also "again" and "back"). Many children learn "hot" quite early. Sometimes this is a designation of anything hot. Sometimes it is an all-purpose cry of warning. They learn "more" in the concrete sense of "Give me some more," but not as a term for comparison, as in "more" and "fewer."

The toddler's holophrases serve a number of functions. As the Daddy's shoe example suggests, possession or at least connection is an important feature of the child's early experience. Interjections are ordinarily mere accompaniments to events. However, more than one toddler has been known to bring a visitor her purse and exclaim "Bye-bye" as a clear invitation to depart. In general, young children are liberal with imperatives—commands and demands.

Expressive Jargon. Many children first try to go beyond single-word utterances by way of what Arnold Gesell called **expressive jargon.** This is a flow of gibberish, sometimes studded with real words, which in most cases seems meant to communicate meaning. Indeed, expressive jargon so faithfully mimics the sounds and cadences of adult speech that it often seems, like the comedian's double talk, tantalizingly on the verge of being comprehensible. The practiced listener may, in fact, from the context and from occasional real words embedded in the stream of jargon, be able to have a pretty good idea of what the child is trying to say. Expressive jargon is such a conspicuous phenomenon that we are constantly surprised to find parents who are unaware of it. We interpret expressive jargon as an attempt by the child to leap magically into fully elaborated speech. It soon dies out, presumably for lack of contingent reinforcement, and the child goes back to speaking in single words.

Two-Word Sentences. Once toddlers have a basic stock of words—and their vocabularies grow at a fantastic rate—they discover the trick of joining them into two-word sentences: "Car, backing up" ("Backing up" seems to have been learned as a single unit) or "Baby, crying." We use the comma here to indicate a slight pause, which to us suggests that the child is engaging in a deliberate act of construction. A number of researchers have looked for systematic grammatical or syntactic patterns in two-word sentences (Bloom, 1970; Braine, 1976; Greenfield and Smith, 1976). So far the search has been in vain.

A child is as likely to say "Ball throw" as "Throw ball," and "Cookie eat" as "Eat cookie." They can express location. They can call for repetition "Tickle again"). We will have more to say about the semantic range of the toddler's vocabulary in a later section. In any event, two-word sentences are only a small way station on the road to more fully developed language.

The Emergence of Standard Forms

Toddlers' sentences steadily increase in length; but at first they have little regard for standard word order, and are totally without benefit of articles, conjunctions, prepositions, or indicators of verb tense or noun number. No one has yet traced the appearance of these missing features. One laudable attempt was based on the utterances of three children between twenty months and three years of age (Limber, 1973). However, this account makes no mention of prepositions. It places conjunctions at twenty-seven months, but does not specify which ones. The conjunction "and" is quite easy, whereas "but" or "or" may be more difficult. According to this account, the indefinite article "a/an" does not appear until age thirty-four months, which strains our credulity.

Without any attempt at a strict chronology, then, we mention a few interesting semantic, syntactical, and grammatical features that emerge in toddlerhood and the early preschool years. We begin with "but." For several children we have known, "but" was a way of taking exception. For instance, the child asks, "Can people fly?" and the adult answers, "No, of course not," to which the child rejoins,

Toddlers play together but can communicate verbally
only through the medium of an adult.

"But airplanes!" Or a child asks Father if she can have a piece of candy. The father says yes. And the child exclaims, "But Mommy!" indicating that Mommy has earlier forbidden candy eating.

Of special interest is the emergence of speaking by the rules. English is full of irregularities, notably in the formation of plurals and past tenses. The child begins by learning irregular forms correctly but then, as the rules take hold, switches to the regular but incorrect form. The child at first says "two feet" but later says "two foots" or even "two feets." As with plurals, so with tenses. Toddlers initially use the past tense or irregular verbs correctly, as in "I brought my teddy bear." Then, as the rules begin to govern, the child changes to forms such as "I bringed," "I brang," "I branged," and even "I broughted" (Cazden, 1968). A four-year-old recently informed one of us, "Daddy was boughting a stroller." This substitution of incorrect regular forms for correct irregular ones is called **overregularization.**

A related phenomenon is the misplaced inflection, as in "He pick it ups" and "I walk homed." Notice two things in connection with these errors. First, the child is not learning the rules by blind imitation. Speech models do not normally use these aberrant forms. Second, even though such constructions are errors, they are intelligent errors. The child first learns the rules, and only then how to apply them correctly. Note, too, that nobody teaches the child either the rules or their correct operation. Children learn these things on their own.

It is not only standard grammatical features that take odd twists in toddlers' speech. Several children from different families have produced a set of constructions derived from "each other": "We're hugging our chothers" or "Are you mad at your chothers?"

Two grammatical operations are of special interest. These are *negation* and *interrogation*. Note that these do not begin at the multiple-word sentence stage. "No" is an early and important word in the toddler's vocabulary. But making negative statements is more complex. The toddler seems impelled to express negation in as many ways as possible: "No, I don't not have none" (Bellugi, 1971). This urge to overdo negation persists into the middle years and sometimes into adulthood. It causes despair in schoolteachers, who are constantly inveighing against the use of double negatives. "Whadda?" is probably the first question, closely followed by "Why?" But interrogative sentences are another matter. The child first forms complex questions by prefacing a declarative statement with an interrogative word: "Why he is doing that?" "Is it is a dog?" "May I can have some?" From the outset, children's questions are marked by the correct interrogatory tone of voice.

We have been describing some of the more common features of early language. Not all children manifest all these features. An occasional child bides his or her time, not uttering any words at all, and then begins speaking in well-formed sentences. Indeed, it is reported that one

highly precocious ten-month-old girl's first utterance was made at the dinner table: "I want a taste."

THE LIMITED ROLE OF INSTRUCTION IN LANGUAGE ACQUISITION

The first thing to be said about instruction in the young child's learning of language is that it is virtually nonexistent. As we have seen, the toddler asks for names, and adults spontaneously supply some names for new objects. But many words are learned simply by listening to people talk. Remember, too, that not all words are names of concrete objects. There are words referring to actions, to all kinds of relationships such as kinship, cause and effect, space, and time, to qualities like color and temperature. Some words, such as "know" and "forget," refer to mental operations. The child learns all these, too. In some sense, the words the child uses are acquired by imitation (Bloom, Hood, and Lightbown, 1974). But it is a special kind of imitation, since the child has to single out the relevant aspects of situations to which words refer. Also, the child's first use of a word may lag hours or days behind hearing the word spoken. Here we see the role of *deferred imitation* in language learning.

But imitation plays no role whatever in the child's early word combinations, which bear no resemblance to those used by older children and adults. As children progress, however, they adopt the standard rules for sentence construction used in their particular speech community. This seems a clear case of schematic learning based on modeling. In Chapter

1, you will recall, we described an experiment in which children were selectively exposed to novel linguistic forms. They then used them spontaneously, apparently as a product of modeling (Nelson, 1977). Young children do acquire such linguistic ornaments as tag phrases and stylized openings, from "Don't you agree?" to "As a matter of fact" (pronounced "zmatterfac"). The child simply develops a sense of which constructions sound or, more accurately, *feel* right. There is one kind of correction that parents do offer. This is of mislabelings: "No, sweetie, that's not a kitty; that's a squirrel." Parents rarely try to correct a young child's grammatical and syntactical errors. When they do try, they are unlikely to succeed (Cazden, 1968). McNeill (1966) recorded a widely cited dialogue between mother and child:

Child: Nobody don't like me.
Mother: No, say "Nobody likes me."
Child: Nobody don't like me.

[This exchange is repeated eight times.]

Mother: *No. Now listen carefully; say "Nobody likes me."*
Child: *Oh! Nobody don't likes me.*

It used to be assumed that parents responded to their children's condensed utterances by offering them an expanded, correct rephrasing—the *expansion hypothesis*. Observation soon showed that this seldom happens. In place of the expansion hypothesis we now have the *expatiation hypothesis*, according to which the adult advances the discussion instead of restating the child's utterance. The expansion hypothesis would predict that the child's "Doggy bark" would be met with "Yes, the dog is barking." The expatiation hypothesis

more accurately predicts that the likely response would be "Yes, he's mad at the kitty" or "Yes, but he won't bite" (Cazden, 1968).

In many cases, toddlers' learning requires a transposition of what they hear. Parents, speaking to the child, use *I* to refer to themselves and *you* to refer to the child. Children must learn or be taught that they in turn use *I* in reference to themselves and address others as *you*. One little girl consistently referred to her parents as *we:* "Are we going out tonight?" meant "Are you and Daddy going out tonight?"

Children learn language by hearing it spoken in a concrete context of objects, relations, actions, gestures, events, and feelings. But children extract from the language they hear more than words and the codified rules of sentence construction. They also extract tones of voice expressing playfulness, despair, sympathy, exasperation, puzzlement, disdain, parody, and mockery. They echo their parents' mannerisms and affectations, such as the special way most adults have of talking over the telephone. It is often an embarrassing self-revelation to hear one's own turns of speech coming out of the mouth of one's child.

It follows that even if parents cannot instruct their children in language they nevertheless, as models, teach them how to talk. This means that it is incumbent upon parents to provide good models.

In talking to babies and young children, parents engage in something known as **code switching** (Gleason, 1973; Snow, 1972). Code switching is speaking in a simplified form of one's ordinary dialect so as to make oneself more easily comprehended. The extreme of code switching is the adult version of

Adults generally speak to young children in a simplified form, a practice known as *code switching*. The adults use simple vocabulary, speak slowly, and repeat phrases.

"baby talk," which usually bears little resemblance to the actual speech of toddlers. Ringler (1981) describes the speech of a sample of working-class mothers talking to their one- or two-year-old babies as slower, briefer, and syntactically simpler than their speech addressed to adults, and as emphasizing affirmatives and questions. The mothers' speech is further described as telegraphic. That is, mothers use a simple, concrete vocabulary and a minimum of connectives. Their speech also contained a great deal of redundancy (the same thing said several times, perhaps with varied phrasings). Even five-year-olds code switch when talking to infants or

very young children (Gleason, 1973). However, fathers do much less code switching than mothers (Gleason, 1975). We feel that mothers err too much on the side of code switching, and we recommend that one speak to young children in a reasonable approximation of adult forms.

Two incidental observations are in order here. Toddlers like to be talked to on the telephone, apparently understanding what is said to them and certainly recognizing a familiar voice. In answer to a yes or no question, toddlers can nod or shake their head. Beyond this, toddlers cannot answer back on the telephone, discourse apparently being possible only with a visible interlocutor and not with a disembodied voice. The second observation is that the things toddlers pick up from adult speech include expletives like "Goddam" and "sonofabitch," which the child uses appropriately if uncomprehendingly. These expressions jar on adult ears, but the offense is aesthetic rather than moral. If parents are concerned about the child's use of earthy epithets, then they must curb their use in the child's hearing.

BILINGUALISM

In a multilingual nation like the United States, large numbers of people are interested in the effects on children of bilingual rearing. Some parents would like to preserve their ancestral tongue, whereas others feel that it is to the child's intellectual benefit to be fluent in a second language. At the same time, parents have heard many horror stories about bilingualism and do not want to do anything that might harm their child.

Early studies in this area did indeed conclude that bilingualism put the child at a disadvantage. But these early studies overlooked the fact that most of their bilingual subjects were the children of poor immigrants. In these cases, what was being measured was less a matter of bilingualism than of incomplete cultural assimilation. More recent studies indicate that children raised in families where bilingualism is taken for granted suffer no ill effects. There is even suggestive—but by no means conclusive—evidence that children reared bilingually by parents each of whom consistently speaks only one of the two languages may gain an intellectual edge over monolinguals or bilinguals both of whose parents switch freely back and forth between the two languages (Bain, 1976). In any event, by age two such children have no difficulty receiving a message in one language and relaying it to the other parent in that parent's language.

Let us pause to make clear that structural changes in early language beautifully exemplify Werner's orthogenetic principle of differentiation followed by hierarchic integration (p. 22), or as we prefer to call it, **functional subordination.** Children begin by using single words differentiated out of the surrounding ocean of language and then go on to combine them into structures of ever-increasing complexity and sophistication.

WORDS, WORD MEANINGS, AND DOMAINS OF KNOWLEDGE AND LANGUAGE

Children are remarkably accurate in grasping what kinds of things, actions, properties, and relationships words refer to. They sometimes overgeneralize, as when "Daddy" becomes the designation for all adult males. They sometimes overparticularize, as when "kitty" comes to stand for their cat and no other. But most of the time—assuming they are dealing with matters within their range of comprehension—they show an amazing facility for matching spoken patterns to particular features of a complex environment. Sometimes they even match spoken language to purely mental states and events. However, children may interpret and generalize words in ways surprising to adults. For instance, to many young children "heavy" refers to anything entailing strain or effort. A two-year-old, easing his way down a steep slope, observes, "This is sure a heavy hill." Another, vainly stretching to reach something overhead, says, "The shelf is too heavy." Many children use "strong" in much the same way. They use "strong" and "heavy" interchangeably, as in "Is the ice heavy enough to walk on?" An eighteen-month-old learned "windmill" in association with a shingled, grain-grinding windmill, and then generalized the word in turn to a rambling shingled house, a water storage tank, a television antenna, and a skeletal, water-pumping windmill.

Many word pairs refer to polar opposites of a single dimension of experience, and many toddlers learn the dimension as a whole before clearly differentiating the words that stand for the extremes. For instance, toddlers tend to confuse "hot" and "cold," "open" and "close," "on" and "off," and "up" and "down" (but never, apparently, "in" and "out"). Other idiosyncratic meanings are less systematic. A toddler being handed some water in a glass shouts, "Too much! Too much!" and then, when the adult starts to pour some out, screams in protest. In this case, it seems, "too much" was synonymous with "a lot," whereas the terms overlap only partially in adult usage.

Toddlers may begin by mixing up antonyms (opposites). However, by late toddlerhood and the early preschool years, children not only can use antonyms to draw contrasts, they can invent them as needed. One two-year-old, watching the traffic speed past, exclaimed, "They're sure not slowpokes, they're fastpokes!" The same little boy observed a few days later, "Sometimes nobody eats with me, and sometimes lots-obodies." A child observes, "This thing has an upper part and a downer part." It is not until age six or seven that children can produce antonyms on demand, but they can and do use them freely in context at earlier ages.

An eighteen-month-old referred to all red motor vehicles as "engine," which was his word for fire engine. It is worth noting that this child used redness as the key identifying criterion, but did not yet name colors or respond reliably to color names. We have encountered several children who referred to adults' arm and leg hairs as "threads," apparently not recognizing their kinship with head hair. A child labeled a covered wagon seen on television as "mixer truck," presumably because of a physiognomic resemblance to cement-mixing trucks. This same boy described being bitten by a sand fly as "bump your toe," apparently an all-purpose term for painful experiences (Church, 1978). One little girl, wrestling with the distinction between jet-propelled and propeller-driven airplanes, asked "Does the airplane have a spinning?" (this and "fastpoke" are examples of *neologisms*, made-up words).

A little girl demonstrated on many occasions how the same object can be given different names according to the various functions it could serve. A pillow on the bed was "pillow," but on top of her head it became "hat." She scribbled with a "pencil," but a pencil in her mouth became "cigar" or "pipe" (Church, 1978). One study reports how a two-year-old converted other parts of speech into verbs. He remarked on a "louding" airplane and playfully threatened to "stomach" his mother as he pushed at her belly (Carlson and Anisfeld, 1969).

One useful way of describing vocabulary (and presumably conceptual) development is in terms of **domains.** This term, borrowed from anthropology, is used in the study of language development to group words belonging to a common segment of reality. Among the more widely studied domains are kinship, causation, number, shape, color, and the realm of the supernatural. In the beginning, children's concrete knowledge of the world far exceeds their ability to talk about it. Later on, though, words can frame and focus previously unnoted aspects of reality and relate them to broader domains. These domains include some that lie beyond our senses and, of these, some that do not exist, such as demons and hobgoblins and the Tooth Fairy. We now sample some of the child's emerging domains of language and thought.

Kinship

A favorite domain for study by anthropologists is kinship terms. The toddler undoubtedly has a strong emotional sense that familiar, well-loved people form a group distinct from the rest of the world. However, toddlers lack a vocabulary of kinship, even though kinship terms are used as proper names for relatives. It is only in the late preschool years that children actually begin using and making sense of words like "grandfather" and "grandmother," "aunt" and "uncle" and "cousin."

Causation

In the domain of causation, toddlers know pragmatically how to make a great many things happen. They can turn lights on and off, work faucets, and tune the radio and television. They know that the cat scratches if you pull its tail. But their vocabulary of cause and effect is limited to such expressions as "Make it work" or "Fix it." They simply accept the way things operate without surprise or curiosity, as the natural order of things.

In general, although events may startle toddlers, as when the jack-in-the-box pops forth, or cause them pain, or frighten them, or make them laugh, events do not stir toddlers to wonder. Late in toddlerhood the child asks "Why?" However, this query—when it is a genuine query and not just a way of maintaining contact with or teasing the adult—seems addressed not so much to explanations of how things work as to motives and justifications. The toddler is asking "For what reason?" or "On what grounds?" rather than "By what means?" or "In accordance with what principles?" This unquestioning acceptance of events as they happen is called **dynamism:** It is as though the world were charged with some kind of all-purpose energy that keeps things happening. It is close kin to what in adults is called fatalism. A dynamistic orientation permits what Piaget calls **transductive thinking,** linking into a causal sequence just about any pair of things that happen to occur together. Lightning causes thunder, or sometimes it is the other way around. Transductive thinking is like a learned association, except that no repetition is necessary for the child to sense

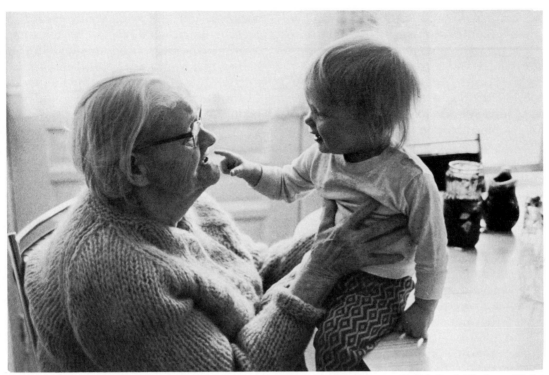

(© Bob Combs/The Image Works)

Toddlers use kinship terms without understanding the vocabulary of kinship. When this child is a couple of years older, however, she will make sense of the term "grandmother."

a causal link between events that happen together, even if only by chance.

It has been said that rational views of cause and effect do not begin to appear until the school years. Throughout the preschool years, children were assumed to think dynamistically, magicalistically, or animistically. **Animism** refers to thinking (or, at least, assuming) that inanimate things are capable of perceiving, feeling, thinking, willing, and spontaneous movement. Thus the boulder rolls down the hillside because it feels like it. One can find plenty of dynamism, transductionism, animism, and magical-

ism in preschool children (and in quite a few adults). However, two recent studies have also demonstrated preschool-age children's capacity for thinking logically about causation. In one study (Koslowski and Pierce, 1981), twenty-nine mothers were asked to keep a record of all causally oriented utterances by their children, who ranged in age from about three to almost six, for periods of one to six weeks. It turned out that children did notice things, and not only the unusual and striking. Also, they thought about them. We quote some of their causality-oriented comments: "The streets are cement-colored, so it didn't rain last night" (contrast this with a four-year-old's remark on a gloomy day, "What's the matter with the sun today? Is it sick?" [United States National Committee, 1979]); "Can planes fly even when they have ice on their wings?"; after putting a piece of food in his mouth, "How did I eat when I was inside your tummy?"

Baillargeon, Gelman, and Meck (1981) built an apparatus in which pushing a rod caused a series of blocks to fall domino-fashion, the final domino striking a lever that toppled a toy rabbit into a bed. Having demonstrated the workings of this mechanism, they asked three- and four-year-old subjects to predict whether various changes in the structure would affect the outcome of pushing the rod. There were twenty-three possible changes. Some of these were relevant—for instance, the position of the rod holder. Others were irrelevant—for example, the color of the rod. The three-year-olds scored from 78 percent to 91 percent correct, and the four-year-olds from 78 percent to 100 percent. In a second study, the middle part of the apparatus was screened from view during questioning. Blocking visual access to the vitals of the gadget lowered accuracy of response. Even so, three-year-olds gave between 65 percent and 87 percent correct answers, and four-year-olds between 70 percent and 96 percent.

It seems to follow that young children, at least when dealing with concrete situations, are capable of thinking quite straightforwardly about cause and effect. It is worth noting that many of the remarks collected by Koslowski and Pierce were questions. Asking questions implies an awareness of one's own ignorance, which is a big step forward. If preschool-age children were as thoroughly dynamistic and magicalistic as Piaget believed, they would not bother to ask questions with self-evident answers. Note, too, that there may be pronounced cultural differences. Children growing up in families in which naturalistic explanations are the norm might answer very differently from children growing up in homes where frequent recourse is made to supernatural forces. We must also be aware that such behavior can be situation-specific: The child who can think quite logically about one kind of problem may be flooded with visions of magic when confronted by a different kind. We shall see plenty of magicalism when we discuss the preschool years.

Number

In the domain of number, toddlers early on learn to count "one, two," with "two" at first standing for any quantity greater than one. They then progress to "one, two, a lot," and then to "one, two, three, a lot." Many two-year-olds can count to five or ten or beyond, but this seems to be a mere recital of a sequence. When toddlers and young preschool children try to count actual things, they are likely to count correctly up to a point and then improvise: 1, 2, 3, 4, 7, 5, 9. Also, they do not adhere to a strict one-to-one correspondence between successive numbers and things counted. They may skip some objects altogether and count others twice or more, so that the final number bears little relation to the size of the collection. What is more, counting and summing seem to be psychologically distinct operations. The ability to count comes before the realization that the last number counted is the total. Thus the child may correctly count five things but, when asked how many there are, reply "Two." By age four, as we shall see later, many children can count and sum accurately. They can even perform some intuitive addition and subtraction. The use of standard units of measurement, like ounces or inches, however, is not likely to appear before the school years.

Time

In the domain of time, it is clear that the baby's or young child's orientation in time is far more advanced than the ability to talk about it. Even infants, as we have seen, develop biological clocks which give a stable sense of recurring routines. Although infants may not anticipate that night will fall, they are not at all surprised when it does. Toddlers know a number of time-related words such as "day," "night," "first," and "now." They show signs of remembering past events, as when the mention of someone whose baby had been ill evokes an association: "Baby sick. Poor Baby." They also anticipate the near future, as when, having been told that there will be a visit to Grandma after a nap, the child bounces awake shouting, "Now go Nana!" Late in toddlerhood, children may use such words as "yesterday," "today," and "tomorrow." However, they mix them up, cannot tell their sequence, and are likely to fasten on a single word, such as "tonight," to designate any point in past or future time.

Toddlers also parrot the adults' "Not now," "Soon," and "In a minute," to indicate delay. To the adult, toddlers are exasperating dawdlers. They are blandly unmindful of time pressures, schedules, and the need to be in a particular place at a time defined by the hands on a clock. The grownup has to make generous allowances of time to lure a toddler away from play and into outdoor clothes. Even as they are being dressed, toddlers may resolutely persist in trying to build a block tower or look at a book. By the same token, of course, adults, wrapped up in their preoccupations and obligations, may seem equally exasperating procrastinators to toddlers.

Toddlers show some grasp of simultaneous activities, as when the adult says, "You go play while I write a letter." They can play synchronously with an adult, taking turns adding blocks to a pile or handing things to an adult engaged in a work project. We shall have more to say about the child's expanding sense of past and future when we discuss cognitive functioning in preschool children.

Space

We described earlier the toddler's concrete orientation to action space. The spatial vocabulary of the toddler comes to include words like "up" and "down," "on," "over," "under," "in," "out," "forward" and "backward," "beside," "next to," "far away," "against," and "around." Toddlers are very sensitive to the car's going *up* the hill and *down* the hill. As we said before, young toddlers do not anticipate that a toy car will roll down an incline, but they delight in seeing this fact demonstrated and in practicing it themselves. There is no reason to expect the child to wonder why a wheeled vehicle should roll down a slope without being pushed. People lived with, adapted to, and even exploited gravity for thousands of years before anybody got around to noticing that there is such a thing.

Shape

The toddler begins learning the special vocabulary of shape and can recognize and name such standard forms as cross, triangle, crescent (called "moon"), heart (called "Valentine" by many children), and star. But note that toddlers' recognition is based on total configuration, or physiognomy, and not on how these figures are composed. Toddlers do not know that a triangle has three sides or a star five points, and they cannot draw these forms.

It is interesting that toddlers learn such seemingly obvious shapes as square and circle relatively late. This seems to be because toddlers see these shapes as concrete objects, like window or ball, rather than as general designs corresponding to nothing special in the world of things.

Toddlers who grow up among written symbols learn very early to recognize letters and numerals as special classes of forms. This is shown by their pointing to a character and asking, "What's this *a*?" or "What's this *1*?" with "a" at first standing for all letters and "1" for all numerals. As we shall see again later, preschool children who cannot yet read may nevertheless be able to tell the difference between writinglike scribbles and cursive script, and between block letters and letterlike nonsense forms.

Color

In the domain of color, many children by age two know the names of all the stand-ard rainbow hues, as well as the achromatic colors black, gray, and white. They may even know such mixed hues as brown, tan, beige, aquamarine, and pink. Toddlers whose parents make no special effort to teach them color names may still learn them from educational and other programs on color TV.

THE FUNCTIONS OF LANGUAGE AS A TOOL AND A TOY

Toddlers' language accompanies and punctuates their play as mood music, as narrative, as commands and instructions and reproaches to self and playthings. Toddlers talk to themselves, to adults, and to inanimate objects. However, they cannot yet talk to each other beyond an occasional angry shout of "No!" or "Mine!" when a possession is in dispute. Toddlers' jokes are usually cheerful commentaries on events and incongruities—"Johnny pants off!" They do not yet include the banter, verbal teasing, and deliberate surprises and manufactured incongruities of preschool and older children. When toddlers do happen on something that strikes them as funny, such as finding their boots on the wrong feet, they will repeat the joke, including appropriate expressions of mock dismay, until something new intervenes to break the spell.

Toddlers also make up sing-song doggerel rhymes ("Lig a loggie, dig a poggie, a la boggie poggie boggie" [Woodcock, 1941]). They memorize and chant or recite commercial jingles and nursery rhymes. They can lie to the extent of denying some misdeed with a vigorous head-shaking "No!" They can play sim-

(© Elizabeth Crews)

Toddlers like to talk to their playthings. At this age children are more likely to talk to inanimate objects than to each other.

ple jokes on their parents, announcing to a homecoming mother that "Daddy go store," when in fact he is in another part of the house.

Toddlers are not so likely to appreciate adults' verbal humor. If an adult, for instance, changes the wording or the sense of a favorite story with some idea of entertaining the toddler, the adult will probably encounter fierce indignation. It is not until children have attained the relative sophistication of the preschool years that they feel sufficient mastery of their language to permit or commit the conscious intermingling of sense and nonsense.

Behavior such as this contributes to what Courtney Cazden (1974) calls **metalinguistic awareness.** Beyond being able to shape language to represent real or imaginary realities, children become aware of language itself as something to be contemplated, manipulated, and played with. The toddler spins out nonsense talk, the preschool child becomes aware of rhyming, and the school-age child becomes adept at punning, alliteration, "secret" languages such as Pig Latin, and codes and ciphers. A high degree of metalinguistic awareness greatly facilitates learning to read. In fact, grasping that language comes in both spoken and written versions is itself an important kind of metalinguistic awareness.

The most obvious and talked-about function of language is *communication*, requesting and giving information. But this definition is too broad. Communication is also a way of sharing experience, of establishing a sense of social closeness and solidarity. It can be used, too, to establish relative status and power. Communication can serve to manipulate other people's emotions, as when we say surprising or shocking or amusing things, when we praise or flatter people, or scold them, or tease them. It is a way of expressing our own emotions. It is a way of alerting people to our inner states, as when we say that we are hungry or sick. It is a way of getting other people to do things for us, or to stop doing things to us. We also communicate with ourselves, as when we try to control our own behavior, even if not always successfully. And communication can serve to transmit misinformation, knowingly or unknowingly. We may deceive other people in order to promote our own interests, to convince them of an ideology, or to protect their feelings. In short, communication is not always a matter of simple fact.

VERBAL REALISM

The ultimate power of language resides in what Piaget called **verbal realism.** Verbal realism is also known as **symbolic realism, nominal realism,** and **linguistic realism.** In Piaget's use of the term, it meant that the child perceives names as inherent in and emanating from the things named. Thus the sun could never be called "moon," since sun and "sun" are one and inseparable, as are moon and "moon." We will use the concept in a somewhat broader sense than Piaget intended.

When we speak, we create realities. People have for thousands of years used words to create phantom entities, from demons to fairies to ghosts to Santa Claus. This power to lend reality to imaginary things is called **reification.** We have already spoken of how some psychologists reify intelligence, and yet others are happy to explain behavior by reference to "instincts," although what an instinct is supposed to be has never been made clear. Verbal realism plays a large part in propaganda and in fallacious thinking. But it is also at the heart of our being able to create fantasies, to write and enjoy fiction—we can live within a fictional world with all the emotional vividness of actual events—and to daydream.

Above all, though, verbal realism makes possible a function of language that most writers on the subject neglect.

This is the use of language, whether in soliloquy or in exchanges with others, to order, organize, and make sense of experience, fitting it into a more or less coherent framework of relationships and principles. With language, we create our private visions of what the world is all about, and it is from these visions that meanings, thought, feeling, action, and anticipations of the future flow. Linguistic realism creates a linguistic imperative. That is, it becomes necessary for us to put our more significant experiences into words. Our thoughts and feelings remain elusive and not yet our own until we have captured them in words and so given them form and substance. Toddlers begin this lifelong process by thinking out loud to an adult. This leads to dialogues that enable the child to formulate, catalogue, and systematize experience. In short, verbal realism can delude us, but it can also permit us to dominate and reshape reality, seriously or whimsically. It is through language that we give form to our own identities. This weaving of a verbal fabric defining self and world is called **thematization** (Merleau-Ponty, 1945). Our well-defined thematizations become part of the cognitive framework that guides our perceiving, thinking, feeling, and action. That is, thematization is another route to schematization. It is the magical quality that verbal realism gives language that motivates people to start speaking and go on speaking.

The child's growing repertoire of language skills opens new realms of activity, making possible the learning, thinking, and social interchange that occupy an ever-increasing part of existence. Toddlers move from the verbal music of infancy toward the still-egocentric poetry of the preschool years and the communicative but often barren prose of adult discourse.

SOCIAL CLASS DIFFERENCES IN LANGUAGE AND THOUGHT

We have ascribed to language an increasing dominance over other cognitive processes. This does not mean that all cognitive functioning is a matter of symbols. Some of our earliest emotional learning may give us an outlook on the world that no amount of verbalization can ever alter. However, the more thorough a job we do of translating experience into symbolic forms, the greater our command of our knowledge and our control over self and world. Linguistic dominance is slower to develop in children from environments in which verbal elaboration is given relatively little emphasis. More specifically, children from lower-class homes do less well in the sphere of language and cognition than do children of the middle class.

The difference shows up quite clearly in a study by Golden, Bridger, and Montare (1974). These investigators compared two groups of two-year-olds of differing social classes on the facilitating effect of language in a simple perceptual discrimination learning task. One group was composed of boys whose mothers had not gone beyond high school. The other group was of boys whose mothers were college graduates. It is important to emphasize that the contrast was not between children from extremely favorable environments and children from the depths of the slums. All came from stable families. The mothers with less educa-

tion were married, typically, to skilled workers, electricians, carpenters, firemen, or policemen.

The task, in brief, was to find a cookie under one of five boxes, on each of which was mounted a relatively unfamiliar identifying object: a valve, a caster, a clip, a switch, and a lock in one set of boxes; and a strainer, a roller, a level, a pole end, and an opener in the other. In one condition, the children were told which object marked the box that covered the cookie. In a second condition, the children were told simply to find the cookie under one of the five boxes. As one might guess, naming the distinctive object helped, but it helped the children of the college-educated mothers more than the other group. The children of mothers high in schooling took an average of some eleven trials to find the cookie when the identifying object was named, compared with an average of sixteen-plus trials for the children of mothers with less schooling. When the cookie was placed under a different box—which was identified by name—63 percent of the children of college-educated mothers made an errorless shift, whereas only 20 percent of the children of mothers with less schooling did so. In the nonlabeling condition, when the children were simply invited to find the cookie, there was no difference between the two groups.

Schachter (1979) compared the linguistic environments in middle-class and lower-class white and black families. He found that middle-class mothers, white and black, placed fewer negative prohibitions ("don'ts") on their children's behavior. They were verbally more responsive to their children's wants or communicative acts than were the lower-class mothers. However, observations made in England (Tizard, 1981; MacLure and French, 1981) do not support the notion of striking social-class differences in conversational exchanges between mothers and children. These observers found that mother-child interactions in working-class homes were quite rich and anticipated most of the patterns that children encounter in school. Although this runs counter to our stereotypes, class differences in highly stratified England may be less serious psychologically than in the more egalitarian United States.

LANGUAGE AND DEAFNESS

It is obvious that deaf children have nothing on which to model their vocal behavior. Deaf babies babble, just as do hearing babies, but deaf babies stop babbling, presumably for lack of feedback. Deaf children can learn to communicate linguistically, but they have to be taught. This brings us to a long-ranging, still unresolved controversy.

Deaf children have been caught in a cross-fire between opposing theoretical camps. On the one hand we have the signers, those who favor teaching deaf children visual-gestural communication—sign language. On the other we have those who favor teaching children visual-oral communication—lip reading and spoken language. There are two traditional arguments in favor of signing: Signing is a "natural" medium of communication for those without hearing; that teaching lip reading and spoken language is an arduous, time-consuming process that does not always work the way it is supposed to. The lip-reading faction argues that sign language isolates deaf children from hearing people except for those few who know sign language, and that sign language itself is a sterile medium of communication.

It is only in recent years that hearing people other than teachers of the deaf have given any great attention to the properties of sign language (Bellugi and Studdert-Kennedy, 1980). It turns out that American Sign Language (which is rendered both ASL and Amsign) is a very rich vehicle of expression. It works differently from spoken language in that signs (which include facial expressions and postural changes) can express a number of components in a statement simultaneously. In contrast, spoken language is of necessity linear.

As we have said, the debate has not been settled. However, there is growing consensus that deaf children should first be taught to sign, which virtually all deaf children are able to do. Thereafter, deaf children can be taught to read lips and to speak aloud, at which some deaf people become quite proficient and others decidedly less so. To the best of our knowledge, no one has yet asked signers to introspect on their own thought processes. We cannot help wondering about the extent that signing, or an internal equivalent of signing, is involved in thinking.

LANGUAGE IN OTHER SPECIES

In the past twenty-five years, we have heard a great deal about "language" in nonhuman animals, notably porpoises and apes. There are three main reasons for studying language in nonhumans.

One is the simple pleasure of observing animals perform humanlike behavior. A second is to explore as fully as possible the cognitive limits of kindred species. Third, there is curiosity about parallels between human and nonhuman processes in acquiring language.

It was thought for a while that porpoises had their own language embodied in clicks and whistles and other vocal sounds. It now appears that porpoises simply have highly ritualized signal calls, just as do many other species, such as birds. Various schemes have been put forth to teach porpoises a communicative code, but we are not aware that any of these has yet borne fruit.

There have been two main approaches to teaching apes to communicate with humans. The first is ASL, or a modified, simplified version of ASL. The other is to give the animal a collection of cut-out shapes, each shape standing for a different word, and to teach it to arrange the appropriate shapes to form messages. (A variant of this method is to display the shapes on the keys of a computer keyboard.) There is no doubt that apes can produce strings of gestures or shapes to make simple sentences. They can even compare two objects and signal such relationships as same, similar, and dissimilar. The question is whether the apes use language spontaneously or only in response to cues from their human interlocutors. The latter is known as the Clever Hans effect (Clever Hans was a "talking" horse, which turned out to be able to answer arithmetic problems by tapping its foot only in the presence of its master, who was unconsciously sending subtle signals that controlled the horse's behavior).

Those who wish to hear both sides of the question can consult the pages of *Science* magazine (Bindra, 1981; Patterson, 1981; Terrace *et al.*, 1981). A generally skeptical approach to the question of nonhuman language can be found in Sebeok and Rosenthal (1981). A highly sympathetic, first-hand account of teaching a gorilla to communicate is given in Patterson and Linden (1982).

THEORIES OF LANGUAGE AND LANGUAGE ACQUISITION

We wish we were able to round off our discussion of beginning language with a clear statement of the theoretical implications of what we have been describing. Unfortunately, linguistic theories are currently in a state of some disrepair. This is because workers in the field keep noticing or discovering new facets of language that had not been considered by theorists. We believe that the most useful thing we can do at this point is to present the leading theories and to point out their chief concepts and shortcomings. Note that these theories deal almost exclusively with simple, concrete, factual, true utterances. Researchers have begun to study extended discourse (Sinclair and Coulthard, 1975); playful language (Cazden, 1974); deception (Sebeok and Rosenthal, 1981); and psychopathology. However, an integrated theoretical framework has not yet been offered to accommodate what is known.

The central issue is the relationship between language and thinking. Some theorists have held that language and thinking are one and the same thing. They believe that any word or assemblage of words is an idea and that ideas exist only when they are given verbal form. Others say that thought is independent of language. They argue that both reality and the cognitive tools with which we operate on it come into being first and then are labeled with words. And, of course, there is Skinner's position that thinking is of no significance anyway, so why bother about it? We will offer our own views on this matter when we have surveyed the various theories. The issue arose with the doctrine of linguistic determinism, and that is where we begin.

Linguistic Determinism

One of the first major modern theories of language was set forth by Dorothy Lee, Edward Sapir, and Benjamin Lee Whorf. This view is known as **linguistic determinism,** but it is generally referred to simply as the **Whorf hypothesis** (Carroll, 1956). In brief, the Whorf hypothesis says that language and culture are one and the same thing. Therefore, the categories provided by the language of one's culture inescapably determine one's powers of perception and thought. In other words, people from different cultures, speaking different languages, perceive and think differently. By now, just about everybody has heard how the Eskimos have an extensive vocabulary to describe different kinds of snow—granular snow, powdery snow, slushy snow, snow that has partially melted and then refrozen—but no word for snow in general. Note how in English, we start out with a generic term like "snow" and then modify it to refer to its sundry manifestations. The Tahitians likewise have many words for coconuts, representing

(© Alex Harris/Archive)

Eskimo children would view a snowy field differently than would, for example, Texan children. The Eskimo language includes more than twenty terms to describe different kinds of snow, whereas English-speakers just use the general term "snow." The idea that categories of language in a culture shape perception and thought is known as the *Whorf hypothesis.*

different varieties and stages of growth, but they have no word for coconuts in general. To the best of our knowledge, there is no Tahitian word for snow of any description, or Eskimo word for coconut.

We know that the Whorf hypothesis is wrong on at least two counts. First, much of culture exists only at the concrete schematic level and never gets verbalized. Our basic sense of time and space are learned unconsciously and are only partly coordinated with formal concepts. We acquire many manipulative skills by practice or through modeling and never think to question where they came from—language itself is a prime example. Many of our tastes, preferences, and values are shaped for us in ways that are never articulated but that can regulate our behavior throughout life. For example, food appears edible or inedible to us according to our cultural experience. Second, people keep finding ways to break out of the limits imposed by language. Children are forever inventing words to cover situations where the standard language and culture have not yet given them the means of expression. Remember neologisms such as "fastpokes" mentioned earlier in this chapter; one little girl, seeking a way to talk about an insect's antennae, referred to them as "prickers." Sometimes circumlocution takes the place of a missing word. For instance, a little girl, lacking the word "stirrup," made up for it by saying, "The things where you put your feet." The growth of dictionaries is testimony enough to the way we create new words to label new things and ideas.

Yet there are two related phenomena that make something similar to linguistic determinism seem attractive. The first is the fact of symbolic realism, our ability to concoct, through symbols and the process of reification, imaginary domains that we treat as though they actually existed. The second phenomenon is our need to formulate our more important experiences, to put them into words, to contain them, to assimilate them to the fabric of our lives. Some experiences are so horrible that they cannot be assimilated, and to accommodate to them would destroy our sanity. This, we suspect, underlies the nightmares and flashbacks that haunt so many veterans of ground combat.

Skinner's Operant Theory

A quite different view of language comes to us from B. F. Skinner (1957). For Skinner, there is nothing special about language. It is simply behavior like any other, learned through the patterning of reinforcements. More specifically, Skinner sees *receptive language*—understanding—as learned through classical conditioning, words learned by association with things until they come to stand for the things. *Productive language*—speaking—is learned on the operant model. This requires active behavior that can be selectively reinforced. Thus when in a state of need, the baby utters various random sounds. Certain of these sounds inevitably resemble words in the baby's native tongue. When such sounds are spoken in the presence of appropriate objects, they will be reinforced by parents, siblings, or other caregivers. For instance, the hungry baby says "na-na-na" and is rewarded with a piece of the banana that happens to be nearby. Although such words at first come out as only crude approximations of actual words, they can be shaped, by giving or withholding reinforcers, to accurate copies of actual words. The caregivers may at first accept "na-na-na" as a satisfactory equivalent of "banana," but at a later period they will withhold reinforcement until the child says the word correctly. Those sounds that are not part of the child's speech community's repertoire will extinguish through lack of reinforcement.

This learning through selective reinforcement would obviously be very slow going, so Skinner has introduced a second mechanism to speed things up a bit. This is imitation. As we have said, the ability to imitate poses something of a mystery (p. 132), and Skinner recognizes this, too. He has therefore given us a theory of how imitation comes to pass.

When the child, at first accidentally, produces a sound resembling something just said by someone else, the other person is likely to hear this as imitation and to reinforce the child. This association between imitation and reinforcement leads to the establishment of imitating as a learned operant.

One serious difficulty with Skinner's theory is that it does not correspond to reality. Parents do not wait around, reinforcers at the ready, waiting for the child to make likely sounds. If indeed children learned to imitate as a way of obtaining reinforcers, one would suppose that they would spend a great part of their waking hours echoing the speech of those around them. They do nothing of the sort. Skinner also violates his own principles by introducing internal mediators and subjective states: meanings, thoughts, ideas, feelings, intentions. Even with these supplementary concepts, Skinner's theory cannot account for children's ability to make sense of statements never heard before. Nor can it explain their ability to put together sensible utterances unlike anything to which they have ever been exposed.

Even though Skinner brought cognitive mediators into his account of language development, he does not allow himself to acknowledge the fact. Therefore, the relationship between language and thinking does not arise. Language is merely one more tool with which to attract reinforcers, and there is no need to invoke anything resembling thought.

Chomsky's Generative Grammar

Noam Chomsky (1968, 1975) has proposed the radical notion that language is not learned at all, but is innate. He ar-

gues that since all languages share key structural features, the underlying structures must be built into human anatomy. Indeed, it is Chomsky's thesis that language is an independent "organ of the mind." Chomsky, on the model of Aristotle's "doctrine of souls" in which each psychological characteristic is the expression of a special soul, leaves to his readers to figure out whether the "organ" is anatomical or vaporous.

For Chomsky there are two levels of linguistic structure, the **deep structure** and the **surface structure.** The deep structure contains general, basic sentence types, whereas the surface structure is what people actually say. A deep structure prototypical sentence is basically a simple declarative sentence made up of noun subject (N), verb predicate (V), and an object or a modifer (N)—N-V-N. To get from the deep structure to the surface structure, Chomsky posits a set of **transformation rules.** These are grammatical and syntactical mechanisms that convert the simple N-V-N structure into a surface structure sentence. Such a surface structure can take the form of a question, a command, a statement referring to past or future or conditional situations, a negative assertion, or a passive construction. For example, the N-V-N structure "The boy hits the ball" can be transformed into "Does the boy hit the ball?" or "Boy, hit the ball!" or "The ball is hit by the boy," and so forth. It is these sentences that we hear spoken.

According to Chomsky, the surface structure is likely to be full of imperfections, whereas the deep structure is in full working order from birth. Thus we have a distinction between **performance,** the surface structure of what people say, and **competence,** the deep structure representing what people are capable of doing given the right circumstances. However, we cannot directly infer the state of the deep structure from the surface structure.

We do not know if Chomsky has ever appreciated the logical bind into which he has gotten himself. If we cannot infer competence from performance, what evidence do we have that it really exists? For a while, there was an attempt to equate competence with receptive language ability, since the capacity to understand is always greater than the capacity to produce. However, it turned out that young children were unable to comprehend a great many grammatical forms (the passive voice received a great deal of attention). This left the deep structure and competence as a hypothetical construct incapable of either proof or disproof.

Chomsky has continued to elaborate his ideas on linguistic competence, but always in terms of innate structures. He has made some slight concession to environmental influences. For instance, he has accepted the idea of a *Language Acquisition Device* (also known as LAD; McNeill, 1970), by which children, having been exposed to language, deduce which of various sets of transformation rules to bring into play. The multiple sets of rules were made necessary to deal with the differences in surface structures among languages and among speakers of the same language.

It is possible that Chomsky's generative grammar will founder on the realization that grammatical structure does not always correspond to semantic (meaning) category. If, at the beginning of a class meeting, the teacher asks, "Is the door still open?" we all recognize that the question is really a command: "Somebody please shut the door." Similarly, the question "Are you going to stand there all day?" is an order: "Get moving!" On the other hand, a declarative statement can serve as a question, as in "You're going to the meeting, of course." The implied rather than literal meaning of an utterance is called its **illocutionary force** (de Villiers and de Villiers, 1978). Some of Chomsky's staunchest followers have fallen from the ranks as they have begun to recognize that language as it is actually used in the real world—*pragmatics*—bears little resemblance to language as described by Chomsky.

Part of Chomsky's thinking is based on Skinner's failure to account for the learning of language. Chomsky concluded that since language is not learned, it must therefore be innate. What Chomsky seems not to have grasped is that psychology recognizes a variety of learning mechanisms besides associative learning, classical or operant. For instance, as we have said, modeling, from social learning theory, gives us a perfectly plausible way of understanding the learning of grammar and syntax as guiding schemata. Be that as it may, Chomsky and his followers avoid the word "learning" altogether, preferring to speak of language development as the "acquisition" of language.

We believe that Chomsky would go along with the linguistic determinists in assigning great weight to the role of language in thinking. However, thinkers like Whorf emphasize the irrational components in linguistic and cultural determinism. In contrast, Chomsky emphasizes the rational properties of language.

Chomsky has never offered an interpretation of the obvious fact that many people much of the time behave and talk irrationally.

Note that in its broadest formulation Chomsky's thesis is beyond argument. There is no denying that human beings, because of their special biological characteristics, are uniquely equipped to become language users. It does not follow, however, that their biological equipment includes a language organ or an LAD containing circuits capable of generating all the rules of grammar for all the languages in the world. What human beings have is a great capacity for learning and for using what they have learned to teach themselves still more.

Chomsky performed a service when he reminded us that language includes grammar and syntax as well as phonemes and morphemes and words. However, he has seemed unable to advance into the domains of semantics, pragmatics, and function.

Piaget on Language

Piaget has given us several important linguistic concepts, such as symbolic realism. However, he has had very little to say about language development or the role of language in cognition. Piaget and Inhelder's (1969) account of language acquisition does not go beyond simple associations between concrete nouns and tangible objects. It seems to take for granted the transition to more complex forms of language. In Piaget's view, we gather, language through the middle years of childhood is merely a set of labels for preexisting ideas. It is as though everything has to be learned first from concrete experience rather than through

language. Thus language does not structure thought. Rather, it is assimilated to the logical structures of thought that the child has already developed.

Piaget seems to accord a new respect to language and symbols when he talks about the stage of formal operations (adolescence and adulthood), when the individual must deal with abstract categories and general relationships. However, he still offers no systematic statement of how symbols can substitute for reality and indeed create new realities. Nor does he show any interest in language other than as a medium of dry factual communication.

Vygotsky on Language, Thought, and Culture

Lev Vygotsky's book on language (1962) was published in English twenty-eight years after it appeared in Russian, in 1934 (the year he died). Unlike Piaget but like Whorf, Vygotsky saw language as giving structure to thought and as regulating cognitive behavior. His emphasis was on communication, with special attention to self-communication and verbal self-regulation. Children at first instruct themselves but act in total disregard of their own instructions. Gradually, however, verbal self-direction and self-control become very effective. A report by Goodman (1981) provides evidence in support of Vygotsky's views. Among preschool children solving jigsaw puzzles, those children who showed a high rate of verbalization, notably of plans, of thoughts, and emotional expletives, were the most proficient puzzle solvers. Where Piaget would allow children to learn by exploring and experi-

(© Michael Weisbrot & Family)

Learning can be accelerated by verbalization. Early and frequent verbal exchanges between parent and child apparently have lasting benefits.

menting with objects and materials, Vygotsky had great faith in the power of language to communicate new knowledge and ways of thinking to children. It seems to us that here one must tread warily. Simple statements of fact or instructions on how to proceed often seem not to penetrate. However, once a person can engage the child in a dialogue, perhaps in association with concrete materials, verbally stimulated learning does indeed take place. More generally, a rich linguistic and cognitive environment early in life appears to have lasting beneficial effects (Stevens, 1981).

Vygotsky was also interested in what William James called the *stream of consciousness,* the flow of words and images that goes through us when we pursue routine, largely unfocused activities. Vygotsky drew a distinction between **inner speech,** talking to oneself, and **outer speech,** talking to others. Inner speech throughout life can be an incoherent jumble of fragments, free associations, fused ideas, and disorganized feelings. When young children are asked to describe a picture or a nonsense shape so that another child can pick its duplicate from an array of similar forms, the descriptions sound very much like inner speech made external (Glucksberg, Krauss, and Higgins, 1975). As they develop, children become increasingly able to adapt their communication skills to suit the needs of the listener.

Vygotsky was extremely interested in the role of culture in cognition. He and his student and colleague A. R. Luria (1976) did research comparing the mental functioning of unlettered Central Asians with that of formally educated people and found striking differences. For instance, when shown depictions of abstract forms, the Asians invariably interpreted them as concrete representations, as of a piece of needlework. The work of Vygotsky and Luria was suppressed by the Soviet government as being open to racist misinterpretations. It was finally published only in 1974, during a political thaw. Luria himself died in 1977, while participating in a project to publish a new selection of Vygotsky's work in English (Vygotsky, 1978).

What we have said is our interpretation of Vygotsky's position. Either he himself did not write particularly clearly, or his translators have not done him full justice. If you should encounter conflicting interpretations, you should be aware that these may very well be correct.

LANGUAGE AND THOUGHT

We now return to our own view of the language and thought controversy which actually covers the wider topic of the role of symbols in cognition (Church, 1961). We must begin by defining our terms. We construe both language and thought very broadly. Language is assumed to include all the symbolic means of representation: words, numbers, maps, charts, diagrams, emblems, and the like. Thought embraces knowledge, beliefs, learning, ideas, perception, reasoning, intuitive jumping to conclusions, and whatever other structures or processes may be contained in the same package. Central to our view is the notion of verbal or symbolic realism. This is a concept that we have adopted from Piaget and elaborated to suit our own somewhat different understanding. We have already spoken of the sense of power over reality that words give us. We quote our elaboration of the concept of symbolic realism:

Word realism can . . . be seen in euphemism, whereby we disguise an unpleasant or indelicate reality with a neutral or pleasant word [you are invited to think of all the different ways people have invented to refer to death or dying without mentioning them by name]; in circumlocution, where we talk all around a touchy topic without ever dealing with it directly; in reification, whereby we treat a hypothetical construct as a substantial thing [Chomsky's "organ of the mind" is a reification; so is "intelligence"]; in our reactions to fiction, in which our emotions can become implicated almost as thoroughly as in real-life happenings; and in the so-called defense mechanisms [such as rationalization and denial].

It is not true that "names will never hurt me." One can flay a person very effectively with words. With words, one can make people blush, one can infuriate them, one can turn their stomachs and make their flesh crawl—with words that need not even describe any factual reality. We can see that word realism works in several ways. First, we can avoid knowledge of a disagreeable reality by refusing to name it, by giving it a name that hides its true nature, or by giving it a name that keeps it neutral and remote. . . . Second, having given voice to a notion, we find that we have created an entity that now dwells in reality on the same footing as other objects. . . . Third, there is a species of negative word realism: lacking a word (or a formulation) for something, we cannot quite believe in the thing itself (Church, 1961).

The power of symbolic realism has to be pitted against the stubborn unchangeability of some of our thinking. We have convictions that are totally impervious to argument. We can know something at one level and its direct opposite at another. We know cerebrally that smoking leads to lung cancer, but many people who know this perfectly well continue to smoke, knowing viscerally that it could never happen to them. Adolescents know about conception and contraception. However, 1 million teenage females turn up unintentionally pregnant every year. Such conflicts between cerebral and visceral (both words are used metaphorically) knowledge, in which gut feelings usually win out, tell us that human thought can never be described totally as either made up of language or free of language.

Varieties of Language-Thought Relationships

In fact, we seem to need four different kinds of language-thought relationships. First, there is *knowledge and thinking acquired independently of language*. Second, there is *thought that involves both language and concrete experience*, as when we try to describe something so that someone else can recognize it. Third, there is *knowledge originally acquired*

through symbols but which has been so thoroughly absorbed that one does not have to reason out the answers to problems; if we ask you what is three times three, you do not have to think, even though learning it may have required many painful repetitions. Fourth, there is *thought that is entirely a matter of and even created by language*, as when we talk about historical events, which are unattainable to us except through words, or about the supernatural. Let us now take a closer look at these four different relationships.

The first, nonverbal knowledge, can come to us from a number of sources. During infancy, well in advance of language acquisition, we learn some of life's most basic lessons in a form that is highly resistant to change. We learn basic trust or mistrust, attitudes that can carry over into adulthood. (The adult form of basic mistrust is paranoia.) The stranger anxiety of the infant may become the stranger anxiety of the adult. Adult stranger anxiety is called *xenophobia*—fear of strangers—and is close kin to prejudice. The behavior that we learn through modeling helps shape our world view and thus our thinking. We form countless associations, through both classical and instrumental conditioning. For instance, we associate the appearances of foodstuffs with their flavors, so that we know how they taste just by looking at them. Note the surprise we feel when, in sampling a new cuisine, we find that we have guessed completely wrong. Sometimes the evidence of our senses seems to contradict what the best minds tell us. We know, in the abstract, that the rising and setting of the sun are caused by the earth's rotation on its axis, but in our heart of hearts we know perfectly well that we see the sun arising and descending. Implicit in what we have said is that the concepts and values of our culture are absorbed and stubbornly maintained regardless of what anybody tells us. They are so deeply rooted as to seem almost innate.

The second kind of thought involves the attempt to formulate our concrete experience in symbols, to capture it and make it our own. By rights, this should involve a working back and forth between formulation in symbols and concrete reality, checking to see how well our ideas fit. When we try to give shape to a completed event, of course, we can check ourselves only against other people's recollections. Whenever something important happens, the witnesses find themselves comparing notes, trying to give the event just the right verbal shape. Such collective formulations are often a study in group myth making, since the final, fully satisfying account of what happened may bear little resemblance to the original. For example, the morning after a big dance, the telephone system is taxed while adolescents exchange impressions until the event has been given verbal shape and so can enter into the body of their experience. Even the commonplace happenings of everyday life get labeled, classified, and filed away in the bin of our personal history. William James called this process of verbalizing one's experience to oneself the *stream of consciousness*. Note that the stream of consciousness does not deal only with the present. Especially when we are operating on automatic pilot, as we do when carrying out routine sorts of activities, the stream of consciousness confronts us with miscellaneous flotsam and jetsam of memories, ideas, feelings, hopes, and plans.

Third, there is thought that depends on past linguistic formulations that no longer have to be made explicit. That is, our thematizations of reality are incorporated into the framework of our knowledge so that answers to problems flow forth automatically and intuitively. If we ask you how much is three times three, your answer is a product not of arithmetic—you do not go through the act of multiplying three by three—but of knowledge. Mastery of any domain of knowledge generally requires a high degree of symbolization to begin with. However, once the knowledge is acquired it can be brought into play with a minimum of verbalization. Thus truly skilled diagnosticians, be they doctors or auto mechanics, know simply by looking, listening, touching, and maybe smelling, what has gone wrong. They may need to do some tests to verify their first, intuitive impression, but they feel confident that their judgment will be vindicated. What you are doing at this moment is reading a verbal account (supplemented by some pictures and perhaps observations) of how people develop. The point of our writing this and your reading it is to start you on the way to knowing so much about the field that you can talk about the settled issues without having to think. Around the settled issues, of course, there are areas of turbulence, and these of course require verbalization and reverbalization, as in the origins of neurosis and psychosis.

Finally, there is thought that consists entirely of symbols. For example, our knowledge of history can by definition never be firsthand. We can examine historic artifacts, but they, too, function as symbols. They must be interpreted, made sense of, and transformed before they can be incorporated into a body of historical knowledge. Our knowledge of distant places can in principle be first-hand, but in practice most of us are fated to learn about the Gobi desert from TV or the pages of the *National Geographic.* Both our examples point to one of the pitfalls of purely verbal knowledge: We have no way of sifting truth from false-hood, actuality from myth.

In addition to talking about things that used to exist or exist only in inaccessible regions, we talk about things that have no existence at all. Word realism permits reification, which makes possible the creation of imaginary realities. Thus we populate our world with ghosts and demons and hobgoblins and poltergeists. We take seriously the notion that people send messages back and forth through extrasensory channels and that people can control the movement of objects by psychokinesis. We explain differences in academic performance in terms of an imaginary something called intelligence. We explain wars as the product of uncontrolled forces called instincts. You will recognize that we are talking once again about phantom environments (see p. 31). History books can give us a phantom past, and politicians can create a phantom geography populated by phantom enemies. Indeed, when they solemnly promise that large numbers of us would survive a nuclear war, they are offering us a phantom future.

We will return in chapters to come to language as it is manifested at various age periods. We now turn our attention to one of life's most delightful periods, the preschool years.

SUMMARY

1. Language development is an especially important phenomenon during toddlerhood. In this phase, we see the emergence of talking, or productive language. Toddlers work hard at talking, but preschool children become aware of language as something to be thought about. It takes about two years to learn the fundamentals of one's native language; further elaboration can continue throughout one's life. Children learn the fundamentals with minimal help, and they make very few mistakes of meaning (that is, mislabeling aspects of reality); they make many mistakes assembling words into sentences. Children can use the resources of language creatively; that is, they can formulate ideas of their own and give them voice.

2. Structural analysis dissects language into its components in order to explain it. It yields four levels: Phonology is the study of the sounds of speech. Children do not learn by hearing and producing individual sounds but are more concerned with the meanings carried by sounds. They hear and speak globally rather than analytically.

3. Phonemes, and the phonetic alphabet, allow all the sounds of a language to be represented; in English, for example, there are forty-odd speech sounds but only twenty-six letters in the alphabet. Morphemes are the smallest sound units that carry meaning. "Misunderstanding," for example, contains three morphemes: *mis, understand,* and *ing.*

4. Prosody is the melodic structure of utterances. It tells listeners our words are a command or a question, conveys playfulness or contempt, anger or joy.

5. Grammar refers to such characteristics of words as tense or number, parts of speech such as nouns or verbs, how we classify sentences, as in affirmative versus negative, the function of words within sentences, such as subject and object, etc. Syntax is the branch of grammar that specifies how words can be assembled to form meaningful utterances.

6. Semantics is the study of what words and longer utterances mean. Pragmatics seeks to identify the means by which we communicate.

7. Where structural analysis dissects language into its components, functional analysis focuses on the uses to which language is put. Language can be employed for various purposes: to stir people emotionally, to tease them or tell a joke; as a weapon; to calm a situation; to make sense of reality; to formulate theories and principles; or to think. We also use language magically.

8. Language learning begins in late infancy, with the development of receptive language; in other words, children can understand before they can speak. (Of course, infants communicate nonverbally as well.)

9. Babies talk in single words at first. Early one-word utterances that imply entire sentences are called holophrases. Some are fusions of commonly linked word groups. The attempt to identify children's first words with any precision seems hopeless; we can be sure a baby has begun to talk only when he or she points to an object and says its name.

10. Toddlers' sentences steadily increase in length, but they initially ignore standard grammar and syntax. Speaking by the rules emerges more gradually. Children acquire their vocabulary and linguistic skills with little help from others. Adults supply names for objects, but many words—notably abstractions—are learned by listening to conversa-

tions. Children apparently develop a sense of which constructions feel right. They learn language by hearing it spoken in a concrete context of objects, relations, actions, gestures, events, and feelings.

11. Children are remarkably accurate in grasping what kinds of things, actions, properties, and relationships words refer to. Sometimes, however, they interpret and generalize words in ways surprising to adults. Vocabulary development can be described in terms of domains, or groups of words referring to related concepts. Toddlers' vocabularies have been studied with respect to domains including kinship, causation, number, time, space, shape, and color.

12. Toddlers begin to use language both as a tool and as a toy. They become aware of language as something they can contemplate, manipulate, and play with. We use language to organize our experiences into a private vision of what the world is all about, and this process begins when we think aloud in toddlerhood. Research indicates that language plays an especially important role in the development of children from better educated families.

13. Deaf children have been caught in a cross-fire between opposing theoretical camps: those who favor teaching them sign language and those who favor lip reading and spoken language. The former have generally prevailed, at least so far as the first language to be taught to deaf children.

14. Whether language can be taught to porpoises and apes is still a matter of debate.

15. There are several linguistic theories in existence, but most of them have serious shortcomings. Whorf states that language and culture are identical, and that people who speak different languages perceive and think differently. Skinner believes that children learn to speak through selective reinforcement (operant conditioning). Chomsky proposes that language is innate, and that children are naturally able to transform the universal key features of language into the specific grammars of their own languages. Piaget, who has provided several important linguistic concepts, merely sees language as a means of communicating ideas. He largely disregards the acquisition process. Vygotsky maintains that language structures thought and regulates cognitive behavior, and that verbal self-direction develops linguistic competence. This theory seems most plausible.

KEY TERMS

animism, 309
code switching, 304
competence, 321
deep structure, 320
domains, 308
dynamism, 308
expressive jargon, 301
functional analysis, 298
functional subordina-
tion, 306
holophrases, 300
illocutionary force, 321
inner speech, 323

linguistic determinism
(Whorf hypothesis),
318
metalinguistic aware-
ness, 313
outer speech, 323
overregularization, 302
performance, 320
phonology, 296
productive language,
299
receptive language, 299
reification, 314

structural analysis, 296
surface structure, 320
thematization, 314
transductive thinking,
308
transformation rules,
320
verbal realism (symbolic
realism, nominal real-
ism, linguistic real-
ism), 314

SUGGESTED READINGS

Church, J. *Language and the Discovery of Reality.* New York: Random House, 1961. A
somewhat dated but still sound introduction to the psychology of language.
de Villiers, P. A., and de Villiers, J. G. *Early
Language.* Cambridge, Mass.: Harvard
University Press, 1979. A more extensive
and detailed account of language intended for the general reader. For a more
technical account of language, see the
same authors' *Language Acquisition.*
Cambridge, Mass.: Harvard University
Press, 1978.

CHAPTER 10

The Preschool Child: Growth, Social Relations, and Play

Somewhere around age two and a half the child moves out of toddlerhood and becomes a preschool child, a status that lasts until age six or so. The label *preschool* is simply a convention. It does not imply that the child attends nursery school or kindergarten, or that this age is mostly a time of preparing to go to school. Further, this convention does not imply a stage. The preschool years are not all of a piece. Just as toddlers may retain many of the qualities of infants, so are young preschool children close kin to toddlers. Half-undressed for a nap, sucking a thumb or pacifier, clutching a teddy bear or a frayed strip of blanket, the two-and-a-half-year-old is fully revealed in tender immaturity. By contrast, the five-year-old seems sophisticated, competent, and self-assured—and is twice as old.

The study of preschool children is rewarding from both a scientific and a personal standpoint. As we shall see, a great many abilities come into flower during this period. But, more than that, children of this age are delightful to work with and know. They have not yet learned the masks and disguises and evasions of later years. They wear their personalities on their sleeves. Their behavior is often colorful and sometimes violent, and because of its transparency, easy to observe and record. Preschool children's growing mastery of language and materials makes communication with them less demanding than with toddlers. But the developing competence with which they express their ideas makes evident the gaps and misperceptions, the miscomprehensions and erroneous assumptions that make their thought processes fascinating to follow, if sometimes baffling. Their utterances, unrestricted by adult considerations of logic, may have a quality of vivid imagination and refreshingly penetrating insight into their own world and even ours—provided that we, on our part, are openly receptive to what children have to tell us.

PHYSICAL GROWTH

During the preschool years, the child's growth rate is leveling off from the first spurt of infancy. In the first two years, the "average" child grows about 14 or 15 inches (35 cm) in length. In the next three years, the child grows 9 or 10 inches (24 cm), a considerable drop in rate. Nevertheless, somewhere between ages two and three, children reach half their adult height.

In the first year, a baby gains some 15 pounds (7 kg). Thereafter, the rate of gain slows to about 5 pounds (2 + kg) per year by age five. Indeed, the weight gain that goes with growth in height may be nearly offset by the loss of baby fat, so that children may not seem to be gaining weight at all. Despite the loss of baby fat, the preschool child's belly is still rounded and the waist is unindented. The child's proportions are changing. In keeping with the principle of asynchronous growth, the legs are growing faster than the rest of the body. At age two, the legs account for 34 percent of total length. By age five, they are 44 percent of body length. This is close to the half-and-half proportions of an adult. As the legs lengthen and head growth slows,

(Philip A. Biscuti/Connecticut College)
Preschool competence in dressing. Note that the heel of the right sock does not match the child's heel.

children lose the top-heavy look of infancy and toddlerhood.

The beginning of this age coincides with completion of the set of twenty baby teeth, and its end with the first shedding of these teeth. As the cartilage and bones of the face develop and the fat pads in the cheeks dwindle, the child's countenance loses its babyish cast and becomes more sharply defined and individualized. Sex differences in rate of

growth are negligible during the preschool years, although boys and girls are likely, with subtle and not so subtle adult and peer encouragement, to follow ever more widely divergent paths of psychological development.

POSTURE AND LOCOMOTION

Along with changes in size and proportion go changes in posture and styles of movement. The posttoddler child can no longer bend double at the waist and, legs straight, touch head to floor. When a preschool child sits on the floor to play, the knees point forward and slightly outward, and the forelegs are folded back along the thighs, with the buttocks resting on or between the heels. The high-stepping toddle of age two becomes a free-swinging stride. The preschool child has lost the toddler's knack of falling limp. Over a couple of years, the preschool child's one-step-at-a-time approach to staircases yields to a continuous movement of ascending and descending. Preschool children learn to scale ladders, jungle gyms, and trees with low branches. They learn to run as well as trot, and to gallop as well as run. Skipping, though, does not usually come until the school years.

When they wake up from sleep, preschoolers may bounce to their feet, kick their feet out from under them and land seated at the edge of the bed, and straighten their bodies and allow themselves to slide to the floor. (Typically, in the United States, the child moves from crib to bed around age three.) Preschool children, like toddlers, may still change

(© Leonard Speir 1983)

Ballet class. Many preschool children readily pick up styles of dancing and execute them in ways ranging from wild burlesque to smooth competence.

direction while running by bouncing off a wall or by hooking the inside hand on a piece of furniture and swinging through the turn. As parents need not be told, the preschool child's fingerprints blossom everywhere imaginable.

Preschoolers try to turn somersaults and cartwheels, most of the time sprawling off center at the top of the turn. They learn to spin about in one place and make themselves enjoyably dizzy. When running along a smooth floor, the child may stop to play with a toy by dropping abruptly onto the knees and sliding to a halt. Out on a walk, the child is likely to move along erratically, with much

swooping and gliding, whirling and flailing and flopping and tumbling, until the adult wonders if the child is capable of walking in a straight line. In fact, when children have a chance to clamber about on a rocky hillside, they are likely to show a surprisingly agile surefootedness. This, of course, does not mean that they need not be watched.

Preschool children, like toddlers, tend to snuggle up to an adult knee or shoulder and gradually drape themselves limply against the adult. However, when children are being carried, they now take some responsibility for holding on. They wrap an arm around the adult's neck or clamp their knees around the adult's waist, helping keep the adult-child totality in balance.

Even more than toddlers, preschool children pick up from people around them or from television the idea of doing exercises and perform a marvelous travesty of calisthenics. Many preschool children pick up styles of dancing, from ballet to ballroom, from teen-age steps to tribal forms, and execute them in ways ranging from wild burlesque to smooth competence.

THE FREUDIAN VIEW OF PRESCHOOL PERSONALITY

For Freud, the preschool years correspond to the **phallic stage** of psychosexual development. (The designation reflects Freud's male-centered view of development.) The focus of gratification has shifted from the mouth (during infancy) to the anus (during toddlerhood), and now to the genitals. During the preschool years, the genitals are supposed to be a source of raw pleasure, uncluttered by the tenderness, concern, and responsibility that are thought to mark the *genital stage* of adolescence and adulthood.

The phallic stage reaches a searing climax in what, for Freudians, is a crucial pattern of events, the **Oedipus complex** (or, in girls, the **Electra complex**) (see p. 12). The successful resolution of the Oedipus or Electra complex, and consequent identification with the parent of the same sex, is for Freudians the foundation for the **superego,** or conscience, for sexual adequacy, and for adjustment to the demands of society. Freud's account al-

erts us to the special relationships that exist between parents and their children of the same or opposite sex.

In the boy's case, briefly, the child desires to possess his mother. Such desires put him in direct competition with the all-powerful and much-loved father. The child perceives the outraged father as threatening him with castration, perhaps delegating the job to the mother. **Castration anxiety** leads the boy to renounce his desire for the mother. In the process he *represses* (forces out of consciousness) all sexual desire and with it all memory. This is the Freudian explanation of **infantile amnesia,** the fact that we can recall only disconnected bits and pieces of our lives before about age six. The boy identifies with his father, internalizing or *introjecting* the father's moral code as a new component of the personality, the superego.

Freud never gave a complete and coherent account of the Electra complex. The Electra complex involves the girl's discovery that she lacks a penis, leading to feelings of inferiority. The girl also wishes to have the exclusive love of her father and to replace the mother. She can express this feeling in action, as in the case of a three-year-old who would squeeze herself between her mother and father when she found them hugging, struggling mightily to push them apart. She can express her feelings in action and words: "Ruth [age 22 months] shows signs of jealousy. Whenever I kiss her father, she runs to him and says, 'My daddy.'" This same little girl at age two years: "My husband, Ruth, and I were having dinner in the dining room, and I went into the kitchen for something. I returned and Ruth said resentfully,

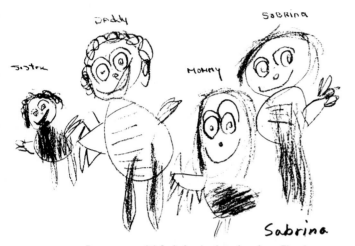

Four-year-old Sabrina's drawing has Electra-like overtones. Note the size of Sabrina and Daddy relative to that of Mommy and Sister.

'Mommy go in the kitchen. Ruthie and her husband are eating. Mommy don't sit with us'" (Church, 1978). Or these feelings can be shown in the child's drawing. The drawing above, by a four-year-old named Sabrina, has strong Electra-like overtones. Note Sabrina's and Daddy's size relative to Mommy's and Sister's. We are not sure whether Mommy's position between Sabrina and Daddy defines Mommy as a barrier to be overcome or removed.

At this juncture, the girl can react in either of two ways. The "normal" response is to identify with the mother, at the same time competing for the father. The girl is said to be moved by **penis envy.** She fantasizes having a baby by the father as a substitute for the missing penis. The penis envy is eventually repressed, and the girl identifies completely with the mother and her role.

The alternative reaction is called the **masculine protest,** a denial of the lack of a penis and the pursuit of an essentially masculine life style, with overtones of lesbianism. Freud believed that girls had less incentive than boys to resolve the Oedipus complex, inasmuch as they are not driven by castration fears to identify with the mother. As a result, the super-ego in women is less developed than in men. This line of thinking has been challenged and rejected by most feminists. At the same time, we should note that some of Freud's most devoted disciples have been women, including his daughter, Anna, and a number of women have risen to eminence in the psychoanalytic movement.

Freud changed his thinking about the origins of the Oedipus and Electra complexes. At first, his patients' tales of rape and seduction by the opposite-sex parent led him to conclude that parents were the instigators of the complexes. He later decided that the patients' recollections were only a device to conceal that they themselves had taken the initiative. In recent years, many psychoanalysts have tended to think that Freud was right the first time. They believe that fathers do indeed lust after their daughters and mothers after their sons, and that some parents—usually fathers—act on these sexual feelings. Even if parents do not make sexual advances to their children, those children can easily read the parents' desires, from which it is easy to imagine an actual liaison.

There are two main patterns that result from carrying an unresolved Oedipus or Electra complex into adulthood. One is a lifelong seeking for a substitute mother or father figure with whom to mate. Certainly affairs with much older partners suggest such surrogate satisfactions of the earlier longings. The other pattern is that of the phallic personality, the seeker after continuous, undiluted sexual satisfaction at whatever cost. This, of course, is the picture of the sexual psychopath—the insatiably promiscuous woman, the man who is a rapist or a Don Juan.

Returning to preschool children, cross-sex parent-child attachment is not hard to find. Also, there is a marked increase in the occurrence of children's fears coinciding with the time of the supposed Electra or Oedipus complex. Psychoanalytic thinkers consider these diverse fears to be manifestations of castration anxiety. Later, we will present the case for a cognitive interpretation of the preschool child's fears.

ERIK ERIKSON'S VIEW OF PRESCHOOL PERSONALITY

We have already seen, in our discussions of infancy and toddlerhood, how Erikson poses a psychosocial crisis for each developmental stage: basic trust versus basic mistrust in infancy, autonomy versus shame and doubt in toddlerhood (Erikson, 1963).

The crisis of the preschool years is *initiative versus guilt*. For Erikson, initiative means a greater eagerness to explore and to undertake new activities. The negative aspect of this period is guilt, the child's realization of possible failure and inability to control the newly felt power and to cope with defeat.

For Erikson, the resolution lies in the child's developing sense of moral responsibility. This is the critical period for children to take pleasure in learning to work with others, to share with and care for them, to learn from and identify with responsible and caring adults. Acquiring

these skills provides a constructive outlet for initiative and sets the stage for future responsibility. What is to be avoided is an immature and inflexible superego that destroys initiative and burdens the child with a crippling sense of guilt.

CHANGING PATTERNS OF SOCIAL RELATIONS

One of the striking features of the preschool years is the changing pattern of relationships with people outside the family—with teachers or day-care workers, with store clerks and librarians, and, above all, with other children, with peers.

As an infant and toddler, the child's sense of an independent identity remained closely intertwined with family identity. Although the family continues as the primary base and frame of reference for a number of years, preschool children begin moving out into the world and slowly finding their place among humanity at large. They are exposed to an ever-increasing number of new people, things, ideas, situations, problems, and roles. This enlarges and complicates the possibilities for identification and identity formation. It is because the child is beginning—however gradually—to form an identity apart from the family that the preschool years are sometimes referred to as the *first adolescence*.

In the preschool child's eyes, the parents continue to be the repository of all wisdom, strength, and virtue. At the same time, the child comes to accept the humanity of people outside the immediate family, if on a somewhat lower plane. Almost from birth on, children are taken on visits to and are visited by numerous people, but to judge by children's behavior toward them and by later recollections, all but the best-known of these outsiders have existed for them as curious, fleeting apparitions without solid identities. Often, for instance, all the children met in a new household are taken for granted as belonging to the same family, and all the new adults are assumed to be the parents of all the children.

Not all children live in relatively isolated nuclear families. Some children from babyhood on have a variety of adult caregivers—grandparents and neighbors, aunts and uncles, nursemaids, baby-sitters, day-care workers—in which case it may be easy for them to accept new adults. Similarly, some children spend a good bit of time in the company of siblings close in age, cousins, and neighborhood children—and, increasingly, in nursery school, day care, or other kinds of group care for young children. These children are likely to show a temporary advantage in social skills over children with less experience.

PEER RELATIONS

Relations with new adults are essentially a transfer of a certain portion of basic trust to them as parent surrogates. With peers, though, children must work out a whole new set of social relations. In doing so, they are not, of course, strictly on their own. There is usually a parent, teacher, or other caregiver around to help establish the ground rules—"No Biting"—but the children do most of the

negotiating in forming friendships. Recall that in toddler play groups aggression was the exception rather than the rule. But note that none of the reports mentions conversations between toddlers. Toddlers talk freely to themselves and to adults, but do not appear to perceive one another as people with whom to exchange ideas. Preschool children, by contrast, do come to be able to talk to one another.

Communication: The Dual or Collective Monologue

Communication among peers does not appear all at once in preschool children. Many messages may have to be relayed through an adult. For instance, instead of asking another child directly why he or she is wearing a bandage, the child seeks the information from an adult.

Preschoolers' early conversations seem to have as their aim less the exchange of information and ideas than the pleasure of affective communication. Piaget calls such conversations **dual,** or **collective** (depending on how many participants there are), **monologues.** What one child says bears no relation to what the other says, each one's utterances being welcome but heard only as the sound that occupies his or her turn to speak. We have a specimen of a dual monologue between two four-year-olds, who are past the age at which such exchanges are common. Their teacher describes them as sitting cozily side by side, swinging their feet, waiting politely in conversational style for their turn to speak, and enjoying a feeling of "comfortable togetherness," but obviously on two different wavelengths:

(Robert M. Sachs)

A preschool conversation. Early conversations seem geared not so much to the exchange of information and ideas as to the pleasure of affective communication.

Jenny: They wiggle sideways when they kiss.

Chris: [*Vaguely*] What?

Jenny: My bunny slippers. They are brown and red and sort of yellow and white. And they have eyes and ears and these noses that wiggle sideways when they kiss.

Chris: I have a piece of sugar in a red piece of paper. I'm gonna eat it but maybe it's for a horse.

Jenny: We bought them. My mommy did. We couldn't find the old ones. These are like the old ones. They were not in the trunk.

Chris: Can't eat the piece of sugar, not unless you take the paper off.

Jenny: And we found Mother Lamb. Oh, she was in Poughkeepsie in the trunk in the house in the woods where Mrs. Tiddywinkle lives.

Chris: Do you like sugar? I do, and so do horses.

Jenny: I play with my bunnies. They are real. We play in the woods. They have eyes. We *all* go in the woods. My teddy bear and the bunnies and the duck, to visit Mrs. Tiddywinkle. We play and play.

Chris: I guess I'll eat my sugar at lunch time. I can get more for the horses. Besides, I don't have no horses now.

Not all preschool conversations are of this kind. Many times the child earnestly tries to give or get information, to communicate, and non sequiturs of the sort that occur in a collective monologue can be frustrating and infuriating. Although the preschool child's communication is far from perfect, a sympathetic and patient adult can often figure out what the child is driving at. A major problem is the young child's egocentrism: He or she simply does not recognize the need to provide the background information the other person needs to be able to understand. It should not be necessary to point out that dual and collective monologues are not unknown among adults. A classic example is two mothers talking about their young children, neither hearing what the other is saying, which has been dubbed "collective momologue."

As children come to feel more at ease with each other and to communicate more freely, a number of social traits arise: leadership, sympathy, cooperation, and aggression. Before looking at these in turn, it is important to note that children develop stable orientations to social relations. In describing these orientations, we can point to a child's group role, such as leader, follower, or participant, or nonrole, such as outcast or lone wolf. We can invoke such trait dimensions as energetic-sluggish, bold-timid, talkative-reticent, hostile-friendly, independent-demanding, imaginative-pedestrian—the list goes on and on. Note that we are not embracing a dispositionist point of view of behavior. It is just that given a stable physical and social setting, children seem to have rather consistent modes of functioning. If the composition of the group were to change drastically, we would expect the members of the changed group to work out new modes of behavior in relating to one another. Note that there has been a dearth in recent years of new research findings on preschool children's social relations. The focus of recent studies of social relations among young children is largely on *social cognition*, which we have already talked about in Chapter 8 and shall discuss further in Chapter 11.

Leadership

Sustained *leadership* in the preschool years is difficult to achieve just because group organization has a way of shifting from moment to moment. Moreover, the child acting as a leader is liable to lose interest and slip out of the role. Other children try to assume leadership and find that no one is paying attention.

Despite these limitations, a number of preschool children do show consistent leadership in one form or another. Some children impose their will by sheer force—of either character or muscle. Some become "bossy," identifying successfully with adult authority. This is not the same thing as the futile bossiness of insecure children trying to win the respect of their peers. Some children can play on the group like an organ. Some prefer to remain inconspicuous and in the background but still can exert a potent authority as arbiter, adviser, or model. One of the marks of competence in three-year-olds is said to be the ability to play the role of either leader or follower as the circumstances warrant (White and Watts, 1973). Successful leaders, child and adult, must have social-cognitive abilities that enable them to attend to the feelings of those they wish to command. A leader who is too insensitive to followers soon ends up without a following.

Empathy and Sympathy

Sympathy toward peers emerges during the preschool years. We must begin, however, by distinguishing between sympathy and empathy, which we first encountered in Chapter 4. This distinction is often lost, but it is important psychologically. We try to treat empathy not in the limited dictionary definition but in the tradition established by Heinz Werner, Robert Woodworth, and Gardner Murphy, although these distinguished figures were by no means consistent. One of the few contemporary writers who seems to observe the same distinction that we do is Martin Hoffman (1981).

To understand empathy, we must know that the usual description of how we perceive is incomplete. Perceiving is not merely a matter of a sense organ's translating environmental energy into nerve pulses which, upon arrival at the brain, are retranslated into a copy of the original stimulus. We perceive not only with our brains but somatically, with our guts, glands, and muscles. Perception is a psychosomatic event, and **empathy** is the basis of psychosomatic perceiving. Almost everyone knows about the contagiousness of yawns, and how we clear our throats as a way of clearing that of a speaker to whom we are listening. When we strain to help a pole-vaulter over the bar, or to hold back a movie hero tottering on the brink of a precipice, we are perceiving empathically. But empathy need not be visual. Tapping one's foot to music is an empathic reaction, and empathic vomiting is not unknown. How do you react when you smell vomit? Note that empathic reactions may or may not be synchronous with the stimulus. When we try to keep the hero from falling or when we tap our foot, we are reacting synchronously, without any lag between stimulus and response, whereas yawning takes a bit of time. Empathy can be passive, as when we are moved to yawn. Or it can be active, as when we exert "body English" to help the pole-vaulter or to steer a pool ball, a golf ball, or a bowling ball. Our empathy can be misguided. American adults watching a baby being tightly swaddled cannot escape a sense of suffocation. The baby, though, finds swaddling soothing. We can react empathically to inanimate objects, as when we are made uncomfortable by a poorly balanced stack of dishes or by a painting hanging out of plumb. Some theorists have proposed that empathy is the basis

(© Cary S. Wolinsky/Stock, Boston)

A sense of sympathy toward peers develops during the preschool years.

of all our aesthetic judgments (Lipps, 1897). When we plant ourselves in front of a painting or open our ears to a piece of music, we fuse with the work and resonate somatically to its qualities.

Empathy is a primitive, direct way of apprehending the world. **Sympathy** is rooted in empathy. However, it is more detached and has an additional component of intellectual understanding. When one says, "I sympathize with you," the speaker means "I *know* how you feel," not "I am having a great upwelling of almost identical feelings." This does not mean that the cognitive component of sympathy has to be conscious. As we said in Chapter 9, many of our cognitive structures are formed out of concrete experience, without benefit of symbolic representation. Preschool children acquire many intuitions about how other people operate simply by recording the feedback they receive in response to their initiatives. Sympathy reflects declining egocentrism. Note that even toddlers can feel sympathy for people they know well. The toddler may seek to console an unhappy parent or offer a toy to an ailing sibling. Recall, for instance, the toddler who fetched his companion's security blanket.

We can trace the development of sympathy toward peers, beginning with the child's pausing to stare at another child who is in distress. Then the child offers words or touches of comfort. The child may rebuke a playmate who has made a third child unhappy. Children learn to recognize serious situations and to seek out adult help.

Let us not overstate the case. Children are not necessarily consistent in being sympathetic. A child who acts compassionately in one situation may behave quite cruelly in another. This is particularly likely to be true when the mob spirit takes over and the children gang up to taunt and tease a victim. At other times, a usually sympathetic child may simply not understand that another person is in distress, as when witnessing a playmate's tumble. Both children and adults, remember, laugh at the spills and pratfalls of others, at least until it dawns on them that those laughable contortions may signal pain. Authentic sympathy requires understanding of other people's feelings, both positive and negative. It is an important ingredient in leadership.

Cooperation and Prosocial Behavior

Another social behavior that emerges during the preschool age is cooperation. Cooperation takes two somewhat different forms, both increasingly visible during this period. The first is willingness to pitch in and help out, which may be related to the development of sympathy. The second is the ability to coordinate and synchronize one's activities so as to fit into a collective enterprise. A seesaw obviously requires cooperative action by two people. A whirligig may require coordinated pumping by a half-dozen children. The theme of growing cooperation will be evident in the account of play and other activities later in this chapter.

Sympathy and cooperation bring us to the topic of **prosocial behavior,** currently an active field of research. The domain is often measured in terms of *altruism,* the person's willingness to give some of his or her wordly goods for the benefit of others. In a world where hostility and violence sometimes seem to be taking over, many parents are concerned about how to raise their children to be loving and generous.

Paul Mussen and Nancy Eisenberg-Berg (1977) have surveyed the research, including their own, in this field. They conclude that prosocial behavior develops most fully in children who are:

> . . . relatively self-confident and active . . . , advanced in moral reasoning as well as in role-taking skills and empathy. Altruists are likely to be the children of nurturant parents who are good models of prosocial behavior, use reasoning in discipline, maintain high standards, and encourage their children to accept responsibility for others early.

Predictions can also be made about the conditions under which predispositions to prosocial behavior are likely to be translated into action. Children become more helpful when they feel happy or successful; when they receive direct rewards for helping; after they have been exposed to preaching that stresses reasons for helping; if they are assigned responsibility (p. 159).

We could add some qualifications, but this pretty well sums up the reliable findings.

Aggression

Anger, of course, appears during infancy. However, venting anger on another begins to appear only in toddlerhood and develops rapidly during the preschool years. **Aggression** is highly resistant to both definition and explanation. We define aggression as behavior intended—sometimes unconsciously—to inflict physical or psychological damage on another. As such, it is an expression of underlying hostility. This rules out several common usages of the term. Predatory behavior, designed to secure food, is not aggression. Ritual displays of hostility, as when a dog snarls at an intruder on its home territory, are protective rather than aggressive. To label as aggressive the vigorous, tenacious pursuit of some goal, as when we speak of "aggressive" salesmanship or leadership, is a metaphorical extension and should not be taken literally. Although hostility is the immediate source of true aggression, it may have still deeper roots, such as jealousy or vengefulness or even moral indignation.

There is a continuous debate about the origins of aggressive behavior (Berkowitz, 1974). There are those who, like Freud (1927) and Lorenz (1966), view it as an instinct, part of our biological constitution. Others (Skinner, 1953; Kuo, 1967; Scott, 1958) consider it a learned response that can be reduced or eliminated by lack of reinforcement. Learning theorists seeking to reconcile psychoanalysis and behaviorism proposed the **frustration-aggression hypothesis** (Dollard *et al.*, 1939). According to this hypothesis, aggression is always caused by frustration (inability to reach a desired goal), and frustration always leads to aggression.

Lorenz's account of human aggression as an instinct run wild has been thoroughly discredited on both factual and logical grounds (Montagu, 1968). This does not, however, deny the possibility of a strong biological disposition to act aggressively in provocative circumstances. Nor can we deny that there are in our midst a few individuals so disposed to violence that they constitute a grave threat to almost anyone who comes in contact with them. Such people, however, are too rare to be taken as typical. Their behavior can be explained equally well by reference to biological abnormalities or brutalizing life histories. The frustration-aggression hypothesis in its pure form has likewise fallen into disrepute. Although frustration and aggression are sometimes linked, aggression, as we have said, may have a number of sources. Also, frustration can lead to constructive—and even creative—as well as destructive behavior.

Assuming a biological component in aggression, experiential factors have also been shown to play an important role in its expression. In every culture studied so far, boys are more aggressive than girls (Fincher, 1975; Maccoby and Jacklin, 1974; Whiting and Edwards,

(Paul Seder, Ph.D./Taurus Photos)

A boy playing soldier. Aggressiveness is considered to be an important part of manliness in Western societies, and boys are often encouraged to "stand up for their rights."

1973). At the same time, we know that in our own culture aggressiveness is an important part of manliness. Boys are encouraged, if sometimes ambivalently, to "stand up for their rights." The concept of *machismo* emphasizes aggressiveness. Governments, which are usually run by males, do not always offer role models of patient forbearance.

Sears, Maccoby, and Levin (1957) and Maccoby (1980) have identified a number of relationships between child-rearing practices and levels of aggressiveness in children. Parental aggressiveness serves as a model for children's aggressive behavior. Highly permissive parents have highly aggressive children, appar-ently because getting away with aggressive acts is reinforcing. Parents who physically punish aggression have aggressive children. (Here we are reminded of studies of child battering, pp. 247–251). Parents who restrain aggression with a minimum of punishment have children low in aggression. The highest level of aggression is found in the children of permissive parents who every so often blow up and punish the child physically.

Social learning theorists have carried out a number of experiments on the imitation of filmed or live aggressive models by children. The models typically behaved violently toward a large clown figure (Bandura, 1973). The children, true to prediction, when turned loose on the figure would have at it with full force. We are not sure how seriously we should take children's pummeling of an inflated plastic Bobo doll as evidence of aggression, but they acted just as the theory said they would. Television is also thought to serve as a model for aggressive behavior.

The early literature (e.g., Dawe, 1934) on fighting and quarreling among preschool children still seems to apply quite well to the behavior of young children today. Regardless of their source, preschool children's passions run high, even if, like summer squalls, they come and go quickly. In a flash of rage, if their strength were equal to their feelings, children would inflict severe, even fatal, damage on one another. But at this age, enmities are as unstable as friendships, so that, a moment later, children may be showering endearments on those they were just preparing to annihilate. Although as a rule friendships and enmities shift and change rapidly, in any group there are likely to be one or two children who are universally liked and admired, and another one or two who are just as pervasively disliked and shunned or picked on.

As Dawe (1934) pointed out, during the preschool years boys and girls already show very different patterns of conflict. To begin with, both physical and verbal aggression is far more common in boys than in girls (Maccoby and Jacklin, 1974). Boys become increasingly combative between the ages of three and five, after which a decline sets in. Girls, by contrast, fight less and less after age three. Girls also are more likely to use their tongues than their fists as weapons (Maccoby and Jacklin, 1974). Both sexes try to settle property disputes by snatching the contested article and fleeing with it.

In general, conflicts develop from grim, almost wordless tugs of war of the kind observed in toddlers, to physical violence punctuated with angry cries and shouts, to violence redirected to an enemy's property (as when a hat is trampled into the dirt), neutral objects, or scapegoats. Physical clashes give way to more "civilized" verbal exchanges, including threats of violence and insults.

At younger ages, preschool children quarrel mainly over possessions. Then, unprovoked attacks and retaliation appear. Such attacks are probably a form of exploration, midway between teasing and simple curiosity about how the victim will respond. Later in the preschool years, and at subsequent ages, social difficulties become the main source of conflict—who will play with whom, what will they play, who will take which roles, who will be included and who excluded, and who dislikes whom.

However, if we pay close attention, we will discover that much of what looks and sounds like aggression is really a form of play—nonliteral behavior again. We note a lunchtime conversation which reveals half-playful aggression. This aggression is reinforced by four-year-olds' liking for experiments with language and by a species of cooperative competition in which each child builds upon the others' ideas in an effort to surpass them in outrageous fantasy. The butt of the aggression tends to be lost in the shuffle:

John: We'll cut off his arms.

Ellie: We'll saw off his legs.

Don: Let's hang him up in a tree and tickle him.

John: Let's poke him full of black and blue marks.

Ellie: Let's cut off his hair and put it in the sandbox.

Don: Let's cut out his grunties.

John: Let's smear him all over with grunties.

Ellie: Let's make him eat lots of grunties.

John: We'll wrap it up in some paper— not cellophane—some yellow paper, and then tie some string around it.

Television, Modeling, and Aggression

During the 1960s, a vast government-sponsored research program on the effects of television on children was carried out. The chief hypothesis to be tested was that watching television violence made viewers more prone to violence. The controversial report (Liebert, Neale, and Davidson, 1973; Lyle and

(© Michael Kagen/Monkmeyer Press Photo)

Children watching TV. One well-controlled study of television's impact on young children showed that programs emphasizing aggression caused a decline in both tolerance of delay and obedience to group rules.

Hoffman, 1972) found a small relationship between watching violence on television and behaving violently. However, there was widespread criticism of the report and of subsequent research studies meant to bolster or rebut its findings. In this case, the natural experiment had just too many uncontrolled variables to permit any firm conclusions to be drawn. At the same time, most observers were willing to accept that violent TV programs can stir up violence in people who are already inclined that way.

An unusually well-controlled study provides an excellent summary of the evidence and directly assesses the impact of TV on young children (Friedrich and Stein, 1973). Children enrolled in a nine-week nursery-school program were exposed daily during the middle four

weeks to violent television shows ("Batman" or "Superman"), or to prosocial ones ("Mister Rogers' Neighborhood"), or to neutral cartoons. The children's free play behavior before and after the viewing period provided evidence of change. Those children who watched programs emphasizing aggression showed a decline in both tolerance of delay and obedience to the rules of the class. However, aggressiveness increased only in those children who had scored above the mean in aggression in the pre-viewing period. Those who watched prosocial programs had an increased level of task persistence and a somewhat higher level of obedience to the rules and tolerance of delay than children who watched the neutral shows. These effects showed up most clearly in the brightest children. Increased prosocial interpersonal behavior, such as helpfulness and cooperation, appeared only in low-SES children. The researchers presented only change scores (post-treatment minus pretreatment scores). Therefore, we have no way of knowing whether high-SES and low-SES subjects had comparable levels of prosocial behavior to begin with.

In a study by Singer and Singer (1979), preschool children's television viewing was monitored over a year. Although there was a significant correlation between the amount of viewing of TV shows featuring a high level of violence and aggressive behavior in children's play in school, the parents' role was an important part of this correlation. Children of parents who did not monitor their children's television viewing, whose orientations and values were traditional, and whose cultural interests were limited were more likely to exhibit aggression. Children whose parents encouraged them to view prosocial programs and were involved in other cultural interests manifested little aggression. In addition, these children appeared to be more imaginative in their play, and imaginative play was found to be a positive way of coping with stressful situations (Singer and Singer, 1980).

In 1982, two supplementary reports on the effects of television viewing were published (National Institute of Mental Health, 1982a, 1982b). The contributors to these volumes concluded that the evidence is "overwhelming" that *excessive* TV violence was the direct cause of aggressive behavior among children and adolescents. It is worth emphasizing, too, that the reports pointed to TV's potent influence on prosocial behavior, even though this influence has not been fully exploited.

Besides the question of TV's influence on prosocial and antisocial behavior, it is a potential source of knowledge, beliefs, values, feelings, and models for behavior in general. Young children's ability to discriminate between reality and fantasy is still shaky. They are convinced that what they are watching on TV are real events. It is only at about age four that children begin to wonder aloud about how the people got inside the set and how they are to get out again. One four-year-old saw his grandmother on a talk show. The next day, he told his schoolmates that Grandma was in the TV set but would be out in time to pay her weekly visit. Research on how young children come to understand the conventions of television and to make sense of its messages is still in an early stage (Jag-

lom and Gardner, 1981; Meringoff *et al.*, 1983). We urge you to stay abreast of developments in this fascinating area through the current literature.

In terms of influence, there is the further fact that time spent watching TV cannot be spent doing other things. However, we actually know very little about how TV shapes children's characters and abilities. We do know that themes from TV programs are often found in young children's dramatic play. We also know that for many parents TV is a cheap and untiring electronic baby-sitter. Some people believe that watching television facilitates learning to read. The repeated juxtapositions of spoken and printed words, especially on commercials, would seem to promote the kinds of associations helpful in reading. The general literature suggests that television contributes little or nothing to learning to read (Whitehurst, Novak, and Zorn, 1972; Quisenberry, 1982). However, Singer and Singer (in preparation) point out that studies of the relationship between TV viewing and reading have typically failed to control for intellectual level and SES. The Singers find a dual pattern: TV viewing facilitates learning to read in low-SES or low-IQ children, but it impedes reading in bright or high-SES children. The Singers confirm observations by Gerbner *et al.* (1977) that watching TV violence helps instill in children a vision of the world as a "mean and scary" place in which to live. Finally, we are forced to wonder about TV's role in breeding materialism, faith that life's highest rewards lie in the possession and consumption of abundant tangible things. Certainly television is used to sell salvation as well as toothpaste (which often promises sexual salvation), but a form of salvation that does not conflict in the slightest with the pursuit of material wealth.

PLAY AND OTHER ACTIVITIES IN THE PRESCHOOL YEARS

Preschool children's social behavior, at home or in school, revolves in good measure around *play*. So it is now time to examine in more detail what this play consists of, what it means to children, what it tells us about them and their world, and what it tells us about *us*.

As we said in connection with toddlerhood, play is used to describe whatever

(© Nancy Hays/Monkmeyer Press Photo)

Children develop their social, cognitive, and manipulative skills while playing together.

young children do that cannot be classified as the serious business of life. But as is true with so many categories, the boundaries are blurred. For one thing, as we shall see in a moment, the child can subvert seriousness with playfulness. For another, play is a serious business for the child. In the course of playing, children hone their social, cognitive, and manipulative skills. And in a preliminary way, they develop some of the practical skills they will need and practice as adults.

Play is intertwined, as both cause and effect, with the child's social cognition, the ability to understand and adapt to other people's inner workings. In play, children become aware that other people have inner workings, and they learn how to relate the signals people emit to those inner workings. In this chapter we merely show social cognition in action. In Chapter 11, we shall have a go at dissecting it.

The Changing Qualities of Play

Play changes in a number of ways during the preschool years (Garvey, 1977). First, it becomes more *playful*, allowing the child to detect and experiment with the multiple possibilities of situations. Some people are lucky enough to retain their playfulness throughout their lives.

Children try to eat with the handle of a spoon or fork. They may want to wear their clothes turned back to front, or wear a shirt as trousers. The boy, urinating, traces curlicues in the toilet bowl (and sometimes, too, outside it). Children feign hunger at bedtime and fatigue at meals. They "forget" how to do things and make "mistakes" so that they have to begin a project all over again. They make an extravagant show of effort helping to pick up their playthings at the end of the day. They experiment with strange combinations of foodstuffs—one four-year-old boy invented a concoction of milk, mashed potatoes, and chocolate ice cream, which he called, for reasons unknown, "Mexican soup."

Second, despite the playfulness, there seems to be a new earnestness in preschool children's play. It is as though children are seriously trying on roles as a way of learning and experiencing the life styles they represent.

A third change is a growing awareness of the distinction between reality and fantasy. Early in the preschool years, children are likely to become so absorbed in their play that they forget that it is play. They become genuinely angry when the meanings they have assigned to the situation are not recognized by others. One little girl, making "cakes" in the sandbox, became so involved in her fantasy that she actually bit off a mouthful of sand (which cured her of that particular fantasy). Later in the preschool years, children draw a fairly distinct line between the world of make-believe and the real world in which power is exercised and irreversible consequences follow from actions (one four-year-old to another: "Let's pretend we're not playing pretend."). Young children have very little idea of how the real world works. For instance, they know nothing about where money comes from or how it functions beyond paying for things. They do know, however, that reality falls very little under their influence.

Fourth, the child's expanding emotional range and newly found cognitive powers make for greater imagination, both in the sense of playing with ideas and possibilities and of imagining en-

tities and situations unlike anything the child has ever experienced. Even when children do not invent them, the dragons and gnomes of fairy tales require a certain maturity to be understood and appreciated. Televised fantasies, of course, do not tax the child's capabilities in the slightest.

Changing Patterns of Play

Most of children's play with peers can be classified reasonably neatly along two dimensions. Both dimensions are developmental, but the appearance of a new pattern does not mean the disappearance of old ones. The new pattern is in addition to those already present.

The Social Dimension of Play. The first dimension of play is the *social*, describing with whom the child plays. Play with parents comes first, as in "the game." As infancy progresses, the baby becomes capable of *solitary play*, exploring space and objects and his or her own body. Play with peers, as we have seen, begins in toddlerhood. Toddlers sometimes engage in *parallel play*; that is, they play separately side by side but obviously aware of and taking pleasure in the other's company. However, there is accumulating evidence that toddlers also engage in social interchanges, handing each other toys or food, copying each other's actions, and sometimes battling for a plaything. We propose calling such nonverbal exchanges **interactive play.**

The next pattern, found in the early preschool years, is **associative play.** Children begin to do things in groups: A flock may congregate in the sandbox, crowd into a rocking boat, or swarm over the climbing structures, shrilling together in an expression of shared feeling. Associative play may also be manifested by a number of individual children all doing the same thing. In a play group, one can witness epidemics of telephoning, grotesque lurching about and falling to the floor, or water play—no sooner has one child begun something than everybody wants to do it. Social psychologists refer to such a pattern as **behavioral contagion,** the spread of an activity or a mood or an impulse through a group. We interpret behavioral contagion as a manifestation of empathy.

Next, as children learn to coordinate their activities, they engage in **cooperative play.** Now roles may be assigned, plans discussed and decided, and verbal exchange is the rule. Finally, although usually not until late in the preschool years or early in the school years, children engage in **competitive play,** as in games that have rules that decide who wins and who loses.

The Content Dimension of Play. The second dimension of play patterns refers to *content,* what one plays with or at. The earliest content of play seems to be **social-affective,** taking pleasure in the manipulation of social relations and feelings. The baby at first is on the receiving end of social-affective play, as when parents talk or croon to the infant, nuzzle its belly, or try other means to elicit a positive emotional response. Babies, in turn, learn to arouse parental emotions in a spirit of play, by simply smiling, by calling for attention, initiating a particular game, pretending not to hear, feigning distress so as to be petted and reassured, and by teasing. Social-affective play reflects the universal satisfaction found simply in being in communication with other people.

(David Strickler/Monkmeyer Press Photo)

As children learn to coordinate their activities, cooperative play emerges. Note the child's typical preschool posture—forelegs on the floor folded under the thighs, buttocks resting on the heels, knees outward.

Quite early in life, the baby begins to enjoy nonsocial stimulation. This produces something akin to aesthetic experience. This kind of enjoyment is called **sense-pleasure play.** Like social-affective play, sense-pleasure play originates in the environment. Patterns of light and color and movement and sounds and rhythms and tastes and odors and textures and consistencies attract attention and provide pleasure. Young infants can do little to initiate interesting physical events in the outside world, and it seems likely that the first form of sense-pleasure play that the baby controls is babbling. The body continues to be a source of sense-pleasure stimulation as well as experience, as when the baby begins to masturbate. Babies explore the textures of cereal, the possibilities of mud and water, the feel and taste of snow. Molding clay, scribbling, and covering paper with colored paint are all forms of sense-pleasure play. So are swinging, bouncing, rocking, humming, listening to music, and smelling flowers or other aromatic things. Solo dancing is sense-pleasure play. Dancing with a partner is a blend of social-affective and sense-pleasure play.

Once the baby has begun to reach out, to grasp and manipulate, we see the beginning of **skill play.** Skill play consists of the persistent, repetitive exercise of newly developed abilities, from batting a suspended doll and making it dance, to removing and reinserting the nipple, to dropping things from the feeding table, to creeping and walking, to carrying things, to piling blocks, and so on through the child's burgeoning repertoire. Obviously, there is often an element of sense-pleasure play in skill play, but there are abundant instances when the only point of an activity seems to be the practicing of a skill. This does not imply that children practice skills with any future benefit in view or even that they are motivated to become competent. They seem to be moved by the intrinsic fascination of the just-barely-able-to, which acts on people of all ages. At all ages, too, an already perfected skill is constantly exercised for the sheer enjoyment of being able to—the expert driver takes pleasure in his or her adroitness on the highway.

The dominant motif of the preschool years is **dramatic play** (also known as **symbolic** or **pretend play**). Here the child takes on roles and acts out themes drawn at first from family life, and then increasingly from the outside world, including the world of fantasy. We saw the beginnings of dramatic play in late infancy

and toddlerhood, but it is during the preschool years that it reaches full flower.

It is our conviction that dramatic play contributes heavily to social cognition. However, from the children's point of view, the satisfactions of dramatic play seem to lie in the magical sense of power and participation that are not yet theirs in real life.

In dramatic play, children put themselves—sometimes literally—into other people's shoes. We see children dressing up and wielding props as they play the role of mother or baby or doctor, serving tea, putting out a fire, digging a ditch, waiting on customers in the grocery store, and simultaneously being pilot and airplane, steam shovel and operator.

Roles that involve visible and clearly functional activities seem to appeal most to children. The jobs of housekeeper, filling station attendant, carpenter, or bulldozer driver can be grasped instantly, at least in their externals, and imitated. Although it may chagrin the white-collar or professional father or mother, it is not surprising that the child finds the role of accountant or attorney drab and unappealing. The doctor, of course, does something of obvious significance tantalizingly touched with mystery and thus qualifies as a model. Children's literal adherence to the externals of a role, with little comprehension of its essence, shows up in the mistakes they make. For example, a three-year-old, playing doctor with a doll as patient, says, "Now I have to test her kneeflexes." A four-year-old reports, "I'm afraid I have to tell you that I took out Jimmy's tonsils. It's all right, though—I put in some new ones." A child turns to the teacher and says, "You know, I'm really desperate! Tell me how to play I'm desperate."

In group dramatic play, young preschool children change roles rapidly, with no apparent sense of strain. Switching sometimes meets the needs of the evolving game and sometimes it simply means that they have tired of the old role.

Children sometimes become so caught up in their roles that they want to carry them over into everyday life. One little girl insisted for several months that she was a particular comic-strip character. She later became a cowboy and was unwilling to go swimming until she had been assured that cowboys sometimes exchange their daily attire for things like swimsuits. This leads us to the fact that as children grow older they demand increasingly realistic props for their dramatic play, which coincides with a sharpening of the boundaries between reality and fantasy.

For the young preschool child, a block can serve as a doll, a train, a building, or a cow. Three-year-olds can people and furnish a universe with sticks and stones and paper and rags, although they make little effort to shape them into representational images. The four-year-old, to be an effective astronaut, wants some key accessory—a helmet and visor or some such. Five-year-olds are likely to feel dissatisfied in their roles unless they can wear the full regalia of the part they are playing. This reversion to literalness seems to reflect a need for role-relevant props to buttress their belief in their own fantasy. Without all the trappings, reality asserts itself.

Dramatic play extends into the middle years in such games as cowboys and Indians, cops and robbers, and pirates and victims. In adolescence, it seems to be part and parcel of everyday life, a large part of which adolescents spend role

(© Myron Papiz)

Dramatic play reaches full flower during the preschool years. Its attraction seems to lie in the marginal sense of power and participation it yields—qualities not yet available in real life.

playing. In adulthood, we still have a great deal of role playing, which can be intensified in amateur and professional theatricals. The pervasiveness of role playing in adult life is suggested by the relief people express at day's end when they say, "Thank heaven I can be myself!"

The next content category is **ritual games**—"The Farmer in the Dell," "London Bridge," "Ring around a Rosie." These games follow their fixed development to an unvarying climax and then end. Ritual games used to be the province of school-age children, but in keeping with the acceleration of development in many spheres, preschool children now play them.

Finally, intersecting with competitive play, there are competitive games. However, except for the board games mentioned earlier, preschool children do not yet play competitively. This does not mean that rivalry and winning and losing are beyond them. It is just that they cannot take competition light-heartedly and nonliterally. Preschool children hate to lose. They will fudge or want to change the rules and demand endless exceptions and opportunities to change their moves when they have made a mistake.

It should not be necessary to point out that all these varieties of play extend into adulthood. Social-affective play, for instance, is found in banter, teasing, practical jokes, flirtation, and the game of love. Sense-pleasure play has its counterparts in adult aesthetic experience, in the enjoyment of art or music, in the appreciation of spectacles, in the contemplation of natural beauty, such as a sunset or a vista or waves breaking on a shore, or in watching the flames in a fireplace.

Reflections of the Adult World in Play

Since so much of children's dramatic play is modeled on the behavior of familiar adults, we can often gather from childish reenactments the special qualities and meanings that the adult world holds for young children. Even though children may not understand adult behavior, they can be very sensitive to its emotional nuances.

It can be a revealing and chastening experience to have our gestures, pos-

tures, mannerisms, affectations, foibles, and turns of speech reflected back to us through the play of our children. Needless to say, we sometimes encounter reflections of parental tenderness, humor, good sense, and compassion. But the most striking insights come when we find ourselves projected as a scolding or whining voice, as a monument of pomposity, as a mean-spirited tyrant, as a sleeping ogre who, if disturbed, snarls and gnashes its teeth.

Much of the child's play is an unconscious caricature of adult ways, but a caricature that may be closer to the truth than we like to admit. Sometimes, of course, the parody becomes conscious, as in the following exchange between two four-year-olds perched atop a jungle gym and convulsed by their own wittiness:

Jack: It's *lovely* to see you!

Danny: I'm so happy to see you!

Jack: How *are* you? How have you *been*?

Danny: Sorry I have to go so quick.

Jack: I hope you have a good time falling down and bumping your head.

The caricature is less conscious, but no less telling, in a speech by a four-and-a-half-year-old as she tucks her doll into bed: "We like to have her, but I just want her to stop the nonsense. She wets the bed all the time. You *wicket* girl! You bad, *wicket* girl!" Let it be noted that this child was not necessarily mimicking the behavior of particular adults. In some cases, dramatic play is a fairly faithful copy of actual events. In other cases, though, it seems to represent the child's generalized perception of adult ways.

Children seem to be very sensitive to the status value both of different roles in the world and of different children in their group. The behavior of a four-year-old girl with marked leadership qualities exemplifies this dual sensitivity. A boy of low standing in the group had been trying persistently to join a game of house in which the little girl was the mother. Finally, with subtle skill, she let him in and expelled him again in one swift, smooth movement: "O.K. You be the daddy. Finish your breakfast and I must drive you to the station. Here's your briefcase and you must get on the train. G'by!"

The Child in the Family

So far, we have been celebrating children's newly found ability to communicate among themselves. Let us now look at the child's play and other doings at home, in contact primarily with parents, siblings, and pets. Children look at picture books, blow soap bubbles, and listen to records. They cut out and paste, draw and paint, sail toy boats, and think about things. Children also spend time just observing and absorbing their surroundings.

Preschool children go with their parents on excursions to the park or the zoo, to special events, and on picnics. They play rough-and-tumble games, go sledding, and slide on the ice. (In the Netherlands and Scandinavia, of course, children of this age are likely to be expert skaters.) They splash in water at the beach or under a fire hydrant or hose. Preschool children happily immerse themselves in water that feels to adults to be barely above freezing. They build sand castles, dig tunnels, listen to stories

that adults make up or read to them, study leaves and stones and insects, and work mechanical toys. Today's children are liable to spend long periods watching television and being imprinted with whatever influences it may have.

Parents and children hold conversations on such recurrent themes as tastes and preferences, feelings, age, shared adventures, the existence and nature of God, elimination and other body functions, accidents and sickness and surgery and death, animals and Santa Claus—in sum, a huge array of things, real and unreal. Children like to confront parents with hypothetical situations introduced by "What if": all the world were covered by water, people could fly, there were only men in the world, the sky fell down, it were always dark, and so on endlessly.

A question that pops up frequently in parent-child conversations is "Where did I come from?" This, of course, expresses only one of children's many curiosities about sex, but it is probably the best place to begin a child's sex education. Even in today's supposedly liberated atmosphere, many parents find it hard to talk to their children about sex.

We favor openness in such matters up to the limit of the child's interest and ability to comprehend and retain. Parents will know that they are reaching the limits when the child's attention wanders, or when remarks on totally unrelated topics start to appear.

The limits of comprehension are shown in children's *birth fantasies*, the theories they dream up to account for what goes on in the womb during gestation and how the baby gets out of the mother's body. Even children whose well-meaning parents have told all are likely to remain confused (Bernstein and

Cowan, 1975). Among the notions put forth by young children are that babies are assembled bit by bit, that babies come from the baby store, that babies get into the mother's tummy by being eaten like food and are expelled as in elimination, and that the mother's egg has a shell like that of a chicken egg. Children have from time to time expressed a belief that babies emerge through the navel, the anus, and the mouth. Bernstein and Cowan's findings have been further extended by Goldman and Goldman (1982). They studied notions of where babies come from in youngsters aged five to fifteen in Australia, North America, England, and Sweden. They classified their data according to Piaget's four stages of cognitive development plus two transitional stages. Among younger children, they found artificialisms ("Jesus makes them in a factory" [American five-year-old]; "A seed in mother's tummy where she has an apple. . . . No, it's something white, maybe mashed potatoes" [Swedish five-year-old]). Even youngsters who knew about sexual intercourse were likely to think of the sperm as containing a complete baby in miniature. As Formanek and Gurian (1982) have found, adult explanations are as likely to confuse as to enlighten. For instance, the word "seed" commonly used to describe sperm is taken by children to mean something like an apple or an orange seed, as apparent above.

Among the helpful things children can learn and remember are the differences between boys and girls and the names for intimate anatomy. From time immemorial little boys and little girls have been instructing each other about anatomical sex differences, but it helps if they have names for the distinguishing features. In some preliterate societies, children regularly witness parental intercourse, and this seems to do them no harm. Some authorities have suggested that Western parents allow their children to watch them make love, but we have no way of knowing what the impact of such an experience would be on children growing up within our cultural framework.

There is no point in worrying about children's masturbation unless it seems to verge on the obsessive. However, visiting adults may be upset to see a child masturbating, and it is probably a good idea to suggest to children that they do their masturbating in private.

For parents who find it hard to talk about sex with their children, there are a number of books designed to help. We recommend that parents looking for such a book do a lot of comparison shopping and buy only those that feel congenial.

Manipulation and Mastery of Tools and Materials

Preschool children interact with things as well as people. Before you object that things cannot be part of a human interaction, let us remind you that children's actions upon things produce feedback and, therefore, information—imagine a baby exploring the properties of a balloon.

In children's dealings with things, we can see a steady progression toward increasing appropriateness, ingenuity, imagination, and skill. This is in keeping

(© Suzanne Szasz/Photo Researchers, Inc.)

Out of activities such as driving nails, children gradually learn to manipulate and master materials to produce constructions and creations of their own.

with a general shift from impulsive behavior under the control of environmental stimuli toward planned, internally directed action. Of particular interest is the way children use raw materials to shape new products. Here we see the *orthogenetic principle*—differentiation followed by hierarchic integration—at work. During the differentiation phase, the child explores the properties of the material and practices the skills needed to shape it. At first, squeezing and pounding and poking a ball of clay is sufficient. Learning to use scissors to cut paper is at first an end in itself. Driving nails is a self-contained activity. As the child gets a sense of the materials and the skills needed to shape them, there gradually emerge integrated constructions that represent the functional subordination of all the part processes into a totality: clay is the raw material of sculpture; paper can be put to a thousand uses; nails and wood can be formed into a crude approximation of an airplane.

Children find raw materials everywhere. Cleaning tissues are not merely things with which to blow one's nose or wipe up spills. They can be bunched together and fastened with rubber bands to make a doll. They can be wrapped around a doll to make clothing. They can be spread over a recumbent doll as blankets. Paper clips, pipe cleaners, cotton wool, gummed labels and reinforcements, scotch tape, paper bags, string and yarn, metal foil, adhesive tape, drinking straws, rollers from toilet paper and paper towels, toothpicks, water, sand, clay, scraps of lumber, and glue—all are grist for the preschool child's mill.

In shaping materials, children make use of such tools as scissors (the small, blunt-nosed kind); saws (the kind that really cut); hammers, staplers, and sometimes screwdrivers and wrenches. It is important that tools be of good quality and that they be in functioning condition. It is also important that children be given guidance in the use of tools with which they might injure themselves.

A paper cutout made by a Chinese preschool child.

Given such guidance, most children can be trusted to use tools properly. In other cultural settings, children are given greater scope in the use of cutting utensils. Chinese preschool children, for instance, use sharp pointed scissors skillfully and carefully to make very precise paper cutouts. A three-year-old Chinese girl's cutout of a rabbit is shown above.

With adult inspiration, children make abstract collages out of old wallpaper, newspaper, tissue paper, leaves and twigs, sea shells, sand, bits and pieces of wood, and sculptured library paste. They make constructions out of empty matchboxes, cereal boxes, tissue boxes, and folded paper, decorated with paint, sand, buttons, sequins, trimmings, scraps of cloth, and the like. Preschool children do not perform especially well on the Unusual Uses Test (Pepler, 1980; Goodnow, 1969; Guilford, 1967), designed as a measure of creativity, which asks the subject to think of all possible ways to use a common object, such as a brick. But in their everyday activities, preschoolers are in no way bound by the conventional uses for which things were originally made, so they in fact demonstrate whatever qualities the test was meant to measure.

Drawing and Painting

The development of children's drawing and painting tells us very little about children's perceptual processes. The representation of three-dimensional objects and spaces on a two-dimensional surface poses problems that humankind collectively took thousands of years to solve, and it is too much to expect that four-year-old children will be able to give us an accurate depiction of things as they see them. Children's drawings and paintings can tell us something about how children organize the world emotionally (Gardner, 1980). The first representations are of people, which tells us what children find significant. Even when other sorts of objects, such as trees and houses appear, the human figure still towers high above them. Before children attempt representation, their choices of colors and qualities of stroke can reveal anything from chronic rage to serene harmony.

Children behave quite differently according to the kinds of media they are given to work with. Using poster paint laid onto large sheets of manila paper with a wide brush, children experiment with pure form and color, giving little thought to the depiction of objects. With a fine-grained medium, such as a pencil or a ball-point pen, children are likely to attempt pictorial representation, at first, as we have said, usually of a person. Even with paint, children eventually pass from color masses and blendings to representation. When they first begin to paint pictures, they may have trouble sticking to their original goal. Accidental effects keep suggesting new possibilities, so that what begins as a picture of a horse may turn into a picture of a house, which may then be transformed into a boat or revert to an exercise in abstract design. Thus what looks like a meaningless jumble of forms and colors may actually be the result of successive superimposed intentions. For the adult to ask "What is it?" serves no purpose and may even hinder a child's efforts, suggesting as it does that every creation has to be a picture of something. What one can say instead is "Tell me about your picture," which children are generally able and happy to do. By age five, many children paint well-planned, elaborate scenes showing complex events and activities with detailed settings and backgrounds of grass, trees, buildings, fences, animals, sky, clouds, and sun or moon and stars.

To trace the evolution of children's depictions in its purest form, however, one does well to stick with line drawings made with pencil or ball-point pen (Goodnow, 1977). Children's first drawings of people consist of a roughly circular line enclosing marks standing for eyes, nose, and mouth, which, assuming one can recognize them, may be in almost any spatial arrangement. Even before going on to further anatomical elaboration, children may draw an upturned or downturned mouth to indicate happiness or sadness.

The next step in children's representations comes with the addition of ears and hair. The latter is drawn as either a zigzag or a series of loops across the top of the head. Next, stiff, sticklike arms sprout straight out from either side of the head, ending in a knob of fist or a sunburst of fingers (if they should number five, it is probably by accident). Then legs grow downward, either directly from the head or from the arms near the head. The legs, like the arms, are jointless and end in balls of feet. The torso is likely to appear first as a disconnected scribbled mass between the legs. To the oversensitive adult eyes, this may look like an attempt to draw the genitals. In fact, it seems to occur to very few preschool children to depict the sex organs. The torso then takes shape as a crude oval or rectangle with the legs appended. For a while, the arms may still grow out of the head. When they are moved to the trunk, it may be only approximately in the region of the shoulders. Head and torso are likely to remain joined directly, without benefit of a visible neck, for some time. Children may mean to show the figure in action, but they either have to say in words what the person is doing or suggest it by drawing in some additional object, such as a shovel or a car. To represent walking or running or sitting overtaxes the child's skills. Clothing and scenery begin to appear around age four. As children develop, drawing styles diverge. Some children draw the human figure as an assemblage of discrete parts, while others draw it as an amoeba-shaped whole.

In general, well into the school years, heads loom disporportionately large, and people tower over nonpeople. Even though one figure overlaps another, both are usually shown in their entirety, as though the near figure were transparent. When children try to draw four-walled houses, they strive mightily to show all four walls, and usually end up settling for three. Painting and drawing are among the most enjoyable experiences of

3½ YEARS

4 YEARS

6 YEARS

5 YEARS

(By permission of LaGuardia House Nursery and Susan Wagner Day Care Center)

These drawings, by children from three and a half to six, show the development of representational ability. The drawings by the younger children are rough approximations of the human form, while the older children depict people and scenery in considerable detail.

the preschool years and contribute to many aspects of development, including, we suspect, reading.

Working with Other Materials

Similar patterns of development can be observed in the use of a variety of materials, from clay to building blocks.

At first, clay is something to be squeezed, pounded flat, rolled out, broken into pieces, made into pellets, and recombined. The child pokes holes in it and indents it with the impressions of familiar objects, such as forks, buttons, and sea shells. It is usually only late in the preschool years that children see the nonliteral possibilities of clay as a medium of representation. Whether treated as clay or as the raw material of sculpture, clay is a source of sheer sensual pleasure.

Blocks, too, are at first treated literally, as mere blocks, not as the stuff of houses, highways, skyscrapers, control towers, rocket ships, and launching pads. Three-year-olds are mainly concerned with problems of balance and size—how big a structure can be put together before the inevitable collapse. By age four, though, children can indeed functionally subordinate blocks in the construction of representations, and block structures are functionally subordinated to dramatic play. The four-year-old's block structures are usually sprawling, loosely hung together, and easily toppled. By age five, children can build well integrated, neatly balanced, ornately intricate constructions that may reach to impressive heights and cover wide areas. These structures often form the core of dramatic play that stretches over several days and even weeks. Such structures vary in compass from cityscapes with cars and trucks and airplanes to enclosures within which children and dolls can enact elaborate dramas. Obviously, block play on this scale requires an abundance of blocks, in a wide assortment of sizes and shapes, such as is usually found only in well-equipped preschools.

Preschool children's carpentry develops in much the same way. Three-year-olds are content just to saw and hammer, and four-year-olds casually nail together crude, ramshackle boats and airplanes. But five-year-olds can—not that all of them do—plan, measure, join together carefully, smooth, and paint. If necessary, they can return to the same project day after day.

Especially when playing with older children, preschoolers become involved in such enterprises as staging a play or a circus. Projects of this kind involve such interesting subsidiary activities as making and arranging scenery, learning parts, creating costumes, making posters, and making and selling tickets. Though some of these activities may lie beyond their competence, preschool children pitch in and do what they can.

Now that we have looked at the social and emotional lives of preschool children, it is time to turn our attention to their cognitive functioning. Remember that these categories—conation, affection, cognition—are merely convenient devices for talking about behavior. They do not stand for distinct parts or aspects of the person. We hope it is obvious that all such partitionings are arbitrary and to some degree false.

You are thus put on notice. Although we shall be discussing an abstraction called cognition that does not exist, what we are really talking about is children's congress with the environment and with themselves, about how things appear to them and what kind of sense things make for children, what children think about and how they think.

If we accept that what the child reacts to initially is the physiognomies and demand qualities of objects and situations, then we can understand that feelings are always an important ingredient of so-called intellectual functioning. It turns out, for instance, that many children fear being sucked down the bathtub drain. The parent may not even suspect this until one day the child announces, "I wouldn't fit, would I?" Indeed, a capacity for emotional involvement is at the heart of intellectual development. In effect, intellectual development means translating emotional reactions into ideas, giving them shape and order and meaning. In the same way, intellectual development brings with it new capacities for feelings and even passions about the objects of cognition, and such feelings play an intrinsic role in our thinking (Church, 1973).

Remember, too, that among the objects we cognize are those mysterious, elusive, appealing, irritating, perverse things called people. A large part of our lives is spent trying to reach some sort of accommodation with people close to us, and all too often the result is reciprocal frustration. It is interesting that cognitive theorists have taken so long to discover the field of social cognition. Mathematicians, natural scientists, and philosophers may spend their days engrossed in abstractions, but most of us much of the time are concerned with disentangling the perplexities of social relations. As we talk about preschool children's cognitive functioning, bear in mind the affective context in which children and their families operate.

SUMMARY

1. The period from age two and a half to age five is known as the preschool years. During this phase, the child's growth rate levels off from the first spurt of infancy. The child's proportions change. The legs grow faster than the rest of the body and approach the proportions of the adult. Early in this period, the set of twenty baby teeth is completed, and toward the end of the phase, the first of these teeth are shed.

2. Preschool children develop more advanced postures and locomotions. They sit on the floor with knees forward and slightly outward; they ascend and descend stairs in a continuous movement; and they become able to run and climb.

3. For Freud, the preschool years correspond to the phallic stage of psychosexual development, during which boys live through the Oedipus

complex and girls the Electra complex. Erikson describes the developmental conflict of the preschool years as initiative versus guilt.

4. The preschool years mark the dawn of children's formation of an identity apart from the family. They begin to come to terms with the full humanity of the new adults and children they encounter on a day-to-day basis. With peers, they must work out a new set of social relationships. Early conversations between young children may take the form of dual or collective monologues in which each child's utterances are unrelated to what any of the others say. As children come to communicate more effectively, a number of social traits emerge—leadership, sympathy, cooperation, and aggression. Aggression in children has been studied extensively; it has been correlated with such factors as excessive parental permissiveness, harsh punishment, and violent television programs.

5. Preschool children's social behavior revolves around play. Play changes in a number of ways during this period. It allows children to experiment with the multiple possibilities of situations; it assumes a certain earnestness; it reveals a growing awareness of the distinction between reality and fantasy; and it is broadened by new powers of imagination. Patterns of play can be classified along social and content dimensions. The dominant motif of the preschool years is dramatic play, which reflects the child's perceptions of the adult world. Children at this age engage in other activities, notably conversing with their parents. "Where did I come from?" is a recurrent question that parents should be prepared to answer.

6. Preschool children display a steady progression toward appropriateness, ingenuity, imagination, and skill in their manipulation and mastery of materials. Their first drawings and paintings are representations of the human figure. These evolve from rudimentary faces to more complete bodies, and eventually clothing and scenery are added. The young preschooler plays with other materials, such as clay and building blocks, because of their physical properties. Only toward the end of the preschool years does the child use them as media of representation.

KEY TERMS

aggression, 345
associative play, 351
behavioral contagion, 352
castration anxiety, 337

competitive play, 352
cooperative play, 352
dramatic play (symbolic or pretend play), 353
dual (collective) mono-

logue, 340
Electra complex, 337
empathy, 343
frustration-aggression hypothesis, 345

SUGGESTED READINGS

Chukovsky, K. *From Two to Five.* Berkeley: University of California Press, 1963. A Russian psychologist's view of the preschool child. Rich in anecdotes. The cultural contrasts are striking and intriguing.

Fraiberg, S. H. *The Magic Years.* New York: Scribner's, 1959. This psychoanalytically, clinically oriented classic offers a vivid portrayal of child life.

Isaacs, S. *Social Development in Young Children.* New York: Schocken Books, 1972 (originally published, 1933). A classic presentation of meticulously recorded observations. These observations are seen from a psychoanalytic viewpoint in terms of social relations, aggression, sexuality, and educational issues.

Maccoby, E. *Social Development.* New York: Harcourt Brace Jovanovich, 1980. A survey of current knowledge and thinking in the domain of children's social development, with special attention to the preschool years.

Zigler, E., and Child, I. L. *Socialization and Personality Development.* Reading, Mass.: Addison-Wesley, 1973. An exhaustive and integrated discussion of theories, disciplines, and major areas of children's social development.

CHAPTER 11

The Preschool Child: Cognition

It is now time to look at preschool children's cognition, the various ways in which they acquire and use information about themselves and their environments. Let us remind you of what we said a few pages ago. Cognition, conation, and affection are a more or less arbitrary way of carving up the person for study. The boundaries have been further blurred by the fast-growing domain of social cognition and we shall blur them further in this chapter.

THE PREOPERATIONAL STAGE

Piaget designated the preschool years—more precisely, ages two to seven—as the **preoperational stage** of logical development. The preoperational stage is defined both positively, in terms of new capabilities, and negatively, in terms of what the child is not yet capable of.

On the positive side, the preoperational stage is marked by the child's blossoming capacity for symbolic thinking. The child begins to use such mental symbols as words and images, internal representations of reality. Piaget lumps together words and images under the label of *signifiers*. Basic to symbolic functioning is **deferred imitation.** This is the ability to perceive an event, store it away, and then reproduce it later in word or action. Deferred imitation is a conspicuous part of acquiring a vocabulary: Words pop out of the baby's mouth that parents know he or she has not heard for days. Other forms of symbolic thinking are dramatic play and representational drawing. Both of these depend on deferred imitation. Dramatic play begins as reenactments of scenes from everyday life, and drawing is the depiction of things previously seen—preschool children rarely try to draw from life or to copy pictures.

The negative definition of preoperational thought emphasizes preschool children's limitations. One of these is egocentrism. Egocentrism certainly does not end with the preoperational stage, but it is much more profound at the beginning of the period than at the end. For instance, when children of preschool age are asked if they have a brother or a sister, they will answer (assuming it is so) yes. But then when asked if that sibling has a brother or sister (meaning the child being interviewed), the child answers no. According to Piaget (1928), it is only around age nine that 75 percent of children are able to adopt the sibling's point of view and realize that they are their siblings' brothers or sisters, as well as the other way around.

Another limitation is **centration.** This is the inability to take account of more than one feature of a situation at a time. **Decentration,** characteristic of the stage of concrete operations that follows the preoperational stage, is the contrasting ability to recognize and coordinate two or more aspects of a situation. For instance, in Piaget's famous experiment on the *conservation* of liquid volume, a container full of liquid is poured into a new, differently proportioned container. The preoperational child cannot grasp that the quantity of liquid remains the same. Centering on either the height or width of the new container, the child will see the volume as having changed. The child who can decenter, though, will understand that the different height and width of the new container offset each other, and the quantity remains the same.

(Whether children actually reason this way is open to question. But when they are asked to justify their judgments after the fact, they often do so in some approximation of these terms.)

Preoperational children are further hampered by their sometimes primitive ideas of cause and effect, about which we will talk more later. Most fundamentally, they (and older children and adults) are liable to mistake coincidence for causation.

In sum, the preoperational stage is defined negatively by the child's inability to perform the operations of the concrete-operational stage. We have already mentioned decentration. Another characteristic of the concrete operational stage is **seriation.** This is the ability to arrange things in a logical sequence. Yet another is **reversibility,** awareness that some operations work backward, as subtraction undoes addition, and division reverses multiplication. We will talk more about these and other capacities in due course.

FANTASY AND REALITY

A major development of this period is learning to draw a boundary, never final or hard and fast, between fantasy and reality. We mentioned in connection with dramatic play that children move from total absorption in the fantasy roles they assume to a half-suppressed awareness that make-believe is only pretending, to the use of lifelike props to fortify their acceptance of their own fantasy. For the young preschool child, fact and fancy are likely to be interchangeable. During this period, the line between the two be-

comes better defined, as when a four-year-old asked his father of a cut-out paper boat he had tried to sail in the family tub, "Would this *really* float on *pretend* water?" Feelings, thoughts, and wishes continue to flow out into and influence the objective world, animating and coloring and shaping it in ways that adults may find surprising. Let it be said that in some respects preschool children are in perfectly good contact with the objective world. They recognize people and places and limits, they make appropriate use of the tools and playthings available to them, they observe certain safety precautions, and so forth. But, around and between and within objects, all sorts of magical potentialities lurk.

Young preschool children, as we have said, believe that the cartoon characters and real people they see on television are equally real and are inside the television set. It is only at about age four or five that children begin to wonder how the people got in there and how they will get out again. Children also believe for a time that they can turn off a television program and later turn it on again at the point of interruption, as when one marks one's place in a book. Children also take it for granted that the musicians heard playing on radio or record player are in the machine. More than one four-year-old has been observed examining a record player from every angle "trying to find where they keep the musicians."

Preschool children nourish a firm conviction that they can magically influence events by an application of will, just as they see adults "making" the car go. Professional magicians—or illusionists, as they prefer to be called—are said to find preschool children an unresponsive audience. This seems to be because, in the

Reality and fantasy become increasingly—but not completely—differentiated during the preschool years.

child's own magical scheme of possibilities, there is nothing more remarkable in sawing a woman in half and then reuniting the pieces than in the unanalyzed wonders of everyday life.

Fantasy is related to, but different from, both humor and lying. The preschool child's humor is mostly a matter of burlesque, of playing tricks on people, and of talking nonsense (Groch, 1974). It is nonliteral behavior, performed with a clear understanding that it is a conscious toying with reality. But one cannot be sure whether the preschool child will take a whimsical fantasy literally or as a joke. For instance, one father thought to entertain his children by telling them that when he went to have a flu shot—which is briefly painful—he tried to run away, kicked and screamed in protest and had to be restrained by two nurses, and then fainted from the agony of the shot. This account was thoroughly enjoyed by his school-age child, but his four-year-old became quite upset, oblivious to the tone of nonliteral, playful melodrama.

In other instances, the child is extremely sensitive to the adult's emotional tone regardless of what the adult is actually saying. One father returned home from a day at work muttering and cursing about the foul weather they had been having, whereupon his preschool-age son, on the verge of tears, cried out, "I didn't do it!"

Lying

Lying in elaborated form does not appear until after the preschool years. However, because the child's world is a mélange of real and fantastic, adults uninstructed in the ways of children may feel a child is playing free and easy with the truth. At first, the lies children tell seem to be an effort to remake reality so that it conforms to a more desirable state of affairs. It appears that when children first tell lies they are trying as hard to deceive themselves as other people. By age four, however, children seem really to be trying to deceive their parents. That is, four-year-olds are likely to know that lies are nonliteral statements meant to be taken literally. They deny that they performed certain misdeeds, such as using mother's fountain pen to punch holes in cardboard. They claim falsely that they have executed tasks such as washing their hands before dinner. Or they try to place responsibility for a misdeed on a sibling, the family cat, or persons unknown. Late in the preschool years, children can make up accounts of behavior designed to gain credit for themselves or to discredit others, in at least a half-serious expectation of being believed.

When preschool children lie or try to say nothing, they are at a double disadvantage. First, they are likely to think that their thoughts, even unspoken ones, are perceptible to the omniscient adult, and it is only a matter of time until the adult notices. This does not imply a body image of oneself with a transparent head through which an adult can read thoughts inscribed on ticker tape coiling through the brain. It seems simply to be the product of feedback: Sensitive parents do indeed seem able to read their children's thoughts and intentions. Second, in keeping with a general human urge to share knowledge and ideas, children feel a potent urge to reveal their inner thoughts. Even when no guilt is involved, children find it very hard to keep secrets from spilling out—"You know what, Daddy? I have a secret. . . ."

Some preschool children fantasize heroic powers and exploits with which to win the admiration of friends and family. In small doses, such fantasies are harmless. When they become the rule, however, they may signal that the child is not getting enough attention for ordinary achievements and is being driven into fantasyland in search of self-redeeming actions. The treatment is obvious: more loving attention and praise in the realm of everyday reality.

By the late preschool years, it becomes the child's turn to be morally outraged by the parents' white lies. The child's outrage can be embarrassing, as when he or she screams at full volume, capable of being heard even over the telephone, "You're telling a lie, Mommy!" At this age, children cannot distinguish between lies told to protect other people's feelings and those told for personal advantage. Parents can, of course, try to explain the distinction, but we doubt that they will have much success.

Imaginary Companions

It is during the preschool years that **imaginary companions** most often appear. (We use the term broadly and loosely to encompass not only imaginary human and animal playmates but also imaginary kingdoms, identities, and playthings, as well as real playthings endowed with imaginary life.) One study indicates that 15 to 30 percent of children between ages three and ten have imaginary companions (Schaefer, 1969). Our inquiries among college students suggest that the incidence may run as high as 50 percent. (We are speaking, of course, only of remembered imaginary companions.) According to somewhat ancient findings, imaginary companions first appear between ages two and a half and six and usually disappear when the child goes to school (Ames and Learned, 1946).

Imaginary companions are often experienced with all the vividness and solidity of real people, and families may find themselves making extravagant adjustments to the visitor in their midst, taking care not to kick or sit on the companion and setting an extra place at table. It is generally assumed that imaginary companions fulfill some otherwise unmet need in the child's life—for a friend, a scapegoat, an extra conscience, a model, or as a means of escape either from tensions or from too dull a reality. Loneliness may be a factor, since only and first-born children are more likely to have imaginary companions than are children with older siblings (Manosevitz, Prentice, and Wilson, 1973). Frances Warfield's (1948) autobiographical account of her imaginary friend, Wrinkel, provides an excellent description of the phenomenon itself and of one of the many functions an imaginary companion may serve. Wrinkel's behavior expressed the resentments and frustrations of a well-behaved girl who was hard of hearing. She was afraid to acknowledge her handicap and hence was unable to ask people to speak louder.

> Wrinkel came along at this time [*age six, according to her recollection*]. I wanted a close friend. Also, in my world of aunts and sisters, a boy was interesting.
>
> Wrinkel was invisible and inaudible, which left him free to do and say whatever he wanted. The first time he entered a room he found the exact center of the ceiling and drove in a large invisible staple. He tossed an invisible rope ladder through the staple, festooning it over the tops of pictures, curtain poles, and chandeliers, and climbed over people's heads, listening to their talk and making nonsense of it.
>
> Wrinkel was smarter than anybody—smarter than my sister Ann. For one thing, he was a boy. For another thing, though he could hear as perfectly as Ann could, he didn't care whether he heard perfectly or not. He chose to hear, and to act on what he heard, strictly as he had a mind to. . . .
>
> When people talked and talked and Wrinkel didn't make sense of what they said, that wasn't because he didn't hear it. It was because he liked to make nonsense by weaving his own name in and out of their sentences. . . .
>
> He killed people off for me all the time. He killed off all the ones I didn't like—the ones who cleared their throats pointedly or raised their voices at me, as if they thought I might not hear them. He killed off deadpans, when they mumbled some question at me (pp. 7-9).

Not all imaginary companions, it should be emphasized, are as pleasant to have around as was Wrinkel. Sometimes they are distinctly unwelcome, like the invading hallucinations of a schizophrenic, and seem to be the incarnation of some deep-rooted dread or guilt. On the other hand, imaginary companions need express no motivating force whatever. Some simply appear on the scene, do what they do, and depart, sometimes fading away, sometimes dying a melodramatic death in a car crash or at the hands of pirates.

LANGUAGE IN THE PRESCHOOL YEARS

As we have suggested, cognitive development is closely bound up with progress in the mastery of language and symbols. We should bear in mind, of course, that language as it is absorbed by children may either liberate their thinking or constrict it by embalming experience in stale formulas and clichés; by providing false or nonexistent conceptual entities and explanations; by shunting certain fascinating topics like sex or death into the realm of euphemism or the unspeakable; and by deceiving children into thinking they have understood something just because they have labeled it and catalogued it. At its best, though, language can free children's thinking by providing them with useful ideas, forms, and operations.

What we have tried to convey so far is that children's "cute sayings" are far more than that. They give us insights into the structure of the child's cognitive and emotional life.

The linguistic skills of preschool children are expanding and elaborating. Preschool children acquire, at their own level, some of the skills of the contemplative philosopher. They bring language

(© Elizabeth Crews)

As they play and experiment with language, preschool children expand and elaborate their linguistic skills.

to bear on their busy taking in and digesting of the world. They enter the realm of vicarious experience provided by literature, as they listen to and discuss stories and go through the motions of reading, "saying" the text as they turn the pages. And they play and experiment with language, discovering sound patterns and such intriguing characteristics as cadence and rhyming.

Children's experiments with sounds and meanings are an example of what Courtney Cazden (1974) calls **metalinguistic awareness.** This mouthful refers to the fact that preschool children not only use language, they become aware of language as an independent entity with its own characteristics and possibilities. Being aware of printed or written language is another aspect of metalinguistic awareness, and the knowledge that speech can be translated into graphic shapes is the first step in becoming able to read.

We have to remember that language development is a lifelong process and can never be said to be complete. We keep on learning new words, and we learn more about the scope and limits and shadings and complexities of meaning of the words we already know. Having learned to read, we learn to read at ever higher levels of sophistication as we learn about metaphor and imagery and allusion and reading between the lines. We learn to recognize irony and contempt and bitterness and light-heartedness in the ways words are combined. We learn to read critically and skeptically, carrying on a running debate with the author. We learn the special languages and metalanguages of painting and poetry and politics. We learn both the special vocabularies and the logics of such fields as mathematics, chemistry, and economics. We learn about long-gone events (or their phantoms), distant places, and the adventures of fictional people. And we learn about forces lying beyond direct perception. Even operations that seem wordless, as when we make or look at pictures or react emotionally, are conditioned by language.

We now look at the way preschool children use language, including lingering immaturities.

Egocentrism and Communication

Although preschool children become increasingly able to assume other people's viewpoints, they remain decidedly egocentric. The collective monologue epitomizes egocentrism, with the participants neither knowing nor caring that no information is being conveyed. But there are lots of situations in which children do care about getting an idea across, and then their egocentrism may do them in.

They may leave out essential features of which the listener is ignorant, or they may provide too much irrelevent information, drowning the message in distracting "noise."

In language as in other spheres of functioning, children may not be able to stick with a single thought from beginning to end of an utterance. We recall a three-year-old boy who, having bowled over a little girl as he charged across the playroom, turned to her and said, "You should watch where you got what was coming to you!"

During the preschool years, children become more adept at shaping their thoughts to other peoples', at describing events coherently, and at using language to coordinate group activities in pursuit of some agreed-on goal. They lapse less often than before into blind self-assertion. They exchange ideas and feelings. And they know, as we can tell from their questions, that adults have information that they themselves do not but are genuinely interested in obtaining.

Adults who wish to establish communication with a preschooler will find themselves frustrated if they try such gambits as "What did you do today?" The child has been busy living his or her life, not keeping a mental record, and is at a loss for an answer. But if adults simply make themselves available, speech will sooner or later come pouring forth from the child, sometimes in unbearable volume.

It is a sign of diminishing egocentrism that five-year-olds can switch codes (Gleason, 1973). *Code switching*, in case you have forgotten, means simplifying one's language when trying to communicate with a listener of limited understanding. Mothers not only simplify language when talking to young children,

(© Michael Weisbrot & Family)

Although asking "What did you do today?" may leave a preschool child at a loss for an answer, if adults simply make themselves available for communication, speech will sooner or later pour forth.

they raise the pitch of their voice. The younger the child, the higher the pitch becomes. The code in which mothers address small children has been dubbed "motherese."

Description, Narration, and Memorization

Preschool children's descriptions and narrations are rambling, loose-jointed, and circumstantial. They include endless detail, relevant or not, and skip over essentials. It takes a nicely attuned listener to make sense of what the child is trying to say and to know what questions to ask for further clues. Beginning late in the preschool years and continuing into the

school years, children's accounts of plays, movies, or television dramas consist of fragments linked by the all-purpose "'n' then." The sequence of the child's narrative may correspond hardly at all to the actual sequence of events. But before we come down too hard on the limitations of preschool children in grasping complex events, we should note that when adults compare impressions of movies they have seen, their interpretations may vary widely.

Poulsen *et al.* (1979) have studied the development of what they call the "story schema." This is the set of rules that dictates how a tale is to be recounted. Four- and six-year-olds were given two sets of picture stories, one in sensible order and

(© Elizabeth Crews)

A conversation between two preschoolers. Descriptions and narrations at this age are rambling, loose-jointed, and circumstantial.

the other scrambled. As long as the pictures provided a guide to the story sequence, both four- and six-year-olds could tell a structured story. When confronted with the scrambled stories, the six-year-olds tried to find a storylike pattern in the series. In contrast, the four-year-olds simply described the pictures one by one.

Young children memorize things in wholesale bunches. Understanding is by no means necessary to the process. Children memorize yard after yard of nursery rhymes, fairy tales, advertising jingles, and prayers, and there is no reason to suppose that they have any understanding of these. The distortions of older children are instructive. We have

all heard of the hymn "Gladly the cross-eyed bear" (Gladly the cross I'd bear), the patriotic refrain of "Three chairs for the red, white, and blue," and the Pledge of Allegiance: ". . . to the Republic of Richard Stands . . . one naked individual. . . ." (Readers outside the United States might want to know that the original reads "to the Republic for which it [the flag] stands" and "one nation indivisible.") Such distortions are not unknown in preschool children. A four-year-old in a Head Start program was heard to recite the Lord's Prayer as: ". . . and lead us not into Penn Station. . . ." Note that all these distortions illustrate the mechanism of assimilation, reshaping unfamiliar material so as to make it fit preexisting cognitive structures. Preschool children cannot paraphrase or summarize the passages they memorize. They can only recite them. If they are interrupted part way through a recitation, they may find it impossible to resume where they left off, and so are obliged to go back and begin again from the beginning.

Some Speech Immaturities

The speech of many preschool children shows vestiges of baby talk. Sounds and syllables may be misplaced, as in "aminal," "hangerburg," and "pisghetti." Three- and four-year-olds may still be having trouble with pronouns. They may mix "he" and "she," not because they fail to differentiate the sexes but because they forget which pronoun goes with which sex. "We" may be learned as the first person plural, but it may also function as a collective designation for the parents, who often speak to the child in terms of "we." Thus, as we said earlier, the child's "Are we going out tonight?" is likely to mean "Are you and Daddy going out tonight?"

Obscenity and Profanity

Preschool children become masters of scatology (obscene language, especially references to excrement), and they early learn the shock value of certain words. Observe, however, that the preschool child's "bad language" deals almost entirely with superficial anatomy and elimination, for which reason it is often called "toilet talk." It is only in the middle years that children begin in earnest to appreciate and exploit the special vocabulary of sexuality and its feelings and varieties, usually, of course, in its four-letter forms.

Preschoolers may have little or no idea what some words mean, but they know very well that they can agitate their parents by saying them. Preschool children, like toddlers, also pick up from the people around them such words as "hell" and "damn," which they use aptly, if ignorantly, to express displeasure. In general, adult outrage at the child's use of taboo words only intensifies their value for the child and serves as effective contingent reinforcement for more of the same.

Invented Forms

Preschool children occasionally compensate for gaps in their vocabulary by stretching the meaning of familiar terms to cover new situations. We have seen this at work in the use of "strong" and "heavy" to express strain or effort. Sometimes, as we pointed out in Chapter 9, children simply invent new words to communicate what they want to say. Such words are called **neologisms.** A three-year-old girl hoped that the new baby would be a "boy-girl. You know, a girl with a penis." Neologisms seem to occur often as a way of stressing a contrast: "This thing has an upper part and a downer part"; "They're sure not slowpokes, they're fastpokes"; "Sometimes nobody eats with me and sometimes lots-of-bodies." Having spotted a berry and then being unable to find it again, a four-year-old remarked, "I must have undiscovered it" (note that "undiscovered" exists as an adjective, but not as a verb). For some preschool children, the very sensible opposite of "O.K." is "no-kay." Observe that preschool children are aware of and put into words the relationship of opposites, but it is usually not until the school years that children can supply antonyms on demand.

Preschool children produce such assertions as "I am so being hāve" (I am so behaving); we are reminded of a sign on a gate: "Be ware of dog." In general, the verb "to be" has a dual meaning for many preschool children, a duality formalized in some languages, such as Spanish and the Scandinavian tongues. To describe an activity, such as making believe, the child says, "He bēs a bear"; but to describe a state or an attribute, the child says, "He is sad."

Some inventions are downright poetic: "Rounder is wider than longer"; "You don't look like you are"; one little girl liked to "secret around in the night." Held up in traffic, a boy complained to his mother, "Look at that old truck busying up the street so we can't get through." (Many children seem totally unable to understand why their car has to wait for the ones in front to move.) Sometimes the emotional meanings of a term dominate the strict semantic ones. For instance, one child climaxed a torrent of spluttering invective with " . . . you—you—you wrong number!"

In spite of the metaphorical quality of these utterances, we know that children of this age cannot understand metaphors and other figures of speech, just as they miss irony and sarcasm (although the more common emotional shadings are quite apparent to young children). Analogies, however, may occur to the child. For instance, a four-year-old watching a cow being milked commented, "It's like a water pistol," and a three-year-old, watching Mother hold some garment against Father's body to check the size, asked, "Is Daddy a paper doll?" Chukovsky (1963) gives an example of how children can become entangled in their own analogies. The child asks, "Mommy, the nettle bites me?" The mother replies, "Well, in a way. . . ," and the child continues, "Then why doesn't it bark, too?"

We quote from a four-year-old girl who produced this joyous combination of sounds, worthy of Lewis Carroll himself:

> There's nothing true about that so don't be so glee. I'm not full of glue, I'm just appearing to. Thumbly, thumbly, glantering damously. Clitter clatter, sing the clitter clatter and the violins some time over . . . . Sing the songs of meener, with the doors of the clitter and the marches too in the dark of the pleasantly opter.

We should recall here the notion of metalinguistic awareness (Cazden, 1974), the way children become aware of language as something to be manipulated and played with. Judith Schwartz (1981) gives these examples of word play, the first from a four-year-old and the second from a five-year-old: "San Diego, San-diego, Sandi Ego, San Diego, Sandi Ego, eggs aren't sandy!"; "I'm gonna telly 'cause you put jelly in my belly and made me smelly."

Late in the preschool years, one finds the beginnings of philosophical wisdom, as when a four-and-a-half-year-old observes, "It doesn't matter, just the way it doesn't matter which sock your foot goes into."

Equivalences and Contrasts of Meaning

A favorite subject matter of cognitive psychology is concept formation. Since no two authorities seem able to agree on the meaning of "concept," we prefer instead to speak of **equivalence** (Klüver, 1936). This is the degree of resemblance that enables two things to have the same name, or of dissimilarity that requires separate names for things. Equivalences do not, of course, require words. The male stickleback fish courts a rounded block of wood for all the world as though it were a female stickleback. Other equivalences are wholly dependent on language, as when we say that coal and a muscle are both sources of energy.

The child's equivalences may surprise the adult. Remember the toddler (in Chapter 9) who generalized the name "windmill" to apply to a house, a water tank, and a TV antenna.

Children from an early age accurately differentiate the sexes. We are not sure what cues they use. Older research indicated that young children relied on hair style and clothing to tell males and females apart. In today's unisex world, however, these are no longer trustworthy guides. The old orientation is revealed in a four-year-old girl's account of the family that had just moved in across the street, including the fact that the family included a young baby. Asked whether the baby was a boy or a girl, the four-year-old replied, "I don't know. It's so hard to tell at that age, especially with their clothes off." Even a five-year-old, looking at a photograph of a naked girl with a boyish hairdo, identified it as a boy.

Some especially verbal children may be able, by age five, to define words, particularly concrete nouns, and usually in terms of action qualities: "car"—"You ride in it"; "banana"—"You eat it." Some five-year-olds can specify the nature of an equivalence: An orange and a peach are alike "because they're both juicy"; a suit and a dress are alike "because they keep you warm." Even earlier, children can articulate nonequivalence: "Doggie bark, kitty meow." A child's ability to talk about similarities and differences is far from absolute and depends on the nature of the contrast or resemblance. For instance, children are likely to have trouble with such an obvious-seeming difference as that between bread and cake.

Syntactic Structures

Students of language development are, of course, curious about how children master grammar and syntax, the rules for making meaningful utterances. One approach is simply to sample the child's spontaneous speech. Another is to test the child's understanding of statements phrased in various ways. The child is asked to act out, with the help of props, the events described by the utterance.

Of special interest is children's comprehension of passive-voice sentences: "The man was bitten by the dog" rather than "The dog bit the man." Although preschool children never or practically never use passive-voice constructions, it is worth finding out if they can understand them. For instance, Strohner and Nelson (1974) compared responses to active-voice and passive-voice statements controlled for two other variables. The first was whether the relationship between subject and object was reversible: "The boy follows the girl" is reversible ("The girl follows the boy"), whereas "The boy throws the ball" is not ("The ball throws the boy"). The second variable was the probability of the relationship between subject and object: "The girl feeds the baby" is highly probable, whereas "The baby feeds the girl" is improbable. Briefly, four-year-olds pay little attention to sentence structures. They grasp instead at whatever semantic features seem to make sense, whereas five-year-olds respond to the structure, taking note of irreversibility and low probability.

Similar findings emerge from a study by Wetstone and Friedlander (1973), comparing responses to logically ordered sentences versus sentences with elements misplaced: "Show the clown to Mommy" versus "Show to clown the Mommy." Four-year-olds reacted to the unfamiliar constructions just as they did to the straightforward ones, whereas five-year-olds were perplexed by the mixed-up sentences. Another variation is found in a study by Ehri and Galanis (1980). They compared responses by four-year-olds to two sorts of compound sentences linked by the connectives "before" and "after." In one kind of sentence, the sequence was arbitrary ("Before he ate the apple, he ate the pear"). In the other kind, the sequence was logical ("After he got undressed, he went to bed"). When the components of the sentence are in an arbitrary order, four-year-olds pay attention to the sequence and disregard the conjunction. For instance, in the arbitrary specimen above, the four-year-old would be likely to say that the apple was eaten first because the eating of the apple comes first in the sentence. However, when logic was at stake, four-year-olds, somewhat surprisingly, did become sensitive to the conjunction and recognized illogical constructions. ("After he ate the banana, he peeled it").

Research on children's understanding of "before"/"after" constructions has led some observers to conclude that "before" is easier to grasp than "after." However, Goodz (1982) pointed out that in test sentences using "before," order of mention and order of occurrence were more likely to match than in sentences using "after." When mention and occurrence coincide, preschool children have no trouble understanding "after."

(© Jean-Claude Lejeune/Stock, Boston)

Acquiring the ability to move from concrete reality to general principles is an important step in intellectual development.

KNOWING AND THINKING

In a moment, we shall look at children's command of specific cognitive domains. First, though, we should examine four general characteristics of immature cognition that seem unrelated to particular ages.

The first of these is the concrete basis of abstract thinking. As we shall see, intellectual development requires that we become able to wrench our thinking away from the particularities and the immediacies. It takes a long time before

an individual can stand back and view things against a framework of general principles. Here we must enter a caution. Abstract thinking is essential to mature behavior, as when we force ourselves to study in hopes that what we learn will be useful to us at some future date. But we must beware of *empty abstractions*, forcing concrete reality into an ill-fitting mold of abstractions, as when we assume that all human development can be accounted for in terms of operant conditioning principles. We must also beware of what the sociologist C. Wright Mills called "crackpot realism," in which one reasons with beautiful logic from premises that are hopelessly in error. Reasoning from the premise that social-class differences are the product of biological differences and that the poor are to blame for their own poverty is an example of crackpot realism.

The second characteristic of immature cognition is realism, which we have encountered before in its guises of picture realism and word realism, but about which more remains to be said. The third characteristic is egocentrism, which we have also met before. The fourth is a pair of attributes posited by Werner (1948), rigidity and lability, which we shall discuss shortly.

The Concrete Basis of Abstract Thinking

Most formal measures of cognitive functioning ask children to detach themselves from the personal, the emotional, and the pragmatically relevant. Children are asked instead to focus their attention on the abstract, logical, formal, analytical properties of things. Children's lives, however, are normally rooted and enacted in human relations, particularly family relations, and these are the concrete prototype of all their understanding. Thus when children are given a formal classification test consisting of blocks that offer a number of abstract bases for grouping—color, shape, size—they may ignore these and instead base their arrangement on the intimate, concrete scheme of their own existence and group the blocks into families, large blocks being the father and mother, and smaller ones the children. Here the child relies on the attribute of size, but not as a basis for separating the blocks: Differing sizes go together to make a set.

We cannot infer that the child has any intellectual understanding of family organization. (We have already seen that young children will accept any grouping of people in one location as a family, as long as it includes children.) A four-year-old who meets his or her teacher's spouse is likely to ask, "Mrs. Jones, are you Mr. Jones's mommy?" and the next moment, with no sense of paradox, "Mr. Jones, are you Mrs. Jones's daddy?" We have the indignant retort of a five-year-old to the information that people in the same family are not supposed to marry: "They can, too! My mommy married my daddy!"

Five-year-olds can sort blocks on the basis of such attributes as size, shape, and color, but they cannot use these properties consistently and systematically, and they may be unable to make explicit the basis of their groupings. Unsystematic grouping by attributes leads to two different sorts of classification, the *cluster* and the *chain*. In a cluster grouping, one key block serves as the point of reference, with the other blocks all relating to it in terms of some similarity but without regard for how the subsidiary blocks relate to one another. For example, if the key block, A, is a large red triangle, then block B may be attached to it because B is a triangle, Block C because it is red, and D because it is large. In chain groupings, B is related to A on the basis of some common feature, C to B on the basis of some shared attribute, D to C, and so on.

Inhelder and Piaget (1964) report that their subjects rarely attempted any sort of classification before age five. Instead they used the blocks to make structures or designs ("**graphic collections**"). In their first attempts at grouping, the children used shifting criteria, as in chains and clusters.

We have erected this conceptual edifice only to watch it begin to dissolve.

Arranging objects in interesting patterns on a flat surface is an emotionally satisfying task for preschool children.

What we have reported is the conventional wisdom. However, Markman, Cox, and Machida (1981) have hypothesized that the primitive groupings observed in preschool children are an artifact of the test situation. Specifically, the need to arrange blocks or other objects on a flat surface induces a need to make emotionally satisfying patterns. When three-to-four-year-old children were asked to sort objects into plastic bags, their sorting began to approximate more mature groupings. This came about without benefit of feedback, modeling, or any other training. How general this finding will prove it is still too soon to tell.

Realism

Closely allied to the blurring of fact and fantasy is what Piaget called *realism*. This term should not be understood in any of its everyday usages, whether hardheaded adherence to the evidence or, as in the "realist" movement in art and literature, emphasis on the sordid side of existence. Instead it simply says that in immature thought there is a single reality encompassing objects, thoughts, dreams, wishes, and beliefs. Note that the fantastic is not excluded. Realism simply stresses the intermingling of what most adults consider distinct kinds of reality.

As adults, we come to order reality into different levels. We recognize that dreams are real, but real in a different sense from automobiles or chewing gum. However, the young child draws no such distinctions. To the preschool child, dreams are real events taking place in real space. Children may even balk at sleeping in their own room because it contains too many dreams. One preschool child expressed puzzlement about dreams on logical grounds: "How can I see the things in dreams unless my eyes are open?"

Verbal Realism. Piaget proposed several specialized forms of realism. We have already spoken of *verbal* (or *nominal* or *symbolic* or *word*) *realism*, according to which words and statements can have the same reality as solid objects and can shape and modify other realities. *Reification* describes the process by which words create imaginary concrete realities. Many people are likely to take these as seriously as the practical issues of everyday life. Religious beliefs assume the existence of supernatural entities, and people live lives of self-denial in hopes of being rewarded in the after-life. Any given religious system exists by virtue of the words that describe it. We believe in heaven and hell because people have postulated their existence, named and described them, and told us which kinds of behavior will land us in one place or the other. Indeed, wars have been fought over fine points of religious doctrine, and in every war the combatants insist that God is on their side. Leprechauns, trolls, and zombies are all words made facts. So, too, are memory and the mind. Reification is made possible only by verbal realism.

Recall that word realism also manifests itself in our need to put our experience into words. It shows up in *euphemism*, whereby we attempt to mask a disagreeable reality by renaming it, and in *circumlocution*, whereby we avoid a painful topic by alluding to it without ever saying what it is. Verbal realism is at work when we find ourselves paralyzed by having lost a word. We have verbal wild cards for such occasions, but we are not really satisfied with "whatyamaycallit," "thingamajig," and "doodad." And it is verbal realism that permits us to participate in literature to the point where we can weep over the hero's misfortunes and gloat over the villain's downfall.

Picture Realism. We have also spoken of *picture realism*, treating pictures as though they were real things. Recall that six-month-olds demonstrate their sensitivity to depth cues in pictures by trying to grasp the "near" side of a pictured lattice (Yonas, Cleaves, and Petterson, 1978). Older babies and young children pet the pictured animal, sniff at the pictured flower, and listen for the ticking of a pictured watch. A three-year-old boy was learning to recognize the makes of cars by such features as the shape of radiator grilles. One day he saw a picture in profile of an unfamiliar make and asked its name. Having been told, he said, "I wonder what the front looks like," and lowered his head to the page in full confidence that he would be able, from the correct angle, to see the car's grille. Picture realism has been documented by Daehler, Perlmutter, and Myers (1976).

Moral Realism and Immanent Justice. In addition, there is **moral realism.** This is the assumption that the rules of right and wrong, virtue and evil, have their own existence as part of the natural world. The young child has no notion that moral rules are human inventions and conventions. The child attributes to them the same solidity, permanence, absoluteness, and inescapability found in all the other forces of nature.

A by-product of moral realism is **immanent justice** (yes, we have spelled "immanent" right; spelled thus, it means "built in"). Immanent justice is the idea that misdeeds carry within themselves the mechanisms by which they will be punished. Piaget has made up a number of stories to test for immanent justice. For instance, two boys cross a river and steal apples from Farmer Smith's orchard. As they return home, the bridge collapses under them and they both drown. What made the bridge fall down at just that moment? For the preschool child, the answer is obvious: It was the boys' naughtiness that caused the bridge to give way.

Another by-product of moral realism is the idea that the seriousness of wrongdoing is to be judged strictly in terms of the seriousness of the outcome, with no allowance made for motives or extenuating circumstances. In tests for moral realism, the child who, for instance, breaks a dozen dishes while trying to aid an ailing parent is judged more harshly than one who breaks a single dish while trying to raid the family money jar. However, more recent research calls for modification of this general statement. Elkind and Dabek (1977) have pointed out that kindergarten-age (and older) children distinguish quite clearly between acts leading to personal injury and those leading merely to property damage. Rule, Nesdale, and McAra (1974) have shown that kindergarten-age and older children do in fact take account of intentions when these are made unambiguously plain. Feldman and colleagues (1976) gave children information about motives or intentions (good or bad) either before or after information about outcomes (likewise good or bad). Four-to-five-year-olds based their judgments on the feeling tone associated with the last bit of information given, whether it be motive or consequence.

As we shall see again shortly, moral realism and immanent justice fit in with the child's belief that everything has a humanlike cause and that there is no such thing as chance events or causally unconnected coincidence. For instance, Weisz (1980) had children play a game drawing cards, so that individual scores were as nearly random as possible. Kindergarten kids took it for granted that scores varied directly with skill in card drawing.

Egocentrism

We have already pointed out that young children are more egocentric than older children and adults. They have only a limited ability to take account of other people's perspectives because young children find it hard to be simultaneously aware of self and world. But the egocentrism of preschool children is far from absolute. An example of behavior intermediate between egocentrism and mature relativism is to be found in a three-year-old girl's asking her father what a mark on his cheek was. He replied, "Do you suppose I nicked myself shaving?" She said, "I don't know. Here, you look" and used her father's nose to turn his head in the direction of the mark.

Note that two different sorts of egocentrism can be identified: (1) spatial, relating to how things appear from different vantage points; and (2) social, which is further subdivided into cognitive, relating to other people's knowledge; and emotional, relating to feelings, attitudes, and motives.

Flavell (1977) has summarized much of the literature on how egocentrism yields to awareness of other people's outlooks. As said earlier, an eighteen-month-old who wants to show someone a picture takes up a position alongside the person so that they share the same view. By age two, the child simply turns the picture so that its face is toward the other person. The two- to three-year-old knows whether an object on one side or the other of a screen is visible to another person. A group of Flavell's associates (Masangkay et al., 1974) used a picture of a turtle drawn in side view that could be placed on a table between experimenter and child. When the turtle was seen by the child as standing right-side-up, it was, of course, seen by the experimenter as lying on its back. A few three-year-olds consistently judged the experimenter's view correctly (the right-side-up and inverted positions were varied randomly over trials), and almost all four- and five-year-olds could do so.

Another aspect of egocentrism is the ability to judge other's feelings in various situations. It is difficult to distinguish between children's judgments about how others feel and how the child would feel in a similar situation. A study by Hughes, Tingle, and Sawin (1981) compared kindergarten children with first- and second-graders on their judgments of the feelings of characters in slide stories. The older children were sensitive to psychological and behavioral cues, whereas the younger ones reacted mainly to the kinds of situations in which the characters found themselves. The authors comment, "However, younger children showed increased understanding about others' emotions following reflection on their own reactions to the others' feelings."

In a study of cognitive egocentrism, Mossler, Marvin, and Greenberg (1976) showed children two short sound films. One film showed a child entering his grandmother's house. The other showed the child asking for a cookie. In both films, a key item of information was given via the sound track: the relationship of grandchild and grandmother in the first film, and the fact of requesting a cookie in the second. The subject's mother, who had not been present during the first showing of the films, was then brought into the room. Mother and child were shown the two sequences with the sound turned off. Next the child was asked about the mother's understanding of the films, including the two facts that could be known only through hearing the sound track. If the child answered correctly that the mother could not know these two items of information, he or she was asked to explain why. The explanations were scored nonegocentric if they mentioned either the mother's absence during the first showing or the lack of sound during the second. The situation seemed to be hopeless for two-year-olds, and only one three-year-old out of twenty was able to give nonegocentric explanations. However, 60 percent of the four-year-olds and 85 percent of the five-year-olds gave relativistic (i.e., nonegocentric) explanations.

It is worth repeating that we are all egocentric to some degree all our lives. Although we may recognize intellectually that other people have viewpoints different from our own, it can be very hard to identify with another person's spatial, cognitive, and emotional outlooks. And do not delude yourself that psychologists do appreciably better at reading other people's minds than do nonpsychologists. Psychologists know cerebrally about the dangers of egocentrism, but viscerally they are all too likely to be trapped in their own comfortable frames of reference.

Rigidity and Lability

Werner (1948) proposed two related characteristics of immature thought that at first seem mutually antagonistic but which in fact complement each other. The first of these is **rigidity**. This is the inability to shift psychological vantage points and take a fresh look at situations. Rigidity can be likened to assimilation without accommodation: The individual has only a few categories into which to stuff all of experience, and cannot construct new, more adaptive categories to accommodate novel experiences. Things must either fit the existing categories or be ignored, denied, or destroyed.

The second characteristic is **lability**—instability or volatility or changeability. At first this may sound like the opposite of rigidity. However, rigidity describes the person, and lability describes the environment. Rigidity is a way of coping with a labile, unpredictable, seemingly capricious and even perverse world. When the world is unmanageable, one can find a security of sorts in sticking close to familiar ways, to routines and rituals and stereotyped reactions, and by blocking out all the complexities that threaten one's peace of mind.

We usually associate rigidity with advanced age and people who live in the phantom environment of the past. Rigidity can persist and even increase with age, but this applies to people incapable of learning, integrating their learning, and adapting to new circumstances. The rigid person is unable to tolerate ambiguity, to live with the fact that there are no known answers to some problems, that indeed some problems defy definition. Rigid people are great dichotomizers. They divide every issue into two parts. Having dichotomized the world, they invariably opt for the safest position. The nature-nurture controversy represents such a dichotomization. Behavior is completely the product of heredity or it is completely the product of experience.

We have spoken of rigidity and lability as cognitive characteristics. However, it should be obvious that we are talking about an emotion-laden aspect of functioning. A labile world is a grave threat to one's personal integrity, and those who seek safety in rigidity achieve it only at great emotional cost. It means the renunciation of playfulness, since playfulness means the exploration of new possibilities. It is possible that there are two kinds of rigidity in children. One simply reflects children's limited knowledge and cognitive skills and gives way to more flexible processes as children achieve improved understanding of how things work. The second kind of rigidity would be primarily emotional, reflecting a partial failure of basic trust. Recall that it is an erratic meeting of needs that leads to mistrust. This is another way of saying that the world is labile in fact and not just in perception.

DOMAINS OF KNOWLEDGE AND THOUGHT

Having looked at some general attributes of immature thinking, let us now go on to look at functioning in various domains of knowledge and thought during the preoperational period. The first of these domains, self-awareness, is so important that we assign it a separate section.

Self-Awareness in Preschool Children

The description of self-awareness in infancy and toddlerhood was a relatively simple matter. We could speak of self-discovery, a sense of a separate identity, of abilities, playfulness, role playing, and of basic trust and autonomy and negativism. By the preschool years, however, children begin to reflect on their own self-knowledge, and to relate it to other people's inner lives. Body boundaries become more sharply defined, and the total body schema becomes better integrated. Preschool children do not yet grade themselves on competences the way older children do. However, they are certainly aware of all-or-none abilities. A three-year-old, asked by an adult if she knew how to read, was able to reply, "Of course not. I'm only three years old." The mother of a five-year-old was moved to cry out in exasperation, "Vicky, you're acting just like a child!" to which the little girl, in some confusion, rejoined, "But I am a child." The following comments by a boy aged four years, two months gives us further insight into developing self-awareness:

> [In the barber's chair] Can you see your hair when you're not looking in the mirror? [Next night in bed, calls father into room] When I hold my nose and close my mouth [demonstrates]—see, I can't breathe. But when I hold my nose and open my mouth, then I can still breathe.

Johnson and Wellman (1979) questioned children aged three to five about their knowledge of brains. Children of all three ages knew that both they and the experimenter had brains. Most knew that the brain is inside the head and not visible. Although the four- and five-year-olds knew that dolls do not have brains, three-year-olds were likely to think that dolls do.

A five-year-old asks his teacher, "What is my back like, Miss Williams?" ["Nice, like other backs," etc.] "*No!* Different. Mine!" ["Yes, but most backs are alike."] "Like Mr. Stone's? Wide?" ["Like his and other people's."] "Oh." [He is thoughtful and somewhat dashed.]

On another occasion, this same child had also discovered that "You can't see your own face, can you?" Here we are reminded that experience of the body is a blend of direct perception, mirror views, and the interpretation and integration of internal sensations, including one's own thoughts, vaguely formulated or clearly worded.

The behavior of preschool children indicates that not all regions of the body are equally well represented in the self-image. When children wash their face, they wash only the frontal surface, and when they wash their hands, they wash only the palms and palm side of the fingers. Adults have to step in to wash ears and necks and backs of hands and the spaces between the fingers. Older preschool children become very modest about exposing their bodies, even when their parents set no particular example in this regard. One four-year-old girl, seeing a painting of a nude, asked, "Isn't she embarrassed?" Note the picture realism. Another four-year-old girl, being bathed by an adult male sitter, apparently sensed there was something unseemly in being exposed to this unfamiliar man and reacted by covering her nipples. The same behavior was observed in an eight-year-old girl who, after trotting around the pool in the altogether, became aware of a man on the premises and shielded her nonexistent bosom.

A boy almost five years old inspects his belly while dressing after a nap and comments:

> You know a thing? There is something funny about my skin. It fits all smooth mostly, but when I do this, there are extra skin in crumples. What is that for? [It's loose so you can move and stretch, etc.] No, it is not loose or it would show. It would hang down. It would be too big. [Like a rubber band.] Would it break if you pulled it too much? [Can stretch a lot.] I had this same skin when I was a baby. It fits very nice. It is me.

(Robert L. West)

A heightened awareness of their bodies and physiological processes is part of preschoolers' developing self-awareness.

The same child on another occasion was even more introspective:

> Sometimes I wonder about the blood in me. Inside me it is all wet and blood and moving and lots of insides, but outside is all dry and careful and you would never know about the inside part by looking at the outside part. Not unless you got a hole in you and some of the blood came out. All the people are like that. Their skins keep them in, but underneath their skins is such a lot. . . . It is so funny to think of you being all wet inside and all dry outside. Everybody is like that. I am. Why, Miss Williams,

you are. [Laughs.] Did you ever think about it? [Teacher offers to show him anatomical picture.] A picture that would be for you would be for me, too? Then we are alike. You and me are alike.

Later on, he carries his thinking one step further: "Your insides is like if another person lived inside your skin." The same child muses on language and speaking:

> A voice is a fast thing, isn't it? Are other sounds voices of things? [The reader is urged to dwell a moment on this insight.] Is the day got a voice, a sound? Where is your voice? It comes out of your mouth. *Does* it, *is* it, *in* your mouth? [Here he begins to elaborate on his idea, half in play, half in earnest.] Are all the words stored up someplace in your mouth? How can you get food in if all these words are in your mouth? How much space does a word take? Words are thin little things. But some of them make a big noise. A sound—is it bigger than a word?

This child conveys in his reflections how children develop a sense of shared experience. Such experience includes the recognition not only that adults have the same kind of bodies but also that these omnipotent and infallible people have feelings, doubts, and frailties akin to the child's own. This does not mean that preschool children have perspectives like those of an adult. Children can hardly be expected to grasp the economic context within which adults are obliged to operate. Nor can they understand the complex needs and coping strategies that adults evolve. It means only that children have flickers of understanding and become increasingly skillful communicators, if only because they begin to realize that communication is problematical.

Preschool children generally know the names of all the major external parts of the body. Some can name such joints as wrist and ankle, and such adornments as eyebrows and eyelashes. Four-year-olds can usually say that they smell with their nose, taste with their tongue (or mouth), and touch with their fingers. They tell us that their eyes are to see with and their ears to hear with. They have some vague idea of digestion and accept that the fluids they drink are discharged as urine. However, many children do not take seriously the notion that food is transformed into feces. Many four-year-olds know about the air and breathing, and about the beating of the heart. A classic study by Gellert (1962) showed that young children have very limited knowledge about their inner organs, how they are arranged, or how they function. Four-year-olds may know that germs cause illness, but they have no idea what a germ is.

Fears. Preschool children typically develop a number of specific fears. Freudians explain such fears as more or less disguised expressions of castration anxiety associated with the Oedipus complex. In our view, fears are better accounted for in terms of children's widening knowledge and deepening understanding. The more sharply defined the boundaries of the body, the more vulnerable to damage or intrusion the body becomes. The more one knows about all the menacing possibilities that exist—in real reality or in phantom reality—the greater is the need to watch one's step. Note the gradations of threat and the fact that they are unrelated to either the reality or the likelihood that they will

affect the child. Ogres and fires can both destroy. Kidnappers can separate children from their families and perhaps even revamp the children's identities. Thieves can rob them of their most precious possessions. Note, too, that a more advanced bodily awareness rules out some earlier fears. We have already spoken of how the child stops worrying about being sucked down the bathtub drain once he or she has recognized that the body is too big to fit in the drain.

Body Intactness. Out of deference to Freud, we begin with the topic of fear lest the body be diminished or mutilated. This is not an altogether new concern (recall the toddler's aversion to broken playthings). However, it becomes especially acute late in the preschool years. The comic-aggressive lunch table conversation quoted earlier (p. 347) suggests how themes of mutilation enter the thinking of preschool children. Humor, of course, is one way of handling anxiety, as we see in the behavior of medical students who play macabre jokes as a way of coping with the sometimes sickening things they have to do.

Preschool children may even protest when a familiar adult appears without his or her accustomed glasses. It is as though the glasses were an integral part of the person, and to be without them a disfigurement. The passage that follows expresses how a child's feelings about a visit to the dentist, blended with anticipations of a coming tonsillectomy, seem to produce anxiety about staying intact:

> Once there was Stuart with a tooth and in it was a hole. So it was fixed. The man had many little streams there, very nice. There was a pain, a bright pain. It was bright

(© Michael Weisbrot & Family)

Children often acquire a number of specific fears at this age. The more one knows about all the menacing possibilities that exist—in reality or phantom reality—the greater appears the need to watch one's step.

when he pushed with a noise and a bar. But there was no blood. No blood. . . . Can I get a hole in my hand like the hole in my tooth? Will it have to be filled with a loud noise? . . . The queen was in the garden hanging up her clothes, there came along a big thing to snap off her nose. . . . Her nose was not. It bled and bled and she died. Humpty Dumpty did die, too. He fell off and couldn't put together again. . . . When I have my tonsils out—what will happen when I have to have my tonsils out? Will it bleed? Will I be dead? Why do I have my tonsils out?

I do not like myself not to be myself, and that is what will happen if even my littlest tonsils is taken away from me. . . . Sad it was to have a nose taken off. So it will be sad to have a tonsil taken out. Blood, blood, blood. When the nose—the tonsils is out.

Another four-year-old faced with a tonsillectomy asked, "You can't live without tonsils, can you?"

Death. It is in this age period that children learn about death and come to fear it. This fear is not rooted in children's abstract knowledge. It is simply an awareness—perhaps reinforced by the death of a grandparent—that people do die and that it could happen to them. What dying means is likely to be uncertain and variable.

The child's first contact with death may very well be with a dead insect or mouse found in the street, and death may mean simply that "You put it in the garbage." But there is a growing sense of a universal, inescapable human mortality. Children's fears of death are at first likely to be focused on the parents. There may be a period when the child constantly asks, with considerable anxiety, "When are you going to die, Mommy?" and "Are you going to die soon, Daddy?" Children then come to realize that they themselves are mortal, although they find it hard to imagine the blank finality of being dead. In games, and sometimes in everyday functioning, death is reversible: "Bang! You're dead. Now you must be alive again." A four-year-old brought home a dead squirrel to his mother, exclaiming excitedly, "Look! I found a squirrel!" "But it's dead." "Well," said the boy earnestly, "Let's leave it on the mantel until it gets alive again."

One child asked, "If you woke up in the morning and you were dead, would it hurt?" Another put it this way: "Being dead is like being blind, only *all* the time, and the same feeling all over, everywhere, like blind in the eye." Although the best analogy in life to being dead may be that of a continuing sleep, the child who is told this is likely to become terrified of going to bed. A four-year-old boy's reaction to a joking remark by his mother shows how easily fears can be stirred up: "My mommy is going to have a new baby and she says it is going to have to be a girl because we already have enough boys at our house. So if the new baby is a boy, she will have too many boys and she will have to get rid of me!" (*Listen! The Children Speak*, 1979, p. 35).

Middle-class American parents try to shield their children from knowledge of death. This shielding is made easier by the separation of the generations. Many children never have a chance to know their grandparents or other old people well, and so are not exposed to dying. The general improvement in living conditions has meant that relatively few children or young adults die anymore. Automobiles kill more people than any of the major diseases except those associated with aging, and homicide is more of a menace to young males than is any disease.

Thus parents may even deny the fact of death ("Grandpa's gone on a long trip"). They may try to disguise their own feelings, but children, with their acute emotional sensitivity, are not likely to be fooled. The unusual behavior of the adults, the air of mystery and exclusion, and the morbid atmosphere with which we surround death tells them that something is seriously wrong. Their piecing together of fragments of knowledge may produce fear and bewilderment far greater than they would feel in response to simple honesty about what has happened and how their parents feel about it.

The tendency to conceal death from children rests on the same assumption of childish innocence that leads adults to try to insulate children from other realities: sex, money, disagreements and animosities among adults, insanity, depravity, and the hard facts of power. In all these areas, in the authors' view, children benefit from being given as much information as they can understand and manage, rather than inventions and evasions that needlessly complicate and confuse their feelings. This does not deny to parents the right to say, "I'll tell you more about it when you're older." As we have said, parents have to be able to judge the timeliness of information. Of course, by the time the child reaches the preschool years, the parents no longer have a monopoly on information.

Irrational Fears. The sense of vulnerability that accompanies heightened self-awareness is often expressed in specific fears at age four to five. A classic study shows how patterns of fearfulness change with age and how widespread fears are in the late preschool years (Macfarlane, Allen, and Honzik, 1954).

As we have said, children's fears do not have to correspond to either the reality or the magnitude of the threat. It is as easy to be afraid of ghosts or witches as of cars and ocean currents. Real things may be feared all out of proportion to their occurrence. Kidnappers are rare, but this does not reduce the child's fear of being abducted. Moreover, the many agencies and injuries that the child learns to fear may imply that the world at large is a fearsome place. The swaying curtains in the bedroom may take on monstrous aspects, and unnamed terrors, including bad dreams, may lurk under the bed or in closets or dark corners.

On the school playground, children who snarlingly declare themselves to be a tiger, or who pronounce their undulating arms to be snakes, may provoke genuine panic in their playmates. The fright may be tinged with skepticism, but the children are not eager to test the reality.

Awareness of Growth and Continuity. A further aspect of self-knowledge is children's growing awareness of themselves as changing with the passage of time.

Time is beginning to move—as we know, it slips away with ever-increasing velocity as we get older—and the child begins to sense the transitory nature of experience. As one child put it, his birthday had come and gone and there was nothing left, but he was older.

It sometimes appears that children suspect that growing older brings with it not only the promise of competence and privilege and freedom but also responsibility and loneliness. This might explain otherwise seemingly unaccountable spells of babyishness, sulking, clinging, whining, and weepiness—in a word, regression. The penalties of growth may be made especially prominent by the birth of a sibling, but even children without siblings show a certain amount of *growth ambivalence.* They want very much to be competent, but they also like to play at being a baby, asking the adult to "Feed me" or "Dress me." Children of preschool age delight in looking at the family photograph album, marveling at pictures of themselves in earlier incarnations.

One way preschool children cope with the problem of an ever-changing identity is to assume a new one, become somebody else. One four-year-old boy we knew spent a number of months earnestly, doggedly, and skillfully being a particular nine-year-old whom he had heard of but never met. There is no reason to think that he ever convinced anyone else that he was anybody but himself, but he nevertheless managed for a time to awe his peers with his patronizing manner and references to the school he attended, where they had real "lissons."

Part of the temporal dimension of identity lies in the ability to do something now in anticipation of a future reward (Mischel and Metzner, 1962). In experimental situations in which the subjects can choose between an immediate small reward and a delayed larger reward, preschool children in general already show ability to delay gratification.

Cause and Effect

Piaget has proposed a sequence of how children come to understand cause and effect, a subject we touched on in connection with toddlerhood. We have pointed out that young children do not inquire closely into cause and effect but seem to take ordinary events for granted. Children obviously may be angered or frightened or amused by departures from expectation, but they do not seem to question why things worked out as they did. Children ask about motives—for what reason?—but not about processes (how does it work?). To turn on a TV set and watch the screen light up into a segment of life complete with sound effects, to hold a piece of ice in one's hand and watch it melt, to trust a tool to the support of a magnetic holder, to follow the budding of a flower, these are not expressions of scientific laws but simply the way things are. Children, let us add, can manage dealing with such things pragmatically. It is their understanding that is limited.

Dynamism. The most primitive form of causal thought is *dynamism*, about which little can be said because everything is simply taken for granted. It is as though the world were imbued with a nameless but all-purpose sort of energy that governs all events and makes causal speculations pointless. Consider super-

stitions: Children in the middle years—and some adults—firmly believe that a black cat crossing one's path will bring bad luck, or that breaking a mirror will cause seven years' misfortune. But the believer in these superstitions never seems to wonder about the mechanisms involved: By what means, by what sequence of events, according to what principles will the black cat's passage make terrible things happen? It may be dynamism that makes people mistake coincidence for causation: A boy struck a utility pole with a stick at the exact moment of a power failure and was thoroughly and guiltily convinced that he had blacked out the city.

Finalism. Dynamism is soon joined by **finalism,** according to which the effect causes the cause. For instance, the sun goes down so that we can have darkness and go to sleep. Both dynamism and finalism exemplify what Piaget called **transductive thinking,** which sees events as linked, but with no particular temporal ordering. Transductive thinking is contrasted with both inductive and deductive thinking. In *inductive thinking,* we generalize from one or more particular instances to form a rule or principle, which may or may not be correct. In *deductive thinking,* we reason from a set of principles to try to find concrete relationships, as when an astronomer deduces the location of a previously unknown planet from irregularities in the orbits of the known planets. Transductive thinking simply joins up things that are close in time or space, or in some way equivalent, and makes one the cause of the other. For instance, it used to be thought that the cure for a disease ought to resemble the disease (Nisbett and

Ross, 1980); thus turmeric, which is bright yellow, was believed to be a cure for jaundice. If a parent regularly returns from work at nightfall, the parent's coming can bring the darkness, or the darkness can cause the parent to return.

Such causal connections—and all associations among things that coincide only by chance—illustrate a primitive tendency that Heinz Werner (1973) called **syncretism,** a fusion in thought of elements that are appropriately thought of separately.

Animism. The next step in causal thinking is known as *animism*, the child's assumption that almost anything can have humanlike powers. Thus events are caused by the action of autonomous entities endowed with capacities for feeling, thought, purpose, and spontaneous movement. This applies to inanimate objects as well as to human beings and animals. It seems clear, in the tenderness and concern that children can lavish on dolls and toy animals, that children often perceive things animistically. But children's animism is unstable. Children shift back and forth between an animistic orientation and a pragmatic one, just as they shift back and forth between fantasy and reality. At one moment, a doll may be an animate participant in a child's play, only to be casually tossed aside, lifeless and inert, a moment later.

A four-year-old boy we knew conveyed something of the animistic outlook when he spoke of "discouraged songs" and "tired songs" and "happy houses," when he asked whether it hurts the ground to have holes dug in it, and when he told how the hands of his clock moved in response to changes in his activities. Piaget (1965) gave us the example of a child referring to an "angry mountain."

(© Hanna W. Schreiber/Photo Researchers)

The dramatic play of young children often reflects animistic thinking.

In a widely cited study, Wayne Dennis (1953) demonstrated that adults ascribe life to natural phenomena like clouds, the moon, the sea, and fire. Poets easily slide into animistic metaphors, personifying storms and other aspects of nature.

Artificialism. The next kind of causal thinking is **artificialism.** This is the assumption that events are caused by the action of some humanlike agent or entity or force that wills things to happen in fulfillment of its own purposes, even if these purposes are sometimes obscure. Thus the child's early causal questions are likely to ask about personal agents and their motives or reasons: "Who did it?" and "Why?" For example, a child, noticing the ground blanketed with pine needles, asked, "Why did they put these here?" making quite clear the assumption of a conscious, purposeful agency. Chukovsy (1963) quotes a child who wants to know "Why do they put a pit in every cherry? We have to throw the pit away anyway." There is a much-told anecdote of a little boy sitting on a hill with his father, watching a colorful sunset, and then, as it begins to fade, begging, "Daddy, please do it again!"

Note that most of the remarks cited so far are spontaneous. However, the concepts of dynamism, finalism, transductive thinking, animism, and artificialism are derived from children's attempts to answer questions dreamed up by adult investigators. There is a strong likelihood that in artificial test situations children are asked to reflect on things in which they have little interest, and which they lack conceptual tools for thinking about. Piaget, with his maturationist bias, would probably have said that these children were not yet maturationally "ready" to learn more advanced modes of thinking. Indeed, it might be very difficult to teach sophisticated thinking to young children, but there is every reason to suspect that children growing up among sophisticated, articulate adults might through modeling learn advanced thinking at an earlier age than Piaget would have thought possible. Recall (see p. 309) that Baillargeon, Gelman, and Meck (1981) showed children an apparatus in which dominoes could be set tumbling, with the last domino tripping a lever that dumped a toy rabbit onto a bed. Most of the three- and four-year-olds knew the difference between superficial changes that would not affect the gadget's operation and essential changes that would make a difference. Recall, too, that Koslowski and Pierce (1981) had mothers keep records of their three- to-five-year-olds' spontaneous observations and questions having to do with causation. They found quite a few hard-headed observations, such as asking, "How did I eat when I was inside your tummy?" From such findings we must conclude either that the causal progression seen by Piaget was a product of irrelevant methods or else that children outgrow primitive thinking much faster than they used to.

Children infer cause from coincidence only when there is very little else to go on, as with the boy and the blackout described above. When there is a simple, easily perceptible causal relationship, as in blowing out a candle with a hand-held hair dryer, children as young as three can easily identify cause and effect (Shultz, 1982).

Naturalism. The more primitive forms of causal thinking are said to be joined eventually by **naturalism.** This is the realization that there are impersonal, stable forces that govern events in the natural world, including some portion of human behavior. Naturalism, of course, is the stuff of science.

Note that for the postdynamistic child, every event has to have a sensible cause. There is no room in the young child's thinking for chance, random events, or mere coincidence. Recall that Weisz (1980) found that five-year-olds thought that success in a random card-drawing game was determined by skill, just as believers in immanent justice think that wickedness will set punitive forces in motion. If a picnic is planned for Saturday and on Saturday it rains, there has to be a reason: The child is being punished for some misdeed, or a capricious deity is playing dirty tricks, or even perhaps the all-powerful parents have arranged for the rain so that they can escape the nuisance of taking the children picnicking. As we have suggested, these primitive forms of causal reasoning may never be completely outgrown.

A predominantly primitive outlook permits the creation of the phantoms and hobgoblins that befuddle serious, rational thinking, and so must be shed. It is obvious, though, that adults never fully grow out of the magical world of childhood. We like to think that this is as it should be. Most of our verbal play requires that we be able to straddle the worlds of magic and reality, as children are beginning to do when they deliberately toy with the idea of growing up in reverse, starting as an adult and ending up as a baby, and even when they collaborate in the prefabricated fantasies of an animated cartoon. For the adult, music and art and literature and love, and even science and mathematics, have no meaning without magic. Without magic, we are cut off from our roots in universal human experience and wander forever homeless.

Time

Time is a dimension of cause and effect. More generally, though, it provides one of the frameworks within which we orient and organize and coordinate our lives. We regulate our behavior in keeping with clocks and calendars and schedules. We remember and anticipate and plan. But we also have a **personal time** that is only partially correlated with formal time schemes, as when time drags or flies, when we feel relaxed or under pressure to meet a deadline, or when we feel that we are losing time, wasting time, saving time, or using time wisely. Personal time is closely related to our sense of our own mortality, and having goals or a direction or a mission is an intimate part of our self-awareness. In our experience of personal time, we fantasize time machines, fountains of youth, getting a fresh start, and eternal bliss or damnation in an afterlife. The concept of time is itself a reification. We reify time doubly by trying to capture it in such images as Old Father Time, the Grim Reaper, and relentlessly flowing rivers.

However, young children who have no knowledge of history, whose own clearly remembered past can be measured in hours (except for occasional flashes that may reach back six months or so), and whose future is a vague abstraction that has to be accepted on adult say-so, may understandably have some difficulty coming to terms with formal time schemes. Even when children have learned some key words, these words may not yet hold their conventional meanings. Thus it should not be thought strange that a three-year-old left with a sitter while his mother went shopping for a few hours should announce to his homecoming father, "Mommy'll be back soon. She went out for a couple of whiles." A four-year-old told a playmate insistently, "It is not today! My mommy said it was Monday!" An understanding of the sequence yesterday-today-tomorrow may be delayed until the school years, although one preschool child announced to her dumfounded parents, "Today is yesterday's tomorrow." (We have heard of a variant: "Yesterday, today was tomorrow.") What is clear is that preschool children are thinking about and trying to make sense out of time relations, whereas toddlers simply take them for granted.

Designations of time gradually become more precise during this period. Many children learn the days of the weeks, the seasons of the year, and in which seasons some of the major holidays fall. Clock time eludes all the preschool children we have ever heard of, although some children can name the hours at which various routine activities are supposed to take place.

Many preschool children are fascinated to learn about their own unremembered past. They enjoy looking at their baby pictures and beg their parents to tell them about "when I was little." Children begin forgetting their past almost as quickly as they live it. This is not to say that all is forgotten. Children remember a fair number of isolated facts and events, largely in the form of what are called **eidetic images** (Giray *et al.*, 1976). Eidetic images are vivid recollections of past experiences, akin to what is called photographic memory (although eidetic images can be auditory or tactual as well as visual). Children can recall some things very graphically. For instance, they may remember the design on a bib worn at dinner at a certain restaurant some months before or a friend crying as they drove past a certain spot. However, they totally lose the context: where the restaurant was or that it was there that the child first tasted lobster, or that it was on the way to go swimming that the friend had an attack of separation anxiety and burst out crying. Eidetic images lack both context and continuity: No links connect one image to the next. Nevertheless, parents can often use their preschool-age children as memory storage devices, eliciting from them a forgotten name, or what kind of clothes someone was wearing when last seen. Children can retain emotion-charged associations. For instance, a little girl was knocked over by an aggressively friendly dog which tried to rest its front paws on her shoulders, and it was several years before she would let another dog come within reach.

In our view, the continuous past of the first six or so years of one's own life is lost to memory not because it is repressed but because it is submerged in constant reworkings of one's knowledge of self and world. We constantly become—especially in our early years—new and transformed versions of ourselves, capable of recapturing former modes of existence only in special circumstance—dreams, hypnosis, or in response to special cues. These cues may be the taste or odor of some forgotten substance from the past (witness Marcel Proust's stream of memories set off by the taste of a cake dipped in tea); an old photograph or letter; a visit to the haunts of our childhood; or the rediscovery of a once-cherished plaything (remember the sled "Rosebud" in the powerful film *Citizen Kane*).

Children have a hard time realizing that their parents once were little and seem to entertain two quite contradictory notions about the parents' past. On the one hand, the parental past seems to stretch into the dim mists of prehistory. This is implied in the often-heard request to "Tell me how it was in the olden days," as though the parents had known giants and dragons. On the other hand, children find it almost unthinkable that the world was ever essentially different from the way it is now. They listen incredulously when a parent says that he or she remembers some now-taken-for-granted technological first—the first moon landing, say. A statement by one four-year-old suggests that he planned to grow up backward in time so as to join those who were already mature: "Pretty soon this will be the olden days and I'll be a man." Numerous children expect to catch up with their parents and marry them, which lends some credibility to talk of Oedipus and Electra complexes. Chukovsky (1963) quotes a child who asks, "Mother, who was born first, you or I?"

Preschool children are far more aware of their own growth than of changes in adults. This is not only because developmental change is faster in childhood than adulthood, but also because parents emphasize and celebrate their children's development in size and competence, while minimizing or trying to ignore the changes taking place in themselves. Just as the parents' lives seem to stretch back into the far-distant past, so do they promise to last changelessly into the perpetual future. Children may know, but with very little conviction, that their parents will someday be *very* old, but the remoteness of this state of affairs leaves plenty of time for catching up. We have a record of one five-year-old's disillusionment on this score:

> It would be funny if I was big and you were little. I wouldn't pay any attention to you and I'd make you do things you didn't like to. But I guess I won't ever be able to do that to you 'cause I won't ever be able to catch up to you. I won't ever be able to be the same age as you at the same time.

This child's discovery of the universal uniformity of time contains a deeper realization: Growth is regular and follows a stable pattern. Younger children do not share this sense of stability. Many children, for instance, believe that birthdays cause a dramatic transformation and are very much let down on the day after a birthday to find that nothing much has changed. Even though children have long since achieved object permanence with regard to many things, their world is still infused with a dynamistic magic that makes metamorphoses possible.

Rheta deVries (1969) did a study in which she disguised a cat with masks representing a dog and a rabbit. Three-year-olds accepted the seeming transformations as real, while older children were skeptical but frightened. Some other quotations illustrate belief in rather drastic transformations. A four-year-old girl asked, "When I grow up to be a big man like my daddy, will I have a penis?" Chukovsky (1963) gives two more examples of acceptance of metamorphosis. A child asked, "Daddy, when you were little, were you a boy or a girl?" Another child, trying to feed cabbage to chickens and having been told that chickens do not eat cabbage, explained, "I'm giving it to them so that they may save it for after they become rabbits."

Note that we have not cited experimental findings on preschool children's memory. Such research deals for the most part with memorizing lists of words or groups of pictures or lists of word pairs, and seems to have little application to everyday life. However, one important concept from the field of memory research is worth mentioning. This is what is called **elaboration**, creating a context for the ideas and relationships to be remembered. A child learning the word pair "cat–apple" might link them by saying, "The cat ate the apple." Preschool children do not elaborate spontaneously, but they can be taught to do it. Elaboration improves retention of learned material, and some preschool children learn to transfer elaboration, applying it in new learning situations (Pressley, 1982).

Space

We have already seen how, in infancy and toddlerhood, spatial relations are linked to the baby's own actions and migrations. Babies have no notion of how things and places are located relative to one another. We have described the space of the older infant and the toddler as *action space.* The preschool child moves gradually away from action space into **map space,** in which locations and directions and distance are linked in a coherent overall pattern.

Norman Maier (1936) performed a classic experiment using a swastika-shaped maze. Each arm of the maze ended in a room that was made distinctively different from those at the ends of the other three arms. Children, by moving from the particular playthings and furnishings found in one room to those in another, were given a chance to learn every possible route inside the maze. Children were deemed to have learned all the routes when they could lead the experimenter unfailingly from say, the red room to the blue room and from the blue room to the yellow room, and so forth. Knowledge of the maze as an organized whole, rather than as a collection of unrelated routes, was tested by requiring the child to go from one famil-

(© Burk Uzzle/Magnum)

Building a trellis with blocks. The preschool child's sense of space moves gradually toward a more coherent overall pattern linking locations, directions, and distances.

iar room to another, but they had to do so on the previously unknown outside of the maze, without any of the familiar clues to be found within the maze. Not until the late preschool or early school years were children able to form the mental map—the *schema*—necessary to solve this task.

A study by Nancy Hazen (1982) partially contradicts Maier's conclusion. However, Hazen used a much simpler maze, three square chambers, with doorways in every wall, joined at the corners to form a boxy V (see Figure 11.1). Hazen taught her two- and three-year-old subjects one of two routes through two

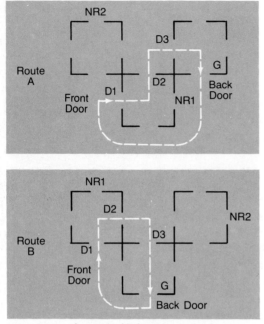

FIGURE 11.1 Layout of laboratory playhouse used by Hazen to study spatial orientation. Routes A and B are indicated by dashed lines. Location of the goal room is marked by *G*. Detours 1, 2, and 3 are marked *D1*, *D2*, and *D3*. New routes 1 and 2 are marked *NR1* and *NR2*.

linked structures, and then asked them (1) to traverse the route backward, (2) to make detours around barriers that interrupted the normal pathway, and (3) to return to their starting point via a new route. Most of the three-year-olds and some of the two-year-olds gave evidence of having mastered this area of space.

Even though they have not yet made the transition to map space, preschool children who have a fair amount of exposure to maps may try to draw them. Figure 11.2 shows maps drawn spontaneously by two five-year-old children, a boy and a girl, of their own dwelling places, together with the actual layouts. We should take a moment to stress that children growing up in favorable

surroundings are learning, in their drawing and painting, map making, and being read to (where they have a chance to grasp the relation between printed marks and spoken words), to organize two-dimensional space in ways that may be denied to children growing up in less favorable environments. It is our suspicion that such a difference in experience with two-dimensional patterns accounts for much of the difference in the ease with which children learn to read.

Dart and Pradhan (1967) used mapping ability as a way of classifying cultures. Only those cultures in which children of school age could imagine and draw a familiar piece of terrain as seen from above were considered ready to learn scientific ways of thinking. Dart and Pradhan found mapping very difficult or even impossible for adolescents in non-Western societies. One would judge that people in these societies are too concretely tied to action space to be able to perform the act of abstraction required for map making.

The concepts of size and quantity can be viewed as special cases of spatial extent and organization. Ordinal numbers—first, second, last—can refer to temporal organization, spatial organization, or both simultaneously. When children line up in the order in which they will have a turn in pinning the tail on the donkey, or when turns in a table game are dictated by the clockwise spatial disposition of the players, both time and space are involved.

Beyond map space lies **abstract space** of the kind found in geometries of two or more dimensions. Such notions seem to be completely beyond the grasp of preschool children, and most school-age children as well. However, experience with computer-generated shapes may

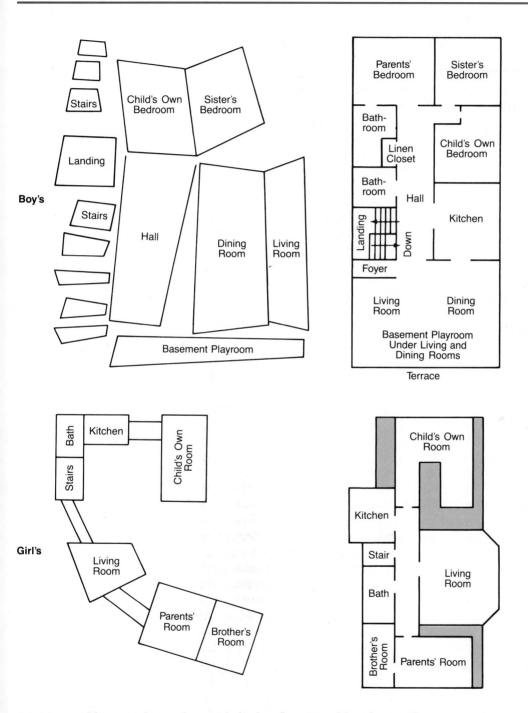

FIGURE 11.2 Maps made spontaneously by two five-year-olds, a boy and a girl, of their own homes, together with the actual layouts. Both maps are greatly simplified.

lead to a radical change in children's understanding. Note that "space-blind" adults, who have trouble with both action space and map space, can excel in their command of abstract space.

Our much-quoted preschool spokesman, aged four and a half, can be observed trying to untangle a temporal idea which he has understood as spatial:

> Miss Williams, what is the end of the world? . . . I don't see how it is a *place*, because my mommy says the world is round, and so there could not be any place where the world stops, or where you could fall off. It goes around, and then when you get to where you start, it goes round again.

What we have been talking about so far is space as a container, space defined by coordinates such as up and down and north, south, east, and west. But space also applies to objects, which are oriented in space and may have spatial attributes such as head and tail, top and bottom, front and rear, and left and right. Eve Clark (1980) has studied understanding of these spatial terms in three- and four-year-old children. For instance, *top* and *bottom* are consistently understood before *front* and *back*. However, when confronted with a "horizontal" object, such as a book or a watch lying flat on a table, children apparently find *top* and *bottom* hard to apply. When told to place a finger on the designated face of a plain block, three-year-olds did much better on *top* than on *bottom*. Here we must note two things. First, the bottom face of a block resting on a surface is invisible, and young children might have doubts about whether the unspoken rules of the situation might forbid lifting the block. Second, *bottom* refers not only to a spatial position but also to an intimate portion of the anatomy, and this could inhibit some children. Once children had mastered *in front of* and *in back of,* they could apply these terms equally well both to objects that have a well-defined front and back (a truck, a donkey) and to objects that do not (a ball, a box).

Number and Quantity

Piaget's account of the number capacities of preoperational children is somewhat misleading. In Piaget's version, preschool children's sense of quantity does not go much beyond a lot and a little. When asked to compare two rows of poker chips in terms of equality or inequality, children are guided more by the length of the rows than by the number of chips each row contains. A lump of clay is likewise seen as changing in amount as it goes through various manipulations, such as being rolled into a sausage or being cut in two. In other words, variations in spatial arrangement seem to be more important in the child's judgment of quantity than are such empirical checks as counting the chips or weighing the clay. Nor do young children reason along the lines that since nothing has been either added or taken away, the original must be quantitatively unchanged.

Once again, it appears that preschool children's numerical abilities vary with test conditions and family background. A number of studies by Rochel Gelman and her associates (Gelman and Gallistel, 1978) show that, given the right conditions, children from age three onward do a rather good job of estimating the number of items contained in a row. At a one-second exposure, most three-year-olds could accurately identify two or three items. At a minute's exposure most could count five things. Note that Piaget did not instruct his subjects to count. He told them only to judge whether two arrays were equal or unequal. But it appears that with small numbers of items, preschool children do not have to count. That is, they **subitize,** perceive the number of things immediately, without having to enumerate them. Three-year-old subjects were of two kinds: those who still functioned at the toddler level of one, two, a lot, and those who could count accurately up to five or more.

We have compared the counting and summing abilities of four-year-olds from middle- and lower-class backgrounds (Church, 1970). Middle-class four-year-olds could accurately count ten blocks, and a few could count as many as twenty. They were indifferent to the spatial arrangement of the blocks. They carefully set each block aside as it was counted, maintaining a clear one-to-one relationship between blocks and numbers. The children from less favored backgrounds obviously understood the concepts of counting and summing, but their upper limit was five blocks. Beyond that number, they reverted to toddlerlike behavior, counting some blocks more than once, skipping others, and using numbers pretty much at random.

It seems, then, that preschool children, given the right sort of experience, can achieve higher levels of numerical skill than Piaget was prepared to grant them. However, we have yet to meet a preschooler who could cope with such abstract standard units of measurement as yards and pounds and minutes and miles per hour.

These conclusions are called into ques-tion by a study by Ginsburg and Russell (1981). These investigators compared black and white middle-class and lower-class four- and five-year-olds on seventeen tests of elementary arithmetic. At the four-year-old level, they found differences associated with social class on four tests, and with race on two. By age five, two of the social-class differences had disappeared, leaving middle-class children doing better than lower-class children on tests of conservation of number and of equivalence between groups. At age five, there were statistically reliable but small differences in favor of white children on tests of seriation (arranging rods according to size) and of the unit rule (understanding the effect of adding or subtracting one element). The unit-rule test was the only one that showed a sex difference—girls scored higher than boys.

The Domain of People: Social Cognition

We return briefly to the topic of social cognition, which we discussed in toddlerhood and to which we shall return in the middle years. Remember that social cognition goes on at several levels. Children know that people have inner lives, including states such as hunger and pleasure, traits such as kindness and selfishness, processes such as hearing and seeing and thinking, goals and purposes, and attitudes toward categories of people and things. Children know about particular people's proclivities, abilities, and sensitivities. Social cognition also means awareness of the external constraints on behavior: Mommy may want most awfully to buy you that shiny new plaything, but if she does not have the

(© Ruth Silverman/Stock, Boston)

A chat between friends. Social congnition continues to develop in the preschool years, and children know that people have inner lives with distinct proclivities, abilities, and sensitivities.

money to spare, she simply cannot do it. And it involves the ability to deduce how receptive another person is likely to be at this moment to a particular kind of message. It even means knowing how to induce a receptiveness. The little boy's "Mommy dear" and the little girl's "Daddy darling" can often work wondrous transformations. Social cognition implies a reduction in egocentrism in two senses. First, it means being aware that other people's views of the world do not necessarily coincide with one's own. Second, it means sharpened self-awareness as a general guide to what goes on in other people (Flavell, 1977; Flavell and Ross, 1981).

Much of what we have said in past sections of this chapter might easily have gone into a section on social cognition. Note that the preschool child's social cognition ranges from blank insensitivity to a fairly acute understanding. Re-

call the preschool child's failure to detect the playfulness of his father's fanciful account of having a flu shot. Children's becoming aware of the possibility of lying, and their reactions to other people's lies, are a study in social cognition. Young children's code switching when talking to still younger children implies a suspicion that babies cannot cope with normal language (Gleason, 1973). However, we must bear in mind that preschool children are far from having escaped from egocentrism, and their awareness of other people's states, needs, and feelings is of necessity limited.

LEARNING AND COGNITION

Traditional learning theories have relied heavily on associationism, as in classical and operant conditioning, and have tried to describe learning as the acquisition of responses without any need for cognitive mediation. However, there have been exceptions, and these are discussed below.

Probability Learning

Probability learning derives from behaviorism, but it has a link to cognition. We begin with the notion of **schedules of reinforcement.** We have already spoken of how reinforcement (which generally means reward) leads to learning. What we have not yet talked about is that the learner does not have to be rewarded on every trial for learning to take place. Reinforcements can be spaced out in various ways, and the patternings of reinforcements are called schedules. For purposes of probability learning, we are concerned only with schedules in which a given proportion of responses is rewarded, although not in a regular ordered way. There can be bursts of reinforcement interspersed with dry patches of nonreinforcement. In probability learning, the subject has a choice of levers to press (or buttons to push, the exact operant being unimportant), both set to differing schedules. Let us say that one lever rewards the learner with a jelly bean on 70 percent of the presses, and the other lever on 30 percent of the presses. The learner soon discovers, through trial and error, that neither lever pays off 100 percent of the time, and that one lever is more profitable than the other. There are many possible ways of reacting to this discovery, but for the moment we need to be concerned with only two. One way of coping with the differential payoffs by the two levers is called **matching,** pressing the 70 percent lever 70 percent of the time and the 30 percent lever 30 percent of the time. A more sophisticated strategy is called **maximizing,** pressing the high-yield lever every time. A bit of simple arithmetic shows why it is more rewarding to stick with the 70 percent lever 100 percent of the time. If one matches, one is rewarded 70 percent of the time (on average) on the 70 percent lever, and 30 percent on the 30 percent lever: $.7 \times .7 = .49; .3 \times .3 = .09; .49 + .09 = .58$, which is rather less than the .70 one would obtain by pressing the 70 percent lever every time.

In a study of probability learning in children from age three to age eighteen, Morton Weir (1964) found that three-year-olds were the group most likely (70 percent) to adopt the more "intelligent" maximizing strategy. From the 70 percent level at age three, maximizing dropped to 66 percent at age five, to 20

to 25 percent at ages seven to fourteen, and climbed back above the 50 percent level only at age eighteen. It has been observed in a number of studies that older or brighter children "fail" in very simple problem-solving situations because they reject the obvious solution. They instead go questing for nonexistent subtleties, trying out some of the innumerable other possible strategies we mentioned.

Winefield (1980) did a partial replication of the Weir study, looking at maximizing in youngsters at ages six, ten, and eighteen. Like Weir, he found that few of his subjects maximized. However, because he chose a narrower age range, he missed the high rate of maximizing in three-year-olds.

Reversal and Nonreversal Shifts

Another area of learning that seems closely related to cognitive processes is that of **reversal** and **nonreversal shifts,** also known as *intradimensional (IDS)* and *extradimensional shifts (EDS)*. The subject, animal or human, begins by learning to choose a rewarded object on the basis of some attribute dimension—for example, size, shape, color. Let us assume that the subject is rewarded for choosing the biggest object, without regard to shape or color. Once the subject has learned the correct response, the experimenter changes the rules. This can be done in two ways. The rewarded feature may be another position on the same dimension—little instead of big—in which case we have a reversal or intradimensional shift. Or the basis of the reward can be located on a new dimension—color or shape—in which case we have a nonreversal or extradimensional shift. It turns out that EDS is much easier to learn that IDS. That is, it seems to be easier to switch to a whole new dimension of responding than to change to a new position on the same dimension. It appears that some sort of cognitive mediation is required to make an IDS.

Tracy Kendler (1964, 1972; Kendler and Kendler, 1970) has proposed that verbal formulation of what must be done is the secret of making an IDS. She has shown that kindergarten-age children who are required to explain their responses do better on reversal shifts than those who are not required to give explanations. However, there must be alternative processes. For one thing, animals without any known linguistic abilities can learn IDS. Further, children who verbalize incorrectly can make IDS. The puzzle remains unsolved.

Learning Set or Learning to Learn

A third kind of learning with cognitive overtones is called **learning to learn** or **learning set,** first described by Harry Harlow and his wife Margaret (Harlow and Kuenne, 1949). A learning-set experiment tests for the subject's ability to learn not a simple discrimination but how to generalize a principle from one learning task to a new one, independent of any particular stimulus array. This is most easily illustrated by *oddity learning*.

The subject is presented with a group of objects, one of which differs from the others in some significant way—let us say the only red block in a group of blue ones. The principle, then, is to pick the one item that is different from a group of items. One tests for learning of the principle by presenting a new collection of objects, with an odd member that differs in some new way: the block that is smaller than the others. The subject immediately applies the oddity principle and chooses the object that is different.

Learning to learn is important because it demonstrates that monkeys and people learn not just that a particular object is the correct one but also the relationship to other objects that makes it correct. Gelman (1969) has shown that training in oddity problems, with number of dots and length of rods as the relevant dimensions, teaches five-year-olds to attend to a variety of features—to *decenter*. Oddity training teaches conservation of number and length, and in many children generalizes to conservation of volume.

PERCEPTION

Although we have so far been talking chiefly about knowing and thinking, we should bear in mind that knowledge is initially built upon perception. By the time children reach the preschool years, their perception begins to be modified and even distorted by knowledge, by the residue of prior experience that gives us a set of expectations to which we are inclined to assimilate new kinds of experience. And let us not forget that the accumulated body of experience includes the residue of verbal experiences that play their part in shaping our vision of reality.

We get clues to children's perceptions from explicit verbalizations, from concrete behavior with objects in the course of the day's activities, and from responses to specially contrived test situations. Children give voice to such discoveries as that distant objects look smaller than near ones, as shown by the child's ability to mask a distant person with a finger. (This discovery is essential to the use of perspective in drawing, and its implications eluded artists up to the time of the Renaissance.) A five-year-old girl asks about a stained-glass window brightly lighted from behind by the setting sun, "Would it burn you if you touched it?"

We know further that some "self-evident" properties of reality are by no means obvious to preschool children. Both everyday experience and formal experiments show that young children cannot reliably predict whether a cube of wood or iron will float or sink in water. Once they have discovered empirically which of the objects will float and which will sink, children invoke wildly irrelevant explanations, such as that things sink or float because they are dull or shiny. Nor do children anticipate that to put a solid object into a container full of water will cause an overflow. We can learn something about children's perceptual abilities by watching them assemble jigsaw puzzles, build with blocks, and draw pictures.

Now let us look at some formal approaches to the study of perceptual development. Bear in mind that children's object-sorting behavior, discussed earlier, can also be considered as a perceptual phenomenon: Children *see* the qualities that link objects into classes. Inhelder (1953) has shown that if young children are asked to draw a line representing the water surface in an outline drawing of a beaker, they draw the line parallel to the bottom of the cup. This is so whether the cup is upright or tilted (see Figure 11.3). It turns out that many college students, women more often than

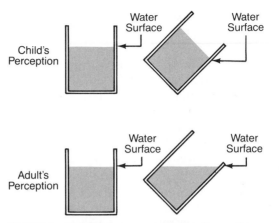

FIGURE 11.3 Drawings representing the water surface in an outline drawing of a beaker. The top figures show the child's perception; the bottom ones, the adult's.

men, do exactly the same (Thomas and Jamison, 1975). This raises the question of whether preschool children are sensitive to parallelism. A study by Eugene Abravanel (1977) indicates that they are. In a matching task, using a pair of parallel lines as the model to which a second figure, chosen from an array, was to be matched, three- and four-year-old children reliably preferred another pair of parallel lines, even when it was oriented differently from the model and the nonparallel alternatives were aligned to match the model.

Four-year-olds are sensitive to the up-down orientation of abstract forms. Given a choice of two possible orientations, they consistently choose one of the two as "correct" (Ghent, 1961; Wohlwill and Wiener, 1964). The preferred orientation is usually reversed beginning around age six, perhaps in conjunction with learning to read, since some of the forms resemble letters of the alphabet. Note that many early readers confuse letters that are mirror images of each other, such as *b* and *d* and *p* and *q*. (One sometimes, but rarely, finds reversals around the horizontal axis, as between *b* and *p* and *d* and *q*.) Cairns and Steward (1970) report a sharp decline in letter reversals after age four. This occurs especially in children who know the names of the letters and have a well-defined knowledge of left and right. (Note that one can teach four-year-olds about their own left and right, but one cannot teach them to *transpose*, identify left and right on a person facing them; instead of transposing, they assign their own left and right to the person, mirror-fashion.) Eleanor Gibson and her associates (Gibson, 1970) have found that most four- and five-year-olds from favored backgrounds can readily tell the difference between cursive script and scriptlike scribbles, and between block letters and letterlike nonsense shapes.

It is worth digressing a moment to point out that children brought up in close association with the written and printed word show early inclinations both to read and write (Hechinger, 1982). Many primary-grade teachers believe that young children are incapable of learning to write and so postpone instruction for a year or two. However, a number of educators (Burrows, Jackson, and Saunders, 1966; Temple, Nathan, and Burris, 1982; Graves, 1982) have found that children want to write and that their almost indecipherable scrawls are often the underpinnings of true writing, on which teachers could build. These educators believe that children learn to write in the same way they learn to talk, through modeling. They take as their models adults, older siblings, TV, highway signs, and so forth. Such early attempts at writing may take an even earlier form of hieroglyphiclike pictorial messages. Figures 11.4, 11.5, and 11.6 give an idea of how spontaneous writing may evolve. The pictorial shopping list (Figure 11.4) is by an almost three-year-old girl. Her mother, about to go shopping, is making a list. The child nearby takes a small piece of paper and says, "I want to write my own list." Mother: "Let's see, what do we need?" Child: "Let's see." Mother: "Carrots, cucumbers." Mother writes and the child draws as they speak. Child: "Lettuce, cheese." Mother: "Two cans of soup, squash, toilet paper, fish." Child: "Apples and bananas." When finished, Mother: "O.K. now, let's go." The child shows her list to her mother and puts it in her own small shopping bag.

Figure 11.5 is an example of the scrawl-type writing noted by Temple, Nathan, and Burris (1982). It is a message written by a four-and-a-half-year-old boy to his older sister when they were both coming down with the measles. It says, "No, I will not let you come in here unless you want something." Just three weeks later, the same boy was able to write the second message (Figure 11.6). This one needs no translating. It is worth noting that this child had not yet started school.

McGurk and Power (1980) have studied the relative potency of information given visually and tactually. Preschool children were invited to explore objects by touch while viewing them through a lens that severely distorted the objects' shape. The children reliably assigned the objects the shape given by the false visual information. Adults likewise will accept false visual information that con-

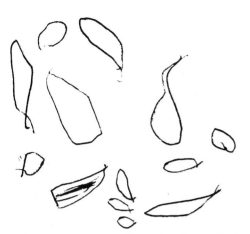

FIGURE 11.4 A pictorial shopping list made by a girl almost three. "Listed" are carrots, cucumbers, lettuce, cheese, apples, and bananas.

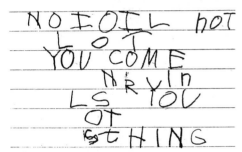

FIGURE 11.5 The scrawl-type writing of a four-and-a-half-year-old boy to his sister as both were coming down with measles: 'No, I will not let you come in here unless you want something.'

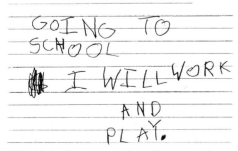

FIGURE 11.6 A message from the same boy—who has not yet started school—just three weeks later.

flicts with true information derived from the sense of touch.

PERCEPTION OF PICTURES

Note that many of the stimuli we have been talking about—parallel lines, forms in search of an orientation, letters—have been meaningful two-dimensional patterns. Now we are talking about a particular sort of two-dimensional arrangement called pictures. We have seen that pictures and the things they stand for initially tend to be interchangeable. That is, pictures are perceived realistically. We know that picture recognition begins in late infancy, and that toddlers recognize pictures of things, of individuals including themselves, and of gross emotional states such as sadness or happiness. Toddlers can identify pictures of familiar objects, such as a horse or a particular make of car, taken from an unfamiliar angle, such as looking down from above. We know that children are at first indifferent to whether a picture is upside-down or right-side-up (Hunton, 1955). Awareness of inversion may come in two stages. First, the child perceives an image as an upright picture of an upside-down object: "Mommy standing on head." Later, the child realizes that the entire picture is inverted.

We have not been able to find out whether children recognize real things seen for the first time, such as animals in the zoo, on the basis of having previously seen and named them in pictures. We do not know very much about the perception and comprehension of actions, relationships among people, and overall themes and meanings in pictures. Jean Berko Gleason (1981) has done a small pilot experiment following the referential communication model of Glucksberg, Krauss, and Higgins (1975). You will recall that two children can both see the same set of designs but cannot see what the other sees. It is the task of one child to describe one particular design in a fashion that allows the other child to select it from an array. Gleason used pictures rather than designs. In one phase of the study she was herself a participant in the game. Successful acts of communication were reinforced with a piece of candy for both sender and receiver. In the role of participant, Gleason was able to model the ideal way to describe pictures. Her four-year-old subjects started out at a rather primitive level of communication. However, under the influence of reinforcement and modeling they became quite expert at picture description. Gleason's aim was the improvement of communication skills, but she demonstrated incidentally that four-year-olds can apprehend pictured meanings at a quite sophisticated level. Wohlwill (1962) showed that children's awareness of size and distance in pictures can be changed more easily than adults' by modifying the amount of information contained in the picture.

Still to be explored are the effects of color versus black and white; natural color versus arbitrary color (gray elephants as contrasted with pink ones, for instance); photographs versus drawings; line drawings versus shaded drawings; naturalistic versus stylized representations; and many other dimensions of depiction. Our ignorance is both surprising and a little frightening in a society that uses pictures as a major me-

dium of communication. Some years back, the Eastman Kodak company launched a program intended to cultivate what it called "picture literacy," but we have never heard of any results.

TEACHING CONCRETE OPERATIONS TO PRESCHOOL CHILDREN

For a great many years, Piaget and his disciples resisted the notion that cognitive development could be accelerated through the teaching of more advanced thinking strategies than occurred spontaneously to children. The fact that every study in this area always turned up some three-, four-, and five-year-olds who apparently were capable of performing concrete operations was written off as an expression of individual differences or of inevitable errors of measurement. There was never any attempt to find out whether these children had life experience consistently different from those who operated at more primitive levels. It often seemed that attempts to teach concrete operations to preschool children were deliberately designed to fail. Such studies have been criticized as being too rigid in both training methods and measurement of results (Kohnstamm, 1970; Kuhn, 1974).

Late in Piaget's life, three of his co-workers (Inhelder, Sinclair, and Bovet, 1974) published a book reporting some limited successes in teaching concrete operations to preoperational children. In his preface to the book, Piaget conceded that such teaching would work, but only if the child was already on the verge of making the transition anyway. By that time, it was too late. Practically everyone in the field was convinced that such acceleration was possible, and that it was only a matter of finding the best way of making it happen.

Gelman (1969) was one of the pioneers in this field, emphasizing the importance of getting children to pay attention to the relevant features of situations. There have by now been a great many studies. Typical is one by Field (1981). Three- and four-year-olds were given training in concepts of number and length. They were taught three rules by which to decide whether number and length had been conserved after a perceptual change. All the children learned the rules. But the older children were better than the younger at generalizing them to new problems. Some 79 percent of the children who could generalize the principle could still do so on follow-up testing two and a half or five months later. Among the three-year-olds who learned the principle without generalizing it, 70 percent had lost the rule on follow-up.

We would like to see longitudinal studies comparing the experiences of children who acquire concrete operations early with those who do not. It would seem to make sense to incorporate measures of concrete operational thought in all cognitive tests addressed to preschool children.

Permit us to remind you that we are using Piaget's stages only as a convenient framework for describing and discussing behavior in successive age periods. We do not take the stage concept literally. How children progress in various areas of functioning is very much a product of the stimulation they receive. And our understanding of what children of various ages can and cannot do is very

much at the mercy of the test instruments we use to assess competence.

A SCHOOL FOR THE PRESCHOOL CHILD

The rather sizable body of material we have described in this chapter and the preceding one carries a great many implications about how best to care for children's needs in a preschool setting. We do not intend to try to expand at any length on these implications. However, it does seem to us that many of today's preschools are in some confusion about what they should be doing for children and how to go about it.

A bit of history is in order. Philanthropic day nurseries have been serving young children and their families for more than 150 years. These nurseries, however, were available only to children of the poor, of the ill, of mothers who were obliged to work, or of neglectful or abusive parents. With a few glowing exceptions, these institutions were custodial in nature, keeping children safe, healthy, fed, and busy until their parents were able to resume their care.

The modern nursery-school movement has two main antecedents. One of these is the work of Maria Montessori, an Italian physician who, just after the turn of the century, set up educational institutions for poor children. The Montessori method emphasized motor skills, cultivation of the senses, and preparation for conventional academic studies (Lewis, 1977). The child was placed in a "prepared environment," which was intended to match each individual's readiness to learn. The teacher's job was to judge children's readiness and then provide appropriate learning materials for the child to interact with. Interestingly enough, when the Montessori method came to the United States, it was an educational approach for the children of affluent families. The second major influence on the preschool movement was John Dewey's pragmatism and progressive education. The concept of progressive education took hold just after World War I, and was practiced in the leading college and university laboratory schools. Progressive education emphasized the "whole child" and preached the doctrine of "learning by doing," which meant that experience is a better teacher than any amount of simple telling by a pedagogue (Franklin, 1981).

The tax-supported day care that a great many people now take for granted is a relatively new phenomenon. In general, it has been government policy not to encourage women to join the labor force and perhaps displace male workers. Governments have, therefore, emphasized the importance of the family and the care of young children within its structure. There have been a couple of exceptions in past eras. In the late 1930s, the Works Progress Administration (WPA) offered early childhood programs as a service to families stricken by the Great Depression. As the economy began to improve, helped along by the war in Europe, these schools were disbanded. Then, during World War II, under the Lanham Act, preschools were established for children of women employed in defense industries. These too were drastically reduced in number when the crisis was past.

The federal government entered the

(© Michael Weisbrot & Family)

Native American children in a contemporary day-care center.

field of early childhood education again in the 1960s, in the wake of the civil rights movement and as part of the War on Poverty. The Head Start program for preschool children began in 1965 as a way of providing intellectual "enrichment" for children from "culturally deprived" backgrounds so as to prepare them for the demands of the primary grades. The notion of government-supported day care has spread steadily. It was backed by the argument that it would help families to seek gainful work instead of drawing welfare, while providing quality care for their children. Added to that was the huge rise in numbers of working mothers, single-parent families with the parent working, and other family compositions that required care for young children outside the home.

More or less simultaneously, theoreticians of both the Piagetian and behaviorist persuasions were offering new approaches to preschool education and trying them out in a number of experimental programs. Many of the newer programs have been packaged commercially and can now be bought and practiced in units. Bartlett (1981) describes twenty-seven programs designed just to foster language development. These were culled from a much larger but uncounted number. One can now identify approaches to preschool education stemming from the psychoanalytic approaches of both Freud and Erikson, from Skinnerian neobehaviorism, from Montessori, from Piaget, and from the "traditional," Dewey-based cognitive-emotional interactionist approach (Biber, Shapiro, and Wickens, 1977; Boegehold *et al.*, 1977; Shapiro and Weber, 1981; Stevens and King, 1976).

It may not be safe to generalize, but it is our impression that a good deal of nursery-school education is a mix of "traditional" and "enrichment" practices, with very little regard for theory. Meanwhile, cutbacks in federal funding pose a threat to the continuation of care for young children. These cutbacks are forcing an increasing proportion of working mothers to form parent cooperatives or to patronize privately run "mom and pop" and franchised schools of uncertain quality.

The trend since the 1960s toward early coaching in academic skills in preparation for the formal schooling to follow strikes us as largely misguided. We feel that much of the academic force-feeding and pressure found in a number of preschools is poorly managed and potentially a menace to sound intellectual and social development. We particularly deplore the attitude that children have to be prepared to survive in conventional schools. No amount of academic cultivation in the best preschool can stand up to the deadening effects of the average public school. At the same time, however, some preschool educators, trying to protect children against forcing, may underestimate their intellectual capabilites and block them from learning things within their capacities but outside the accustomed province of the nursery school. Such views are founded on the critical-periods assumption of biologically fixed and universal timetables for the maturation of learning abilities. This assumption is at best quite fragile and leads to the equally groundless belief that everyone who, for example, has not learned to read by age seven is some sort of lost soul. This view overlooks the distinction between forcing formal learning and permitting and encouraging genuine curiosity and discovery.

It is our opinion that preschools

(Donna J. Harris/The Merrill-Palmer Institute)

For most preschoolers, formal learning should proceed from concrete transactions with people, other living creatures, things, and materials.

should concern themselves with all aspects of development, fostering but not forcing, and exercising full sensitivity to each child's interests and level of development. We further believe that, for most preschool children, formal learning should proceed from concrete transactions with people, other living creatures, things, and materials. The good teacher will ensure that learning takes place through sound planning, astute choice of materials and activities, and alertness to the child's reactions.

A good preschool maintains close liaison with parents and can serve as a valuable source of parent education—and of education of teachers by parents. What we favor is a core that parents from a variety of backgrounds can accept. It is important that preschools serve all constituencies in our multiethnic, multiracial, ideologically pluralistic society.

On this note, we take leave of the preschool years and direct our attention to the middle years of childhood. You are invited to read what follows in a new frame of mind. From now on, we will be talking about the sorts of things that you can remember for yourself from your own past. The chances are that your preschool years are for the most part a closed book, but the pages of the middle years are wide open for those who will take the trouble to peruse them.

SUMMARY

1. According to the Piaget, preschoolers are in the preoperational stage of cognitive development. On the positive side, they become capable of symbolic representation, including deferred imitation. On the negative side, preoperational thought is limited by egocentrism, centration, and the absence of concrete operations. A major development at this stage is learning to draw a boundary between fantasy and reality. Conscious lying emerges as a behavior—primarily in the form of denial of misdeeds. Children at this age may invent imaginary companions.

2. The language preschool children use gives us insights into the structure of their cognitive and emotional functioning. Preschool language is often egocentric. Preschool children's descriptions and narrations are rambling and circumstantial—full of endless detail and lacking essentials. They memorize nursery rhymes, commercials, and prayers without any clear understanding. Their speech often contains remnants of baby talk, misplaced sounds and syllables, and confused pronouns.

3. Preschool children may compensate for their limited vocabularies by inventing new words, or neologisms. They note and use equivalences and are increasingly able to express the salient features of objects, actions, and relationships. Research indicates that sensitivity to the demands of complex syntactical structures does not generally develop until age five.

4. It is difficult for preschool children to think abstractly; their lives are grounded in close personal relationships. Older preschoolers are somewhat better able to think objectively. These children may successfully perform groupings such as clusters and chains.

5. In Piaget's terms, preschool children are "realistic." They think that there is one reality that encompasses objects, thoughts, dreams, wishes, and beliefs. Piaget described specialized forms of realism— verbal, picture, and moral. Preschoolers have reached a level of egocentrism that is less profound than that of earlier ages. They are increasingly able to judge the feelings of others. Another characteristic of preschool thought is rigidity, or having only a limited number of ways of responding. Children behave rigidly in an attempt to control their environment, which they perceive as inherently labile.

6. By the preschool years, all the components of adult self-awareness are in operation in a preliminary fashion. This developing self-awareness is almost a special part of the child's growing awareness of the world in general. Body boundaries become more sharply defined, but not all regions of the body are equally well represented. Differentiation of sensations is imperfect. Preschoolers have little or no knowledge of their internal organs.

7. The child's growing knowledge of self and world is accompanied by a number of fears. Fear for body intactness and fear of death are common to many preschoolers. Individual children also often develop specific irrational fears. Increased self-awareness at this stage is also reflected by the child's realization that he or she is changing with the passage of time.

8. Piaget has described a sequence of how children come to understand cause and effect. These levels of understanding appear in a stable sequence, but once a new form emerges, it coexists with the others rather than superseding them. The most primitive form of causal thought is dynamism. It is accompanied first by finalism, then by animism, artificialism, and finally by naturalism.

9. Time provides one of the frameworks in which we operate. In addition to formal time schemes, we have a sense of personal time. Preschoolers have trouble in understanding time relations, but these do become a matter of interest. Space is another basic framework, and the preschool child moves from action space toward map space, in which locations are linked into an overall pattern. Abstract space is not understood until much later. Preschool children tend to have highly labile notions of number and quantity in general; given an advantaged background, preschoolers appear to have more numerical skill than Piaget believed. Although their awareness of others' states, needs, and feelings is necessarily limited, preschool children are beginning to know about others' psychological workings.

10. The study of learning in the United States has deemphasized cognition. Some exceptions are studies of probability learning, reversal and non-reversal shifts (IDS and EDS), and learning set, or learning to learn.

11. By the time children reach the preschool years, their perception is modified—and sometimes distorted—by knowledge. They are not yet able to grasp many properties of reality that are obvious to adults. Indicators of perceptual development include spontaneous comments and actions, and responses to test situations.

12. As the number of working women with young children has risen dramatically in recent years, interest in preschools (nursery schools and day-care centers) has grown. Rather than stressing intellectual skills, preschools should concern themselves with all aspects of development, proceeding from the individual child's unique concrete transactions. The ideal atmosphere is one of involvement, with extensive interchange among children and teachers.

KEY TERMS

abstract space, 400
artificialism, 394
centration, 368
decentration, 368
deferred imitation, 368
eidetic images, 397
elaboration, 398

equivalence, 378
finalism, 393
graphic collections, 381
imaginary companions, 372
immanent justice, 383
lability, 386

learning to learn, 406
map space, 399
matching, 405
maximizing, 405
metalinguistic awareness, 373
moral realism, 383

SUGGESTED READINGS

Cazden C. B. (ed.). *Language in Early Childhood Education*. Washington, D.C.: National Association for the Education of Young Children, 1981. Many examples of preschool language, plus educational implications.

Ginsburg, H., and Opper, S. *Piaget's Theory of Intellectual Development*. 2d. ed. Englewood Cliffs, N.J.: Prentice-Hall, 1979. Piaget's theoretical writings are highly obscure and are best approached through an interpreter. This is one of several books giving a good introduction and is recommended here for its description of the preoperational stage. Geared primarily to the advanced reader.

Pulaski, M. A. S. *Understanding Piaget*. Rev. ed. New York: Harper & Row, 1980. A lay reader's guide to the sometimes obscure logic of the most renowned of child psychologists.

Siegl, L. S. and Brainerd, C. J. (eds.). *Alternatives to Piaget: Critical Essays on the Theory*. New York: Academic Press, 1978. As the title suggests, several leading thinkers examine weaknesses in Piaget's theory and propose alternatives.

The Middle Years of Childhood: Social, Emotional, and Physical Development

The period of life from age six to age twelve has been given a variety of labels, each pointing to what the labeler considers an essential characteristic of these years. To call them the *middle years* is to suggest a period of relative tranquillity between the turbulence of the preschool years and the upheavals of adolescence. To label this period the *school years* calls attention to a state of mental maturity that permits children to absorb a certain amount of systematic learning, more or less akin to what is taught in schools. To refer to it as the *gang age* points to the cardinal importance of affiliation and identification with peers—the gang. Freudians call this period **latency,** a time of supposed sexual quiescence between the Oedipus complex and the sexual reawakening of puberty. We shall question this designation in a later section. The middle years begin with the loss of the first baby teeth and end about the time that the permanent teeth (except for the wisdom teeth) are all in, so that we can call this the *age of the loose tooth.*

To Piaget and his followers, the middle years constitute the stage of **concrete operations.** For some observers, this period is noteworthy for the strong *ritualism* found in children's games, chants, and superstitions. Although children of this age are capable of playful, imaginative thinking, they can also be surprisingly concrete and literal. For instance, a first-grade teacher was explaining to the class that, for a forthcoming special assembly, the girls might want to wear dresses and the boys coats and ties. There was an uneasy silence until one little boy finally raised his hand and asked: "Should we wear pants, too?"

AN OVERVIEW OF CHILDHOOD— YESTERDAY AND TODAY

The middle years are perhaps the age that adults know least about. One reason is that middle-years children turn their backs on adults and band together in a society of children. Parents, caught up in their own concerns, tend to be satisfied to let these newly competent children go their way. And the children do, clustering for the most part into same-age and same-sex groups. At this age, the values of one's peers become considerably more important than those handed down by adults. What is more, middle-years children learn to keep their thoughts from adults. They stop thinking out loud and, besides, practice deliberate guile and deception.

Another factor in adult ignorance about the middle years of childhood is that adults take this age for granted, as though it had no secrets. Adults are concerned with how to civilize or educate their middle-years children, but it seldom occurs to them to wonder what their children are like, what the children themselves think about and are concerned with.

Yet when we stop to think about it, the middle years are easily accessible to adults. It is at this age that people begin to have organized, continuous memories rather than the piecemeal, episodic ones of the preschool years. We learn some of life's most vital lessons as babies—basic trust, attachment, identification, language—but we cannot recall the events that taught us. We can bring back snatches of early childhood, but the special flavor of that time is gone. Our school years, by contrast, are our own and can be evoked readily by the proper cues: the way we worked a loose tooth about with our tongue, the reluctance to break the last thread holding it in place, putting the now-fallen tooth under the pillow for the Tooth Fairy to exchange for a gift; the pungent and unchanging smell of chalk dust and disinfectant in a schoolroom; the memory of the books (and comics) we read; the recollection of the jokes, riddles, and rhymes of childhood; or remembering a special friend with whom we shared confidences and escapades. When parents reminisce, it is about their children's preschool years. But when adults harken back to their own childhoods, it is the middle years that they recall.

Middle-years children themselves recognize the special quality of this age. When asked what the best age is to be, preschool children and adolescents wish to be either older or younger, whereas school-age children like their own age period best. At no other age do they have as much freedom and as few responsibilities. This has not always been the case. According to Ariès (1962), childhood itself is a relatively recent invention. In earlier times, children past age seven or so were expected to act like adults. Well into this century, and still in some societies, poor children were expected to be fully productive members of the household. Six-year-olds worked in the mills and the mines and the fields, or at home in cottage industries. (We mention only in passing that hundreds of thousands of orphaned, abandoned, and runaway children lived by their wits in the city streets [Riis, 1971; Ward, 1978]). The "chores" that today's mid-

(Photograph by Lewis Hine/ The Bettman Archive)

A child laborer. In past centuries and well into this one, the children of poor families were required to work like adults in mills and mines, on farms, or in cottage industries at home.

dle-years children are expected to perform are vestiges of the life-and-death demands made on children in past centuries.

However, even when children were workers, they still found time to be children. Pieter Brueghel's sixteenth-century painting *Children's Games* and a twelfth-century Chinese painting, *One-Hundred Children at Play*, show children engaged in already venerable pastimes. Many of these activities would not look out of place on today's playgrounds or streets.

As far as we can tell, children have always spent as much time as possible in the company of their peers. From them children learn firsthand about friendship and enmity, about jealousy and betrayal, about social structures, in-groups and out-groups, leadership and followership, justice and injustice, loyalty and heroism and ideals. But even as they are becoming members of a distinct society of children, they also, sometimes unwittingly and sometimes grudgingly, learn the ways and standards of adult society.

Over the millenia, child society evolved its own special culture. This culture seems to be disappearing, but one can still find traces of it. One still finds children jumping rope and playing stickball and roller-skate hockey on the streets and sidewalks, in the parks and playgrounds. Vanishing fast are the traditional games, rhymes, jokes, riddles, tricks, superstitions, factual and mythical lore, and skills. These were all transmitted virtually intact from one childhood generation to the next, with no help from adults and often in spite of them.

The traditional childhood culture was in fact two cultures, one for boys and one for girls. The male ethos emphasized toughness, daring, disdain for the weaker sex—in a word, *machismo*. Boys used to be dirt-streaked ragamuffins. Girls identified rather more strongly with adult values and, at least when they could be observed, maintained facades of "goody-goody" virtue. We know, of course, that both boys and girls exchanged quantities of sexual misinformation with their playmates. However, it seems that boys were far more likely to experiment with mutual masturbation, not to mention fellatio and anal intercourse. Boys were more likely than girls to smoke and to sample alcohol. Boys and girls had different games. Girls played jacks and hopscotch and jumped rope. Boys played marbles, cops and rob-

bers, and stickball. The sexes did join forces to play games like hide-and-seek and tag. Among the components of children's culture listed by the Opies (1970a, 1970b) are playful utterances, from satirical rhymes to tongue twisters, puns, and tangle talk ("The next song will be a dance sung by the female gentleman sitting at the corner of the round table"); stock wisecracks for standard occasions; various tricks, including some that cause pain; standard jeers and forms of insult ("Roses are red, Violets are blue, If I had your face, I'd join the zoo"); riddles; and counting-out rhymes and rituals.

If one can believe accounts like Joyce Cary's *House of Children* (1955) or the authors' own memories, children used to drift through life in a misty, half-focused, dreamlike, dissociated state. The children of yesteryear used to harbor endless superstitions and magical beliefs, were prone to dread and terror, and were genuinely moved by ghost stories and horror movies.

Today's children seem increasingly like the savvy, wisecracking kids who figure in television sitcoms. We have the story of a seven-year-old and her four-year-old sister, listening outside their parents' bedroom door to the strange sounds coming from within. The four-year-old asks, "What do you suppose they're doing?" and her sister replies, "Oh, *you* know. They're mating."

A more intellectual and socially aware variety of the new breed seems to be epitomized by *Children's Express*. This publication began as a newspaper, evolved into a magazine, and is now a syndicated column with reporters aged ten to thirteen and editors aged fourteen to nineteen. Among the topics dealt with in *Children's Express* are television programming, children in institutions, sex education, parental brutality, divorce, drug use and alcoholism in children and adults, and nuclear warfare. A pair of reporters and an editor journeyed to Thailand and Cambodia to interview children in refugee camps.

The accompanying newspaper article (Schanberg, 1982) describes the wish lists of first- to eighth-graders attending a private school in New York. It is worth emphasizing, as does the original article, that this school, as a matter of policy, has a particularly heterogeneous student body, considerably more so than most comparable schools. It is integrated both economically and ethnically. Note how the focus of concern shifts from the private and personal in the early grades to the more general—unemployment, poverty, war and peace—in the upper grades. Note, too, the emergence of introspective self-evaluation in the older children.

Whether one feels pleased or displeased about the change in children, it seems to be there and is probably irreversible. Children study the gaudier illustrations in sex magazines. Boys and girls dance the latest steps at mixed parties. Some even venture into necking and petting, and, late in this period, a few attempt sexual intercourse. The transformation seems to have begun when parents moved in on child life, often with a desire to give their children every advantage, and also, we suspect, to try to recapture their own childhood—ironically, even at the cost of their children's. For numerous middle-class children, life is a highly organized and tightly scheduled round of music lessons, dance lessons, horseback riding lessons, Little League practice and games, visits to the orthodontist, and other activities. Many schools now have elaborate after-hours programs for youngsters whose parents are at work. For poor children whose families meet the legal requirements, there are school-age programs under the aegis of day care. The programs are typically a mixture of doing homework assigned by their regular school, academic remediation, and activities not offered during their school day, but all too many programs are only babysitting, and absenteeism is high among older middle-years children. The children attend in the afternoons during the school year and full time during the summer, when field trips play a large part in the program. For those who can afford it, the after-school activities of the school year give way to summer school or camp. A number of camps, too, are no longer places where one swims and hikes and communes with nature and makes wampum in arts and crafts. They have become specialized schools. These include music camps, remedial schools, athletic training camps, psychotherapeutic environments dedicated to removing the flab from overweight kids or emotional problems from the more clearly neurotic, and, more recently, computer camps for children as young as six.

One of the first people to comment on the changing character of childhood was neither a psychologist nor a sociologist, but a novelist. The plight of contemporary children was amusingly and poignantly set forth in Robert Paul Smith's *"Where did you go?" "Out." "What did you do?" "Nothing."* (1957). Smith made the point that children no longer collected butterflies or seashells but bought collections already mounted, classified, and labeled. According to Smith (1958),

If Brothers Could Cook

By Sydney H. Schanberg

There are times when it's appropriate for the journalist to step aside and let others say it better for him.

Just before Thanksgiving, the 185 children of the Manhattan Country School, which runs through the eighth grade, were asked by their teachers to write down what they are thankful for or, subjunctively, "would be" thankful for if they could make such things happen.

Since this is a private school, perhaps its students have more blessings than some others, but it is a school integrated both economically and racially where two-thirds of the children are on scholarship—so their thoughts seem reasonably representative of children in this city and, I felt, worth sharing.

Not surprisingly, the younger children's wish lists (like their Santa Claus lists) at times had a materialistic bent, and their comments tended to be more self-oriented and more involved with their immediate wants—while the older students seemed more thoughtful and more concerned with others. But the younger ones also exhibited an active sense of humor—and that, too, is something to be thankful for.

Some examples from the lower grades:

"I would be thankful if my gerbils came back to life, and if it snowed, and if my cat would stop stealing my socks."

"I am thankful for the fact that my brother is still smaller than I am."

"I would be thankful if I had lots of money, and a bigger house, and all the stickers in the world, and if I could go to Boston, and if I were magic or Superman and could jump like Tarzan."

Some youngsters were very pragmatic, going right for life's crucial things.

"I would be thankful if I was better at spelling."

"The world would be perfect as long as there was no homework."

"I would like to have my ears pierced because I have wished for it for a long time, but I only want to change a little, because I like my life like it is."

"I'd be thankful if my brother could make his own dinner."

Others were serious, even plaintive, in their desires.

"I would be thankful if my sister didn't roughhouse with me because it hurts, and if I had a puppy or a kitty or a teddy bear."

"I would be thankful if I had a few more friends in my class and my father wouldn't be so strict on my brother."

"I would be thankful if I could make my own decisions."

"I would be thankful if I were not so much of a loner."

As the ages of the children rose, their

childhood lore was no longer being transmitted from child to child. For this reason, Smith felt compelled to tell chil-

dren all the things they used to tell one another.

More recently, David Elkind (1981),

remarks became more worried about the problems of the immediate world around them.

"I would be thankful on Thanksgiving if all the graffiti in Manhattan would be cleaned off the walls and ground."

"I would be thankful if people were not unemployed."

"I'd be thankful if there would be no killing or stealing and the kids on my block would stop setting fires."

"I would be thankful if everybody had food to eat and a place to stay and a doctor to check them out. People should not have to sleep on the street."

"I would be thankful if President Reagan could experience what it was like to be poor."

Occasionally, the thoughts were wishful, idealistic and realizable only on a much more perfect planet. Students said they would be thankful, for example, "if children could have their rights . . . if the whole world became one nation and there were everlasting peace . . . if people would cooperate and be more reasonable and loved each other more . . . if everyone would be treated equally, man, woman, boy or girl, everybody treated equally regardless of their color."

In the higher grades, seventh and eighth, some children became introspective and self-aware.

"Sometimes I am very selfish. I really don't realize it, but I am very fortunate. I would be thankful if people were as lucky as me."

"I am thankful for knowing that I am not perfect and that I have to improve myself in certain areas, but knowing that there are more things I am good at than bad."

Finally there were those among the 12- and 13-year-olds who searched for wisdom and, more elusive, sanity.

"If the world was full of machines and no one was around to feel or give love to one another, the world would be nothing."

"I am thankful for poems to express my feelings."

"I am thankful for having all five senses."

"I am thankful for having to go home and be safe."

"Many people are lonely and have nothing to live for. I am living today. I have something to live for."

There's really nothing a columnist can add to that.

Neil Postman (1982), and Valerie Suransky, (1982) have deplored what they perceive as rushing children pell-mell into precocious maturity. Like many other observers, Elkind deplores the pressures to achieve placed on children, the lack of opportunities to do tradition-ally childish things, and the manipula-tion of children as sex objects in adver-tising. (The fashion ads in the *New York Times Magazine* and other media have long been referred to as "kiddy porn.")

We do not know how childhood is far-ing in other lands. It certainly is not a wholly lost way of life in the United States, but what we will have to say about this period will have to be inter-preted in the light of the changing real-ity.

PHYSICAL DEVELOPMENT IN THE MIDDLE YEARS

The middle years are not all of a piece. Over a six-year span, a great deal of growth and maturation takes place. However, growth is at a much slower rate than at earlier and later age periods. While the Freudian notion of sexual la-tency seems to be contradicted by the facts, there is another sense in which the concept of latency can be applied to the middle years. We refer to the middle years as a period of **growth latency.** This is a time when growth slows down in comparison with the periods preceding and following it. The school-age child is on a plateau of growth between the first spurt of infancy and the one that foretells puberty.

The average six-year-old is slightly over 3.5 feet (105 cm) tall. There is, of course, considerable variation associ-ated with dietary and other health-re-lated factors and with race. By the time the average child's adolescent growth spurt begins (at age ten or eleven for girls, twelve or thirteen for boys), he or

she is nudging the 5-foot (150 cm) mark. During this same period, the child's weight doubles, from 40 to 80 pounds (18 to 36 kg). Muscular strength in boys dou-bles in the middle years. Girls used to lag behind boys in strength, but recent changes in girls' sex roles may have nar-rowed the gap.

Since girls begin their adolescent growth spurt a couple of years sooner than boys do, we run into a problem of classification. By fifth, sixth, or seventh grade, many girls have reached puberty, so that while they are psychologically still middle-years children, physically they are mature young women. The physical-psychological contrast becomes evident when one watches a girl, bosom bouncing, skip rope.

Striking changes come about in the cast of the facial features during the mid-dle years. From birth to adolescence, the brain case grows faster than the face. Babies and young children, you will note, have a small face topped by a high forehead. The fat pads of infancy dwin-dle during toddlerhood and the pre-school years, and by the beginning of the middle years, the child's face is rela-tively lean and the features well defined.

It is the successive losses of baby teeth and the emergence of permanent ones that distinguish the changing face of the middle-years child. The baby teeth are shed and replaced in approximately the same order in which they first appeared, beginning with the lower front teeth and moving upward and symmetrically to the rear. Six- to seven-year-olds are noted for their gap-toothed grin. When permanent teeth grow in to fill the gaps, they loom disproportionately large. Eight-year-olds are distinguished by out-sized, "tombstone" front teeth. It is only

(© Stephen Shames, 1981/Woodfin Camp & Assoc.)

Many girls reach puberty by the fifth, sixth, or seventh grade, although in terms of mental development they are still middle-years children.

in adolescence, when the nose and the chin are fully developed, that the face at last catches up to the teeth in size. Later losses and replacements are not so conspicuous, since they occur farther back. However, the shedding of baby teeth and the eruption of permanent ones go on until age ten or twelve.

A number of workers in the area of physical development have proposed the notion of **growth ages.** These "ages" provide separate measures for the various asynchronous components of physical development. Thus children's chronological age can be compared with their Height Age, Weight Age, Grip Age (the strength of their grip), Dental Age, Carpal Age (bone ossification as determined by x-rays of the hand and wrist), and so forth. Such comparisons give indices of development. We have analogies in such concepts as mental age and reading age.

In theory, the patterns yielded by measures of growth ages can predict future development. In practice, however, so many factors of health, diet, exercise, and endocrine function—not to mention psychosomatic influences—enter into the total growth process that individual predictions have to be made with great caution. Our general knowledge may, however, help to reassure the early-blooming girl that she will not grow up to be a giant, and the late-blooming boy that he is not doomed to life as a shrimp. Youngsters have to be reminded that almost everybody ends up by definition in the normal range.

MOTOR SKILLS IN THE MIDDLE YEARS

In describing the many motor skills that appear during the middle years, we anticipate to some degree our later discussions of middle-years activities.

In the past, there were strong cultural pressures leading to different patterns of mastery in boys and girls. It is only in recent times that we have learned to view without dismay boys cooking and sewing (despite a long tradition of master chefs and tailors) and girls using hand tools and power tools in shop. Girls are joining boys in increasing numbers in learning to play baseball and football (or whatever other sports the culture favors) instead of being confined to the "gentler" sports of volleyball and gymnastics. Boys, in turn, but probably in lesser numbers, are enrolling in modern dance classes and other traditionally "female" activities.

Middle-years children learn to swim and dive and, given the opportunity, to snorkel and scuba-dive. They learn to roller-skate, ice-skate, hang by their knees from exercise bars or tree branches, vault over barriers, and chin themselves. Both boys and girls learn to jump rope, snap their fingers, wink one eye, and whistle. They learn to make

(© Alice Kendell/Photo Researchers)

A young gymnast practices her skills on the rings. Motor skills flower during the middle years, and some children become accomplished athletes during this period.

themselves cross-eyed, to see double, contort their faces into horrendous shapes, and rub their bellies while patting their heads. They turn somersaults and cartwheels. They learn to cross their arms and clasp their hands and be perplexed as to which finger is which. A fortunate few become able to wiggle their ears. School-age children learn to slide needles through the upper layer of skin without hurting themselves. They ink themselves with mock tattoos. They practice and master tongue twisters. They learn to carve wood with a knife and to chop wood with a hatchet.

Children become proficient at controlling various modes of locomotion. They used to ride scooters, although we have not seen one in years. The latest vogue (which may have vanished by the time you read this book) is roller-skating, a fad not only for middle-years children but also for adolescents and young adults. Most middle-years children cannot afford the Walkman radios with which older skaters block out the sounds of cars and pedestrians and in time with which they cavort through the streets. Children learn to ride two-wheeled bicycles, and the more affluent graduate to mopeds and trail bikes. Given the right conditions of affluence and climate, kids operate snowmobiles. Depending on the opportunity, middle-years children can learn to ride horses, sail sailboats, or operate power boats. Many children, through observational learning, can manage an automobile competently by the late middle years. We have not heard of any middle-years airplane pilots, but nothing would surprise us.

Farm children, of course, learn appropriate skills, from milking cows to fishing eggs out from under reluctant hens. They drive tractors and other farm machines and take part in planting and harvesting. In some parts of the country, the school year is adjusted to free farm children during the times their labor is needed most. It should be noted that the multiplying skills of the middle years are coupled with potential dangers to the child and to others. For example, if firearms are kept in the house, they should be safely locked away. Too many serious, even fatal, accidents have occurred when suitable precautions have not been taken.

(© Rick Smolan/Stock, Boston)

Middle-years children become proficient at controlling various modes of locomotion.

THE SOCIETY OF CHILDREN

As we have said, it is during the middle years that children embrace and revel in their status as children. They neither yearn backward to babyhood nor aspire forward (with some exceptions to be noted) to adolescence and adulthood. Although school children live within adult society, they maneuver their way through it, preoccupied with the concerns of childhood. Theirs is psychologically a separate world. Even though children and adults intermingle in space, they take as little heed of each other as do squirrels and pigeons feeding in close proximity. It is fascinating to walk down a city block, ideally after the evening meal in summertime. One can observe child and adult societies carrying on their activities in and around each other, but oblivious of each other except when they collide. Children step aside for passing cars without breaking the rhythm of their game. The driver of the car slows down for the children, but without really noticing what they are doing. Strolling adults are unaware that they are walking through a game of stickball or stoopball at a crucial moment, while the children barely pause to let the alien adults pass.

The conversations and the greetings of the adults blend in the observer's ear with the shouts, chants, and jeers of the children, but the two sets of sounds do not interpenetrate. And along the shifting boundaries between these two societies are strung the younger children. The toddlers and younger preschoolers are the responsibility of the adults. However, the older preschool children and young middle-years children are the charges of older brothers and sisters, who keep watch on them with a bored but remarkably efficient eye. Some of these younger children on the fringes start to join in with the gang. Instead of hanging back and keeping out of the way, they edge in closer, watching, listening, taking in, imitating doggedly. They participate whenever allowed to, as when they retrieve a stray ball, gratefully accepting whatever crumbs of attention and recognition come their way. The full-fledged older gang members enjoy great prestige and authority in the eyes of these younger hangers-on.

By age eight or nine, the transition to the gang is usually complete, and with it the adoption of the gang's values, manners, and speech patterns. Parents are often distressed to find that their recently loving and outgoing child seems to have lost his or her affectionate and confiding nature and become a stranger to the family. While children are consolidating their attachment to the gang, they are likely to be taciturn and sullen with their parents. When they do speak out, they are likely to be insolent. They affect odd mannerisms, gaits, and postures. Their speech is likely to be slurred and careless and peppered with curse words and obscenities. As we shall see, this is a passing phase. Nevertheless, it is one in which a basic shift in loyalties takes place.

In one sense, the immersion in being a child and the strong peer-group affiliation of the middle years look like time out from the process of development. From another standpoint, these attachments to the peer group seem necessary and valuable in finding an identity. Preschool children take their identities from their parents and other authority figures. With their preschool identity as a base, middle-years children are ready to begin the quest for an independent identity and existence. School-age children can perceive and judge their parents with some degree of objectivity. They know that the parents have frailties and imperfections. Children begin to realize, however dimly, that their parents cannot be counted on for perpetual psychological and material support, and that they are going to have to find stability in themselves. This is too frightening an enterprise to be undertaken individually. The gang thus serves as an intermediate reference point. Each member upholds

School-age children live in a psychologically separate world; by eight or nine, they are generally one of the gang—and faithful to its values, speech patterns, and manners.

and fortifies the others' "Declaration of Independence" from total reliance on adults. This apparent time out is in fact a moving away from the parents toward a self-sufficient identity.

The Structure of the Peer Group

The gang may have many degrees of organization. These range from a loose cluster of children playing in the schoolyard or the street to well-defined pairs or groups of friends; from clubs founded for the sake of having a club to special-purpose clubs such as ball teams or delinquent gangs. We might point out that children of this age can play in pairs or

groups, but not in threes. When three children play, two of them almost inevitably band together against the third.

Probably the first real acts of affiliation are the sharing of a secret and the formation of best-friends attachments. The child's "best" friend may change from day to day, or best friends may accumulate: "You know what? I have four best friends." Genuine affiliation with a stable group, culminating in love for the secret society, is found in the middle middle years. By the later middle years, clubs and gangs are less likely to exist primarily for the sake of belonging or for the formal rites they practice. They are more likely to be organized around particular kinds of activities and functions. The older school child is likely to be involved, and can handle (although not without strains and conflicts), multiple affiliations.

Children who live close together play together. If they all go to the same neighborhood school, school and place of residence jointly reinforce the geographical basis of peer-group structure. Geographic divisions in many American communities correspond closely to ethnic and economic divisions. Therefore, neighborhood affiliations may help perpetuate in children's groups the same homogeneity, segregation, and prejudices that prevail in adult groupings. Affiliations are often made within the home block. Outside "our block," a child may be in alien or even hostile territory.

Depending on the number of children available, the neighborhood play group with its unannounced but regular meetings before and after the evening meal, may either include a variety of kids playing together or break down into subgroups, divided according to sex and age. In some areas, there is direct continuity between childhood play groups and adolescent street-corner society.

Children's neighborhood affiliations may be partially offset by other factors. Schools may draw children from several neighborhoods (although we suspect that busing has little influence on choice of playmates). Adults may foster visiting relationships. And after-school activities or summer camp may provide the chance to meet new children in an organized setting. In some thinly populated suburbs where neighborhood groups cannot easily form, the telephone may become a major medium for maintaining contact among peers. Here we

must note an age difference. Younger school-age children transact their business and hang up. Older children (and adolescents) hold protracted, often whispered and furtive, exchanges. We should also remember that in the suburbs there is much adult-sponsored organization of children's activities. Adults may steer their children toward those organizations and activities that seem socially most advantageous.

Certain individual children—usually the more outgoing and energetic, full of ideas for things to do, and, sometimes, the best-looking, strongest, wittiest, and most mature—become especially popular and exercise some power of leadership. However, children of this age are in many respects hard-headed pragmatists. When it comes to engaging in particular activities—a game of baseball, say, or staging a play—they look for leadership to those children competent in that activity.

Group organization and status rankings are measured by a technique called **sociometry** (Hallinan, 1981). Each member of the group is asked to choose another member as a partner in a number of varied activities, from going to camp to doing homework. From the pattern of choices, one can construct a diagram representing the status hierarchy within the group. The arrows standing for choices will converge on the stars. Those on the receiving end of few or no choices can readily be identified as the outcasts. Reciprocal choices imply friendships. However, there are problems in determining just what activities correspond to lasting friendships. Furthermore, group relations in the middle years are decidedly unstable. As slight a shock as a vacation period can produce a marked reorganization. Even the new boys and girls do eventually gain admittance to the group, and almost any event, such as being hurt in a car crash, can make the pariah suddenly the object of everyone's awed admiration.

The Sex Cleavage

An important structural feature of the peer group is the **sex cleavage,** the fact that boys and girls tend to form separate groupings. This used to be so during the full range of the middle years but, along with other aspects of childhood, it is changing, especially among the older middle-years children and even among the middle middle-years children. Nevertheless, a nine-year-old boy, enumerating the guests who were coming to a party and asked whether girls were to be invited, replied emphatically, *"No* girls!"

Segregation by sex does not become pronounced until about age eight. Nowadays, though, eleven- or twelve-year-olds and even ten-year-olds have mixed-sex parties, including dancing and some furtive necking in secluded corners. Indeed, if adult vigilance is relaxed, the merry-makers will put out the lights and make smooching the rule. Even at its peak, however, the sex cleavage is not absolute. Brothers and sisters sometimes play together, especially when there are no other playmates available. If the after-dinner play group is small, distinctions of both sex and age are lost in the interests of having enough children to play the usual games. Unrelated boys and girls sometimes find themselves with no same-sex playmates around, and they manage very well together. The probability that the play will include some sexual exploration is high.

(© Jean-Claude Lejeune/Stock, Boston)

Segregation by sex does not become pronounced until about age eight. This polarizing of boys and girls reflects the views of traditional adult society.

In recent years we have seen an assault on the sex cleavage by girls demanding the right to participate in organized athletics. Although there has been considerable resistance on the part of male team members, coaches, and fathers, little by little the barriers to integration are being eroded.

The sex cleavage is partly a matter of differing tastes and interests and preferences, of course. But at a very basic level it is built into the childhood culture, probably as a reflection of traditional adult views on the inferiority of the opposite sex. This held true both of males' view of females and females' view of males. It seems to be the case that men and women, even when they are in love, do not like each other very much. The divorce rate appears to tell us that they find it next to impossible to live together in any sort of harmony, with, of course, many exceptions. But even as parents make a conscious effort to avoid sex typing their children, the peer group, which is in some ways more conservative than parents, does a very effective job of socializing its members into conventional views of the sexes.

Note that there is a certain asymmetry in the sex cleavage. Virtually all boys go through a period when they reject the opposite sex (with the possible exception of their mothers). They vehemently take vows of total, permanent celibacy (which is not to be confused with chastity). This may reflect a deep-seated male fear of the female, expressed in the dual image of woman as a fragile vessel to be placed on a pedestal and worshiped from afar and as a Delilah who, given half a chance, will castrate the male and drain him of his manhood. Girls also express contempt for boys, but they nevertheless nourish throughout childhood dreams of romantic love, marriage, parenthood, and living happily ever after. Their fantasies of domesticity seem not to conflict with other fantasies of a glamorous and lucrative career. However, it is left conveniently vague who will play the male roles in fulfilling the girl's romantic fantasies. It is certainly no one bearing the slightest resemblance to the male ruffians the girl knows in the flesh.

The Functions of the Peer Group

We have already of necessity mentioned a primary function of the peer group, solidarity in breaking free of adult domination. Recall that it is not simply parents whose authority is challenged by the peer group, but the adult world in general. On the lips of school-age children, "the grownups" is a term of scorn. The teacher who asks the class to identify some wrongdoer meets a wall of silence masking outrage that the children should be asked to violate the group's code against snitching.

Children frequently invoke gang authority to counteract parental authority: "Aw gee, Mom, all the other kids..." (are going on a particular outing, are allowed to stay up later, receive bigger allowances, travel after dark without an escort, watch a forbidden television show). Gangs sometimes do things that seem expressly designed to provoke adult retaliation just so they can outrun or outwit it. It is a lot more fun to steal corn from a field or apples from a pushcart if you are seen and chased. Adults who view such behavior either disapprovingly or indulgently ("Kids will be kids") are missing the true psychological point: "I can stand up to adult authority and survive."

Note that the child's "Declaration of Independence" is provisional and partial. Children do not suddenly stop loving their families or taking pleasure in family doings. Furthermore, we cannot take the child's behavior at face value. Much of children's behavior is role playing, doing and saying things to see how they feel, doing what is expected of them by peers, and living up to an image. This of course applies to all the other children whom the child sees as sitting in judgment (Minuchin, 1977). If children turn strongly against their families, it is probably an indication of the strength of the bonds that the child is trying—part of the time—to escape. If children are all bravado and self-assertion, it is because they have to cover up their doubts and anxieties. Children resist public displays of parental affection, but the child who is obviously and deeply loved is envied by those peers whose own needs for warmth have not been fully met.

Childhood society is a proving ground where children learn to function apart from adults. As such, it has its dangers. Because children cannot stand up to adults by themselves, they are doubly dependent on the gang for support and reassurance. The child's bid for independence may thus turn into a new enslavement, bought at the cost of strict conformity and complete subservience to the group (Asch, 1940; Berenda, 1950; Hartup, 1970). The need to conform is epitomized in one eight-year-old's lament: "Everybody in my class has poison ivy except me."

Such subservience to the group has two dangers. The first and most immediate danger is that pressure from the gang may force children, against their better judgment, into dangerous, foolish, or immoral acts. We are not speaking here of such minor transgressions as trying out smoking or stealing apples or experimenting with sex, which, however adults may view them, are a normal part of gang activity and appear to have no ill effects on children. What we have in mind is the serious acts of degradation or violence into which the mob spirit sometimes leads children's gangs. It is gangs of middle-years children, sometimes in concert with young adolescents, who stone the windows of passing trains and drop large rocks from overpasses onto the cars below. It is often in the gang that children are seduced into experiments with alcohol or drugs, sometimes to the point of becoming addicted.

The second, long-term danger of submission to the group is failure to grow out of it, to be able to think and judge and behave individually. This is not a hazard for most children who, it should be remembered, are simultaneously learning several sets of cultural norms in addition to the gang's: the parents', the school's, and perhaps those of a much larger culture embodied in stories, music, television, poetry, the movies, and works of art. Children may also be exposed to several different and conflicting parental cultures, those of their own family and of the families of their friends. A number of children grow up to be adults who feel threatened and disoriented and somewhat guilty if obliged to take a stand without knowing the "right" way of thinking as set by group opinion. They feel doubly bad if they suspect that their own feelings run counter to the group's. It is, of course, normal to experience some discomfort or anxiety when we are ignorant of or in conflict with group standards, but a mature identity permits us to know what our own opinions are and to stand by them confidently even in opposition to the group.

Let us note a contrary danger. Some children, meeting persistent rejection by the group, may be driven to take refuge in an inappropriate identification with adults. The "good boy" or the "good girl," who may appear to adults to be a model child, may be missing out on an important part of experience, with possible repercussions to come. Such a child's estrangement from peers may be made worse by adult acceptance and approval, as he or she comes to be known as a "goody-goody," "Mama's boy" (or girl), or "teacher's pet." In sum, then, the multiple identifications of the middle years can be quite painful. But permanent identification with either peer or adult culture can produce undesirable consequences. Children who can shift identifications to suit the needs of the situation—who can practice a certain amount of duplicity—have the best chance of working through to an independent identity.

A fascinating series of studies by Muzafer Sherif and his colleagues (1961) showed how completely the gang's mores can dominate individual members' values and thinking. The research was done with summer campers who were assigned to various activities and projects. The researchers demonstrated how they could manipulate group values, creating and undoing cooperative and competitive orientations, and producing and removing prejudice by varying group composition and goals, and by placing goals in a competitive or cooperative framework.

The group often casts children of low status in the role of **scapegoat.** This is a convenient object on whom children higher in the pecking order can vent all their negative emotions. By the magic of scapegoating, one can even assign blame for one's own misdeeds and thus free oneself from guilt and responsibility.

The ultimate badge of group membership is the nickname. The gang is quick to seize on any idiosyncrasy of constitution, manner, speech, or skill. Thereafter it treats the child in terms of this trait. Nicknames express the stereotype that the group holds of various members: Skinny, Fatso, Four-eyes, Dopey, Professor, Limpy—the total frankness of children often startles adults. Most children wear their nicknames proudly, even unflattering ones, because they symbolize their identity as a member of the group. Any recognition, even contempt or ridicule, is better than being left out. The outcasts or scapegoats would rather have the gang persecute them than act as if they did not exist. Even the label "Stinky" means that the gang has acknowledged the child's existence. Children's sense of self and self-worth comes largely from the way others, children and adults, treat them. Needless to say, self-regard also depends on demonstrated competence, and one of the features of this age is becoming able to judge one's own abilities, first by concrete comparison with others, and later by measuring oneself against abstract standards, a set of ideals.

A sense of personal power comes from effectiveness in social dealings. It is this power that group membership gives, even in driblets. The powerless individual is highly dangerous. It is those who feel ineffectual—the "nobodies" and "nothings"—who become the snipers, the assassins, the ones who go to insane extremes to make people notice them. We also know, from the behavior of people in high places, that too much power can often breed pathology. But power in moderation—from provoking contingent feedback in infancy to finding acceptance from one's peers—is essential to mental health and a secure sense of identity.

Finally, the gang provides companionship. We turn now to the sorts of things middle-years children—in the gang, in smaller friendship groups, and sometimes alone—like to do.

THE ACTIVITIES OF MIDDLE-YEARS CHILDREN

Middle-years children are everywhere. They ride their bikes all over town. They explore woods and fields and ponds. They go fishing. They scavenge for treas-

ure in old dumps. They investigate junk-
yards, abandoned buildings, and construction sites. They scale fences and
take shortcuts through yards and alleys.
They play on the sidewalks, in the playgrounds and parks, and in the streets.
They build clubhouses in vacant lots and
tree houses where they can. They fly
kites, play catch, and make snowmen.
They set up refreshment stands. They
stage shows. They make collections and
hold exhibitions of what they have collected. One middle-years boy we know
used his collection of old bottles sal-
vaged from abandoned garbage heaps as
the basis of a thriving roadside business.

School-age kids congregate at all
events and spectacles, shinnying up
lampposts to get a better view of things
or sitting on the platform's edge while
the politician practices oratorical magic.
They turn up at fires and smash-ups and
to watch the drowned body brought
ashore. They go to movies in pairs or in
packs. Outdoors, they play both traditional games like dodgeball, stickball,
jump rope, or hopscotch, and variations
on such adult sports as baseball, football, soccer, and hockey.

They continue the pattern of dramatic
play begun years earlier as they play
space explorers, Martians, war, cops and
robbers, and games fashioned after the
latest movie or television idol. Playing
doctor, of course, continues into the
school years.

Indoors, they sprawl singly or in small
groups in front of the television set, consuming endless snacks. We use the word
"sprawl" advisedly: Middle-years children drape their bodies into strange postures, which they seem to find restful.
Even as the television set flashes and
blares, the child may be reading a comic

*(© Mark and Evelyne Berheim/Woodfin
Camp & Assoc.)*

(© Leonard Speier)

**Popular games of childhood: Chinese check-
ers and an Ivory Coast version of checkers that
requires skill in counting and reasoning.**

book, switching attention back and forth with no apparent strain. Children play games like poker and authors. They practice magic tricks. They play Monopoly and checkers—some learn chess. Ping-pong has been much in vogue ever since the United States resumed relations with China. Today's American children are addicted to homegrown and Japanese video games. Some authorities fear that video-game addiction is causing children's personalities to come unglued ("TV Games . . . ," 1982). Others think the mania is fading fast. Children spend long periods listening to records. Many are photography buffs and use photographic equipment expertly. They talk among themselves about the eternal topics of childhood, exchanging sex lore (much of it imprecise) and discussing death and torture and team standings. They compare parents and their virtues and shortcomings, they talk about their teachers, and they compare anatomy. They enjoy frightening each other with talk about far-fetched menaces: Every banana conceals a deadly tarantula; one is in constant danger of being struck by a meteorite or captured by extraterrestrials. And, of course, every town or neighborhood has its haunted house. Nowadays, children talk seriously about the threat of nuclear war and how to prevent it. Many join in demonstrations for peace along with their families or in groups.

In solitude, children do things like putting their collections in order. A special word needs to be said about children's collections. Initially, they have no theme. Children simply accumulate pocketfuls and drawerfuls of miscellaneous objects with which every parent of a middle-years child is familiar. They range from faded seashells to electronic scrap to broken bits of jewelry to pieces of stuff so far gone that it is unrecognizable. But no matter how disorderly the child's aggregations seem to adults, to the child every object merits the designation of "very valuable." In fact, the objects that the child collects often take on highly charged magical properties.

As children mature, their collections become more specialized: stamps or coins neatly arranged in albums; movie magazines or comic books and records stacked in some sort of order; rocks, miniature cars, or dolls arrayed on a shelf; and even birds' nests. Collections seem to serve a deep psychological purpose by helping children master and give order to a world that often seems beyond comprehension and control. The collection becomes a microcosm that is the child's private realm. The room of a boy now grown is layered like an archeological dig with remnants of past collections: models, stamps, coins, boxes of assorted rocks, comic books, baseball cards, and no end of lists. The room of a girl now grown is similarly layered with tattered dolls, horse and dog figurines, Nancy Drew books, pictures of entertainment stars, autographs, and ticket stubs. Today's girls, of course, have rooms furnished more like those of boys as interests cross the barriers of sexual stereotypes.

A sense of magic and **ritualism** runs through much of what middle-years children do. They are fascinated by codes, ciphers, and "secret" languages like Pig Latin. Note that these emphasize both communication within the in-group and exclusion of the out-group. Again, their function is largely ritualistic. The child who has mastered a code is hard put to think of anything worth encoding. But they also contain a touch of the magic found in the special priestly languages of many societies, and the most banal message takes on a mystical tinge when translated into a secret language.

Mastery of childhood rituals reinforces the sense of participation in group ways and of satisfaction that one is in the know, that one has the key. The sense of membership in an exclusive body is demonstrated by the following ritual: Two children find themselves saying the same thing at the same time (which they naturally attribute to extrasensory perception). They instantly hook their little fingers together, make a silent wish, and then recite the prescribed formula before they break the hold with a ceremonial flourish. They then remain mute until a third person speaks to one of them and so breaks the spell. If they forget and speak without this release, the wish is lost. All the other children are aware of their role and of their power to enforce silence on the main participants until they choose to free them. One assumption of the game is that the principals should not be liberated too quickly. If anyone speaks to them too soon, this is felt as desecration of the magic moment, to be greeted by the indignant and almost equally ritualistic cry of "No fair!" The Opies (1970a) give several English and Scottish versions of the speaking-together ritual.

Young children play their games, just as they recite their sayings and perform their rituals, according to ironclad rules that permit no variation. Note the overtones of moral realism, which we described as part of the preschooler's thinking. Later in the school years, the absolutism of the early years mellows somewhat, permitting more flexible adaptation to circumstance. Children become able to accept the sorts of departures from the norm that are known as local ground rules.

Children also observe individual rituals that serve the same magical needs. Such rituals include obsessive humming and compulsive counting (including counting repeated things like freight cars, counting by fives or tens, and counting backward), avoiding or stepping on sidewalk cracks, touching every lamppost, and so on without end. These rituals are common to many children, but there are idiosyncratic rituals as well. One adult recalls how he had to be in bed and under the covers before the door swung shut or else the (imaginary) mice under the bed would bite his toes. A woman recalls how she had to get upstairs before the basement toilet stopped flushing, lest she be captured by some obscure bogeyman. In general, such rituals serve to ward off a threat, nameless or specific.

There are games and chants that go back to the Middle Ages and beyond to Roman and Druidic times and perhaps even earlier. These have been handed down through generations of almost-adolescent elders to awestruck juniors, whom they initiate, providing much of the cement for middle-years solidarity. A picture book published in France in 1657 (Stella, 1969) shows such (all-male) pastimes as butterfly chasing; riding a stick horse; playing with dolls; playing with pets; top spinning; riding a see-saw; blowing soap bubbles; swinging; playing marbles; kite flying; pitching pennies (or some seventeenth-century French equivalent); ninepins; tossing quoits; doing handstands; playing king

(© Bonnie Freer/Photo Trends)

Traditional games, passed on from generation to generation, have long been the favorites of middle-years children.

of the mountain; piggy-back fighting; shooting craps; playing leapfrog; field hockey; human wheelbarrow; and using slings, darts, and bows and arrows. Some of these same games are shown in the Han dynasty Chinese *Scroll of a Hundred Sons* dating from 200 B.C. (Fawdry, 1977). As we have said, however, the chain of cultural transmission is weakening, and the culture itself is losing out to commercial and urban pressures. We should therefore be grateful that the Opies have recorded a large part of the vanishing heritage in their charming books on children's lore, language, and games (Opie and Opie, 1970a, 1970b).

To recall the games and chants and rituals of childhood is, like the evocative loose tooth, another effective passport to our own childhood. And when, comparing recollections, someone offer a minor variation in the wording of a rhyme, we feel a thrill of moral indignation at this intolerable unorthodoxy. Our indignation is a further clue to the relative rigidity of this childhood culture and to the unthinking way we learn it as a given.

As we suggested earlier, many of the ritual games that once characterized middle childhood, games like "London Bridge," "Farmer in the dell," and "Ring-around-a-rosy," have been ceded to preschool children. Even at this age, they are not played as often as before. More durable middle-years games are dodgeball, tag, stickball, blindman's buff (sometimes rendered "bluff"), hide-and-seek, and, in some areas, marbles and hopscotch (observable in India as in Indiana, and called *Klassike* in its Russian version). You are invited to supply your own favorites. In all probability, all the traditions will soon be lost in favor of the video games on which children of all ages spend their lunch money and allowances.

Many games are played to the accompaniment of ritual chants like those that go with "London Bridge" and "Ring-around-a-rosy." There are chants for skipping rope ("Mabel, Mabel, set the table") and for ball bouncing ("One, two, three, a nation"). Closely allied are the counting-out rhymes: "Eeny, meeny, miney, mo," "One potato," and so forth. There are rhymed guessing games: "Buck, Buck, you lousy muck, How many fists have I got up? One, two, or none?" This particular specimen has been traced back to Nero's day *(Bucca, bucca, quot sunt hic?)*. One decides who will go first by "Junk and a po." Some chants are reserved for special occasions: "Ladybird, ladybird, fly away home,"

"Last one in is a rotten egg," "I scream, you scream, we all scream for ice cream," "It's raining, it's pouring, the old man is snoring." Some are magical incantations ("Rain, rain, go away"). Others are taunts: "Susie's mad, and I'm glad, and I know what will please her," "God made the French, God made the Dutch, Whoever made you Never made much," "Cry, baby, cry, stick your finger in your eye," "Lucy is a fool, And a donkey in school, If she had a longer tail, I'd hang her up for sale."

Other sorts of middle-years behavior are less formalized and ritualistic than these, but are no less closely bound up with traditional childhood culture. There are the ever-recurring jokes and riddles. These seem wholly threadbare to adults but they come as revelations to each new wave of children as the essence of sophisticated wit. Generation after generation finds fresh such antiquities as "Why does the chicken cross the road?" and "Why do firemen wear red suspenders?" One of us drove a nine-year-old to the Saturday matinee during a downpour and found himself being asked, "Why is a ghost like a rainstorm? [pause] They both come down in sheets." This was followed by "What's the difference between elephants and fleas? [pause] Elephants can have fleas, but fleas can't have elephants."

There are fads and fashions in children's jokes. Some of them endure, whereas others seem to come and go in cycles. Traditional children's humor is still with us. However, it is being supplemented by adult-produced humor, much of it manufactured for sale in the middle-years market—children control more money than most people realize. Even story-telling, that time when adult and child can be together, enjoying the sounds and content of books or adult made-up tales, is being delegated to the telephone—Dial-A-Story.

Although children are almost certainly brighter than they used to be, their brightness is not always manifested in ways that adults appreciate. For instance, many of the children who used to delight in browsing in the library nowadays spend a great deal of time punching instructions into a computer.

SEX ROLES AND SEX DIFFERENCES

We have already pointed to a number of ways that middle-years boys and girls differ from each other, in the values that govern their gangs, the games they play, and the things they collect. We have pointed to the sex typing that goes on in the family and in the gang. And we have pointed to changing conceptions of sex roles and society's gradual coming to terms with these changes. In the past, girls have tended to remain more parent-oriented, modeling peer-group culture on adult values and practices. The male peer culture has been more clearly distinct from, and even at odds with, the values professed (if not always practiced) by adults. Nevertheless, as should be obvious, boys are not uninfluenced by various adult models, for better or for worse. Indeed, a small minority of boys does not conform to the code of the pack. These seem to be boys who are studious, who read a lot, and who prefer having one or two close friends to the gregariousness of the gang. They like to relive the Robin Hood and King Arthur legends. Singly or in pairs, they invent private countries, planets, or historical events that they can draw or write about or, when they can round up a willing cast, stage in makeshift but no less heroic dramatizations. Such fantasy play should not be confused with the prefabricated fantasies of adherents of "Star Trek" and similar cults.

The ability of girls in past eras to blend peer identification with family identification reflected what Ruth Benedict (1938) called **continuity of sex-role development.** That is, girls have traditionally moved smoothly from childhood into their long-established adult roles as wife, parent, homemaker, and all the associated subsidiary functions. This probably still holds true for some number of girls. However, we must be aware that both adult roles and childhood indoctrination are undergoing profound changes.

Boys, by contrast, have usually shown marked **discontinuity of sex-role development.** In the peer group, they learn the style of the frontiersman, the two-fisted he-man, warrior, roughneck, free-swinging playboy. The sex role of the male child bears little resemblance to the life he is likely to lead as husband, father, citizen, and worker. There are still some occupations that embody the frontiersman style, but even these are usually combined with domesticity, for which boyhood offers precious little preparation. Families with limited resources are likely to make practical demands on their children from an early age, but domestic chores are far more likely to fall on girls than on boys. In general, however, sex-role continuity is greater among the less affluent.

We must also take note of transitory reversals of sex-role identification. There have always been tomboys, girls who prefer the seeming promise of freedom

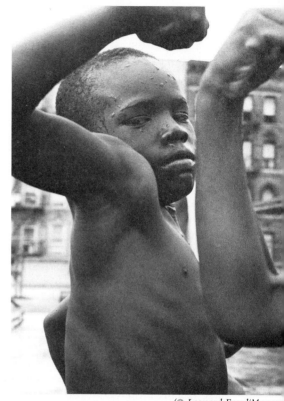

(© Leonard Freed/Magnu

There is little sex-role continuity between the macho styles that boys learn in their peer groups and the demands they will face as husbands, fathers, citizens, and workers.

and excitement in the male role. The girl may have a hard time winning acceptance from her male contemporaries, but no social stigma attaches to being a tomboy. Some people view tomboyishness as a precursor of adult lesbianism, but to the best of our knowledge, tomboys grow up to play a full spectrum of adult roles.

The boy dubbed "sissy," by contrast, is the butt of considerable contempt, expressing a deeply rooted belief that sissies inevitably grow up to be gay. We know of no factual foundation for such a belief. Indeed, some sissies we have known played the role precisely because they found great excitement in close contact with girls, indicative of strong early heterosexuality.

Boys have problems both ways, whether conforming to the conventional male role or shunning it in favor of sissyhood. The boy's largely female caregivers expect him to meet their standards of decorum, yet if he fails to exhibit a certain amount of rebelliousness, aggressiveness, and even ruthlessness, adults—women and men—are made uneasy and feel that "something is missing." Adult expectations for boys include the parts of both Little Lord Fauntleroy and Tom Sawyer. The boy is taught obedience, generosity, and kindness, but if he does not stand up for his rights, he is scorned as a weakling. Boys are expected to be ambitious and to strive for tangible achievement. At the same time, if they do not show a touch of hooliganism, they raise suspicions that they may be lacking in "the right stuff." Let us remember, though, that adults are usually not aware that they are teaching their children sex roles. They believe, rather, that they are simply witnessing, now with satisfaction and now with trepidation, the natural unfolding of male and female character.

The long-term effect of cultural enlightenment is to make males more feminine and females more masculine. Historically, as the level of sophistication rises, men become capable of feeling and expressing greater tenderness, of taking an interest in household affairs. They come to view women as equals rather than as chattels or mere sex objects, and become receptive to aesthetic experience. In parallel, women act in less dependent and capricious ways, become more analytical and logical, assert their right to sexual equality, and enter traditionally masculine occupational fields. Both women and men feel a growing freedom to define their own individual life styles independent of traditional conceptions of "normal" sex roles.

This is not to say that in the future all psychological sex differences will be abolished. It does imply that some of our assumptions about appropriate sex-linked behavior can be harmful. We brutalize boys when we expect them to act like cave men in the setting of a humane, intellectually advanced society. We brutalize girls when we expect little from them in the way of intellect and creativity, asking them to be passive, docile, and subservient, and denying them the right to develop to the full their own abilities and interests.

HOME AND FAMILY

In order to make certain features of the child's behavior stand out, we exaggerate them. In the process, we risk distorting or caricaturing them. Thus both child and authors overdo the "Declaration of Independence" from the family. In fact, home and family continue throughout this age period to be important emotional refuges and sources of love, learning, entertainment, and companionship. (Obviously, either severe economic hardship or emotional disruption makes some homes and families unrewarding. However, we are speaking here of the sorts of families usually described as normal, which, with all their ups and downs, are on balance sources of gratification.)

We must recall that the transition from family to gang is gradual. Six-year-olds, after all, retain many babyish characteristics, including a taste for silliness and a tolerance of and even desire for cuddling. They are likely to be but fringe members of the gang, imitating the ways of the older kids with literal dead seriousness and doing their bidding. The six-year-old is still likely to blab to the adults about the gang's activities and secrets. The young school-age child still cries easily. But even the cocksure twelve-year-old, fiercely independent and scornful of all things childish, finds comfort in the family and enjoys displays of affection more than he or she can admit.

We must also remember that part of peer-group life is lived at home. Singly or in small groups, children become involved in such ventures as model-building projects (sometimes grandiose in conception and hurried in execution), jewelry making, writing and staging plays, playing table games (usually on the floor), drawing pictures, and even doing homework. As we have said, they share marathon feasts while watching television. Nowadays, for those who can afford the accessories, the television screen has become a playing field for everything from logic games to intergalactic warfare. Children stay to dinner at a friend's house, they sleep over, and they take friends along on family outings.

Children have brothers and sisters as well as friends, and we need to take a moment to look at sibling relations. Granted that every family and every relationship is unique, we can risk some generalizations. We spoke earlier of the pervasiveness of *sibling rivalry*. This notion finds support in the behavior of mid-

dle-years children with siblings close in age or older. Home contacts between two siblings who are both in the middle-years age span are likely to be marked by baiting, bantering, bickering, battling, belittling, and bedlam. Just to keep the record straight, though, outbreaks of friction occur in the midst of periods in which brothers and sisters engage in joint activities, compare notes on people and events, share more or less harmoniously in family chores and in whole-family enterprises, and band together in defiance of adult authority.

If there are two siblings of the same sex who are fairly close in age, the older often takes the role of mentor to the younger. Sometimes this is accepted and welcomed, sometimes not. When the siblings are in different periods of development, the gulf is likely to seem unbridgeable. An adolescent brother or sister is inclined to be haughtily critical of the grubby, noisy, ill-mannered, sassy middle-years child. The adolescent may express doubts about their common parentage, or sometimes descend to eruptions of rage and perhaps even slaps and blows. The middle-years child shrewdly hacks or picks away at the adolescent's new and precarious dignity, commenting caustically on his or her preoccupation with physical appearance, with the opposite sex, with social standing, and on the length of time the adolescent spends in the bathroom. A brother or sister of preschool age, on the other hand, is seen by the middle-years child as constantly underfoot or tagging along, disturbing or wrecking the older child's most precious possessions, and receiving favors and indulgences from the parents such as the older child was never granted at this age. The elder child is highly jealous of the

(© Elizabeth Hamlin/Stock, Boston)

When siblings of the same sex are fairly close in age, the older often assumes the role of mentor to the younger.

hard-won prerogatives of his or her age, while the younger one resents them as preferential. Note that the middle-years child is likely to be right about the younger child gaining privileges at an earlier age. With each successive child, parents become less controlling and more permissive, and younger children do gain privileges faster. A much younger sibling—an infant or toddler—is likely to be tolerated and even treated with affection.

Parents, all too aware of the turbulence of sibling relations at home, are often thoroughly startled to learn how the children close ranks in family solidarity when an outsider threatens or abuses one of them. The terms "kid brother" and "big sister" may be used disparagingly, but they also carry considerable affection, which is supposed to be hidden from the gang.

For all their insistence on freedom and privacy from adults, for all their disrespect and defiance, and for all the fault they find with their parents and parental ways, children do not suddenly stop loving their parents. Indeed, as in displays of sibling solidarity, the same children who themselves criticize their parents freely will not tolerate the slightest slur on them from outside the family. Parents cannot hope to remain high on a pedestal, but they can learn to climb down gracefully, conceding their human fallibility, and find a new, more relaxed way of being a parent.

Let us stress that there is no sight more pathetic than a parent trying to be a "pal" to his or her child (not that there is any lack of things they can enjoy doing together). There are almost always plenty of peers around to serve as pals. Children need their parents as parents, which means as adults and not as pseudochildren. Parents sometimes have to exercise authority in a way that no pal can. Parents can no longer expect unquestioning obedience, and have to be prepared to back up their authority with solid logic or overriding necessity. But occasions arise when the need for authority is inescapable. At such times, parents will be grateful that they have not yielded to fantasies of egalitarianism.

Children need their parents to turn to when they feel cut off from the gang in one of its periodic realignments, when they are sick, or at other vulnerable moments. They need them as ethical and moral advisers, as sources of information, and simply as sources of family feeling. Being a member of the gang requires constant role playing, the assumption of the required poses, which can be a strain. Children probably do not realize why, but they feel an occasional need to escape from the strain of constant role playing, to relax, to be themselves, trading news, jokes, and confidences with the family. At bedtime, they may welcome a frolic, being read to (even though they may be proficient readers), and cuddling.

Thus middle-years children are simultaneously forming at least two patterns of identification, with their family and with the peer group (Minuchin, 1977). And, of course, they may also identify with folk heroes or heroines, fictional characters from literature or, nowadays, more likely TV or the movies, whatever models the world offers. The important point is that parents are the primary models for children, and it is likely to be their values that prevail when there is serious conflict with gang values. Some lessons may have to be taught explicitly. Children may argue heatedly against some rule at home, only to be overheard the next day passing it along as gospel to a friend. Sometimes the child's conversion to adult values follows a change in concrete behavior. In one case that we know of, the girls in a fifth-grade class had ganged up on one of their peers and were making her life a torment. When word reached the parents of one of the ringleaders, they commanded her, to the accompaniment of tears of resentment mixed with guilt, to be friendly to the victim and to invite her home to play the

next day. In no time at all, the victim had been integrated into the group and stood high in its esteem. As most adults realize, their preaching sounds fatuous to the children it is meant to influence, but parents cannot on that account abandon their notions of conduct and morals. In fact, a strong parental stand on values can be reassuring to children. No matter how much they grumble, they welcome firm parental backing which can, if necessary, be invoked in resisting pressures from the gang. Many a child, even in this emancipated era, has taken refuge in the assertion, "My mom won't let me!" There is also evidence that the children of parents who make their values known are likely to rank high in self-esteem (Coopersmith, 1967; Sears, 1970).

As children develop during the middle years, the pattern of both privileges and responsibilities obviously has to shift. As children become more competent, they have a right to expect greater freedom to roam, a bigger allowance, later bedtime. But, by the same token, they have to accept new responsibilities consistent with their more mature status. In general, American middle-class families have underestimated the capabilities of children. We hope the time is coming when children will be given opportunities to acquire practical competences and to exercise them in the discharge of family duties. We are not advocating a return to the days of child labor, but we do favor placing demands on children. We further hope that the era is arriving when privileges and responsibilities are not assigned on the basis of sex. Boys as well as girls can learn to shop, cook, clean up after meals, sew, do housework, and mind the baby. Girls as well as boys can learn to change faucet washers, shovel the walks and driveway after a snowstorm, and mow the lawn in summer. In keeping with the same trends, children can be given an increasing voice in family decisions—whether to take on a pet, how to spend a vacation—with parents of necessity having the final say. As children share in family duties, in family prosperity or hard times, in decision making, they develop a sense of the bonds of reciprocity that tie together a family and, by extension, communities and societies.

No matter how strong the bonds between family and child, the child is going to go through periods of estrangement. These may be so severe that the child experiences what are called **foundling fantasies,** suspicions, or even firm convictions, that the parents with whom they live are not their true parents. Children having foundling fantasies believe that they were born to a family of high estate and through some ghastly combination of circumstances have fallen into the hands of strangers.

Another issue that arises during these years and is related to the child's "Declaration of Independence" reflects what Margaret Mead (1942) called the **immigrant personality.** This term describes the cluster of attitudes that second-generation Americans have toward the alien, old-fashioned, often highly restrictive ways of their parents. Typically, the children of immigrants have been ashamed of the old-country ways (and language) and have striven to be as unlike their parents and as super-American as they could manage. Middle-years children, even of native-born parents, are in an analogous situation. They are alienated not from the culture of a distant

place but from that of a distant time, the past in which their parents were formed. Their immigrant personality consists in repudiating the ways of the past in favor of all that is new and up to date. For generations, children have been telling their parents that times have changed, meaning that the old rules no longer apply. In fact, times have been changing so fast that many parents have lost faith in the validity of their own standards. But while parents have to adapt to changing social climates, they also have to know that there are some enduring basic human values, and that it is their business to try to instill these in their children.

At the same time, parents have to recognize children's commitment to the peer group and its mores and understand the importance of the group for the child's development toward independence. Obviously, adults have to combat the group's more pernicious teachings, but in full awareness of the constructive aspects of group affiliation. The peer culture is a mixed blessing, but we do not know of any substitute for it or shortcut to the benefits it brings. Here, as at all ages, parents must be prepared to let children try out some enterprises that the parents know to be doomed, to let them make some mistakes and, we hope, to learn from them. And it is the job of parents to support children through the pain of failure and help them learn the lessons it teaches—without rubbing it in.

SEXUAL LATENCY

As we mentioned early in this chapter, the middle years in Freudian theory are a time of sexual latency following the repression of Oedipal or Electral strivings and all associated sexuality and memories. Sexual energy is said to be "deflected either wholly or partially from sexual utilization and conducted to other aims" (Freud, 1938). In Freudian terms, the sex cleavage of the middle years, accompanied by a lavish show of indifference and even animosity toward the opposite sex, would be an example of **reaction formation.** This defense mechanism entails going to the opposite extreme to protect oneself against unwanted wishes and feelings. The upsurge of intellectual curiosity observable in middle-years children would be thought of as **sublimation,** a redirection of id energies into socially acceptable channels. The child's rituals, chants, and literal adherence to rules and formulas would be viewed as magical devices for controlling forbidden impulses and feelings. These include the anxieties and hostilities associated with the traumatic climax of the Oedipal or Electral drama. What Freud failed to see was that middle-years children, and most particularly those of his own Victorian and post-Victorian time, learn to hide their sexuality from disapproving adult eyes.

Erikson also described this as a period of delay which allows the child to attend whatever "school" his culture provides. Erikson sees the crisis of the middle years as *industry versus inferiority.* Children must prepare to assume adult responsibilities, developing a sense of pleasure in mastering and using the skills of their culture. According to Erikson, inferiority is a product of repeated failures, leading to a general sense of oneself as inadequate, incompetent, and worthless.

Children, regardless of any theory, are very much aware of sex during this period. They are capable of sexual arousal. They are eager to acquire information and to pass it along to their peers. Most of their actual sexual activities are with members of the same sex, although generations of girls and boys have proposed, "I'll show you mine if you'll show me yours." We suspect an increase in heterosexual activity, but we have no way of verifying it. There is a steady traffic among children in off-color stories that may be poorly comprehended but are sure to elicit titters and giggles. Children likewise giggle together as they pore over the dictionary, looking up words referring to sexual functions. They read the sex magazines with lavish displays of nudes of both sexes and, if not of sexual intercourse, at least strong suggestions of various forms of coupling. We should also note the sexual component in the teasing and tussling that goes on between girls and boys.

Parents who have grown up under restrictive conditions may feel uncomfortable talking to their young children about such sensitive matters. Yet most parents want their children to know the facts of sex, to understand them, and to grow up to enjoy sex wisely and thoroughly. Their first problem is to know for themselves what the morally and psychologically relevant standards are for the conduct of adult sexuality. This is something they have to decide for themselves. Today's culture provides answers ranging all the way from total sexual license with anyone at any age to a harsh puritanism that says that sex should be enjoyed minimally, and then only in the narrow context of procreation, disarranging one's nightclothes as little as possible.

(© Donald Dietz/Stock, Boston)

Middle-years children are aware of sex and eager to acquire information on the subject and pass it along to their peers.

Moreover, parents must examine their own feelings about masturbation. However, whatever parents feel, myths should not be propagated. Masturbation is not "unnatural." It will not be punished by stunted growth, mental deficiency, warts, or hairs growing on the palm of the offending hand. It will not cause a boy's penis to drop off or make a girl sterile. These are some of the explicit threats that have been used and, as a result, many children experience some anxiety and guilt in connection with their sexual investigations of their own body.

Believers in the importance of preserving children's innocence tend to wax ag-itated at the thought of middle-years sophistication. Childhood innocence is, of course, a myth, and the best treatment for loss of innocence is to make sure that children are fully and accurately informed. There is no evidence that anyone has ever been injured by a full knowledge of sexual functioning. We are not prepared to say when the right moment comes for which kinds of sexual experience. We condemn coercion in human relations, sexual and otherwise, including the subtle psychological kind that pressures people to act contrary to their own inclinations.

The ultimate meaning of childhood sexual experience lies in how it influences the person's self-image relative to other people. This, in turn, is influenced by the values assigned by the culture to various sorts of interpersonal relations. The parents can provide models of adult love and affection. However, the internal and external forces acting on the child are so numerous that the role of the parents has to be limited to serving as models, providing full information, and offering guidelines to values.

If, then, sexual latency does not exist, does it follow that Freud and his disciples were completely off the mark in their perception of the middle years? Not quite. We have already mentioned the slowing down of growth during this period and suggested that the label of growth latency makes sense. But the fact of growth latency by itself would be of little psychological interest. What makes it a useful notion is that it is accompanied by—draw no inferences about cause and effect—a certain comfortable integrity. Children of this age seem to feel at peace with themselves and each other. One thing about the middle years has not changed. They can still be described, with only a few reservations, as the halcyon years of childhood.

In Chapter 13, we turn to cognitive functioning during the middle years.

SUMMARY

1. During the middle years of childhood, between the ages of six and about twelve years, children cluster into same-age and same-sex groups. Peer values and associations assume paramount importance. From their peers, middle-years children learn about social structures, leadership, justice and injustice, loyalty, and idealism. Children form a dual identification, with the standards of both the peer group and adult society. These sets of standards overlap in some areas and conflict in others.

2. The middle years are known as a period of growth latency because, although there is substantial physical development, it occurs more slowly than during earlier and later stages. During the middle years, the average child grows in height by about 50 percent, his or her weight doubles, and muscular strength doubles in boys and increases somewhat less in girls. The loss of baby teeth and the appearance of permanent ones distinguish the changing facial features of the middle years.

3. Motor skills flower in the middle years. Children become proficient at many types of physical activities, skills, and games. They learn to use tools and to control various modes of locomotion.

4. Peer-group structure is variable; such groups generally consist of children who live close together. Group membership has two sides: belonging and exclusion. The sex cleavage, or the fact that boys and girls tend to form separate groups, is an important structural feature of the peer group.

5. The peer group functions to create solidarity in breaking free of adult domination. Children may use their gang to show that they can stand up to adult authority and survive. However, excessive subservience to the group may force a child to commit dangerous or foolish acts or may impair his or her ability to think, judge, and behave independently.

6. Middle-years children begin to acquire collections of objects—at first haphazard and disorderly, then more deliberate and specialized. Collections seem to be a device by which children can order and dominate reality. They are fascinated by codes and secret languages, and they have a large stock of ritual games and riddles.

7. Among middle-years children, peer-group affiliation has generally been stronger among boys than among girls. Girls tend to display continuity of sex-role development. They have traditionally moved smoothly from childhood into established adult roles. In boys, however, sex-role development shows a marked discontinuity.

8. The home and family continue to be important emotional refuges and sources of learning, entertainment, and companionship during the middle years. Sibling rivalry is pervasive among children, but brothers and sisters will close ranks when an outsider abuses or threatens one of them. As children mature, the pattern of privileges and responsibilities must shift. Problems of identification are reflected in foundling fantasies and the immigrant personality.

9. According to Freud, the middle years are a period of sexual latency. Erikson describes the crisis of this period as industry versus inferiority. Regardless of theory, children at this age are aware of and eager to acquire information about sex. Ideally, parents should decide for themselves what, when, and how to explain sex to their children.

10. During the growth latency that characterizes the period, children appear to feel at peace with themselves and each other.

KEY TERMS

concrete operations, 420

continuity of sex roles, 442

discontinuity of sex roles, 442

foundling fantasies, 447

growth ages, 427

growth latency, 426

immigrant personality, 447

latency, 420

reaction formation, 448

ritualism, 438

scapegoat, 436

sex cleavage, 433

sociometry, 432

sublimation, 448

SUGGESTED READINGS

Cary, J. *A House of Children*. New York: Harper, 1955.

Golding, W. *Lord of the Flies*. New York: Coward-McCann, 1954.

Hughes, R. *A High Wind in Jamaica* (also published as *The Innocent Voyage*). New York: New American Library, 1965 (originally published, 1929).

　　Three British views of childhood ranging from a slightly sentimentalized reminiscence (Cary), through a more complex and probably more accurate novelistic view (Hughes), to a morality tale, Freudian in outlook, about the destructive forces that drive us in the absence of full socialization (Golding).

Minuchin, P. P. *The Middle Years of Childhood*. Monterey, Calif.: Brooks/Cole, 1977. An excellent overview of the middle years. See especially the section on the peer group.

Smith, R. P. *"Where Did You Go?" "Out" "What Did You Do?" "Nothing."* New York: Norton, 1957. Sheer fun, with some serious undertones.

Smith, R. P. *How to Do Nothing with Nobody, All Alone by Yourself*. New York: Norton, 1958. Ditto. A guide to a vanishing culture.

The Middle Years of Childhood: Cognitive Functioning

In Chapter 12, we saw how middle-years children withdraw some of their emotional involvement with the family and reinvest it in the outside world. Something analogous happens in the domain of cognition. Children begin to take an interest in the world at large. Let us not overstate our case. Children still spend much of their time at the level of personal involvements, and this is probably their central concern. Even so, personal involvements mean the sharing of ideas, and the ideas middle-years children share are increasingly ideas about how the world works. They begin to substitute a naturalistic world view for a magicalistic one. They learn to appraise human behavior objectively as well as affectively. They become steadily less egocentric and more capable of taking account of other people's points of view. They are intrigued by the sphere of nonhuman nature—animals, plants, weather, landscapes, rocks, catastrophes. They become able to think about things distant in time and space. They want to know about the mechanics of things, how they work and how they are made. They still enjoy fantasy, but it is no longer blended hit or miss with reality. If fantasizing in public is discouraged or ridiculed, children can keep their fantasies private. They are learning, however imperfectly, to think systematically,

(© Julie O'Neil/Stock, Boston)

Applying makeup for a play. Middle-years children begin to acquire the skills, tricks, competences, and procedures that mark them as initiates of the world at large.

in terms of organizing schemes and principles and logic. Above all else, they want to know.

Children are hungry for both knowledge and know-how. They want information, even if they do not discriminate well between information and misinformation. And they also want to acquire the skills and tricks and competences and procedures that are the badge of the initiate. But their magicalism has not disappeared. Children may think that abilities like playing a musical instrument are merely a matter of knowing the right trick. This may be one reason that children balk at practicing: They had expected a magical transformation. The same forces that move childhood rituals partly govern their approach to formal learning and give it some of the same flavor. For instance, children may consider it a major achievement to memorize the Gettysburg Address, even though they know next to nothing about its occasion. At the same time, they may ask, "You know the Gettysburg Address? [pause] 1270 Elm Street, Gettysburg, Pennsylvania."

THE STAGE OF CONCRETE OPERATIONS: THE PIAGETIAN VIEW

Piaget describes the middle years as the stage of **concrete operations.** Most generally, this means that children have some capacity for abstract, rational thought, but that they still need concrete props. They can manipulate objects much better than ideas. There are seven new competences—operations—that define this stage.

Perhaps the most important of these new competences is **decentration.** This is the ability to take account of more than one feature of a situation at a time. Decentration is associated with a second capacity, **conservation.** As we have said, conservation refers to the understanding that quantity does not change simply because a mass or a collection is rearranged spatially. For instance, when one pours a beakerful of water into a tall, thin container, the amount of water may look different, but we know logically that it is unchanged. Decentration allows the child not to become fixated on only one part of the situation. For instance, if the child notices only that the water level has risen in the new container, he or she may conclude that the amount of water has increased. If, on the other hand, it is seen that the column of water is much thinner than before, it may be concluded that the quantity of water has diminished. When the child can note that the increased height and the decreased diameter offset each other, he or she is said to compensate.

Piagetians used to treat **compensation** as the chief or only mechanism of conservation. It is now accepted, however, that there are at least two other operations that can support conservation judgments. One of these is **reversibility,** the understanding that some operations can be reversed mentally or in fact. For instance, subtraction reverses addition, and division reverses multiplication. Note that reversibility applies mainly to the realm of ideas, and only in a limited way to the world of real events. One can indeed combine hydrogen and oxygen to make water, and water can then be broken down into hydrogen and oxygen. One can run a film backward so that the diver emerges from the water and sails back onto the springboard. But one cannot break an egg more than once. In serving conservation, reversibility tells the child that if the water were to be poured back into its original beaker, or if any other original situation were restored, the quantity would be the same as before. Therefore, quantity has been conserved. The second way besides compensation of arriving at conservation is called **necessity.** One can learn to apply a test: If nothing is added and nothing is taken away, then the quantity must of necessity remain the same. However, an intuitive sense that there have been no important changes can also point to conservation.

Yet another concrete operation is **seriation.** This is the ability to place things in a sensible order, such as arranging a set of rods according to increasing or decreasing length. When preoperational children try to copy a model array of rods, they are likely to arrange the tops of the rods along an ascending or descending line, but without noticing that the bottoms of the rods form a totally disorderly zigzag. Middle-years children master such arbitrary series as the alphabet (in fact, so do many preschool children) and such logical ones as the number series. Not only can they count indefinitely, they can count by twos, by fives, and by tens; they can count backward; and they can figure out the rules of complex series like 1, 2, 4, 7, 11, and so forth. However, Walkerdine and Sinha (1981) have detected one problem that many children have in understanding numbers. They have trouble coming to terms with odd numbers. According to Walkerdine and Sinha, this is because they understand "odd" in the sense of "peculiar" or "weird" rather than its intended sense of "not even," and therefore

conclude that odd numbers are somehow tainted.

The stage of concrete operations is further marked by **transitivity.** This is the ability, given a set of relationships, to infer still another that was only implied. Thus if Linda is taller than Sue, and Sue is taller than Maria, who is taller, Linda or Maria?

Finally, we have the very important operation of **classification,** the ability to group objects on the basis of a common trait. What the concrete operator cannot yet do is conjure up a formal matrix whereby things can be classified simultaneously along several dimensions. Classification can be studied using either abstract objects like blocks, or miniature versions of everyday objects, or symbols. We have already seen how even abstract forms can be used for concrete kinds of groupings, as when the child arranges blocks in "families."

Children's classifications of real-life objects go through a developmental change during this period, a change which, as we shall see, is closely paralleled in language development. At first, children group objects together because they form some kind of functional entity. Thus a child may form a group of a dinner plate, a cigar, and a newspaper, explaining, "After dinner, Daddy likes to smoke a cigar and read the newspaper." Such groupings based on common situational contexts are called **syntagmatic.** At later ages, children become able to group things on the basis of more formal, abstract attributes. The plow, scissors, and knife go together because they are all implements for cutting. The radio, book, and semaphore flags go together because they are means of communication. The watch, ruler, and thermometer go together because they are measuring instruments. Such groupings on the basis of abstract attributes are called **paradigmatic.** Words arranged to form a sentence are a syntagmatic group. Words grouped together because they represent a common domain or belong to the same part of speech are arranged paradigmatically.

DOUBTS ABOUT THE STAGE OF CONCRETE OPERATIONS

We have said that Piaget's theory of developmental stages has been called into question. Most fundamentally, the actual behavior of children lacks the consistency one would expect if they were in a "stage" of development. That is, performance on one measure of concrete-operational thought does not necessarily correlate with performance on another measure. In sum, children seem to function at varied levels of maturity.

Another difficulty is that readiness for concrete-operational thinking is supposedly determined by biological maturity, which means that such thinking is impossible for anyone younger than, say, age six. But in fact, as we saw in Chapter 11, appropriate teaching methods allow preschool children to master at least some concrete operations. We might note that readiness theorists have long held that one cannot teach preschool children to read. Such theorists seem undaunted by the fact that large numbers of preschool children have learned to read.

Finally, critics have been pointing out that Piaget's thinking about cognition was too narrowly focused on cognizing in the realms of physics and mathemat-

(© Jo Berndt, 1982/The Picture Cube)

Scouting is one of the many adult-sponsored activities that seem to be replacing traditional children's groupings and doings.

ical logic, to the neglect of the human sphere. It is true that Piaget studied moral judgment (remember moral realism and immanent justice, p. 383) but somewhat superficially. Children's lives, of course, are overwhelmingly concerned with human relations. Children think about, worry about, and fantasize about relationships. And now we have a whole new field of study called social cognition, a field so new that its practitioners are not yet sure what it consists of.

Although Piaget himself attached great importance to his stages, his contribution to our understanding of development can easily be detached from the stage framework. We have already pointed to a number of useful nonstage concepts such as egocentrism, realism, and artificialism. In the same way, we can speak of centrated thought—thought that focuses on only one aspect of a situation at a time—without regard to the age at which it is found. We can also use terms like "unseriated" and "syntagmatic" as descriptions unrelated to age. What this amounts to is a merger of Piagetian and Wernerian thought, converting what were age-bound behaviors in stage theory to polarities of primitive and sophisticated functioning after the manner of Werner. This would in no way preclude our looking for patterns of cognitive functioning, but such patterns might turn out to be more useful for describing group and individual differences than for describing age differences.

For example, Abravanel and Gingold (1981) studied correlations among water-surface representation (recall that the primitive response is to draw the water surface parallel to the bottom when the container is tilted), the rod-and-frame test (we'll explain in a second), and IQ. To understand the rod-and-frame test, you must recall what we said earlier about field dependence and independence. Young children rely on the environment for clues to their orientation in space, whereas older children rely on internal clues. The rod-and-frame test is made up, not too surprisingly, of a rod that the experimental subject is supposed to adjust to a vertical position and a frame that surrounds the rod and gives the subject an external indicator of verticality, even though the frame itself may be tilted. Those who judge verticality by the frame are said to be field dependent, whereas those who project a standard of verticality outward from their own bodies' spatial orientation are said to be field independent. The young

are supposed to be more dependent than the mature, and girls more so than boys. IQ you know about. Studying fourth-graders in Washington, D.C., the investigators found, first, that only about 30 percent of their subjects drew the water surface in a tilted vessel correctly. Here we see pronounced individual differences. There were no sex differences. There was a sizable average deviation from true vertical in rod settings, indicating much field dependence. The expected sex difference was reversed, with boys' settings deviating from the vertical more than girls'. Correct drawing of the water surface was correlated with a high level of field independence. The correlation was greater for girls than for boys. High-IQ girls did better on the water-surface test than low-IQ girls. However, IQ was unrelated to performance in boys.

It is impossible to draw any hard and fast conclusions from such a study, but it has the virtue of showing us that relationships among various areas of functioning are likely to be complex. We may be forgiven for suspecting that many relationships that prove to be statistically reliable in one study will turn out not to exist in further studies, as in the case of sex differences in field dependence.

Still other questions have been raised regarding Piagetian views of middle childhood, including the order of emergence of concrete operations, its concept as a structured whole (Brainerd, 1974), the cross-cultural applicability of Piaget's views (Berry and Dasen, 1974), and so on. Again, there are numerous opinions, although even one of Piaget's warmest adherents has questioned the fit between Piaget's theory and the facts (Flavell, 1981).

BEYOND CONCRETE OPERATIONS

Let us look at some aspects of cognition that Piaget did not deal with. For instance, Piaget had little if anything to say about motivation. Robert W. White (1959) has proposed the notion of **effectance** or **competence motivation.** This concept says that we take pleasure in mastering our environment, in becoming skillful and competent. Research by Susan Harter (e.g., 1974) shows clearly that children take pleasure in problem solving. Fifth- and sixth-graders from favored backgrounds, given an anagrams task, smiled more (indicating pleasure) when they arrived at the correct solutions than when they were stumped, and the harder the task, the greater the smiling when the problem was solved.

Kreutzer, Leonard, and Flavell (1975) have studied children's understanding of conditions that aid or impede remembering. For instance, children were asked whether it would be easier to remember a variety of things set in a story context or simply presented as a list. They appreciated that having a context would facilitate remembering. They also agreed, correctly, that it would be easier to remember a set of colored pictures than uncolored ones. They knew that the amount of time spent studying something would affect their recall. Some age differences appeared. To test for awareness that short-term memory is fleeting, subjects were asked if, having been told a phone number, they could better keep it in mind if they dialed it immediately or went to get a drink of water first. Only kindergartners failed to realize that waiting to dial while getting a drink of water might result in forgetting the

(© Elizabeth Crews)

Making a clay pot. The concept of competence motivation is exemplified in the pleasure middle-years children take in developing skills and competences.

number. It was only at the third-grade level that children fully appreciated that word pairs consisting of antonyms (words that are opposite in meaning) would be easier to recall than pairs of unrelated words.

Older children were better able than younger ones to compare their own powers of remembering with other people's. Older kids acquired strategies for remembering. Such strategies include rehearsal—repeating material to oneself—and grouping things by categories instead of trying to retain a series of unlinked items. They learned standard mnemonic devices, such as "Thirty days hath September. . . ."

Kreutzer and associates (1975) studied another aspect of remembering that is often overlooked. We ordinarily think of remembering as referring to the past—remember last summer? In fact, however, it can also refer forward, as in "Remember (or don't forget, or remind me) to put away the meat loaf when it cools." Ceci and Ambinder (1983) have dubbed this **prospective memory.** The researchers asked children how they could be sure to remember to take their skates to school the following day. Four categories of response emerged: placing the skates where they could not be missed, writing oneself a note as a reminder, making a special effort to keep the skates in mind, and asking somebody else (guess who) to remind them. Using the skates or a note as a reminder was scored as *planful* behavior, whereas counting on one's own or somebody else's remembering was judged to be *nonplanful*. The chief developmental finding resided in the relatively large number of kindergartners and first-graders who failed to come up with any reminder strategy whatsoever. It is important to note, though, that at least some of the youngest children were able to produce mature, planful responses to all these problems.

Early in the middle years, children become able to perform imaginary acts involving tools, such as pretending to drive a nail or cut a piece of paper (Overton and Jackson, 1973). Preschool children either fail to perform the desired action or else use a body part to represent the tool: The fist becomes the hammer; fingers take the place of blades. Six-to eight-year olds, by contrast, perform these imagined acts as though they were actually holding and manipulating an invisible tool.

Still another accomplishment of this age is increasing *awareness of one's own comprehension or failure to comprehend* (Markman, 1977). In one experiment, children in grades one through three were taught how to play a game, but with one important particular omitted—how to tell who had won. After the defective instructions had been given, the children were asked a series of ten questions designed to test their acceptance of the instructions as adequate. The score for each child was the number of questions asked before the child became aware that something was missing. First-graders had an average score of 8.92, indicating a very low level of awareness that they had been given faulty instructions. The average score of third-graders was only 3.08. This score suggested that these children, if they did not immediately recognize that the instructions were flawed, rather quickly came to realize it.

Middle-years children's knowledge comes to be organized in ever more logical structures. Unlike preschoolers, for whom almost anything is possible, middle-years children are surprised when their logical expectations are violated. As we have said, stage magic is wasted on preschool children, who see nothing remarkable about the illusionist's pulling yards of fabric out of a thimble. The middle-years child is startled and fascinated by this incongruity, and may consult countless books on magic to find out how it was done.

Middle-years children become aware of their own *body processes*—respiration, circulation, digestion, sensation, sleep, and the private nature of dreaming. Note that preschool children are aware of things like their own breathing or heartbeat, but as isolated phenomena to be amused by but not to try to understand. Middle-years children learn about bacteria and viruses and diseases and may have bouts of hypochondria, imagining they have caught infections they have heard about (a condition many adults never outgrow). When city children first learn where meat comes from—meat ready for cooking or eating has little resemblance to its source—they may be quite disturbed. A number of children go through a period of partial or total vegetarianism.

The material world becomes sufficiently well organized during this period for children to be able to detect both anomalies and new relationships. They see the burst of the fireworks and notice that it takes a second or two for the sound to reach them. The concept of gravity is a major revelation, and the idea of weightlessness triggers off new bouts of fantasy. Children are fascinated by space travel and space exploration and space fantasies. They also delight in the realities of and imaginings about the world beneath the sea.

It is typical of middle-years children that they are much concerned with problems of justice and injustice, especially when it concerns them personally. Remember that "It's not fair!" is one of the rallying cries of this age. In addition, starting in the middle of this period, children think more and more about justice in society at large. Although their knowledge is still rudimentary, they become increasingly aware of economics, politics, and international relations, of widespread poverty, exploitation, and war (recall the Thanksgiving wishes re-

ported in Chapter 12). Needless to say, the children of the poor have always been aware of poverty and exploitation and injustice. Such awareness is now becoming common in all strata of society. Late in the middle years, children can talk about social issues with a good deal of sophistication. Following a demonstration against nuclear weapons on June 12, 1982, a nine-year-old boy was quoted as saying, "This is very important. If there is a nuclear war, a lot of us children will die, and some of us could be very important to the future of America." A twelve-year-old boy said, "We all want to be here in ten years" (McFadden, 1982). A growing number of children is concerned with *children's rights*. These issues involve such matters as **status offenses**—actions, such as truancy, that are criminal when committed by children but not by adults; incarceration of children without trial, including those deemed psychologically incompetent; the right of children to have a say in custody cases; and, perhaps the most startling, the right of children to divorce their unfit parents.

Note, of course, that children of this age cannot always put their passions aside in favor of rational analysis. Their thinking is still liable to throw up chunks of egocentrism, realism, ignorance glossed over with made-up facts, non sequiturs, and just about every logical fallacy known to philosophers. Most particularly, as a number of studies have shown, children fail to integrate their experience, to see the connections between and among things. For a laboratory example, Kasdorff and Schnall (1970; Schnall, 1968) show children a series of slides depicting an object in various phases of being transformed: a square

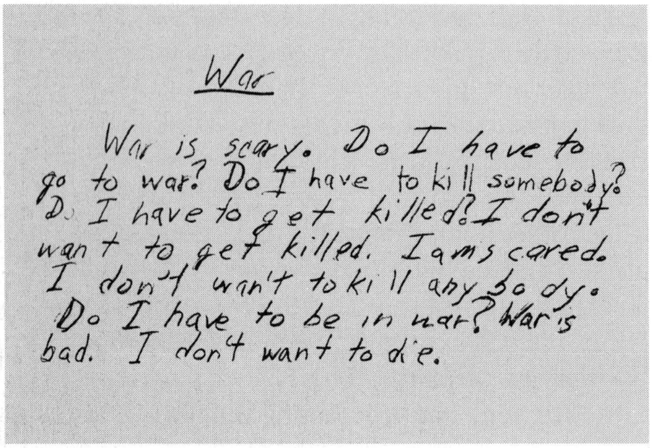

> War
>
> War is scary. Do I have to go to war? Do I have to kill somebody? Do I have to get killed? I don't want to get killed. I am scared. I don't won't to kill any body. Do I have to be in war? War's bad. I don't want to die.

> WAR AND PEACE
>
> War is common thing but peace is better because war is a feud and peace is not figting or complaining. Some kids like playing and war and soldgier.

> Money
>
> Money is important. At stores you can buy things with money if you have it. Money is just a paper with a special shape and special printings on it. But everybody knows that they can buy something with it The person they buy something from also knows that they can buy something with it and so it goes on and on

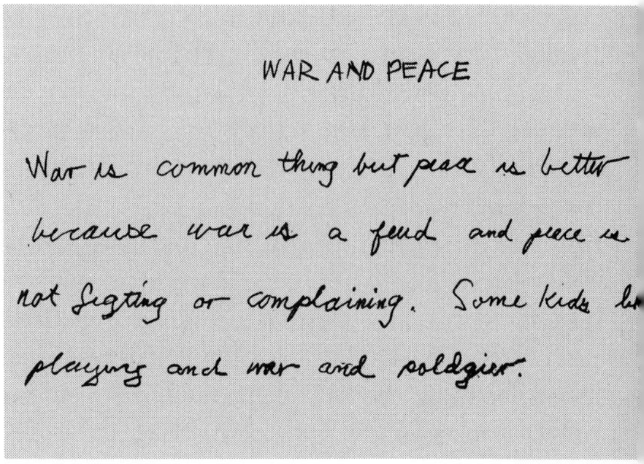

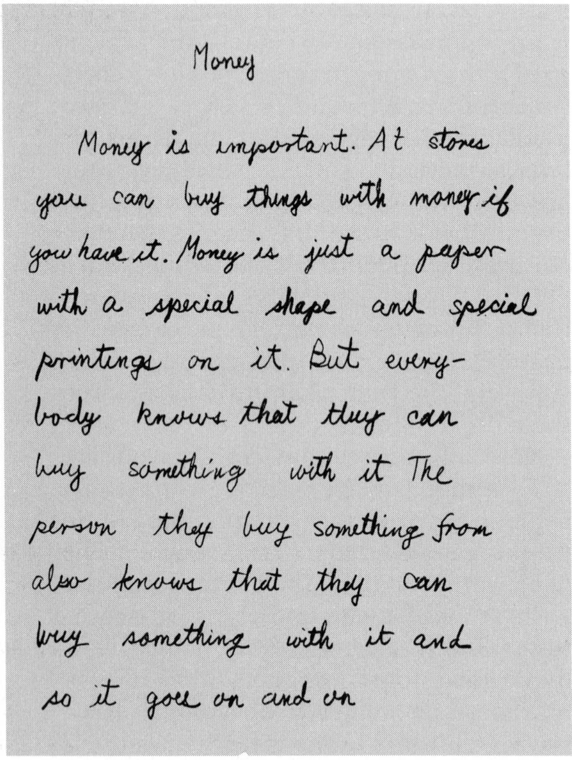

FIGURE 13.1 Social Forces Explained by Nine- and Ten-Year-Olds

becoming a triangle, a red object turning blue. Typically, children see a disconnected series of discrete objects, rather than a process.

However, we cannot help being impressed by the way today's children leave off playing to march in favor of the environment and various liberation movements and against nuclear power and warfare. Even if they do not think clearly about the issues and even if their motives are sometimes murky, they display humane intuitions, collecting funds for the families of injured firefighters, gathering food and clothing for disaster victims, and performing clerical chores for sundry social agencies.

The growing objectivity and skepticism of middle-years children have consequences beyond the realm of factual knowledge. They become able to judge their own performance by stable, external standards (Stipek and Hoffman, 1980). When children say, "Isn't this a junk drawing?" they may be fishing for a compliment, but they are also learning

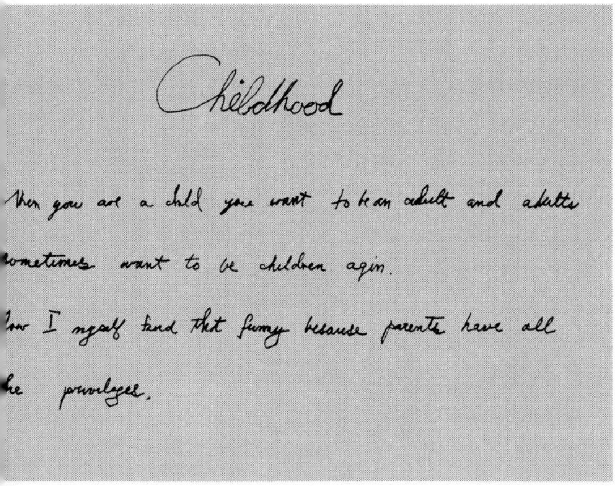

Childhood

When you are a child you want to be an adult and adults sometimes want to be children again. Now I myself find that funny because parents have all the privileges.

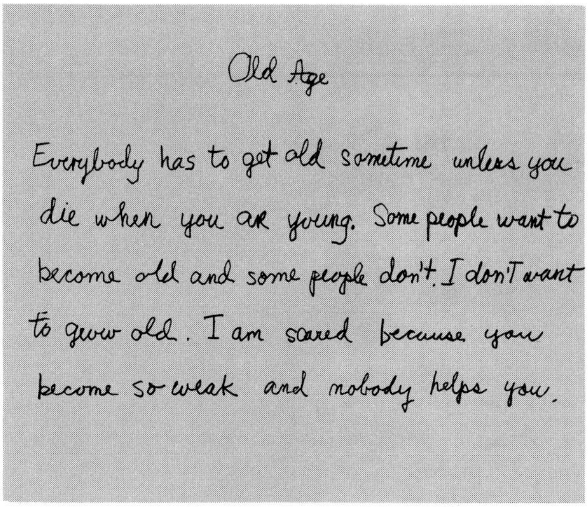

Old Age

Everybody has to get old sometime unless you die when you are young. Some people want to become old and some people don't. I don't want to grow old. I am scared because you become so weak and nobody helps you.

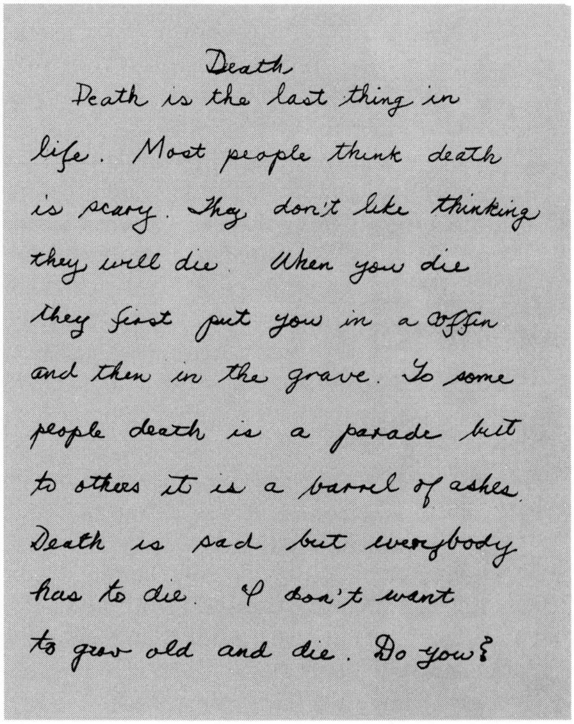

Death

Death is the last thing in life. Most people think death is scary. They don't like thinking they will die. When you die they first put you in a coffin and then in the grave. To some people death is a parade but to others it is a barrel of ashes. Death is sad but everybody has to die. I don't want to grow old and die. Do you?

FIGURE 13.2 Childhood, Old Age, and Death Described by Nine- and Ten-Year-Olds

to define criteria for judging the quality of drawings. Children come to understand norms, as in athletic abilities or academic performance. They more or less automatically perform rank orderings of themselves and classmates on every conceivable attribute, from looks to eating capacity to dancing ability (Ruble *et al.*, 1980). Another by-product of children's new critical detachment is that they turn the judgmental tables on adults. At younger ages, children were transparent objects of adult appraisal. Now they can return the adult's scrutiny and do their own judging, a gift that adults may find unsettling.

SOCIAL COGNITION

Much of what we have said so far belongs, of course, under the heading of **social cognition.** But social cognition is still a somewhat amorphous field of investigation. Its practitioners do not always agree among themselves about just what is to be studied. Flavell (1977) quotes Tagiuri (1969), who lists, as aspects of social cognition, intrapersonal attributes such as intentions, attitudes, emotions, ideas, abilities, purposes, traits, thoughts, and perceptions, and such interpersonal relations as friendship, love, power, and influence. To this catalogue Flavell adds social structures with their roles, rules, and institutions; social customs; moral imperatives ("thou shalt . . . ," "thou shalt not . . ."); the self; the difference between the constant personality and shifting moods; the difference between intrapersonal dispositions and external stimulus conditions; the possible split between expressed feelings and true feelings; and egocentrism. Damon (1981) gives as the components of social cognition coordinated social intentions (exchanges, sharing, reciprocity, conflicts, manipulations); relationships (friendship, authority); justice; social conventions; communication; higher-order social groupings (institutions, organizations, nations); learning acquired through others; collaborative problem solving; and norms and expectations (as defined, for instance, in sex roles). As you can see, there is rather more here than we can possibly deal with.

Most generally, social cognitive development deals with the child as psychologist (and to some extent sociologist). That is, the child is considered to be someone groping toward an understanding of human behavior. The favored method of studying children's psychological insights has been to ask subjects to write descriptions of people they know and like or dislike. This technique has been criticized because it requires children to construct verbal formulations of things that they may know only intui-

tively, at the gut level. Ideally, we should find ways to observe children's concrete social transactions. In so doing, we should record techniques of communication and manipulation, understandings and misunderstandings, the achievement of individual and shared goals, expressions of feelings, and so forth. Thus we might get a picture of what children can do socially rather than of what they can say about people. Something of this sort goes on in what is called **discourse analysis,** which tries to classify conversational patterns. However, the categories applied by the discourse analysts strike us as more logical than psychological.

The picture of children's social cognition arrived at through asking children to describe people they like and do not like is simple enough. Up to about age seven, children rarely mention anything about other people that could be classed as psychological. They refer to externals: physical appearance, dress, belongings. They may mention concrete behavior that implies a personal trait, as giving the child gifts may imply generosity, but they do not name dispositions. Then, children begin using global trait names such as "bad" and "nice." By age ten, children can refer to such traits as cruelty or fearfulness. Even so, they are likely to rely more on behavioral generalizations than on trait names—"He's always fighting" rather than "He's very aggressive." At this point, development pretty well comes to a halt for most people. Their vocabularies increase, but their social perceptions do not seem to improve markedly. Obviously, a few people go on to develop an elaborate and subtle understanding of human character. Several novelists come to mind, and some psychotherapists are said to be exquisitely attuned to other people's inner states.

Newman (1982) suggests that what is required in social cognition is not knowledge of how people's minds work but a command of the culture's concepts. He illustrates this with interpretations by children from the first to the sixth grade and by college students of a "Sesame Street" sequence in which one character, Ernie, deceives another, Bert. In sum, Ernie is eating a banana and Bert expresses a desire to have part of it. Ernie promises to share the banana with Bert, turns his back, and finishes off the banana. He then hands Bert the skin, saying, "See, I took the inside part and here's the outside part for you." Bert faints. Newman asked his subjects if Ernie lied to Bert. All but one first-grader said that Ernie told a lie, whereas half the third- and fourth-graders said that Ernie's promise was both a lie and the truth. This view was concurred in by seven out of twelve sixth-graders and ten out of twelve college students. Five fourth-graders were able to articulate the difference between edible and inedible parts of a banana. Some third- to sixth graders knew that Ernie had set up an incorrect expectation in Bert. Only college students could specify the distinction between literal and implied truth.

Inasmuch as the field is still in flux, we have chosen five areas of research in social cognition to talk about. These are egocentrism, altruism, prejudice, moral judgment (including authority as a subtopic), and locus of control.

Egocentrism

Let us begin by saying again that Piaget's view of the young child as pro-foundly egocentric has been considerably modified by more recent research. Piaget's original test for egocentrism was to have a child sit before a three-dimensional mock-up of a mountain landscape and identify which photograph showed the scene from the standpoint of a doll that was moved around the model. A number of critics have pointed out that to most people one mountain view looks pretty much like another, and it is unreasonable to expect a young child to differentiate among various perspectives. It was further pointed out that choosing photographs was not necessarily the best indicator of the child's understanding. Borke (1975) made up a more familiar expanse of scenery, and also made it rotatable. To identify another's point of view, the children turned the display until the requested vantage point coincided with their own. In these conditions, 79 percent of three-year-olds and 93 percent of four-year-olds responded nonegocentrically.

Note, however, that this and kindred studies are addressed to **spatial egocentrism.** This is the inability to figure out what it is possible or impossible for another person to see. Such studies do not deal with **social egocentrism,** the inability to understand and make allowances for other people's states of mind. Everyday observation tells us that middle-years children are better judges than preschool children of what other people know, think, and feel. We also know that there are distinct limits to children's ability to transcend their own ways of thinking and feeling about things. The reasons for adult behavior, for example, often elude children. In the same way, adults often forget what it is like to be a child. They may be so thoroughly egocentric with regard to children's behavior that they are outraged when children act like children rather than like adults. Note again that egocentrism does not imply selfishness. It is possible to be lovingly generous and thoroughly egocentric, as when a small boy saves up his allowance so that he can buy his mother a pocket knife for her birthday. We hereby name such behavior **egocentric generosity.** It can be observed at all ages.

We do not know what experiences help children overcome their egocentrism or whether there are ways to accelerate the process. We know only that there are marked individual differences among both children and adults in the ability to take account of others' abilities and limitations, tastes, sensitivities, and vulnerabilities. The ideal, of course, is not to become a mind reader but to recognize that there are obstacles to reciprocal understanding and communication between people. Once we accept our own unconquerable egocentrism, we become sensitized to the kind of feedback that tells us whether we are communicating effectively.

Altruism

In a series of studies, Rushton and associates (Emler and Rushton, 1974; Rushton, 1975, 1979; Rushton and Owen, 1975; Rushton and Wiener, 1975) have examined the development of **altruism** (selfless regard for the welfare of others) in middle-years children. In summary, they found, as we might expect, that altruism increases with age; that it is related to the child's level of moral development (of which more shortly); that it is affected by the experimenter's portrayal of the supposed beneficiary as either sympathetic or neutral; that it is enhanced by exposure to an altruistic same-sex model; that it is unresponsive to or negatively affected by preaching; and that it is not correlated with performance on tests of cognitive development or "intelligence."

How such studies reflect real-life behavior is hard to say. Common sense suggests that altruism is influenced by the person's egocentrism or lack thereof, by the examples to which he or she has been exposed, by the immediate situation, by unknown factors in individuals' personal make-ups, and by child-rearing practices (Hoffman, 1975). Hoffman puts particular stress on the operation of empathy. However, empathy can produce helpful or unhelpful behavior, depending on how much egocentrism is mixed in. If we all set out to live by the Golden Rule, we might end up making our neighbors very unhappy by performing all kinds of services for them that they would be more than glad to do without. Children's increasing awareness of social issues, concern for the victims of injustice and oppression, and involvement in helping others can be taken as indicators of growing altruism.

Prejudice

Prejudice has fallen out of favor as a subject for research, although the newspapers make clear that it is far from a dead issue. Even college students, who would probably deny any trace of prejudice in their thinking, betray their unspoken biases in experimental settings (Coates, 1972). Several mechanisms seem to operate in the development of prejudice, with *stranger anxiety* and the *discrepancy*

(© Telegraph Sunday Magazine, by John Marmuras, 1980/ Woodfin Camp & Assoc.)

Children are keenly aware of their parents' prejudices and often come to adopt their stereotypes about women and minorities.

prejudice carries the seeds of a self-ful-filling prophecy: Our stereotypes tell us that the members of thus-and-such a group have thus-and-so characteristics. We treat them accordingly; and lo and behold, they turn out to have precisely those characteristics.

Note that prejudice is not a one-way street. We usually think of a majority group being prejudiced against a minority, but it works the other way round, too. Hindus are prejudiced against and persecute Untouchables, and Untouchables are prejudiced against Hindus and would undoubtedly persecute them if they were given the chance. Most reasonably aware parents today would hesitate to verbalize prejudiced attitudes to their children. However, in talking about a despised group, no matter how honeyed the words, they will reveal, by tone of voice, by gesture, by body language, their true feelings. Children will also be aware, even though they do not keep score, of who their parents' friends are, the degree of welcome accorded visitors of various backgrounds, and other such indicators. Children also absorb the lesson of which sorts of people are cast in what kinds of roles. We match stereotypes of ethnic groups with stereotypes of occupations.

We can rephrase stereotyping in Piagetian terms. Stereotypes are merely a special variety of schema. Our receptiveness to new information consonant with the schema can be seen as assimilation. By contrast, our reluctance to accept information, no matter how compelling, that is inconsistent with the schema can be seen as a failure of accommodation. Accommodation comes hard, but accommodation there is. Little by little, we are coming to see once-scorned minorities

hypothesis as two key components. (The discrepancy hypothesis says that we react negatively to substantial departures from the familiar, even though we may find lesser differences attractive.) Explicit awareness of racial differences appears as early as the preschool years (Morland, 1966). Prejudice can also arise through modeling and can be rationalized and strengthened by a culture's verbal stereotypes. Once we have formed a stereotype, evidence that confirms our views is very easy to perceive, whereas contrary evidence is likely to go unnoticed. There is the further problem that (and, in the case of women, a subjugated majority) as full human beings, with the same sorts of virtues and failings as everybody else.

Moral Judgment

Piaget approached the study of moral judgment by posing pairs of situations for children to think about. He analyzed responses in terms of the extent to which children took account of intentions, punishment, authority, and other factors. He was not concerned with what children would actually do in his hypothetical situations but with the reasoning behind their answers. Here are two Piagetian examples:

> There was a little boy called Julian. His father had gone out and Julian thought it would be fun to play with his father's ink-pot. First he played with the pen, and then he made a little blot on the tablecloth.

> A little boy who was called Augustus once noticed that his father's ink-pot was empty. One day when his father was away he thought of filling the ink-pot so as to help his father, and so that he should find it full when he came home. But while he was opening the ink-bottle he made a big blot on the tablecloth (Piaget, 1965, p. 122).

The question then is asked, which child was naughtier, Julian or Augustus. In describing children's responses to such situations, Piaget brought into play such concepts as intentionality, immanent justice, punishment, and moral realism. Piaget's characterizations of children's moral reasoning did not mesh with his system of cognitive stages. However, he did propose two distinct levels of moral judgment. According to Piaget, younger children have an attitude of **ob-jective responsibility,** judging misdeeds solely according to their observed (and hence objective) consequences without regard to the actor's underlying motives. In the cases given above, young children would find Augustus naughtier than Julian because he made a bigger inkblot. His intention to help his father would count for nothing. Children older than ten or so, by contrast, evidence what Piaget called **subjective responsibility.** This is the ability to take into account subjective motives and extenuating circumstances. Thus Augustus would be adjudged the less wicked because his motives were pure.

Piaget also studied how children think about rules. He was interested not in the rules handed down by adults but those that govern children's games and are "elaborated by children alone." Piaget drew an analogy with moral reasoning because morality, too, is governed by rules. Here again, as we saw earlier, Piaget found rigid absolutism and moral realism. It is only late in the middle years that children can accept that rules are merely conventions to guide the orderly conduct of the game, and that they can be modified by common consent to suit varying conditions.

Nucci and Nucci (1982) found that children throughout the age range from seven to fourteen judged misbehavior in terms both of concrete consequences and of conformity to the rules. Children drew very little distinction between moral principles and the conventions of proper behavior.

Lawrence Kohlberg's Studies of Moral Development. Kohlberg (1978, 1981) claims to have done what Piaget could not: fit moral development into Piaget's cognitive-developmental framework. Kohlberg proposes three levels of moral development corresponding roughly to the preoperational, concrete-operational, and formal-operational stages of cognitive development. Each level is subdivided into two stages.

Level I is dubbed the *preconventional.* At this time, the child is responsive to cultural norms but is moved by the concrete consequences of various courses of action, such as reward, punishment, or tit for tat. Stage 1 is called the punishment-and-obedience orientation. Preschool children are at first made moral by their fear of punishment and deference to power. Stage 2 is the instrumental-relativist orientation. It is marked by a hard-headed pragmatic concern with maximizing satisfaction. If need be, the child can exchange satisfactions with others on a quid pro quo, "you-scratch-my-back-and-I'll-scratch-yours," basis.

Level II is called the *conventional.* Here one observes the expectations of the group, both passively conforming to accepted norms and actively promoting them. Stage 3 is the interpersonal concordance or "good boy–nice girl" orientation. Here one seeks the approval of others. Children in this stage can take account of intention to the extent of saying that someone means well. Stage 4 is the law-and-order orientation. The child is respectful of authority, fixed rules, and the social order as it exists.

Level III is named the *postconventional,* or *autonomous,* or *principled.* At this level, the individual seeks to find or to formulate general moral principles that are independent of any particular culture's teachings. Stage 5 is the social-contract, legalistic orientation. "Right action tends to be defined in terms of

general individual rights and standards which have been critically examined and agreed upon by the whole society" (Kohlberg, 1978, pp. 50-51). We quote so that we cannot be accused of quarreling with our own paraphrase when we ask why such guides to action are anything other than conventional. Stage 6 is the universal-ethical-principle orientation. At this stage, the individual has achieved the ultimate conscience, guided not by rules but by a coherent, consistent body of principles. (Kohlberg cites the Golden Rule as an example.)

Kohlberg's scheme has been highly influential, especially in educational circles. It has provided the foundation for what is called **values clarification,** attempts to arrive through discussion at the essential issues involved in what are called **moral dilemmas** (Beyer, 1978; Scharf, 1978a, 1978b). A moral dilemma that almost everyone has heard of features the man whose wife is dying of a rare disease. The local pharmacist has a cure for the disease, but he charges an arm and a leg for it, and the distraught husband feels that he cannot afford to part with an arm and a leg. The moral dilemma here is whether the husband should ignore the law and steal the medicine or let his wife take her chances. The moral dilemmas typically involve only two choices, although in the real world the range is usually more complex. It is noteworthy, too, that the druggist does not seem to be trapped in a dilemma, even though he or she seems to place a higher value on money than on human life.

Kohlberg's views have provoked some harsh criticism. For instance, his Level III seems to reside mainly in the realm of the theoretical, since practically no research subject seems to attain it. In a recent publication of Kohlberg and his associates (Colby, Kohlberg, Gibbs, and Lieberman, 1983), Stage 6 seems to have been dismissed from consideration because of its rarity. Some critics quarrel with Kohlberg's scoring system and the wide scope it leaves for subjective interpretations (Kurtines and Greif, 1974). Others note the large discrepancy between what people say and how they behave, which is what really counts (Alston, 1971).

The central issue, it seems to us, is how one defines the moral domain. Kohlberg, as far as we can tell, defines it only by implication. What we find in various moral dilemmas is an overwhelming concern with property rights. The moral dilemmas proposed cover a wide range (Scharf, 1978c), from throwing a paper airplane in class to a boy who violates his father's taboo on tree climbing to rescue a neighbor's kitten, from euthanasia on request to capital punishment, from using drugs to espionage. However, the one recurring, insistent theme is property rights. Apparently it would threaten children's innocence to talk about exploitation, the abuse of power, pollution and depletion of the environment, corruption in high places, or the morality of nuclear warfare.

Kohlberg tells us that individuals construct their own moral codes in keeping with their cognitive capacities. Youniss (1981) takes issue with this view. He proposes instead that people construct their moral codes socially, through discussion and debate and the emergence of consensus. Shweder (1981) takes issue with the rationalism of Piaget, Kohlberg, and Youniss alike, saying that the two mechanisms of moral learning are enculturation and the imposition of authority. The second of these mechanisms may derive from the castration anxiety postulated by Freud as a key to the development of the superego. We agree that modeling and conditioning play an important role in teaching children the culture's code of conduct (including the principle that one is not always expected to practice what one preaches). However, we would like to say that the basis for morality in general is love, attachment, and basic trust. If one thinks of morality as putting other people's needs on a par with one's own, then its most obvious source is intense emotional involvement with people. We think both Kohlberg and Youniss are right about later development. One would hope that a great deal of thought is devoted to sorting out moral issues. But one would expect a large part of such thinking to take place in the context of bull sessions rather than in solitude. However, there is no reason to believe that cognitive maturity automatically brings moral maturity into being. All too many cognitively advanced people are perfectly willing to sell their intellectual skills to the highest bidder, with little regard to the moral issues involved.

Authority. Closely implicated in moral reasoning are relationships to authority. William Damon (1977) has proposed a six-stage model describing the evolution of authority-obedience relationships. The first is based on *attachment* and *identification*, and it is marked by convergence of the desires of the authority figure and the child. The second is based on *physical attributes of the authority figure*, such as size, and is characterized by a pragmatic sense that obedience is likely to pay off in rewards. The third is

(Bobbi Carrey/The Picture Cube)

Authority relationships are closely implicated in moral development.

based on the authority figure's *strength or social power*, and obedience arises out of respect for the seemingly omnipotent authority. The fourth derives from the *manifest superiority* of the authority, and the child obeys from a sense that obedience will buy protection. In the fifth stage, the authority figure is seen as superior, but as a result of *special preparation* rather than innate qualities, and obedience is founded on respect and on faith in the authority's concern. In the final stage, authority is parceled out among a variety of figures, depending on the situation. In addition, authority is based on an *agreement between the ruler and the ruled;* authority and obedience can continue only as long as they appear reasonable to the individual doing the obeying.

Moral Judgment in Everyday Life. It used to be that children judged misbehavior far more strictly than did adults, and favored torture or execution as a fitting answer to almost any degree of mis-

conduct. We suspect that such harshness represents children's concern about keeping their own impulses in check. Such moralism still exists among children, but it is our impression that children, along with the rest of society, are becoming more tolerant of lesser infractions. In the peer group, of course, children may be governed by moral codes that adults would consider intolerably constricting. Needless to say, the peer group's code can be quite relaxed in areas where society would like to place restraints, as in smoking or sexual play, but it becomes murderously strict in areas like snitching to the grownups.

Obviously, children violate both adult codes and gang codes and, like adults, find devices for avoiding guilt. They become masters of denial (which may include loss of memory of the misdeed), rationalization, and self-justification. In general, the defense mechanisms against guilt entail using the magic of words either to abolish a reality or to reshape it into something acceptable. This process is greatly facilitated by children's literal-mindedness. The letter of the law is more important than its spirit. Children argue legalistically for the narrowest possible interpretation: "You said not to run. I was only walking fast." Note, though, that both children and adults have double standards so that they judge other people's infractions rather more harshly than their own. Thus children who regularly play free and easy with the truth are outraged if they discover that an adult has told a lie.

A great many social psychologists and sociologists would argue that moral codes play a minor role in most people's behavior. Instead, a substantial part of the population plays the game of **situa-**

tionism, adapting their standards to the conditions of the moment, with little or no regard to principle. Indeed, for a great many adults it appears that the single guide to conduct is one vital anti-principle: Don't get caught.

The somewhat less cynical and opportunistic values that most parents probably want for their children are first learned primarily as feelings picked up from parents and other models. In favorable conditions, they take shape also as ideas. In the final analysis, being good probably consists mainly in being able to control one's own behavior. However, no one has yet resolved all the possible ambiguities. If one accepts self-sacrifice as an important part of morality, there will still arise instances in which one's own welfare seems rather more important than someone else's, and it seems likely that selfishness will sometimes prevail over principle.

Locus of Control

Locus of control lies at the intersection of cognition and personality and is an important dimension of self-awareness. It refers to the extent to which one feels in control of events or is the passive, helpless plaything of external forces. Thus the child who has failed a test can blame it on internal factors, saying that he or she did not study hard enough or is too dumb to learn or, externally, saying that the teacher made the test too hard or graded the child's paper unfairly. If a child does well on a test, internal localization would be implied by a statement about how hard the child had studied, and external localization by a remark that the test was ridiculously easy.

The study of locus of control has been formalized in what is called **attribution theory**—one attributes performance to either situational (external) or dispositional (internal) factors (Weiner *et al.*, 1971). It is not hard in real life to find people projecting blame for their failures on circumstances beyond their control or hogging credit for an achievement that could never have happened without other people's contributions. In the laboratory, children can be asked to judge stories or can be given problems to solve (anagrams are a perennial favorite) in which task difficulty can be manipulated or the child can be given differing kinds of feedback (true or false) about his or her performance relative to that of other children. In attribution theory, both internal and external forces are of two kinds. The two factors in internal determination are ability and effort. In external determination, they are task difficulty and luck (paranoids might be able to think of other external determinants).

Here we must pause a moment to prevent possible confusion. Attribution theory is used in social psychology to refer to two related but distinct things. It means what we have just said it means. But it also points to the fact that we make judgments about other people. These judgments are based on anything from the person's name to reading an account of his or her psychoanalysis. That is, this sort of attribution theorist is interested in how we ascribe attributes to people, not how we assign credit and blame.

In general, development seems to proceed in the direction of internal locus of control. That is, people become increasingly able to take responsibility for the events in their lives. There are, of course, complications. Sometimes external factors are truly to blame. People do not have to feel guilty if their houses are destroyed by a tidal wave. The passengers are hardly accountable when an airliner crashes. One may sometimes be called upon to do things that simply lie outside the scope of one's powers. Thus the developmental ideal seems to be the ability to appraise with a level head all the factors, internal and external, that operate in situations.

Some people, children and adults, feel helpless to control their own destiny. In today's parlance, they are said to be suffering from **learned helplessness** (Dweck and Goetz, 1978; Seligman and Beagley, 1975). This notion comes to us from animal psychology. Rats are subjected to stressful electric shock. One group can learn to escape the current, either by working a switch or by moving to another part of the cage. The other group is unable to escape the current and can only wait miserably for it to end. Now the two groups of rats are dumped into a pool of water. The rats that were exposed to inescapable shock simply sink beneath the surface and drown. Their experience in the shock cage has taught them the lesson of learned helplessness—since all control is localized externally, there is no point in struggling. The rats who were able to escape shock, by contrast, struggle to escape from the water also. They still localize control internally and therefore seem to think themselves masters of their fate. They are wrong, of course. After a while, exhausted by their own struggles, they, too, sink beneath the surface and perish. (They have to be allowed to drown because time spent struggling is the key measure.) Some psychologists have found an analogy between learned helplessness and various degrees of depression in people.

LANGUAGE IN THE MIDDLE YEARS

By the beginning of the middle years, children have mastered some key fundamentals of language, but they still have a long way to go. They do not yet understand figures of speech or irony or sarcasm. This does not mean total literal-mindedness, although literalism

(© Jean-Claude Lejeune/Stock, Boston)

Middle years children learn to read and write at ever-higher levels of sophistication.

can be a problem in communication. Middle-years children understand perfectly well such nonliteral language as jokes and lies (although they are quite gullible and will accept as true all but the most outrageous assertions). They also are sensitive to at least some of the unspoken implications of utterances. Middle-years children learn to read and write, and learn to do so at ever-higher levels of sophistication.

Everyday Language

Let us first look at children's language as it is manifested in everyday life. We will then consider instruments for the formal study of language and what these tell us about linguistic development in the middle years.

At the heart of the middle-years child's cognitive status is the ability to detach word from object and see the word as symbol. Preschool children are trapped in verbal realism, and they find it hard to disentangle symbol and object. Of course, people never completely outgrow verbal realism. It is word realism, let us remember, that makes some topics unspeakable, driving people to euphemism and circumlocution. Politicians talk about "police actions" instead of "wars," or children assuage their guilt by talking about "borrowing things" instead of "stealing." It is word realism that allows politicians to frighten us with fabricated bogey men. But it is also word realism that allows us to participate vicariously in stories, to respond to poetic evocations, and to enjoy playing with language. Verbal realism is a mixed blessing, but a blessing all the same. Without it, language would be logical but totally flat, lacking color or vitality or half-hidden meanings sporting just beneath the surface. Its logic and starkness would not even guarantee its accuracy or veracity.

Middle-years children come to realize, though, that words and the things they are supposed to stand for exist on quite distinct levels. This differentiation of levels gives children new freedom to manipulate symbols, as seen in the delight they take in playing with words and meanings. Children who have an opportunity to learn about them are typically fascinated by rhymes, alliteration, tongue twisters, codes and ciphers, anagrams, foreign words and phrases, and the split meanings of puns and double-entendres ("Why does Mrs. Santa Claus have trouble getting pregnant?" "Santa comes but once a year"). Akin to punning is playing with the ambiguities of language, as in "I simply can't bear it. It's much too heavy" or "You want me to take my vitamins? O.K., I'll take them to my room." Children play with the notion of nonexistence, as in the poem about "The Little Man Who Wasn't There." They love big words and use them liberally, with only the vaguest idea of what they mean. They comprehend broad travesty and burlesque, and a favorite occupation of some children is composing playlets satirizing television programs and commercials.

Levels of meaning are incompletely differentiated, and for many children language is only partially differentiated into words. Even the compositions of college students reveal such gems as "alot," "alittle," and "anotherwords" (try saying the last aloud). Such lack of differentiation may be a factor in difficulty in learning to read, since the divisions of words on a page may correspond only partially to the sound groupings the child hears and uses. Traces of immature language persist throughout this period. They can be heard in double negatives and in past tenses of irregular verbs: "Harriet baby-sitted with us over the weekend." (College student to friend: "He hitted me real hard!")

Mostly, though, middle-years children become increasingly able to dominate language, to make it do their bidding. As at other points of near mastery, they practice their linguistic skills tirelessly. They try reading and writing backward, from right to left, and writing with their nondominant hand. As children make progress in reading, the mechanics are functionally subordinated to meanings, so that it takes an effort to see the letters themselves. For instance, the Stroop color-word technique employs color names printed in ink of a color different from the color named, so that "red" might be printed in blue ink, and "blue" in green. The more proficiently children read, the harder they find it to name the color of the ink (Comalli, Wapner, and Werner, 1962; Sichel and Chandler, 1969).

Middle-years children are fascinated by coded talk and writing. Their codes, ciphers, and secret languages have a largely ritual function, including that of emphasizing communication within the in-group and exclusion of the out-group. Beyond such ritual, the child who has mastered a secret language is hard put to think of anything to say in it. Secret modes of communication contain a touch of the magic found in the special priestly language of many societies. Even the most commonplace message takes on mystical significance when couched in pig Latin or laboriously transcribed into code or cipher. The irony, of course, is that these "secret" languages are known throughout childhood society, and even the ciphers are variations on a few simple themes.

In these days of computer-competent children, computerized cryptography, and, we are told, children who know how to invade commercial computer records and drain off funds for their own accounts, the systems of past generations of children may seem hopelessly antiquated. Nevertheless, here is a widely-used cipher:

A	B	C	D	E
F	G	H	I	J
K	L	M	N	O
P	Q	R	S	T
U	V	W	X	Y

FIGURE 13.3 The symbol for each letter (Z is squeezed out in this system) is simply the set of lines wholly or partially enclosing that letter. Thus, ⌐ = A, ⊐ = K, ☐ = S, and Γ = X. The reader can figure out the following message, using these rules:

If one wanted to be particularly sneaky, one could start the alphabet at the lower-right-hand corner. It is apparently beyond the cognitive scope of most middle-years children to think of assigning the letters at random to the various

Middle-years children learn to recognize and react to a number of conventional symbols.

(© Robert Eckert/Stock, Boston)

locations. A variation on this cipher consists of four three-by-three matrices, with otherwise identical spaces differentiated by a dot, a diagonal, an X, and an *. This scheme permits all twenty-six letters and the ten digits besides. Just as every child used to learn some version of this cipher, so did they all learn pig Latin. Nowadays, we suppose, they communicate by interactive video.

Middle-years children pick up foreign words and phrases and take special pleasure in using them, as in *bon jour* or *bonne nuit, beaux rêves*. They are abundant users of slang, much of it scatological and much of it taken over from teen-agers. We refrain from giving examples because they go out of date too rapidly.

Beyond language, children learn to recognize a great many conventional symbols, such as the Star of David, symbolizing Judaism; the Cross, symbolizing Christianity; flags symbolizing nations; the three balls emblematic of the pawn shop; and the striped pole announcing the barbershop. Children may grasp even more subtle symbolism: The police officer symbolizes authority; the expensive car, high status. Note a distinction between symbols and signs. Symbols, whether words or emblems, change meaning according to context. Depending on the circumstances, the police officer can symbolize either a respected or feared authority, can stand for violence, or for oppression. Signs, like traffic lights and road signs and the beam from a lighthouse, have a single fixed meaning that consists of a specific course of action.

Children also learn about such advanced symbolic devices as maps, diagrams, charts, graphs, and even blueprints. They become proficient in the basic manipulations of numbers, such as multiplication and division, the understanding of decimal and ratio fractions, and perhaps even extracting square roots. Note that all these burgeoning symbolic skills imply new levels of metalinguistic awareness. As an index of sophistication in the use of computers, children have gone into the business of writing computer programs.

Techniques for the Formal Study of Language Development

A number of techniques, some of them used in IQ tests, reveal systematic changes in language ability during the middle years. Let us survey a few of the better-known approaches.

Vocabulary Tests. One of the most venerable tests associated with IQ is the so-called vocabulary test. It is assumed that the normal child's vocabulary increases with age, and the brighter the child, the greater the increase. Vocabulary-test scores do indeed correlate well with other measures of mental ability and are generally considered the most useful single assessment tool for linguistic development. However, from a developmental point of view, vocabulary tests have at least three major flaws.

First, there is a cultural bias built into the very concept of the test, regardless of the choice of words to be defined. Children from groups in the cultural mainstream are taught to define words. However, children from other subcultures may not learn to make words an object of formal analysis and are likely to take word meanings for granted. The choice of words to be defined can, of course, contribute still another dimension of cultural bias.

A second major problem with vocabulary tests is that they simply sample the number of words known. They give very little attention to the qualitative changes that take place in children's styles of defining words. An analysis of these changes would make clear not only that children know more words as they grow older, but also that they acquire more effective strategies for talking about word meanings. Indeed, as a measure of psychological flexibility, one might also want to take note of how many different meanings and uses children can find in the same word. The child is given credit for defining "nail" either as a finger- or toenail or as a fastening device, but no extra credit for knowing both. The scoring manuals for the tests make no mention of the difference between "nail" as a noun and as a verb, or the metaphorical verb in "nailing a criminal."

To return to styles of definition, younger middle-years children may seize on a single feature or function which, while accurate enough, is insufficient to define the class of things named. Thus "bicycle" may be defined as "It's got pedals" or "You ride on it." Later in the middle years, a bicycle becomes "Something that you ride on [for lack of the word *vehicle*], and it's got two wheels, and these pedals that you push, and handlebars to steer with." By the end of the middle years, a linguistically competent child may tell the tester that "A bicycle is a two-wheeled, pedal-propelled vehicle."

The third major problem with vocabulary tests is that they are supposed to measure both the size of children's vocabularies and the difficulty level of the words children can deal with. In practice, difficulty is judged by rarity of use rather than by conceptual difficulty. Thus "contumely" and "traduce" are seldom heard or seen and so rank high in difficulty on vocabulary tests, but they do not stand for anything hard to understand. "Contumely" simply means "abusive language," a notion with which most people beyond the cradle are familiar. "Traduce" means "to slander or defame" or, in the common parlance, "to bad-mouth." Words like "parasite" and "synopsis," by contrast, are more common and easy to use, but may be harder to define.

Similarities and Differences. Also taken from intelligence tests is the task of specifying how two seemingly unlike things resemble each other, or two similar things differ. In general, it is easier to say how things differ than how they are alike. Specifying differences is an act of analysis, and specifying similarities an act of synthesis. Even the toddler can tell us that "Doggie bark, kitty meow." But this order of precedence is not absolute. We have already said that the child may have trouble articulating the difference between bread and cake, and many children find it hard to pin down the difference between "house" and "barn."

A fairly stable sequence can be observed in the detection and specification of similarities, through the administration of verbal classification or concept-formation tests. These ask the subject to group words, rather than solid objects, according to common features. The five- or six-year-old may misconstrue the task and, asked in what way a cat and a mouse are the same, reply "The cat chases the mouse." You will recognize the concrete, syntagmatic, action-bound nature of such a response. At a more advanced level, children seize on peripheral, nondefining characteristics of the two things being compared. They say that "A cat and a mouse both have whiskers" or "They both have four legs," or that an apple and a peach are alike because "You eat them both." At a still more advanced stage, childen are able to name abstractly, formally, paradigmatically, the class of things to which the two objects belong. They can make explicit that apples and peaches are fruits, that bicycles and boats are means of transportation, and that cats and mice are animals.

Note that among non-Western children and adults, syntagmatic groupings are the rule (Cole *et al.*, 1971). This does not mean that people from the poor countries are unable to produce paradigmatic groupings. Rather, they consider such abstract arrangements foolish, unrelated to the workaday world of survival and family life. We Westerners nourish a faith that, even though we cannot point to any practical applications of our mental gymnastics, such exercises somehow contribute to intellectual superiority.

In any event, the ability to define words or to link words paradigmatically should not be thought of as some kind of general mental mechanism that develops in the brain or elsewhere in the child. A child's level of competence varies with the sorts of materials to be thought about. It is much easier to deal with concrete nouns like "shoe" than with abstract ones like "justice." It is easier to manipulate nouns than adjectives like "proud." It is easier to say how a boat and an airplane are alike than to specify the similarity between salt and water, the numbers thirty-six and sixty-four, or first and last. The child who can say that a pear and a banana are both fruits may still respond to a pairing of salt and water with "They make salt water"; or to the pairing of coal and paper with "Paper is white and coal is black" or "You can write on paper with a piece of coal." Children may have special difficulty finding similarities between opposites like first and last. It requires considerable sophistication to appreciate that, in order to be opposites, things must belong to a common dimension or domain.

The Detection of Absurdities. Another form of verbal problem found on some intelligence tests calls for the detection of absurdities or incongruities. For example, "They looked out and saw that it was raining, so they decided to leave their umbrellas at home" or "The man found a shirt that fit him, but he decided to buy it a size smaller in case it should shrink." To young middle-years children, the obvious illogic contained in such statements may be anything but obvious. In the context of an IQ test, there is no opportunity to explore a child's response and try to reconstruct his or her thought processes. It is possible that if children were presented the relevant information one item at a time, they could connect the items and see the absurdity of the mismatched elements.

Seven-year-olds are shown pictures of absurd situations. Beginning at age eight, children are asked to deal with purely verbal descriptions. As might be expected, there is steady improvement with age in performance on the absurdities task.

Proverb Interpretation and the Understanding of Metaphors. During the middle years, children have trouble comprehending *metaphors*. A metaphor is the designation of something by a nonliteral label that implies a point of resemblance, as when the Emperor of Ethiopia referred to himself as the Lion of Judah. Metaphors are a poetic device to make something more vivid than would a prosaic, literal label. Other figures of speech, such as similes, hyperbole, or personification, are likewise wasted on middle-years children. They can understand dead metaphors (metaphors that have been used so much that their metaphorical origins have worn off, like the "dead" in "dead metaphor") from their contexts, just as they understand other nonfigurative words. For instance, children know perfectly well what is meant by "a sweet person," but they deny any connection to the sweetness of sugar (Asch and Nerlove, 1960).

Proverbs, many of which are phrased metaphorically, make generalizations about conduct. Asking children to interpret proverbs (e.g., "The leopard cannot change his spots") reveals how they make sense of both literal and figurative statements (Billow, 1975; Richardson and Church, 1959; Winner, McCarthy, and Gardner, 1980). Proverbs can be worded either literally ("Absence makes the heart grow fonder") or figuratively

("You can't teach an old dog new tricks"; "Don't wash your dirty linen in public"). They can be either prescriptive, pointing out desirable courses of action ("Look before you leap"; "He who hesitates is lost") or descriptive ("Every cloud has a silver lining"; "It's an ill wind that blows no good"). Whether literal or metaphorical, prescriptive or descriptive, any proverb stands for a whole class of antecedent-consequent relations, a set of situations and what follows or should follow from them.

Young middle-years children interpret all proverbs as literal statements about particular situations or events. Children's responses sometimes suggest an undifferentiated image. Thus "Every cloud has a silver lining" becomes "A big bright thing shining in the sky." Children may convert a proverb into a story, adding, rearranging, or omitting information. For instance, a nine-year-old boy defined "A stitch in time saves nine" as "Well, there was this boy, about nine years old, and he got a cut and had to have some stitches."

When children do begin to sense the two-layered, metaphorical meaning of proverbs, they fail to see that there has to be a structural correspondence between the highly concrete metaphor and the broader, more general literal statement it implies. Thus each term in the original requires a matching term in the paraphrase. When children first attempt to deal with proverbs as metaphors, they respond physiognomically to dominant features of the proverb. For instance, a nine-year-old boy rendered "An ounce of prevention is worth a pound of cure" as "Well, if something is too heavy for an old person, you could help him carry it." Here "ounce" and "pound" seem to

make weightiness the central theme. Some interpretations show a misunderstanding of particular words. Another nine-year-old said that "Absence makes the heart grow fonder" means "It makes your heart grow weaker, I guess." The chief misunderstanding here does not seem to be of "fonder," which could probably take on a variety of meanings depending on context. Rather, it seems that the key to this child's interpretation is "absence," which means, to this child and many others, sickness, by a process of you're - absent - from - school - because-you're-sick. Sometimes emotional and moral associations shape interpretations. A number of middle-years children have difficulty with "Revenge is sweet," not because it is a metaphor but because they believe that finding pleasure in hurting people is wrong. Children try to soften their interpretations, as in "You don't revenge too hard" or "It means the same thing as forgive." It is not until the late middle years that children give translations from concrete metaphor to general literal meaning that show close structural correspondences, so that "You can't teach an old dog new tricks" comes out as "When people are used to doing things a particular way, they find it hard to change."

Twenty Questions. A favorite technique for studying verbal thinking is the game Twenty Questions, which can be played by having the child either figure out what the experimenter is thinking or guess which of an array of pictures is the "right" one.

According to studies in this area, there seem to be three main developmental steps in children's approach to Twenty Questions. The first is simply to guess at what the experimenter has in mind. Next comes a disguised form of guessing: Children describe the guessed object instead of simply naming it. The most mature strategy is called **constraint seeking.** The child asks questions that rule out whole categories of possible answers and thus narrows the field to a manageable spectrum of remaining possibilities.

The Word Association Test. The **Word Association Test,** as almost everyone knows, consists of a series of stimulus words presented one at a time. The subject is instructed to reply as fast as possible with the first thing that occurs to him or her. The Word Association Test was invented by the well-known Swiss psychoanalyst Carl Jung as a way of probing emotional difficulties. Extremely unusual responses (e.g., "mother"—"butcher") or long delays in responding are supposed to point to areas of emotional concern.

However, it has been found that the Word Association Test can be used to study normal language development as well as emotional troubles. Systematic changes can be traced through the middle years. Young middle-years children typically produce syntagmatic associations, just as they produce syntagmatic classifications. A typical syntagmatic response would be "sister"—"fights." Characteristically, in syntagmatic associations, stimulus and response words belong to different parts of speech. In the example given, "sister" is a noun and "fights" a verb. In a syntagmatic association such as "fire"—"hot," we have a noun coupled to an adjective. By the end of the middle years, children are more likely to give paradigmatic associations, in which the response word stands in an abstract, formal relationship to the stimulus word. The most common logical relations between stimulus and response are opposition ("black"—"white"); coordination ("chair"—"couch"); subordination ("gem"—"diamond"); and superordination ("table"—"furniture"). In paradigmatic associations, stimulus and response belong to the same part of speech.

There are some highly predictable pairings regardless of age. "Black" almost invariably evokes "white." However, the reverse does not hold. "White" is most likely to elicit a syntagmatic "snow" or "paper." There are some ambiguities. Pairings like "pencil"—"paper," "knife"—"fork," and "chair"—"table" meet the formal requirements for paradigmatic responses, but psychologically they may represent highly concrete syntagmatic associations. In any event, a number of studies have shown a consistent rise in the proportion of paradigmatic responses by American children over a span of more than half a century, indicating a rise in verbal competence.

Communication among Children. Communication among children in everyday life is far from perfect (as among adults), but it is adequate. Two children may end up using their fists to settle a fine point of fact or logic, but most of the time they make themselves understood with words. In the laboratory, one can introduce impediments to communication and watch how children devise strategies for overcoming these impediments.

The typical procedure for studying what are called **referential communication skills** (Glucksberg, Krauss, and Higgins, 1975) is, as we have said before, to seat two children on opposite sides of a table with a screen blocking their view of each other's doings. Thus whatever information is transmitted between them has to be verbal. Both children are provided with the same set of objects or pictures or designs. One object is designated for one child and he or she is given the job of describing the object in a way that enables the second child to pick it out of his or her set. There are a couple of constraints. For one thing, the objects are selected so as to be unnamable. They can be talked about only through a description. They may all belong to a common category, such as faces, that has a name, but the key object must not be identifiable in terms of a single label. A second constraint is that the sets, although made up of the same objects, are not arranged in the same order. This is to prevent the use of such strategies as "It's three from the left and down two."

Progress in communication during the middle years shows up in a shift from physiognomic, highly personal, egocentric, inner-speech characterizations of stimuli (a face may be described as "It looks like my cousin Tom"; a nonsense figure may be described as "It looks like two dogs having a fight") to highly differentiated description that zeroes in on just that combination of features that distinguishes the target object. For instance, faces can be varied so that they are presented full face, three-quarter view left or right, or profile left or right. The eyes and mouth can be shown open or shut, hair can be long or short, the ears exposed or covered, and so forth. The skilled communicator might say something like, "It's the one where you can see both eyes, except they're shut, the straight-line mouth, and the long

hair." The child on the receiving end will, as in Twenty Questions, progress from guessing to asking constraint-seeking questions like "Which way is the head turned?"

A related task is to have a child teach another to play a game that an adult has just taught to the first child (Flavell *et al.*, 1975). Here the chief problem in communication between younger middle-years children is persistent egocentrism. The young child who is doing the teaching seems to take it for granted that his or her pupil already has access to the purpose and procedures of the game. Older middle-years children, by contrast, assume that the other child is ignorant of the game, although they may make use of analogies with other games familiar to both teacher and learner.

Other Findings from Research on Middle-Years Language

One interesting but puzzling study is concerned with the relationship between time sequences in sentences and an aspect of cognition less obviously tied to language, *transposition* (Feldman and Barsky, 1975). Transposition means several things, but in this context it refers to understanding that left and right are transposed for two people facing each other. Until about age seven, children cannot grasp that their own left is opposite the other person's right, and their right opposite the other's left. This is shown by the simple task of asking the child to point to the other person's left or right hand. In Feldman and Barsky's study, transposers and nontransposers were compared in their understanding of time relations in sentences, which we have already discussed with reference to complex sentences connected by "before" and "after." Nontransposers could understand time sequences only when the order of mention corresponded with the order of occurrence, as in "The baker read a book and then he made a cake and then he lit a candle." Transposers could understand, but nontransposers could not, sentences in which the order of mention was reversed from the order of occurrence, as in "Before the clown rolled the ball, he ate the pizza." Johnson and Chapman (1980), studying children's understanding of causal connectives, also found that many six-year-olds assimilated order of occurrence to order of mention. However, they did not investigate ability to transpose. We are not clear about why transposing should be related to sentence comprehension, but there it is.

In another study, young middle-years children were divided into conservers and nonconservers (Sinclair, 1967). Their task was to compare a short, thick pencil with a long, thin one. Conservers typically gave coordinated descriptions, saying, in effect, "This one is short but fat, and that one is long but thin." Nonconservers, by contrast, gave run-on descriptions, such as "This one is long and that one is short, and this one is thin and that one is fat." Sinclair attributes the difference to conservers' ability to decenter, to take account of two dimensions, length and thickness, at a time. The nonconservers' centrated descriptions do not tell the listener whether length and thickness are systematically related.

There is a growing body of evidence showing what we should have known all along, that what children remember from a narrative or an extended description (assuming that they understand it to begin with) is the *sense* of what is said rather than the words used to say it. Thus in tests of recognition of material to which they have been exposed, subjects accept paraphrases that do not change the meaning. However, they reject sentences very similar in wording and structure to the original but conveying a slightly different meaning. In other words, substance prevails over form. One component in such understanding is the ability to draw inferences—that is, understanding things that are not explicitly stated but are strongly implied. There is a striking improvement between ages six and ten in the ability to make correct inferences, although a majority of six-year-olds are already sensitive to some obvious implied meanings (Paris and Upton, 1976). For instance, to say that a boy hears his father chopping wood in the barn implies, although it does not say so, that the father is wielding an axe. Johnson and Smith (1981) studied the inferences drawn from written material by third- and fifth-graders. Both groups could grasp the implied meanings contained in a paragraph. But fifth-graders could, and third-graders could not, carry their inferences over to a series of related paragraphs. According to the authors, the third-graders' difficulty was partly a matter of memory, but even more a matter of failing to integrate their inferences. It is our opinion that this is two ways of saying the same thing: Studies of remembering tell us that if one is to retain material, one must "process" it. Processing usually means rephrasing it in one's own words and establishing associations with established knowledge to make it a part of one's own cognitive framework.

From time to time, people have been

amused by children's failure to understand a key feature of American life: money. Entertaining anecdotes are told of how all money comes from Daddy who, when he needs to replenish his funds, runs out and "catches a check." Berti and Bombi (1981) report that it is not until about age eight that children have a coherent sense of how money and merchandise are related in buying and selling. Younger children insist that *every* transaction must conclude with the giving of change.

A study by Saltz, Dunan-Markiewicz, and Rourke (1975) falls in the domain of verbal social cognition, since it asks children's judgments of characters created by the experimenters. As we might expect, children find it hard to cope with human complexity, real or invented. For instance, eight-year-olds deny that one can simultaneously be a father (which is perceived as a positive attribute) and a drunkard (which is perceived as bad). In general, value judgments and feelings take precedence over fact and logic in the reasoning of young children, but middle-years children are increasingly able to sort out and reconcile seemingly incompatible attributes.

It should be clear by now that the distinction between cognition and language is an artificial one. Without denying the importance of the pragmatic, emotional, and preverbal and nonverbal cognitive foundations of the early years, we must recognize that language and other kinds of symbols play an increasingly intimate part in cognitive processes. They extend and enrich them so that eventually we can use language to transcend immediate experience and move about accurately in predominantly symbolic domains.

All told, then, the world of the middle-years child includes isolated domains or segments of experience that are logically organized and about which the child can reason maturely. However, the world as a whole has not yet come together as a coherent, integrated system. Clouds of magicalism surround and sometimes invade the more orderly realms of thought. As we said earlier, this is not necessarily bad. We need occasional infusions of magic to charge up humdrum reality. The trick is knowing where to stop.

SCHOOLS, SCHOOLING, AND EDUCATION

We are not prepared to offer either a psychology or a philosophy of education. We presume to think that we know how to raise individual children to be bright, well informed, thoughtful, compassionate, interested, and perhaps even creative. But when we contemplate taking a cohort of three and a half million five-year-olds and nourishing them intellectually through thirteen or seventeen years of schooling, our heads reel. At best, we can offer some thoughts about cognitive cultivation and then suggest some ways of thinking for your consideration.

Let us begin by observing that education and schooling are not synonymous, and schooling is not always educational (Macchiarola, 1982). Education can go on not only in schools but also in the family, in books of fiction and nonfiction, in newspapers and magazines, on television and in movies, in the playground, in the bushes, and in the gutter. This brings us to two related observations:

(© Leonard Freed/Magnum)

(© Davis Pratt/Photo Researchers)

(© Lynn McLaren/Photo Researchers)

Schools in other settings: (Top) An orthodox Hebrew school in the United States; (Left) Learning to read in Iran; (Above) Learning to count in Tanzania.

First, the graduates of our most prestigious educational institutions, when placed in positions of power and public trust, have sometimes conducted themselves with almost unrelieved stupidity and immorality. Our second observation in turn comes in two parts. First, many of our most valued citizens have had very little schooling—Mark Twain comes to mind. Second, many of our brightest lights were, as children, written off as hopeless clods and dunces. Ronald Illingworth (1973) has compiled a list of people who, if they were going to school today, would be classified as problem children with severe learning disabilities. The roster includes Albert Einstein, Claude Bernard, Carl Jung, Alfred Adler, Gregor Mendel, Charles Darwin, Thomas Edison, Galileo Galilei, Edouard Manet, Pablo Picasso, Paul Gauguin, Auguste Rodin (who could not even get into art school), Hans Christian Andersen, Honoré de Balzac, Jean de la Fontaine, Oliver Goldsmith, Leo Tolstoy, Emile Zola (who earned a zero in literature), Beatrice Webb, Johann Heinrich Pestalozzi, Mahatma Gandhi, Winston Churchill, and G. K. Chesterton. These eminent figures, as children, had trouble reading, spelling, doing arithmetic, and just about everything else connected with school. This is not to say that maladjustment in school is diagnostic of genius—or even that all these people were necessarily gifted. However, it sometimes seems that creativity and group schooling do not mix.

We have asked a great deal of our schools, and disappointment may have been inevitable. Starting about 150 years ago, we decreed that schools should make every normal child into a literate, patriotic American citizen who, according to his or her rank in the social order, could function well in the world of commerce. Needless to say, there were different emphases in the education provided for males and females, even when they shared the same classrooms. But the general goals were pretty much the same. The schools went further. They offered not only a chance to maintain one's social rank but even to improve it. Obviously, this could not be for everyone, but those who managed to stand out were to have been duly rewarded (de Lone, 1979). Over the years, our definition of literacy expanded until it included the elements of a liberal education for all comers.

The Civil Rights Movement of the 1950s and 1960s made us aware that our original commitment to educate everybody and to give everybody, through education, an opportunity to rise through the system, had defined "everybody" in a rather peculiar way, excluding a sizable proportion of the population. The schoolhouse doors were opened a little wider to admit those who had been excluded. Much to our surprise, we learned that another sizable segment of our population was not in the least hospitably disposed toward the newcomers, and many schools became racial battlegrounds. At about the time the schools were making room for a new constituency, many of their old customers took off for the remote suburbs. The cities' tax bases were weakened, school budgets were cut, and many school systems began to come apart at the seams.

However, sociological factors are not everything. For us, the really basic problem is that too many children are uninterested in learning. More precisely, they are not interested in learning what the schools have to teach, at the time and place at which schools want to teach it. Without openly acknowledging the problem of missing motivation, the schools have adopted various strategies for getting children to learn. All these work to some degree, but each exacts a price. One strategy is coercion and is exemplified in authoritarian classrooms in our own country and in the educational systems of many countries of Europe. Coercion is effective in teaching more children more knowledge than any other approach, but the price is high.

Note that well-loved, well-brought-up children dutifully learn the things that schools teach them, but not because they care particularly about what the schools have to offer. They are just in the habit of doing what the grownups tell them to do. As they begin to exchange insights in the peer group, they develop ways to outwit the adults and make themselves look good, avoiding censure and winning praise. Children come rather quickly to perceive that knowledge and understanding are not what school is about. Rather, the important things, beyond docile comportment, are course units, grades, diplomas, certificates, and, eventually, degrees. Children become adept at scholarly gamesmanship. They find respite from the tedium of the classroom in each other's company, where they can discuss the really important things in life, such as movies, TV programs, liaisons and fallings out, and league standings, among other things.

We believe that our caricature is a fairly accurate portrayal of most schools. We must insist, though, that there are occasional schools that truly engage pupils' interest and emotions, that open their eyes to the larger realities, and make the labor involved in learning seem truly worthwhile. Such schools seem to have four characteristics. They have a strong administration with humanistic values and high intellectual standards. They have teachers who are devoted and well informed. They offer a diversity of programs so that every individual can find an appealing channel into the world of learning. And they have budgets large enough to pay their staff a decent wage, have a comfortable, well-functioning physical plant that includes

(© Richard Sobol/Stock, Boston)

Working on the school computer. Schools are still trying to figure out how to make the most effective use of computers.

computers, laboratories, studios, shops, and athletic facilities, and to buy necessary learning materials and equipment. It is perfectly true that throwing money at the educational system will not produce high-quality schooling. But it is likewise true that if we wish to offer decent educational opportunities to all our children, not just those whose parents can afford private schools and not just those who come equipped with a built-in desire to learn, we cannot do it cheaply. It is also worth mentioning that schools generally recognized as superior have their share of turned-off students, time-killers, truants, vandals, and troublemakers. To the best of our knowledge, no school has ever come close to satisfying the whole potential range of students and families.

We have suggested that a major obstacle to universal education is that most children have very little interest in learning the things that the school wants to teach them. Another factor of no small importance is that parents can be openly hostile to a great many things that schools consider worth teaching. One cannot overstate the role of ideology in shaping our children's schooling. All parents would doubtless agree that they want their children to learn history, but it turns out that they want their children to learn the parents' own special version of history. They want their children to learn science, but in a way that does not threaten religious beliefs. As this is being written, we hear public figures inveighing against the teaching of "secular humanism." Parents believe that the schools should teach brotherhood, but in a way that does not challenge prejudice. The topic of sex education splits parents into warring factions.

It is not only parents that generate controversy in their opposition to controversy. The agencies of government, too, do not want the schools teaching facts and ideas that undermine the established order. Since most educators are employees of the state and know on which side their bread is buttered, they are not likely to insist on topics their employers are likely to find distasteful.

In the face of such pressures, it is little wonder that most of our public schools—and many of our private ones—offer pallid, flavorless curricula that further al-

ienate children from education. All too many schools have failed in even the simplest of their tasks, that of providing a safe, comfortable, enjoyable environment. All over the country, the already sizable problem of truancy is made worse by children who are afraid to go to school lest they be robbed, beaten, or raped.

SOME POSSIBILITIES FOR EDUCATION

There have been critics who considered the schools so awful that they proposed doing away with them altogether. Paul Goodman (1964) correctly pointed out that the ideal model for learning is language acquisition, which, as we have seen, depends hardly at all on instruction but very heavily on modeling. We agree most profoundly in principle with Goodman's thesis. However, modeling works only with the behavior one has an opportunity to observe, and what children can be expected to learn from their exposure to everyday life is the mainstream culture and its values, including the implicit (and sometimes explicit) Social Darwinism and racism that inform much of our thinking.

Thus we are not prepared to abolish schools, but we are willing to think radically about a new order in education. We agree with radical critics who say that schooling should not be compulsory. (You may find this hard to swallow, but you can try thinking it through.) We agree that a school has to be so attractive and rewarding to children that they will do everything short of battering down the doors to get in. Indeed, in the best schools that we know, the children hate to leave at the end of the day.

Each community and each family will inevitably impose its dominant ideology on its schools, and children will in varying degrees absorb it. But there is a saving note here. Schools are not the only educational institutions around. Unless parents are willing to keep their children cloistered, the school will have to compete with the ideas dished out by peers, libraries, periodicals, and, of course, the all-but-inescapable tube. From such sources, children can glean all kinds of information that might never find its way into the classroom.

In our thinking about a design for a school, we want to retain the subject matter-centeredness, the child-centeredness, and the social utility-centeredness of earlier approaches, at the same time giving to each a somewhat different meaning. Our approach is child-centered in that we favor giving children an education that is personally relevant and contributes to full development. Our central goal is children who want badly to understand themselves and the world they live in. If in addition they take joy in learning for its own sake, that is all to the good. We hope that children will learn to find pleasure in playing with ideas, whether in looking for solutions to real-life problems or in producing purely aesthetic objects. We want children who can absorb knowledge into their very organic make-up, in line with Michael Polanyi's (1958) concept of **personal knowledge.** One of us has summed up the goal of personal education as

> . . . multiplying our perspectives on reality; by informing us about a far greater range of phenomena than we can ever know from personal experience; by teaching us the sets of principles according to which different realms of knowledge cohere; by teaching us techniques of logical, psychological, and stylistic analysis; and, most centrally, by equipping us with the symbolic systems—verbal, mathematical, diagrammatical, representational, expressive—by which we master reality conceptually and shape new realities in imagination (Church, 1962).

Our approach is not child-centered in the sense, sometimes encountered, of schooling being a continuous process of individual or group psychotherapy, or the romantic naturalist sense that children should be sheltered against instruction and left to find their own way. Our approach is, however, child-centered in that we have to take account of how children think and learn, and of individual children's styles of thinking and learning. There is a common subject matter—the world—for all children. This does not imply, however, that they all have to learn the same things at the same time and in the same way.

We are thus subject matter-centered in that children's egos and feelings of self-worth are not at stake, so that they are free to pay attention to the demands of the learning task without being distracted by irrelevant emotions. This is not to say that learning should be emotion-free, but that emotions should originate in the subject matter and how children understand it. Children need to be helped to feel competent and worthy so that negative feelings do not obstruct communication with reality.

We wish we were in a position to decree that the schools teach the world as

A child-centered education takes into account how children in general think and learn as well as the cognitive styles of individual children.

the best modern minds view it in the light of the best available empirical evidence. At the moment, however, we see no escape from the political realities of fear, superstition, bigotry, and hostility to advanced styles of thinking. What the schools can teach is practical skills and practical problem solving.

A profound social change is under way, and we can foresee one possible benefit to the educational enterprise. We think that we detect a spreading awareness that it makes no sense to set apart ages five to twenty-one as the period of life that is to be devoted to schooling, to preparation for the serious business of real life, earning a living, and forming a family. Instead, sizable numbers of people have come to realize that children need to be given more opportunities to participate directly in the family's and community's work, to acquire competence and learn responsibility from an early age. Along with this notion goes the realization that any age is a good time for learning, most particularly if the individual is painfully aware of gaps in his or her knowledge and understanding. Experience is not necessarily the best teacher, but it often does an excellent job of making us aware that we badly need enlightenment.

SUMMARY

1. Middle-years children typically turn their attention toward the world at large. Piaget describes the middle years as the stage of concrete operations, during which children have a limited capacity for abstract thought but can deal with objects quite fully. Several new competences define this stage—conservation, decentration, compensation, reversibility, seriation, transitivity, and classification.

2. Piaget's model has been questioned on several accounts. For one, children actually appear to function at varied levels of maturity; performance on one measure doesn't necessarily correlate with performance on another. Also, children become capable of various operations at much younger ages than Piaget's theory would allow. Finally, critics note that Piaget focused rather narrowly on cognition in physics and mathematical logic to the neglect of the human sphere, with which children's lives are overwhelmingly concerned. Piaget's ideas about development can be reformulated independent of his framework of stages, however.

3. During the middle years, children advance cognitively in many ways. They take active pleasure in problem solving, and their powers of memory improve. They can perform imaginary acts; they become increasingly aware of their own comprehension or lack thereof; they develop a more objective and relativistic view of the world; they begin to locate themselves in time; they become aware of their body processes; they are intrigued by irregularities and new relationships; they begin to think about social concepts; and they can judge their own performance.

4. Several dimensions of social cognition, or the understanding of human functions and relations, have been studied in middle-years children. Egocentrism decreases, while altruism begins to emerge. The development of prejudice can be related to the mechanisms of stranger anxiety and the discrepancy hypothesis. Piaget believes that moral judgment in children shifts from an objective orientation to a subjective orientation, while Kohlberg proposes that it progresses from a preconventional level to a conventional level and then in a few cases, to a postconventional or principled level. In general, moral judgment among children is far more stringent than among adults. Also during the middle years, locus of control generally moves from the external toward the internal, that is, toward taking responsibility for the events in one's life.

5. At the beginning of the middle years, children have usually mastered the fundamentals of language. The cognitive status of school children

depends largely on their grasp of symbols, which help them to outgrow verbal realism. They discover the freedom to manipulate symbols, and they take delight in playing with words and meanings. They are fascinated by coded language and alphabets. They also learn to recognize many conventional symbols and signs.

6. A number of techniques have been used to reveal changes in language during the middle years. These include vocabulary tests, specifying similarities and differences, the detection of absurdities, interpretation of proverbs and metaphors, the game of Twenty Questions, and the Word Association Test.

7. Other studies have found correlations between language comprehension and other cognitive competences, such as transposition and conservation. Children tend to remember the sense of what is said to them, rather than the words used to say it. Basically, the middle-years child is at home with isolated segments of experience. He or she organizes these logically and can reason about them in a mature fashion. The world as a whole, however, still remains an imperfectly integrated realm.

8. We have asked a great deal of our schools, and disappointment may have been inevitable. Basically, too many children are not interested in learning what the schools have to teach at the time and place at which schools want to teach it. Children soon perceive that school is about scholarly gamesmanship—grades, diplomas, degrees—not knowledge and understanding. Some schools truly engage pupils' interests and emotions, but most offer pallid, flavorless curricula. If education is to improve, it must take into account how children think and learn, as well as individual children's styles of thinking and learning. Children needn't learn the same things at the same time in the same way. And education need not be only or even primarily for children.

KEY TERMS

altruism, 468
attribution theory, 474
classification, 458
compensation, 457
competence motivation
 (effectance), 461

concrete operations, 457
conservation, 457
decentration, 457
discourse analysis, 466
egocentric generosity,
 468

learned helplessness, 475
locus of control, 474
moral dilemmas, 471
necessity, 458
objective responsibility,
 470

SUGGESTED READINGS

Flavell, J. H., and Ross, L. (eds). *Social Cognitive Development*. New York: Cambridge University Press, 1981. A summary of current knowledge and
speculation about the development of social cognition.

Minuchin, P. P. *The Middle Years of Childhood*.
Monterey, Calif.: Brooks/Cole, 1977. An
excellent integration of all aspects of development during the middle years.

CHAPTER 14

Adolescence and the Transition to Adulthood

The middle years of childhood end with a change that may at first go unnoticed. Beginning around age ten or eleven in girls and twelve or thirteen in boys (boys lag about two years behind girls), the rate of growth starts speeding up. The growth latency of the middle years yields to the **pubescent growth spurt.** The onset of the growth spurt, which can often be determined only in retrospect, marks the beginning of *adolescence,* the period that, in Western societies, falls between childhood and adulthood. The key biological event of adolescence is **puberty,** the manifestation of sexual maturity, the ability to reproduce. Puberty is marked by the **menarche** (pronounced men-AR-kee), or first menstruation, in the girl, and the production of sperm in the testes of the boy.

Following puberty, physical growth slows down and eventually stops, somewhere around age nineteen in females and twenty-one in males. At this point, the young person has reached full biological maturity. Biological maturing is accompanied by changes in behavior. These changes vary from moving directly into adulthood in some societies to the Western version of an extended adolescence with all its agonies, joys, and complexities.

The tale of contemporary adolescence is neither simple nor stable. The manifestations of adolescence keep changing, and students of this age repeatedly find themselves stranded by the shifting currents. Thus, although much of what we shall have to say is drawn from formal research, it will also reflect our personal contacts with young people, our students' accounts of the behavior of their younger brothers and sisters and cousins, information gained from people who work with adolescents, and from journalistic sources. The biological aspects of adolescence are reasonably well documented. It is the behavioral aspects that tend to elude systematic description. As we have suggested, the very nature of adolescence changes from era to era, and a given era seldom lasts very long. Moreover, adolescents are reluctant to reveal their inner selves to the prying psychologist. They will fill out questionnaires, but even when guaranteed anonymity they are likely not to tell the whole story. In addition, there are ethical restraints on research into the more sensitive areas of adolescent behavior. These restraints may even have the force of law; in 1978, the United States Supreme Court upheld a school administration's ban on a student newspaper's proposed inquiry into the students' sex lives, even though identities would have been protected.

A final complication is that adolescence is not all of a piece. There are vast differences between twelve-year-olds, trying to come to terms with bodily changes and with the often ambiguous role expectations that accompany these changes ("I am still a child but I no longer really feel like a child") and eighteen-year-olds, faced with awesome decisions about accepting or deferring adult freedoms and responsibilities, and finding a place in the community of adults.

BIOLOGICAL AND CULTURAL ADOLESCENCE

Adolescence is usually defined in terms of biological change. The changes we have alluded to, and which we shall discuss in more detail, are human universals, acknowledged in all societies as indicators of a new status. In traditional societies, the new status is adulthood, to be confirmed ceremonially and then taken for granted. In technologically advanced societies, however, the new status is adolescence, neither childhood nor adulthood. To distinguish this culturally ordained status from the universal of **biological adolescence,** we designate it **cultural** or **psychological adolescence.** Since these two adolescences have, in our society, a common beginning and considerable overlap in time, many people have a hard time maintaining the distinction.

The prolonged postponement after puberty of full adult status is a relatively recent phenomenon in Western societies (here we must include countries like Japan, China, Australia, and New Zealand). Up until a few hundred years ago, the physical fact of puberty meant, as it still does in tribal societies, automatic eligibility for adulthood. Indeed, as we said earlier, even middle-years children were expected to work side by side with adults as productive members of the economy. Beginning with the sons of royalty and the nobility, who had no economic function but who might be called upon to be warriors, and spreading gradually to the male offspring of the merely affluent, there was increasing acceptance of delay in adopting adult status. To occupy the time of economically surplus but energetic young men, the university came into existence, to be followed in due course by the secondary school. Adolescents now had a role, that of student.

It is in the role of student that young people constructed an identity separate

(© Michael Hayman/Stock, Boston)

Adolescence has become an accepted stage of identity since World War II, and most young people appear comfortable with it.

from that of the adult world. With the coming of industrialization and related radical social changes, countless new occupational roles opened up, and schooling was further rationalized as a necessary preparation for full participation in a technology-based economy. Instead of following automatically in the footsteps of their parents, young people had a choice of careers and the promise of upward social mobility. With adulthood deferred, young people were obliged to elaborate their identities as students into identities as adolescents. Their status was fundamentally ambiguous, and this ambiguity helped generate the awkwardness and self-consciousness that were accepted as built-in features of the adolescent years.

Since World War II, adolescence has come to be taken for granted as a status for practically all young people, the way youngsters are from the time of pubertal changes until that ill-defined moment when they merge into the world of adults. Young people have seemed for the most part content with this immature status, especially as new privileges accrued to the role.

Cultural adolescence is buttressed by many rationalizations. We have already mentioned the notion that a long apprenticeship is necessary to master the technology by which we now wring a living from the earth. However, the most basic one is that the way young people behave is a direct product of their physiology, that the emotional upheavals characteristic of adolescence mirror biological ones. This view includes the notion that there is an inevitable strain between adolescents' sexual maturity and their mental and emotional immaturity. There are people who rationalize adolescence as an essential time out, an interval for sowing one's wild oats, especially if one happens to be male.

We are skeptical of all such reasoning. Only a very few occupations in our society require a real understanding of how technologies work. One can operate a highly sophisticated piece of high-technology gear without having the slightest notion of what makes it tick. How many cooks could tell you how their microwave ovens operate? How many television viewers could fabricate a TV set? The biological view falls short on two counts. First of all, the emotional upheaval it sets out to explain is by no means a universal of psychological adolescence (Bandura, 1964; Offer, 1982). Second, none of the traditional adolescent traits is to be found in societies in which cultural adolescence has never taken shape. The time-out, wild-oats view of adolescence is probably a product of parental wishful thinking. Many

parents, looking at their adolescent offspring, may see in them an embodiment of all the parents' wasted opportunities, failed hopes, and lost dreams, and seek to recapture vicariously, through the young, all the glories to which they once aspired.

We would propose instead that psychological adolescence is the product of a self-fulfilling prophecy. We expect immature behavior, treat young people in terms of our expectations, and find that they behave immaturely. It is our opinion that the basic reason for psychological adolescence is economics. Our economy, as it is now organized, has no real function for most of its 32 million citizens aged thirteen to nineteen. It therefore assigns young people to a status with its own subculture, in part self-generated, in part perpetuated by custom, in part imposed by law, and in part produced by shrewd manipulation of young people by commercial interests. Let us not appear to cast adolescents in the role of innocent victims. They protest restraints and confinement and demand all sorts of rights and opportunities, but large numbers secretly welcome prolonged immaturity and postponement of the need to assume adult responsibilities. In fact, adolescents experience an intensified version of the growth ambivalence that has marked development ever since toddlerhood.

PUBERTY RITES

In preliterate societies, there is no equivalent for our concept of cultural adolescence. Most commonly, we find that the young person on the threshold of maturity goes through a ritual, beginning as a child and ending as an adult. The rituals by which adulthood is recognized or conferred are variously called **puberty rites, rites de passage** (anthropologists prefer to retain the French term), and **initiation ceremonies** (Brown, 1975; Munroe and Munroe, 1975; Muuss, 1970). They may be carefully timed to coincide with puberty, or children of approximately the right age are rounded up and initiated, or they may be timed to suit the individual's sense of readiness.

At their simplest, puberty rites may consist of nothing more than a haircut or a change of costume. More complex rituals may involve elaborate tattooing, periods of isolation or fasting, or a quest for a vision or revelation. Some ceremonies are ordeals that serve at least partly as a test of character: circumcision with a sharpened stick, surgical removal of the clitoris, having one's teeth filed to a point, enduring torture without crying out, or the infliction of lesions that will leave scars considered to enhance beauty. Young men may have to demonstrate their manhood in mortal combat. The scalp at the belt or feasting on the heart and genitals of the man one has just slain may be the ultimate sign of full-blown masculinity. Such rites de passage seldom last more than a few weeks (admittedly, these may be very vivid and memorable weeks), and even the longest of them are negligible when compared with the seven or ten or more years we allot to this transition.

There is one clear exception to this description of absence of cultural adolescence in preliterate societies. This is found in the Masai, a pastoral people in Kenya and Tanzania (Saitoti, 1980). The young Masai male, following circumcision at about age sixteen, assumes the status of warrior. The warrior's job is defending the people, the land, and the herds of cattle against human enemies and wild beasts. Warriors are allowed to accumulate property and to have sex, but they may not marry. Warriorhood ends in what we would consider early adulthood, usually as a result of the warrior group's having become too large. The older members are squeezed out of the group into the status of elder, which they occupy for the rest of their lives. It appears that warriors, once upon a time, were indeed warriors. Nowadays, their warrior functions seem to be minimal, and they pass their time drinking, playing games, making love, and occasionally engaging in the sort of hooliganism that distresses proper citizens all over the world. As we understand Saitoti, the warriors' sex partners seem to be preteen groupies, teeny-boppers, and one another's mothers. The governments of Kenya and Tanzania are doing their best to abolish warrior status and persuade young males to go either to school or to work. So far, they have had little success.

Note that traces of puberty rites persist in our own society. The Jewish bar mitzvah and the Christian confirmation began as puberty rites. The "sweet sixteen" birthday party and the more formal debut both announce to the world that the young woman is available for marriage, although these latter rites seem to be dying out. Other micro-rites are more a function of the state than of the family or community. Many young people nowadays look to the driver's licence, working papers, or passport as a badge of maturity.

PHYSICAL GROWTH

Youngsters sprout up in the two or so years before puberty, and especially in the year that culminates in puberty. This year before puberty is called the **maximum growth age (MGA).** Puberty marks the peak of the growth-rate curve. After puberty, as we have said, the rate of growth slows down, with girls reaching their full height at about nineteen, and boys at about twenty-one. Nobody knows for sure just when growth stops, but annual increments beyond the ages given are too small to be measured accurately. Changes in body proportion, of course, go on lifelong. During physical adolescence, height increases about 25 percent and weight by anywhere from 50 to 100 percent—obviously, growth in weight is more variable than growth in height.

During the middle years, children gain slightly over 2 inches (5 cm) a year in height and from 4.5 to 5 pounds (2 + kg) in weight. During the maximum growth age, girls grow about 3.5 inches (9 cm) and gain about 11 pounds (5 kg). Boys grow 4 or 5 inches (11 cm) and put on 12 or 14 pounds (6 + kg) in the course of the MGA. Boys are somewhat bigger than girls except between the ages of nine and fifteen, when the earlier maturing of girls sends them shooting past their male counterparts. But let us note that in both sexes there are early maturers and late maturers and a vast number of individual growth patterns.

Down through the years, Americans have become taller on average, and American males have become heavier. Adolescent and adult females are, on average, a few pounds lighter than their counterparts of sixty years ago, reflecting changes both in diet and in concepts of beauty. These averages conceal socioeconomic and cultural differences. Male children of the rich are no bigger than they used to be. Average size will in all likelihood stop increasing once the less-favored segments of society catch up.

BIOLOGICAL MATURING

Biological adolescence begins with **pubescence** (so called after the fuzz that appears on the pubic mound), a series of changes over a period of about two years, of which the growth spurt is only one manifestation. Pubescence culminates in puberty, the beginning of sexual maturity, the capacity for reproduction.

Pubescence is initiated by an increase in activity of the pituitary gland, a growth-regulating endocrine gland, recessed in the base of the brain, that secretes several hormones. The pituitary is at the center of the endocrine network, communicating with the rest of the body via hormones in the bloodstream. Secretions from the pituitary regulate other growth-governing endocrine glands, notably the thyroid (located at the base of the throat); the adrenals (attached to the kidneys); and the sex glands, or gonads (the ovaries in the female and the testes, or testicles, in the male).

Other changes that take place during pubescence include, as we have said, the first appearance of pubic hair as a downy tuft on the forward face of the pubic mound. Development of the breasts in girls and the growth of underarm hair in both sexes are other signs of pubescence. In boys, this period is marked by the growth of the penis and testes until both become pendulous. The boy's beard begins to grow, at first as fuzz above the corners of the mouth and gradually as true facial hair. Girls, too, may have a sprinkling of facial hair on the upper lip, and hairs may sprout around the nipples. These manifestations in no way detract from the girl's femaleness.

Puberty

In girls, **puberty** is relatively well defined by the *menarche,* or first menstruation. Menstruation tends at first to be skimpy and irregular. From this fact some authorities have arrived at the notion of **adolescent sterility,** which says that girls cannot conceive until several years after the menarche. It is true that young adolescent girls are less likely to conceive than older ones and, having conceived, are less likely to carry a baby to term. But enough freshly postpubertal girls do become and stay pregnant to make reliance on a hypothetical adolescent sterility a less than safe method of birth control. Authorities now speak of **adolescent subfecundity** rather than adolescent sterility. Fecundity refers to the probability of giving birth (Frisch, 1980, 1982).

In boys, puberty is marked by several signs. The most reliable of these is probably the presence of sperm in the urine, which, of course, can be detected only under the microscope. The most publicly noticeable sign of puberty is the **change of voice.** The boy's voice deepens steadily during pubescence, but it sometimes shifts embarrassingly from its normal bass or baritone to a falsetto soprano squeal. The shaft of the penis becomes longer and thicker and the glans (the head of the penis) grows until, in some cases, it emerges completely from the foreskin. (Needless to say, if the boy has been circumcised, this does not apply.) The penis is capable of erection from birth onward, but until pubescence, erection is likely to be in response to direct stimulation or irritation. Around the time of puberty, the penis begins to tumesce very readily, either spontaneously or in response to sexually provocative sights, sounds, smells, language, and the like. Now erection is accompanied by a strong and unmistakable urge to ejaculate. The first ejaculation may come in the form of a **nocturnal emission,** known popularly as a "wet dream." The testicles and *scrotum,* the sac containing the testes, grow, and the skin of the scrotum becomes deeply wrinkled. Since sperm cells need a constant temperature, slightly below that of the body as a whole, to survive, an effective thermostat is built into the testicular structures. When the surrounding temperature goes down, the testes are drawn closer to the groin as a source of body heat. When the surrounding temperature goes up, the testes are lowered away from the groin.

Age at menarche has been studied more intensely than puberty in boys, and there are interesting historical, geographical, and personal variations. In contemporary societies, the median age at menarche varies from 12.4 years in both black and white Cubans to 12.8 in Californians to 18.8 in the Bundi of New Guinea (Johnston, 1974). For several years, students marveled at the dramatic rise in age at menarche from 13 or 14 in classical Greece and Rome to almost 18 in northwestern Europe in the mid-nineteenth century, and its steady decline thereafter. As it turns out, we were marveling at a nonexistent phenomenon. The original source of the erroneous data, John M. Tanner, has taken a second look and discovered that the mean age at menarche was never much more than 16, and that the pattern of rise and fall is by no means clearcut (Tanner, 1981). Wyshak and Frisch (1982) present evidence of a decline from about age 16.5 in 1840 to just under age 13 today. If we accept the idea that this downward trend is related to improved living conditions and diet, the puzzle of why age at menarche should have risen from 13 or 14 in ancient Greece and Rome to about 16 in the mid-nineteenth century still remains.

A number of environmental factors are known to have an influence. Good diet accelerates and poor diet delays development. The same relationship holds with health in general. In fact, obese girls menstruate earlier than lean ones (Johnson, 1974; Frisch, 1976). Even atmospheric pressure plays a role. Girls in sea-level regions of California menstruate earlier than girls in mile-high Denver. However, the myth that girls in tropical climates menstruate earlier than those in northern climates has long been dispelled (Zacharias and Wurtman, 1969). Regular muscular exertion retards menarche, which may explain the less than voluptuous contours of female gymnasts (Frisch *et al.*, 1981). Young ballerinas who adhere to a sylphlike physical ideal are also likely to have delayed menarche or irregular menstruation (Frisch, Wyshak, and Vincent, 1980). The daughters of women who were exposed to the atom bombing of Nagasaki show delayed menarche in direct relation to the extent of their mother's exposure. Girls in large families menstruate later

than girls in small families. Finally, there is the question of whether exposure to erotic stimulation can accelerate sexual maturing. It would fit our psychobiological view of development (p. 31) if it did, but the evidence is slight.

The one major fact that we know about boys' age at puberty comes from the age at which boys are released from choirs because of the change in their voice. (At one time, it was not uncommon to make permanent sopranos out of choirboys by castrating them.) In Johann Sebastian Bach's eighteenth-century boys' choirs, boys had to be let go at an average age of eighteen, except during a period of war and privation, when they matured considerably later. Presumably, nutrition affects puberty in boys as well as in girls. Nowadays, the average age at which boys are released from choirs is 13+ (Sullivan, 1971).

Other Somatic Changes in Adolescence

Sexual maturing includes development both of the **primary sex traits,** the reproductive apparatus, and of the **secondary sex traits,** predictable changes associated with sexual maturing but not directly involved in reproduction. The secondary sex traits (or characters) include breast development in girls, pubic and armpit hair in both sexes, facial and, later, chest hair in boys, and the change of voice. Girls, too, have a change of voice, although it is less pronounced than in boys.

Other somatic changes seem not to be directly related to sex, although the intricacies of maturation make any simple statement suspect. Girls' hips widen as the pelvis grows. Girls more than boys

(© Jerry Berndt, 1979/Stock, Boston)

The age of onset of puberty varies widely among girls, and depending on the progress of their peers, early or late maturers may feel that they are out of place.

develop a layer of subcutaneous fat that rounds and softens the contours of face and body. Boys' shoulders broaden, and boys develop a leaner, more angular and muscular appearance than girls. (This may be changing as girls show increasing interest in body-building activities.) In both sexes, the skin becomes coarser, with larger pores. The sebaceous glands in the skin become more active, producing an oily secretion that may contribute to the formation of blackheads. Acne of all kinds is a source of great embarrassment to adolescents. The composition of sweat changes during adolescence, and body odor becomes stronger. Adolescent self-consciousness has many origins, but one of the more important is awareness of the odors of sweat and menstruation. Adolescents are a special target of advertisements for deodorants and perfumes.

Before puberty, girls have higher blood pressure than boys, but after puberty this relationship is reversed. It will be interesting to see if changes in sex-role expectations, particularly in the direction of high achievement by the female, will be reflected in equalization of blood pressure between the sexes.

A characteristic of somatic changes during adolescence is **asynchrony,** the fact that bodily changes seem to be out of phase with one another. Arms and legs may seem to sprout with no regard for overall proportions and harmony, giving many youngsters a long-legged, gawky, coltish look. During pubescence, the left and right sides of the body may even grow at different rates, although by puberty they usually have returned to approximate balance. Facial proportions also change, as the nose and the chin become more prominent. What may look to adults like odd body proportions probably inspired the designation of the years around puberty as the "awkward age." However, plenty of adolescents use their awkward-appearing bodies quite gracefully. Awkwardness and clumsiness are probably symptoms of insecurity and self-consciousness rather than of somatic incompetence.

Early Maturing and Late Maturing

Individual differences in age at puberty may occasion some social dislocations. The early-developing girl may feel out of place among her undeveloped age-mates, although, as we suggested earlier, she may still be a middle-years child devoted to middle-years pastimes (Faust, 1960). One early blossomer recalls feeling self-conscious to the point of trying to conceal her postpubertal status from her friends. At the same time, she was amused that she could feel her breasts bouncing when she skipped rope. The late-maturing girl, by contrast, is very likely to feel a lost soul among the surrounding hips and bosoms (Faust, 1960).

The early-maturing boy, because of his superior size and strength, is usually at a temporary social advantage, although he may soon find himself overtaken and surpassed. The late-maturing boy may suffer the most of all. He is likely to be made a butt of jokes, a scapegoat, an object of scorn and ridicule (Weatherly, 1964). A classic study by Mary Cover Jones (1965) has shown that personality differences between early-maturing and late-maturing boys may persist into middle age. With all due allowance for individual differences and overlaps between the groups, early-maturers were found to be poised, responsible, successful, and conventional; late-maturers were active, exploratory, insightful, independent, and impulsive.

Now that we have seen some of the major changes that take place in the adolescent's body, it is time to consider cultural or psychological adolescence.

CULTURAL ADOLESCENCE

Cultural adolescence refers to the fact that the larger society believes that people of a given age are naturally endowed with certain psychological characteristics. This cultural assumption becomes a self-fulfilling prophecy, for adolescents do indeed behave much as their elders expect them to. Thus the larger culture's view of adolescence is taken over by adolescents themselves and incorporated into their self-image. The ways of adolescents—their characteristic values, beliefs, thought patterns, tastes and preferences, activities—crystallize to form a subculture. Indeed, there are a number of adolescent subcultures associated with social-class differences, sex, life goals, and so forth. Our generalizations cannot possibly fit all young people.

Furthermore, adolescent subcultures change, and we can never be sure that we are abreast of current trends. Individual adolescents may switch personalities rapidly. This is an expression not of psychopathology but of role playing, a constant trying out of all the possible life styles that young people encounter or fantasize. As we attempt to delineate the ways of adolescents, we proceed with caution and you are urged to exercise due skepticism.

The Adolescent Subculture

The traditional image of the adolescent is almost wholly a male one. Writers such as Johann Wolfgang von Goethe (*The Sorrows of Young Werther*), Thomas Mann (*Tonio Kröger*), and James Joyce (*A Portrait of the Artist as a Young Man*) have depicted the adolescent male as moody, romantic, idealistic, and given to inner turmoil, or **Sturm und Drang** (roughly translated, "storm and strain" [Hall, 1904]). This tormented young man was prone to periods of disillusioned depression, or **Weltschmerz** ("world pain"). He was full of daydreams (more often heroic than erotic), surrendered himself totally to music and poetry, took long solitary walks in the rain, and, in moments of despair, toyed with thoughts of suicide. Such fantasized suicide is, of course, a very special kind that permits the deceased to hover about invisibly, relishing the grief and remorse that others feel "after I'm gone." This adolescent had very few friends to whom to bare his soul, and kept his most intimate thoughts for his diary. Such adolescents still exist, but they seem to be a decreasing minority and hardly prototypical.

The realities of life keep adolescents shuttling between the larger culture of family, school, and, perhaps, job, and that of the peer group. Unlike middle-years children, who withdraw from adults into a society of children, adolescents think of the peer group as a new adult society, the wave of the future that will overwhelm and erase the old order. To help guard this feeling, adolescents maintain a conspiracy of silence about their own and each other's pasts. The very thought of their recent immaturities is too agonizing to bear, and they firmly block out any possibility that any such immaturity could still be part of their nature. This emphasis on being grown up—"sophisticated"—does not, of course, lessen friction with the world of chronological grownups. Indeed, the separation of adult and adolescent spheres is at least partly the doing of grownups, who are moved by either disdain or fear or hostility.

Whether to emphasize their differences from adults or simply to assert their own special identity, adolescents immerse themselves in the peer culture. The peer culture expresses itself in a variety of ways. Most obviously, adolescents are recognizable by such externals as the way they wear their hair, their choice of clothing, and their speech, which is marked by its own special intonations and vocabulary. Adolescents are kept busy coining new slang. There seems to be a continuing need for novel ways to express enthusiasm and contempt, for colorful names for the latest intoxicants, and for assorted activities, from studying to sleeping to making love.

Adolescents have a community of tastes in music, dance steps, movies, food and drink, and reading. We are not quite sure who makes up the audience for "young adult" books promoted because they deal with the "real problems" young people have to cope with, but such books sell well. As this is being written, there is a bumper crop of science-fiction and horror (and sometimes combined sci-fi-horror) movies that seems tailored specifically to youthful audiences, although adults appear to enjoy them just as much. We have given up trying to keep track of the styles of music with which young people seek to induce trancelike states.

There are recognizably adolescent patterns of recreation. We suspect that the soft-drink commercials on TV do an excellent job of capturing an idealized spirit of adolescent play; it is highly physical, action oriented, covertly sexy, and beach centered.

The adolescent culture mandates attitudes. The prevailing one, among males and females alike, seems to be *machismo*. There are certainly numerous adolescent feminists, but many females seem still to be drawn to the assertive, even brutal he-men. Male bonding seems to be very much a part of adolescent society. Needless to say, females form friendships among themselves, but such ties have yet to be celebrated in the same way as the bonds of manhood.

One would predict that a society that treasures *machismo* would be largely anti-intellectual, and this seems to be the case. Most adolescents believe in schooling as a path to later success in life, but there seem to be few young people who are excited by ideas. Needless to say, there is little in the experience of most high-school students to stoke their intellects (Owen, 1981).

We must recognize, though, that ide-alism is very much a part of the adolescent attitudinal system, even if sometimes heavily disguised. Adults tend to associate youthful idealism with "liberal" thinking in such fields as politics, economics, foreign affairs, religion, and civil rights. But young conservatives are likewise pursuing an ideal, that of free-market economics and a minimum of governmental intervention in the conduct of life. The young people who undergo religious revelations or conversions are also questing after an ideal of perfect virtue; this applies equally whether the young person seeks salvation in a fundamentalist cult, a mainstream religion, or one of the many fringe movements that have flowered in recent years. We must further recognize that young thugs and hoodlums are often questing after the ideal of perfect manhood. Most (but far from all) adults find the *macho* ethic somewhat laughable, but it is an attempt to define an ideal state.

Finally, the adolescent culture can be defined in terms of its beliefs. Adolescents have a consuming interest in sexual matters, and most seem to assume that they are very well informed about the facts of life. The research into adolescents' sexual knowledge and beliefs is not too satisfactory. However, investigator after investigator reports that adolescents show abysmal ignorance of essential items of information, most notably in the area of avoiding pregnancy (*Teenage Pregnancy*, 1981). Belief in supernatural entities and forces seems to be rampant, not only among adolescents, but also among young adults. There is every reason to think that youngsters' recurrent ventures into witchcraft, black magic, and devil worship are in a spirit

Male bonding and machismo, dominant themes of the adolescent experience, create problems for boys and girls alike. Boys are under pressure to renounce intellectual concerns and conceal their emotions, while girls may enter relationships marked by contempt for females.

of mockery. But large numbers of young people seem to believe quite seriously in extrasensory perception and telekinesis (controlling material objects by an act of will), visitors from outer space, and reincarnation. Many adolescents seem to believe in luck as a material force exerting a superhuman influence on events. We suspect that there is a strong element of magicalism in young people's passion for independent means of transportation—cars, bicycles, motorcycles, surf boards, hang gliders, and so forth. These machines enable one to transcend the mundane, to speed under one's own power at one's own convenience to whatever enchanted destination one selects.

It is worth stressing that not all of the adolescent subculture is the invention of adolescents. Shrewd adults have long recognized that adolescents constitute a distinct market and have become adroit manipulators of tastes and interests. Cosmetics, clothes, conveyances, jewelry, books and magazines and comic books, radios, record and tape players and records and tapes, video games, video equipment, and so on ad infinitum—all can be shaped to lure the adolescent customer into the store and to insinuate new artifacts and values into the adolescent subculture.

It used to be that adolescents hurried toward adulthood, with a view to bringing into being their own version of utopia. Nowadays, they are held back by assorted forces. Some adolescents fear that, far from taking over and transforming the system in which they have so little faith, they will become the system's slaves. Many adolescents shy away from the involvements and responsibilities of adult life which they have seen as draining and burdensome. The adolescent culture has become so powerfully institutionalized that for a number of young people it has come to seem a permanent way of life. Some are in a position to have such benefits of adulthood as sex and money and wheels without the annoying clutter of careers, spouses, children, mortgage payments, and political participation. For such young people there is little incentive to assume the status of adulthood. Finally, a slack economy makes it hard for those young people who want to find jobs or launch a career. The seemingly logical response is to remain in school and prepare for one of the careers that promise to have openings for some time to come. Unfortunately, the costs of advanced schooling are rising rapidly, and many adolescents and their families simply cannot afford post-high-school education.

The Adolescent Peer Group

Adolescents have always been group minded, but today's youth culture seems more self-consciously communal than ever before. Young people talk less about popularity than they used to, but it is vital that one be liked and accepted as a member of the group. It is likewise essential that one be attuned to the latest trends.

There are loners, male and female, but most adolescents seek the safety, warm companionship, and reciprocal reinforcement of group belonging. Even those who feel estranged from the available groups may still feel pressure to maintain membership. This pressure may come from peers, whose sense of solidarity is threatened by would-be defectors, or from misguided parents who worry unduly about the young person who "doesn't have enough friends." During adolescence, the cliques into which young people form become ever more homogeneous and stratified by social class and academic ambitions. Increasingly, individual friendships are based on shared tastes, interests, and goals. As adolescents become more mobile—by age sixteen or seventeen many of them have, or have access to, a car—they can maintain friendships over an ever-wider geographical range. As they travel about the country and abroad, driving or hitchhiking, they help to cement today's worldwide youth culture.

The dependence of the adolescent on peer-group values and standards is probably even more slavish than that of the middle-years child. The greater the wall between adolescents and adults, the more elaborate the peer culture becomes and the more the adolescent has to turn to it for support and identity. Adolescents seize upon and display all the trademarks of their kind, so that nobody can possibly miss them. Conformity is the rule. It extends to matters of dress, adornment, hair styles, tastes, posture, gait, vocabulary, and intonation. Both the individual and the group are eager for innovations, but innovations consonant with the established, basically conservative youth culture.

When adolescents wish to assert their individuality, they are likely to do so by carrying whatever fad is prevalent one more step toward its ultimate utterness. Partly because they want to stand out, and partly to reassure themselves about the solidity of the peer culture, adolescents are always striving for vividness and extremes, as in their slang. But only the strongest leaders will dare to pioneer a really novel fad, such as wearing one's hair in a Mohawk cut and dyed blue.

Young people's dependence on group belongingness to tell them who they are, and their submissive conformity to group ways to affirm their membership, can produce highly injurious results, as in the case of street gangs. The use of alcohol, drugs, and cigarettes may be in response to group pressure. It is not enough to say that young people should have sufficient moral character to resist pressures and temptations; failure to conform to the group's mores can produce feelings of guilt and inadequacy at least as severe as those that result from acting contrary to conscience. Thus the group can place the adolescent in a no-win situation in which any of the courses open will lead to painful consequences. What is interesting is that not only can a single strong leader sway the group to act against its own better feelings, but in some cases no leader is needed. Even though each individual is opposed to a course of action, they all respond to a sensed group demand that the course of action be followed.

It is worth noting that, according to the latest figures derived from a poll of 16,000 high-school students, cigarette smoking and hard-drug use are on the decline (U.S. Department of Health and Human Services, 1981). However, marijuana smoking is as common as ever, and many young people seem to have discovered methaqualone (Quaalude), which is reputed to have aphrodisiac properties.

The Popularity Neurosis. Adolescent dependence on group approval is so strong that it has been labeled the "*popularity neurosis*" (to which not all adults are immune). It is only some adolescents who, late in the period, define abstract standards of conduct against which to measure their own behavior. Most adolescents most of the time act in ways that they think will make other adolescents like them. Adolescents' concern about having a "good personality" is often less a search for inner strength than for the tricks that will win them acceptance. The devices are legion: being a star athlete, playing a musical instrument, cultivating a sense of humor, augmenting one's vocabulary, participating in many activities. The commercial world has capitalized on this need with the promise of all kinds of ways to win popularity. We were surprised to read the other day that there are still innumerable customers for a mail-order course in body-building for those tired of being stigmatized as "97-pound weaklings."

The need for popularity stems in large part from the lessons parents teach their children: It is important to get along with people, to have people like you, to be well adjusted, to hearken to the voice

(© Hiroji Kubota/Magnum)

The desire to be popular is a driving force for many adolescents, reflecting an all-consuming need to be validated by others.

Our generalizations, let us remind you, do not apply to all young people equally, and to some hardly at all. Also, much of what we say applies only to outward behavior and may not do justice to adolescents' actual feelings. Indeed, adolescents' inner feelings, like adults', may be very much at variance with what outward behavior would lead us to believe. Remember the developmental principle of duplicity, our ability to think one thing and do another. Adolescents have not yet mastered all the tricks by which we mask our true feelings from others, but they have moved a long way in that direction.

Adolescent Activities. In cities, adolescents live a sizable part of their group lives on the telephone in intense, interminable conversations, to the point where families that can afford it may be driven to have two or more telephone lines. Young people also go to school-sponsored dances, and there is an effective grapevine that tells where the dances are. However, the point of going to a dance is usually less to dance than to hang out, smoke, drink, and entice a member of the opposite sex into a dark corner. Private parties are plentiful, but the ones most favored are those held when the parents are not at home. Armed with forged ID cards, adolescents gather in bars, rock clubs, and discotheques. They go to the movies, concerts, and plays. They visit museums and special exhibits, study, engage in sports, and watch television. One friendship group of teenage girls liked to sit in a cathedral, listening to the organist practicing, and surrendering to the atmosphere of solemnity. The less affluent use the basketball and handball courts, play-

of public opinion. The need becomes particularly acute in terms of the adolescent's in-between stage of self-knowledge. Adolescents cannot be satisfied with what they think about themselves; they need someone out there to validate their self-perceptions. Nor can they appraise themselves in terms of what they produce—jokes, insights into events and people, a drawing, or a poem—unless it meets with fervent acclaim. Adolescents treasure their own subtleties, but they are insensitive to other people's, and unless their audience is noisily appreciative, they doubt the sincerity of the applause.

(© Jim Anderson/Woodfin Camp & Assoc.)

"Cruising" has long been a favorite adolescent pastime, especially for males.

grounds where they can hold baseball and football games, and public swimming pools.

The picture is somewhat different in the suburbs and small towns. Adolescents take part in many of the same activities as their city counterparts. Certainly the family phone may be monopolized by adolescents. However, there are fewer resources available to them, and they spend much time in local hangouts—a lunchroom, drug store, bowling alley, community recreation hall, the shopping mall, or wherever they can find a resting place.

Another important element of adolescent suburban and small-town life is the automobile. Males typically are infat-

uated with cars, motorcycles, and cross-country vehicles. Some will spend countless hours customizing their wheels to make of them a personal statement, a projected image of individuality. Cruising about in cars has long been a favored pastime, especially, but not exclusively, among males. The point of cruising is to collect some members of the opposite sex with whom one drives to the hangout for idle talk and perhaps something to eat or drink, to the drive-in for whatever sexual play can be accomplished, or sometimes to a deserted lane for total sex. These fantasies go unfulfilled much of the time. The most usual pattern is just riding around headed nowhere in particular, sometimes at high speed but often at a leisurely pace, watching the scenery go by, shouting and whistling at girls or using enticing gestures to capture the attention of boys, or talking about everyday matters. Sometimes, under special conditions of emotion or intimacy, adolescents talk about shared convictions and concern with such profundities as life, death, human nature, religion, war and peace, justice and injustice, and the meaning of it all.

We have no way of estimating their numbers, but it is clear that there are a great many young people who are simply marking time. For whatever reason, a sizable proportion of today's young people suffer from chronic *boredom*, in school and out. We have always had the street-corner gangs of slum society, bunches of kids who have nothing to go home to and no money to do anything else. But now the phenomenon of "hanging out" has spread to the affluent suburbs and small towns, where young people congregate in parks, in playgrounds, on sidewalks, on beaches, or in shopping centers, and numbly watch the world go by. The hangers-out have the air of burned-out cases, people who have tasted life to the full and have nothing more to look forward to (Freedman, 1982). We suspect that many of them sense that there are not going to be any meaningful roles for them to play as adults, and so have given up on different forms of striving, including school work. It seems to us that these bored, and probably resentful, young people are a social powder keg in our midst. Bored people turn to simple-minded forms of excitement—stoning cars and trains, vandalism, and arson. There have been many occasions in recent years where bands of rowdy youths of various backgrounds have run wild, smashing property and attacking people at random. Once such activities take hold, they can erupt into an epidemic.

Our description of herd life has elements of caricature, but it is essentially true. As we have said, however, it is not equally true for all adolescents. Some young people fit the stereotype hardly at all. Some youngsters participate very little in herd life, either because they have overriding interests or because the various herds will not make room for them. Solitude need not be the only alternative to herd life. Some young people dislike the mindlessness of group activity. They prefer more direct, individualized friendships. The capacity for sentimental attachments is suggested by this contract drawn up by two high-school seniors, one male and one female: "We, the undersigned, do hereby solemnly swear that twenty years from today, February 14, 1994, at 9:00 PM, we will meet at the Southeast corner of 16th St. and Third Avenue /signed/signed/." Some young people are genuine scholars, deeply involved in one or more areas of academic or creative learning. Such young people may be brought together in specialized schools catering to one or another category of giftedness. If circumstances do not throw them together, they seek each other out. A number of youngsters look for ways to translate their idealism into concrete action. They can be found tutoring slum children, rehabilitating rundown housing, and working in campaigns for assorted causes. And, of course, there are young people who hold jobs or serve as interns for future professional employment and have little time for the frivolities that engage many of their age-mates.

THEMES IN ADOLESCENCE

From time to time, we have tried without success to construct a taxonomy, a system of categories, of adolescence. Instead of a taxonomy, we point to some recurring themes in adolescent behavior.

Almost all adolescents feel stirrings of *romanticism*, responding to or fantasizing sentimental visions of pure love, fulfilled or thwarted. Adolescents fantasize not only about love, but also about heroism and death, various forms of religious purity, and political movements. Romanticism is simply one more manifestation of **idealism,** the belief in the perfectibility of self and society.

Idealism inevitably leads to *disillusionment*, the realization that reality can never measure up to the ideal. Disillusionment is felt as *Weltschmerz*, "world pain," referring to the reality that betrays our dreams of what ought to be. The inner conflict between the ideal of purity and the all-too-human baser urges that afflict all adolescents is one of the sources of *Sturm und Drang*. Even the need to eat and drink and eliminate can be felt as a threat to cravings for perfect nobility. Disillusionment may be the occasion for another adolescent theme, that of *theatricality*. Perhaps to lend significance to lives that are often felt as aimless, adolescents may melodramatize even the most trifling of emotional events. Adolescents fall madly in love at every opportunity, and are easily plunged into suicidal despair by some minor setback.

There are some adolescents who work hard to make sensuality a way of life. The dedicated pursuit of pleasure (and avoidance of pain) is known as *hedonism*.

Some people make a virtual career of hedonism, and others dream of it as a lifelong ambition. For a fair number of young people, drugs are a shortcut to life lived according to the pleasure principle. The other side of the coin of hedonism is *boredom*. As we said earlier, chronic boredom is a fact of life for many young people, and occasional boredom is a plague for almost all. Recall that it is boredom that accounts for a large part of the destructive and antisocial behavior in which some adolescents engage.

Mixed in with their nobility and idealism, most adolescents have a streak of the *psychopath*, an unfeeling and even brutal disregard for the welfare of other people. Here we can see one sign of the persistence of egocentrism into adolescence and adulthood. The adolescent's wishes and concerns loom so large that they blot out the existence of other people's needs. The culture of some adolescent groups dictates psychopathy as a way of life, resulting in destructive behavior, but this is partly role playing, measuring up to the group's expectations. We suspect that the mask of toughness rather often conceals a quite normal capacity for caring and fellow feeling.

Whatever roles they play, most adolescents have an intermittent commitment to *conventionalism*, accepting the values, goals, and practices of the larger society. It is an expression of many adolescents' ambivalence that they scorn the success ethic that dominates American culture yet want very badly to make it big.

THE SEARCH FOR IDENTITY

It is during infancy that babies begin to define themselves as persons separate from their environment. From that time on, the definition of the self is constantly refined, elaborated, and revised. In adolescence, the young person confronts the task of forming an identity as an adult. This involves finding the answer to such questions as who I really am, what I am really capable of doing that justifies my claim to adulthood, what I truly believe in and value, and what I will make of my life. In sum, the adolescent must find the meaning of his or her own existence.

Erikson's View of Adolescence

For Erikson (1959, 1968), the adolescent suffers from an **identity crisis.** The successful resolution of this crisis is the formation of a coherent, stable sense of oneself as estimable, competent, and responsible. The young person arrives at such a definition of the self through role playing, experimenting with the numerous life styles offered by a complex society. Erikson recognizes that the wide choice of roles offered by modern society may in itself be a source of perplexity to young people. Furthermore, although we pride ourselves on our open society, the young person knows that not all roles are equally accessible to everybody. Some roles are open only to those with certain qualifications of knowledge or skill, whereas others are open only by virtue of family wealth or special connections. In times of economic constriction, even the best-prepared and best-connected young people may find themselves shut out from many of the more desirable economic roles.

The alternative to forming an identity is **role confusion** (also called **role diffusion**), indicating that the adolescent, bewildered and overwhelmed by pressures

(© Linda Swartz/The Picture Cube)

According to Erikson, the adolescent identity crisis is resolved when a coherent sense of the self is achieved through role playing—trying on the various life styles offered by one's society.

and demands, may withdraw from the effort to shape an identity or else simply toy with the various options. To exemplify role confusion, Erikson quotes Biff in Arthur Miller's play *Death of a Salesman:* "I just can't take hold, Mom. I can't take hold of some kind of life."

Marcia's Adaptation of Erikson's Theory

James Marcia (1966, 1980) has recast Erikson's theory of identity formation to yield four stages of identity development. These are derived from the concepts of **crisis** and **commitment.** Crisis refers to the process of wrestling with the problem of who one is, what one believes in and values, what one wants to be, and how to become what one wants to be. Commitment refers to the state of having resolved the issues of identity formation. We can use the presence or absence of crisis and commitment to generate a four-celled table thus:

Table 14.1 Marcia's Scheme of Identity Formation

| | | Commitment | |
		Absent	Present
Crisis	Absent	Identity Diffusion	Foreclosure
	Present	Moratorium	Identity Achieved

In each cell of the table, we find an **identity "status."** The desirable line of development is from the upper left, Identity Diffusion, to lower left, Moratorium, to lower right, Identity Achieved. Let us look at each of the four statuses.

Identity diffusion describes the condition of the youngster to whom it has never occurred to question his or her own identity. *Moratorium* describes the young person in the throes of wrestling with the question of identity but who has deferred an immediate resolution. *Identity achieved* describes the status of those who have been through crisis and arrived at a satisfactory integration of possibilities. It is this status of identity achievement that Marcia considers the most mature. *Foreclosure* is a dead end. It describes the status of the young person who has incorporated unquestioningly the values and goals ordained by the family and by society at large. Note that neither Erikson nor Marcia would find the acceptance of conventional values unsatisfactory, but he and Marcia seem to feel that something is missing in the lives of young people who have never seriously questioned the established order and thought through the issues before deciding that the status quo is a fair approximation of the ideal.

Sally Archer (1982) has applied Marcia's scheme to 160 lower-middle-class suburban sixth- to twelfth-graders. She studied identity development in four areas: vocational plans, religious belief systems, political philosophy, and sex-role preference. There were no sex differences, and the expected developmental progression was present, although on a far-from-striking scale. Status in the four identity domains is shown in Table 14.2 It is obvious that this sample of youngsters showed its greatest maturity (moratorium and identity achievement) in the realm of vocational planning, and its most pronounced conservatism (foreclosure) in the matter of sex roles. There was apparently some questioning of religious beliefs, but it seems that only three of

Table 14.2 Frequencies of Identity Statuses × Content Area Across Grade Level (Sexes Combined)

	Identity Status			
Content Area	Identity Diffusion	Fore- closure	Mora- torium	Identity Achieved
Vocational plans	57	61	20	22
Religious belief system	60	72	7	21
Political philosophy..	142	15	1	2
Sex-role preference ..	12	132	6	10

these 160 young people had any inkling of political awareness.

The Reflected Self

Adolescents, like people at every age, define themselves at least partly in terms of how other people regard them. They see themselves mirrored in the responses of peers of both sexes (Elkind, 1980). This expressive feedback tells adolescents both about how their behavior is being received and about the impression their physical attributes make. The body is one of the core components of the self, and a sense of its comeliness is a vital ingredient in self-acceptance. Logically, one should be able to determine the attractiveness of one's body by studying it in a looking glass, and adolescents do, indeed, spend long hours searching their reflections for clues to the self. Younger adolescents typically scrutinize their features as though waiting for them to reveal a message. Older adolescents spend hours before the mirror, trying out hair arrangements and facial expressions and postures, worrying a pimple on the chin. They are trying to gauge how best to achieve maximum impact—that is, to communicate to the world what one's True Self is like. The mirror serves as a place to rehearse the role playing, the gestures, the intonations, and hairdos which, on the morrow, will win the stunned admiration of one's friends. But adolescents' perception of their reflection is subject to all sorts of strange distortions. Both assets and liabilities can be exaggerated or played down, and what the adolescent sees in the mirror is an unreliable guide to how others will react.

We should not have to add that the adolescent whose ego is on trial is simultaneously serving as a mirror and sounding board to the other youngsters. They are all caught up in a complex pattern of feedback loops carrying messages in all directions.

The body must be attractive. It must be of the right size, neither too tall nor too short, neither too fat nor too skinny. Physical strength is important, in the past primarily for males, but increasingly for females as well. It makes a difference whether one feels graceful or clumsy in the use of the body, whether one commands the usual motor skills, and, in general, whether one is physically able to accommodate the group's activity patterns.

Few adolescents feel truly in control of their own functioning. Most tend to be trapped between impulses that they have not yet succeeded in making a part of themselves and what often seem like unreasonable or capricious adult constraints. But lack of control also carries the hidden blessing of lack of responsibility. Adolescents become masters of the mechanisms of defense by which they can evade both objective and subjective guilt. Like adults, adolescents learn to rationalize their behavior with all the guile of a legal expert—note that rationalization uses verbal realism to reshape the reality of deeds and motives. Adolescents project blame onto forces beyond their control or onto an environment that does not understand the real, interior adolescent (One teenage girl to another: "So I said to him, 'How do you know this is the real me you're talking to?' ").

Personal values are yet another component of the self. Some adolescents quietly assimilate the values professed or

(© Margaret Thompson/The Picture Cube)

Adolescents spend a great deal of time studying their reflections in mirrors. Their perceptions of their appearance, however, can be oddly distorted.

practiced by their parents or by adult society at large. Others, in blind revolt, **counteridentify** with adult values and try to be as unlike their parents as possible. And there are those who seriously try to think out their own individual codes of conduct: These are the minority whom Kohlberg (1978) would classify as *postconventionalists,* those who can go beyond what everybody knows and think for themselves.

The choice of one's life work, insofar as one has a choice, is an important part of adolescent identity. Young people seem to feel ambivalent about materialism, rugged individualism, and high achievement, but most dream of having a career.

ADOLESCENT SEXUALITY

We now turn to adolescent sexuality, which is yet another major component of the adolescent's personal and social identity.

Freud's View of Adolescence

Freud regarded adolescence as the **genital stage** of psychosexuality. The latency of the middle years is ended, and there is a resurgence of sexual drives. Now, however, sexual urges are intermingled with capacities for loving, caring, tenderness, respect, and protectiveness toward the young. Masturbation usually increases during adolescence, and young people seek anxiously for partners with whom to have sex. Some adolescents experiment with homosexuality, but most end up firmly heterosexual. Note, however, that in certain settings—sexually segregated boarding schools, the military, prison—homosexuality may be accepted as standard practice.

The Freudian view of female sexuality says that the libido shifts from the clitoris to the vagina, the region in which women feel stimulation most intensely. Freud (1949) himself disparaged women who responded only to clitoral stimulation, and his followers have stressed that one cannot consider oneself fully feminine until one reliably experiences vaginal orgasm. Masters and Johnson (1966) found that clitoral stimulation was a source of considerable pleasure for most women.

Sexual Attitudes and Behavior

The attitude of today's young people toward sex may be summed up in a graffito in the New York subway:

> Lynette
> I'm
> cool
> 13 today & not a virgin any more

It is not easy to study adolescent sexuality, as many researchers will attest. Many adolescents, as we said earlier, consider inquiries into their sexual attitudes, beliefs, values, and practices an invasion of privacy. Even in conditions guaranteeing anonymity, they may overstate their sexual activity or minimize it or deny it. Because their long-term research shows a coherent pattern, we rely chiefly on the findings of John F. Kantner and Melvin Zelnick, of Johns Hopkins University, who periodically survey large samples of young people (de Witt, 1980). The trend is to earlier and more widespread sexual activity. In 1979, 70 percent of some 900 males aged seventeen to twenty-one had had intercourse, and about half the sample of 1,700 teenage females said they were sexually active. Another source (*Teenage Pregnancy*, 1981) states that there was a two-thirds increase in sexual activity during the 1970s. This same source states that the average age at which sexual activity begins is sixteen, and that by age nineteen, 80 percent of males and 70 percent of females have had sex. Yet another source (Hass, 1979) reports that teenagers are learning to try a great variety of sexual practices. A similar sexual revolution has been documented in Israel (Antonovsky, 1980). Kibbutz youngsters, according to this source, are more liberal than their nonkibbutz counterparts, and kibbutz girls are decidedly more emancipated than adolescent females who do not live on a kibbutz.

There used to be distinct social-class differences in extent of sexual activity and in the forms of sex practiced. For instance, it used to be thought that lower-class males were far more experienced than middle-class young men. At the same time, middle-class boys masturbated freely, whereas lower-class boys rejected masturbation as unmanly. Such differences are fast disappearing. The 1979 Kantner and Zelnick survey,

(© Frank Siteman, 1981/The Picture Cube)

Today young girls are as keenly interested in sex as boys and are increasingly taking the initiative in sexual relationships.

mentioned above, found that sexual activity among black teenage women grew from 54 percent in 1971 to 66 percent in 1979, while sexual activity in white teenage women increased in the same period from 26 percent to 47 percent.

As the newspapers keep telling us, fewer young people today marry than formerly. Those who do marry do so at later ages. They have fewer children, and those who have children start having them at ever later ages (U.S. Bureau of the Census, 1980). In 1970, the Census Bureau was aware of 523,000 unmarried couples living together. By 1979, the figure had almost doubled, to 1.3 million.

It has long been taken for granted that females are less highly sexed than males, and that females develop full sexual responsiveness slowly, in many cases becoming capable of orgasm only as they approach middle age (Kinsey and associates, 1953). Today's girls and young women are giving the lie to such beliefs. It is not merely that they have sex, but they enjoy it, have little trouble achieving orgasm (a number of girls first experience orgasm while masturbating [Hass, 1979]), and crave sex as avidly as males. In fact, the sexual awakening of females seems to be a reawakening. According to Conway (1979), from medieval times to the nineteenth century, female sexuality was viewed as fiercer and more insatiable than that of the male, and far more difficult to control. Starting with the writings of Aristotle, hysteria was understood as sexual desire pressing the womb against the other organs, causing a great assortment of physical symptoms ("hysteria" comes from the Greek *hystera*, "womb"). The treatments for hysteria included "sweet things" placed at the entrance to the vagina, burning a feather under the nose, and sniffing smelling salts. The preferred way of dealing with rampant female sexuality in the nineteenth century was to marry the girl off so that she could be satisfied. However, when a husband was not readily available, young women diagnosed as oversexed were often treated by cauterization or removal of the clitoris, or by removal of the ovaries.

One of the widely reported (although not easily verifiable) side effects of female sexual liberation is an increase in impotence among adolescent and young-adult males. It would seem that the thinking habits instilled through generations are not easily cast off. The male was traditionally the pursuer and the female the elusive, if seductive, prey. The young man who finds his erstwhile prey not only available on demand but in some cases predatory and clamoring for more is not always able to rise to erotic occasions. Here we must take note of the mismatch between male and female sexual capabilities. The fully responsive female may continue to have orgasm after orgasm, whereas the most virile of males is limited in his capacity for repeated couplings (Masters and Johnson, 1966).

The Darker Side of Sex

The two areas of adolescent sexuality about which we are best informed are those in which sex may turn out to be less than beautiful. The first of these is venereal disease. There seems to be an ineradicable reservoir of syphilis, a growing incidence of gonorrhea, an influx of previously rare diseases carried by voyagers from far places, and now an epidemic of incurable genital herpes. Although herpes is not thought to be fatal or crippling, it apparently can cause sterility, is disagreeable to experience, and casts a pall on the individual's sexual self-image.

Young people have made light of gonorrhea because it can be cured with penicillin. Two facts make a casual attitude toward gonorrhea inappropriate. The first is that some 80 percent of females, and perhaps 20 percent of males, who contract gonorrhea are free of symptoms and do not even know that they have the disease. Symptom-free victims can transmit the disease and may themselves suffer severe damage of the reproductive tract; it is usually only after the damage is done that the gonorrhea is diagnosed. The second fact is that strains of gonococcus resistant to penicillin have, predictably, evolved. So far, the drug makers have managed to catch up with new strains of disease agents, but the race is by no means won.

The definition of venereal disease has been enlarged to include vaginal inflammations of unknown origin. These, too, can be transmitted to the male and may cause damage to the woman's reproductive system.

The second problem area of adolescent sexuality is unplanned pregnancy. According to Jaffe (1979), there are more than a million teenage pregnancies a year. This figure is not quite as alarming as it sounds. More than half these pregnancies are found in seventeen- to nineteen-year-olds who, in many societies, would be considered grown women. Furthermore, some number of teenage pregnancies are wanted: Some 14 percent of unmarried youngsters and 49 percent of married ones welcomed pregnancy (*Teenage Pregnancy*, 1981). Some teenagers are married, and many young women want a baby of their own. Unmarried young women who intentionally have babies may do so for unsound reasons, but the situation is rather different from that of the youngster who simply "gets caught." Of each year's million or so teenage pregnancies, about 59 percent lead to live births, 27 percent end in abortions, and 14 percent end in miscarriages. About 45 percent of live births to teenage mothers are to unmarried youngsters; 27 percent of births to married teenagers are to mothers who married during pregnancy (*Teenage Pregnancy*, 1981).

There are several reasons given by adolescents for not using contraceptives. One is that they find them aesthetically displeasing. Some young males say that the use of contraceptives implies disrespect for the partner. This applies especially to condoms, which double as contraceptives and VD-prevention devices. For some young people, the use of contraceptives mars what they would like to think of as a "spontaneous" experience. Some young people hesitate to procure contraceptives because a number of doctors and pharmacists make known their disapproval and may refuse to prescribe or sell contraceptives to young people. Many youngsters are misinformed about the risks of pregnancy and think they are having intercourse during a "safe" time of the month. Even teenagers who know all the facts about becoming pregnant

may still be unable to believe that pregnancy could really happen to *them*.

Between 1971 and 1979, the proportion of sexually active teenage women who used contraceptives increased from 50 percent to 70 percent (*Teenage Pregnancy*, 1981). During this time, use of intrauterine contraceptive devices and of the pill declined. The use of condoms, diaphragms, foam, withdrawal, douches, and the rhythm method increased. Needless to say, the last three contraceptive techniques are far from reliable. Until 1982, there was great emphasis on the potentially harmful side effects of the pill. In 1982, it was announced that the benefits of the pill, notably in reducing the risk of several kinds of cancer, seem to outweigh the dangers. We now have the contraceptive sponge. It is still too early to understand its role in adolescent sexual behavior.

We have a few data from a survey of 184 mothers ages twelve to fifteen in three midwestern cities (Miller, 1981). These mothers were interviewed within the first few months after giving birth and again when their babies were about twenty months old. Of these mothers 85 percent were black, 11 percent white, 3 percent American Indian, and 1 percent Hispanic. Eighty-eight percent were living at home, most of the white youngsters with both parents and most of the black mothers with their mothers. A number of the teenage mothers were living in unsatisfactory housing. Their complaints included unsafe neighborhoods (39 percent); rats and mice (27 percent); cramped living quarters (26 percent); delays in making repairs (26 percent); and lack of protection against break-ins (24 percent).

Only 28 percent of the young mothers

realized during their first month that they were pregnant. When they did become aware of their pregnancy, 80 percent were dismayed, 4 percent unbelieving, and 16 percent pleased. Forty-six percent had prenatal care beginning in the first trimester (three-month period) and another 48 percent from the second trimester. There was no detectable relationship between prenatal care and the babies' well-being. This had been the second pregnancy, but the first birth, for eleven of the mothers. Eighty-five percent of the mothers had been instructed in birth control methods, and 19 percent knew about female fertility. Ninety percent were taking precautions against another pregnancy: 75 percent were using contraceptives, and 15 percent were abstaining from sex. Two mothers had already become pregnant again by the time of the first interview. Eighty-five percent of the youngsters were in school. Most foresaw a rather bleak future, but most also clung to a hope that things would be better. They seemed to be quite hard-headed about their needs—for advice, for medical care, for food stamps—and the ways in which these were and were not being met.

THE INTEGRATED SELF

It is from such strands—values, roles, reflections in the peer-group's regard, competences, vocational aspirations, body awareness, and sexuality—that young people weave an integrated sense of who they are. The roles they play increasingly resemble those of adult life. Some **role playing** is based on culturally defined types: the tough guy, the sweet young thing, the swinging playboy or playgirl, the woman of the world, the bored sophisticate, the man's man. Young people who identify with particular careers begin to play the roles and affect the mannerisms associated with occupational stereotypes. Movies, TV, and literature provide abundant models for the proper conduct of journalists, doctors, lawyers, and people in other high-prestige callings.

It is often the case that adolescents, like the preschool child playing cowboy, seize on the externals of a role and miss its essence. In the course of shifting from role to role, the adolescent girl may decide to try out a new hair style or hair color, or to speak in a lazy, insolent drawl, or to affect a saintly manner. Similarly, the boy may decide to wear his shirt casually unbuttoned to the waist or to wear a black T-shirt with the sleeves hacked off, to greet whatever is said with a cynical, sneering grunt, or to assume an air of unaccustomed humility and submissiveness. Parents are likely to react by asking, "Who are you being today?" The adolescent is taken aback that adults should fail to recognize that the new self now on display is the true and final one. Adolescents easily forget that the roles they played earlier were equally valid at the time, and, when reminded of them, are likely to disclaim them totally and contemptuously: "That was ages ago! I was only a baby then!" However amusing role playing seems, it is a vital mechanism in adolescents' coming to term with themselves. It is a way of trying out possible identities until they find the one that is consistently comfortable.

COGNITIVE FUNCTIONING IN ADOLESCENCE

According to Piaget, young people at about age eleven enter the final and most mature stage of cognitive development, the stage of **formal operations** (Inhelder and Piaget, 1958). Central to the stage of formal operational thought is the ability to think and operate symbolically and reason abstractly. Formal operational thinkers can imagine possibilities that lie outside of the immediate environment. They can order information into sensible patterns and form multiple classifications: For example, they can devise a matrix into which blocks can be sorted, taking simultaneous account of size, shape, and color. They can formulate and test hypotheses.

To demonstrate the problem-solving abilities of younger and older children, Inhelder and Piaget (1958) experimented with the pendulum problem (see Figure 14.1). Children of different ages were given strings of differing lengths and objects of differing weights that they could hang from a rod, forming a pendulum. The children were told that each of the

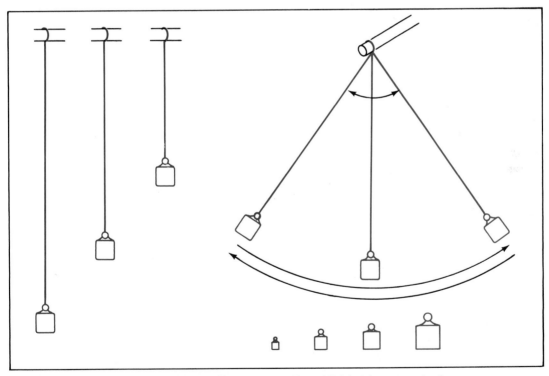

FIGURE 14.1   Illustration of the Pendulum Problem. The child is given a set of weights *(pictured at bottom)* and a string that can be shortened or lengthened *(as pictured at left)*. The task is to determine which factor(s) account for the speed with which a pendulum traverses its arc (After Inhelder and Piaget, 1958).

pendulums would complete its arc at a different rate. What Inhelder and Piaget wanted to find out was how children of different ages would explain the difference in rate, that is, how thought processes develop. The possible causes for the differing times the pendulum took to move through its arc included: weight of object; length of string; height from which the object was released; and force of push. It was only starting at age fourteen that young people could approach the pendulum problem systematically, taking account of all the variables. For younger children, the process was too complex. At age fourteen and above, the subjects were able to figure out the correct solution, that the time it takes for the pendulum to travel through the arc depends on the length of the string.

It was Inhelder and Piaget's position that younger children did not have the systematic understanding of physical relationships needed to think or reason in a scientific manner. However, Siegler, Liebert, and Liebert (1973) were able to teach ten- and eleven-year-olds to solve the pendulum problem. They thus demonstrated that with training such thinking is not beyond the grasp of younger children.

Siegler continued his exploration of scientific thinking in children. He used subjects who were much younger than children Piaget thought capable of scientific thought. For example, Siegler devised a series of experiments involving a balance scale (1978). A balance scale operates just like a seesaw. If one seesaw rider is markedly heavier than the other, the heavier person must sit closer to the center of the seesaw (the fulcrum or leverage point) to compensate for the difference in weights. In this way, the seesaw will balance. Thus, whether riding

a seesaw or using a balance scale, we have to be aware of two components in keeping both sides of the scale in balance: (1) how much weight is on each side; and (2) how far the weight is from the fulcrum, or leverage point. The product of the weight times the distance must be the same on both sides for the scale to be in balance. As we see in Figure 14.2, two units of weight that are six distance units away from the fulcrum will be in equilibrium with a six-unit weight that is two distance units away from the fulcrum.

In working with children and the balance scale, Siegler was interested in how children of different ages would figure out the concept of balance. He showed his subjects drawings of various combinations of weights and distances and asked them to say how the scale would behave. He predicted that children would first attend to only one part of the formula, in all probability to weight. When they started to take account of distance, they would fail to do so accurately. Only sometimes would they be able to predict whether the scale would be in balance or, if not, which side would go up or down.

Siegler observed a developmental trend of the kind he anticipated. However, he does not make clear how many children discovered for themselves the strict logical relationship of weight and distance. Siegler tried to specify the mechanisms of thought by which children arrived at incorrect or accidentally correct solutions. Unfortunately, these do not permit adequate descriptions of children's behavior. It was not until adolescence that youngsters could actually calculate the numerical relationship between weight and distance. Even then, training was needed.

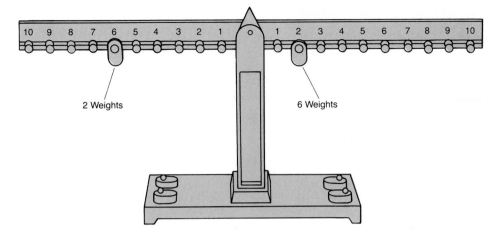

FIGURE 14.2   A Balance Scale of the Sort Used by Siegler.

To discuss the concept of formal operations more fully would require a course in logic. Almost everyone is agreed that Piaget has set standards for adolescent thinking that only a tiny minority of adolescents ever achieve. Indeed, Flavell (1977), in a moment of candor rare among authors, expressed this rather neatly:

> If the presence of either *A* or *B* or both implies the presence of both *C* and *D*, does the absence of *C* necessarily imply the absence of *B?* Trying to solve logical problems like these hurts my head and I do not always get them right, even when I take a lot of time and care (p. 118).

What does the research evidence tell us about thinking in adolescents? A series of studies by Roberge and Flexer (Flexer and Roberge, 1980; Roberge, 1976; Roberge and Flexer, 1979a, 1979b, 1980) indicates that there is clear improvement with age on tests of formal operational thinking. However, performance on differing sorts of tasks is quite inconsistent. This suggests that various formal operations do not cluster into a coherent pattern that can be identified as a stage. Edith Neimark (1975, 1979) has surveyed the literature and con-

cludes that the stage of formal operations has been inadequately defined. She, too, observed that subjects' level of performance depended very much on the nature of the task. Formal operational thinking often coexists in the same individual with egocentrism, animism, magicalism, and the gambler's fallacy (a belief that the odds shift in one's favor every time one loses). Even Piaget (1972) has conceded that there may not be some general level of thinking that permits formal operational thinking regardless of the problem, that individuals may differ with regard to the areas in which they function best, that formal operational thinking may not appear at all in some cultural settings, and that special training may be required before the individual can perform formal operations.

It is clear that Piaget's original conception of the stage of formal operations, like that of earlier stages, is based on subjects' approaches to problems in the domains of logic, mathematics, and the physical sciences. Flavell (1977, 1981) and Neimark (1975) have pointed out that we should redefine formal operational thought so that we could recognize it at work in such domains as art, music, history, medical care, business management, and police work. Practitioners in these fields are often called on to exercise a great deal of knowledge and skill, but no one has yet catalogued the sorts of mental operations they engage in or looked to see if there are common features connecting disparate domains.

Nisbett and Ross (1980) have helped open up a whole new area of research into problem solving. The problems with which they confront subjects usually involve estimates of probability, cause and effect, prediction, and how various distorting factors may influence judgments. A more or less typical problem goes like this:

> [I am a professor of psychology. I have a friend who is a college professor.] He likes to write poetry, is rather shy, and is small in stature. Which of the following is his field: (a) Chinese studies or (b) psychology?

If your answer to this question was 'Chinese studies,' you are guilty of two errors. The first is stereotyping. There is no legitimate reason to think that Sinologists are smaller, shyer, or more poetic than psychologists. The second error is the disregard of probabilities. We do not know how many Sinologists there are in the United States, but we would guess the total at under a thousand. On the other hand, there are more than twenty thousand college teachers of psychology. Further, a professor of psychology is far more likely to know other psychologists than to know teachers of Chinese studies.

SEX DIFFERENCES IN BEHAVIOR

We now return to a topic upon which we touched earlier (see p. 441) but will now discuss in more detail. This is the matter of sex differences in behavior. It should be emphasized that no one can question the existence of such differences. The focus of controversy is whether, and to what extent, such differences are determined by genetic endowment or by experience. On the side of genetics, the only difference between male and female human beings is that females have two X chromosomes and males an X and a Y. The male's Y chromosome controls the formation of the testes and so is implicated in hormonal differences between the sexes. Otherwise, the only known practical consequence of genetic sex differences is the male's greater vulnerability to sex-linked recessive traits such as hemophilia or red-green color blindness (see p. 57). Hormonal differences are very likely to entail differences of temperament, but it is hard to see how they would affect cognitive functioning.

It is said that girls rely on the right cerebral hemisphere—the physiognomically oriented, intuitive half of the brain. Boys, however, are said to rely on the left hemisphere, and they are rational, logical, and factual. We are skeptical of all generalizations about functional differences in the hemispheres. Roger Sperry (1982), who won a Nobel Prize for his studies of split-brain patients, warns us against jumping to sweeping conclusions about hemispheric differences. Gevins and associates (1979) claim to have shown that the differences in activity in the two hemispheres of the brain are produced by the muscle activity required by a task and not by the associated mental processes that accompany the task, as in manipulating blocks to copy a design. This is not to deny the role of biological forces in shaping sex differences in behavior, but to insist that we have not yet identified them.

Popular perceptions of psychological differences between males and females often reflect stereotypical thinking. The notion that girls are more concerned with social relations while boys are more interested in ideas is a myth.

On the experiential side, there are definite sex-role stereotypes for both males and females. These stereotypes include interests, traits, and abilities. As everyone knows, little girls are interested in dolls and dramatic play with domestic themes, whereas boys like guns, high adventure, and everything mechanical. Everyone knows, too, that girls are sweet and gentle and quiet, and that boys are rough and noisy and assertive. Girls are good with words, boys with numbers. And so forth.

The first problem in explaining these differences between the sexes is to find out if they really exist. As we said a moment ago, there obviously are differences. The trick is to be specific about what they are. People keep reporting sex differences in various experimental situations, and other observers keep finding that the earlier observations cannot be repeated. If there are systematic differences, they should have stabilized by adolescence.

Maccoby and Jacklin (1974a) have written a book surveying all the information then available on psychological sex differences. Their findings were summarized in a magazine article (Maccoby and Jacklin, 1974b). They proposed three categories: myths, facts, and unsettled questions.

The myths are many: Girls are more

concerned than boys with *social relations,* and boys are more concerned with *things* and *ideas.* Girls are more *suggestible* than boys. Girls have less *desire to succeed* than boys. (Maccoby and Jacklin make clear in their book, but not in their article, that achievement motivation in girls is more often accompanied by ambivalence and inner conflict than in boys.) Girls have *lower self-esteem.* Girls do better at *simple, rote tasks,* and boys at *high-level tasks* demanding new adaptations. Girls are *less affected by environmental conditions* in development than are boys. Girls are *auditory,* boys *visual.*

In reviewing Maccoby and Jacklin's second category of factual sex differences, one should bear in mind that there is always considerable overlap between males and females. It seems to be a fact that young males are more physically *aggressive* than females, although male aggressiveness declines with age. Girls are said to have greater *verbal ability,* although an examination of Maccoby and Jacklin's tabulation of studies does not reveal a clear pattern. Boys surpass girls in *spatial visualization,* and boys do better in *math and science.*

This last observation leads to an area of debate. Camilla Benbow and Julian Stanley (1980) published test results of 10,000 seventh- and eighth-graders indicating that boys consistently scored higher than girls in mathematical reasoning. They attributed the difference to genetic factors and hypothesized that mathematical ability depends very heavily on spatial ability.

The subjects in Benbow and Stanley's research were participants in six talent searches conducted between 1972 and 1979 by an organization called the Study of Mathematically Precocious Youth. To begin with, all the youngsters were given a test of mathematical achievement on which all (boys and girls) scored in the top 5 percent. They were then given the verbal and math parts of the Scholastic Aptitude Test (SAT-V and SAT-M), one of the leading college admissions tests usually taken by high-school juniors and seniors. The boys each time outscored the girls on the SAT-M. The average differences ranged from 32 points to as high as 116 points (the maximum score on the SAT is 800, but the group means in this study all fell below 600).

There is a puzzling aspect of Benbow and Stanley's findings. If boys and girls scored equally well on the first test of achievement, why should they perform at different levels on the second? Despite its name, the SAT is an achievement test, that is, it measures what has been acquired through exposure to relevant instruction. Why should the SAT-M be treated as the crucial measure rather than the original test?

Predictably, a great many people took exception to Benbow and Stanley's conclusions. Chipman (1981) raised the same problem we have just referred to, that the two groups performed equivalently on one test but not on the other. Which test is to be considered the true indicator of ability? Egelman and his associates (1981) pointed out that even if the observed sex difference was genetic in origin, this would not preclude environmental modification. PKU and diabetes are both genetic conditions, but they can be corrected by environmental measures. Kelly (1981) reports on an international study of performance in science and math on which boys generally did better than girls. However, girls scored higher than boys in Japan, Hungary, Belgium, the Netherlands, and Italy. Luchins and Luchins (1981) state that their research shows social conditioning to be at the root of any observed sex differences, and say that there is no known gene for spatial ability. Stage and Karplus (1981) point to sex stereotyping by teachers, and stress that the relationship between spatial and mathematical abilities is still only speculative. Moran (1981) says that the search for genetic determinants of behavior is motivated more by political and economic considerations than by scientific ones. Tomizuka and Tobias (1981) say that girls are reluctant to volunteer for special programs like the one from which the subjects were drawn. To join such enrichment classes is to risk ostracism by less gifted peers They further question the validity of the tests for assessing basic abilities.

In a more extended comment, Tobias (1982) points out that the parents of mathematically gifted girls tend to be unaware of their daughters' abilities. By contrast, the parents of mathematically gifted boys almost invariably know that their sons are well endowed and so give them every encouragement to further development. For instance, many boys crammed for the talent search exams, whereas very few girls did so. Since 1972, the number of boys outscoring the highest-scoring girls has been declining. In 1979 and 1980, only one boy outperformed the leading girl. Many of the girls who dropped out of the program reported that the class meetings were dull and their male classmates were "little creeps."

Since it appears that even those sex differences that have been established through extensive research may be disappearing as the culture changes, we have to be skeptical about the remaining areas of differences, which Maccoby and Jacklin labeled their third category, unsettled questions. These include: which sex is more fearful; which more active; which more competitive; more dominant or compliant; more nurturant and "maternal"; and which more passive. The authors barely mention sex differences in sexuality, but, as we said earlier, whatever differences there may once have been seem to be disappearing.

Plomin and Foch (1981) question whether there are any psychologically significant sex differences. They tested 216 seven-year-old boys and girls for verbal abilities, spatial abilities, memory, and perceptual speed (such as picking out all the triangles from an array of shapes). They found that the differences among individuals of the same sex were far more pronounced than differences between the sexes.

A change has come about in our thinking about masculinity and femininity in the past decade. People used to think of masculine and feminine as the two poles of a single dimension: The more masculine you were, the less feminine, and vice versa. Nowadays, people think of masculine and feminine as two distinct dimensions. This way of thinking says that people can be either high or low in both masculinity and femininity, or just about any mixture imaginable. This doctrine of **androgyny** (Bem, 1974) says that we can all develop as much as we wish—and as circumstances will let us—both masculine and feminine components in our nature. ("Androgyne" comes from Greek *andros*, "man," and *gyné*, "woman.") Note, however, that the concept of androgyny still accepts masculinity and femininity as meaningful and useful dimensions for describing personality.

What is the evidence for pervasive sex typing? We have already seen, in Chapter 8, that sex typing is well advanced in toddlerhood. Among preschool children, boys play more with blocks, toy vehicles, and uniformed male figurines than do girls. Girls play more with dolls, domestic furniture, toy animals, and water than do boys. Girls do more painting (Clark, Wyon, and Richards, 1969; Cramer and Hogan, 1975). Boys play outdoors more than girls do, and use more space in their play (Harper and Sanders, 1975). Boys and girls spend approximately equal periods of time playing with jigsaw puzzles, sawing and hammering, and listening to music (Clark, Wyon, and Richards, 1969).

We get a clue to the subtleties of early sex typing from the furnishings found in children's bedrooms. Harriet Rheingold and Kaye Cook (1975) catalogued and counted the furnishings and playthings in the rooms of forty-eight boys and forty-eight girls under the age of six. The total number of items did not differ for boys and girls. However, the girls' rooms had a greater number of dolls, floral designs, and ruffles. Boys' rooms had more educational and art materials (charts of numerals or letters, typewriters, equipment and supplies for art work). They also had more sports equipment, toy animals, and spatial-temporal objects. (The last are "items relating to the properties of space, matter, energy, and time, including shape-sorting toys, outer-space toys, magnets, clocks, etc."—remember the possible connection between spatial and mathematical abilities.) Boys' rooms contained dolls, too, but rarely female or baby dolls or dolls with joints that permit easy dressing and undressing. There were no quantitative differences with respect to books, furniture, musical objects (radios, record players, instruments), stuffed animals,

(© Margaret Thompson/The Picture Cube)

The media are powerful influences in socializing girls into their culturally approved roles, emphasizing, for example, that physical beauty and attracting male approval are more important than other accomplishments.

and jointless male dolls. The Rheingold and Cook approach has now been formalized as a way of assessing sex typing in the family.

What are we to make of these patterns of differences, nondifferences, and ambiguities? Outside the sphere of reproductive behavior, there is very little that we can confidently attach to biology. So far, we have very few women professional football, basketball, and baseball stars, but their day may be coming. In the realms of feelings and intellect, of tastes and interests, differences are as easily related to conditions of rearing as to biological factors. Yet we cannot say that socialization practices alone account for whatever nonreproductive differences exist. It seems perfectly plausible that males and females should have evolved to perform quite different functions in family life. But we know that some women make imperfect mothers, and that males can play the mother role, too. If we alter our sex-typing practices, as many of us have already begun to do, it is probably because we do not want to deny to either boys or girls the opportunity to explore a full range of human possibilities and to adopt that combination of life styles they find most congenial.

It makes no sense to tell a girl that she should forget about being a mathematician because she is a girl. Nor does it make any more sense to tell a boy that he cannot be a day-care worker because he is a boy. We are learning, slowly, to let children find out for themselves where their inclinations lie, and, as long as their inclinations are not harmful to other people, to encourage them to follow those inclinations. Obviously, parents urge their children to investigate as wide a range of possibilities as they can manage. The seeming change is that parents no longer strongly define possibilities in terms of conventional sex roles.

THE TRANSITION TO ADULTHOOD

Biological and cultural adolescence have a common starting point in the pubescent growth spurt. Biological adolescence clearly ends when the young person reaches full physical maturity. But when does psychological adolescence end? The answer is more subtle. We approach it by looking at adolescents' relations with the world of adults.

Adolescents and Their Parents

This book has witnessed a gradual transition. Parents are all-important in the life of the infant, but with the passage of time they recede ever farther into the background. Even as late as their children's adolescence, though, parents still have an important role to play.

Some unknown number of adolescents get along beautifully with their parents. They identify strongly with their parent's values and work cooperatively with them to complete the passage to adulthood. This probably applies most often to second and subsequent children. First-borns often have to blaze trail and teach their parents the art of parenting, including how to cope with an adolescent.

In a large—but still unmeasured—proportion of cases, however, relations between adolescents and their parents are anything but serene. On the adolescent's side, behavior may range from sullen sulkiness to haughty contempt to expressions of animosity to screaming denunciations of parental inadequacy. The adolescent's ultimate weapon is the cry, "I didn't ask to be born!" On the parents' side, feelings may vary from blind, almost murderous rage to consuming guilt to utter bewilderment. But on both sides, remember, there is usually an unshakable component of love. If parents do no more than serve as emotional punching bags for their children, they are still helping them come to terms with complex feelings.

The central problem, for both parents and children, is *letting go*. Issues such as dating, sex, use of the car, observance of curfew, or money may sometimes be the focus of discussion and argument (Kinlock, 1970), but these are likely to be smoke screens that obscure the real issue: how to sever the bonds so that the adolescent can assume adult autonomy. In all matters, adolescents want to be free and unconfined. At the same time, they are coming to understand that they are enmeshed in a network of reciprocal ties that inevitably restricts their free-

Although some adolescents get along beautifully with their parents, for many the relationship is anything but serene.

dom. It may be this very inevitability, rather than any particular restriction, that they are battling.

Beginning with toddlerhood and the first drive to autonomy, the long, painful process of cutting the bonds goes on. Not all bonds, and not for good, but enough to allow the young person to assert his or her adulthood. It is important to remember that the stronger the attachment, the more violent may be the process of getting detached. Thus when a young person tells a parent "I hate you," the underlying message may be "I'm afraid I love you too much."

It is not only bonds of affection that tie parents and children together. There is also sheer habit, the innumerable taken-for-granted relationships and ways of acting that accrue over time. The long history of authority, by which parents have the final say in decisions, plays its part. There is still the largely unexplored factor of economic dependence and independence. To what extent can one think of oneself as an independent adult while still receiving significant financial support from parents? Does supporting the young person financially confer on parents an extension of their habitual authority? We know of no general answers to these questions, but we know that financial independence can be a burning issue in some families. We have known young people who were forced to assert their independence by leaving home and going on welfare. The matter becomes particularly acute in periods when jobs are hard to find.

Most parents want their children to be better persons than they themselves have managed to become, but this desire—or even expectation—sets a trap. If parents exhort their young to practice virtue, the young person's awareness of the imperfect parents' shaky moral position is aroused. It is in such circumstances that we hear the adolescent battle cry of "Hypocrisy!" It is probably true that parents do not always practice what they preach, but they are not being hypocrites. "Hypocrisy" means trying to appear better than one is. Parents preaching to their young are not trying to hide their own moral shortcomings but to share "the benefit of their experience." Parents want to teach the lessons they had to learn the hard way, from life itself, sometimes too late for it to do them any good. Unfortunately, these lessons are not likely to make much sense to adolescents, who lack the very experience that would make them meaningful. Furthermore, adolescents, knowing that the world has changed, are profoundly doubtful that their parents' experience can have any relevance to their own lives. It later comes as a shock to each generation of adults to discover that they are repeating all the parental mistakes from which they had once thought themselves immune.

Among the lessons parents try to communicate to their children is that the world is a complicated, often treacherous and heartless, place in which to make one's way. They are all too vividly aware of the adolescent's weaknesses, inadequacies, and fallibility, and know with great certainty that he or she is not yet ready to cope with the harsh demands of adult life. What parents have forgotten is that no one is ever fully prepared for the trials of independence, and that everybody has to do a lot of on-the-job learning. Adolescents themselves know at some level that they are not fully ready to tackle life on their own, but they cannot stand the thought of continued dependence.

If we have painted a picture of an eager adolescent straining to break away from the determined clutches of his or her elders, we have told only half the story. Parents very badly want their offspring to grow up, to move out into the world. But the imminent reality alarms them and makes them want to postpone the inevitable. Adolescents likewise are genuinely eager to assert their mature freedom, but when they stand at the threshold, they are not quite sure that they want to confront the terrors, known and unknown, that lurk on the far side.

This situation can be summed up as the ultimate dual growth ambivalence, which we first mentioned in speaking of toddlerhood, and which we have shortened to the more manageable **dual ambivalence**. The young person feels ambivalent about each step in development. He or she welcomes the challenges and the associated privileges, but at the same time hesitates out of fear both of failure and of losing the advantages of immaturity. Consciously, the adolescent refuses to acknowledge the possibility of failure, but it repeatedly crops up as a chilly, menacing presence. Yet another source of anxiety is that adult privileges themselves are not uniformly inviting. Much as they rail against parental control, adolescents are often glad to have external backing in dealing with the powerful forces waiting to be unleashed. Independence carries with it the threat of loneliness. Self-reliance means that there is no one to help with the dirty work.

Concern about the young person's readiness to cope is probably the main ingredient in the negative side of parental ambivalence, but it is not the only one. There may be more than a little envy that the young person still has a whole life to lead, and a resentment that they, the parents, are approaching the end of the line. They may share Bernard Shaw's sentiment that youth is wasted on the young. In any event, dual ambivalence puts parents into what Gregory Bateson (Bateson *et al.*, 1956) called a **double bind** or, as it is now referred to, **a no-win situation.** If the parents urge the young person to leave the nest, they are liable to be accused of trying to get rid of their child. If they suggest, ever so gently, that the young person might want to defer independence just a little bit longer, they are accused of infantilizing the youngster ("You're treating me just like a baby!"). The parental double bind does not mean that what parents do is unimportant. If young people are going to develop their own set of durable values, they will probably have to begin by contesting the values of their parents. Parents may feel that a defense of their values is a futile exercise. However, a serious discussion forces the youngster to think more deeply about his or her basic assumptions. Parents are unlikely to go about cultivating conflict, but they

can stand up to it courageously when it comes in their interactions with their adolescents.

Conflict between the generations is not always bad, and lack of conflict is not always good. One way to achieve a seemingly idyllic peace is through tyrannical domination of the child. Some children are permanently squashed by tyrannical parents. Such a child's decorous behavior is a symptom of an impoverished capacity for autonomy. Wise parents know when to regulate and when to let the child try things out. The older the child, the greater the freedom to make mistakes.

Obviously, the parents of adolescents have to stand firm against clearly disastrous courses of action. In the case of ambiguously risky ventures, parents may have no choice but to hope for the best. Besides which, parents do not always know in advance about their offspring's projects, which may be cooked up on the spur of the moment. If a youngster lands in jail or the hospital, ends up stranded penniless on some remote shore, is unintentionally headed for parenthood, or is unable to cope with debts, then parents can only do their best to help salvage the situation and, in sympathetic cooperation with the young person, try to figure out what went wrong. The newspapers tell us that a certain number of young people are going to get into serious trouble. What they do not need from their parents is self-righteous moralizing, "I told you so" or "I warned you," or giving up on them too soon.

Parents fear the "empty nest" effect, rattling around in quarters that have suddenly grown too big when the children have left. We can say from personal experience that fears of an empty nest are largely groundless. The nest is not always that empty. Once young people have made the break and established their independence, they are free once more to let their love shine through. Most children return to establish a new adult-to-adult relationship with their parents. Parents find it highly gratifying to know their adult children as friends. In addition, children sometimes like to regress a little, and come back to the nest once in a while to be looked after and taken care of.

Parents find it extremely hard to let go completely. A few years ago, one of us had lunch with a colleague, a woman of forty, long married and the mother of two children. "Would you believe it!" she asked in some amazement. "Just before I left the house, my father called. He said the forecast was for heavy rain, so I should be sure to wear my boots."

Parents help and hinder their adolescent's transition to adulthood. But there are other forces that the adolescent has to contend with in the larger society. There are customs and traditions, laws, and economic conditions that bear directly on the adolescent's assuming adulthood.

Adolescents and Society

Adolescents are most vividly aware of their parents' concerns as barriers to maturity, but they know also that society at large has an interest in the matter. As we said earlier, most adolescents welcome society's badges of maturity: working papers, the driver's license, the voter registration card. Now the adolescent is ready to take the final step to independ-ence, and new obstacles become apparent.

Customs. The first problem that adolescents come up against as they prepare to assume maturity is that society has some pretty rigid ideas about the nature of adolescence. A number of adults stereotype young people (except their own kids, of course), defining them as disrespectful, unreliable, and lacking in common sense. If, for example, during a job interview, adult skepticism about the young person's ability gets him or her all flustered, this becomes the fulfillment of the adult's prophecy. The youngster's nervous reaction is clear evidence to the doubting adult that the young person is inept and unstable. There are, of course, adults who are understanding and helpful and young people who are poised and can present themselves with confidence.

Perhaps the most damaging aspect of the adult world's view of the young person is sex stereotyping. Many of today's young people are being reared with androgynous self-concepts. They feel free to have both traditionally masculine and feminine components in their personality. Young people so reared find it hard to deal with an older generation that still has many fixed ideas about the proper roles of male and female. It is not merely that young women are going to find it hard to get hired for male-typed jobs, or young men for female-typed ones. They may find it hard to get hired at all if they do not conform to the employer's image of femininity or masculinity. Unless the young person comes equipped with high-level occupational credentials—or, obviously, with powerful connections—he or she may be steered into the traditionally sex-typed divisions of whatever organization is willing to offer a job.

Laws. There are several legal hurdles between adolescence and full adult freedom. Receipt of a driver's license is conditioned not only on competence but also on age. The underlying assumption is that a young person may be able to drive but cannot exercise needed judgment until a certain chronological age. Below a certain age—fourteen in most places—one cannot obtain working papers. Laws defining the age of consent may have lost all meaning. Technically, however, anyone who has sex with a person below the age of consent is guilty of statutory rape. Marriageable age is still determined by law, although it, too, is meaningless for young people who simply live together. Youngsters are supposed to stay in school until they are fourteen or sixteen, depending on where they live. Nowadays many youngsters drop out of school by simply becoming full-time truants. About 10 to 20 percent of young Americans do not make it through high school; almost 1 million youngsters of high-school age (of a total enrollment of some 33 million) drop out each year (U.S. Bureau of the Census, 1980).

In most jurisdictions, people under sixteen accused of a crime can seek the protection of children's court. The rules of procedure are far more relaxed in children's court than in courts for adults, but so are the safeguards of the defendant's rights. Note, however, that many states are changing their laws in response to violent crimes committed by children and young adolescents. No longer can youngsters who commit violent crimes be sure that they can take refuge as juvenile offenders with the rel-

ative protection of children's courts. For young people, there is a whole category of crimes that simply does not apply to adults. Known as **status offenses**, these misdeeds are considered illegal if engaged in by persons below a certain age but not by persons above that age. Truancy is the most obvious example. Running away from home is a status offense. Here again, the flood of runaways has grown to such proportions that most big city police departments do not even try to deal with them. The young person can be jailed for incorrigibility, sometimes merely on the request of a parent. There is also an ill-defined set of behaviors, any one of which can mark the youngster as a Person in Need of Supervision (PINS). In New York City, PINS are sometimes jailed along with criminals, even though the PINS may have done nothing remotely criminal by adult standards.

As all young people know, the law specifies the age at which they are permitted to buy alcoholic beverages. However, adolescents easily circumvent this law. Forged ID cards are just one of the ways. New York State, alarmed at the number of car crashes involving drunken eighteen-year-olds, has raised the drinking age to nineteen. Letters to newspapers have asked whether it might not make better sense to raise the driving age to nineteen since eighteen-year-olds seem to have no difficulty obtaining all the alcohol they want. Movie ratings of X and R have no legal status that we know of, but in many communities the police stand ready to back up theater owners who want to enforce the ratings. The voting laws define eligibility by age. The law also specifies the age at which people can enter into binding contracts.

(© Tyrone Hall/Stock, Boston)

Finding work—a difficult enough task for adults in a thriving economy—can be close to impossible for teenagers during a time of recession. Even relatively unskilled jobs are much in demand.

Economic Influences. The law and economic considerations merge to make two kinds of insurance rates applicable to young people. The law allows insurance companies to charge according to risk categories—the greater the risk, the higher the premium. Statistics indicate that males below the age of twenty-five have a disproportionate number of automobile accidents, and their auto premiums are set accordingly. In most states, employers are obliged by law to carry worker's compensation insurance for their employees. For younger workers, who are statistically more accident-prone than older workers, the rates may be prohibitively high, effectively barring youngsters from risky occupations.

The young person's chances of employment are considerably enhanced if he or she has salable skills. It is easy enough for adolescents to acquire skills in vocational schools. What is much harder is predicting which skills will be in demand when it is time to enter the job market. Even relatively unskilled jobs, like being a busboy or waiting on tables, are very much in demand. In urban areas like New York City, restaurant jobs are the mainstay of aspiring actors and dancers, and to a lesser extent artists and writers and musicians, and the competition is fierce. Many college degree holders are happy in a recessionist economy to find themselves behind the wheel of a taxicab.

THE END OF CULTURAL ADOLESCENCE

Throughout this chapter, we have been playing with the question of when cultural adolescence can be considered to have come to an end. The answer is not a matter of age but of self-concept. Venturing into the adult world, adolescents half-consciously brace themselves against the high probability that they will meet with a challenge or a rebuff, from bartenders, waiters, druggists, and other adults who may view adolescents negatively.

Thus young people move almost defiantly in spheres that older people take for granted. They try not to appear ill at ease, but that is how they feel. Gradually, with practice, adolescents become increasingly relaxed, and they feel at home doing adult things. They become objectively more competent and subjectively more self-confident on the job. Then, one day, they notice a difference. They no longer expect slights, rejections, or insults. They take it for granted that they belong in the adult world, doing casually the same things that adults do. Most important, though, long-standing adults also take the new adults for granted. They do not think it odd that these young people should ask to participate in everyday adult activities. This is the key. Adolescence ends when the young person feels comfortable playing the role of adult. And the young person

feels comfortable when other adults accept him or her as one of themselves. Note that older people may still joke with younger ones about the latters' youth, about being a greenhorn or still wet behind the ears, but they do it as banter among people who are fundamentally equals. The adolescent at this point has joined the adult peer group and has left adolescence behind. Note that it is usually the young person's own parents who are the last to acknowledge the successful transition to adulthood. Parents can never quite escape their children's past, the one-time need to be protected, cherished, nourished, and fretted over. Parents will continue to remind their grownup children to go to the bathroom before they leave on a trip. Parents persist in fixing up "care packages" to help their self-supporting adult offspring survive.

Adults look back on their own adolescence in two quite disparate ways. There are those adults for whom adolescence seems in retrospect a time of torment, to be escaped from as fast as possible and to be banished as completely as possible from memory. Any reminder of the adolescent years brings feelings of frustration, humiliation, and despair. There are, by contrast, those adults who look back on adolescence as a time of lost splendor, of perpetual fun and games, of carefree revelry. These people would have been delighted to have adolescence go on forever. They entered adulthood only because circumstances forced them to. They still retain a largely adolescent outlook. Those at the extreme wear their hair in keeping with the latest adolescent fashions, dress themselves as much like teenagers as their adult roles will permit, and identify with passing teen fads in music, dance, and drug use. Some people do not want cultural or psychological adolescence ever to end.

At this point we conclude our discussion of normal psychological development. Adulthood, however, does not mean the end of development. Development goes on lifelong, ending only on one's deathbed. However, a single book cannot do justice to the entire life span. We have tried to give you a reasonably full account of the first couple of decades. If you are curious about what lies ahead, you will have to seek out a book dealing with adult development and aging.

But our task is not done. We have given you only the story of normal development. It is clear, though, that some people do not grow up normally or grow up to be normal. In Chapter 15, we give you a brief introduction to patterns of disturbance in development.

SUMMARY

1. Beginning at around age ten in girls and twelve in boys, a child's growth rate begins to accelerate. This pubescent growth spurt signals the beginning of adolescence, the period of transition from childhood to adulthood. The basic definition of adolescence is a biological one, but in technologically advanced societies, adolescence has taken on cultural and psychological meanings.

2. In preliterate societies, cultural adolescence does not exist. The young person on the threshold of maturity goes through a ritual, beginning as a child and ending as an adult. Vestiges of these puberty rites, rites de passage, or initiation ceremonies persist in our society.

3. The year before puberty is called the maximum growth age. During adolescence, height increases about 25 percent, and weight increases by anywhere from 50 to 100 percent.

4. Biological adolescence begins with pubescence, which is initiated by an increase of activity in the pituitary gland. During pubescence, the first pubic hairs appear, the breasts develop in girls, the penis and testes grow pendulous in boys, and the boy's beard begins to grow. Pubescence culminates in puberty. In girls, puberty is marked by the menarche, or first menstruation. In boys, it is marked by the presence of sperm in the urine and ready erection of the penis, along with strong urges to ejaculate. Somatic changes during adolescence are characterized by asynchrony. Individual differences in reaching puberty may lead to social difficulties.

5. The institutionalization of adolescence in Western societies has generated an adolescent subculture with its own prescribed ways of feeling and acting. Most adolescents strive to be widely liked and to be abreast of the latest trends. The dependence of the adolescent on group approval is so strong that it has been labeled the "popularity neurosis." Of course, some adolescents do not participate in this stereotypical herd life.

6. Certain themes seem to recur in adolescent behavior. These include romanticism, idealism, disillusionment, theatricality, hedonism, psychopathy, and conventionality.

7. In adolescence, the young person confronts the task of forming an identity as an adult. Erikson sees the central crisis of adolescence as one of identity versus role confusion. James Marcia has recast Erikson's theory to yield four statuses of identity development: diffusion, moratorium, identity achieved, and foreclosure. Adolescents largely define themselves according to the responses of their peers and worry a good deal about their appearance.

8. Adolescent sexuality is a major component of the adolescent's personal and social identity. Freud regarded the period as the genital stage of psychosexual development. The trend among adolescents is toward earlier and more widespread sexual activity. Social-class differences in sexual values have greatly narrowed, and a sexual reawakening among women has been underway. Unfortunately, the incidence of venereal disease is high among adolescents, and use of contraceptives low.

9. Adolescents use role playing to try on different identities; this is a vital mechanism in their coming to terms with themselves.

10. According to Piaget, adolescents enter the final stage of cognitive development, the stage of formal operations. They can organize information into systematic patterns, reason abstractly, and formulate and test their own hypotheses. Only a tiny minority of adolescents ever achieve the full extent of formal operations that Piaget described, however.

11. There is no question that sex differences in behavior exist; the question is their origin—genetic endowment or experience. Genetically, the sexes differ with regard to only one chromosome. Hormonal differences are likely to entail differences in temperament but not in cognitive functioning. In any case, it appears that even those sex differences—as in mathematical ability—that have been established through extensive

research may be disappearing as the culture changes. People think of masculine and feminine as two distinct dimensions nowadays, not two poles of one dimension, and parents no longer define their children's possibilities exclusively in terms of conventional sex roles.

12. As adolescents approach adulthood, the central problem for both parents and children is letting go—severing the bonds so the adolescent can assume adult autonomy. The stronger the attachment, the more violent may be the process of detachment. Adolescence ends when a young person feels comfortable playing the role of adult and is accepted by older adults.

KEY TERMS

adolescent sterility, 503
adolescent subfecundity, 503
androgyny, 531
asynchrony, 505
biological adolescence, 499
change of voice, 503
commitment, 516
counteridentify, 519
crisis, 516
cultural or psychological adolescence, 499
double bind (no-win situation), 536

dual ambivalence, 535
formal operations, 525
genital stage, 519
idealism, 515
identity crisis, 516
identity status, 517
maximum growth age (MGA), 502
menarche, 498
nocturnal emission ("wet dream"), 503
popularity neurosis, 511
primary sex traits, 504
puberty, 498
puberty rites, rites de

passage, initiation ceremonies, 501
pubescence, 498
pubescent growth spurt, 498
role confusion (role diffusion), 516
role playing, 524
secondary sex traits, 504
status offense, 538
Sturm und Drang, 507
Weltschmerz, 507

SUGGESTED READINGS

Joyce, J. *A Portrait of the Artist as a Young Man*. New York: B. W. Huebsch, 1916 (available in a number of editions). The epitome of classical adolescence.

Muuss, R. E. *Theories of Adolescence*. 4th ed. New York: Random House, 1982. A comprehensive picture of different theoretical perspectives on development during adolescence.

Owen, D. *High School*. New York: Viking, 1981. A 24-year-old enrolls in high school. A sometimes funny, often depressing picture of administrative disorientation, faculty incompetence, and student hostility or indifference.

Salinger, J. D. *The Catcher in the Rye*. Boston: Little, Brown, 1951. A fictional account of a young adolescent under stress. A classic.

Wright, R. *Black Boy*. New York: Harper & Row, 1965 (originally published, 1945). An eloquent autobiography of growing up as a black in the Jim Crow South.

CHAPTER 15

Disturbances in Development

This book is about normal psychological development. It depicts the way people with reasonably sound constitutions grow up in reasonably favorable environments. It includes the normal "problems" that large numbers of parents and children have to face. Sometimes, however, the developmental process goes seriously awry. This book would be incomplete if we failed to mention some of the major abnormalities that occur in childhood, along with what we know or suspect about their causes and remedies. The study of abnormal development is important for practical and theoretical reasons. We hope, on a practical level, to relieve human misery. On a theoretical level, we again hope that our theories will lead us to increased understanding of normal as well as disturbed development. Having said this, we are confronted with a problem. This is defining what we mean by normal and abnormal behavior.

There are three basic ways of defining what it means to be psychologically normal. The first is the **symptom-free definition:** As long as a person has no serious psychiatric symptoms—inability to learn, disordered thinking, hallucinations—or combination of symptoms, he or she can be considered normal. The second is the **social-modal definition:** As long as the person behaves pretty much like most other members of his or her social group, observing its values and conventions, he or she is considered normal. The third is the **creative-minority definition:** Only those people who have transcended the cultural myths and artificial restraints that hobble the thinking of ordinary people can be considered truly normal. Here we are moved to think of Abraham Maslow's (1950) **self-actualizing person** as the ideal of normality, the person who has fulfilled all his or her developmental potentialities. Note that the first two concepts permit all but a handful of people to qualify as normal. The third concept refers to only a small portion of the population.

We reject the symptom-free and the creative-minority concepts of normality. We know that it is possible to be free of symptoms of psychiatric disturbance and still be hopelessly, even murderously, deranged. Indeed, psychiatry has a decidedly poor record at predicting who will go off the deep end and in what circumstances. The creative-minority concept offers us no reliable way of distinguishing between creative nonconformists and unconventional psychotics.

The social-modal concept is far from perfect, of course. We accept it only by elimination. Our culture imposes a great many blinders. A total identification with any culture's assumptions and beliefs might well qualify as a special form of lunacy. But we are saved from complete subservience to cultural dogma by our capacity for duplicity. We can conform outwardly in public and indulge our own ideas and tastes in the company of like-minded familiars—or, if necessary, in solitude.

From this standpoint, it follows that any form of psychopathology can be described as a failure of identification with the larger society. For instance, a child can identify thoroughly with his or her family. However, if the family is a bunch of misfits, society will judge the child to be, too. On the other hand, identification with the family is a necessary first step to identifying with the society at large. There are two main obstacles to identi-

(© Alan Carey/The Image Works)

Research shows that even severe organic damage need not necessarily prevent sound psychological development.

fication: organic impairments and disturbed family relationships.

Organic impairments, notably defects in the nervous system or the endocrine system, may make a child incapable of forming normal attachments and elaborating these into a sense of identity. However, there is a good deal of research indicating that even quite severe organic damage need not prevent sound development (Sameroff and Chandler, 1975; Werner and Smith, 1982). It would appear that, most of the time, organic impairments interfere with identification because parents think they make normal communication with the child impossible. In these cases, either parents view the damaged baby as incapable of normal feeling and cognition, or the baby seems deformed and unlovable. When parents see organic damage as an obstacle to normal communication, they (sometimes jointly with medical personnel) set up a self-fulfilling prophecy.

There are any number of reasons that bonds of attachment and identification may fail to form. For a long time, when things went wrong with children's development, it was the custom to heap all the blame on inadequate mothers. We now recognize that this view is misguided in at least two ways. First, fathers also bear a share of responsibility for the psychological well-being of their children even if the father's dealings with a child are far less than the mother's. Second, the baby is an important stimulus to outpourings of positive parental feeling. If the baby does not look quite right to the parents or have the right activity level, or the right kind of responsiveness to parental stimulation, then the parents may feel rejected. They may become anxious or hostile. These feelings make normal interactions difficult. We know that each failure of communication can feed into a vicious circle and make the next exchange that much more likely to fail. At the ultimate, repeated failures of contact and communication add up to a chronic pattern of neglect, rejection, or abuse. Note, though, that even under the least favorable conditions, all but a small minority of children form some sort of identification and come to reasonable terms with the world.

We cannot hope, within the compass of a short chapter, to cover the whole field of behavior pathology in childhood. Those who wish to explore further are referred to more inclusive sources (e.g.,

Lachenmeyer and Gibbs, 1982). We shall point out only a few of the more common or most intensively studied conditions that arise during childhood and adolescence. We shall deal only briefly with treatment procedures, partly for lack of space, partly for lack of expert qualifications, and partly because there are still so many unknowns. Therapies for children and adults are proliferating furiously, and we cannot even pretend to keep up with each movement. The kinds of conditions we will discuss fall into four categories: retardation, neurosis, sociopathy, and psychosis.

DISTURBANCES IN INFANCY AND TODDLERHOOD

We have already, in Chapter 4, spoken of the various conditions to be found in newborn babies. Newborns, you will recall, show abnormalities associated with genetic disorders (such as *Down's syndrome*); with unfavorable conditions in the prenatal environment (such as *rubella*), which may cause blindness or deafness or brain damage); with prematurity; with damaging events during the birth process (such as *cerebral palsy*); or with unknown causes. However, while these conditions can be recognized as abnormal, they are of very little help in predicting the course of development. We can safely state that babies with marked congenital abnormalities are, on a group basis, more likely to grow up to have some sort of psychological impairment than those who are not physically flawed. However, we cannot say that any individual baby's future is full of either

promise or gloom. Obviously, ethics demand that we do everything we can for infants who appear to be at risk for developmental abnormalities, even though our interventions spoil our research plans.

A disorder of infancy that seems to be quite clearly of nonorganic origins is **failure to thrive.** Failure to thrive is associated with disturbed relations between babies and their parents in which parental efforts at communication cannot be timed to the baby's needs. The parents lack the self-control necessary to adapt to the baby's rhythms, and the baby lacks the means to bring the parents under control. There is so far insufficient research on what becomes of failure-to-thrive infants.

DISTURBANCES IN THE PRESCHOOL YEARS

Very few major psychological disorders seem to be tied specifically to the preschool years. Some children, of course, carry with them the afflictions of earlier periods, including prenatal life and birth. But as we have said, most of these are amenable to some sort of treatment. Those disorders that first become apparent in the preschool years seem to have been present from early life, and become manifest in response to the new demands of this age.

In a survey of middle-class mothers of some 200 four-year-olds, the problems emphasized involved such everyday matters as the children's resisting bedtime, shyness or lack of assertiveness with peers, stubbornness and disobedience, whining and nagging, temper outbursts, and fighting or quarreling with siblings (this last was mentioned in 92 percent of the cases) (Chamberlin, 1974). One might expect problems of delayed language acquisition or problems of sphincter control, such as bed-wetting, to be prominent. In fact, these were rarely mentioned.

A more comprehensive study of mental health problems in childhood and adolescence was that of Achenbach and Edelbrook (1981). These investigators surveyed a large sample of youngsters from age four to age sixteen. Their sample consisted of a cross-section of boys and girls, half of whom had been referred to clinics for various psychological problems and half of whom had not. The two groups were matched for both socioeconomic status and sex. They were grouped into seven age levels, each encompassing a two-year span. We are concerned here only with the four- to five-year-old group. This group consisted of fifty boys and fifty girls referred to clinics and fifty boys and fifty girls who had had no such referral. What the investigators found was a much higher incidence in the clinic group of the following behaviors: acting too young; bragging; inability to concentrate; obsessions (preoccupation with some area of concern); hyperactivity; overdependence; complaints of loneliness; confusion; excessive crying; cruelty to animals; cruelty to other people (especially among clinic boys); daydreaming; destructiveness (especially among clinic boys); disobedience; poor peer relations; lack of guilt; fearfulness; and being prone to jealousy.

Such observations, interesting as they are, do not tell us much about the nature of psychopathology in the preschool years. For one thing, many of the "symptoms" are perfectly normal preschool-age behavior, even when more clinic children than nonclinic children seem to suffer from them. There is nothing remarkable about bragging, overdependence, disobedience, or having fears in four- and five-year-olds. We suspect that the parents who reported these as characteristics of their children did not know enough about preschool children to be able to judge what is normal. Indeed, Gibbs (1982) cites a sizable body of research indicating that much childhood psychopathology may reside only in the eye of the parent. Ironically enough, parents with the most education are the most likely to see behavior as pathological; it is as though they had learned just enough to be hypersensitive to children's childishness, but not enough to see it as normal. Even in the case of clearly abnormal behavior, such as cruelty to animals, we do not know whether it is part of a larger pattern or simply a deviation found in otherwise normal children.

Fears and Phobias

There is a marked increase in fears and phobias during the preschool years. Freudians interpret the fearfulness of this age as an expression of castration anxiety associated with the Oedipus complex. We, however, view this increase as tied to the child's growing knowledge both of the body and its vulnerability and of the world and its menaces. Obviously, older children have a still greater range of knowledge. However, they also have improved understanding and can put their knowledge of all the dreadful things that can happen into some kind of perspective. Also, as we have seen, older children are less prone than preschoolers to fear imaginary things. Thus we see a peak of fearfulness late in the preschool years and a decrease thereafter.

Children may express their fears openly, or they may try to hide them. Adult lack of sympathy may lead the child to attempt to conceal fear, but suppressed fearfulness is likely to come out in nightmares, in a generalized timidity, or in somatic symptoms such as chronic stomach aches. Some children seem to focus a formless sort of dread into fear of some particular thing—high places, elevators, men with beards, or cats, among others. Focusing fear in this way appears to give it a shape and so make it more manageable except, of course, in the presence of the thing feared. Such a fear is called a **phobia.** Among the better known phobias are *acrophobia* (fear of high places); *agoraphobia* (fear of open spaces); *claustrophobia* (fear of being shut in); and *ailurophobia* (fear of cats).

Even when phobias have a sensible origin, as when a disagreeable experience with a dog leads to a fear of all dogs in all circumstances, phobias tend to be highly irrational and resistant to evidence that they are unfounded. The consensus seems to be that one should avoid reinforcing a phobia (O'Leary and Carr, 1982). The child with a school phobia should be made to go to school (Lachenmeyer, 1982). The adult with acrophobia must somehow be made to endure high places. Many people are seized with panic when they have to drive across a high bridge. It is said that people with agoraphobia may become totally housebound rather than expose themselves to the terrors of wide open spaces. When the phobia attaches to tangible objects,

it may yield to the behavior modification technique of **desensitization.** This technique was pioneered some sixty years ago by Mary Cover Jones (1924), a student of John B. Watson's. Desensitization consists in exposing the subject very gradually to the feared object in unusually pleasant conditions. One might play the individual's favorite music, or provide favored food and drink, talk on topics that the individual holds dear, encourage relaxation, and, little by little, bring the feared object within touching range.

Speech Defects

In the preschool years, when the fundamentals of language are being established, speech defects are not uncommon. Some of these are due to impaired hearing, and some to problems in the speech apparatus that make articulation difficult. However, the great majority are simply a matter of immaturity. Most children correct their speech defects just in the course of living.

Sometimes, though, defects persist. When children continue using baby talk long after their contemporaries have left it behind, it may be a sign of one of several conditions: The parents may be talking baby talk and thus providing inappropriate models. They may be overprotecting their children. Perhaps they are overindulging them and making babyhood too attractive to leave. When the child first begins to talk, parental baby talk is almost inevitable—remember code switching and motherese, in which adults and older children simplify their speech in talking to babies and young children. Once the child is well launched in speaking, however, it is time for the parents to resume normal adult language. If a child reverts to baby talk after having spoken in a more mature manner, this regression may reflect emotional strain, lasting or transitory. In such cases, one cannot treat the baby talk itself. Instead, one has to look for the source of stress, such as the birth of a new baby in the family.

Probably the most frequent form of speech disorder in young children is **stuttering.** (Speech specialists no longer draw a distinction between stuttering and stammering.) Theories to account for stuttering have been of two kinds. Psychological theories treat stuttering as a symptom of emotional distress. Physiological theories emphasize disruptions in brain circuits. Neither sort of theory has been able to marshal a great deal of convincing evidence.

Stuttering has been brought under partial control in the laboratory (Fillenbaum, 1963). It is possible that in natural stuttering, as well as in stuttering induced artificially in the laboratory, the critical factor is a disturbance of feedback. Studies indicate that a smooth flow of speech is dependent on the speaker's listening to and monitoring his or her own speech. The speaker is usually unaware of this process until something interferes with it. Normally, the lag between speaking and hearing oneself speak is infinitesimal. Stuttering can be induced experimentally in anyone simply by producing a lag of about one quarter of a second between the time people speak and the time their voices come back to them. This is accomplished by having a person speak into a tape recorder which, after the predetermined interval, plays the person's voice back to him or her through headphones.

This observation accords well with those made way back in the 1930s and 1940s by Wendell Johnson and still accepted by many leaders in the field (Shapiro and DeCicco, 1982). Johnson and his associates (1942) proposed that a large part of stuttering in children is created by adults who, overreacting to normal speech hesitations and gropings, force children to become self-conscious about their speech. This can be crippling for the child. We have an analogy in the story of the centipede who had gotten along perfectly well until an admiring ant asked him which leg he moved first, thereby rendering the centipede paralyzed. Other views have been proposed, but they have found scant empirical support (Perkins, 1980; Shapiro, 1980). It appears that the most effective therapy for stuttering is to help stutterers live more comfortably with their stuttering. Few cures are reported. Therapy with very young children may even be counterproductive simply because it leads to crippling self-consciousness of the kind described.

Whatever other emotional or neurological factors underlie stuttering, there is every reason to think that it can be created. Hence, it is not a good idea to tell preschool children that they can talk better, that they should try to talk more slowly, or that they should repeat themselves and "this time say it nicely." Children expect reactions to the substance of what they say, not to how they say it. Children whose parents provide good models of speaking generally end up talking just fine.

Moderate Mental Retardation

Severe mental retardation may be evident in infancy, although as we have seen, it is not a good idea to make such

Retardation in all its varied forms may be traced to genetic, prenatal, and perinatal factors, and to postnatal rearing conditions. Disentangling all these possible causative forces is no easy matter. Regardless of cause, behavior modification techniques can help (O'Leary and Carr, 1982), if only by raising the child's level of self-esteem.

Infantile Autism

A most profound psychological disturbance may appear during the preschool years in the form of **childhood schizophrenia,** an early form of the disorder that we shall discuss more fully under adolescence. In addition to the fairly classical, adultlike schizophrenia occasionally found in young children, a special variety has been recognized which can appear any time from infancy through the preschool years. This is known as **infantile autism,** a condition first defined by Leo Kanner (1943, 1944). A fairly stable pattern of symptoms is associated with autism. Most prominent is the avoidance of human contact, physical, visual, or verbal. Autistic children may remain mute, but even when they speak it is in ways that do not communicate. They may simply parrot things said to them (*echolalia*). Instead of answering a question, autistic children may simply repeat it, sometimes over and over. They may recite rhymes or other word clusters picked up from the people around them. They often produce meaningless utterances (or they seem meaningless to other people). Autistic children relate well to inanimate objects, and some show great mechanical proficiency. They may show the characteristics of *idiots savants*, persons of se-

(© Elizabeth Crews)

A child with Down's syndrome builds sand castles. With special training, Down's syndrome children can often lead active and productive lives.

judgments lightly. In the preschool years, moderate mental retardation may beome apparent. Mild mental retardation may remain hidden until the child has to cope with the special demands of schooling. However, freed from the necessity of conforming to the somewhat artificial learning demands of the school, large numbers of "retarded" people blossom into normality (Werner and Smith, 1982).

verely limited intellectual ability who can perform dazzlingly well in a particular area. Both idiots savants and autistic children may show great gifts for mental arithmetic, know the day of the week on which any particular date fell for centuries back, have marked artistic or musical talents, or perform prodigious feats of memorization.

Autistic children seem to take comfort in highly repetitive, ritualistic activities, such as switching a light on and off, repeatedly flushing a toilet, or watching a phonograph turntable spin. Autistic children themselves may like to spin or twirl or roll machinelike, or they may adopt ritualized, often-repeated gestures or mannerisms. Like the fictionalized Jordi (Rubin, 1960), many autistic children carry a "jiggler" with them at all times. This typically is a toy tied to the end of a string so that it can be taken out and jiggled in moments of tension. Autistic children show little interest in sex and rarely masturbate. In general, it would seem that they have identified with the nonhuman world. They treat other people—without hatred or malice—as though they are only another kind of thing. At the extreme, we get the child who seems to have become a machine, as in Bettelheim's (1959, 1967) case of Joey the Mechanical Boy. Autistic children also fiercely resist even the slightest change in the arrangement of their familiar environments.

Autistic males outnumber autistic females three to one. A large majority are first-born children. Their parents, in many cases, are described as highly intelligent but emotionally constricted.

There is general agreement on what we have said so far. However, there is spirited debate on two issues. The first is whether autism is genetic (or at least or-

(© Meri Houtchens-Kitchens/The Picture Cube)

A six-year-old autistic boy. Whether autism is caused by a genetic defect or by parental rejection and a failure of attachment has been the subject of intense debate.

ganic) in origin (Morgan, 1981; Rimland, 1964) or stems from parental rejection and a failure of attachment (Bettelheim, 1967, 1974). The second issue is how best to treat the condition. Bettelheim (1967, 1974) favors immersing the child totally in a carefully designed human and physical environment aimed at reestablishing a capacity for human contact and communication, and, eventually, giving the child a well-defined sense of self. Bettelheim has had some notable successes in restoring children to normal functioning. He has also had some failures.

The second treatment approach comes from behavior modification or behavior therapy. Behaviorally oriented therapists begin by grouping autism with schizophrenia and retardation as "developmental disabilities," on the basis of their similar symptoms. Behavior therapists define developmental disability as a deficit in adaptive behavior, the ability to modify one's actions in keeping with circumstances (O'Leary and Carr, 1982). The first aim of behavior therapy is to eliminate such autistic behavior as head banging, self biting, tantrums, and aggression. This is done by reinforcing constructive behaviors that are incompatible with the destructive behaviors. If this does not work, the unwanted behaviors may be punished by spanking, electric shocks, or "time out" (the behavior therapist's term for solitary confinement). The therapist uses a combination of instruction, modeling, and praise or material rewards for desired behaviors. Parents and teachers are also taught to function as therapists. Controlled studies are few. However, the available evidence suggests that behavior therapy works best if it is begun early (before age thirty months), if the treatment can be continued over a long period, if the child has a nonverbal IQ of at least 60, and if the child can be kept in an approximately normal, noninstitutional environment.

We do not pretend to understand the riddle of infantile autism. It is possible that there is some unknown organic deficit leading to unresponsiveness in the infant to which the parents, in turn, react with withdrawal or rejection. In any event, some autistic children recover spontaneously and grow up to lead reasonably normal lives.

BEHAVIORAL DISTURBANCES IN THE MIDDLE YEARS

School-Related Problems

A number of difficulties emerge during the middle years that are related to starting grade school. At this time, formal instruction in reading, writing, and arithmetic usually begins, accompanied by new demands for effort and achievement, and also for an unprecedented immobility, silence, and attentiveness.

In recent years, much attention has been given to children who suffer from what are called "**learning disabilities**" (Farnham-Diggory, 1978; Sapir and Wilson, 1978). About 10 percent of school-age children are afflicted. They are mostly boys who have average to above-average IQs. There is often a family history of similar difficulty.

The reported symptoms of learning disability are diverse. A major symptom is said to be clumsiness. Learning disabled children are often reported to be poorly coordinated in both gross and fine motor activities. They are likely to have trouble catching a ball, tying shoelaces, or writing with a pencil. Some learning disabled children have speech difficulties. Others may suffer from memory problems, difficulties in coordinating vision and action, or defective ability to process information and make sense of what they see and hear. They can be either overactive or lethargic.

A special form of learning disability is *dyslexia*, or reading difficulty. Manifestations include inability to associate printed letters and words with spoken sounds; reversal or rotation of letters (for instance, confusing *d* and *b*, or seeing E as Ǝ); and difficulty in integrating letters or syllables to form words. Dyslexia may be accompanied by *dysgraphia*, writing problems. The dysgraphic child's words are often placed so poorly on the page as to be illegible. It was long supposed that dyslexia in American children was related to the peculiarities of

English spelling. However, research by Stevenson and his associates (1982) shows that reading disabilities are also found in children learning to read Chinese and Japanese.

According to some observers, learning disorders are thought to be an expression of **minimal brain damage (MBD).** This is a structural or functional abnormality of the brain that does not show up with the usual neurological diagnostic techniques. MBD is regarded by others, including the authors, as an untestable hypothesis that by means of reification (i.e., giving it a name) gives an illusion of explaining something (Leung, 1975). Learning disabilities in general and dyslexia in particular have also been attributed to junk foods or food additives (preservatives, flavorings, colorings). One study blames them on high levels of lead and cadmium in the body (Pihl and Parkes, 1977). Some cases may be due to undetected problems in eyesight or hearing, slow maturation, malnutrition, or psychological or social problems. It is important to bear in mind that many dyslexics become fully competent readers and writers, if only at a somewhat later age than is usual. Among the remedies that seem to help some dyslexics is having lots of practice with large type. Those who cannot organize regular printed matter may be able to manage when the type is big and there is plenty of space between words and lines.

Emotional interferences with learning are sometimes called **learning blocks.** They appear in the context of parental overambition and pressure, which can turn children away from the learning process and make it extrinsic to their own needs and wishes. Some children try hard to measure up to their parents'

(© Meri Houtchens-Kitchens/The Picture Cube)

One school-related behavior disorder is hyperkinesis, or hyperactivity, the inability to sit still and focus attention.

expectations, but the strain of trying simply increases the irrelevant emotion in the situation. Each failure becomes more frustrating. This leads to new anxiety and confusion and makes the next failure all the more likely. For some children, failure may be a weapon with which to punish overdemanding parents.

Another school-related problem, again found most often in boys with normal or high IQs, is **hyperkinesis** or **hyperactivity.** This is an inability to sit still and focus attention in school and school-like situations. Hyperkinetic children are often impulsive. They are easily distracted and often distract their classmates (Stewart and Olds, 1973).

Like learning disability, hyperkinesis has been explained by MBD, poor nutrition, environmental pollutants, and so forth (Kolata, 1978). The evidence on food additives is elusive (Brozan, 1980; Brunner, Vorhees, and Butcher, 1981). However, there is some reason to believe

(Weiss, 1981) that risky amounts of toxic food dyes are allowed in foods and may affect behavior. Halverson and associates have tried to relate various forms of problem behavior to the presence of minor physical anomalies (Halverson and Victor, 1976). These include unusually large head circumference, epicanthic folds of the eyelids, widely spaced eyes, a curved fifth finger, and wide gaps between the first and second toes. One study (Waldrop et al., 1978) found that the number of minor physical anomalies in newborn boys (girls were not studied) correlated .86 with problem behavior at age three. However, a study by Jacklin, Maccoby, and Halverson (1980) does not bear out these findings. Even if an organic basis for hyperactivity can be established, we must remember that the course of development depends heavily on a continuing two-way interaction between the child and other people.

Children diagnosed as hyperactive are often treated with drugs. How effective such treatment is we cannot judge from the conflicting reports we have seen. One of the favored drugs is the stimulant amphetamine, which nonmedical users know as "speed." Amphetamine is said to have a paradoxically soothing effect on hyperactive children because of some atypical characteristic of such children's brains. However, Rapoport and his associates (1978) have shown that amphetamine has identical effects on normal and hyperkinetic boys. Amphetamine given to normal boys between the ages of six and twelve produces a rapid drop in activity level, faster reaction time, improved memory, and increased vigilance. About five hours after receiving the drug, children show a marked "rebound" effect. This consists of excitability, talka-tiveness, and, in a few subjects, euphoria (exaggerated feelings of well-being). A number of subjects suffered from insomnia, and a few had stomach aches and mild nausea. Such reactions have been attributed to the wearing off of the drug. However, Rapoport suggests that the rebound is caused by delayed chemical reactions. Swanson and Kinsbourne (1979) report that the drug Ritalin seems to improve attention, concentration, and learning, but only as long as the drug is active. They point to a phenomenon known as *state-dependent learning:* Material is retained and is usable in the condition in which it was learned, but evaporates when the state changes. Thus the individual under the influence of tranquilizers, alcohol, or other drugs may learn and remember, only to forget what was learned as soon as the intoxicant wears off. The learning may return when the state is resumed. It is as though the drugged person was separate from his or her undrugged self.

Delinquency and Crime

Juvenile delinquency has been with us for some time, usually as a gang phenomenon and often under adult direction (consider Fagin, Oliver Twist, and the Artful Dodger). However, in recent years there have been several new trends in childhood criminality. One trend has been toward greater youthfulness in criminals. This could be accounted for in part by the exploitation of children by adult criminals. It is theorized that children caught in activities like running numbers, drugs, or weapons are unlikely to be punished. However, a number of states and cities have modified their ju-

(© *Charles Gatewood/Stock, Boston*)

Girls are now arrested twice as often as boys, though 75 percent of the arrests are for status offenses: truancy, running away from home, disobedience, or promiscuity.

venile offender statutes to remove this particular weakness.

A second trend has been toward greater ferocity and violence by child criminals. These children, in pairs or small groups, prey on people who look defenseless, such as the very old. They rob, beat, and sometimes rape and kill them. Such behavior may indicate profound psychopathology, but at least some child criminals voice considerable hostility toward the "haves" of society. Delinquent behavior in children from fa-

vored backgrounds almost always expresses hostility toward the parents or, through them, toward society at large. We remind the reader once again that failure of identification may be an important factor in all kinds of psychopathology.

A third trend in juvenile delinquency has been the increasing involvement of girls. According to *Today's Girls: Tomorrow's Women* (1979), in the period 1960 to 1975 arrests of girls under eighteen for violent crimes rose 503 percent; for possession of weapons, 410 percent; and for crimes against property, 420 percent. These seemingly huge percentages reflect the fact that arrests of girls for serious crimes before 1960 amounted to very small numbers. Arrests of girls are now twice as frequent as arrests of boys. However, 75 percent of girls' arrests are for status offenses. We defined status offenses in Chapter 14 as misdeeds that are considered criminal only if committed by someone below a stated age: truancy, running away from home, disobedience, or, in the case of girls, promiscuity.

Runaways, both middle-years and adolescent girls and boys, often support themselves as heterosexual or homosexual prostitutes. Although prostitution is against the law, most police forces seem to have given up on fighting it. Some observers feel that the child prostitute is unable to form stable positive relationships. However, in such cases it is almost impossible to distinguish cause and effect. Bracey (1982) speaks of the juvenile female prostitute as being victimized several times over: by her pimp, perhaps by her customers, and by society if she has the bad luck to be arrested and charged. A serious complication of life as a prostitute is the threat of venereal disease. There are more than a million new cases of gonorrhea each year. The greatest increase is in the ten- to fourteen-year-old group, which between 1970 and 1977 experienced a 95 percent increase (*Today's Girls: Tomorrow's Women,* 1979).

There are a number of varieties of delinquent, but two deserve special mention. The first kind is the **acting-out delinquent.** Such an individual freely expresses his or her impulses, particularly hostile ones. "Acting out" refers to the uninhibited, deliberate, and often malicious indulgence of urges that normal people try to control. Unbridled impulses lead to battering, rape, and sometimes homicide. We have said that vandalism is often the product of boredom. Some vandalism, however, expresses a free-floating rage against society or some of its segments. We cannot find either single causes or reliable patterns in the early life histories of children who act out. However, Werner and Smith (1977), who have collected longitudinal data on all the children born in 1955 on the island of Kauai, in Hawaii, report that such children can be spotted as early as age two. Authors of a Freudian bent have speculated about an unconscious need for punishment in children who act out. They rather often get caught, and it seems plausible that basically they may want to be punished. Acting-out children are normally intelligent. They have rather strong emotions that, even though predominantly negative, make them different from the sociopathic delinquent.

The **psychopathic** or **sociopathic** or **antisocial personality** is the second variety of delinquent to which we want to call attention. These labels refer to chronic antisocial behavior expressing a near-total lack of fellow feeling for other people. There seem to be two likely reasons for the sociopath's defective conscience. One is failure to identify with sound parental models. The other is identifying with parents who themselves model sociopathic styles of behavior.

Psychopaths or sociopaths are remarkable for their emotional blandness in regard to actions that would profoundly shock normal people. Although psychopaths are indifferent to other people's feelings, they often understand them well enough to do an expert job of manipulating them. Psychopaths know how to talk in terms of the accepted values. They can be quite charming in their short-term personal relations. They make glib promises and resolutions but may at the same time be picking the pocket of the person they are talking to. They are profoundly egocentric and seem incapable of seeing their own responsibility for anything that goes wrong. Psychopaths score in the normal range on IQ tests, but their thinking is essentially superficial. Despite normal learning ability, they seem not to profit from their own mistakes. This means that they are repeatedly caught repeating their past blunders. They seek to manipulate people with stock formulas, and, even though this works for a while, people do catch on. When they do, the psychopath cannot adapt to the change and goes on with the same nonfunctional manipulations. Psychopaths seem never to be discouraged by a history of failed scams—they are foolishly, incurably optimistic.

Psychopaths steal even when they are sure to be caught. They lie even when there is no earthly reason for them to do so. Some psychopaths can be murderously violent (although most are not), but even their violence has a shallow, unfeeling quality. They do not particularly wish other people ill. It is just that others' needs and feelings are of no great significance. Their own desires are paramount and absolute.

Although children are rarely labeled as psychopaths or sociopaths, the foundations for a sociopathic outlook are laid down early. Not all psychopaths are delinquents or criminals. Some are simply unpleasant characters who exploit and betray their friends and families but stay within the law. Some become marginal personalities. Some settle down to shallow respectability. A few become financially successful, but it is doubtful that such people ever become able to establish satisfying interpersonal relationships.

Patterns in Childhood Psychopathology

Using the technique of cluster analysis, which permits one to detect patterns of intercorrelation, Achenbach (1982) has identified three broad categories of problem behavior. First, there is overcontrolled or internalizing behavior. Here we find such symptoms as compulsions and obsessions, irrational guilt, low self-esteem, and psychosomatic disturbances. Second, there is undercontrolled or externalizing behavior. Here we find all the varieties of acting out and aggression. The third category is mixed, or hostile withdrawal. This category includes such symptoms as bed-wetting and confused thinking.

A finer analysis of the symptoms found in twelve- to sixteen-year-old boys has yielded six profile-types of disturbed behavior. First, there is the *schizoid* type. Schizoid behavior is marked by clinging to adults, expressing fear of one's own impulses, perfectionism, or hallucinations. Second, there is the *uncommunicative* type. Children exhibiting such behavior may be confused, withdrawn, self-conscious, shy, timid, or moody. Third, we have the *immature-aggressive* type. Such a child acts too young, cries, wets the bed, whines, argues, screams, or fights. Fourth, there is the *hyperactive* type. Such children are characterized by an inability to concentrate, disobedience in school, impulsiveness, and nail biting. Fifth, we have the *uncommunicative-delinquent* type, marked by destructiveness, disobedience, a taste for unsavory companions, lying, cheating, stealing, and fire setting. Sixth, there is the *delinquent* type. Delinquent children are characterized in Achenbach's analysis primarily by poor school work. These last data have already taken us into adolescent psychopathology, a description of which we now continue.

BEHAVIORAL DISTURBANCES IN ADOLESCENCE

The excesses of normal adolescent behavior often reach such emotional extremes that some people would say that adolescence itself is a form of psychopathology. However, it is important to recognize that some adolescents are deeply troubled individuals whose ability to function may be severely limited. Thus, we are talking about problems ranging from the almost normal to the neurotic and the psychotic.

Running Away

One fairly common expression of adolescent unhappiness is running away from home. As far as we can tell, there are nowadays three sorts of running away. The first of these is the lark, running away temporarily from adult authority in order to go on a spree, often with a companion. When the money runs out, the young person telephones home collect, professes contrition, and asks to be retrieved.

The second kind of running away is also temporary but has a more serious purpose. It seems to be a way of saying as concretely as possible to unheeding parents that they are mistreating the young person badly and causing him or her grave distress. This sort of running away may embody repeated flights and reconciliations. It appears to occur most often among females.

The third form of running away expresses a grim determination, come what may, to escape from all that makes life unbearable at home: parental authority, the boredom of small-town life, ostracism by peers, the demands of school, any of the things that drive young people to desperation. We consider this last kind of running away to be at least marginally pathological because the young person has usually not thought through the practical consequences of his or her decision. Running away in this manner is an escape into a fantasyland. The lucky young person may find a friend's house or a hostel to serve as a base, if only temporarily, from which to build a life. Some hostels offer counseling and try to reconcile parent and child. Failing a reconciliation, hostels try to place the youngster in school, find him or her a job, or do whatever else is possible to keep the young person occupied and off the streets. The less lucky—and more numerous—young runaways, unfamiliar with big-city ways and the few legitimate job opportunities that exist, simply drift until picked up by one of the professional predators. The desperate young person may begin by getting hooked on drugs, but the ultimate fate of all too many is prostitution.

We lack the research that tells us about the long-term fate of young runaways. We do not know what proportion of them eventually finds conventional employment, goes back to school, and launches a career. Some may rise in the world of prostitution or drug dealing which, at the top, offer rich material rewards. Some may become thieves or confidence artists. Some, we are sure, deteriorate and end up as derelicts. Those who study Skid Row report that its denizens are younger all the time. The worst off are the addicts, for whom no degradation is too big a price to pay for drugs.

Delinquency

Adolescent delinquency may be simply an extension of the delinquent behavior found in middle-years children. Adolescents, too, act out their impulses or behave sociopathically. The chief new feature of adolescent delinquency is what is called **socialized** or **subcultural delinquency.** What appears to members of the mainstream culture as criminal behavior is, in some subcultures, taken for granted as a normal adjustment to reality. Young people growing up in and identifying with such a subculture do not even think of right and wrong in the dominant culture's terms. Right and wrong are not what the law says. They are what their subculture's view of reality dictates. Smuggling or burglary or prostitution may be passed down from generation to generation as a family trade. A criminal way of life may be simply the young person's cultural heritage.

We do not know whether today's reform schools for young males offer any sort of preparation for a noncriminal life. Rector (1979) says that intended rehabilitation for delinquent females expresses sex-role stereotyping at a low level. Female inmates are trained to find careers as cooks, maids, seamstresses, or beauticians.

It is not certain that running away and delinquency qualify as mental or emotional disturbance. There are, however, conditions found in adolescence that are readily identifiable as neurotic or psychotic. We now look at these.

Neurotic Reactions in Adolescence

For unknown reasons, the incidence of various neurotic conditions shifts with the times. For instance, in years past *hysteria* was thought of as a common neurosis of adolescence. Hysteria refers to a bodily malfunction in the absence of any detectable physical cause. Thus young people used to develop hysterical blindness or deafness, paralysis of a limb, or loss of feeling in some region of the body. There was a thriving hysteria industry, with learned accounts of the disorder's origins, of methods to distinguish between true hysteria and malingering in soldiers, and of ingenious procedures for proving that the malfunctioning organ system was basically in good working order. Now, as far as the literature shows, hysteria is a rare occurrence.

The most common forms of neurosis in today's adolescence seem to be *phobias*, which, as we have seen, can begin as early as the preschool years and continue lifelong, and **anorexia nervosa.**

Anorexia nervosa is an inability or refusal to eat. It is most common among adolescent girls and has often been interpreted as a disguised resistance to growing up and accepting a heterosexual role. It formerly was an affliction of the well-to-do, but it now seems to occur at all levels of society. Jane Brody (1982) lists the symptoms as a dreadful fear of getting fat, a mistaken belief by the anorexic that she is fat, and a weight loss of 25 percent or more. Anorexia is likely to be marked by absence of menstruation (menstruation generally stops with a weight loss of about 10 percent [Frisch, 1980]). The anorexic also experiences slowed pulse, low blood pressure and body temperature, hyperactivity, and, in some cases, a growth of fine hair all over the body. Male victims lose their sexual drive.

Most anorexics eat as little as possible. Some, however, stuff themselves full of their favorite foods and then vomit everything out again. Some stop eating altogether and have to be tube-fed. Some die.

Minuchin, Rosman, and Baker (1978) see anorexia as a product of disturbed family relations, specifically unspoken hostilities that are masked by rigidity. These writers favor treating the whole family, confronting it with its shortcomings with a frankness that borders on the brutal. They claim a remarkable success rate of 86 to 88 percent.

A similar success rate is claimed by a system of long-term individual psychotherapy known as the nurturant-authoritative approach (Levenkron, 1982). This approach does not try to encourage or force the patient to eat, as does the method of Minuchin and his associates. It emphasizes self-starvation as an attention-getting device that compensates for a broad sense of inadequacy. Inasmuch as some anorexics recover without professional treatment, we are not sure how much various therapies contribute beyond the spontaneous cure rate.

At the opposite pole from anorexia is the once-common condition of **bulimia**, or compulsive overeating. Bulimia may begin long before adolescence. It often appears to be an expression of an oral infantile personality hungering for love and support. It has somatic consequences in obesity and metabolic changes. Current usage often defines bulimia as the variety of anorexia that involves gorging followed by vomiting and purging. This usage may prevail, but it should not blind us to the fact that some adolescents and adults are neurotically voracious eaters who do not promptly unload what they have ingested.

Various psychosomatic disorders may appear in adolescence or even at younger ages. **Psychosomatic disorders** are anatomical changes associated with prolonged psychological distress. All strong emotions entail bodily changes. When individuals are subjected to chronic strain their organ systems begin to break down. Among the more prominent psychosomatic disorders are migraine headaches, asthma, eczema, and gastric ulcers. Note that reacting psychosomatically to emotionally charged situations is perfectly normal. It is only when persistent or recurring stress leads to tissue damage that one is said to be suffering from a psychosomatic illness.

Psychotic Reactions in Adolescence

Psychosis refers to those psychological conditions in which individuals lose most effective contact with the outside world and become unable to control their own behavior in ways that are generally considered rational. In adults, the two most common forms of psychosis are the so-called *mood disorders* (notably *manic-depressive psychosis*) and *schizophrenia* (see below). True manic-depressive psychosis, marked by recurring cycles of energetic excitement and black depression, is quite rare in adolescence. However, a fair number of adolescents become profoundly depressed, some to the point of wanting to kill themselves.

Depression and Suicide in Adolescence.
As defined by psychiatrists, **depression** covers quite a few states of mind. Most obviously, there is sadness, the sort of feeling we associate with loss: of a loved one, of a romance, of a period of our lives. A more intense sort of sadness is grief. Depression also includes despair and hopelessness, feelings of impotence or worthlessness, self-hatred and self-contempt. It includes such delusions as that one's internal organs are rotting away. Depression may appear as guilt for misdeeds or inadequacies. It may take the form of fierce anger turned inward.

Some authorities treat depression as the result of *learned helplessness* (Seligman and Beagley, 1975). Learned helplessness, you will recall, describes the reaction of rats that have been exposed to inescapable electric shock. When placed in a tank of water, they simply give up and drown without a struggle (see p. 475). We do not know how valid the analogy is, but some number of adolescents no doubt despair of ever meeting the unrealistically high standards set for them by their parents. However, the variety of states encompassed within the concept of depression makes any simple explanation unlikely.

Adolescent depression of varying kinds

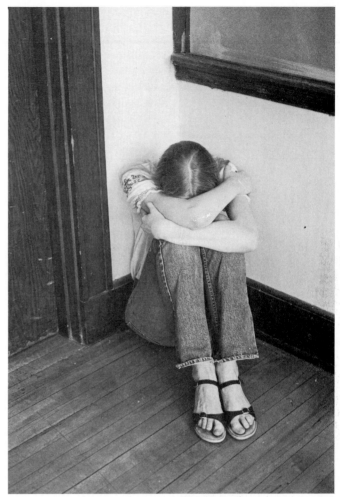

(© Peter Vandermark/Stock, Boston)

Depression comprises a wide variety of states, from a sense of loss to despair and self-contempt. During deep depressions, some adolescents attempt or commit suicide.

and depths can be triggered by a single major reversal, such as failure to get a coveted job or the end of a romance. It can be the result of a series of lesser setbacks, such as a scolding by the parents and a broken date and a quarrel with a friend. It can reflect adolescents' perception of the broader society as inhospitable, even hostile, offering no handholds with which to get a grip on adult life. It can express *Weltschmerz,* adolescents' pain at the gap between the ideal and reality. Or, when it suits adolescents' role playing, they can easily talk themselves into a fit of depression. Even though some cases of depression may be nothing but romantic posturing, most are real and serious. It is out of deep and enduring depression that some adolescents attempt or commit suicide.

Between 1970 and 1978, among fifteen- to twenty-four-year-olds, the suicide rate per 100,000 went up from 13.9 to 20.8 for white males; from 11.3 to 14.8 for black males; and from 4.2 to 5.0 for white females; it declined from 4.1 to 3.2 for black females. The suicide rate is decidedly lower among females of all ages (U.S. Bureau of the Census, 1980).

Suicide in adolescence is much lower than that found at later ages. Suicide among white males increases steadily with age to a peak at ages eighty to eighty-four. The suicide rate for white females reaches a peak at ages forty to forty-nine. The peak for nonwhite males comes at ages twenty-five to twenty-nine. For nonwhite females, there is a peak in suicide rate between ages twenty-five and thirty-nine, with a second similar peak in the early fifties. (All figures are from *The World Almanac,* 1982.)

One final statistic. According to Weiner (1980), adolescent females are three times more likely to attempt suicide than adolescent males, although the actual rate for death by suicide is three to four times higher among males than females. Adolescent suicide is always dreadful, but its incidence is somewhat less alarming than some people would have us believe. There is some reason to think that suicide is contagious. Whenever a major public figure commits suicide, there is a subsequent rise in fatal one-car crashes. Many people suspect that these are usually deliberate rather than accidental. A TV program on adolescent suicide was shot on location in a suburban community where three adolescents had killed themselves a short time before. Such minor epidemics and the attendant publicity may give the impression that multitudes of adolescents are doing away with themselves. In fact, even in the most vulnerable group, our 14 million teenage males, there are under 3,000 suicides a year. Experts on suicide caution us not to dismiss failed attempts as mere attention-getting gestures of no real significance. At least some of those who fail keep right on trying until they finally succeed. Thus a suicidal gesture may be a cry for very badly needed attention.

Most adolescents, of course, are strong, healthy, vigorous people with considerable resilience and vitality and a powerful urge to live. However, this assertion must be qualified by saying that many adolescents seem to have a limited awareness of their own mortality, as is evident in the risks they take.

Schizophrenia. *Schizophrenia* is a condition of severe psychological disturbance that is thought to reflect a split between mind and emotion. It can occur as early as the preschool years, but it is during adolescence that a true schizophrenic breakdown is most likely. Indeed, schizophrenia used to be known as *dementia praecox,* insanity of the young.

Like the mood disorders, schizophrenia is actually a label that embraces several kinds of psychoses. All have in common a distortion of normal emotional responding. They all also are marked by ideas about reality that are greatly at odds with what most people think. Schizophrenics may harbor *delusions,* unfounded beliefs such as that one is being bombarded by x-rays or being controlled by radio messages from some mysterious source. Schizophrenics may believe that their bodies are being corrupted by strange diseases. These beliefs may take the more concrete form of *hallucinations.* These are imaginary but nevertheless vivid experiences of seeing, hearing, tasting, or smelling things that are not there. Some schizophrenics are *paranoid.* They believe that they are being persecuted, or being poisoned, or plotted against, or spied on. Some schizophrenics spend at least part of their time in total apathy and inactivity, or in a semistuporous state of immobility called *catatonia.* Schizophrenics may withdraw from human contact. They may show grossly inappropriate emotional reactions such as giggling at news of disaster or flying into a rage over some trifle.

Some schizophrenics seem to be happy in their fantasy worlds. Some seem to lack any emotion. Some are at constant war with their surroundings. Others appear to seethe with bottled-up passions. Schizophrenics may feel harried by their enemies. They may be verbally abusive. They may take pleasure in behaving outrageously. Schizophrenics seem to have a sense of themselves as grotesque, and when they turn violent, it seems to be in an attempt to destroy a world which reflects back to them an unbearable self-image. When they simply turn away from the world, it is to avoid seeing a painful reflection.

Schizophrenics are increasingly being treated with drugs outside the hospital setting. Unfortunately, the ataractic (tranquilizing) drugs may have serious physical and behavioral side effects, such as uncontrollable grimacing. A great many schizophrenics recover spontaneously, especially those who develop symptoms during adolescence. A few schizophrenics are lethally dangerous. One of the great puzzles of legal psychiatry is how to distinguish between dangerous schizophrenics, who have to be kept locked up, and harmless ones who can safely live in the community. Numerous patients have been locked up for years as potentially dangerous without ever doing a bit of harm. Others, as one can read in the newspapers, are let go as harmless and then embark on a killing spree.

We have already mentioned the ongoing debate about whether schizophrenia is organic or psychological in its origins (see p. 72). The debate is further complicated by the diversity of conditions grouped together in a single category, and by the difficulty of finding agreement on which symptoms and syndromes are to be studied. Some experts, following Szasz (1961), question whether any such thing as schizophrenia even exists. We prefer to leave that question to others and refer you to such authorities as Shapiro (1982).

PSYCHOPATHOLOGY OF THE ENVIRONMENT

Even if one takes a strongly biological view of disturbed behavior, one is forced to acknowledge that some environments are more conducive to sound emotional and intellectual development than

(© J. R. Holland/Stock, Boston)

For many children poverty is a handicapping condition. It affects nutrition, sanitation, medical care, and shelter. It can weaken and demoralize parents.

others. Werner and Smith (1982) have shown quite convincingly how biological factors interact with rearing conditions to shape various psychological outcomes. Here we want to mention briefly some environmental conditions that make normal development difficult.

Poverty is a handicapping condition for many children. It involves, at the physical level, such matters as nutrition, sanitation, access to medical care, and protection against the elements. It can have a weakening and demoralizing effect on adults and limit their ability to function well as parents. Note that where poverty is the rule, people tolerate it rather well. Poverty is most damaging when there is a great contrast between rich and poor, perhaps made worse by crowding in urban slums.

Emotional and intellectual deprivation likewise impair development. Note again that these notions are relative ones. In communities where advanced intellectual achievement is not considered particularly advantageous, routine intellectual skills are all that a child need be exposed to and acquire.

Parental neglect, rejection, and abuse are injurious to children. Neglect and abuse may simply be a perpetuation of a subcultural orientation to child rearing. The parents were neglected or abused when they were children. They in turn raise their own children according to the model provided by their own parents and by the community at large. No one has yet figured out how to break this chain of cultural transmission.

Divorce can have a devastating effect on children. We say this in full recognition that growing up in a home where the parents hate each other can likewise have a destructive impact on children. In fact, the damage worked by divorce can be avoided if the parents can conduct themselves with a bit of rationality. If they can refrain from using the children as pawns in a game of custody based less on the children's welfare than on parental vanity or greed, they can avoid subjecting the children to an agonizing split of loyalties. If they can handle property disputes with a degree of generosity, they can avoid inflicting needless deprivations on the children. There is one subtle factor at work in divorce that parents may miss altogether. This is the guilt felt by many children who, in their egocentrism, jump to the conclusion that they are to blame for the parents' falling out.

At any age, divorce represents a breaking up of a familiar frame of reference and so can be seriously disorienting. The younger the child, the more disruptive the loss of the familiar reference points. On the other hand, an older child from long habit takes the family structure for granted and is all the more likely to feel shocked that the foundations are collapsing. Older children, too, are more likely than younger ones to feel uncomfortable about the parents establishing new sexual and marital liaisons. This is true even of emancipated young people who have a relatively casual view of sex.

RECOVERY FROM PSYCHOPATHOLOGY

We have touched in Chapter 7 on the topic of recovery from psychopathology. Both Skeels (1966) and Dennis (1973) have shown that children removed at an early age from a demonstrably pathogenic environment can grow up normally. Studies of closet children suggest that victims of isolation and abuse can, with a great deal of loving patience, be helped toward normality.

We are aware of only one reasonably well-controlled longitudinal study of the later development of psychotic children. Goldfarb and his associates (1978) followed up seventy-eight children, fifty-nine boys and nineteen girls, who had been in a residential treatment home for disturbed children. They had been admitted to the home at an average age of 7.2. They stayed in the home for a mean of four years. They were followed up for an average of 8.7 years after discharge from the residential home. When last seen, they were 19.9 years old on average. The subjects were predominantly white and Jewish. They represented a normal socioeconomic spread. They were institutionalized for a variety of behavioral disturbances, but 69 percent of the male subjects and almost half of the female subjects showed signs of neurological malfunction as well. Their IQs clustered in the 70 to 89 range, with twelve children having IQs below 46 and nine above 110.

The children were evaluated three times: at admission to the residential home, at discharge from the home, and at the final point of follow-up. These three evaluations yielded four significant kinds of scores: One indicated that some children functioned poorly throughout— from admission to the home to follow-up. The second indicated that some children showed little or no improvement when discharged but were functioning normally at follow-up. The third indicated improvement at discharge but regression at follow-up. The fourth indicated improvement at discharge that was maintained through the follow-up evaluation.

The second and fourth scores describe lasting improvement. Nine of the children scored 2 and nineteen scored 4. In other words, 36 percent of the sample were functioning normally at age twenty. A third of these children had shown no great improvement at time of discharge and so must be assumed to have improved with little reference to the treatment they had received in the residential home.

Children without neurological malfunction did somewhat better than those who showed signs of such impairment. There were no social-class differences in rate of improvement. Females fared slightly better than males, especially in the score-2 group. Those with high IQs did better than those with low IQs. It is obvious that some children benefit from intensive residential treatment, but there are still many unanswered questions.

Let us close these pages on the note that we owe it to our children to provide the best possible environment to permit their full physical and psychological development, and to become in turn the parents of a still better generation.

SUMMARY

1. There are three basic definitions of psychological normality: the symptom-free, the creative-minority, and the social-modal. The last, which the authors accept by elimination, suggests that as long as people behave like most other members of their social group, observing its values and conventions, they can be considered normal. By this token, psychopathology can be described as a failure of identification with the larger society.

2. Identification with the family is a necessary first step to identification with the society at large. Organic impairments—defects in the nervous or endocrine system—and disturbed family relationships can impede identification. Although severe organic damage can make normal communication with a child difficult, it need not prevent sound development.

3. Attachment and identification can fail to occur for any number of reasons; ultimately, however, all but a small minority of children form some sort of identification and come to reasonable terms with the world under even the least favorable conditions.

4. Behavior pathologies during childhood and adolescence fall into four categories: retardation, neurosis, sociopathy, and psychosis. Babies with marked congenital abnormalities are more likely to grow up with psychological impairment than babies not physically flawed, but this relationship is far from inevitable. A disorder in infancy not of organic origin is failure to thrive.

5. A marked increase in fears and phobias occurs during the preschool years. Fears can be expressed or hidden. Speech defects are not uncommon at this stage, but most correct themselves in the course of time. Children may revert to baby talk. Stuttering is the most common speech disorder; no great evidence has been amassed to explain it. Helping the stutterer live more comfortably with stuttering appears to be the most effective therapy—that is, reacting to what is said, not how; few cures are reported.

6. Freed from the somewhat artificial learning demands of school, many "retarded" people blossom into normality. Behavior modification can raise a retarded child's level of self-esteem.

7. In general, autistic children appear to have identified with the non-human world. Infantile autism remains a riddle; a still-unknown organic deficit may cause it.

8. A number of difficulties related to starting school appear during the middle years. These include learning disabilities, dyslexia, learning blocks, and hyperkinesis, or hyperactivity. Juvenile delinquency is a problem that increasingly affects children at ever younger ages. Two major types are acting-out delinquency, or the free and deliberate expression of hostile impulses, and psychopathic (or sociopathic) delinquency, the absence of conscience and emotional ties, and indifference to others.

9. Some adolescents are deeply troubled individuals. In addition to running away, delinquency—most commonly of the socialized or subcultural variety—is characteristic of the period. Common adolescent neuroses include phobias and anorexia nervosa, an inability to eat that occurs predominantly in girls. Adolescents may suffer from psychosomatic disorders, which are physiological manifestations of chronic distress. Suicide in adolescence is much lower than that found at later ages; rates are higher among males.

10. Schizophrenic breakdown is most likely to occur during adolescence. The schizophrenic is liable to be affected by delusions or hallucinations. Schizophrenics may withdraw from human contact or display inappropriate emotional reactions.

11. Rearing conditions have considerable impact on behavior disturbances. Environmental conditions that make normal development difficult (poverty—particularly when great differences exist between rich and poor and the poor live under conditions of crowding in urban

slums—emotional and intellectual deprivation, parental neglect, rejection and abuse, and divorce) are all injurious to children (as is growing up in the cross-fire of parental hatred). Intensive residential treatment is beneficial for some children, but there are still many unanswered questions.

KEY TERMS

acting-out delinquency, 558

anorexia nervosa, 561

bulimia, 562

childhood schizophrenia, 552

creative-minority definition of normality, 546

depression, 563

desensitization, 550

failure to thrive, 548

hyperkinesis (hyperactivity), 555

infantile autism, 552

learning blocks, 555

learning disabilities, 554

minimal brain damage, 555

phobia, 550

psychopathic, sociopathic, or antisocial personality, 558

psychosis, 562

psychosomatic disorders, 562

self-actualizing person, 546

social-modal definition of normality, 546

socialized or subcultural delinquency, 561

stuttering, 551

symptom-free definition of normality, 546

SUGGESTED READINGS

Golding, W. *Lord of the Flies*. New York: Coward-McCann, 1954. A morality tale, Freudian in outlook, about the destructive forces that drive us in the absence of full socialization.

Redl, F., and Wineman, D. *Children Who Hate*. Glencoe, Ill.: Free Press, 1951. A classic account of acting-out delinquency.

Lachenmeyer, J. R., and Gibbs, M. S. (eds). *Psychopathology in Childhood*. New York: Gardner Press, 1982. A technical treatment of issues in the origins, diagnosis, and treatment of children's disturbances.

MacLeod, S. *The Art of Starvation*. New York: Schocken Books, 1982. A first-person account of anorexia that shows only partial agreement with current theories.

Shapiro, S. A. *Contemporary Theories of Schizophrenia*. New York: McGraw-Hill, 1982. An overview of a complex psychological disturbance and the theories that underlie its origins and treatments.

GLOSSARY

abstract space Space as conceived in formal geometries of two or more dimensions; rarely accessible before adolescence. (Ch. 11)

accommodation One of the two contrasting processes in equilibration in which the child modifies or reorganizes established ideas about the world or, if necessary, forms new ones. (Chs. 1, 6)

acrophobia Fear of high places. (Chs. 6, 15)

acting-out delinquency The free, deliberate, and often malicious indulgence of impulse, frequently expressed as acts of aggression, including vandalism. (Ch. 15)

action space The young child's orientation to space, defined less by its formal relationships and coordinates than by its possibilities for movement. Cf. abstract space, map space. (Chs. 8, 11)

active wakefulness A waking state characterized by considerable movement of the arms and legs and twisting of the head and trunk in neonates. (Ch. 4)

adolescent sterility The notion proposed by some authorities that adolescent girls cannot conceive until several years after menarche (q.v.). Most authorities now speak of adolescent subfecundity (q.v.) instead. (Ch. 14)

adolescent subfecundity The fact that young adolescent girls are less likely to conceive than older adolescents and, having conceived, are less likely to carry a baby to term. (Ch. 14)

affect (affection) Feelings and emotions. (Ch. 1)

afterbirth The placenta with its attached membranes and cord, expelled after the birth of the baby. (Ch. 3)

aggression Behavior, motivated by hostility (sometimes unconscious), meant to inflict physical or psychological damage on another. (Ch. 10)

agitation A neonatal state marked by distress and crying. (Ch. 4)

agoraphobia Fear of open spaces. (Ch. 15)

ailurophobia Fear of cats. (Ch. 15)

alert inactivity A waking state in which the neonate is comfortable and ready to make contact with the world. Occurs usually after the baby has been fed and changed. (Ch. 4)

alphafetal protein (AFP) A component of fetal blood that can cross the placental barrier into the mother's bloodstream. Its presence in large quantities in maternal blood may signal neural tube defects or other fetal abnormalities. (Ch. 3)

altruism Selfless regard for the welfare of others. (Chs. 10, 13)

amniocentesis Drawing samples of amniotic fluid directly from the womb between the sixteenth and twenty-second weeks of pregnancy. Shed fetal skin cells from the fluid can be karyotyped (q.v.), and gross anomalies such as Down's syndrome detected, as well as the sex of the fetus. (Ch. 3)

amnion The inner membrane of the double-walled sac filled with amniotic fluid in which the fetus floats. (Ch. 3)

amniotic fluid The fluid that surrounds the fetus in the womb. (Ch. 3)

anal-aggressive character From Freudian theory, a messy, disorganized, verbally hostile person, as if still in rebellion against toilet training. (Ch. 1)

anal-retentive character From Freudian theory, a meticulous, precise, miserly, emotionally constipated person, as if too well toilet-trained. (Ch. 1)

anal stage The second psychosexual stage, according to Freud, coinciding with toddlerhood, when anal functions provide the main channel of gratification. (Chs. 1, 8)

androgyny The idea that masculinity and femininity are not the poles of a single dimension but are distinct dimensions. This way of thinking permits us to characterize people as any combination of masculine and feminine. (Ch. 14)

anecdotal record A descriptive account of a behavioral episode that illustrates special aspects of functioning. (Ch. 1)

anencephaly The lack of a brain in the fetus; leads to death immediately after birth. (Ch. 3)

animism The assumption that inanimate things are capable of perceiving, feeling, thinking, willing, and spontaneous movement. According to Piaget, one of the earliest forms of causal thinking. (Chs. 1, 9, 11)

anorexia nervosa An inability or refusal to eat, seen mostly in adolescent girls; may produce severe emaciation and even death. (Ch. 15)

anoxia Deprivation of oxygen; associated in the neonate with partial strangulation, with premature separation of the placenta, or with delayed breathing. Capable of producing brain injury and perhaps cerebral palsy (q.v.). (Ch. 3)

antecedent variable See independent variable.

Apgar Score A score derived from rating the neonate on five scales: breathing effort, muscle tone, heart rate, reflex irritability, and color. Ratings range from zero (poor) to two (good), and scores range from zero to ten. (Ch. 4)

apnea Unusually long interruption of breathing (Ch. 3)

artificialism The successor to animism (q.v.) in causal thinking. In Piaget's scheme, the assumption that events are caused by the action of some humanlike agent or entity or force that wills things to happen in fulfillment of its own purposes. E.g., "Why do they have thunder?" (Ch. 11)

assimilation The more primitive of the two contrasting processes in equilibration (q.v.) in which the child tries to fit a new phenomenon into already established schemata, if necessary distorting perception of the object to fit existing ways of thinking. (Chs. 1, 6)

associationism The idea that development is the product of learning and that learning consists of associations between things that coincide in space or time. (Ch. 1)

associative play Play in which a number of children are all doing the same thing, such as swinging or telephoning, but with little if any interchange. (Ch. 10)

assortative traits (discontinuous traits) Physical characteristics that vary qualitatively, such as eye color. Such trait variations are thought to be governed by the variations in a single gene. Cf. distributive traits. (Ch. 2)

asynchronous growth The principle that various parts of the body grow at different rates at different times; particularly noticeable in adolescence. (Chs. 1, 14)

attachment The powerful emotional bonds of affection that develop between child and the parents that, in time, can be generalized to a wide array of other individuals. Essential to identification (q.v.). (Chs. 1, 5)

attribution theory A theory of locus of control (q.v.) that says that people attribute their performance to either situational (external) factors or dispositional (internal) factors. Situational factors are either task difficulty or luck; dispositional factors are either ability or effort. This version of attribution theory should not be confused with another that deals with how we make judgments about personal attributes. (Ch. 13)

autogenous development Behavioral development resulting from growth and maturation rather than from learning. (Chs. 1, 5, 7)

autonomy versus shame and doubt The second stage in Erikson's scheme of psychosocial development, consisting of resistance to external influence, even beneficial influence, on the behavior of the toddler, who is striving for independence; shame and doubt is the result of a failure to develop autonomy and has a negative influence on future development. (Ch. 8)

aversive conditioning Learning to abstain from actions that produce unpleasant consequences. To those who control the consequences, aversive conditioning is synonymous with punishment. (Chs. 1, 5)

aversive reinforcers Punishment, or disagreeable consequences of action. (Chs. 1, 4)

Babinski response The upward and outward fanning of the toes in response to having the sole of the foot stroked from back to front; normal in neonates, abnormal in older persons, where downward curling of the toes is normally seen. (Ch. 4)

Babkin response A reflex produced by pressing on the palms when the neonate is supine (lying face up), in which the baby's head turns to the midline, the mouth opens, and sometimes the head is raised. (Ch. 4)

basic needs A baby's essential material and psychological needs. Psychological needs include love, attention, play, contact, stimulation, and discipline and control—all essential for sound development. (Ch. 5)

basic trust versus basic mistrust The first of Erikson's eight stages of psychosocial development. The infant learns either that the world is a good, stable, predictable, manageable place, as a result of having her or his physical and psychological needs reliably satisfied, or that it is a source of pain, misery, threat, frustration, and uncertainty, as a result of not having these needs met. (Ch. 5)

battered child syndrome Describes the effects of abuse and brutality practiced on infants and children by their caregiver(s). (Ch. 7)

behavioral contagion The spread of an activity, mood, or impulse through a group; the foundation of associative play. (Ch. 10)

behaviorism (learning theory) A psychological theory that focuses on observable behavior and on how environmental stimuli and reinforcers affect, mold, and control actions, learning, and development. (Ch. 1 *et passim*)

behavior modification A method of treatment designed to change or modify maladaptive behavior; disregards the original causes of behavior; based on principles of operant conditioning (q.v.). (Chs. 1, 15)

biological adolescence The physical changes that occur during adolescence and culminate in biological maturity; includes reaching sexual maturity and one's adult size. Cf. cultural or psychological adolescence. (Ch. 14)

biological clocks Semiautonomous internal regulators of daily and perhaps seasonal cyclic rhythms (such as activity and repose) that seem to be set initially by recurring events in the environment, like day and night and the family's schedule and routines. A general phenomenon common to virtually all species. (Ch. 5)

birth fantasies Children's invented explanations of how babies are conceived and born. (Ch. 10)

blastocyst A hollow sphere of cells with an inner cell mass at one side from which the embryo will develop. (Ch. 3)

breech presentation The buttocks-first emergence of the baby at birth. Cf. vertex presentation. (Ch. 3)

bulimia Compulsive overeating; may cause obesity and metabolic changes. The term is sometimes applied to a form of anorexia marked by gorging followed by induced vomiting or purging. (Ch. 15)

bursting of the bag of waters A sign of impending labor. The rupture of the membranes enclosing the fetus releases a stream of amniotic fluid through the vagina. (Ch. 3)

carcinogen An agent capable of producing cancer. (Ch. 3)

case history An integrated word portrait of an individual compiled from all the sources available. (Ch. 1)

castration anxiety According to Freud, a boy's feelings for his mother during the phallic stage of psychosexual development result in fear that his penis will be cut off by his father in retaliation. This fear causes a repression (q.v.) of all sexual desire. See Oedipus complex (q.v.). (Chs. 1,10)

catatonia A form of schizophrenia marked by semistuporous immobility. (Ch. 15)

cathexis In psychoanalytic theory, the investment of emotional energy in a channel of gratification and the gratifying objects associated with that channel. At each psychosexual stage, one's supply of libidinal energy is said to be invested or cathected in the relevant channel and its objects. (Ch. 1)

centration Piaget's term for the child's tendency to focus on only a single aspect of an object or situation; the child is thereby unable to take other relevant attributes into account. Cf. decentration. (Ch. 11)

cephalocaudal growth gradient The principle that the head end is the focus of early elaboration, with later foci moving toward the tail (head-to-tail). (Ch. 1)

cerebral palsy A condition of poor muscular control produced by injury to the motor centers of the brain before or at birth. (Ch. 3)

chain A grouping in which each successive object is related to the one that went before it, but without any overall scheme of organization. (Ch. 11)

change of voice The deepening of the voice associated with changes in the speech apparatus early in adolescence. Taken as an indicator of puberty in boys. (Ch. 14)

checklist A precoded list on which the observer simply marks the occurrence of a given behavior. (Ch. 1)

childhood schizophrenia An early form of schizophrenia in which the child has a seriously disturbed image of self and world. (Ch. 15)

chorion The outer membrane of the double-walled sac filled with amniotic fluid in which the fetus floats. (Ch. 3)

chromosomal anomalies Abnormalities in the constitution of the chromosomes. They are genetic but usually not hereditary. They are associated with the action of external agents, such as X-rays, viruses, and toxic chemicals, on the chromosomes in the mother's ova. (Ch. 3)

chromosomes The rodlike bodies in the cell nucleus, visible under the microscope during cell division; they carry the genes. Human beings normally have twenty-three pairs of chromosomes or forty-six in all. (Ch. 2)

circumlocution The avoidance of a painful topic by talking around it without ever saying what it is; a manifestion of verbal realism (q.v.). (Ch. 11)

classical (or Pavlovian) conditioning After a neutral stimulus is repeatedly paired with one that produces a response, the previously neutral stimulus by itself will produce the response. (Ch. 1)

classical experiment See formal experiment.

classification The ability to group objects on the basis of a common trait. (Ch. 13)

claustrophobia Fear of being shut in. (Ch. 15)

cleft palate A split in the roof of the mouth, a deformity produced during the embryonic period. (Ch. 3)

clinical approach An idiographic approach (q.v.) which explores the inner motivation, thoughts, feelings, conflicts, and skills of an individual through interviews, tests, and other means. (Ch. 1)

clinical method, Piaget's A method of studying children's behavior that combines observation, questioning, and formal and informal tests. (Ch. 1)

closet children Children who are raised under conditions of severe isolation. (Chs. 7, 15)

cluster A grouping in which one key object serves as the point of reference and the other objects all relate to it in terms of one or another similarity, without regard to how they relate to one another. (Ch. 11)

code switching (motherese) Simplifying one's language when trying to communicate with a listener of limited understanding; mothers also raise the pitch of their voices in such communication with their young children. (Chs. 9, 11)

cognition   The processes by which we make sense of the world so that we can act effectively; the psychological processes involved in knowing, including perceiving, thinking, remembering, and language. (Chs. 1, 6)

cognitive theories   Theories of psychological development, such as those of Piaget and Werner, that emphasize the role of cognitive processes in behavior. Contrasted with motivational theories, such as Freud's, and associationist theories, such as behaviorism. (Ch. 1)

colic   A major cause of crying in young babies that takes the form of several hours of intense screaming, usually in the evening; other symptoms are a swollen belly, doubling up of the body, and breaking wind. It almost always ends at age three months. (Ch. 4)

collective monologue   See dual monologue.

colostrum   A substance secreted from the mother's breasts for a day or two after birth; thought to be good for the baby. (Ch. 3)

commitment   Marcia's term for having resolved the issues of identity formation in adolescence. (Ch. 14)

comparison groups   In place of a control group (q.v.) and an experimental group (q.v.) in an experiment, two comparison groups are used, each receiving a contrasting but related treatment. (Ch. 1)

compensation   In conservation (q.v.), the awareness that a change in one aspect of a situation can be offset by a change in another so that the total quantity remains the same. (Ch. 13)

competence   Chomsky's term for people's underlying linguistic capacities, which are thought to be much greater than what they actually say (cf. performance); competence resides in the deep structure (q.v.). (Ch. 9)

competence motivation (effectance)   White's concept that we take pleasure in mastering our environment and in becoming skillful and competent, and that intellectual curiosity is an important human characteristic. (Chs. 1, 13)

competitive games   Games in which there are rules, and score is kept to determine who wins and who loses; usually begin late in the preschool years or early in the school years. Cf. ritual games, social games. (Ch. 10)

conation   Will; that is, drives, motives, and intentions. (Ch. 1)

concordance   The observed percentage of cases in which both twins share a trait. (Ch. 2)

concrete operations, stage of   The third stage in the development of logical thinking, according to Piaget from the age of approximately seven to eleven, when the child can solve problems by manipulating concrete objects. Marked by conservation (q.v.), compensation (q.v.), seriation (q.v.), reversibility (q.v.), classification (q.v.), transitivity (q.v.), and decentration (q.v.). (Chs. 1, 12, 13)

conditioned response (CR)   A response attached through association to a conditioned stimulus. (Ch. 1)

conditioned stimulus (CS)   A formerly neutral, arbitrary stimulus that has been associated to a particular response. (Ch. 1)

congenital anomalies   Abnormalities present at birth. May be of either genetic or environmental origin. (Ch. 3)

conservation   The understanding that quantity does not change simply because a mass or a collection is rearranged spatially. (Ch. 13)

constancy   The fact that objects preserve their identities and various properties such as size, shape, and color in a wide range of observing conditions. (Ch. 6)

constraint seeking   A strategy of questioning whereby the answers received will rule out whole categories of possibilities and thus permit the efficient acquisition of information, as in the game of Twenty Questions; the ability to ask such questions increases as children get older. (Ch. 13)

contact comfort   Harlow's term for the peace, pleasure, and security derived from physical contact with other people or with soft, warm, cuddlesome objects. (Ch. 5)

contingent reinforcement   The process of reinforcement in which the individual receives direct and immediate feedback (q.v.), or reinforcement, following a particular behavior. Contributes significantly to the individual's sense of competence. (Chs. 4, 5, 7)

continuity of sex roles   The preparation offered by one's childhood role for one's sex role as an adult; such continuity used to be the rule for girls, who could move smoothly from childhood into their long-established adult roles as wife, mother, and homemaker. Cf. discontinuity of sex roles. (Ch. 12)

continuity theory   The belief that changes in behavior represent the result of incremental changes rather than the emergence of truly novel behavior. Cf. discontinuity theory. (Ch. 1)

continuum of caretaking casualty   The idea that the degree of impairment varies inversely with the adequacy of parenting. It implies that good care can go a long way toward overcoming organic handicaps. (Ch. 3)

continuum of reproductive casualty   The idea that the more severe the congenital problems, the more severe the later psychological problems. (Ch. 3)

control group   A group of subjects in an experiment carefully selected to be equivalent to the experimental group (q.v.) except in exposure to the independent variable. (Ch. 1)

conventional level The second of three levels of moral judgment, according to Kohlberg, characterized by a seeking of approval and an acceptance of and an active promotion of the norms of society. (Ch. 13)

convergent thinking Following a set routine to a single correct answer, as in an arithmetic problem. Cf. divergent thinking. (Ch. 2)

cooperative play Play in which children discuss, plan, and assign roles necessary to a joint venture. (Ch. 10)

correlational studies Methods of assessing the degree of relatedness between two or more variables. (Ch. 1)

correlation coefficient A numerical indication of how closely subjects' distribution of scores on one variable is associated with their distribution on another. (A value of $+1.0$ indicates a perfect correlation; 0.0, no correlation; and -1.0 a perfect negative, or inverse, correlation.) (Ch. 1)

co-twin control studies Tests popular in the 1930s and 1940s in which one of a pair of identical twins was given special training to see if it gave him or her a developmental advantage over the other twin. (Ch. 7)

counteridentification A phase of rebellion against one's models—a phenomenon unknown in other species. Cf. identification. (Chs. 1, 5, 14, 15)

crawling An early form of locomotion, usually beginning around seven months, in which babies pull or otherwise propel themselves with the torso touching the ground. (Ch. 5)

creative-minority concept of normality A definition of normality that suggests that only those people who have transcended the cultural myths and artificial restraints that hobble the thinking of ordinary people can be considered truly normal. (Ch. 15)

creeping A form of locomotion, beginning around nine months of age, in which infants advance on all fours with the torso clear of the ground. (Ch. 5)

cretinism Defective functioning of the thyroid gland associated with an inborn error of metabolism (q.v.). If not detected and treated early, can cause retarded physical and mental development. (Ch. 3)

crisis In Marcia's usage, the process during adolescence of wrestling with the problem of identity. The presence of crisis is associated with either moratorium (q.v.) or identity achieved (q.v.); its absence is associated with identity diffusion (q.v.) or foreclosure (q.v.). (Ch. 14)

critical period The time of an organ system's most rapid growth, during which it is most sensitive

to growth-inducing forces and most vulnerable to damage. (Ch. 3)

critical-periods hypothesis An attempt to draw a parallel between the critical periods (q.v.) of prenatal development and postnatal behavioral development. In this view, there are biologically defined periods for such functions as attachment, toilet training, and learning to read. If these functions are not stimulated during the appropriate critical periods, they may be permanently impaired. (Chs. 5, 7)

cross-sectional method Compares the performance on the same measure(s) of groups of children representing successive ages; one of two approaches (cf. longitudinal method) to studying age differences in behavior. (Ch. 1)

cruising In the course of learning to walk, the baby side-steps while supporting itself with items of furniture and shifting its grip from support to support. (Ch. 5)

cultural or psychological adolescence The definition of adolescence as a distinct age period with its own special folkways, attitudes, styles, and problems. Cf. biological adolescence. (Ch. 14)

cultural bias The use of materials, as in intelligence testing, that are familiar to one cultural group but remote from the experience of another. (Ch. 2)

Cyclops effect Behavior indicating that despite an awareness that they have two eyes, babies at first experience seeing as being centered between the eyes. (Ch. 6)

death wish See Thanatos.

decentration Piaget's term for the ability to take account of more than one aspect of a situation at a time. Cf. centration. (Chs. 11, 13)

deductive thinking Reasoning from a set of principles to try to find concrete relationships; an astronomer deduces the location of a previously unknown planet, for example, from irregularities in the orbits of the known planets. Cf. inductive thinking. (Ch. 11)

deep sleep (regular sleep) A neonatal sleep state marked by even breathing and a minimum of grimacing and body movement. (Ch. 4)

deep structure Chomsky's term for the hypothetical fundamentals of grammar shared by all languages—the general basic sentence types (cf. surface structure) plus the transformation rules for imposing alternative grammatical structures. A prototypical deep-structure sentence is a simple declarative, composed of noun subject, verb predicate, and an object or a modifier. (Ch. 9)

defense mechanisms Ploys and stratagems employed by the ego to reduce the anxiety caused by severe inner conflicts. (Ch. 1)

deferred imitation Piaget's term for the child's ability to perceive an event, store it away, and reproduce it later in word or action. (Chs. 8, 11)

delayed-reaction experiment Studies popular early in the century testing ability to remember the location of a concealed object. (Ch. 6)

delinquent type In Achenbach's scheme, a type of disturbance marked primarily by poor school-work. (Ch. 15)

delusions False beliefs held despite demonstrable evidence to the contrary, such as the idea that one is being controlled by radio messages from a mysterious source. (Ch. 15)

demand qualities or **characters** Expressive properties in the physiognomy (q.v.) of objects that elicit emotional and behavioral reactions even in the absence of learning; for babies, crevices demand poking, for example. (Ch. 6)

dementia praecox An obsolete name for schizophrenia (q.v.). (Ch. 15)

denial A defense mechanism that consists in blocking the obvious from awareness. (Ch. 1)

deoxyribonucleic acid (DNA) The organic molecule, shaped like a double helix, that composes genes and stores and replicates genetic information. (Ch. 2)

dependent variable (outcome variable) The variable in an experiment that is expected to change in response to manipulation of the independent variable (q.v.); in other words, the effect. (Ch. 1)

depression Prolonged and stubborn feelings of sadness, impotence, worthlessness, and even self-rage. (Ch. 15)

deprivation Lack of emotional and intellectual stimulation, of good models, and of needed discipline. Originally discussed in terms of maternal deprivation, later expanded to include lack of many kinds of beneficial experiences. (Ch. 7)

desensitization A behavior therapy technique designed to reduce anxiety or remove a phobia by pairing a pleasant experience, such as relaxation, with increasingly close contact with the threatening object or situation. (Ch. 15)

development The orderly sequences of biological and psychological change that occur in the course of the life cycle. (Ch. 1 *et passim*)

discontinuity of growth rate Body size increases at different rates at different times; there are two major growth spurts, one right after birth and the other during pubescence. (Ch. 1)

discontinuity of sex roles The lack of preparation offered by one's childhood role for one's sex role as an adult; such discontinuity exists for boys in Western cultures, who among their peers practice he-man warrior styles that bear little resemblance to the lives they will actually lead as husbands, fathers, citizens, and workers. Cf. continuity of sex roles. (Ch. 12)

discontinuity theory The belief that truly novel forms of behavior emerge in the course of development. Cf. continuity theory. (Ch. 1)

discontinuous traits See assortative traits.

discourse analysis The attempt to classify conversational patterns. (Chs. 9, 13)

discrepancy hypothesis An attempt to describe the baby's general reaction to novelty, according to which small deviations from the familiar are attractive, but greater departures produce fearfulness. (Chs. 5, 13)

dispositions Fixed underlying traits considered to determine behavior. (Ch. 1)

distributive traits Traits that vary quantitatively, such as height, rather than qualitatively; they are regulated by more than one gene and are highly sensitive to environmental influences. (Ch. 2)

divergent thinking Speculating about possible ways of dealing with problems that may have many solutions—or none at all; thinking of all the uses to which an object could be put is an example. Cf. convergent thinking. (Ch. 2)

domains Common segments of reality, each with its special vocabulary and logic; kinship, causation, color, number, and the body are examples. (Ch. 9)

dominant trait A trait that develops given the presence of a single gene, which suppresses the expression of the counterpart gene inherited from the other parent. Brown eye color is a dominant trait. Cf. recessive trait. (Ch. 2)

double bind (no-win situation) A situation in which any of the options available entails unfavorable results. (Ch. 14)

Down's syndrome (formerly Mongolism; also called Trisomy-21) A condition associated with an extra chromosome, number 21, and marked by an extra fold of skin over the eyelid and, in the absence of special training and stimulation, mental deficiency. (Ch. 3)

dramatic play (symbolic, fantasy, or **pretend play)** The acting out of scenes and events from everyday life or from imagination; children act out roles and behaviors taken from the models with whom they identify. (Chs. 8, 10)

drowsiness See light sleep.

dual ambivalence The combination of growth ambivalence (q.v.) on the part of both child and parents. (Chs. 8, 14, 15)

dual or **collective monologue** An early form of conversation: children speak in turn, but each on a different topic, with little or no attention paid to what the other is saying. (Ch. 10)

duplicity People become able to observe, judge, criticize, and regulate themselves; in addition, they can think one way and act another, as the situation demands. (Ch. 1)

dynamism An unquestioning acceptance of events as they happen, as though the world were charged with some all-purpose energy that keeps things happening. (Chs. 1, 9, 11)

dysgraphia A learning disability involving difficulty in writing; words are often placed so poorly on the page as to be illegible. (Ch. 15)

dyslexia A learning disability involving specific problems in learning to read and spell. Symptoms include inability to associate words and letters with spoken sounds, reversal or rotation of letters, and difficulty integrating letters or syllables to form words. (Ch. 15)

echolalia The compulsive parroting of what one hears; characteristic of the speech of some autistic children. (See infantile autism.) (Ch. 15)

ecological validity The question of whether tasks and treatments used in the laboratory resemble or have any relevance to real life. (Ch. 1)

ecological view The view that organisms can be understood only in relation to their environments. (Ch. 2)

ectoderm The outer layer of the cell mass from which the skin and nervous system develop. (Ch. 3)

ego In psychoanalysis, the rational, reality-oriented functions; the practical strategies that can attempt to satisfy the id's strivings for gratification. (Ch. 1)

egocentric generosity Well-intended acts that reflect the actor's tastes with little regard to those of the intended beneficiary, as when the baby offers a parent a bite of the baby's saliva-soaked toast. (Chs. 6, 8)

egocentric-relativistic polarity Development from a condition of egocentrism (q.v.) to one in which one can take account of other people's outlooks. (Ch. 11)

egocentrism A low level of self-awareness which leads the individual to assume that his or her view of reality is the one universal view, and thus to fail to realize that other people's ways of viewing things may be radically different. (Chs. 1, 6, 11, 13)

ego psychology The school of psychoanalysis that emphasizes people's rational capacities. (Ch. 1)

eidetic images Vivid recollections of past experiences, akin to photographic memory, though eidetic images can be auditory, tactual, olfactory, gustatory, or proprioceptive as well. Children retain a fair number of eidetic images, which usually fade or disappear with age. (Ch. 11)

effectance See competence motivation.

elaboration Creating a context for the ideas and relationships to be remembered; preschool children do not elaborate spontaneously but can be taught to do so. Elaboration improves retention of learned material. (Ch. 11)

Electra complex The female version of the Oedipus complex (q.v.), never satisfactorily formulated by Freud. (Chs. 1, 10)

embryo In human prenatal development, the organism during the period from about two to eight weeks when its organ systems are taking rudimentary shape. (Ch. 3)

embryonic period The period from two weeks until about eight weeks after conception. It is during the embryonic phase that the various organ systems have their critical periods (q.v.) and are subject to serious damage by the action of teratogens. (Ch. 3)

empathy A form of perceptual participation in which the boundaries between self and world are lost; a close behavioral link between person and environment, as though the material boundaries were blurred. A neonate moves its arms and legs in synchrony with an adult's speech, for example. Another example is contagious crying among neonates. Cf. sympathy. (Chs. 4, 6, 10)

empty organism Skinner's metaphor for the idea that past and present reinforcement contingencies rather than mental structures and processes govern our behavior. (Ch. 1)

enculturation The various mechanisms by which we communicate to a child the shared meanings of the group; often outside the sphere of anyone's awareness, it is the work of many agencies beside the parents, including television, peers, and schools. Cf. socialization. (Ch. 5)

endoderm The inner layer of the cell mass from which the mouth, throat, and digestive tract develop. (Ch. 3)

enrichment Providing children with extra linguistic, intellectual, and emotional stimulation, as well as, in some cases, improved diets and medical and dental care. (Ch. 7)

environmentalism The doctrine that emphasizes the supreme role of experience in shaping people's behavior. (Ch. 1)

equilibration The restoration of cognitive equilibrium, according to Piaget, lost as the result of the difference between a child's expectations of something and the thing's actual nature. When the idea and the object have been brought to terms with each other, first through assimilation (q.v.) and then accommodation (q.v.), equilibration has occurred. (Chs. 1, 6)

equivalence Klüver's formulation of the idea of category, in terms of similarities and differences among aspects of reality. A shared name suggests equivalence among objects, whereas different names suggest nonequivalence. (Ch. 11)

Eros Freud's term for the sex drive. (Ch. 1)

errors of dysjunction Errors in cell replication during the formation of germ cells whereby the gamete ends up with abnormal chromosomes or an abnormal number of chromosomes. (Ch. 3)

ethnocentrism An unquestioning acceptance of one's own society's ways as the only truly human way. Cf. egocentrism, relativism. (Ch. 5)

eugenics The attempt to improve a species through controlled breeding. (Ch. 3)

euphemism The use of inoffensive words or phrases in place of a disagreeable reality; a manifestation of verbal realism (q.v.). (Ch. 11)

euphenics The attempt to improve a species by manipulating the genetic material itself. (Ch. 3)

euthenics The attempt to improve a species by improving the environment in which the young are reared. (Ch. 3)

event recorder An electronic checklist, with the observer pressing precoded buttons. (Ch. 1)

expansion hypothesis The assumption that parents respond to children's condensed utterances by offering them an expanded, correct rephrasing; observation shows this seldom happens. Cf. expatiation hypothesis. (Ch. 9)

expatiation hypothesis The view that parents respond to a child's utterance by carrying the discourse forward; for example, an expatiation of "Doggie bark" would be "Yes, but he won't bite." Cf. expansion hypothesis. (Ch. 9)

experimental group The group of subjects in an experiment exposed to an independent variable. Cf. comparison groups, control group. (Ch. 1)

expressive jargon A toddler's flow of gibberish, sometimes studded with real words, that faithfully mimics the sounds and cadences of adult speech. (Ch. 9)

extinction The gradual decay of a conditioned association if no reinforcement is forthcoming. (Ch. 1)

factorial theory A theory that assumes the existence of different kinds of intellectual abilities (factors) and tests for each separately. (Ch. 2)

failure to thrive A disorder of infancy marked by deficient physical development in the absence of any organic cause; it may be associated with disturbed relations between the baby and the parents or with parental discord. (Chs. 7, 15)

false positives Test results that indicate that something is wrong when, in fact, nothing is. (Ch. 3)

familial hypercholesterolemia (FH) A recently discovered enzyme deficiency disease caused by an error of fat metabolism that leads to arteriosclerosis (fatty deposits in the blood vessels and hardening of the arteries) and heart attacks in children and young adults. (Ch. 3)

feedback Our behavior produces changes in the environment, and these changes provide information that tell us how effectively we are behaving. The information we receive from the environment in response to our own actions is called feedback. (Chs. 1, 5)

feral children Human children erroneously thought to have been raised by wild animals. (Ch. 7)

fetal alcohol syndrome (FAS) Growth deficiency, slow motor and intellectual development, small head size, heart defects, and mild anomalies of the face and limbs in the babies of mothers who drink heavily during pregnancy. (Ch. 3)

fetal period In human prenatal development, the period from about age eight weeks to birth. During this time, the rudimentary organ systems laid down during the embryonic period are taking more mature form, and the unborn baby is growing at a rapid rate. (Ch. 3)

fetus The unborn child from about eight weeks after conception until term, about thirty-eight weeks after conception. (Ch. 3)

field dependence Reliance on external rather than internal cues for orientation in space and for preserving one's identity. Cf. field independence. (Ch. 5)

field independence Reliance on internal rather than external cues for orientation in space. Normal development entails a shift from field dependence (q.v.) to field independence, indicating an increasing awareness of self. (Ch. 5)

finalism Causal thought in which the effect is thought to cause the cause; the belief that things occur to ensure their outcome, such as the sun setting so we can have nighttime to go to sleep. (Ch. 11)

fine (small-muscle) motor activity Activity involving controlled use of the hands (and sometimes the feet and toes), as in reaching for, grasping, and manipulating objects. Cf. gross motor activity. (Ch. 5)

fixation In psychoanalytic theory, continuing to seek gratification appropriate to an earlier stage of psychosexual development, as the result of too much or too little gratification at that stage. (Ch. 1)

fontanels Six soft spots in the neonate's skull that are openings covered with a tough, resilient membrane just beneath the skin. They permit some skull compression during birth, and allow space for the brain's rapid growth afterward. (Ch. 4)

foreclosure In Marcia's usage, the situation of a young person who has incorporated unquestioningly the values and goals ordained by the family and society at large. (Ch. 14)

formal experiment Research procedure that attempts to isolate a causal agent. Typically employs an experimental group that receives a treatment designed to produce change and a control group that, in the absence of treatment, is expected to show no relevant change. (Ch. 1)

formal operations stage The final stage in Piaget's scheme of logical development, beginning at approximately eleven years of age, characterized by the ability to think and operate symbolically, reason abstractly, and formulate and test hypotheses. (Chs. 1, 14)

foundling fantasies Children's suspicions—even firm convictions—that they are of noble birth and that the parents with whom they live are not their true parents. (Ch. 12)

fraternal twins (dizygotic, or **DZ)** Twins who come from two different eggs. (Ch. 2)

frustration-aggression hypothesis The idea, proposed by learning theorists seeking to reconcile psychoanalysis and behaviorism, that aggression is always caused by frustration and that frustration always leads to aggression. (Ch. 10)

functional analysis Analysis of the uses to which language is put. (Ch. 9)

functional subordination The integration of differentiated parts into a coherent whole—for example, words into sentences. Also called hierarchic integration. (Ch. 1, 9)

galvanic skin response (GSR) or **psychogalvanic response (PGR)** An increase in the skin's electrical conductivity caused by light sweating. Observable from birth on in periods of stress. (Ch. 4)

gametes Reproductive cells (sperm in males, ova in females) that contain half the normal complement of chromosomes. In humans, each gamete contains twenty-three chromosomes. (Ch. 2)

Ganzfeld A homogenous surface that fills the field of view and gives the impression, according to adult subjects in experiments, of a space-filling fog. (Ch. 6)

generative grammar Chomsky's view that a grammatical system made up of a very few parts can generate an infinite number of meaningful statements. (Ch. 9)

genes The primary units of heredity; composed of DNA, constituents of the chromosomes. (Ch. 2)

genetic counseling Expert advice on reproductive matters for parents or prospective parents. Family health histories, chromosomal studies, and, if necessary, chromosomal and biochemical studies of fetal tissues determine the likelihood of a genetic flaw in the offspring. (Ch. 3)

genetics The study of the mechanisms by which characteristics are transmitted from one generation to the next. (Ch. 2)

genital stage In Freud's scheme of psychosexual development, the final stage, which begins with the physiological changes of puberty and is characterized by a mixture of sexuality with love and concern for others. (Chs. 1, 14)

genotype The individual's underlying genetic make-up, which does not necessarily correspond to phenotype (q.v.): it may include genes for recessive traits that are not realized but are transmissible or that may appear under changed environmental conditions. (Ch. 2)

gentle childbirth Management of pregnancy and birth according to the precepts of Lamaze and Leboyer, making the transition from prenatal to postnatal life as stress-free as possible. Also

called prepared childbirth (q.v.). The modern-day version of "natural childbirth" (q.v.). (Ch. 3)

germinal period The first two weeks after conception, when the zygote (q.v.) becomes a blastocyst (q.v.) which, after traveling down the Fallopian tube, embeds itself in the uterine lining. (Ch. 3)

Geronimo response A reaction to the visual cliff (q.v.) in which the subject seems determined to leap into space. (Ch. 6)

gestation period The period of prenatal development from the moment of conception until birth, estimated to last about 266 days. From the mother's point of view, pregnancy. (Ch. 3)

gonad The sex gland (ovary or testis) in which gametes are produced. (Ch. 2)

grammar and syntax The rules by which words are shaped and combined to form correct sentences. (Chs. 9, 11)

graphic collections Groupings into patterns and structures without regard for logical considerations. (Ch. 11)

grasping reflex The neonate's firm gripping of a rod or finger pressed against its palm or fingers. The grip is so firm that some neonates can hang by their hands for as long as a minute. This reflex gives way to voluntary grasping at three to four months of age. (Ch. 4)

gross (large muscle) motor activity Activity involving movement of the large muscles of the arms and legs and the ability to control the whole body, as in posture and locomotion. Cf. fine motor activity. (Ch. 5)

growth Increases in size and changes in body proportions. (Ch. 5)

growth ages Separate measures for the various asynchronous components of physical development, such as mental age, reading age, height age, weight age, grip age, dental age, and carpal age (degree of bone ossification), yielding various indices of growth. (Ch. 12)

growth ambivalence The ambivalence children feel about growing up, first manifested in toddlerhood. Progressive urges, the desire for mastery and competence, and the desire to try out new challenges conflict with a conservative streak—the desire to avoid risks and challenges. (Chs. 8, 14)

growth gradients The directional components in physical and behavioral developmemt: cephalo-caudal (q.v.) or head-to-tail, and proximo-distal (q.v.) or near-to-far. (Ch. 1)

growth latency Describes both the slowing down of growth during the middle years of childhood and the middle years themselves as a period of relative serenity. Cf. latency. (Ch. 12)

habituation Loss of responsiveness to a frequently repeated stimulus. (Ch. 4)

hallucinations   Imaginary but vivid experiences of seeing, hearing, feeling, tasting, or smelling things that are not there. (Ch. 15)

harelip   An opening in the upper lip, a teratogenic deformity produced during the embryonic period. (Ch. 3)

hemophilia (bleeders' disease)   A sex-linked disease, caused by a recessive gene on the X chromosome, in which the blood fails to clot properly. It is found predominantly in males, whose much smaller Y chromosome lacks a corresponding gene to counteract it. (Ch. 3)

hierarchic integration   See functional subordination.

holophrasis (pl. **holophrases**)   An utterance consisting of a single word or word-fusion that functions as a complete sentence. (Ch. 9)

HOME Scale   A technique for quantifying the sources of favorable psychological stimulation in the child's family environment. (Ch. 7)

Huntington's disease   A hereditary progressive deterioration of the central nervous system, marked by grimacing and dancinglike movements, which may not appear until middle age. (Ch. 3)

hydrocephaly   An excess of cerebrospinal fluid within the cranial cavity, resulting in an enlarged skull and forehead and atrophy of the brain. (Ch. 3)

hyperactive type   In Achenbach's scheme, a type of disturbed behavior marked by an inability to concentrate, disobedience in school, impulsiveness, and nail biting. (Ch. 15)

hyperkinesis (hyperactivity)   A type of overactivity that makes children—usually boys—unable to sit still and focus attention in school and similar situations; often involves impulsiveness, distractibility, and distraction of others. (Ch. 15)

hypothesis formation   Deducing a possible new relationship from known facts and ideas. (Chs. 1, 14)

hysteria   Any bodily malfunction—as in hysterical blindness, deafness, paralysis or loss of feeling—that exists in the absence of any detectable physical pathology. (Chs. 14, 15)

id   In psychoanalytic theory, the source of a person's drives and impulses. Its functioning is said to be ruled by the pleasure principle (q.v.). (Ch. 1)

idealism   An image of and desire for a perfect social order. May assume diverse forms. Idealism is prevalent in adolescence. (Ch. 14)

identical twins (monozygotic, or MZ)   Twins who come from the same egg, and, therefore, have identical genetic make-ups. (Ch. 2)

identification   A generalized form of modeling in which we think, feel, and act in harmony with people close to us; referred to in both psychoanalytic and social learning theory. (Ch. 1)

identity achieved   In Marcia's usage, this is characteristic of adolescents and adults who have been through the stage of "crisis" (q.v.) and have achieved a satisfactory integration of possibilities. (Ch. 14)

identity crisis   An acute need to redefine and integrate one's sense of who and what one is, believes in, values, and aspires to. (Ch. 14)

identity diffusion   In Marcia's usage, the condition in which it has never occurred to someone to question his or her identity. (Ch. 14)

identity status   In Marcia's scheme, any of the four steps toward forming an adult identity. Defined by the presence or absence of crisis and commitment: identity diffusion (q.v.), moratorium (q.v.), identity achieved (q.v.), and foreclosure (q.v.). (Ch. 14)

identity versus role confusion   In Erikson's scheme of psychosocial development, this is the crisis of adolescence. Identity describes a condition of knowing and accepting who and what one is, what one believes in and stands for, and how one will meet the future; role confusion describes the failure to develop a strong identity. (Ch. 14)

idiographic study   Study of the functioning of one particular, unique, idiosyncratic individual. Cf. nomothetic approach. (Ch. 1)

idiots savants   Persons of severely limited intellectual capacity who perform dazzlingly well in a particular area, such as mental arithmetic or music. (Ch. 15)

illocutionary force   The implied rather than literal meaning of an utterance. (Ch. 9)

imaginary companions   Imaginary playmates, animal or human, and imaginary kingdoms, identities, and playthings, as well as real playthings endowed with imaginary life and treated as autonomous psychological entities. Appear most often during the preschool years. (Ch. 11)

immanent justice   The idea that misdeeds carry within themselves the mechanisms for their own punishment. (Ch. 11)

immature-aggressive type   In Achenbach's scheme, a type of disturbed behavior marked by acting too young, crying, wetting the bed, whining, arguing, screaming, or fighting. (Ch. 15)

immigrant personality   The cluster of attitudes that second-generation Americans have toward the alien, old-fashioned, often highly restrictive ways of their parents. As used here, it refers to alienation in time rather than geography from past generations' codes. (Ch. 12)

implicit perception   Awareness of the hidden parts of partially visible objects. (Chs. 5, 6)

impression record   A method of naturalistic observation that summarizes the total flow of events, with typical events and the emotional atmosphere treated in some detail. (Ch. 1)

imprinting In animal behavior, the bond that forms between the mother and newly hatched fowl, who follow the first moving object they encounter and show strong emotional attachment. (Ch. 5)

inborn errors of metabolism A group of inherited genetic disorders, some treatable and some fatal, caused by particular enzyme deficiencies. (Ch. 3)

independent (treatment) variable The experimental manipulation that is expected to cause a behavioral change as measured by the dependent variable (q.v.). (Ch. 1)

indicator responses Physiological changes, as in heartbeat or breathing rate, associated with changes in stimulation, indicating that a stimulus is having an impact. (Ch. 4)

inductive thinking Generalizing from one or more particular instances to form a rule or principle, which may or may not be correct. Cf. deductive thinking. (Ch. 11)

industry versus inferiority Erikson's definition of the developmental crisis of the middle years of childhood. Children are said to be oriented toward achievement, and if their abilities do not measure up to those of their peers, they develop feelings of inferiority. (Ch. 12)

infantile amnesia Our ability to remember only isolated fragments of early childhood; in Freudian theory, the result of repression associated with the resolution of the Oedipus or Electra complex. In the cognitive view, infantile amnesia is caused by radical reorganizations of cognitive structure that block out earlier ways of experiencing. (Chs. 1, 10)

infantile autism A special variety of childhood schizophrenia characterized by unresponsiveness to human stimulation, failure to talk, or compulsive parroting of what is heard, a fascination with the inanimate, and, most important, avoidance of human contact—physical, visual, or verbal. (Ch. 15)

infantilization Holding back the child's progress when the conservative side of a parent's ambivalence toward growth gains the upper hand. (Ch. 8)

initiative versus guilt In Erikson's psychosocial stages, the conflict of the preschool years, marked by the ability to act on one's own, without being told, versus feelings of sinfulness. (Ch. 10)

inner speech Vygotsky's term for the fragmented, loosely organized speech forms used in talking to oneself. Cf. outer speech. (Ch. 9)

instrumental conditioning The organism's actions produce effects, forming a learned associ-

ation between action and outcome. When the effects are favorable to the organism, they are called rewards or reinforcement. All effects can be thought of as informative feedback. Cf. operant conditioning. (Chs. 1, 4)

intelligence quotient (IQ) A measure of the rate of mental development, originally obtained by dividing mental age by chronological age and multiplying by 100, and now derived from deviations from age-group averages. The average IQ is 100. (Ch. 2)

intentionality/purposiveness Describing behavior that shows some degree of planning and foresight. (Ch. 6)

intention movements Obligatory movements that are preludes to action, such as the toddler's rocking back and forth from foot to foot to set himself into forward walking motion. (Ch. 8)

interactionism The view that development has both genetic and experiential components, inextricably entwined. (Ch. 2)

interactive play Nonverbal social exchanges between young children, such as handing each other toys or food or copying each other's actions. (Ch. 10)

intersensory effects The progressive coordination, through experience, of information received through the various senses. Cf. synesthesia. (Ch. 6)

interview The clinical investigator's basic tool, consisting of a series of factual or attitudinal questions asked orally in order to obtain information from the subject. The interview allows the subject to elaborate on answers and gives the interviewer more opportunity to explore answers than does the questionnaire. (Ch. 1)

introjection The unconscious incorporation of ideas or attitudes into the personality. (Ch. 10)

irregular sleep A neonatal sleep state marked by quick, uneven breathing, much movement, changes of facial expression, and possibly starts, tremors, and twitches, as well as rapid eye movements (REMs) (q.v.). (Ch. 4)

karyotype To make visible and sort the chromosomes of a cell in order to detect gross anomalies, such as Down's syndrome. (Ch. 3)

knee-jerk (patellar) reflex An involuntary forward kick that occurs when the leg is relaxed and the base of the kneecap is tapped. (Ch. 4)

kwashiorkor A protein deficiency disease that can lead to brain damage, most often seen in individuals weaned prematurely from the breast and given a high-starch, low-protein diet. (Ch. 5)

labile (unstable)/stable worlds The progression, according to Werner, from perceiving one's environment as unstable, disordered, unpredictable, and teeming with magical possibilities, to the mature view of reality as stable, comprehensible, predictable, and manageable, thus permitting flexibility of behavior. (Ch. 11)

lability Like rigidity (q.v.), a characteristic of immature thought—volatility as a response to the perception of one's environment as essentially unstable, disorderly, unpredictable, and unmanageable. (Ch. 1)

labor The process by which the baby is expelled from the mother's body. (Ch. 3)

labor pains Pain accompanying contractions of the uterus during labor. (Ch. 3)

language acquisition device (LAD) In McNeill's version of Chomsky's theory, the child is born with a LAD, prewired with several sets of grammatical rules, all of them variants on a presumed "deep" grammar common to all languages. The actual speech to which the child is exposed activates the set of rules that matches what the child hears, and the child begins to speak his or her native tongue. Therefore, experience merely liberates capacities the child already has. (Ch. 9)

language of behavior Spontaneous behavioral expressions of the infant's conditions, such as distinguishable cries for hunger, fatigue, and pain, coupled with the feedback a caregiver receives (cessation of cries, gurgles) when the nature of the need has been correctly perceived and satisfied. (Ch. 5)

lanugo A coating of fine, downy hair that covers the fetus's body, some of which may still be present at birth, growing low across the brows or far down the back. (Ch. 4)

latency Freud's idea of a period of supposed sexual quiescence between the Oedipus complex and the sexual reawakening of puberty. (Chs. 1, 12)

learned helplessness The attitude that since all control is localized externally (see locus of control), there is no point in struggling. (Chs. 13, 15)

learning A mechanism of development by which we acquire and integrate new information, including ideas about space and time; facts, knowledge, and ideas; understanding of relationships; and understanding how people function. May take place spontaneously, out of our own experience, or be mediated through the teaching of other people. (Chs. 1, 11)

learning blocks Emotional interferences with learning that appear in a context of parental overambition and pressure. (Ch. 15)

learning disabilities A variety of problems related to difficulty with school learning. (Ch. 15)

learning theory See behaviorism.

learning to learn or **learning set** Generalizing principles from one learning situation to another instead of learning only a specific response to a specific stimulus. (Ch. 11)

libido The supposed specialized sexual energy that underlies our erotic motives. (Ch. 1)

lightening The easing of pressure on the mother's upper abdomen that occurs when the head of the fetus turns downward and rests in the lower part of the uterus; this occurs sometime during the four weeks before birth. (Ch. 3)

light sleep (transitional sleep or **drowsiness)** An intermediate state between deep sleep (q.v.) and irregular sleep (q.v.), in which the baby moves little and the eyes open and close; rapid eye movement (REM) (q.v.) may also be present. (Ch. 4)

linguistic determinism (the **Whorf hypothesis)** Language and culture are one and the same, so that the categories provided by the language of one's culture inescapably determine one's powers of perception and thought. (Ch. 9)

lochia The disintegration and shedding of the uterine lining after birth in a ten- to fourteen-day process that resembles menstruation. (Ch. 3)

locus of control The extent to which one feels that one controls events or that one is the passive, helpless plaything of external forces. (See attribution theory.) (Ch. 13)

longitudinal method A way of studying developmental change by following the same individual(s) over an extended period. Cf. cross-sectional method. (Ch. 1)

looming effect In babies as young as two weeks, when what looks like a large object (actually a projected shadow) rapidly "approaches" (that is, expands symmetrically) on a collision course, babies throw back the head, raise the arms, and probably cry. If the approaching shape grows asymmetrically, suggesting a noncollision course, the baby will observe it unemotionally. The baby must be propped up for this effect to occur. Could be considered an early index of sensitivity to depth. (Ch. 4)

manic-depressive psychosis Mood disorder (q.v.) marked by recurring cycles of energetic excitement and black depression. (Ch. 15)

map space The notion of how things and places are related to each other spatially, which begins to develop in the late preschool or early school years; the child forms integrated schemata, not merely of routes and pathways, but of whole regions of familiar space. Cf. action space. (Chs. 8, 11)

masculine protest The girl's denial of the lack of a penis (see penis envy) and the pursuit of an essentially masculine life style, with overtones of lesbianism. First defined by Adler. (Ch. 10)

matching In probability learning (q.v.), distributing one's responses according to the percentages of reinforcement; for example, pressing a lever that gives positive reinforcement 70 percent of the time 70 percent of the time, and pressing a 30-percent lever 30 percent of the time. Cf. maximizing. (Ch. 11)

maturation   The often subtle anatomical and physiological reorganizations through which the individual passes in the course of development. Puberty is the most dramatic expression of maturation. (Chs. 1, 5)

maximizing   In probability learning, a pattern of response in which the subject maximizes the amount of positive reinforcement received, by pressing, say, only the high-payoff lever. Cf. matching. (Ch. 11)

maximum growth age (MGA)   The twelve months before puberty, during which time growth is most rapid. (Ch. 14)

means-end relationships   A beginning awareness of cause and effect, one of the key achievements of the sensorimotor period. (Ch. 6)

mechanisms   Real or hypothesized explanations of how things happen; mechanisms clarify principles (q.v.). (Ch. 1)

meiosis (reduction division)   A special final stage of cell division undergone by gametes (q.v.): individual chromosomes do not double and separate; instead, the chromosome pairs simply separate, with one member of each of the twenty-three pairs going to a new cell. (Ch. 2)

menarche   (pronounced men-ar-kee)   The first menstrual flow, marking puberty in girls. (Ch. 14)

mental age (MA)   An intelligence test score stated in terms of the age group whose average performance is most like that of the child being tested. (Ch. 2)

mesoderm   The middle layer of the cell mass from which the skeleton, muscles, and supporting tissues develop. (Ch. 3)

metalinguistic awareness   Awareness of language and its possibilities for contemplation, manipulation, and play. (Chs. 9, 11)

minimal brain damage (MBD)   Hypothetical abnormality of brain functioning too slight to be detected by the usual neurological tests. Invoked as an explanation of both learning disabilities (q.v.) and hyperkinesis (q.v.). (Ch. 15)

mitosis   The process of successive cell divisions in which the forty-six chromosomes split lengthwise so that there are ninety-two chromosomes within the cell. These chromosomes migrate in pairs to opposite ends of the cell, which then divides in half, forming two cells with the normal complement of twenty-three pairs of chromosomes each. (Ch. 2)

modeling   Teaching and learning by example; observational learning in which the learner picks up whole styles and categories of behavior rather than particular acts and action sequences. For instance, modeling provides the best available explanation for how we learn linguistic rules. (Chs. 1, 10)

mood disorders   Psychoses (q.v.) marked by disorders of feeling but not of thought. (Ch. 15)

moral dilemmas   Situations in which each of the available options involves a violation of a moral principle. (Ch. 13)

moral realism   The assumption that the rules of moral conduct are a part of nature rather than human conventions. (Chs. 6, 11)

moratorium   In Marcia's scheme, the situation in which a young person wrestles with the problem of identity but defers an immediate resolution. (Chs. 14, 15)

Moro response   The neonatal version of the startle in adults: a loud noise, bright light, or abrupt loss of support causes the neonate to stretch its arms and legs wide, cry, then hug the extremities inward against the trunk. (Ch. 4)

morphemes   The smallest sound units that carry meaning. (Ch. 9)

mosaicism   A chromosomal abnormality, accompanied by various physical abnormalities, characterized by a person having two kinds of cells, each with a different complement of chromosomes, such as XX/XO or XXY/XO. (The O stands for a missing chromosome.) (Ch. 3)

motherese   See code switching.

motor copy   Imitation of actions and gestures as a form of communication between toddlers. (Ch. 8)

mutagen   An agent, such as a virus, chemical, or radiation, capable of producing genetic mutations. (Ch. 3)

natural childbirth   A method that emphasizes educating the prospective mother to understand and participate in the birth process, exercises to limber her body and ease delivery, no use or only sparing use of anesthetics, and the participation of the father throughout pregnancy and birth. Cf. gentle childbirth. (Ch. 3)

natural experiment   The study of conditions that happen to occur naturally, as opposed to being deliberately set up as an experiment; the experimenter assesses their impact on the affected individual(s), who can be compared with an untouched "control" population. (Ch. 1)

naturalism   Mature causal thinking: the realization that there are impersonal, stable forces and principles that govern events in the natural world, including some portion of human behavior; this viewpoint accepts coincidence and accident as well. (Chs. 1, 11)

nature-nurture controversy   The never-ending debate about whether group and individual differences in behavior have their origins in biological (nature) or experiential (nurture) differences. (Ch. 2)

necessity The understanding that if nothing is added to or subtracted from a quantity, it must of logical necessity remain the same. (Ch. 13)

negativism Resistance to control by other people; an expression of the toddler's striving for autonomy, manifested by his or her refusal of parental commands, requests, and offers of help. Often merely a ritual or playful nay saying, not to be taken seriously. (Ch. 8)

neobehaviorism Behaviorism as formulated by Skinner. (Ch. 1)

neologisms Invented words. (Chs. 9, 11)

neonate A baby in the first few weeks after birth. (Ch. 4)

neurosis Disturbed functioning which permits an ordinary life but with considerable pain for self and others. (Ch. 15)

nocturnal emission ("wet dream") The ejaculation of semen during sleep. Women also have erotic dreams accompanied by orgasm, but we have no information about the age at which they begin. (Ch. 14)

nominal realism See verbal realism.

nomothetic approach Studying people with a view to generalizing about human characteristics. Cf. idiographic study. (Ch. 1)

nonliteral behavior Behavior that does not mean what it seems to mean; for example, babies enjoy the mock fright that comes when parents say "Boo," then smile. (Chs. 5, 11)

norm In psychological testing, the expected average performance for a given individual or group of people on the basis of age or background, derived from the scores of representative samples drawn from the population at large. Cf. normative studies. (Chs. 1, 2)

normative studies Research aimed at establishing the average age at which specified forms of behavior appear. Cf. norm. (Ch. 1)

no-win situation See double bind.

nystagmus The jerky eye movements seen in neonates and adults after being spun on a turntable; suggest an effort to anchor oneself in the visual environment to compensate for the disorientation of being spun around. (Ch. 4)

objective responsibility Judging wrongdoing in terms of the magnitude of its consequences, without regard for intentions or motives. (Ch. 13)

object permanence or **object concept** Awareness that an object can exist independent of one's being able to perceive it; at earlier ages, the baby shows no awareness that vanished objects may continue to exist. Object permanence develops in a series of steps beginning between six and eight months of age. (Ch. 6)

observational learning Acquiring skills or information by observing a model in action. Often seems to take place without any particular attention being paid to the model. Differs from imitation in that the observer can learn from the model's mistakes without having to repeat them. Closely related to modeling (q.v.). (Chs. 1, 9)

oddity learning A learning situation in which the subject has to respond to the stimulus that is different from the rest of the set. Once learned, the response can be transferred to new dimensions of difference. Exemplifies learning to learn (q.v.). (Ch. 11)

Oedipus complex A series of events, according to Freud, coinciding with the preschool years, during which a boy directs his sexual strivings toward his mother and feels rivalry toward his father. Normally resolved when the boy, moved by castration anxiety, renounces his pursuit of the mother and identifies with the father, internalizing the father's moral code as the superego, or conscience. The resolution is accompanied by repression (q.v.) of all sexuality and also of all memory of the past, accounting for infantile amnesia (q.v.). (Chs. 1, 10)

operant conditioning Learning through reinforcement of a set of instrumental acts (the operant) all of which produce approximately the same consequences. More flexible than instrumental conditioning (q.v.). (Ch. 1)

operationalize To define research variables in terms of concrete, observable manipulations and behaviors. (Ch. 1)

oral-acquisitive character In psychoanalysis, a clinging, demanding, selfish, helpless, babylike person. (Ch. 1)

oral stage The first of Freud's psychosexual stages, coinciding with the period of infancy, in which the mouth is the main channel of gratification. (Chs. 1, 5)

organismic-developmental approach Werner's developmental framework, stressing the child's growth from rigid and undifferentiated thinking to flexible, stable, and integrated thinking. (Ch. 1)

orthogenetic principle Development proceeds, according to Werner, from a state of global, undifferentiated functioning toward increasing differentiation followed by integration. An important aspect of the organismic-developmental approach (q.v.). (Chs. 1, 10)

outcome variable See dependent variable.

outer speech Vygotsky's term for the well-articulated speech forms used in talking to others. Cf. inner speech. (Ch. 9)

overregularization The substitution of incorrect regular forms for correct irregular ones. For example, *foots* as the plural of foot. (Ch. 9)

ovum (pl. ova) The female reproductive cell, or gamete. (Ch. 2)

paradigmatic associations Perceived relationships of items based on common abstract attributes; for example, plow, scissors, and knife are all instruments for cutting. Cf. syntagmatic associations. (Ch. 13)

parallel play Two or more children playing side by side, obviously taking pleasure in each other's companionship, but without any real exchange. (Chs. 8, 10)

paranoia The erroneous belief that one is being persecuted, poisoned, plotted against, or spied on, or that one is constantly at the center of everybody's attention. (Ch. 15)

patellar reflex See knee-jerk reflex.

Pavlovian conditioning See classical conditioning.

penis envy In Freudian theory, the girl's desire to have a penis like the male's. See masculine protest. (Ch. 10)

performance Chomsky's term for what people actually say, which may be a very poor indicator of their underlying competence (q.v.). (Ch. 9)

perinatal Referring to the period immediately before, during, and immediately after birth. (Ch. 3)

perinatal disorders Disorders related to events during or immediately after birth. (Ch. 3)

personal knowledge Polanyi's notion that formal learning becomes worthwhile as it relates to the individual's conduct of life. (Ch. 13)

personal time A perception of the passage of time in one's own life, which is only partially correlated with formal measurements of time. We feel that time drags or flies, that we are relaxed or under pressure, that we are losing, wasting, or saving time or using it wisely. (Ch. 11)

phallic character From psychoanalytic theory, a sexual exploiter interested only in getting pleasure and not in giving it. (Chs. 1, 10)

phallic stage The third of Freud's psychosexual stages, corresponding with the preschool years, when the source of gratification shifts to the genitals, which supposedly provide pleasure uncluttered by the tenderness and concern and responsibility characteristic of the genital stage of adolescence and adulthood. The Oedipus and Electra complexes (q.v.) take place during the phallic stage. (Chs. 1, 10)

phantom environment Living in the past; failing to adapt to changing circumstances; also, an imaginary reality created through the manipulation of symbols. (Chs. 1, 9)

phantom limb An example of the persistence of a schema; even though an arm or leg is lost, a phantom limb continues to be experienced. (Ch. 1)

phenomenalism Accepting the surface appearance of things without wondering about their deeper structure, as in the "floating island" phenomenon. (Ch. 6)

phenotype The observable trait or characteristic. Cf. genotype. (Ch. 2)

phenylketonuria (PKU) An inherited enzyme deficiency that can cause mental retardation unless diet is controlled. (Ch. 3)

pheromones Airborne chemical messages secreted by a plant or animal which affect the behavior of other organisms. (Ch. 4)

phobia A chronic, irrational fear of a real or invented menace. (Ch. 15)

phocomelia The "seal flippers syndrome"—the stunted arms and incompletely differentiated fingers associated with, among other possible agents, the drug Thalidomide; a deformity produced during the embryonic period. (Ch. 3)

phonemes The units of sound of which language is composed. (Ch. 9)

phonetic drift The tendency, by late infancy, for a baby's babbling to take on the intonations and cadences of its native tongue. (Ch. 6)

phonetics The sound patterns in spoken language. (Ch. 9)

phonology The study of speech sounds and, often, of the structure and function of our vocal and auditory apparatus. Includes phonetics, which deals with phonemes, morphemes, and prosody. (Ch. 9)

physical cognition Knowledge about the workings of the physical world, and also about mathematical and logical relationships. (Chs. 6, 8)

physiognomic perceiving Reacting to the global properties of things rather than to specific attributes; that is, to overall expressive qualities rather than detailed features. (Ch. 6)

picture realism Children's confusion between pictures and the things they portray. The child's "smelling" the picture of a flower is an example. (Chs. 6, 11)

placebo effect A psychosomatic (q.v.) cure: the fact that illnesses are sometimes cured or ameliorated by sham drugs with no intrinsic curative properties. (Ch. 2)

placenta The disk-shaped fleshy slab implanted in the uterus through which the fetus's circulation interlocks with the mother's. The baby is connected to it by the umbilical cord. (Ch. 3)

placental barrier The permeable surface of the placental blood vessels, where all transactions between the bloodstreams of the mother and the fetus take place. (Ch. 3)

plantar (sole of the foot) **response** A reflex that changes with development. If one strokes the sole of the neonate's foot, its toes fan up and outward in the Babinski response (q.v.). Later in development (except in conditions of brain damage or stupor), the normal response to this stimulus is for the toes to curl downward. (Ch. 4)

play The spontaneous activity of children, essential to sound development, but with no goal or motive other than the satisfaction derived from the activities themselves. (Chs. 8, 10)

pleasure principle In psychoanalysis, the unbridled seeking for immediate gratification that governs the id (q.v.). (Ch. 1)

pleasure smile A smile of contentment in neonates, awake or asleep, in well-fed, placid repose. Cf. social smile. (Ch. 4)

polygenic (multigene) **inheritance** Describes traits that are governed by the interaction of many genes with one another and with the environment. (Ch. 2)

popularity neurosis A desire, common in adolescents and adults, to be widely liked to a degree that approaches the pathological. (Ch. 14)

positive reinforcers Rewards or need-satisfying consequences. (Chs. 1, 4)

postconventional level The highest of three levels of moral judgment, according to Kohlberg, when morality is based on individually defined principles without regard to conventional views of right and wrong. (Chs. 13, 14)

pragmatics The techniques we use and the rules we follow to communicate; includes gestures, pointing, facial expression, turn-taking, and prosodic manipulation. (Ch. 9)

pragmatism An outlook, associated with Dewey, that would have discarded much of traditional education in favor of knowledge appropriate to contemporary life, including practical skills. (Ch. 5)

preconventional level The first of three levels of moral judgment, according to Kohlberg, characterized by a punishment-and-obedience orientation and a pragmatic concern with maximizing satisfaction. (Ch. 13)

premature birth Birth after a gestation period of less than 37 weeks, instead of the usual 40, or with a low birth weight under 2,500 grams, or about 5 pounds. (Ch. 3)

preoperational stage The second stage in Piaget's scheme of the development of logical thinking, lasting from about ages two to seven years; marked by internal representation, as through symbolic play, images, drawing, and the use of words. (Chs. 1, 8, 11)

prepared childbirth A modern philosophy surrounding childbirth that incorporates the teachings of Lamaze and Leboyer, emphasizing preparations for birth; education, exercises, and care of the body; and comfort for the baby immediately after delivery to minimize the presumed trauma of birth. Cf. gentle childbirth, natural childbirth. (Ch. 3)

primary adualism The primitive intermingling of self and surroundings. (Ch. 1)

primary-process thinking Magicalistic thinking, immune to fact or logic. Cf. secondary-process thinking. (Ch. 1)

primary sex traits The reproductive organs: the penis and testes in the male and the ovaries, uterus, and vagina in the female. Cf. secondary sex traits. (Ch. 14)

principles Systematic statements describing what happens in development, but not how it happens. Cf. mechanisms. (Ch. 1)

probability learning In a learning situation in which different courses of action have different likelihoods of producing a reward, the subject modifies his or her behavior to take account of the differing probabilities. See matching, maximizing. (Ch. 11)

productive language Talking, as contrasted with receptive language (q.v.), understanding other people's utterances. (Chs. 6, 9)

profile A set of numerical scores on related subtests, as in a factorial test of intelligence. (Ch. 1)

projection A defense mechanism by which one attributes one's own secret urges to others. (Ch. 1)

projective test A measure that asks the subject to make sense of unstructured or unorganized stimulus materials, such as ink blots, permitting many interpretations that are thought to reveal personality traits. (Ch. 1)

prosocial behavior Constructive and cooperative social behavior such as altruism. (Ch. 10)

prosody The melodic structure of utterances. (Ch. 9)

prospective memory The vocabulary of remembering applied to the future, as in "Remind me to call Alice." (Ch. 13)

prospective studies Studies that look forward in time rather than back, such as the study beginning at birth of the effects of premature birth on later development. (Ch. 3)

proximodistal growth gradient The principle that says that development proceeds from the central axis of the body outward, toward the periphery and extremities (near-to-far). (Ch. 1)

psychoanalysis The psychological theory and method of treatment formulated by Freud that emphasizes the role of the unconscious and instinctual drives in normal and abnormal development and behavior. (Ch. 1)

psychobiological view The belief that human development is produced by interactions between biological processes and meaningful psychological stimuli. (Ch. 2)

psychological adolescence See cultural adolescence.

psychometric test A measure that yields a numerical score (or a profile, a set of scores) that can be compared with norms derived from a supposedly representative sample of the population at large. (Ch. 1)

psychopathic or **sociopathic** or **antisocial personality** A type of pathological personality that develops early in life; the individual lacks a conscience, depth of feeling, or empathy for others. Possible causes include failing to identify with sound parental models or identifying with parents who themselves exhibit such behavioral styles. (Ch. 15)

psychosexual stages In psychoanalysis, a series of changes in which motivational expression changes but not the underlying motives themselves. Psychosexual development refers to shifts in the channels or zones of the body through which id gratification is sought and obtained, and in the change of objects that serve as gratifiers. The oral, anal, phallic, and genital stages express the successive changes in the developing individual's sexual motivation. (Ch. 1)

psychosis (pl. **psychoses**) Any behavior disturbance so severe as to make the ordinary conduct of life all but impossible. (Ch. 15)

psychosocial stages Erikson's formulations of the eight stages through which a person passes as the developing ego interacts with the social forces around it. At each stage there is an emotional conflict that must be resolved for healthy development. (Ch. 1)

psychosomatic disorders Pathological body changes associated with prolonged psychological distress; migraine headaches, asthma, eczema, and gastric ulcers are examples. (Ch. 15)

psychosomatic reactions Physical reactions to psychological stimuli; blushing, sexual arousal, or laughter are examples, in addition to psychosomatic illness. Cf. placebo effect. (Ch. 2)

puberty The point in life at which sexual maturity—the ability to reproduce—begins; marked by menarche (q.v.) in girls and the production of sperm in the testes in boys. (Ch. 14)

puberty rites, rites de passage, initiation ceremonies The formal rituals by which adulthood is recognized or conferred. (Ch. 14)

pubescence The period of about two years immediately prior to puberty, marked by an increase in the rate of physical growth, changes in facial and body proportions, and the maturing of primary and secondary sex traits (q.v.). (Ch. 14)

pubescent growth spurt The increase in the rate of physical growth that marks the end of growth latency and the beginning of pubescence. (Ch. 14)

push-back response Lying prone (face down) with bottoms of feet in contact with a solid surface, the neonate's feet push against it, sometimes with enough force to move its body. At a slightly older age, this occurs when supine (face up). (Ch. 4)

quasi-experimental design A research method that uses comparison groups (q.v.) in an experiment instead of an experimental group (q.v.) and a control group (q.v.). (Ch. 1)

quickening The mother's experience of fetal movements, first felt as mild flutterings and later as solid kicks. (Ch. 3)

range of reaction The various ways in which a gene can express itself, depending both on environmental conditions and on the workings of the neighboring genes. (Ch. 2)

rapid eye movements (REMs) The quick movements of the eye under the closed eyelid during sleep; REMs frequently accompany dreaming in older children and adults. (Ch. 4)

rating scale A technique by which the observer assigns numerical values to traits, such as emotionality or quiet versus active play. (Ch. 1)

rationalization A defense mechanism whereby one invents justifications for unjustifiable behavior. (Ch. 1)

reaction formation A defense mechanism that involves going to the opposite extreme from one's true feeling in order to protect oneself from these unwanted wishes. (Chs. 1, 12)

realism Failure to distinguish among orders or levels of reality; experiencing a dream as an event in the real world, for example. (Chs. 1, 6, 11)

reality principle In psychoanalysis, the principle that governs the ego; involves taking into account what is already possible or the means of making gratification possible to resolve the conflicts between the strivings of the id and the demands of reality. (Ch. 1)

receptive language The ability of a baby to understand other people's utterances, even though the baby cannot yet talk. Cf. productive language. (Chs. 6, 9)

recessive trait A trait that appears only when the two controlling genes are both of the same kind. Blue eye color is a recessive trait. Cf. dominant trait. (Ch. 2)

reduction division See meiosis.

referential communication skills The ability to describe an object verbally so that a listener can identify the described object from among an array. (Ch. 13)

reflexes Predictable, unlearned, automatic, and involuntary responses to particular forms of stimulation. Some are physiological, some serve no known function (but help reveal neurological impairment), and some are complex behavioral responses to stimulation. (Ch. 4)

regression In psychoanalytic theory, reacting to excessive frustration by returning to the behavior of an earlier stage. (Ch. 1)

regular sleep See deep sleep.

reification The process by which words create imaginary concrete realities; a manifestation of verbal realism (q.v.). Examples include ''intelligence,'' ''instinct,'' ''memory,'' and ''language acquisition device''. (Chs. 2, 9, 11)

reinforcement   Reward, feedback, or punishment produced by an instrumental act, which serves to strengthen learning. (Chs. 1, 4)

reinforcement contingencies   In operant conditioning (q.v.), the learned associations between behavior and reinforcement that govern subsequent behavior. (Chs. 1, 4, 9)

relativism   The opposite of egocentrism; ability to take account of other people's differing needs, wants, and perspectives. (Ch. 1)

reliability (significance)   A statistical indication of the probability that an observed relationship is real rather than a product of chance. A probability of .05 or less (that is, anything smaller than a 1-in-20 chance) is usually accepted as ruling out a chance relationship, meaning that the observation is significant or reliable. (Ch. 1)

repression   A defense mechanism by which one blocks unwanted ideas and cravings from consciousness. (Chs. 1, 10)

restricted range   The problem of meaningless correlation coefficients that occurs when subjects are from a narrow or restricted range; a few misrankings will conceal whatever actual relations exist. (Ch. 2)

retrolental fibroplasia   A thickening of the inside of the eye that results in blindness, caused by giving premature babies excessive quantities of pure oxygen. (Ch. 3)

reversal and **nonreversal shifts (intradimensional and extradimensional shifts, IDS and EDS)**   Learning situations in which the experimenter changes the rules after the subject has learned a response. In reversal or intradimensional shifts (IDS), the newly rewarded feature may be another position on the same dimension—little instead of big, for example. In nonreversal or extradimensional shifts (EDS), the new reward can be based on a new dimension—say, color or shape instead of size. EDS is much easier to learn than IDS. (Ch. 11)

reversibility   The understanding that certain operations can be reversed, mentally or in fact; that subtraction reverses addition, for example. (Chs. 11, 13)

Rh factor   A blood protein found in most people. Rh incompatibility between mother and fetus was once a source of damage to the newborn, but problems can now be prevented by treating the mother with gamma globulin. (Ch. 3)

rigidity/flexibility   According to Werner, the progression from the safety achieved by adhering to rigid, ritualistic behavior patterns to more flexible and adaptive patterns of thought and behavior. (Chs. 1, 11)

ritual games   Games with a set procedure that run their own set course to an unvarying climax and then end, such as "London Bridge." Cf. competitive games. (Ch. 10)

role confusion (role diffusion)   Erikson's term for the adolescent's inability to form a stable, satisfying identity; overwhelmed by unmanageable feelings and by the pressures and demands of adulthood, some adolescents are unable to find themselves or their place in the world. (Ch. 14)

role playing   Acting the part of some person or category of people with whom one temporarily identifies. An important mechanism of learning, from the toddler's make-believe to the adolescent's adopted personalities. (Ch. 1)

romantic naturalism   A world view, first set forth by Rousseau, suggesting that the ideal condition for humans is that of happy, noble savages living in a state of nature. (Ch. 5)

rooming in   The practice of having the newborn baby live in its mother's hospital room, with the mother beginning immediately to take care of her child. (Ch. 3)

rooting response   A reflex of the neonate to seek out nourishment when hungry and in contact with a responsive adult body; searching with the mouth, as though for a nipple, clutching at whatever it touches, and actively propelling itself with the trunk, arms, and legs. (Ch. 4)

running record   A method of naturalistic observation using a continuous narrative account to capture the events that occur within a given period of time. (Ch. 1)

scapegoat   A person of low status on whom those higher in the pecking order can vent their negative emotions. (Ch. 12)

schedules of reinforcement   In experimental situations, reinforcements can be given every time a subject makes a desired response, or they can be given only to some proportion of responses. The various patterns according to which reinforcements are dispensed are called schedules. (Ch. 11)

schema (pl. schemata)   Piaget's term for a mental structure representing some aspect of reality; generally lies outside awareness but becomes apparent when violated. (Chs. 1, 5, 6)

scheme   According to Piaget, the mental pattern that underlies the performance of a skilled action, as for sucking or grasping. (Chs. 1, 6)

schizoid type   In Achenbach's scheme, a type of disturbed behavior marked by clinging to adults, expressing fear of one's impulses, perfectionism, or hallucinations. (Ch. 15)

schizophrenia   A group of psychotic conditions marked by serious distortion of the emotions and disturbances of cognition. (Ch. 15)

scrotum   The sac containing the testes and related structures. (Ch. 14)

secondary-process thinking   Pragmatic thinking that takes into account what is possible or how things can be made possible. Cf. primary-process thinking. (Ch. 1)

secondary sex traits   Physical characteristics, other than the reproductive organs, that are related to sexual maturing but not directly involved in reproduction. In the male, they include the growth of chest and facial hair; in the female, breast development. In both sexes, pubic and armpit hair develops and the voice deepens. Cf. primary sex traits. (Ch. 14)

selective record   A method of naturalistic observation whereby one's description focuses on some preselected form of activity, such as sharing, block building, dominance, or parent-child interaction. (Ch. 1)

selective reinforcement   By reinforcing only some kinds of behavior and not others, one can shape the organism's patterns of actions. For Skinner, a major mechanism in learning to talk. (Ch. 9)

self-actualizing person   Maslow's term for an individual who has creatively fulfilled his or her potentialities. (Ch. 15)

self-fulfilling prophecy   The idea that an expectation of an outcome helps produce that outcome. (Ch. 6)

semantics   The study of the meaning of words and sentences; that is, the way words "stand for" states of affairs. (Ch. 9)

sense-pleasure play   Nonsocial stimulation that produces something akin to early aesthetic experience. Light, color, movement, sound, rhythm, etc. attract attention and provide pleasure. Babbling, dancing, or masturbation are manifestations of sense-pleasure play. (Ch. 10)

sensorimotor stage   In Piaget's scheme of the development of logical thinking, this is the first stage, lasting from birth to approximately two years of age, when the child is involved in the exploration and manipulation of materials and is under the control of external stimuli. (Chs. 1, 6, 8)

separation anxiety   A child's distress when separated from the parents. (Ch. 5)

seriation   The ability to put things in a sensible order, such as one of increasing or decreasing length, and to learn such conventional series as the alphabet and such logical ones as the number series. (Chs. 11, 13)

sex cleavage   The tendency of middle-years boys and girls to associate primarily with members of their own sex. (Ch. 12)

sex-linked recessive traits   Traits carried by genes on the X chromosomes for which there are no corresponding genes on the smaller Y chromosomes. These traits are recessive in females, who have two alleles (differing forms of the same gene) for each such trait, but dominant in males, who have no offsetting second gene. Examples are hemophilia and red-green color blindness. (Ch. 2)

sex typing   Behavior directed toward the child that communicates society's expectations of how the child should fulfill the roles associated with maleness and femaleness. (Chs. 5, 8)

shoving, shaping, and showing   The three teaching strategies adopted by mothers given the task of teaching their babies how to reach an object behind a transparent screen. Shoving refers to manipulating the baby's hand, shaping to moving the object by stages from full accessibility to inaccessibility, and showing to demonstrating the action. (Ch. 6)

showing   One of the first signs of labor; the emergence from the vagina of a small blood-spotted clot of mucus that had formed in the cervical opening of the uterus and is released as the cervix relaxes and dilates in preparation for birth. (Ch. 3)

sibling rivalry   Adler's concept of the competition, jealousy, and hostility that exist among children in the same family. (Chs. 8, 12)

sickle-cell anemia   A disease marked by sickle-shaped red blood cells that can impede circulation, causing pain, sickness, and even death. Found predominantly in blacks of West African extraction and in people from the Mediterranean and Middle East, it is thought to be a mutation that survived because it confers partial immunity against malaria. (Ch. 3)

significance   See reliability.

signifiers   Piaget's term for the mental symbols (words or images) that a child uses to represent reality. (Ch. 11)

situationism   Adapting one's moral standards to the conditions of the moment, with little or no regard to principle. (Ch. 13)

size-distance constancy   The tendency to perceive objects as maintaining their size despite variations in distance from the viewer (applies only in horizontal plane). (Ch. 6)

skill play   The persistent, repetitive exercise of newly developing abilities, which is apparently motivated by the intrinsic satisfaction of mastering skills. (Ch. 10)

social-affective play   The earliest type of social play, taking pleasure in the manipulation of social relations and feelings. Such play begins with the adult, when he or she talks or croons to the baby to elicit a positive emotional response. Babies, in turn, learn to arouse parental emotion in a spirit of play. (Ch. 10)

social cognition   Awareness of one's own and others' perceptions, feelings, thoughts, intentions, values, capacities, and the like, including the action of external and internalized social forces. (Chs. 8, 11, 13)

social Darwinism   A doctrine that teaches that wealth and power are distributed through a population in terms of differing degrees of biological fitness. Thus the social order is to be understood as a product of evolution. (Ch. 2)

social egocentrism Limited ability to judge others' reactions (emotional social egocentrism) and/or limited awareness of others' psychological processes in general (cognitive social egocentrism). (Chs. 1, 11, 13)

social games Play patterns, formal (peekaboo, this little piggy) or informal (tickling, nuzzling, chasing), the main point of which is pleasurable reciprocal social stimulation. (Ch. 5)

socialized or **subcultural delinquency** Delinquency in a child who grows up into a ready-made delinquent culture within his or her own society; sanctioned by the culture, such behavior does not evoke guilt or condemnation from other members of the culture. (Ch. 15)

socialization The conscious and deliberate teaching of socially desirable attitudes and behavior to children. Cf. enculturation. (Ch. 5)

social learning theory A theory of identification that postulates learning without reinforcement and deals with learning from models. (Ch. 1)

social-modal concept of normality A definition of normality based on adherence to the behavioral norms set by one's social group. (Ch. 15)

social smile The baby's smile that appears at about six weeks of age in response to a human face or voice. Cf. pleasure smile. (Chs. 4, 5)

sociometry The study and measurement of interpersonal relationships in a group of people; members are asked which partner they would choose for various activities, yielding a diagram representing the status hierarchy within the group. (Ch. 12)

somatic cells Body cells, that is, the cells that constitute the bones, nerves, glands, muscles, etc., of the organism, as contrasted with gametes (q.v.). (Ch. 2)

spatial egocentrism Limited ability to understand how differing vantage points in space affect what one can perceive. (Chs. 1, 13)

sperm The male reproductive cell, or gamete. (Ch. 2)

spherical model A scheme devised by Schaefer to assess a parent's behavior toward a child by observing acceptance-rejection; psychological control–psychological autonomy; and firm control–lax control. (Ch. 7)

spina bifida A congenital defect in which the covering of the spinal nerves fails to develop properly. (Ch. 3)

stage theories Developmental theories, such as Freud's and Piaget's, that see the life span compartmented into periods each of which has an identifying feature that serves to organize behavior into a coherent whole. (Ch. 1)

standardization In psychological testing, trying out test items on a large number of subjects and modifying or rejecting them, if necessary, in an effort to ensure the validity of test scores using the items. (Ch. 2)

state An individual's physiological or psychological condition, such as being drowsy, asleep, alert, or crying. (Ch. 4)

state-dependent learning Learning that is retained and usable only in the condition in which it was acquired; when the state changes, as when a drug wears off, the learning evaporates. (Ch. 15)

state stability The stability of sleep and waking patterns from day to day, important in evaluating the behavior of newborns and infants. State *instability* refers to inconsistent patterns of sleep and alertness. (Ch. 3)

status offenses Actions, such as truancy, that are criminal when committed by children but not by adults. (Ch. 13)

stepping reflex When the neonate is held vertical with feet lightly touching a firm surface, the feet and legs move up and down as though walking. (Ch. 4)

stimulation-induced maturation Maturation at least partly controlled by environmental factors. (Chs. 1, 2)

stranger anxiety A pronounced fear of unfamiliar people or places, beginning anywhere from five months to one year of age. (Ch. 5)

strange settings (strange situations) A room or rooms constructed within a laboratory, used to measure attachment through the baby's reactions to a variety of manipulations. (Ch. 5)

structural analysis Analysis of the components of language; comprises phonetics (q.v.), grammar and syntax (q.v.), semantics (q.v.), and pragmatics (q.v.). (Ch. 9)

Sturm und Drang The storm and strain produced by conflicting internal forces, characteristic of adolescence. (Ch. 14)

stuttering Severely nonfluent speech—probably the most troublesome form of speech disorder in young children—thought to be caused by emotional distress, disruptions in brain circuits, or disturbed feedback. (Ch. 15)

subitize To perceive the number of things in a collection directly, without having to count them; with small numbers of items, preschool children do not have to count. (Ch. 11)

subjective responsibility The ability to take into account subjective motives and extenuating circumstances when judging wrongdoing. (Ch. 13)

sublimation A defense mechanism by which unacceptable impulses (id energies) are redirected into socially acceptable channels. (Chs. 1, 12)

sucking response Part of the rooting response (q.v.): touching a baby's lips or cheeks causes its head to turn toward the stimulus and its mouth to try to take in the stimulating object; if it's a milk-producing nipple, the baby will begin a fairly well-coordinated sequence of sucking, swallowing, and breathing. (Ch. 4)

sudden infant death syndrome (SIDS) The sudden and inexplicable death (also called crib death) of apparently healthy infants. (Ch. 3)

superego In psychoanalysis, the father's moral code, internalized by the boy as part of the process of identification that resolves the Oedipus complex. Roughly equivalent to conscience. (Chs. 1, 10)

suppression A process by which one deliberately forces back unwanted ideas and cravings from consciousness. (Ch. 1)

surface structure Chomsky's term for the superficial aspects of grammar in which languages differ. Cf. deep structure. (Ch. 9)

swaddling Wrapping up the baby snugly, mummy-fashion; this calms the infant. (Ch. 4)

swimming reflex Supported horizontal on the belly, the neonate makes swimminglike movements. (Ch. 4)

symbolic realism See verbal realism.

sympathy The ability to share in other people's feelings without submerging one's own identity in an empathic fusion with the other person. Cf. empathy. (Ch. 10)

symptom-free concept of normality A definition of normality based on the absence of serious psychological disturbance, such as inability to learn, disordered thinking, or hallucinations. (Ch. 15)

syncretism A tendency of primitive thought toward global, undifferentiated perceiving and thinking about things that are appropriately thought of separately. (Ch. 11)

syndactyly Failure of the digits to separate, a deformity produced during the embryonic period. (Ch. 3)

synesthesia Stimulation in one sense modality produces effects in another; babies must overcome synesthesia and learn to distinguish among the different kinds of information carried by the senses. Cf. intersensory effects. (Ch. 6)

syntagmatic associations Perceived relationships based on common situational contexts; for example, dog—barks. (Cf. paradigmatic associations.) (Ch. 13)

Tay-Sachs disease An enzyme-deficiency disease, found almost exclusively in Jews of Eastern European extraction, for which no treatment is known. (Ch. 3)

teratogen An agent capable of deforming the unborn baby, such as radiation or protein deficiency. (Ch. 3)

teratology The study of prenatal developmental anomalies. (Ch. 3)

Thanatos Freud's term for the death wish, or the unconscious destructive urges that are at work within us. (Ch. 1)

"the game" According to J. S. Watson, the first social game, consisting of an alternation between the adult's speaking to the infant and the infant's reaction, typically smiling, wriggling, and straining to vocalize. (Ch. 5)

thematization The weaving of a verbal fabric defining self and world; the process of giving verbal order and coherence to one's knowledge, which helps form the schemata that guide thought and action. (Ch. 9)

theory A set of systematic statements about how facts are related. A theory attempts to make sense of reality by relating known facts and predicting new ones. (Ch. 1)

time sampling Schedules of observation arranged so that all subjects will be observed for comparable periods; used when comparing the incidence of specific behaviors. (Ch. 1)

transductive thinking Finding a causal relationship between objects or events simply because they are close in time or space or in some way equivalent, with no thought of further elaborating the nature of the link. (Chs. 9, 11)

transformation rules Grammatical and syntactical mechanisms that convert deep structure (q.v.) into a surface-structure (q.v.) sentence, with forms such as a question, command, reference to past or future or conditional situations, negative assertion or passive construction. (Ch. 9)

transitional sleep See light sleep.

transitivity The ability, given a pair of relationships, to infer still another that was only implied; for example, if X is taller than Y, and Y is taller than Z, who is taller, X or Z? (Ch. 13)

transposition The ability to identify the right and left sides of another person in a face-to-face position. (Chs. 11, 13)

treatment variable See independent variable.

umbilical cord A rubbery tube enclosing a vein, which carries fresh blood from the placenta to the unborn baby, and two arteries, which carry waste-laden blood to the placenta. (Ch. 3)

uncommunicative-delinquent type In Achenbach's scheme, a type of disturbed behavior marked by destructiveness, disobedience, a taste for unsavory companions, lying, cheating, stealing, and fire setting. (Ch. 15)

uncommunicative type In Achenbach's scheme, a type of disturbed behavior marked by confusion, withdrawal, self-consciousness, shyness, timidity, or moodiness. (Ch. 15)

unconditioned response (UR) A reaction that is automatically triggered by a particular stimulus. (Ch. 1)

unconditioned stimulus (US) A stimulus that automatically triggers a particular response. (Ch. 1)

unconscious In Freudian theory, our motives may lie outside awareness. This fact is sometimes reified into the notion of "the" unconscious, an alter ego that lurks in subterranean darkness and controls us like a puppet master. (Ch. 1)

values clarification The attempt to arrive, through discussion, at the essential issues involved in moral dilemmas (q.v.). (Ch. 13)

verbal realism (nominal, symbolic, or word realism) The acceptance of words and statements as endowed with the same reality as solid objects, able to shape and modify other realities. (Chs. 1, 6, 9, 11)

verifiability The requirement that a theory be formulated in such a way that one can see whether it is consistent with the facts discovered through hypothesis testing. (Ch. 1)

vernix caseosa A moist, cheeselike substance that protects the fetal skin before birth and dries to a chalky cast after birth. (Chs. 3, 4)

vertex presentation The usual head-first position in which babies emerge at birth. Cf. breech presentation. (Ch. 3)

visual cliff effect A baby's disinclination to cross a clear, plastic-covered "cliff" suggests innateness or very early development of sensitivity to depth in humans and some other species. Babies too young to avoid the drop-off show cardiac changes when placed on the glass over the deep end. (Ch. 6)

visually guided grasping Reaching out to grasp objects given visually, at a distance, rather than those that happen to come in contact with a hand. Usually well established by the fourth month. (Ch. 5)

wariness A guarded reaction to strangers, beginning at around three months, that shows that infants distinguish them from familiar people in their lives; implies the beginnings of a schema, or internal representation, of the primary figures in the baby's life. (Ch. 5)

Weltschmerz World pain: the feelings associated with disillusionment, the discovery that the world will not live up to one's ideal image. Characteristic of adolescence. (Ch. 14)

Whorf hypothesis See linguistic determinism.

wisdom of the body Cannon's belief that organisms know spontaneously how to match the intake of particular nutrients to the body's tissue needs. (Ch. 5)

word association test A test that requires the subject to respond to a stimulus word with the very first thing he or she thinks of. (Ch. 13)

word realism See verbal realism.

xenophobia Fear and distrust of foreigners or strangers. (Chs. 5, 9)

zygote The single cell resulting from the fusion of the sperm and egg that will become a new individual. (Ch. 2)

BIBLIOGRAPHY

Abel, E. L. Fetal alcohol syndrome: Behavioral teratology. *Psychological Bulletin*, 1980, *87*, 28–50.

Abravanel, E. The figural simplicity of parallel lines. *Child Development*, 1977, *48*, 708–710.

Abravanel, E., & Gingold, H. Perceiving and representing orientation: Effects of the spatial framework. *Merrill-Palmer Quarterly*, 1981, *23*, 265–278.

Achenbach, T. M. Empirical approaches to classification. In J. R. Lachenmeyer & M. S. Gibbs (Eds.), *Psychopathology in childhood*. New York: Gardner Press, 1982.

Achenbach, T. M., & Edelbrock, C. S. Behavioral problems and competencies reported by parents of normal and disturbed children aged four through sixteen. *Monographs of the Society for Research in Child Development*, 1981, *46*(1, Serial No. 188).

Acredolo, L. P. Development of spatial orientation in infancy. *Developmental Psychology*, 1978, *14*, 224–234.

Acredolo, L. P. Laboratory versus home: The effect of environment on the 9-month-old infant's choice of spatial reference system. *Developmental Psychology*, 1979, *15*, 666–667.

Acredolo, L. P., & Evans, D. Developmental changes in the effects of landmarks on infant spatial behavior. *Developmental Psychology*, 1980, *16*, 312–328.

Adelson, J. (Ed.). *Handbook of adolescent psychology*. New York: Wiley-Interscience, 1980.

Ainsworth, M. D. S. *Infancy in Uganda*. Baltimore: Johns Hopkins University Press, 1967.

Ainsworth, M. D. S. Object relations, dependency, and attachment. *Child Development*, 1969, *40*, 969–1026.

Ainsworth, M. D. S., & Bell, S. M. V. Attachment, exploration and separation: Illustrated by the behavior of one-year-olds in strange settings. *Child Development*, 1970, *41*, 49–67.

Ainsworth, M. D. S., Bell, S. M. V., & Stayton, D. J. Individual differences in strange situation behavior of one-year-olds. In H. R. Schaffer (Ed.), *The origins of human social relations*. London: Academic Press, 1969.

Ainsworth, M. D. S., Bell, S. M. V., & Stayton, D. J. Individual differences in the development of some attachment behaviors. *Merrill-Palmer Quarterly*, 1972, *18*, 123–143.

Ainsworth, M. D. S., Bell, S. M. V., & Stayton, D. J. Infant-mother attachment and social development. In M. P. M. Richards (Ed.), *The integration of a child into a social world*. Cambridge: Cambridge University Press, 1974.

Allport, G. W. *The use of personal documents in psychological science*. New York: Social Science Research Council, 1942.

Almy, M., & Genishi, C. *Ways of studying children* (Rev. ed.). New York and London: Teachers College Press, 1979.

Alston, W. P. Comments on Kohlberg's "From is to ought." In T. Mischel (Ed.), *Cognitive development and genetic epistemology*. New York: Academic Press, 1971.

Ambrose, J. A. The development of the smiling response in early infancy. In B. M. Foss (Ed.), *Determinants of infant behavior*. New York: Wiley, 1961.

Ames, L. B., & Learned, J. Imaginary companions and related phenomena. *Journal of Genetic Psychology*, 1946, *69*, 147–167.

Amsterdam, B. Mirror self-image reactions before age two. *Developmental Psychobiology*, 1972, *5*, 297–305.

Anastasi, A. *Differential psychology* (3rd ed.). New York: Macmillan, 1958. (a)

Anastasi, A. Heredity, environment, and the question "how?" *Psychological Bulletin*, 1958, *65*, 197–208. (b)

Anastasi, A. *Psychological testing*. New York: Macmillan, 1982.

Anderson, D. R., & Bryant, J. (Eds.). *Watching TV, understanding TV*. New York: Academic Press, 1983.

Anisfeld, M. Interpreting "imitative" responses in early infancy. *Science*, 1979, *205*, 214–215.

Antonovsky, H. F. *Adolescent sexuality*. Lexington, Mass.: Lexington Books/D. C. Heath, 1980.

Apgar, V. Perinatal problems and the central nervous system. In Children's Bureau, Department of Health, Education, and Welfare, *The child with central nervous system deficit*. Washington, D.C.: U.S. Government Printing Office, 1965.

595

Archer, S. L. The lower age boundaries of identity development. *Child Development*, 1982, *53*, 1551–1556.

Ariès, P. *Centuries of childhood.* New York: Knopf, 1962.

Asch, S. E. Studies in the principles of judgments and attitudes: II. A determination of judgments by group and ego standards. *Journal of Social Psychology*, 1940, *12*, 433–465.

Asch, S. E., & Nerlove, H. The development of double function terms in children. In B. Kaplan & S. Wapner (Eds.), *Perspectives in psychological theory.* New York: International Universities Press, 1960.

Asher, S. R., & Gottman, J. M. (Eds.). *The development of children's friendships.* New York: Cambridge University Press, 1981.

Azrin, N. H., & Foxx, R. M. *Toilet training in less than a day.* New York: Simon & Schuster, 1974.

Baillargeon, R., Gelman, R., & Meck, B. Are preschoolers truly indifferent to causal mechanisms? Paper presented at meetings of the Society for Research in Child Development, 1981.

Bain, B. Verbal regulation of cognitive processes: A replication of Luria's procedures with bilingual and unilingual infants. *Child Development*, 1976, *47*, 543–546.

Ball, W., & Tronick, E. Infant responses to impending collision: Optical and real. *Science*, 1971, *171*, 818–820.

Bandura, A. The stormy decade: Fact or fiction? *Psychology in the Schools*, 1964, *1*, 224–231.

Bandura, A. *Aggression: A social learning analysis.* Englewood Cliffs, N.J.: Prentice-Hall, 1973.

Bandura, A. Behavior theory and the models of man. *American Psychologist*, December 1974, pp. 859–869.

Bandura, A. *Social learning theory.* Englewood Cliffs, N.J.: Prentice-Hall, 1977.

Bandura, A., & Walters, R. H. *Social learning and personality development.* New York: Holt, Rinehart and Winston, 1963.

Bartlett, E. J. Selecting an early childhood language curriculum. In C. B. Cazden (Ed.), *Language in early childhood education* (Rev. ed.). Washington, D.C.: National Association for the Education of Young Children, 1981.

Bateson, G., Jackson, D., Haley, J., & Weakland, J. Toward a theory of schizophrenia. *Behavioral Science*, 1956, *1*, 251–264.

Bayley, N. *Manual for the Bayley Scales of Infant Development.* New York: The Psychological Corporation, 1969.

Bee, H. L., Barnard, K. E., Eyres, S. J., Gray, C. A., Hammond, M. A., Spietz, A. L., Snyder, C., & Clark, B. Prediction of IQ and language skill from perinatal status, child performance, family characteristics, and mother-infant interaction. *Child Development*, 1982, *53*, 1134–1156.

Bell, S. The development of the concept of object as related to infant-mother attachment. *Monographs of the Society for Research in Child Development*, 1970, *41*(2).

Bell, S. M. V. The effectiveness of various maternal responses as terminators of crying. Paper presented at meetings of the Society for Research in Child Development, 1971.

Bellugi, U. Simplification in children's language. In R. Huxley & E. Ingram (Eds.), *Language acquisition.* London and New York: Academic Press, 1971.

Bellugi, U., & Studdert-Kennedy, M. (Eds.). *Signed and spoken language: Biological constraints on linguistic form.* Deerfield Beach, Fla.: Verlag Chemie, 1980.

Belsky, J. Mother-infant interaction at home and in the laboratory: A comparative study. *Journal of Genetic Psychology*, 1980, *137*, 37–47.

Belsky, J., & Steinberg, L. D. The effects of day care: A critical review. *Child Development*, 1978, *49*, 929–942.

Bem, S. L. The measurement of psychological androgyny. *Journal of Consulting and Clinical Psychology*, 1974, *42*, 155–162.

Benbow, C. P., & Stanley, J. C. Sex differences in mathematical ability: Fact or artifact? *Science*, 1980, *210*, 1262–1264.

Benedict, R. Continuities and discontinuities in cultural conditioning. *Psychiatry*, 1938, *1*, 161–167.

Bennett, E. L., Diamond, M. C., Krech, D., & Rosenzweig, M. R. Chemical and anatomical plasticity of brain. *Science*, 1964, *146*, 610–619.

Berenda, R. W. *The influence of the group on the judgments of children.* New York: King's Crown Press, 1950.

Berezin, N. *The gentle birth book.* New York: Simon & Schuster, 1980.

Bergmann, G. Sense and nonsense in operationalism. *Scientific Monthly*, 1954, *79*, 210–214.

Berkowitz, L. Some determinants of impulsive aggression. *Psychological Review*, 1974, *81*, 165–176.

Berkowitz, L. (Ed.). *Advances in experimental social psychology* (Vol. 12). New York: Academic Press, 1979.

Bernstein, A. C., & Cowan, P. A. Children's concepts of how people get babies. *Child Development*, 1975, *46*, 77–91.

Berry, J. W., & Dasen, P. (Eds.). *Culture and cognition: Readings in cross-cultural psychology.* London: Methuen, 1974.

Berti, A. E., & Bombi, A. S. The development of the concept of money and its value: A longitudinal study. *Child Development*, 1981, *52*, 1179–1182.

Bettelheim, B. Joey: A "mechanical boy." *Scientific American*, March 1959.

Bettelheim, B. *The empty fortress.* New York: Free Press, 1967.

Bettelheim, B. *A home for the heart.* New York: Knopf, 1974.

Beyer, B. K. Conducting moral discussions in the classroom. In P. Scharf (Ed.), *Readings in moral education.* Minneapolis: Winston Press, 1978.

Biber, B., Shapiro, E., & Wickens, D. *Promoting cognitive growth: A developmental-interaction point of view* (2nd ed.). Washington, D.C.: National Association for the Education of Young Children, 1977.

Billow, R. M. A cognitive developmental study of metaphor comprehension. *Developmental Psychology,* 1975, *11*, 415–423.

Bindra, D. Ape language. *Science,* 1981, *211*, 86.

Birch, H. G., & Lefford, A. Intersensory development in children. *Monographs of the Society for Research in Child Development,* 1963, *28*(5).

Birns, B. Individual differences in human neonates' responses to stimulation. *Child Development,* 1965, *36*, 249–256.

Blank, M., & Bridger, W. H. Cross-modal transfer in nursery-school children. *Journal of Comparative and Physiological Psychology,* 1964, *58*, 277–282.

Block, N. J., & Dworkin, G. (Eds.). *The IQ controversy.* New York: Pantheon, 1976.

Bloom, L. *Language development: Form and function in emerging grammars.* Cambridge, Mass.: M.I.T. Press, 1970.

Bloom, L., Hood, L., & Lightbown, P. Imitation in language development: If, when and why. *Cognitive Psychology,* 1974, *6*, 380–420.

Boegehold, B. D., Cuffaro, H. F., Hooks, W. H., & Klopf, G. J. (Eds.). *Education before five.* New York: Bank Street College of Education, 1977.

Bond, L. A., & Joffee, J. M. (Eds.). *Primary prevention of psychopathology* (Vol. 6). Hanover, N.H.: University Press of New England, 1981.

Borke, H. Piaget's mountains revisited: Changes in the egocentric landscape. *Developmental Psychology,* 1975, *11*, 240–243.

Bornstein, M. H. Psychological studies of color perception in human infants: Habituation, discrimination and categorization, recognition and conceptualization. In L. P. Lipsitt & C. K. Rovee-Collier, *Advances in infant research* (Vol. 1). New York: Ablex, 1981.

Bornstein, M. H., Kessen, W., & Weiskopf, S. The category of hue in infancy. *Science,* 1976, *191*, 201–202.

Bouchard, T. J., Jr., & McGue, M. Familial studies of intelligence: A review. *Science,* 1981, *212*, 1055–1059.

Bower, T. G. R. Stimulus variables affecting space perception in infants. *Science,* 1965, *149*, 88–89.

Bower, T. G. R. *Development in infancy.* San Francisco: Freeman, 1974.

Bowlby, J. *Attachment and loss* (Vol. 1). *Attachment.* New York: Basic Books, 1969.

Bracey, D. H. The juvenile prostitute: Victim and offender. Paper presented at the Second International Institute on Victimology, 1982.

Bradley, R. H., & Caldwell, B. M. The relations of infants' home environments to mental and test performance at fifty-four months: A follow-up study. *Child Development,* 1976, *47*, 1172–1174.

Bradley, R. H., & Caldwell, B. M. Home observation for measurement of the environment: A validation study of screening efficiency. *American Journal of Mental Deficiency,* 1977, *81*, 417–420.

Bradley, R. H., & Caldwell, B. M. Home observation for measurement of the environment: A revision of the preschool scale. *American Journal of Mental Deficiency,* 1979, *84*, 235–244.

Braine, M. D. S. Children's first word combinations. *Monographs of the Society for Research in Child Development,* 1976, *41*(1).

Brainerd, C. J. Structures-of-the-whole: Is there any glue to hold the concrete-operational "stage" together? Paper presented at meetings of the Canadian Psychological Association, Windsor, Ontario, June 1974.

Brazelton, T. B. *Neonatal behavioral assessment scale.* Philadelphia and London: Lippincott and Heinemann, 1973.

Brazelton, T. B. *Toddlers and parents.* New York: Delacorte, 1974.

Brazelton, T. B. *On becoming a family: The growth of attachment.* New York: Delacorte, 1981.

Brazelton, T. B. Behavioral assessment of the premature infant: Uses in intervention. In M. H. Klaus & M. O. Robertson (Eds.), *Birth, interaction, and attachment.* Skillman, N.J.: Johnson & Johnson Baby Products Company, 1982.

Brenner, J., & Mueller, E. Shared meaning in boy toddlers' peer relations. *Child Development,* 1982, *53*, 380–391.

Brody, J. E. Personal health. *The New York Times,* July 14, 1982. (a)

Brody, J. E. Personal health. *The New York Times,* July 21, 1982. (b)

Bronfenbrenner, U. *A report on longitudinal evaluations of preschool programs* (Vol. 2). *Is early intervention effective?* Arlington, Va.: Computer Microfilm International Corp., ERIC reports, 1974.

Bronfenbrenner, U. Toward an experimental ecology of human development. *American Psychologist,* 1977, *32*, 513–531.

Bronson, G. W., & Pankey, W. B. On the distinction between fear and wariness. *Child Development,* 1977, *48*, 1167–1183.

Brown, J. K. Adolescent initiation rites: Recent interpretations. In R. E. Grinder (Ed.) *Studies in adolescence* (3rd ed.). New York: Macmillan, 1975.

Brozan, N. Diet discounted in hyperactivity. *The New York Times,* October 17, 1980.

Brunner, R. L., Vorhees, C. V., & Butcher, R. E. Food colors and behavior. *Science,* 1981, *212,* 578–579.

Burd, A. P., Milewski, A. E., & Camros, J. Matching of facial gestures by young infants: Imitation releasors? Paper presented·at meetings of the Society for Research in Child Development, 1981.

Burrows, A. T., Jackson, D. C., & Saunders, D. O. *They all want to write* (3rd ed.). New York: Holt, Rinehart and Winston, 1966.

Cairns, N. U., & Steward, M. S. Young children's orientation of letters as a function of axis of symmetry and stimulus alignment. *Child Development,* 1970, *41,* 993–1002.

Caldwell, B. M. Mother-infant interaction in monomatric and polymatric families. *American Journal of Orthopsychiatry,* 1963, *33,* 653–664.

Caldwell, B. M. The effects of infant care. In M. L. Hoffman & L. W. Hoffman (Eds.), *Review of Child Development* (Vol. 1). New York: Russell Sage Foundation, 1964.

Campos, J. J., Langer, A., & Karowitz, A. Cardiac responses on the visual cliff in prelocomotor human infants. *Science,* 1970, *170,* 196–197.

Carlson, P., & Anisfeld, M. Some observations on the linguistic competence of a two-year-old child. *Child Development,* 1969, *40,* 569–575.

Carr, H. S., & Watson, J. B. Orientation in the white rat. *Journal of Comparative Neurology,* 1908, *18,* 27–44.

Carroll, J. B. (Ed.). *Language, thought, and reality: Selected writings of Benjamin Lee Whorf.* New York and Cambridge, Mass.: Wiley and M.I.T. Press, 1956.

Case, R. Intellectual development: A systematic reinterpretation. In F. H. Farley & N. J. Gordon (Eds.), *New perspectives in educational psychology.* Washington, D.C.: National Society for the Study of Education, 1980.

Cattell, P. *Infant intelligence scale.* New York: Psychological Corporation, 1940.

Cazden, C. B. The acquisition of noun and verb inflections. *Child Development,* 1968, *39,* 433–448.

Cazden, C. B. Play with language and metalinguistic awareness: One dimension of language experience. *International Journal of Early Childhood,* 1974, *6,* 12–24.

Cazden, C. B. (Ed.). *Language in early childhood education* (Rev. ed.). Washington, D.C.: National Association for the Education of Young Children, 1981.

Ceci, S., & Ambinder, B. "Don't forget to take the cake out of the oven": Prospective memory in laboratory and naturalistic settings. Paper presented at meetings of the Society for Research in Child Development, 1983.

Chamberlin, R. W. Management of preschool behavior problems. *Pediatric Clinics of North America,* 1974, *21,* 33–47.

Chipman, S. Mathematical ability: Is sex a factor? *Science,* 1981, *212,* 114–116.

Chomsky, N. *Language and mind.* New York: Harcourt Brace Jovanovich, 1968.

Chomsky, N. *Reflections on language.* New York: Pantheon, 1975.

Chukovsky, K. *From two to five.* Berkeley and Los Angeles: University of California Press, 1963.

Church, J. *Language and the discovery of reality.* New York: Random House, 1961.

Church, J. Innovations, excellence, and children's learning. *School and Society,* 1962, *90,* 401–404. *Bank Street College of Education Publications,* 1962(65).

Church, J. Techniques for the differential study of cognition in early childhood. In J. Hellmuth (Ed.), *Cognitive studies 1.* New York: Brunner/Mazel, 1970.

Church, J. *Three babies.* Westport, Conn.: Greenwood Press, 1978, originally 1966.

Church, J. *Understanding your child from birth to three.* New York: Pocket Books, 1973.

Clark, A. H., Wyon, S. M., & Richards, M. P. M. Free-play in nursery school children. *Journal of Child Psychology and Psychiatry,* 1969, *10,* 205–216.

Clark, E. V. Here's the *top:* Nonlinguistic strategies in the acquisition of orientational terms. *Child Development,* 1980, *51,* 329–338.

Clarke, A. M., & Clarke, A. B. D. *Early experience: Myth and evidence.* New York: The Free Press, 1976.

Clarke-Stewart, K. A. Recasting the lone stranger. In J. Glick & K. A. Clarke-Stewart (Eds.), *Studies in social and cognitive development: The development of social understanding* (Vol. 1). New York: Gardner Press, 1978.

Coates, B. White adult behavior toward black and white children. *Child Development,* 1972, *43,* 143–154.

Cohen, D. H., & Stern, V. *Observing and recording the behavior of young children* (2nd ed.). New York: Teachers College Press, 1978.

Cohen, S. E., & Parmalee, A. H. Cognitive development in preterm infants: Prediction to 5 years. Paper presented at meetings of the Society for Research in Child Development, 1981.

Cohen, W. Spatial and textural characteristics of the *Ganzfeld. American Journal of Psychology,* 1957, *70,* 403–410.

Cole, M., Gay, J., Glick, J. A., & Sharp, D. W. *The cultural context of learning and thinking.* New York: Basic Books, 1971.

Cole, M., & Scribner, S. *Culture and thought.* New York: Wiley, 1974.

Collins, W. A. (Ed.). *Minnesota symposia on child psychology* (Vol. 14). Hillsdale, N.J.: Lawrence Erlbaum, 1981.

Comalli, P., Jr., Wapner, S., & Werner, H. Interference effects of Stroop color-word test in childhood, adulthood, and aging. *Journal of Genetic Psychology*, 1962, *100*, 47–53.

Condon, W. S., & Sander, L. W. Neonate movement is synchronized with adult speech: Interactional participation and language acquisition. *Science*, 1974, *183*, 99–101. (a)

Condon, W. S., & Sander, L. W. Synchrony demonstrated between movement of the neonate and adult speech. *Child Development*, 1974, *45*, 456–462. (b)

Condry, J., & Condry, S. Sex differences: A study of the eye of the beholder. *Child Development*, 1976, *47*, 812–819.

Conway, J. K. A proper perspective. In *Today's girls: Tomorrow's women*. New York: Girls Club of America, 1979.

Coopersmith, S. *The antecedents of self-esteem*. San Francisco: Freeman, 1967.

Copans, S. A. Human prenatal effects: Methodological problems and some suggested solutions. *Merrill-Palmer Quarterly*, 1974, *20*, 43–52.

Cousins, N. *Anatomy of an illness*. New York: Norton, 1979.

Cramer, P., & Hogan, K. A. Sex differences in verbal and play fantasy. *Developmental Psychology*, 1975, *11*, 145–154.

Curtiss, S. *Genie: A psycholinguistic study of a modern-day "wild child."* New York: Academic Press, 1977.

Daehler, M. W., Perlmutter, M., & Myers, N. A. Equivalence of pictures and objects for very young children. *Child Development*, 1976, *47*, 96–102.

Dale, P. S. *Language development* (2nd ed.). New York: Holt, Rinehart and Winston, 1976.

Damon, W. *The social world of the child*. San Francisco: Jossey-Bass, 1977.

Damon, W. Exploring children's social cognition on two fronts. In J. H. Flavell & L. Ross (Eds.), *Social cognitive development*. New York: Cambridge University Press, 1981.

Darlington, R. B. Duration of preschool effects on later school performance. *Science*, 1981, *213*, 1145–1146.

Darlington, R. B., Royce, J. M., Snipper, A. S., Murray, H. W., & Lazar, I. Preschool programs and later school competence of children from low-income families. *Science*, 1980, *208*, 202–204.

Dart, F. E., & Pradhan, P. L. Cross-cultural teaching of science. *Science*, 1967, *155*, 649–656.

Darwin, C. A. A biographical sketch of an infant. *Mind*, 1877, *2*, 285–294.

Davis, C. M. Results of the self-selection of diets by young children. *Canadian Medical Association Journal*, 1939, *41*, 257–261.

Davis, K. Final note on a case of extreme isolation. *American Journal of Sociology*, 1947, *52*, 432–437.

Dawe, H. V. An analysis of two hundred quarrels of preschool children. *Child Development*, 1934, *5*, 139–157.

De Casper, A. J., & Fifer, W. P. Of human bonding: Newborns prefer their mothers' voices. *Science*, 1980, *208*, 1174–1176.

DeLoache, J. S., & Brown, A. L. Looking for Big Bird: Studies of memory in very young children. *Quarterly Newsletter of the Laboratory of Comparative Human Cognition*, 1979, *1*(4), 53–57.

de Lone, R. H. *Small futures*. New York: Harcourt Brace Jovanovich, 1979.

Dennis, W. Infant development under conditions of restricted practice and of minimum social stimulation. *Genetic Psychology Monographs*, 1941, *23*, 143–190.

Dennis, W. Animistic thinking among college and university students. *Scientific Monthly*, 1953, *76*, 247–250.

Dennis, W. *Children of the Crèche*. Englewood Cliffs, N.J.: Prentice-Hall, 1973.

Dennis, W., & Najarian, P. Infant development under environmental handicap. *Psychological Monographs*, 1957, *71*(7).

de Villiers, J. G., & de Villiers, P. A. *Language acquisition*. Cambridge, Mass.: Harvard University Press, 1978.

de Villiers, P. A., & de Villiers, J. G. *Early language*. Cambridge, Mass.: Harvard University Press, 1979.

DeVries, R. Constancy of generic identity in the years three to six. *Monographs of the Society for Research in Child Development*, 1969, *34*(3).

de Witt, K. Study finds increase in teen-age sex. *The New York Times*, October 17, 1980.

Dietrich, K. N., Starr, R. H., Jr., & Kaplan, G. Maternal stimulation and care of abused infants. In T. Field (Ed.), *High-risk infants and children*. New York: Academic Press, 1980.

Dobzhansky, T. *Genetic diversity and human equality*. New York: Basic Books, 1973.

Dollard, J., Doob, L. W., Miller, N. E., Mowrer, O. H., & Sears, R. R. *Frustration and aggression*. New Haven: Yale University Press, 1939.

Dunn, J., Kenrick, C., & MacNamee, R. The reaction of first-born children to the birth of a sibling: Mothers' reports. *Journal of Child Psychology and Psychiatry*, 1981.

Dweck, C. S., & Goetz, T. D. Attributions and learned helplessness. In J. Harvey, W. Ickes, & R. Kidd (Eds.), *New directions in attribution research* (Vol. 2). Hillside, N.J.: Lawrence Erlbaum, 1978.

Eckerman, C. O., Whatley, J. L., & Kutz, S. L. Growth of social play with peers during the second year of life. *Developmental Psychology,* 1975, *11,* 42–49.

Ehri, L. C., & Galanis, A. H. Teaching children to comprehend propositions conjoined by "before" and "after." *Journal of Experimental Child Psychology,* 1980, *30,* 308–324.

Eimas, P. D., Siqueland, E. R., Jusczyk, P., & Vigorito, J. Speech perception in infants. *Science,* 1971, *171,* 303–306.

Eisenberg, R. B. Auditory behavior in the human neonate: Functional properties of sound and their ontogenetic implications. *International Audiology,* 1969, *8,* 34–35.

Elardo, R., Bradley, R., & Caldwell, B. M. The relation of infants' home environments to mental test performance from six to thirty-six months: A longitudinal analysis. *Child Development,* 1975, *46,* 71–76.

Elardo, R., Bradley, R., & Caldwell, B. M. A longitudinal study of the relation of infants' home environments to language development at age three. *Child Development,* 1977, *48,* 595–603.

Elkind, D. Strategic interactions in early adolescence. In J. Adelson (Ed.), *Handbook of adolescent psychology.* New York: Wiley-Interscience, 1980.

Elkind, D. *The hurried child: Growing up too fast too soon.* Reading, Mass.: Addison-Wesley, 1981.

Elkind, D., & Dabek, R. F. Personal injury and property damage in the moral judgments of children. *Child Development,* 1977, *4,* 518–522.

Emde, R. N., & Harmon, R. J. (Eds.). *The development of attachment and affiliative systems.* New York: Plenum, 1981.

Emde, R. N., Harmon, R. J., Metcalf, D., Koenig, K. L., & Wagenfeld, S. Stress and neonatal sleep. *Psychosomatic Medicine,* 1971, *33,* 491–497.

Emler, N. P., & Rushton, J. P. Cognitive-developmental factors in children's generosity. *British Journal of Social and Clinical Psychology,* 1974, *13,* 277–281.

Engen, T., Lipsitt, L. S., & Peck, M. B. Ability of newborn infants to discriminate sapid substances. *Developmental Psychology,* 1974, *10,* 741–744.

Epstein, R., Lanza, R. P., & Skinner, B. F. "Self-awareness" in the pigeon. *Science,* 1981, *212,* 695–696.

Erikson, E. H. Identity and the life cycle. *Psychological Issues,* 1959, *1,* 1–171.

Erikson, E. H. *Childhood and society* (Rev. ed.). New York: Norton, 1963.

Erikson, E. H. *Identity: Youth and crisis.* New York: Norton, 1968.

Escalona, S. The use of infant tests for predictive purposes. In W. E. Martin & C. B. Stender (Eds.), *Readings in child development.* New York: Harcourt, Brace, 1954.

Escalona, S. K. *The roots of individuality: Normal patterns of development in infancy.* Chicago: Aldine, 1968.

Evans, B. *The natural history of nonsense.* New York: Vintage, 1958, originally 1946.

Fagot, B. I. Sex-related stereotyping of toddlers' behavior. *Developmental Psychology,* 1973, *9,* 429.

Fagot, B. I. Sex differences in toddlers' behavior and parental reaction. *Developmental Psychology,* 1974, *19,* 554–558.

Fagot, B. I. The influence of sex of child on parental reactions to toddler children. *Child Development,* 1978, *49,* 459–465.

Fantz, R. L. Visual perception from birth as shown by pattern sensitivity. *Annals of the New York Academy of Sciences,* 1963, *188,* 793–814.

Farley, F. H., & Gordon, N. J. (Eds.). *New perspectives in educational psychology.* Washington, D.C.: National Association for the Study of Education, 1980.

Farnham-Diggory, S. *Learning disabilities.* Cambridge, Mass.: Harvard University Press, 1978.

Faust, M. S. Developmental maturity as a determinant in prestige of adolescent girls. *Child Development,* 1960, *31,* 173–184.

Fawdry, M. *Chinese childhood.* Woodbury, N.Y.: Barron's, 1977.

Feldman, N. S., Klosson, E. C., Parsons, J. E., Rholes, W. S., & Ruble, D. N. Order of information presentation and children's moral judgments. *Child Development,* 1976, *52,* 326–334.

Feldman, S., & Barsky, L. H. Development of deictic skills: I. Linguistic performance. Paper presented at meetings of the American Psychological Association, 1975.

Feldman, S. S., & Ingham, M. Attachment behavior: A validation study in two age groups. *Child Development,* 1975, *46,* 319–330.

Field, D. Can preschool children really learn to conserve? *Child Development,* 1981, *52,* 326–334.

Field, T. (Ed.). *High-risk infants and children.* New York: Academic Press, 1980.

Field, T., Widmayer, S., Stringer, S., & Ignatoff, E. Teenage lower class black mothers and their preterm infants. *Child Development,* 1980, *51,* 426–436.

Field, T., Woodson, R., Greenberg, R., & Cohen, D. Discrimination and imitation of facial expressions by neonates. *Science,* 1982, *218,* 179–181.

Field, T. M., & Widmayer, S. M. Developmental follow-up of infants delivered by Caesarean section and general anesthesia. *Infant Behavior and Development*, 1980, *3*, 253–264.

50-Year sterilizing in Virginia decried. *The New York Times*, February 22, 1980.

Fillenbaum, S. Impairment in performance with delayed auditory feedback as related to task characteristics. *Journal of Verbal Learning and Verbal Behavior*, 1963, *2*, 136–141.

Fincher, J. *Human intelligence.* New York: Dutton, 1975.

Fitzgerald, H. E., & Brackbill, Y. Classical conditioning in infancy: Development and constraints. *Psychological Bulletin*, 1976, *83*, 353–376.

Flavell, J. H. *Cognitive development.* Englewood Cliffs, N.J.: Prentice-Hall, 1977.

Flavell, J. H. On cognitive development. Presidential address to the Society for Research in Child Development, 1981.

Flavell, J. H., Botkin, P. T., Fry, C. L., Wright, J. W., & Jarvis, P. E. *The development of role-taking and communication skills in children.* Huntington, N.Y.: Robert E. Krieger, 1975. (Originally published, 1968.)

Flavell, J. H., & Ross, L. (Eds.). *Social cognitive development: Frontiers and possible futures.* New York: Cambridge University Press, 1981.

Flexer, B. K., & Roberge, J. J. IQ, field dependence-independence, and the development of formal operational thought. *Journal of General Psychology*, 1980, *103*, 191–201.

Formanek, R., & Gurian, A. *Why? Children's questions.* Boston: Houghton Mifflin, 1982.

Foss, B. M. (Ed.). *Determinants of infant behavior.* New York: Wiley, 1961.

Foss, B. M. (Ed.). *Determinants of infant behavior* (Vol. 4). New York: Barnes & Noble, 1969.

Fraiberg, S. H., with the collaboration of L. Fraiberg. *Insights from the blind.* New York: New American Library/Meridian, 1977.

Frankenburg, W. K. Early screening for developmental delays and potential school problems. In C. Brown (Ed.), *Infants at risk.* Skillman, N.J.: Johnson & Johnson Baby Products Company, 1981.

Franklin, M. B. Perspectives on theory: Another look at the developmental-interaction point of view. In E. K. Shapiro & E. Weber (Eds.), *Cognitive and affective growth.* Hillsdale, N.J.: Lawrence Erlbaum, 1981.

Fraser, B. G. The tragedy of child abuse. *Compact*, 1974, *8*, 10–12.

Freedman, D. A. Congenital and perinatal sensory deprivations: Their effect on the capacity to experience affects. *Psychoanalytic Quarterly*, 1975, *44*, 62–80.

Freedman, S. G. Summertime, boredom, a fatal derailment. *The New York Times*, July 10, 1982.

Freud, S. *Beyond the pleasure principle.* New York: Boni and Liveright, 1927.

Freud, S. *The basic writings of Sigmund Freud.* New York: Random House, 1938.

Freud, S. *An outline of psychoanalysis.* New York: Norton, 1949.

Friedrich, L. K., & Stein, A. H. Aggressive and prosocial television programs and the natural behavior of preschool children. *Monographs of the Society for Research in Child Development*, 1973, *38*(4).

Frisch, R. E. Fatness of girls from menarche to age 18 years with a nomogram. *Human Biology*, 1976, *48*, 353–359.

Frisch, R. E. Pubertal adipose tissue: Is is necessary for normal sexual maturation? Evidence from the rat and human female. *Federation Proceedings*, 1980, *39*, 2395–2400. (a)

Frisch, R. E. Fatness, puberty, and fertility. *Natural History*, October 1980, pp. 16–27. (b)

Frisch, R. E. Malnutrition and fertility. *Science*, 1982, *215*, 1272–1273.

Frisch, R. E., Gotz-Welbergen, A. V., McArthur, J. W., Albright, J., Witschi, J., Bullen, B., Birnholz, J., Reed, R. B., & Hermann, H. Delayed menarche and amenorrhea of college athletes in relation to age of onset of training. *Journal of the American Medical Association*, 1981, *246*, 1559–1563.

Frisch, R. E., Wyshak, G., & Vincent, L. Delayed menarche and amenorrhea in ballet dancers. *New England Journal of Medicine*, 1980, *303*, 17–19.

Frodi, A. M. Paternal-baby responsiveness and involvement. *Infant Mental Health Journal*, 1980, *1*, 150–160.

Gallup, G. G. Chimpanzees: Self-recognition. *Science*, 1970, *167*, 86–87.

Gallup, G. G. Self-recognition in primates. *American Psychologist*, May 1977, pp. 329–338.

Gardner, H. *Artful scribbles.* New York: Basic Books, 1980.

Gardner, J., & Gardner, H. A note on selective imitation by a six-week-old infant. *Child Development*, 1970, *41*, 1209–1213.

Garvey, C. *Play.* Cambridge, Mass.: Harvard University Press, 1977.

Gellert, E. Children's conceptions of the content and functions of the human body. *Genetic Psychology Monographs*, 1962, *65*, 293–405.

Gelman, R. Conservation acquisition: A problem of learning to attend to relevant attributes. *Journal of Experimental Child Psychology*, 1969, *7*, 167–187.

Gelman, R., & Gallistel, C. R. *The child's understanding of number.* Cambridge, Mass.: Harvard University Press, 1978.

Gelman, R., & Spelke, E. The development of thoughts about animate and inanimate objects. In J. Flavell & L. Ross (Eds.), *Social cognitive development*. New York: Cambridge University Press, 1981.

Gerbner, G., Gross, L., Eleey, M., Jackson-Beeck, M., Jeffries-Fox, S., & Signorielli, N. *Violence profile no. 8: Trends in network television drama and viewer conceptions of social reality 1967–1976*. Philadelphia: Annenberg School of Communications, University of Pennsylvania, 1977.

Gerbner, G., Ross, C. J., & Zigler, E. *Child abuse: An agenda for action*. New York: Oxford University Press, 1980.

Gesell, A., & Thompson, H. Twins T and C from infancy to adolescence: A biogenetic study of individual differences by the method of cotwin control. *Genetic Psychology Monographs*, 1941, *24*, 3–121.

Gesell, A., Thompson, H., & Amatruda, C. S. *The psychology of early growth*. New York: Macmillan, 1938.

Gesell, A. L. *The mental growth of the preschool child: A psychological outline of normal development from birth to the sixth year, including a system of developmental diagnosis*. New York: Macmillan, 1925.

Gevins, A. S., Zeitlin, G. M., Doyle, J. C., Yingling, C. D., Schaffer, R. E., Callaway, E., & Yeager, C. L. Electroencephalogram correlates of higher cortical functions. *Science*, 1979, *203*, 665–668.

Ghent, L. Form and its orientation: A child's-eye view. *American Journal of Psychology*, 1961, *74*, 177–190.

Gibbs, M. S. Identification and classification of child psychopathology. In J. R. Lachenmeyer & M. S. Gibbs (Eds.), *Psychopathology in childhood*. New York: Gardner Press, 1982.

Gibson, E. J. The ontogeny of reading. *American Psychologist*, 1970, *25*, 136–143.

Ginsburg, H., & Opper, S. *Piaget's theory of intellectual development* (2nd ed.). Englewood Cliffs, N.J.: Prentice-Hall, 1979.

Ginsburg, H. P., & Russell, R. L. Social class and racial influences on early mathematical thinking. *Monographs of the Society for Research in Child Development*, 1981, *46*(6).

Giray, E. F., Altkin, W. M., Vaught, G. M., & Roodin, P. A. The incidence of eidetic imagery as a function of age. *Child Development*, 1976, *47*, 1207–1210.

Gleason, J. B. Code switching in children's language. In T. E. Moore (Ed.), *Cognitive development and the acquisition of language*. New York: Academic Press, 1973.

Gleason, J. B. Fathers and other strangers: Men's speech to young children. Paper presented to the Georgetown Rountable, 1975.

Gleason, J. B. An experimental approach to improving children's communicative ability. In C. B. Cazden (Ed.), *Language in early childhood education*. Washington, D.C.: National Association for the Education of Young Children, 1981.

Glick, J. Cognitive development in cross-cultural perspective. In F. D. Horowitz (Ed.), *Review of child development research* (Vol. 4). Chicago: University of Chicago Press, 1975.

Glick, J., & Clarke-Stewart, K. A. (Eds.). *Studies in social and cognitive development: The development of social understanding* (Vol. 1). New York: Gardner Press, 1978.

Glickman, B. M., & Springer, N. B. *Who cares for the baby?* New York: Schocken Books, 1978.

Glidewell, J. C. (Ed.). *The social context of learning and development*. New York: Gardner Press, 1976.

Glucksberg, S., Krauss, R., & Higgins, E. T. The development of referential communication skills. In F. D. Horowitz (Ed.), *Review of child development research* (Vol. 4). Chicago: University of Chicago Press, 1975.

Golden, M., Bridger, W. H., & Montare, A. Social class differences in the ability of young children to use verbal information to facilitate learning. *American Journal of Orthopsychiatry*, 1974, *44*, 86–91.

Goldfarb, W. Psychological privation in infancy and subsequent adjustment. *American Journal of Orthopsychiatry*, 1945, *15*, 247–255.

Goldfarb, W., Meyers, D., Florsheim, J., & Goldfarb, N. *Psychotic children grown up*. New York: Human Sciences Press, 1978.

Goldman, B. D., & Ross, H. S. Social skills in action: An analysis of early peer games. In J. Glick & K. A. Clarke-Stewart (Eds.), *The development of social understanding* (Vol. 1). New York: Gardner Press, 1978.

Goldman, R. J., & Goldman, J. D. G. How children perceive the origin of babies and the role of mothers and fathers in procreation: A cross-national study. *Child Development*, 1982, *53*, 491–504.

Golinkoff, R. M., & Harding, C. G. The development of causality: The distinction between animates and inanimates. Paper presented at the International Conference on Infant Studies, 1980.

Goodman, P. *Compulsory mis-education*. New York: Horizon Press, 1964.

Goodman, S. H. The integration of verbal and motor behavior in preschool children. *Child Development*, 1981, *52*, 280–289.

Goodnow, J. *Children drawing*. Cambridge, Mass.: Harvard University Press, 1977.

Goodnow, J. J. Effects of active handling, illustrated by uses for objects. *Child Development*, 1969, *40*, 201–212.

Goodz, N. S. Is before really easier to understand than after? *Child Development*, 1982, *53*, 822–825.

Gottman, J. M. How children become friends. *Monographs of the Society for Research in Child Development*. 1983, *48* (3, Serial No. 201.)

Gratch, G. A study of the relative dominance of vision and touch in six-month-old infants. *Child Development*, 1972, *43*, 615–623.

Graves, D. H. *Writing: Teachers and children at work*. London: Heinemann Educational Books, 1982.

Greenfield, P. M., & Smith, J. H. *The structure of communication in early language development*. New York: Academic Press, 1976.

Griffiths, R. *The abilities of babies*. New York: McGraw-Hill, 1954.

Groch, A. S. Joking and appreciation of humor in nursery school children. *Child Development*, 1974, *45*, 1098–1102.

Gruber, H. E., & Vonèche, J. J. (Eds.). *The essential Piaget*. New York: Basic Books, 1977.

Guilford, J. P. *The nature of human intelligence*. New York: McGraw-Hill, 1967.

Haire, D. *How the FDA determines the "safety" of drugs—just how safe is "safe"?* Washington, D.C., and New York: National Women's Health Network and American Foundation for Maternal and Child Health, 1980.

Haith, M. M. Infrared television recording and measurement of ocular behavior in the human infant. *American Psychologist*, 1969, *24*, 279–283.

Hale, G. A., & Lewis, M. (Eds.). *Attention and cognitive development*. New York: Plenum, 1979.

Hall, G. S. *Adolescence*. New York: Appleton, 1904.

Hall, G. S. *Aspects of child life and education*. New York: Appleton, 1907.

Hallinan, M. T. Recent advances in sociometry. In S. R. Asher & J. M. Gottman (Eds.), *The development of children's friendships*. New York: Cambridge University Press, 1981.

Halverson, C. F., & Victor, J. B. Minor physical anomalies and problem behavior in elementary school children. *Child Development*, 1976, *47*, 281–285.

Harlow, H. F. The nature of love. *American Psychologist*, December 1958, pp. 673–685.

Harlow, H. F. The heterosexual affectional system in monkeys. *American Psychologist*, January 1962, pp. 1–9.

Harlow, H. F., & Harlow, M. K. Effects of various mother-infant relationships on rhesus monkey behaviors. In B. M. Foss (Ed.), *Determinants of infant behavior* (Vol. 4). New York: Barnes & Noble, 1969.

Harlow, H. F., & Kuenne, M. Learning to think. *Scientific American*, 1949, *181*, 36–39.

Harlow, H. F., & Zimmerman, R. R. Affectional responses in the infant monkey. *Science*, 1959, *130*, 421–432.

Harper, L., & Sanders, K. M. Preschool children's use of space: Sex differences in outdoor play. *Developmental Psychology*, 1975, *11*, 119.

Harper, L. V. The young as a source of stimuli controlling caretaking behavior. *Developmental Psychology*, 1971, *4*, 73–88.

Harris, B. Whatever happened to "Little Albert?" *American Psychologist*, 1979, *34*, 151–160.

Harris, D. (Ed.). *The concept of development*. Minneapolis: University of Minnesota Press, 1957.

Harter, S. Pleasure derived by children from cognitive challenge and mastery. *Child Development*, 1974, *45*, 661–669.

Harter, S. A model of mastery motivation in children: Individual differences and developmental change. In W. A. Collins (Ed.), *Minnesota symposia on child psychology* (Vol. 14). Hillsdale, N.J.: Lawrence Erlbaum, 1981.

Hartup, W. W. Peer interaction and social organization. In P. H. Mussen (Ed.), *Carmichael's manual of child psychology* (Vol. 2). New York: Wiley, 1970.

Hass, A. *Teenage sexuality*. Los Angeles: Pinnacle Books, 1979.

Haugh, S. S., Hoffman, C. D., & Cowan, G. The eye of the very young beholder: Sex typing of infants by young children. *Child Development*, 1980, *51*, 598–600.

Hayes, H. T. P. The pursuit of reason. *The New York Times Magazine*, June 12, 1977, pp. 21–23; 73; 75–79.

Hazen, N. L. Spatial exploration and spatial knowledge: Individual and developmental differences in very young children. *Child Development*, 1982, *53*, 826–833.

Hebb, D. O. Heredity and environment in mammalian behavior. *British Journal of Animal Behaviour*, 1953, *1*, 43–47.

Heber, R., Garber, H., Harrington, S., Hoffman, C., & Falender, C. *Rehabilitation of families at risk for mental retardation*. Madison: Rehabilitation Research and Training Center in Mental Retardation, University of Wisconsin, 1972.

Hechinger, F. M. How do children learn to write? *The New York Times*, November 30, 1982.

Helfner, R. M. The etiology of child abuse. *Pediatrics*, 1973, *51*, 777–779.

Hellmuth, J. (Ed.). *Cognitive studies: 1*. New York: Brunner/Mazel, 1970.

Hendin, D., & Marks, J. *The genetic connection*. New York: New American Library-Signet, 1979.

Henig, R. M. Saving babies before birth. *The New York Times Magazine*, February 28, 1982, pp. 18–22; 26; 28; 45–46; 48.

Hetherington, E. M. (Ed.). *Review of child develop-*

ment research (Vol. 5). Chicago: University of Chicago Press, 1975.

Hoffman, M. Developmental synthesis of affect and cognition and its implications for altruistic maturation. *Developmental Psychology,* 1975, *11,* 607–622.

Hoffman, M. L. Perspectives on the difference between understanding people and understanding things: The role of affect. In J. H. Flavell & L. Ross (Eds.), *Social cognitive development.* New York: Cambridge University Press, 1981.

Hoffman, M. L., & Hoffman, L. W. (Eds.). *Review of child development research* (Vol. 1). New York: Russell Sage Foundation, 1964.

Honig, A. S. Infant-mother communication. *Young Children,* March 1982, pp. 52–62.

Honzik, M. P. Value and limitations of infant tests: An overview. In M. Lewis (Ed.), *Origins of intelligence in infancy and childhood.* New York: Plenum, 1976.

Horn, J. M. Duration of preschool effects on later school competence. *Science,* 1981, *213,* 1145.

Horowitz, F. D. Infant learning and development: Retrospect and prospect. *Merrill-Palmer Quarterly,* 1968, *14,* 101–120.

Horowitz, F. D. (Ed.). *Review of child development research* (Vol. 4). Chicago: University of Chicago Press, 1975.

Horowitz, F. D. Intervention and its effects on early development: What model of development is appropriate? In R. Turner & H. W. Reese (Eds.), *Life-span developmental psychology.* New York: Academic Press, 1980.

Hubert, J. Belief and reality: Social factors in pregnancy and childbirth. In M. P. M. Richards (Ed.), *The integration of a child into a social world.* London and New York: Cambridge University Press, 1974.

Hughes, R., Jr., Tingle, B. A., & Sawin, D. B. Development of empathic understanding in children. *Child Development,* 1981, *52,* 122–128.

Hunton, V. C. The recognition of inverted pictures by children. *Journal of Genetic Psychology,* 1955, *86,* 281–288.

Huxley, R., & Ingram, E. (Eds.). *Language acquisition.* London and New York: Academic Press, 1971.

Illingworth, R. Under-achieving children destined for fame. *Proceedings of the Royal Society of Medicine,* 1973, *66,* 1207–1208.

Inhelder, B. Criteria of the stages of mental development. In J. M. Tanner & B. Inhelder (Eds.), *Discussions on child development* (Vol. 1). New York: International Universities Press, 1953.

Inhelder, B., & Piaget, J. *The growth of logical thinking from childhood to adolescence.* New York: Basic Books, 1958.

Inhelder, B., & Piaget, J. *The early growth of logic in the child.* New York: Harper & Row, 1964.

Inhelder, B., Sinclair, H., & Bovet, M. *Learning and the development of cognition.* Cambridge, Mass.: Harvard University Press, 1974.

Irwin, D. M., & Bushnell, M. M. *Observational strategies for child study.* New York: Holt, Rinehart and Winston, 1980.

Isaacs, S. *Social development in young children.* New York: Schocken Books, 1972. (Originally published, 1933.)

Jacklin, C. N., Maccoby, E. E., & Halverson, C. F. Minor physical anomalies and preschool behavior. *Journal of Pediatric Psychology,* 1980, *5,* 199–205.

Jacob, F. *The logic of life: A history of heredity.* New York: Vintage, 1976. (Originally published, 1970.)

Jacobson, S. W., & Kagan, J. Interpreting "imitative" responses in early infancy. *Science,* 1979, *205,* 215–217.

Jaffe, F. S. Teenage pregnancies: A need for education. In *Today's girls: Tomorrow's women.* New York: Girls Clubs of America, 1979.

Jaglom, L. M., & Gardner, H. Decoding the worlds of television. *Studies in Visual Communication,* 1981, *7,* 33–47.

Jensen, A. R. How much can we boost IQ and scholastic achievement? *Harvard Educational Review,* 1969, *39,* 1–123.

Johnson, C. N., & Wellman, H. M. Children's conception of the brain: A developmental study of knowledge about cognitive processes. Cited in R. Gelman & E. Spelke, The development of thoughts about animate and inanimate objects. In J. H. Flavell & L. Ross (Eds.), *Social cognitive development.* New York: Cambridge University Press, 1981.

Johnson, H., & Smith, L. B. Children's inferential abilities in the context of reading to understand. *Child Development,* 1981, *52,* 1216–1223.

Johnson, H. L., & Chapman, R. S. Children's judgment and recall of causal connectives: A developmental study of "because," "so," and "and." *Journal of Psycholinguistic Research,* 1980, *9,* 243–259.

Johnson, R. C., Cole, R. E., Ahern, F. M., Schwitters, S. Y., Huang, Y. H., Johnson, R. M., & Park, J. Y. Reported lactose tolerance of members of various racial/ethnic groups in Hawaii and Asia. *Behavior Genetics,* 1980, *10,* 377–385.

Johnson, W. A study of the onset and development of stuttering. *Journal of Speech and Hearing Disorders,* 1942, *7,* 251–257.

Johnston, F. E. Control of age at menarche. *Human Biology,* 1974, *46,* 159–171.

Jones, M. C. A laboratory study of fear: The case of Peter. *Pedagogical Seminary,* 1924, *31,* 308–315.

Jones, M. C. Psychological correlates of somatic development. *Child Development,* 1965, *36,* 899–911.

Jones, M. C. Albert, Peter, and John B. Watson. *American Psychologist*, August 1974, pp. 581–583.

Jones-Molfese, V. J. Responses of neonates to colored stimuli. *Child Development*, 1977, *48*, 1092–1095.

Kadushin, A., & Martin, J. A. *Child abuse: An interactional event*. New York: Columbia University Press, 1981.

Kamin, L. J. *The science and politics of IQ*. Potomac, Md.: Lawrence Erlbaum, 1974.

Kanner, L. Autistic disturbances of affective contact. *Nervous Child*, 1943, *2*, 217–250.

Kanner, L. Early infantile autism. *Journal of Pediatrics*, 1944, *25*, 211–217.

Kaplan, B., & Wapner, S. (Eds.). *Perspectives in psychological theory*. New York: International Universities Press, 1960.

Kaplan, L. J. *Oneness and separateness*. New York: Simon & Schuster, 1978.

Karmiloff-Smith, A. *A functional approach to child language*. Cambridge: Cambridge University Press, 1979.

Kasdorf, C. A., III, & Schnall, M. Developmental differences in the integration of pictures series: Effects of variations in object-attribute relationships. *Human Development*, 1970, *13*, 188–200.

Kawi, A. A., & Pasamanick, B. Prenatal and parental factors in development of childhood reading disorders. *Monographs of the Society for Research in Child Development*, 1959, *24*(4).

Kaye, K. Infants' effects upon their mothers' teaching strategies. In J. C. Glidewell (Ed.), *The social context of learning and development*. New York: Gardner Press, 1976.

Kaye, K. Discriminating among normal infants by multivariate analysis of Brazelton scores: Lumping and smoothing. In A. J. Sameroff (Ed.), Organization and stability of newborn behavior: A commentary on the Brazelton Neonatal Behavior Assessment Scale. *Monographs of the Society for Rsearch in Child Development*, 1978, *43*(5–6, Serial No. 177).

Kelly, A. Mathematical ability: Is sex a factor? *Science*, 1981, *212*, 118.

Kemler, D. G. Wholistic and analytic modes in perceptual and cognitive development. In T. Tighe & B. E. Shepp (Eds.), *Interactions: Perception, cognition, and development*. Hillsdale, N.J.: Lawrence Erlbaum, 1982.

Kempe, C. H., & Helfer, R. E. *The battered child*. Chicago: University of Chicago Press, 1980.

Kempe, R. S., & Kempe, C. H. *Child abuse*. Cambridge, Mass.: Harvard University Press, 1978.

Kendler, H. H., & Kendler, T. S. Developmental processes in discrimination learning. *Human Development*, 1970, *13*, 65–89.

Kendler, T. S. Verbalization and optimal reversal shifts among kindergarten children. *Journal of Verbal Learning and Verbal Behavior*, 1964, *31*, 428–436.

Kendler, T. S. An ontogeny of mediational deficiency. *Child Development*, 1972, *43*, 1–17.

Keniston, K. *All our children: The American family under pressure*. New York: Harcourt Brace Jovanovich, 1977.

Kennell, J. H., Jerauld, R., Wolfe, H., Chesler, D., McAlpine, W., Kreger, N. C., Steffa, M., & Klaus, M. H. Maternal behavior: Significance of the first post-partum days. Paper presented at meetings of the International Society for the Study of Behavioral Development, 1973.

Kennell, J. H., Jerauld, R., Wolfe, H., Chesler, D., McAlpine, W., Kreger, N. C., Steffa, M., & Klaus, M. H. Maternal behavior one year after early and extended post-partum contact. *Developmental Medicine and Child Neurology*, 1974, *16*, 172–179.

Kessen, W., Haith, M. M., & Salapatek, P. H. Infancy. In P. H. Mussen (Ed.), *Carmichael's manual of child psychology* (Vol. 1). New York: Wiley, 1970.

Keyserling, M. D. *Windows on day care*. New York: National Council of Jewish Women, 1972.

Kinloch, G. C. Parent-youth conflict at home: An investigation among university freshmen. *American Journal of Orthopsychiatry*, 1970, *40*, 658–664.

Kinsey, A. C., and associates. *Sexual behavior in the human female*. Philadelphia: Saunders, 1953.

Klaus, M. H., & Kennell, J. H. *Maternal-infant bonding*. St. Louis: C. V. Mosby, 1976.

Klaus, M. H., & Kennell, J. H. *Parent-infant bonding* (2nd ed.). St. Louis: C. V. Mosby, 1982.

Klaus, M. H., & Robertson, M. O. (Eds.). *Birth, interaction and attachment*. Skillman, N.J.: Johnson & Johnson Baby Products Company, 1982.

Klüver, H. The study of personality and the method of equivalent and nonequivalent stimuli. *Character and Personality*, 1936, *5*, 91–112.

Kohlberg, L. The cognitive-developmental approach to moral education. In P. Scharf (Ed.), *Readings in moral education*. Minneapolis: Winston Press, 1978.

Kohlberg, L. *The philosophy of moral development* (Vol. 1). New York: Harper & Row, 1981.

Kohnstamm, G. A. Experiments on teaching Piagetian thought operations. In J. Hellmuth (Ed.), *Cognitive studies* (Vol. 1). New York: Brunner/Mazel, 1970.

Kolata, G. B. Childhood hyperactivity: A new look at treatments and causes. *Science*, 1978, *199*, 515–517.

Kolata, G. B. Prenatal diagnosis of neural tube defects. *Science*, 1980, *209*, 1216–1218.

Koslowski, B., & Pierce, A. Preschool children's

spontaneous explanations and requests for explanations. Paper presented at meetings of the Society for Research in Child Development, 1981.

Kotelchuck, M. The nature of the infant's tie to his father. Paper presented at meetings of the Society for Research in Child Development, 1973.

Kramer, J. A., Hill, K. T., & Cohen, L. B. Infants' development of object permanence: A refined methodology and new evidence for Piaget's hypothesized ordinality. *Child Development*, 1975, *46*, 149–155.

Krech, D., Rosenzweig, M. R., & Bennett, E. L. Effects of environmental complexity and training on brain chemistry. *Journal of Comparative and Physiological Psychology*, 1960, *53*, 509–519.

Kreutzer, M. A., & Charlesworth, W. R. Infant recognition of emotions. Paper presented at meetings of the Society for Research in Child Development, 1973.

Kreutzer, M. A., Leonard, C., & Flavell, J. H. An interview study of children's knowledge about memory. *Monographs of the Society for Research in Child Development*, 1975, *40*(1).

Kuhn, D. Inducing development experimentally: Comments on a research paradigm. *Developmental Psychology*, 1974, *10*, 590–600.

Kuo, Z.-Y. *On aggression*. New York: Harcourt, Brace, and World, 1967.

Kurtines, W., & Greif, E. B. The development of moral thought: Review and evaluation of Kohlberg's approach. *Psychological Bulletin*, 1974, *81*, 453–470.

Lachenmeyer, J. R. Special disorders of childhood. In J. R. Lachenmeyer & M. S. Gibbs (Eds.), *Psychopathology in childhood*. New York: Gardner Press, 1982.

Lachenmeyer, J. R., & Gibbs, M.S. (Eds.). *Psychopathology in childhood*. New York: Gardner Press, 1982.

Lally, J. R., & Honig, A. S. *The family development research program. A program for prenatal infant and early childhood enrichment: Final report*. Syracuse: College for Human Development, Syracuse University, 1977.

Lamaze, F. *Painless childbirth*. London: Burke, 1958.

Lamb, M. E. Twelve-month-olds and their parents: Interaction in a laboratory playroom. *Developmental Psychology*, 1976, *12*, 237–246.

Lamb, M. E. Father-infant and mother-infant interaction in the first year of life. *Child Development*, 1977, *48*, 167–181.

Lamb, M. E. The father's role in the infant's social world. In J. H. Stevens & M. Mathews (Eds.), *Mother/child, father/child relationships*. Washington, D.C.: National Association for the Education of Young Children, 1978.

Lazar, I., Darlington, R., Murray, H., Royce, J., &

Snipper, A. Lasting effects of early childhood education: A report from the Consortium for Longitudinal Studies. *Monographs of the Society for Research in Child Development*, 1982, *47*(2–3).

Leboyer, F. *Birth without violence*. New York: Knopf, 1976.

LeCompte, G. K., & Gratch, G. Violation of a rule as a method of diagnosing infants' level of object concept. *Child Development*, 1972, *43*, 385–396.

Lepper, M. R., & Greene, D. (Eds.). *The hidden costs of rewards*. Morristown, N.J.: Lawrence Erlbaum, 1978.

Lerner, R. *Concepts and theories of human development*. Reading, Mass.: Addison-Wesley, 1976.

Leung, F. L. The measurement of brain damage in children. *Psychologia*, 1975, *18*, 194–204.

Levenkron, S. *Treating and overcoming anorexia nervosa*. New York: Scribner's, 1982.

Levy, D. M. Advice and reassurance. *American Journal of Public Health*, 1954, *44*, 1113–1118.

Lewis, C. The Montessori method. In B. D. Boegehold, H. K. Cuffaro, W. H. Hooks, & G. J. Klopf (Eds.), *Education before five*. New York: Bank Street College of Education, 1977.

Lewis, M. (Ed.). *Origins of intelligence*. New York and London: Plenum, 1976.

Lewis, M., & Rosenblum, L. A. *The effect of the infant on its caregiver*. New York: Wiley-Interscience, 1974.

Liebert, R. M., Neale, J. M., & Davidson, E. S. *The early window: Effects of television on children and youth*. New York: Pergamon, 1973.

Limber, J. The genesis of complex sentences. In T. E. Moore (Ed.), *Cognitive development and the acquisition of language*. New York: Academic Press, 1973.

Lindzey, G., & Aronson, E. (Eds.). *The handbook of social psychology* (Vol. 3). Reading, Mass.: Addison-Wesley, 1969.

Links, P. S. Minor physical anomalies in childhood autism. Part II. Their relationship to maternal age. *Journal of Autism and Developmental Disorders*, 1980, *10*, 287–292.

Lipps, T. Raumaesthetik und Geometrischoptische Täuschungen, 1897. Cited in G. Murphy, *Historical introduction to modern psychology*. New York: Harcourt, Brace, 1949.

Lipsitt, L. P., & Rovee-Collier, C. K. (Eds.). *Advances in infant research* (Vol. 1). New York: Ablex, 1981.

Listen! The children speak. Washington, D.C.: World Organization for Early Childhood Education, 1979.

Lorenz, K. *King Solomon's ring*. New York: Crowell, 1952.

Lorenz, K. *On aggression*. New York: Harcourt, Brace, and World, 1966.

Luchins, E. H., & Luchins, A. S. Mathematical ability: Is sex a factor? *Science*, 1981, *212*, 116–118.

Luria, A. R. *Cognitive development*. Cambridge, Mass.: Harvard University Press, 1976.

Lyle, J., & Hoffman, H. R. Children's use of television and other media. In E. A. Rubenstein (Ed.), *Television and social behavior* (Vol. 4). Washington, D.C.: U.S. Government Printing Office, 1972.

Lynn, D. B. Fathers and sex-role development. *Family coordinator*, 1976, *25*, 403–409.

Macchiarola, F. J. Making schools work for students. *The New York Times Magazine*, September 26, 1982, pp. 72–83.

Maccoby, E. *Social development*. New York: Harcourt, Brace and Jovanovich, 1980.

Maccoby, E. E., & Jacklin, C. N. *The psychology of sex differences*. Stanford: Stanford University Press, 1974. (a)

Maccoby, E. E., & Jacklin, C. N. What we know and don't know about sex differences. *Psychology Today*, December 1974, pp. 109–112. (b)

Macfarlane, J., Allen, L., & Honzik, M. P. *A Developmental study of the behavior problems of normal children between twenty-one months and fourteen years*. Berkeley and Los Angeles: University of California Press, 1954.

MacLure, M., & French, P. A comparison of talk at home and at school. In G. Wells (Ed.), *Learning through interaction*. New York: Cambridge University Press, 1981.

Maier, N. R. F. Reasoning in children. *Journal of Comparative Psychology*, 1936, *21*, 357–366.

Manosevitz, M., Prentice, N. M., & Wilson, W. Individual and family correlates of imaginary companions in preschool children. *Developmental Psychology*, 1973, *8*, 72–79.

Marcia, J. E. Development and validation of ego identity status. *Journal of Personality and Social Psychology*, 1966, *3*, 551–558.

Marcia, J. E. Identity in adolescence. In J. Adelson (Ed.), *Handbook of adolescent psychology*. New York: Wiley-Interscience, 1980.

Markman, E., Cox, B., & Machida, S. The standard object-sorting task as a measure of conceptual organization. *Developmental Psychology*, 1981, *17*, 115–117.

Markman, E. M. Realizing that you don't understand: A preliminary investigation. *Child Development*, 1977, *48*, 986–992.

Marks, L. On colored-hearing synesthesia: Cross-modal translations of sensory dimensions. *Psychological Bulletin*, 1975, *82*, 303–331.

Martin, W. E., & Stendler, C. B. (Eds.). *Readings in child development*. New York: Harcourt, Brace, 1954.

Marx, J. L. Cytomegalovirus: A major cause of birth defects. *Science*, 1975, *190*, 1184–1186.

Masangkay, Z. S., McCluskey, K. A., McIntyre, C. W., Sims-Knight, J., Vaughn, B. E., & Flavell, J. H. The early development of inferences about the visual percepts of others. *Child Development*, 1974, *45*, 357–366.

Maslow, A. H. Self-actualizing people: A study of psychological health. *Personality Symposia*, 1950, *1*, 11–34.

Mason, M. K. Learning to speak after years of silence. *Journal of Hearing and Speech Disorders*, 1942, *7*, 295–304.

Masters, J. C. Interpreting "imitative" responses in early infancy. *Science*, 1979, *205*, 215.

Masters, W. H., & Johnson, V. E. *Human sexual response*. Boston: Little, Brown, 1966.

McBroom, P. *Behavioral genetics. National Institute of Mental Health Science Monograph 2*. Washington, D.C.: U.S. Government Printing Office, 1980.

McCall, R. B. Childhood IQ's as predictors of adult educational and occupational status. *Science*, 1977, *197*, 482–483.

McCall, R. B., & Kagan, J. Stimulus-schema discrepancy and attention in the infant. *Journal of Experimental Child Psychology*, 1967, *5*, 381–390.

McClintock, M. Menstrual synchrony and suppression. *Nature*, 1971, *229*, 244–245.

McFadden, R. D. A spectrum of humanity represented at the rally. *The New York Times*, June 13, 1982, p. 42.

McGraw, M. B. *Growth: A study of Johnny and Jimmy*. New York: Appleton-Century, 1935.

McGurk, H., & Power, R. P. Intermodal coordination in young children: Vision and touch. *Developmental Psychology*, 1980, *16*, 679–680.

McKay, H., Sinisterra, L., McKay, A., Gomez, H., & Lloreda, P. Improving cognitive ability in chronically deprived children. *Science*, 1978, *200*, 270–278.

McNeill, D. Developmental psycholinguistics. In F. Smith & G. A. Miller, *The genesis of language*. Cambridge, Mass.: M.I.T. Press, 1966.

McNeill, D. *The acquisition of language*. New York: Harper & Row, 1970.

Mead, M. *Growing up in New Guinea*. New York: Morrow, 1930.

Mead, M. *And keep your powder dry*. New York: Morrow, 1942.

Mednick, S. A., et al. (Eds.). *Genetics, environment, and psychopathology*. New York: American Elsevier, 1974.

Mehrabian, A., & Williams, M. Piagetian measures of cognitive development up to age two. *Journal of Psycholinguistic Research*, 1971, *1*, 113–126.

Meltzoff, A. N., & Moore, M. K. Imitation of facial and manual gestures by human neonates. *Science*, 1977, *198*, 75–78.

Meltzoff, A. N., & Moore, M. K. Interpreting "imitative" responses in early infancy. *Science*, 1979, *205*, 217–219.

Meringoff, L. K., Vibbert, M. M., Char, C. A., Fernie, D. E., Banker, G. S., & Gardner, H. How is children's learning from television distinctive? In D. R. Anderson and J. Bryant (Eds.), *Watching TV, understanding TV.* New York: Academic Press, 1983.

Merleau-Ponty, M. *Phénoménologie de la perception.* Paris: Gallimard, 1945.

Metzel, M. N. Teaching parents a strategy for enhancing infant development. *Child Development,* 1980, *51,* 583–586.

Miller, G. A. *Language and speech.* San Francisco: W. H. Freeman, 1981.

Miller, J. The myth of mental illness. *The sciences.* July/Aug 1983, 22–30.

Miller, S. *Children as parents.* New York: Child Welfare League of America, 1981.

Minuchin, P. P. *The middle years of childhood.* Monterey, Calif.: Brooks/Cole, 1977.

Minuchin, S., Rosman, B. L., & Baker, L. *Psychosomatic families.* Cambridge, Mass.: Harvard University Press, 1978.

Mischel, W., & Metzner, R. Preference for a delayed reward as a function of age, intelligence, and length of delay interval. *Journal of Abnormal and Social Psychology,* 1962, *64,* 425–431.

Mitchell, L. S. *Young geographers.* New York: Bank Street College of Education, 1934.

Moerman, D. E. Edible symbols: The effectiveness of placebos. In T. A. Sebeok & R. Rosenthal, *The Clever Hans phenomenon.* New York: Academy of Sciences, 1981.

Mongoloid children in Israel receive unique surgery aid. *The Jewish Week–American Examiner,* week of March 14, 1982.

Montagu, M. F. A. *Prenatal influences.* Springfield, Ill.: Thomas, 1962.

Montagu, M. F. A. (Ed.). *Man and aggression.* New York: Oxford Univ. Press, 1968.

Moore, T., & Ucko, L. E. Night waking in early infancy. *Archives of Diseases in Childhood,* 1957, *32,* 333–342.

Moore, T. E. (Ed.). *Cognitive development and the acquisition of language.* New York: Academic Press, 1973.

Moran, D. J. Mathematical ability: Is sex a factor? *Science,* 1981, *212,* 116.

Morgan, S. M. *The unreachable child: An introduction to early childhood autism.* Memphis: Memphis State University Press, 1981.

Morland, J. A. A comparison of race awareness in northern and southern children. *American Journal of Orthopsychiatry,* 1966, *36,* 22–31.

Moss, H. A. Sex, age, and state as determinants of mother-infant interaction. *Merrill-Palmer Quarterly,* 1967, *13,* 19–36.

Mossler, D. G., Marvin, R. S., & Greenberg, M. T. Conceptual perspective taking in 2- to 6-year-old children. *Developmental Psychology,* 1976, *12,* 85–86.

Mueller, E., & Musatti, T. Almost symbol in action: A cognitive analysis of peer-related play themes. Paper presented at meetings of the Society for Research in Child Development, 1981.

Muir, D., Abraham, W., Forbes, B., & Harris, L. The ontogenesis of an auditory localization response from birth to four months of age. *Canadian Journal of Psychology,* 1979, *33,* 320–333.

Muir, D., & Field, N. Newborn infants orient to sounds. *Child Development,* 1979, *50,* 431–436.

Munroe, R. L., & Munroe, R. H. *Cross-cultural human development.* Monterey, Calif.: Brooks/Cole, 1975.

Murphy, G. *Historical introduction to modern psychology.* New York: Harcourt, Brace, 1949.

Murray, A. D., Dolby, R. M. Nation, R. L., & Thomas, D. B. Effects of epidural anesthesia on newborns and their mothers. *Child Development,* 1981, *52,* 71–82.

Mussen, P., & Eisenberg-Berg, N. *Roots of caring, sharing, and helping.* San Francisco: Freeman, 1977.

Mussen, P. H. (Ed.). *Carmichael's manual of child psychology* (Vol. 2). New York: Wiley, 1970.

Muuss, R. E. Puberty rites in primitive and modern societies. *Adolescence,* 1970, *5,* 109–128.

Muuss, R. E. *Theories of adolescence* (4th ed.). New York: Random House, 1982.

National Center on Child Abuse and Neglect. *Study findings: National study of the incidence and severity of child abuse and neglect.* Washington, D.C.: U.S. Department of Health and Human Services, 1982.

National Institute of Mental Health. *Television and behavior: Ten years of scientific progress and implications for the eighties. Vol. 1: Summary report.* Washington, D.C.: U.S. Government Printing Office, 1982. (a)

National Institute of Mental Health. *Television and behavior. Vol. 2: Technical reviews.* Washington, D.C.: U.S. Government Printing Office, 1982. (b)

Neff, W. S. Socioeconomic status and intelligence: A critical survey. *Psychological Bulletin,* 1938, *35,* 727–757.

Neimark, E. D. Intellectual development during adolescence. In F. D. Horowitz (Ed.), *Review of child development research* (Vol. 4). Chicago: University of Chicago Press, 1975.

Neimark, E. D. Current status of formal operations research. *Human Development,* 1979, *22,* 60–67.

Nelson, K. B., & Broman, S. H. Perinatal risk factors in children with serious motor and mental handicaps. *Annals of Neurology,* 1977, *2,* 371–377.

Nelson, K. E. Facilitating children's syntax acquisition. *Developmental Psychology,* 1977, *13,* 101–107.

Newman, D. Perspective-taking versus content in understanding lies. *Quarterly Newsletter of the Laboratory of Comparative Human Cognition*, 1982, *4*, 26–29.

Newman, H. H., Freeman, F. H., & Holzinger, K. J. *Twins: A study of heredity and environment*. Chicago: University of Chicago Press, 1937.

Nilsson, L. *A child is born*. New York: Delacorte/Seymour Lawrence, 1977.

Nisbett, R., and Ross, L. *Human inference: Strategies and shortcomings of social judgment*. Englewood Cliffs, N.J.: Prentice-Hall, 1980.

Novak, M. A., & Harlow, H. F. Social recovery of monkeys isolated for the first year of life. I. Rehabilitation and therapy. *Developmental Psychology*, 1975, *11*, 453–465.

Nowlis, G. H., & Kessen, W. Human newborns differentiate differing concentrations of sucrose and glucose. *Science*, 1976, *191*, 865–866.

Nucci, L. P., & Nucci, M. S. Children's responses to moral and social conventional transgressions in free-play settings. *Child Development*, 1982, *53*, 1337–1342.

Nyiti, R. M. The development of conservation in the Meru children of Tanzania. *Child Development*, 1976, 47, 1122–1129.

Oden, M. H. The fulfillment of promise: 40-year follow-up of the Terman gifted group. *Genetic Psychology Monographs*, 1968, 77, 3–93.

Odent, M. The milieu and obstetrical positions during labor: A new approach from France. In M. H. Klaus & M. O. Robertson (Eds.), *Birth, interaction, and attachment*. Skillman, N.J.: Johnson & Johnson Baby Products Company, 1982.

Offer, D. Landmarks in the literature: Adolescent turmoil. *New York University Education Quarterly*, *13*, 29–32.

Ogburn, W. F., & Bose, N. K. On the trail of the wolf-children. *Genetic Psychology Monographs*, 1959, *60*, 117–193.

O'Leary, K. D., & Carr, E. G. Behavior therapy for children: Outcome and evaluation. In G. T. Wilson & C. M. Franks (Eds.), *Contemporary behavior therapy*. New York: Guilford Press, 1982.

Opie, I., & Opie, P. *The lore and language of schoolchildren*. London: Oxford Unviersity Press, 1970. (Originally published, 1959.) (a)

Opie, I., & Opie, P. *Children's games in street and playground*. Oxford: Clarendon Press, 1970. (b)

Osofsky, J. D., & Danzger, B. Relationships between neonatal characteristics and mother-infant interaction. *Developmental Psychology*, 1974, *10*, 124–130.

Overton, W. F., & Jackson, J. P. The representation of imagined objects in action sequences: A developmental study. *Child Development*, 1973, *44*, 309–314.

Paris, S. G., & Upton, L. R. Children's memory for inferential relationships in prose. *Child Development*, 1976, 47, 660–668.

Parke, R. D. *Fathers*. Cambridge, Mass.: Harvard University Press, 1981.

Pasamanick, B., & Knobloch, H. Early feeding and birth difficulties in childhood schizophrenia: An explanatory note. *Journal of Psychology*, 1963, *56*, 73–77.

Pasamanick, B., & Knobloch, H. Retrospective studies on the epidemiology of reproductive casualty: Old and new. *Merrill-Palmer Quarterly*, 1966, *12*, 7–26.

Patterson, F. G. Ape language. *Science*, 1981, *211*, 86–87.

Patterson, F. G., & Linden, E. *The education of Koko*. New York: Holt, Rinehart and Winston, 1982.

Pepler, D. J. The effects of play on convergent and divergent problem-solving. Paper presented at meetings of the American Psychological Association, 1980.

Perkins, W. H. Prevention and treatment of stuttering. In P. E. Brookhouser (Ed.), *Childhood communication disorders: Present status and future priorities: Annals of otology, rhinology, & laryngology*, Suppl. 74, 1980, *80*(5, P. 2)

Phillips, J. L., Jr. *Piaget's theory: A primer*. San Francisco: Freeman, 1981.

Piaget, J. *Judgment and reasoning in the child*. New York: Harcourt, Brace, 1928.

Piaget, J. Das Umdrehen des Gegenstandes beim Kind unter einem Jahr. *Psychologische Rundschau*, 1932, *4*, 110–115.

Piaget, J. *The construction of reality in the child*. New York: Basic Books, 1954.

Piaget, J. *The child's conception of the world*. Totowa, N.J.: Littlefield, Adams, 1965. (a)

Piaget, J. *The moral judgment of the child*. New York: Free Press, 1965. (Original American ed., 1932.) (b)

Piaget, J. Intellectual evolution from adolescence to adulthood. *Human Development*, 1972, *15*, 1–21.

Piaget, J., & Inhelder, B. *The psychology of the child*. New York: Basic Books, 1969. (Original French ed., 1966.)

Pihl, R. O., & Parkes, M. Hair element content in learning disabled children. *Science*, 1977, *198*, 204–206.

Play. Washington, D.C.: National Association for the Education of Young Children, 1971.

Plomin, R., & Foch, T. T. Sex differences and individual differences. *Child Development*, 1981, *52*, 383–385.

Polanyi, M. *Personal knowledge*. Chicago: University of Chicago Press, 1958.

Pomeroy, W. B. *Boys and sex*. New York: Dell, 1971.

Pomeroy, W. B. *Girls and sex*. New York: Dell, 1973.

Postman, N. *The disappearance of childhood*. New York: Delacorte Press, 1982.

Poulsen, D., Kintsch, E., Kintsch, W., & Premack, D. Children's comprehension and memory for stories. *Journal of Experimental Child Psychology*, 1979, *28*, 379–403.

Pressley, M. Elaboration and memory development. *Child Development*, 1982, *53*, 296–309.

Preyer, W. *Die Seele des Kindes.* Leipzig: Grieben, 1882.

Provence, S., & Lipton, R. *Children in institutions.* New York: International Universities Press, 1962.

Provence, S., Naylor, A., & Patterson, J. *The challenge of day care.* New Haven and London: Yale University Press, 1977.

Pulaski, M. A. S. *Understanding Piaget* (Rev. ed.). New York: Harper & Row, 1980.

Rapoport, J. L., Buchsbaum, M. S., Zahn, T. P., Weingartner, H., Ludlow, C., & Mikkelsen, E. J. Dextroamphetamine: Cognitive and behavioral effects in prepubertal boys. *Science*, 1978, *199*, 506–562.

Ratcliffe, S. G. The development of children with sex chromosome abnormalities. *Proceedings of the Royal Society of Medicine*, 1976, *69*, 189–191.

Rector, J. M. Justice for young women. In *Today's girls: Tomorrow's women.* New York: Girls Clubs of America, 1979.

Reed, E. W. Genetic anomalies in development. In F. D. Horowitz (Ed.), *Review of child development research* (Vol. 4). Chicago: University of Chicago Press, 1975.

Reinisch, J. M. Prenatal exposure to synthetic progestins increases potential for aggression in humans. *Science*, 1981, *211*, 1171–1173.

Rheingold, H. L. The social and socializing infant. In D. A. Goslin (Ed.), *Handbook of socialization theory and research.* New York: Rand McNally, 1969.

Rheingold, H. L., & Cook, K. V. The contents of boys' and girls' rooms as index of parents' behavior. *Child Development*, 1975, *46*, 459–463.

Rheingold, H. L., & Eckerman, C. O. The infant's free entry into a new environment. *Journal of Experimental Child Psychology*, 1969, *8*, 271–283.

Rheingold, H. L., Hay, D. F., & West, M. J. Sharing in the second year of life. *Child Development*, 1976, *47*, 1148–1158.

Richards, M. P. M. (Ed.). *The integration of a child into a social world.* London: Cambridge University Press, 1974.

Richardson, C., & Church, J. A developmental analysis of proverb interpretation. *Journal of Genetic Psychology*, 1959, *194*, 169–179.

Riis, J. *How the other half lives.* New York: Dover, 1971. (Originally published, 1890.)

Rimland, B. *Infantile autism.* New York: Appleton-Century-Crofts, 1964.

Ringler, N. M. The development of language and how adults talk to children. *Infant Mental Health Journal*, 1981, *2*, 71–83.

Ringlet, N. M., Kennell, J. H., Jarvella, R., Navojosky, B. J., & Klaus, M. H. Mother-to-child speech at age 2 years—effects of early postnatal contact. *Journal of Pediatrics*, 1975, *86*, 141–144.

Roberge, J. J. Developmental analyses of two formal operational structures: Combinatorial thinking and conditional reasoning. *Developmental Psychology*, 1976, *12*, 563–564.

Roberge, J. J., & Flexer, B. K. Propositional reasoning in adolescence. *Journal of General Psychology*, 1979, *700*, 85–91. (a)

Roberge, J. J., & Flexer, B. K. Further examination of formal operational reasoning abilities. *Child Development*, 1979, *50*, 478–484. (b)

Roberge, J. J., & Flexer, B. K. Control of variables and propositional reasoning in early adolescence. *Journal of General Psychology*, 1980, *103*, 3–12.

Rosenblith, J. F., & Allinsmith, W. (Eds.), *The causes of behavior* (2nd ed.). Boston: Allyn & Bacon, 1966.

Rosenfeld, A. The heartbreak gene. *Science*, 1981, *81*, 46–50.

Rosenthal, D., Wender, P. H., Kety, S. E., Welner, J., & Schulsinger, F. The adopted-away offspring of schizophrenics. In S. A. Mednick, et al. (Eds.), *Genetics, environment, and psychopathology.* New York: American Elsevier, 1974.

Ross, H. S. Establishment of social games among toddlers. *Developmental Psychology*, 1982, *18*, 509–518.

Ross, H. S., & Goldman, B. D. Infants' sociability towards strangers. *Child Development*, 1977, *48*, 638–642.

Ross, H. S., & Hay, D. F. Conflict and conflict resolution between 21-month-old peers. Paper presented at meetings of the Society for Research in Child Development, 1977.

Ross, H. S., & Kay, D. A. The origins of social games. *New Directions for Child Development*, 1980, *9*, 17–31.

Ross, J. B., & MacLaughlin, M. M. (Eds.). *A portable medieval reader.* New York: Viking, 1949.

Rothbart, M. K., & Maccoby, E. E. Parents' differential reactions to sons and daughters. *Journal of Personality and Social Psychology*, 1966, *4*, 237–243.

Rousseau, J. J. *Emile: Concerning education* (W. Boyd, trans. and Ed.). New York: Educational Bureau of Publications, Teachers College, Columbia University, 1962. (Originally published, 1762.)

Rubenstein, E. A. (Ed.). *Television and social behavior* (Vol. 4). Washington, D.C.: U.S. Government Printing Office, 1972.

Rubenstein, J. L., & Howes, C. Caregiving and infant behavior in day care and in homes. *Developmental Psychology*, 1979, *15*, 1–24.

Rubin, J. Z., Provenzano, F. J., & Luria, Z. The eye of the beholder: Parents' views on sex of newborns. *American Journal of Orthopsychiatry*, 1974, *44*, 512–519.

Rubin, T. I. *Jordi*. New York: Macmillan, 1960.

Ruble, D. N., Goggiano, A. K., Feldman, N. S., & Loebl, J. H. Developmental analysis of the role of social comparison in self-evaluation. *Developmental Psychology*, 1980, *16*, 105–115.

Ruff, H. A., & Halton, A. Is there directed reaching in the human neonate? *Developmental Psychology*, 1978, *14*, 425–426.

Rule, B. G., Nesdale, A. R., & McAra, M. J. Children's reactions to information about the intentions underlying an aggressive act. *Child Development*, 1974, *45*, 794–798.

Ruppenthal, G. E., Arling, G. L., Harlow, H. F., Sackett, G., & Suomi, S. J. A 1-year perspective of motherless-mother monkey-behavior. *Journal of Abnormal Psychology*, 1976, *85*, 341–349.

Rushton, J. P. Generosity in children: Immediate and long-term effects of modeling, preaching, and moral judgment. *Journal of Personality and Social Psychology*, 1975, *31*, 459–466.

Rushton, J. P. Effects of prosocial television and film materials on the behavior of viewers. In L. Berkowitz (Ed.), *Advances in experimental social psychology* (Vol. 12). New York: Academic Press, 1979.

Rushton, J. P., & Owen, D. Immediate and delayed effects of TV modeling and preaching on children's generosity. *British Journal of Social and Clinical Psychology*, 1975, *14*, 309–310.

Rushton, J. P., & Wiener, J. Altruism and cognitive development in children. *British Journal of Social and Clinical Psychology*, 1975, *14*, 341–349.

Russell, K. P. *Eastman's expectant motherhood*. Boston: Little, Brown, 1977.

Rynders, J. Unpublished data. Cited by S. Scarr-Salapatek. Genetics and the development of intelligence. In F. D. Horowitz (Ed.), *Review of child development research* (Vol. 4). Chicago: University of Chicago Press, 1975.

Sagi, A., & Hoffman, M. L. Empathic distress in the newborn. *Developmental Psychology*, 1976, *12*, 175–176.

Saitoti, T. O. Warriors of Maasailand. *Natural History*, August 1980, pp. 42–55.

Saltz, E., Dunan-Markiewicz, A., & Rourke, D. The development of natural language concepts. 2. Developmental changes in attribute structure. *Child Development*, 1975, *46*, 913–921.

Sameroff, A. J. Can conditioned responses be established in the newborn infant? *Developmental Psychology*, 1971, *5*, 1–12.

Sameroff, A. J. (Ed.). Organization and stability of newborn behavior: A commentary on the Brazelton Neonatal Behavior Assessment Scale. *Monographs of the Society for Research in Child Development*, 1978, *43*, (5–6, Serial No. 177).

Sameroff, A. J., & Chandler, M. J. Reproductive risk and the continuum of caretaking casualty. In F. D. Horowitz (Ed.), *Review of child development research* (Vol. 4). Chicago: University of Chicago Press, 1975.

Sapir, S. G., & Wilson, B. *A professional's guide to working with the learning disabled child*. New York: Brunner/Mazel, 1978.

Scarr, S. *Race, social class, and individual differences in IQ*. Hillsdale, N.J.: Lawrence Erlbaum, 1981.

Scarr, S., Pakstis, A. J., Katz, S. H., & Barker, W. B. The absence of a relationship between degree of white ancestry and intellectual skills within a black population. *Human Genetics*, 1977, *39*, 69–86.

Scarr, S., & Weinberg, R. A. IQ test performance of black children adopted by white families. *American Psychologist*, October 1976, pp. 726–739.

Schachter, F. F. *Everyday mother talk to toddlers*. New York: Academic Press, 1979.

Schaefer, C. E. Imaginary companions and creative adolescents. *Developmental Psychology*, 1969, *1*, 747–749.

Schaefer, E. S. A configurational analysis of children's reports of parent behavior. *Journal of Consulting Psychology*, 1965, *29*, 552–557.

Schaffer, H. R. (Ed.). *The origins of human social relations*. London: Academic Press, 1969.

Schaffer, H. R., & Emerson, P. The development of social attachments in infancy. *Monographs of the Society for Research in Child Development*, 1964, *29*(3).

Schaffer, H. R., & Emerson, P. Patterns of response to physical contact in early human development. *Journal of Child Psychology and Psychiatry*, 1965, *5*, 1–13.

Schanberg, S. If brothers could cook. *New York Times*. Nov. 27, 1982.

Scharf, P. Indoctrination, values clarification, and developmental moral education as educational responses to conflict and change in contemporary society. In P. Scharf (Ed.), *Readings in moral education*. Minneapolis: Winston Press, 1978. (a)

Scharf, P. Creating moral dilemmas for the classroom. In P. Scharf (Ed.), *Readings in moral education*. Minneapolis: Winston Press, 1978. (b)

Scharf, P. (Ed.). *Readings in moral education*. Minneapolis: Winston Press. 1978. (c)

Schein, M. W., & Hale, E. B. The effect of early social experience on male sexual behavior of androgen-injected turkeys. *Animal Behaviour,* 1959, *7,* 189–200.

Schiff, M., Duyme, M., Dumaret, A., Stewart, J., Tomkiewicz, S., & Feingold, J. Intellectual status of working-class children adopted early into upper-middle-class families. *Science,* 1978, *200,* 1503–1504.

Schiff, W. The perception of impending collision. A study of visually directed avoidant behavior. *Psychological Monographs,* 1965, *79*(11).

Schnall, M. Age differences in the integration of progressively changing visual patterns. *Human Development,* 1968, *11,* 287–295.

Schneirla, T. C., & Rosenblatt, J. S. "Critical periods" in the development of behavior. *Science,* 1963, *139,* 1110–1115.

Schwartz, J. I. Children's experiments with language. *Young Children,* July 1981, pp. 16–26.

Scott, J. P. *Aggression.* Chicago: University of Chicago Press, 1958.

Scott, J. P. Critical periods in behavioral development. *Science,* 1962, *138,* 949–958.

Sears, R. R. Relation of early socialization experiences to self-concepts and gender role in middle childhood. *Child Development,* 1970, *41,* 267–289.

Sears, R. R. Sources of life satisfaction to the Terman gifted men. *American Psychologist,* February 1977, pp. 119–128.

Sears, R. R., Maccoby, E. E., & Levin, H. *Patterns of child rearing.* Evanston, Ill.: Row-Peterson, 1957.

Sebeok, T. A., & Rosenthal, R. The Clever Hans phenomenon. *Annals of the New York Academy of Science,* 1981, *364.*

Seligman, M. E. P., & Beagley, G. Learned helplessness in the rat. *Journal of Comparative and Physiological Psychology,* 1975, *88,* 534–541.

Shantz, C. U. The development of social cognition. In E. M. Hetherington (Ed.), *Review of child development research* (Vol. 5). Chicago: University of Chicago Press, 1975.

Shapiro, A. I. An electromyographic analysis of the fluent and dysfluent utterances of several types of stutterers. *Journal of Fluency Disorders,* 1980, *6,* 203–231.

Shapiro, A. I., & DeCicco, B. A. The relationship between normal dysfluency and stuttering: An old question revisited. *Journal of Fluency Disorders,* 1982, *7,* 109–121.

Shapiro, E. K., & Weber, E. (Eds.). *Cognitive and affective growth: Developmental interaction.* Hillsdale, N.J.: Lawrence Erlbaum, 1981.

Shapiro, S. A. *Contemporary theories of schizophrenia.* New York: McGraw-Hill, 1982.

Sherif, M., Harvey, O. J., White, B. J., Hood, W. R., & Sherif, C. W. *Intergroup conflict and cooperation.* Norman, Okla.: University Book Exchange, 1961.

Shinn, M. W. *Biography of a baby.* Boston: Houghton Mifflin, 1900.

Shockley, W. Proposed research to reduce racial aspects of the environment-heredity uncertainty. *Science,* 1968, *160,* 443.

Schultz, T. R. Rules of causal attribution. *Monographs of the Society for Research in Child Development,* 1982, *47*(1, Serial No. 194).

Shweder, R. A. What's there to negotiate? Some questions for Youniss. *Merrill-Palmer Quarterly,* 1981, *27,* 405–412.

Sichel, J. L., & Chandler, K. A. The color-word interference test: The effect of varied color-word combinations upon verbal response latency. *Journal of Psychology,* 1969, *72,* 219–231.

Siegl, L. S., & Brainerd, C. J. (Eds.). *Alternatives to Piaget: Critical essays on the theory.* New York: Academic Press, 1978.

Siegler, R. S. The origins of scientific reasoning. In R. S. Siegler (Ed.), *Children's thinking: What develops?* Hillsdale, N.J.: Lawrence Erlbaum, 1978. (a)

Siegler, R. S. (Ed.). *Children's thinking: What develops?* Hillsdale, N.J.: Lawrence Erlbaum, 1978. (b)

Siegler, R. S. Seven generalizations about cognitive development. Paper presented at meetings of the Society for Research in Child Development, 1981.

Siegler, R. S., Liebert, D. E., & Liebert, R. M. Inhelder and Piaget's pendulum problem: Teaching pre-adolescents to act as scientists. *Developmental Psychology,* 1973, *9,* 97–101.

Sinclair, H. *Langage et opérations.* Paris: Dunod, 1967.

Sinclair, J. McH., & Coulthard, R. M. *Towards an analysis of discourse.* London: Oxford University Press, 1975.

Singer, J. L., & Singer, D. G. Television viewing, family style, and aggressive behavior in preschool children. Paper presented at meetings of the American Association for the Advancement of Science, 1979.

Singer, J. L., & Singer, D. G. Imaginative play in the preschooler. Paper presented at meetings of the American Psychological Association, 1980.

Singer, J. L., & Singer, D. G. Implications of childhood television-viewing for cognition, imagination and emotion. In D. Anderson & J. Bryant (Eds.), *Watching TV, understanding TV.* New York: Academic Press, 1983.

Siqueland, E. R. The development of instrumental and exploratory behavior during the first year of human life. Paper presented at meetings of the Society for Research in Child Development, 1969.

Skeels, H. M. Adult status of children with contrasting early life experiences. *Monographs of the Society for Research in Child Development*, 1966, *31*(3).

Skinner, B. F. *The behavior of organisms: An experimental analysis*. New York: Appleton-Century-Crofts, 1938.

Skinner, B. F. *Walden Two*. New York: Macmillan, 1948.

Skinner, B. F. *Science and human behavior*. New York: Macmillan, 1953.

Skinner, B. F. *Verbal behavior*. New York: Appleton-Century-Crofts, 1957.

Skinner, B. F. *About behaviorism*. New York: Knopf, 1974.

Skodak, M., & Skeels, H. M. A final follow-up of one hundred adopted children. *Journal of Genetic Psychology*, 1949, *75*, 85–125.

Smith, D. W., & Wilson, A. A. *The child with Down's syndrome (mongolism)*. Philadelphia: Saunders, 1973.

Smith, R. P. *"Where Did You Go?" "Out." "What Did You Do?" "Nothing."* New York: Norton, 1957.

Smith, R. P. *How to do nothing with nobody, all alone by yourself*. New York: Norton, 1958.

Smith, S. M., & Hanson, R. 134 battered children: A medical and psychological study. *British Medical Journal*, September 1974, pp. 666–670.

Smith, S. M., Hanson, R., & Noble, S. Parents of battered babies: A controlled study. *British Medical Journal*, November 1974, pp. 388–391.

Snow, C. Mothers' speech to children learning language. *Child Development*, 1972, *43*, 439–465.

Snygg, D. The relation between the intelligence of mothers and of their children living in foster homes. *Journal of Genetic Psychology*, 1938, *52*, 401–406.

Spears, W. C. Assessment of visual preference and discrimination in the four-month-old infant. *Journal of Comparative and Physiological Psychology*, 1964, *57*, 381–386.

Sperry, R. Some effects of disconnecting the cerebral hemispheres. *Science*, 1982, *217*, 1223–1226.

Spinetta, J., & Rigler, D. The child-abusing parent: A psychological review. *Psychological Bulletin*, 1972, *77*, 296–304.

Spitz, R. A. Hospitalism: An inquiry into the genesis of psychiatric conditions in early childhood. *Psychoanalytic Study of the Child*, 1945, *1*, 53–74.

Spitz, R. A. Hospitalism: A follow-up report. *Psychoanalytic Study of the Child*, 1946, *2*, 113–117. (a)

Spitz, R. A. The smiling response: A contribution to the ontogenesis of social relations. *Genetic Psychology Monographs*, 1946, *34*, 57–125. (b)

Spock, B. *Baby and child care*. New York: Pocket Books, 1976. (Originally published, 1945.)

Sroufe, L. A. Drug treatment of children with behavior disorders. In F. D. Horowitz (Ed.), *Review of child development research* (Vol. 4). Chicago: University of Chicago Press, 1975.

Sroufe, L. A., & Waters, E. The ontogenesis of smiling and laughter: A perspective on the organization of development in infancy. *Psychological Review*, 1976, *83*, 173–189.

Stage, E. K., & Karplus, R. Mathematical ability: Is sex a factor? *Science*, 1981, *212*, 114.

Staples, R. The responses of infants to color. *Journal of Experimental Psychology*, 1932, *15*, 119–141.

Stein, Z., Susser, M., Saenger, G., & Marolla, F. Nutrition and mental performance. *Science*, 1972, *178*, 708–713.

Stella, J. *Games and pastimes of childhood*. New York: Dover, 1969.

Stevens, J. H., Jr. Everyday experience and intellectual development. *Young Children*, November 1981, pp. 66–71.

Stevens, J. H., & King, E. W. *Administering early childhood education programs*. Boston: Little, Brown, 1976.

Stevens, J. H., & Mathews, M. (Eds.). *Mother/child, father/child relationships*. Washington, D.C.: National Association for the Education of Young Children, 1978.

Stevenson, H. W., Stigler, J. W., Lucker, G. W., & Lee, S.-Y. Reading disabilities: The case of Chinese, Japanese, and English. *Child Development*, 1982, *53*, 1164–1181.

Stewart, M. A., & Olds, S. W. *Raising a hyperactive child*. New York: Harper & Row, 1973.

Stipek, D. J., & Hoffman, J. M. Development of children's performance-related judgments. *Child Development*, 1980, *51*, 912–914.

Stone, L. J., Smith, H. T., & Murphy, L. B. (Eds.). *The competent infant*. New York: Basic Books, 1973.

Stone, L. J., Smith, H. T., & Murphy, L. B. (Eds.). *The social infant*. New York: Basic Books, 1978.

Stott, L. H., & Ball, R. S. Infant and preschool mental tests: Review and evaluation. *Monographs of the Society for Research in Child Development*, 1965, *30*(3).

Stratton, P. M., & Connolly, K. Discrimination by newborns of the intensity, frequency, and temporal characteristics of auditory stimuli. *British Journal of Psychology*, 1973, *64*, 219–232.

Strauss, M. E., Lessen-Firestone, J. K., Starr, R. H., & Ostrea, E. M., Jr. Behavior of narcotics-addicted newborns. *Child Development*, 1975, *46*, 887–893.

Strauss, M. S., & Curtis, L. E. Infant perception of numerosity. *Child Development*, 1981, *52*, 1146–1152.

Strohner, H., & Nelson, K. E. The young child's development of sentence comprehension: Influence of event probability, nonverbal context, syntactic form, and strategies. *Child Development*, 1974, *45*, 567–576.

Sullivan, W. Boys and girls are now maturing earlier. *The New York Times*, January 24, 1971.

Suransky, V. P. *The erosion of childhood*. Chicago: University of Chicago Press, 1982.

Swanson, J. M., & Kinsbourne, M. The cognitive effect of stimulant drugs on hyperactive children. In G. A. Hale & M. Lewis (Eds.), *Attention and cognitive development*. New York: Plenum, 1979.

Szasz, T. S. The uses of naming and the myth of mental illness. *American Psychologist*, 1961, *16*, 59–65.

Tagiuri, R. Person perception. In G. Lindzey & E. Aronson (Eds.), *The handbook of social psychology* (Vol. 3). Reading, Mass.: Addison-Wesley, 1969.

Tanner, J. M. *A history of the study of human growth*. Cambridge: Cambridge University Press, 1981.

Tanner, J. M., & Inhelder, B. (Eds.). *Discussions on child development* (Vol. 1). New York: International Universities Press, 1953.

Teenage pregnancy: The problem that hasn't gone away. New York: Alan Guttmacher Institute, 1981.

Temple, C. A., Nathan, R. G., & Burris, N. A. *The beginnings of writing*. Boston: Allyn and Bacon, 1982.

Terman, L. M. *Genetic studies of genius* (Vol. 1). *The mental and physical traits of a thousand gifted children*. Stanford: Stanford University Press, 1925.

Terman, L. M., & Oden, M. H. *Genetic studies of genius: The gifted group at mid-life*. Stanford: Stanford University Press, 1959.

Terrace, H. S., Petitto, L. A., Sanders, R. J., & Bever, T. J. Ape language. *Science*, 1981, *211*, 87–88.

Thoman, E. B. A biological perspective and a behavioral model for assessment of premature infants. In L. A. Bond & J. M. Joffee (Eds.), *Primary prevention of psychopathology* (Vol. 6). Hanover, N.H.: University Press of New England, 1981.

Thoman, E. B., Denenberg, V. H., Sievel, J., Zeidner, L. P., & Becker, P. State organization in neonates: Developmental inconsistency indicates risk for developmental dysfunction. *Neuropediatrics*, 1981, *12*, 45–54.

Thomas, H., & Jamison, W. On the acquisition of understanding that still water is horizontal. *Merrill-Palmer Quarterly*, 1975, *21*, 31–44.

Thorndike, E. L. *Animal intelligence*. New York: Macmillan, 1911.

Tighe, T., & Shepp, B. E. (Eds.). *Interactions: Perception, cognition, and development*. Hillsdale, N.J.: Lawrence Erlbaum, 1982.

Tizard, B. Language at home and at school. In C. B. Cazden (Ed.), *Language in early childhood education*. Washington, D.C.: National Association for the Education of Young Children, 1981.

Tizard, B., & Rees, J. The effect of early institutional rearing on the behavior problems and affectional relationships of four-year-old children. *Journal of Child Psychology and Psychiatry*, 1975, *16*, 61–73.

Tobias, S. Sexist equations. *Psychology Today*, January 1982, pp. 14–17.

Today's girls: Tomorrow's women. New York: Girls Clubs of America, 1979.

Tomizuka, C., & Tobias, S. Mathematical ability: Is sex a factor? *Science*, 1981, *212*, 114.

Tracy, R. L., Lamb, M. E., & Ainsworth, M. D. S. Infant approach behavior as related to attachment. *Child Development*, 1976, *47*, 571–578.

Tronick, E. Z. (Ed.). *Social interchange in infancy*. Baltimore, Md.: University Park Press, 1982.

Tronick, E. Z., & Adamson, L. *Babies as people*. New York and London: Collier Books and Collier Macmillan, 1980.

Turner, R., & Reese, H. W. (Eds.). *Life-span developmental psychology*. New York: Academic Press, 1980.

TV games zapping kids' minds? *New York Daily News*, November 10, 1982, p. 28.

United States National Committee, World Organization for Early Childhood Education. *Listen! The children speak*. Washington, D.C.: United States National Committee, 1979.

U.S. Bureau of the Census. *Marital status and living arrangements: March 1979* (Current Population Reports, Series P-20, No. 349). Washington, D.C.: U.S. Government Printing Office, 1980. (a)

U.S. Bureau of the Census. *Statistical Abstract of the United States*. Washington, D.C.: U.S. Government Printing Office, 1980. (b)

U.S. Department of Health and Human Services. *A parent's guide to day care*. Washington, D.C.: U.S. Government Printing Office, 1980.

U.S. Department of Health and Human Services. *Highlights from student drug use in America, 1975–1980*. Rockville, Md.: National Institute of Drug Abuse, 1981. (a)

U.S. Department of Health and Human Services. *Study findings: National study of the incidence and severity of child abuse and neglect*. Washington, D.C.: U.S. Government Printing Office, 1981. (b)

U.S. Department of Health and Human Services. *Caesarean childbirth*. Washington, D.C.: U.S. Government Printing Office, 1982.

U.S. Department of Labor, Employment Standards Administration, Women's Bureau. *Working mothers and their children*. Washington, D.C.: U.S. Government Printing Office, 1977.

Uzgiris, I. C. Patterns of cognitive development in infancy. *Merrill-Palmer Quarterly*, 1973, *19*, 181–204.

Uzgiris, I. C., & Hunt, J. McV. *Toward ordinal scales of psychological development in infancy*. Urbana: University of Illinois Press, 1974.

Valentine, C. W. The colour perception of an infant during its fourth and eighth months. *British Journal of Psychology*, 1913–1914, *6*, 363–386.

Vandenbergh, J. G. Social determinants of the onset of puberty in rodents. *Journal of Sex Research*, 1974, *10*, 181–193.

van Doornick, W. J., Caldwell, B. M., Wright, C., & Frankenburg, W. K. The relationship between twelve-month home stimulation and school achievement. *Child Development*, 1981, *52*, 1080–1083.

Vygotsky, L. S. *Thought and language*. New York and Cambridge, Mass.: Wiley and M.I.T. Press, 1962. (Original Russian ed., 1934.)

Vygotsky, L. S. *Mind in society*. Cambridge, Mass.: Harvard University Press, 1978.

Waldrop, M. F., Bell, R. Q., McLaughlin, G., & Halverson, C. F. Newborn minor physical anomalies predict short attention span, peer aggression, and impulsivity at age three. *Science*, 1978, *199*, 563–565.

Walk, R. D., & Dodge, S. H. Visual depth perception of a 10-month-old monocular human infant. *Science*, 1962, *137*, 529–530.

Walk, R. D., & Gibson, E. J. A comparative and analytical study of visual depth perception. *Psychological Monographs*, 1961, *75*(15).

Walkerdine, V., & Sinha, C. Developing linguistic strategies in young children. In G. Wells (Ed.), *Learning through interaction*. New York: Cambridge University Press, 1981.

Wallace, P. Complex environments: Effects on brain development. *Science*, 1974, *185*, 1035–1037.

Ward, C. *The child in the city*. New York: Pantheon, 1978.

Warfield, F. *Cotton in my ears*. New York: Viking, 1948.

Watson, J. B. *Psychology from the standpoint of a behaviorist*. Philadelphia: Lippincott, 1919.

Watson, J. B. *Psychological care of infant and child*. New York: Norton, 1928.

Watson, J. S. Smiling, cooing, and "the game." Paper presented at meetings of the American Psychological Association, 1970.

Weatherly, D. Self-perceived rate of physical maturation and personality in late adolescence. *Child Development*, 1964, *35*, 1197–1210.

Wechsler, D. *Manual for the Wechsler Intelligence Test for Children—revised*. New York: The Psychological Corporation, 1974.

Weiner, B., Freize, I., Kukla, A., Reed, L., Rest, S., & Rosenbaum, R. W. *Perceiving the causes of success and failure*. New York: General Learning Press, 1971.

Weiner, J. B. Psychopathology in adolescence. In J. Adelson (Ed.), *Handbook of adolescent psychology*. New York: Wiley, 1980.

Weinraub, M. Fatherhood: The myth of the second-class parent. In J. H. Stevens & M. Mathews (Eds.), *Mother/child, father/child relationships*. Washington, D.C.: National Association for the Education of Young Children, 1978.

Weir, M. W. Developmental changes in problem-solving strategies. *Psychological Review*, 1964, *71*, 473–490.

Weiss, B. Food colors and behavior. *Science*, 1981, *212*, 579.

Weisz, J. R. Developmental change in perceived control: Recognizing noncontingency in the laboratory and perceiving it in the world. *Developmental Psychology*, 1980, *16*, 385–390.

Welsh, M. J. Infants' visual attention to varying degrees of novelty. *Child Development*, 1974, *45*, 344–350.

Werner, E. E., & Smith, R. S. *Kauai's children come of age*. Honolulu: The University Press of Hawaii, 1977.

Werner, E. E., & Smith, R. S. *Vulnerable but invincible*. New York: McGraw-Hill, 1982.

Werner, H. The concept of development from a comparative and organismic point of view. In D. Harris (Ed.), *The concept of development*. Minneapolis: University of Minnesota Press, 1957.

Werner, H. *Comparative psychology of mental development*. New York: International Universities Press, 1973. (Originally published, 1948.)

Werner, H. *Developmental processes: Heinz Werner's selected writings* (Vols. 1 and 2) (S. S. Barten and M. B. Franklin, Eds.). New York: International Universities Press, 1978.

Wetstone, H. S., & Friedlander, B. Z. The effect of word order on young children's responses to simple questions and commands. *Child Development*, 1973, *44*, 734–740.

White, B. L. The development of perception during the first six months of life. Paper presented at meetings of the American Association for the Advancement of Science, 1963.

White, B. L. *The first three years of life*. Englewood Cliffs, N.J.: Prentice-Hall, 1973.

White, B. L., & Held, R. Plasticity of sensorimotor development in the human infant. In J. F. Rosenblith & W. Allinsmith (Eds.), *The causes of behavior* (2nd ed.). Boston: Allyn and Bacon, 1966.

White, B. L., & Watts, J. C. *Experience and environment: Major influences on the development of the young child*. Englewood Cliffs, N.J.: Prentice-Hall, 1973.

White, R. W. Motivation reconsidered: The concept of competence. *Psychological Review*, 1959, *66*, 297–333.

Whitehurst, G. J., Novak, G., & Zorn, G. A. Delayed speech studied in the home. *Developmental Psychology*, 1972, 7, 169–177.

Whiting, B., & Edwards, C. P. A cross-cultural analysis of sex differences in the behavior of children aged three through eleven. *Journal of Social Psychology*, 1973, 91, 176–177.

Willerman, L., Naylor, A. F., & Myrianthopoulos, N. C. Intellectual development of children from interracial matings. *Science*, 1970, 170, 1329–1330.

Willis, A., & Ricciuti, H. *A good beginning for babies: Guidelines for group care.* Washington, D.C.: National Association for the Education of Young Children, 1978.

Wilson, G. S., Desmond, M. M., & Verniaud, W. M. Early development of infants of heroin-addicted mothers. *American Journal of Diseases of Children*, 1973, 126, 457–462.

Winchester, A. M. *Heredity: An introduction to genetics.* New York: Barnes & Noble, 1977.

Winefield, A. H. Probability learning in children as a function of age and reinforcement procedure. *Journal of Genetic Psychology*, 1980, 137, 79–90.

Winner, E., McCarthy, M., & Gardner, H. The ontogenesis of metaphor. In R. P. Honeck & R. R. Hoffman (Eds.), *Cognitive and figurative language.* Hillsdale, N.J.: Lawrence Erlbaum, 1980.

Witkin, H. A., Lewis, H. G., Hertzman, M., Machover, K., Meissner, P. B., & Wapner, S. *Personality through perception.* New York: Harper, 1954.

Witkin, H. A., Mednick, S. A., Schulsinger, F., Bakkestrom, E., Christiansen, K. O., Goodenough, D. R., Hirschorn, D., Lunsteen, C., Owen, D. R., Philip, J., Rubin, D. E., & Stocking, M. Criminality in XYY and XXY men. *Science*, 1976, 193, 547–555.

Wohlwill, J. F. The perception of size and distance relationships in perspective drawings. Paper presented at meetings of the Eastern Psychological Association, 1962.

Wohlwill, J. F., & Wiener, M. Discrimination of form orientation in young children. *Child Development*, 1964, 35, 1113–1125.

Wolff, P. H. The cause, controls, and organization of behavior in the neonate. *Psychological Issues*, 1966, 5, 17.

Woodcock, L. P. *Life and ways of the two-year-old.* New York: Dutton, 1941.

The World Almanac. New York: Newspaper Enterprise Association, 1982.

Wyshak, G., & Frisch, R. E. Evidence for a secular trend in age of menarche. *New England Journal of Medicine*, 1982, 306, 1033–1035.

Yang, R. K., & Bell, R. Q. Assessment of infants. In P. McReynolds (Ed.), *Advances in psychological assessment* (Vol. 3). San Francisco: Jossey-Bass, 1975.

Yonas, A., Cleaves, W. T., & Petterson, L. Development of sensitivity to pictorial depth. *Science*, 1978, 200, 77–79.

Youniss, J. Moral development through a theory of social construction: An analysis. *Merrill-Palmer Quarterly*, 1981, 27, 385–403.

Zacharias, L., & Wurtman, R. J. Age at menarche. *New England Journal of Medicine*, 1969, 280, 869–875.

Zamenhoff, S., van Marthens, E., & Grauel, L. DNA (cell number) in neonatal brain: Second generation (F_2) alteration by maternal (F_0) dietary protein restriction. *Science*, 1971, 172, 850–851.

Zazzo, R. Le problème de l'imitation chez le nouveau-né. *Enfance*, 1957, 2, 135–152.

Zeigler, H. P., & Leibowitz, H. W. Apparent visual size as a function of distance for children and adults. *American Journal of Psychology*, 1957, 70, 106–107.

Zelazo, N. A., Zelazo, P. R., & Kolb, S. Walking in the newborn. *Science*, 1972, 176, 314–315.

Zeskind, P. S., & Ramey, C. T. Preventing intellectual and interactional sequelae of fetal malnutrition: A longitudinal, transactional, and synergistic approach to development. *Child Development*, 1981, 52, 213–218.

Zigler, E. F., & Child, I. L. *Socialization and personality development.* Reading, Mass.: Addison-Wesley, 1973.

Zigler, E. F., & Gordon, E. M. (Eds.). *Day care: Scientific and social policy issues.* Boston: Auburn House, 1982.

Zigler, E. F., & Trickett, P. K. IQ, social competence, and evaluation of early childhood programs. *American Psychologist*, September 1978, pp. 789–796.

Zigler, E. F., & Valentine, J. *Project Head Start: A legacy of the war on poverty.* New York: The Free Press, 1979.